D1302486

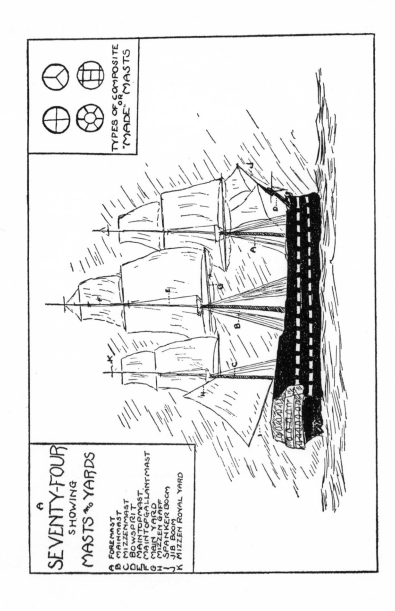

TYPES OF COMPOSITE
"MADE" OR MASTS

A
SEVENTY-FOUR
SHOWING
MASTS AND YARDS

A FOREMAST
B MAINMAST
C MIZZENMAST
D BOWSPRIT
E MAINTOPMAST
F MAINTOPGALLANTMAST
G MAIN YARD
H MIZZEN GAFF
J SPANKER BOOM
J JIB BOOM
K MIZZEN ROYAL YARD

FORESTS AND SEA POWER

THE TIMBER PROBLEM OF
THE ROYAL NAVY
1652—1862

BY

ROBERT GREENHALGH ALBION.

ARCHON BOOKS
HAMDEN, CONNECTICUT
1965

To
J. B. P.

INTRODUCTION

FROM the days when Cromwell ruled England till the battle of Hampton Roads sounded the knell of wooden ships of war, the heads of the English Navy worried over its timber shortage. Not only were the woodlands of England becoming less able to supply oak for the hulls of the King's ships, but in all Britain there grew no trees suitable for the best masts. Dependence on foreign lands for masts, therefore, had to be recognized from the outset; but it was only with the greatest reluctance that England looked to forests beyond the seas for timber to replace her own oak.

The influence of this naval timber situation extended to many diverse fields. It was felt not only in the Navy itself, but in international law, in naval architecture, and in England's foreign, colonial, commercial, and forest policies as well. In this study, the timber problem will be treated in its entirety, in all those spheres of influence and throughout the two centuries when it was a vital factor. The choice of a field so broad and so long involves the obvious risk of scattering effort and diluting the value of the research; but the nature of the subject makes possible a thorough treatment on such a scale. Conditions of timber supply, naval construction, and sea fighting were almost static throughout the period, so that general descriptions will apply to almost any part of the two centuries, with slight exceptions which will be noted. An examination of the records for two hundred years reveals long stretches which contain nothing worthy of more than passing mention. It will be possible, therefore, to concentrate upon the important periods when the problem was most influential.

The years 1652 and 1862 form the best natural boundaries for the period of the naval timber problem. The two centuries included within those dates saw most of the great naval wars in the era of wooden sailing ships. Prior to the beginning of the First Dutch War, in 1652, there was no real naval timber problem, for the naval fighting was carried on for the most part by private ships gathered for the occasion. After the battle of Hampton Roads in 1862, iron definitely replaced wood as the material for naval architecture. The period began definitely late in 1652, with a severe mast crisis which lasted throughout the Dutch wars and was soon followed by a shortage of oak. Its close was equally abrupt, for as late as 1861 there was such alarm over the scarcity of oak that the Navy ordered a larger amount of naval timber than in any previous year of the problem. The important parts of those centuries, so far as this subject is concerned, lay between 1652 and 1677 and between 1775 and 1815. The problem was present during the remainder of the period, but it presented few new aspects during most of the eighteenth century.

Of the various fields in which the effects of the timber problem was felt, the Navy itself was naturally the most important. The timber supply was inseparably connected with sea power. As long as England could maintain control of the sea, the whole world could be searched for timber. The Admiralty, however, could imagine a day when the main fleet might be shattered or sunk by an enemy who could then blockade the coast, so that no materials could arrive from foreign forests for the repair of the old fleet, or the construction of a new one. Admiral Keppel had this in mind in 1778 when he retired to Portsmouth to avoid battle with a superior French fleet. He knew that the supply of masts and naval stores was notoriously low, and declared before his court martial:

Whether we could ever repair the Loss is not very clear to me when I consider the State of our Naval Stores at that time, and the extreme Difficulty of a Supply as long as the French should continue superior in the Channel. It is impossible to say to what such a calamity might not lead. . . . My Courage was never put to such a test as in that Retreat *but my firm Persuasion is that the Country was saved by it.*[1]

That statement is typical of the fears which haunted admirals and naval administrators for two centuries. Fortunately for England, the situation was never realized as it was in France, but the stores were so low at times that such a demand upon them would

---

[1] *Minutes of the Court Martial of Vice Admiral Augustus Keppel, 1779,* p. 106.

have been disastrous. The fear of such a situation was real, even if the situation never materialized, and it was enough to give unusual importance to the timber supply.

Whatever criticism may be made of the naval timber supply, it must be remembered that England gathered oak and masts enough to build the ships which won the control of the seas, so that, on the whole, the supply was a success. It was conspicuous, however, only in the instances where it miscarried. It never produced the extreme consequences that Admiral Keppel and many others feared; but this study will consider three of the occasions when the failure of the timber supply affected the condition and operations of the Navy — the Dutch wars, the American Revolution, and the Napoleonic wars. The effect of a faulty timber supply was often felt in the general condition of ships at sea. For want of oak, moreover, the building or repair program might be so curtailed that the Navy was reduced in strength. "God knows where materials can be had for so many first and 2d rates, however wee shal thinke fitt to propose the building of them," wrote Samuel Pepys, the great Restoration diarist and naval administrator.[1] For want of sound masts, a whole squadron sent on an important mission might be rendered useless, while weak ships, resulting from bad timber, often hampered admirals in their operations.

The influence of the timber problem has been generally neglected by naval historians. The American Revolution episode has been completely overlooked, while the other instances have been treated in a brief and incomplete manner. Even if the timber problem were recognized at its full value, it would, of course, be only secondary in importance to the achievements of the admirals, because, as Mahan wrote, good sailors in poor ships are better than poor sailors in good ships. It will be seen, however, that a lack of oak sometimes made the ships so poor that even Nelson was affected, and the results of such occasions are surely worthy of record. England was not alone in her naval timber problem, for her chief maritime rivals, France, Spain, and Holland, were in a similar situation. That able minister of

---

[1] Magdalene College, Cambridge University, *Pepysian MSS*, 2265, f. 113.

Louis XIV, Colbert, drew up the most comprehensive naval timber policy that the world has seen, but he predicted that France would perish for want of timber.

The relation of ship timber to sea power gave it an importance far above ordinary articles of commerce. This study will follow it into several extra-naval fields where it was influential. Diplomats often made efforts to secure a supply of timber from abroad; England's Baltic policy was chiefly a matter of keeping the sea open at all costs, in order to ensure a supply of naval materials. This policy was taken so seriously that on several occasions English fleets forced their way into the Baltic to protect the supply. It also became a practice of the English to cut off the enemy's supply of timber while maintaining their own. This was one cause for the Armed Neutrality of 1780, an important step in the development of neutral rights. Commercial policy, as well as foreign policy, in the Baltic region was influenced by considerations of naval timber, particularly in the contest between the Baltic and American timber trades. The naval supply of timber was advanced as one cause for the settlement of new colonies, and the English need for timber helped to colonize Canada and northern New England. In all the maritime nations of that period, the preservation of ship timber was the chief aim of a forest policy. In England and in her American colonies, important developments arose from the application of a forest policy to such a purpose.

The chief value of this work would seem to lie in the correlating of these various fields affected by the timber problem. The importance of the need for naval timber in separate fields has been noted by a number of writers, but heretofore there has been no attempt to study the problem as a whole. This treatment will bring out striking instances of cause and effect which may have hitherto escaped notice. The actions of a Swedish king, for instance, helped to colonize the coast of Maine; the fact that fir is of superior quality in northern latitudes was partly responsible for an important development in international law; Napoleon's Berlin and Milan decrees led to the instruction of African savages in the art of lumbering; and partly because many of the members of Parliament owned oak on their estates, Nelson was crippled in his blockade of Toulon.

In addition to coördinating these diverse fields to indicate their interrelationship, an attempt will be made to present an original picture of various steps in the timber supply, particularly of the lumbering operations and the transportation of timber in several regions. A brief explanation of the semi-technical aspects of forestry and naval architecture is included in the study, as many of the terms may be new to the general reader. In connection with the relation of the Navy Board to the timber problem, the study will also show to some extent the conservatism and corruption of an official bureau transacting business in the period under consideration.

Such a treatment calls for an arrangement in which the chronological is subordinated to the topical. The descriptive and explanatory passages have been segregated for the most part in the earlier chapters. The later chapters are more definitely historical in their nature and follow in a general chronological order. This arrangement is adopted for clearness and naturally calls for considerable cross-reference. In the matter of terminology, the English usage has been followed in general. "Timber" will ordinarily be used in the general sense denoted by the American word "lumber." "Masts" will ordinarily include bowsprits, yards, and spars. There is no convenient English word, such as the German *Schiffsmaterial*, to include all forms of ship timber, masts, and naval stores, and the expression "naval materials" will be understood to comprehend those articles.

The study has a present-day application in the close resemblance of the old timber problem to the modern oil situation. Oak, like oil to-day, was a natural product very abundant at the outset, but liable to ultimate exhaustion. The extensive commercial demands for the object encroached on the smaller but more vitally imperative demands of the Navy. For want of an adequate domestic supply, nations sought colonies and exerted diplomatic pressure in those days for ship timber as they do now for oil. Finally, there seem to be evidences of faulty policy in regard to the international and domestic oil situation which closely resemble policies that produced serious results in the supply of masts and oak.

Many individuals have given me valuable advice and assistance in the preparation of this study. My wife, Jennie Pope Albion, collaborated with me in many stages of the work and gave unselfishly of her time, energy, and the results of her training in economics. Without her constant constructive criticism and untiring assistance, this work would not have been completed in its present form. I am deeply indebted to Professor Wilbur Cortez Abbott of Harvard University for his original suggestion that a subject of interest might be found in the relation between the Baltic and American timber trades. I am very grateful, also, for his advice and criticism during his supervision of the work. Mr. W. G. Perrin, librarian of the Admiralty Library at Whitehall, Mr. Edward Fraser and Mr. David Bonner Smith of the Admiralty staff, Captain Alfred Dewar, R. N., and Mr. Hubert Hall, until recently Deputy Keeper of the Records, are among those who assisted me greatly during my researches in England. Mr. A. R. M. Lower of the Canadian Bureau of Historical Publications, who is preparing a study of the Canadian timber trade, was kind enough to exchange notes with me on that subject. Professor Walter Phelps Hall and Mr. Jere H. Wheelwright, Jr., of Princeton gave me valuable suggestions after reading portions of the manuscript. Professor Mark M. Heald explored certain papers for me, and my sister assisted me in the preparation of part of the work. A number of naval officers, shipbuilders, forestry experts, and timber merchants gave me advice in their particular fields. To all these, and to many others, I wish to express my appreciation of their assistance.

PRINCETON, 1926.

CONTENTS

CHAPTER VIII

St. Vincent's Economy and Reform Program — Timber Monopoly opposes new Dockyard Inspection — "Trust" refuses to furnish Oak while Napoleon threatens Invasion — Navy forced to submit — English Woodlands unequal to Dockyard Demands—Napoleon blocks Efforts to secure European Timber — Thwarted Attempts in Holland, Holstein, Adriatic and Black Sea — The Continental System in the Baltic — Effect on Timber Trade — Evasions — Europe almost completely cut off in 1809.

CHAPTER IX

America after the Revolution — New England no longer Dependable, favoring French — Transfer of "Broad Arrow" to Canada — Development of New Brunswick — Shift to Quebec — Encouragement by Monopoly and Baltic Duties — Heavy Timber Exports save England — Pitch Pine from southern United States — Evasions of Embargo and Non-Intercourse — Widespread Attempts in other Continents — South America, Africa and South Seas — Shipbuilding in India — Justification of Imperial Self-sufficiency.

CHAPTER X

Lack of Oak felt in Squadrons blocking Napoleon's Navy — Nelson at Toulon and Cochrane at Ferrol — Extreme Oak Shortage in Dockyards — Improvised Relief Measures — Patching up of Old Ships with Fir — Temporary Force for Trafalgar—Changed Function of the Royal Navy after 1805 — Flimsy Ships in War of 1812 — Extreme Prevalence of Dry Rot — New Features in Last Half Century of Problem — Conservative Opposition to Introduction of Iron — Huge Timber Purchase in last Year of Problem — Influence of Hampton Roads — Review of Problem.

FORESTS AND SEA POWER

A LIST OF THE PRINCIPAL ABBREVIATIONS
USED IN THE REFERENCES

Acts P. C. ....Acts of the Privy Council.

Acts P. C. (Col.) ....Acts of the Privy Council (Colonial Series).

Adm. ....Admiralty.

Adm., Acct.Gen., Misc., Var. Admiralty, Accountant General, Miscellaneous, Various.

B. M. ....British Museum.

B. of T. ....Board of Trade.

C. O. ....Colonial Office.

C. L. R. ....Commissioners of the Land Revenue.

Cal. S. P., A. & W. I. ....Calendar of State Papers, Colonial Series, America and West Indies.

Cal. S. P., Col. ....Calendar of State Papers, Colonial.

Cal. S. P., Dom. ....Calendar of State Papers, Domestic Series.

Cal. Treas. Papers ....Calendar of Treasury Papers.

Corr. de Nap. ....Correspondance de Napoléon.

E. H. R. ....English Historical Review.

F. O. ....Foreign Office.

H. C. J. ....House of Commons Journals.

Hist. MSS Com. ....Historical Manuscripts Commission.

L. & P., Henry VIII ......Letters and Papers, Foreign and Domestic, of the Reign of Henry VIII.

N. B. ....Navy Board.

N. H. S. ....Naval History Society.

N. R. S. ....Navy Records Society.

(Numbers) ....Guns of ship, e.g., *Victory*, 100; *Guerrière*, 38.

Parl. ....Parliamentary.

R. N. ....Royal Navy.

R. O. ....Public Record Office.

V. C. H. ....Victoria County History.

CHAPTER I

TREES AND SHIP TIMBER

"IT will always be said of us with unabated reverence, 'THEY BUILT SHIPS OF THE LINE.' Take it all in all, a Ship of the Line is the most honourable thing that man, as a gregarious animal, has ever produced." [1] Such a superlative from Ruskin is tribute indeed. It was not entirely unnatural for an Englishman thus to place those stout old products of Deptford and Chatham, Portsmouth and Plymouth even ahead of medieval cathedrals. Those "wooden walls" not only formed the nation's first line of defense but, by crushing similar ships of the line from Holland, France, and Spain, had won for England her mastery of the seas and had contributed to her dominant position in the world.

The ship of the line did not depend upon her historic record alone for merit. She had a sturdy beauty, whether rolling in a mid-Atlantic swell or lying proudly at anchor. There was a lofty dignity in her masts, for naval architecture has probably produced no general feature as beautiful as the right angles of the square-rigged ship. There was also an aspect of massive strength in the solid hull of the "seventy-four," that favorite instrument of war by sea for more than a century. Her hull ranged some two hundred feet from the figurehead under the great bowsprit to the ornate windows of the cabin at the stern. She was broad in proportion to her length, for her beams measured more than fifty feet between the bulging sides, which were pierced with two rows of guns and were painted yellow until the more sober, practical styles of the nineteenth century changed them to black. This breadth robbed her of the speed of the little frigates, but it gave her the strength to withstand terrific buffeting in battle.

Much was crowded between the decks of that stout hull. The seventy-four was known as a two-decker, for they did not count

[1] Ruskin, *Harbours of England;* Works, ed. Cook and Wedderburn, xiii, 28.

the musty orlop deck below the waterline, which supported the
cockpit and the cables and covered an even more musty region
occupied by magazines, storerooms, bilge water, and ballast.
The two fighting decks, flanked with long rows of muzzle-loading
guns on wooden trucks, were painted a dull red inside, so that
the sanguinary stains of battle would be less evident. The upper
deck, sheltered by high topsides, rose forward into the forecastle
and aft into the quarterdeck. In those cramped quarters, some
six hundred men lived at sea for months, and sometimes years,
on end.

The ships of the line formed the backbone of the Navy, for they
were the capital ships which could form a line of battle. There
were usually about a hundred of them in the Royal Navy, in addition to several hundred lesser craft, which ranged from frigates
down through sloops and gun-brigs to fireships. Some of the
ships of the line were great, lumbering, three-decked first and
second rates, with ninety or a hundred guns. There were also
a few small fourth rates, "sixty-fours," used ordinarily for convoy duty or for service on distant stations. The bulk of the
battle strength of the Navy, however, lay in the dozens of third
rate seventy-fours. The seventy-four was considered the largest
ship that could sail well and fight well under nearly all conditions,
and its rôle in the growth of British sea power was tremendous.

Probably not more than one man in a thousand who looked at
a ship of the line reflected that her great mainmast had been cut
in the forests of Maine, that the topmast had grown in the
Ukraine, or that the little spars came from some Norwegian moun-
tainside. Nor would he probably know that part of the planking
of those yellow sides had floated down the Vistula to Dantzig,
while the curved frame timbers which gave the shape to the
bulging hull had come from tough, crooked hedgerow oaks in
Sussex. At the most, the casual observer might have some vague
thought of "heart of oak." The ship of the line, so majestic in
its entirety, is less spectacular when divided into its component
parts, but such analysis is essential to an understanding of the
timber problem of the Navy. It will be necessary to consider
first the shapes and forms of wood required for the building of

the ship, and then the range of trees that could furnish timber suitable for the purpose.

The ship of the line was larger than the average country house of the day, and in the matter of materials, the task of the builder of houses was light compared with that of the shipwright. The latter had no recourse to brick or stone, but, until the ultimate introduction of iron, was confined entirely to the use of wood. Even in wood, his choice was limited by considerations of the size and shape of timber, while the inexorable demands of the sea eliminated the wood of most trees as unfit for ship timber. The supply of timber for hulls and for masts presented separate problems throughout the period. With the exception of fir, distinctly different kinds of wood were required for the two purposes. Leaving masts for the present, the timbers of the hull will be considered first.

In many portions of a ship, considerable straight timber could be used. Certain parts of the anatomy, however, required logs of exceptional size and shape. As these could come only from trees of advanced age or peculiar formation, they were very difficult to obtain. This need of large and crooked timber exerted an important retarding influence on the development of naval architecture. In these days when the style in battleships often changes almost before the latest superdreadnought has completed her maiden voyage, it is hard to realize that naval architecture remained almost stationary during the entire "sailing-ship era." More radical progress has been made in every decade since 1860 than in the entire two preceding centuries. There was surprisingly little difference between Phineas Pett's *Sovereign of the Seas,* built in 1637 for the Ship Money Fleet, and the last splendid creations in wooden warships just before 1860.[1]

This static condition was due partly to conservatism, but even more to those large and crooked timbers. They were essential to the construction of a wooden ship, and the cleverest shipwright could not entirely dispense with them. "The limitations of the tree proved the limitations of the ship," declares Jane,[2] who

---

[1] Fincham, *History of Naval Architecture*, p. 54.

[2] Jane, *The British Battle Fleet*, p. 51. For a somewhat different view, see Robinson, *The British Fleet*, pp. 239, 240.

states that Cromwell appreciated the value of the "big ship" but
was unable to go beyond the bounds set by the oak. The dimensions of the largest English ships of the line in the eighteenth
century showed a surprisingly small increase in size, due partly to
the fact that certain parts of the ship's frame already required
the largest oaks available. There was some increase in tonnage,
but the second *Royal George* of 1788 was only twelve feet longer
and two feet wider than the *Royal Sovereign* of 1719. "The size
of our ships seems now to have reached its ultimatum," wrote
Charnock in 1804, "for nature itself in some measure fixes its
limits. . . . Timber, the growth of nature as much as man,
cannot be made to grow larger." [1] Under such conditions ships
did not soon become obsolete, and the *Royal William* took part
in Howe's relief of Gibraltar when over sixty years of age.

The naval architects did not accept these limitations meekly.
By scarphing, or piecing together, they tried to make composite
sticks that would serve, but there were some portions of the ship
where the full strength of a single tree was needed. They might
conceive a great ship, but its proportions would require a stern-
post larger than any available tree could furnish. The French,
with the *Commerce de Marseilles*, tried to go beyond the natural
limits in 1792, only to produce a ship that was notoriously flimsy.
In spite of a constantly increasing difficulty in procuring great
and crooked timber, the ingenuity of the shipwrights was able
to secure a gradual increase in the size of the largest ships; but
it was relatively slight in comparison with the rapid developments
since 1860.

This situation had its effect on the naval warfare of the period.
To-day, battles are won by designers almost as much as by admirals. Then, the admirals fought with almost equal weapons,
for designs were practically common property. Advantages from
speed, construction, and ordnance were incidental in the great
battles, and naval warfare was chiefly a consideration of the
number of ships that could be concentrated, the skill of the admiral in utilizing them, and the discipline and efficiency of the

[1] Charnock, *History of Marine Architecture*, iii, 234. For dimensions of all R. N.
ships to 1804, *Ibid.*, p. 245.

crews. This put a premium on strategy and tactics and on the individual ability of the leaders at sea.

The timbers of unusual size and shape were not only partially responsible for that static condition of naval architecture, but they also made their influence felt in other aspects of naval construction. It was in the supply of such pieces that a timber shortage was first and most severely felt. The construction of ships was sometimes held up for months, and even for years, while the forests were searched for certain pieces. On at least one occasion, the Admiralty was forced to curtail the projected construction of large ships for want of these timbers.[1] The Navy Board might truly claim that it had a two years' supply of timber on hand, so far as the total amount was concerned, yet it could often be charged with equal truth, at the same time, that there was not enough timber on hand to complete a single seventy-four, for some of this timber of exceptional size and shape would be lacking.

These important exceptional pieces were known as "great" and "compass" timbers, and frequent reference will be made to them under those names throughout this study. The great timbers presented a serious problem because they had to come from trees which had passed the stage where it was most profitable to cut them for timber. Oaks were ordinarily felled between the ages of eighty and one hundred and twenty years, when they were between fifteen to eighteen inches in diameter. If allowed to live beyond that age, they were liable to decay at the heart, and landowners, as will be seen later, were reluctant to take such a risk. The Navy, therefore, suffered for want of logs in sizes above the average. Curved or "compass" timber came chiefly from isolated trees that displayed more individuality in shape than those in groves or forests. Grown alone in the hedgerows which separated cultivated fields, the English oak produced good compass timber. The enclosure movement, however, cut down this source of crooked timber when it did away with most of the hedgerows by throwing several fields together.[2] Young saplings could be pinned

[1] See p. 226.
[2] Eleventh Report, Commissioners of the Land Revenue, *H. C. J.*, *1792*, pp. 317–319.

down or tied together in order to produce curved timber in later years, but this presupposed more foresight than was usual with those who grew oaks upon their estates.[1] Straight timber of large size was usually hard enough to procure, but the chief difficulty usually arose in the case of certain pieces which had to be both great and curved.

These pieces of great timber and compass timber were found for the most part in the frame or skeleton of the ship. The backbone was represented by the keel, which rose forward in the stem and aft in the stern-post. Crossing this backbone at right angles were the frames or "ribs" — sixty or seventy in number in a ship of the line. The ribs were in pairs, each rib being composed of a floor piece and several "futtocks" and top pieces of varying curvature. At the bow and stern many special pieces of peculiar shape, such as the breast-hooks, apron, and wing transoms, were required. The decks were supported by beams, which were attached to the ribs by knees. Some of these pieces presented far more of a problem than others. The question was most acute, naturally, in the construction of the largest ships, and where dimensions are given they will be for the first rate, which represented the maximum difficulty. The keel, which was composed of a dozen or more pieces over twenty inches thick, created little trouble, because elm could be substituted for the more valuable oak in portions of the ship entirely below the waterline. The stern-post presented a very stubborn problem. Since it was required to bear the strain of the rudder, it could not be pieced, and a single oak stick some forty feet long and sometimes twenty-eight inches thick was needed. There was considerable difficulty in procuring the large curved pieces for the stem, as well as for the cathead, the heavy crooked timber which supported the anchor. The knees, which were cut from the intersection of large branches with the trunk, also presented a problem, for only the trees raised in isolation tended to have large branches. One of the hardest pieces in the whole ship to procure was the wing-transom knee, which had two thick arms twelve or fourteen feet

NO. 1

A MIDSHIP SECTION OF A 74 GUN SHIP WITH A DEEP WAIST AND TUMBLE HOME SIDES, AS BUILT IN HIS MAJESTY'S DOCK YARDS

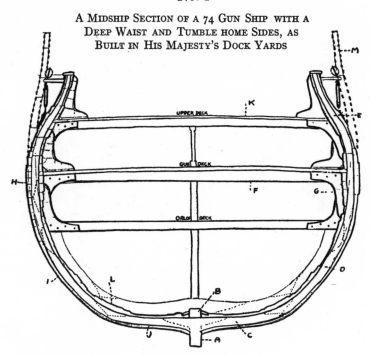

CROSS-SECTION OF A **SEVENTY-FOUR** SHOWING TIMBERS USED IN CONSTRUCTION	A KEEL (ELM) B KEELSON (ELM) C FLOOR PIECE D FUTTOCK E TOP PIECE F BEAM (FIR)	G KNEE H THICKSTUFF I PLANK (BALTIC OAK) J GARBOARD STRAKES (ELM, BEECH) K DECK DEALS (BALTIC OAK OR FIR) L CEILING

FROM 11 CLR; H.C.J., 1792, PLATE 1.

M SNODGRASS PLAN FOR STRAIGHT SIDES TO SAVE COMPASS TIMBER. ENGLISH OAK USED IN ALL PARTS EXCEPT WHERE SUBSTITUTES NOTED

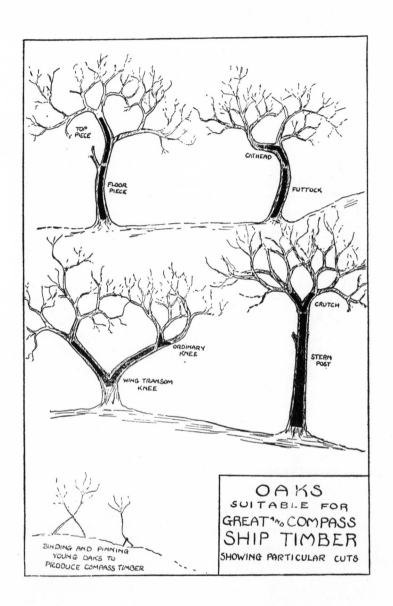

TOP PIECE

FLOOR PIECE

CATHEAD

FUTTOCK

ORDINARY KNEE

WING TRANSOM KNEE

CRUTCH

STERN POST

BINDING AND PINNING YOUNG OAKS TO PRODUCE COMPASS TIMBER

OAKS
SUITABLE FOR
GREAT AND COMPASS
SHIP TIMBER
SHOWING PARTICULAR CUTS

long, whereas most knees had arms not over three or four feet in length.[1]

The relative scarcity of these pieces may be judged from the Navy contract prices of 1804. The unit of timber measurement was the "load" of fifty cubic feet, the equivalent of six hundred American board feet. Roughly, the average oak of timber size contained about a load of timber and made nearly a ton of shipping. It weighed about a ton and a quarter. In 1804, straight oak timber ranged from £4 3s. to £7 16s. a load, according to its size, the oak of average dimensions being about £7. Different pieces of great and compass timber, however, commanded higher prices because of their relative scarcity. Fourth futtocks cost £12 7s. a load; stern-posts, rudder-pieces, and wing transoms, £12 18s.; common knees, £13 2s.; stem pieces, even scarphed three times, £13 4s.; while the most expensive item of all, the wing-transom knees, cost £15 8s., and often they could not be supplied even at that price, which was more than double the average cost of oak.[2] The scarcity of this kind of timber stimulated invention, which was really necessary in view of the almost absolute shortage during the Napoleonic wars. Scarphing and the substitution of iron knees were successfully experimented with, while able constructors devised methods for building with smaller timber.[3]

The other forms of timber that went into the hull presented occasional problems, but these could be met much more easily. There was an outside layer of planking, the "skin" of the ship, and an inner, thinner layer known as ceiling. The term "plank" was ordinarily applied to sawn wood between two and eight inches thick. Anything larger than that was "timber" proper, while the pieces thinner than plank were called "deals," or boards. The heavier type of planking, more than four inches

[1] For contemporary descriptions of shipbuilding, see esp. Bushnell, *The Compleat Shipwright* (1669); Duhamel du Monceau, *Élémens de l'Architecture Navale* (1758); Hoste, *L'Art des Armées Navales* (1727); Knowles, *Elements and Practice of Naval Architecture* (1822); Mazaudier, *Guide Pratique d'Architecture Navale* (1835); Peake, *Rudiments of Naval Architecture* (1851); Sutherland, *Shipbuilder's Assistant, or Marine Architecture* (1766).

[2] Knowles, *op. cit.*, pp. 425–432. See R. O., *Adm., Acct. Gen., Accts. Misc., Var.; Contracts, passim.*   [3] See p. 393.

thick, was commonly known as "thickstuff." Young oaks
could be used for planking, since suppleness rather than size was
required. The chief difficulty in the case of the great and compass
timbers lay in the fact that no adequate substitutes for the precious English oak were available. Other woods, however, could
be used for most of the planking, except that in the trying position "between wind and water." Elm, beech, fir, and Baltic oak
were frequently used for planking below the waterline. For the
decks, deals an inch or two in thickness were employed. These
were usually imported, because it was cheaper to have them sawn
by windmills in the Baltic than by hand in England. Treenails,
or "trunnels," the wooden pins used for fastening the timbers,
were difficult to secure at times, and there were numerous petty
special requirements in the matter of wood, descending even to
tackle-blocks and capstan-bars.

Troublesome as these questions of size and shape might be at
times, the Navy found even more of a problem in deciding what
species of tree and what regions could furnish the best timber.
This second consideration had great importance in the solution
of the timber problem. In taking up the matter of timber qualities, it is necessary to consider not only the relative values of the
various woods as determined by experts to-day, but also the
contemporary opinions held by the Navy Board and the shipwrights during that period. The solution of the timber problem
was strongly affected by the stupid and conservative partiality for
certain woods, and an equally unjustifiable discrimination against
others. This tended to exhaust the supply of the favored timbers
when the drain could have been relieved by using the others.

Strength and durability were the standards by which the Navy
judged the relative merits of different woods available for ship
timber. Differences in weight and cost were of less importance.
Simple tests at the dockyard could determine the strength of
wood. After breaking, bending, and pulling numerous samples,
the shipwrights were able to make accurate tables showing the
amount of strain which each variety of timber should resist.[1]
Weak woods were eliminated without further consideration.

[1] Laslett, *Timber and Timber Trees*, Appendix.

The question of durability was more subtle. Even the stronger timbers might contain elements of decay. The timber problem was closely related to the durability of ships.[1] Unsatisfactory wood could produce speedy decay. This not only reduced the efficiency of the Navy, but it greatly increased the demand for timber to replace the rotten material. Decay could come from external or internal sources. The external decay was usually produced by marine borers; the internal by dry rot. One of the advantages of oak was its strong tannic or gallic acid, which was distasteful to the little *teredo navalis*, or sea-worm. In spite of this acid, these marine borers made leaky sieves of dozens of the King's ships by chewing the planking into veritable honeycombs, especially on the southern stations. Sheathing with tar, hair, and fir boards was an ineffective remedy practised for two centuries. Experiments with lead sheathing during the Restoration were not satisfactory, but the general introduction of copper sheathing into the Navy during the American Revolution finally put an end to this external decay.

The Navy hit upon no such simple remedy for the internal ravages of the dry rot, which was the curse of wooden ships for centuries. Its results were very evident, for it sometimes pulverized whole fleets, and the effects will be noted from time to time throughout this work. There was never a time when at least a few warships were not feeling the effects of its ravages. It was a baffling enemy, and after hundreds of suggestions and experiments on means of checking it, dry rot remained unmastered to the end.

This destructive dry rot was a fungous growth which penetrated the wood with small white cottony fibres.[2] These gradually robbed the timber of its vitality and eventually reduced it to powder. It betrayed itself on the surface by a toadstool growth, which gradually fructified and spread the little white fibres to neighboring timber, which might be sound. The forms

[1] See pp. 84, 85.
[2] On dry rot in general see esp. Britton, *Treatise on Dry Rot in Timber;* Knowles, *Dry Rot;* Dodd, *Practical Observations on Dry Rot in Timber;* Garraud, *Études sur les Bois de Construction;* Hough, *Report upon Forestry,* U. S. Dept. of Agriculture, 1878; Betts, *Timber, its Strength, Seasoning and Grading, passim.*

of dry rot, most common in wooden ships, were the *xylostroma giganteum*, usually limited to oak, producing a large, tough, leather-like excrescence, and the *boletus hybridus*, described as soft, ragged, and white, resembling the nature of a spongy turnip.[1] Samuel Pepys, the diarist, describes gathering "toad-stools . . . as big as my fist" in the rotting ships of the 1677 armament,[2] and when Lord Sandwich visited the ships in reserve at Chatham in 1771, it was necessary to shovel away filth of this sort before the timbers could be viewed.[3]

The dry rot was often more insidious, eating out the heart of the timber, while the exterior remained apparently sound. The most vulnerable part of a ship was the section just above the waterline, known as the wales, or buttocks. There the planking was exposed intermittently to air and water, and the rib timbers, having to bear the heavy guns, were subjected to a severe strain. Beams, knees, futtocks, and planking in this part of the ship were usually the first to decay. Wherever stagnant air collected — as, for example, in the intervals between the rib timbers, in the magazine and bread-rooms, and around the extreme bow and stern — dry rot appeared. It required a moderate mixture of air, moisture, and heat in order to flourish. An excess of any of these elements would kill the spores, so that the timber constantly below the water, or in a dry position freely exposed to the air, was relatively immune. An analysis of dockyard repairs shows a large demand for new knees, beams, futtocks, and planking, while the keel and lower frame timbers ordinarily escaped. Many ships foundered because the frame timbers near the waterline, the only longitudinal support, gave way as the weight of the ship pulled them apart, under an unusual strain.[4] It was in this way that the bottom fell out of the *Royal George* in 1782, and it was probably the cause of the foundering of many warships that were never heard from.

The four principal causes of the origin and spread of dry rot in ships were unseasoned timber, the use of certain foreign woods,

[1] *Quarterly Review*, xii, 230, 231.
[2] Pepys, *Memoires relating to the State of the Royal Navy of England*, pp. 84–86.
[3] Fraser, *Londons of the British Fleet*, p. 259.
[4] N. R. S., *Journals and Letters of Sir T. Byam Martin*, iii, 379.

improper construction, and lack of ventilation. The greatest of these was unseasoned timber, and it was through the necessity of building with green wood that the timber problem made itself felt most consistently in the Navy. The purpose of seasoning was to remove the sap. Wood is composed of long cylindrical cells of many sizes and shapes, interspersed with ducts for the movement of fluid up the tree. During the warmer months of the year, the cells are full of watery sap, which is considerably reduced in the winter. It required two or three years to dry a log properly. The loss of the sap, with the resultant shrinkage of the cells, left the seasoned log about one fourth lighter and somewhat smaller, the sap having been gradually drawn out by the air through the normal ducts. The inner heartwood of the log could become well seasoned and extremely durable. The outer ring of sapwood, which contained the active sap channels, never became sound. Trouble arose when the quest for timber of extra size led to the inclusion of sapwood in order to give a few extra inches of girth.

The effect of unseasoned timber in naval construction was no secret to the Admiralty. In 1609, the Naval Commission of Inquiry, appointed by James I, drafted a report on the matter which bitter experience from two more centuries of rotting green wood could not improve upon. They wrote:

> In buylding and repaireing Shippes with greene Tymber, Planck and Trennels it is apparent both by demonstration to the Shippes danger and by heate of the Houlde meeting with the greenesse and sappines thereof doth immediately putrefie the same and drawes that Shippe to the Dock agayne for reparation within the space of six or seaven yeares that would last twentie if it were seasoned as it ought and in all other partes of the world is accustomed.
> Adde hereunto experience at this day that many Shippes thus brought in to be repaired, subject to miscareinge upon employment, and besides they breed infection among the men that serve in them;

and they advised that the timber be "seasoned in water to sucke out the sappe and after dryed by the ayer and sonne and pyled uppe till thear be fitte use of it." [1] This was sound advice, but it was so poorly followed that fleet after fleet rotted prematurely. The Navy experimented at times with many methods of sea-

[1] Admiralty Library, MSS, p. 141; *State of the Navy*, 1609, f. 60.

soning timber, which will be treated more in detail in later chapters. Provisions were made for a more adequate reserve in the dockyards, and when there was no immediate rush for ships, they were allowed to season in their frames before being planked. Roofs were sometimes built over the building ships to protect the timbers from sun, snow, and rain. A few planks were occasionally left off until the ship was ready for launching, in order to allow a free passage of air into the hold. Timber felled in the winter was often advocated, and sometimes tried, because it contained less sap. At times there were attempts to accelerate seasoning by drying the timber in kilns, but this tended to crack the wood and destroy its resilience and strength. Chemical preservatives such as tar, salt, oil, or Kyan's process of immersion in corrosive sublimate, were tried spasmodically. None of these methods was pursued with sufficient persistence to overcome the evils of construction with green wood.[1]

Faulty seasoning could produce an extreme form of dry rot, even in the choicest English oak. In many respects, however, foreign timber was much more subject to rapid decay. In America and the Baltic, the two regions from which the Navy imported nearly all its foreign timber before 1804, timber was usually floated down the rivers in rafts, sometimes for hundreds of miles. While still dripping from that long wet trip, it was usually loaded immediately into the holds of timber ships. There the wet timber steamed for weeks on the hot passage to England, for timber ships usually traveled during the warmer months of the year. The steaming timber in the hot holds made an ideal nursery for dry-rot spores, and the logs were sometimes covered with fungi before they reached the dockyards. English timber escaped such treatment, for it was carried in lighters or sloops without touching the water. The Navy Board was not interested in the relative qualities of English and foreign trees as they grew in the forests, but they did know that the imported timber was much more susceptible to dry rot by the time the Navy was ready to use it.

In the Navy's estimate of timber values, the foreign wood was

[1] See pp. 82, 101, 392–397.

at a still further disadvantage, because of the uses to which it was put. American or Baltic timber was employed ordinarily only in times of emergency, when there was no time for the requisite two or three years of seasoning. The substitute timber was ordinarily employed only for repairs of old ships already decayed. It was well recognized that, where various sorts of timber, even different kinds of oak, were used together, dry rot was more liable to develop than where a single kind was used throughout, and it was so contagious that a few pieces of decaying timber could soon affect the whole structure. In such instances as the rapid decay of the 1677 fleet, the rotting of the ships built of Stettin oak around 1770, or of those built of Canadian oak forty years later, there was a tendency to make foreign timber the scapegoat.[1] That was an example of stupid loyalty to English oak; but during those periods there was almost as much decay in the ships built of that native oak. Justifiable or not, the supposed susceptibility of foreign timber to dry rot prevented more extensive use of it.

Of the four principal causes of dry rot, the considerations of improper seasoning and the use of foreign woods were intimately related to the timber supply. The third cause, improper construction, was related to the process of seasoning and will be discussed in a later chapter on shipbuilding. The problem of ventilation rested with those in charge of the ships in reserve or at sea, and it will be seen that those who built the ships tried to shift the blame for decay from themselves and the timber they used to the officers in charge of the ships. At all events, the condition and species of timber used in construction had a very close relation to the prevalence of dry rot in the Navy, and every kind of timber was judged by its susceptibility to this form of decay.

Up to 1804, only four kinds of timber — oak, elm, beech, and fir — were used to any extent in the hulls of the king's ships. That was considered the widest possible range by the most broadminded Navy Board, and it was the Navy Board who determined what timbers should be used. Even within those limits there were very strong opinions on the relative value of trees

[1] See pp. 161, 228, 394–397.

from different regions which are especially noticeable in the case of the discrimination against American oak, and the more excusable low opinion of the fir of Scotland. This favoritism went so far that only the oak of one particular county in England was regarded as fit for the best ship timber. After 1804, the shortage created by the Napoleonic wars forced a breaking down of those old prejudices, and after Trafalgar, dozens of timbers coming from every continent were used in the dockyards, and some were even considered the peers of English oak. It is interesting to compare the scores of timbers allowed by Lloyd's to-day with that scant old Navy list of four.

The outstanding feature in the question of timber qualities is the predominance of English oak, already alluded to. In all the maritime countries, oak was considered the ship timber *par excellence*. It is "tough, bending well, strong and not too heavy, nor easily admitting water," wrote Evelyn in his *Sylva*.[1] Oak, moreover, is durable and resilient and it did not splinter easily in action, which was an important consideration in ships of war. The tannic or gallic acid with which it is impregnated helped to preserve it from worms but it was a decided nuisance in corroding all iron with which it came in contact. Above all, oak was available in all the great maritime countries and was the favorite ship timber of every nation, so that in all the great sea fights of the sailing-ship era most of the ships were built of oak.

It was not enough that the King's ships be built of oak. It had to be English oak. The outstanding fact in this whole question of relative timber quality is the persistent and not altogether unreasonable belief held by Englishmen that, above all other timbers in the world, the oak of England was the choicest material for shipbuilding. It was the *Quercus robur*, the most common of the three hundred or more species of oak which the botanists have classified. Ranging from Norway to Sicily and from Ireland to

---

[1] Evelyn, *Sylva*, i, 67. For a general discussion of the relative merits of various timbers for shipbuilding the best accounts are in Evelyn and in Laslett, *Timber and Timber Trees;* Garraud, *Études sur les Bois de Construction;* and Schlich, *Manual of Forestry*, vol. iv. For a more general view, consult any of the numerous manuals of timber and forestry. On the oak, one of the best works is Ward, *The Oak*. Most of the works on shipbuilding discuss the matter of timber.

the Urals, the *Quercus robur* was supposed to reach the condition most applicable to shipbuilding in England.

In determining the quality of trees for timber, environment is a factor second only to heredity. The chief element in environment for trees is the climate, though the soil also is an important consideration. The oak is a tree which improves as it advances southward, requiring a mild and even climate south of 60 degrees north latitude to attain its greatest development. The effect of climate is especially noticeable in the oaks of Italy, where the *Quercus robur* is only one of a half-dozen species. They all produce a tough, horny wood, dark brown in color, and admirably crooked for the shipwright's purposes. The timber of the Italian *Quercus robur*, so different from the large, straight, and comparatively soft wood of its northern forms, is scarcely distinguishable from that of the other species of oaks in Italy. The moderate, humid climate of England was conducive to the growth of excellent oak; but if England enjoyed a climatic advantage over the Baltic in the case of oak, the reverse was true with regard to fir, a fact which, it will be seen, was of extreme importance in the timber problem. Even in England the effect of climate was noticeable, for the oaks of the southeastern counties, Sussex, Surrey, Kent, and Hampshire, were considered superior to any others grown in the island; and even there the favor did not stop. Naval contracts not only constantly discriminated against the oak of Yorkshire and other counties of the north, but often specified "good, sound Sussex oak." To an English shipwright there was no wood in the world superior to Sussex oak.[1]

The prominence of Sussex oak was due not only to the climate, but also to the clayey soil of that region; for the quality of the soil had an effect more limited in range than climate, but equally important in its influence on the quality of the timber. "The nature of the soil has so great an influence on the quality of timber that one can almost judge a tree by feeling and examining the earth which produced it," wrote one of the leading French au-

[1] R. O., Navy Board, *Contracts, passim;* N. B. In Letters (1625), *Thos. Steemson to N. B.*, Oct. 27, 1807; Colbert, *Lettres, Mémoires et Instructions*, vol. iii, pt. 2, pp. 322, 323, 330.

thorities on naval timber.[1] The oak is one of the most fastidious of trees, requiring soil of a special nature in order to flourish and produce the best timber. Subsequent experts have in large measure confirmed the advice given by the Navy Board to John Bridger in 1696, as he was setting out to inspect the timber and masts of the New England colonies:

With us in England, a strong Earth nearest a bright colour'd Clay bringeth the best Timber. Gravelly and Rocky high Grounds no more than marshy low and very wett Grounds seldom produce good Timber — the one being too cold and barren brings trees of no great Stature and most times shaken for want of Root — the other produces trees quick in Growth, free in Substance, spungy, slender and tall, and very little compass among it.[2]

Nearly every work on arboriculture confirms the fact that oak grows best in a rich loam or a clayey soil. One important result of this was that wheat and oak came into rivalry for those rich lands. A tree so discriminating in the matter of soil and climate could not be planted profitably in waste places. That contest will be seen at its height during the Napoleonic wars, when the need of wheat was as vital to England as the need of oak, and the agriculturists protested against the "maritime mortmain" of the oak groves.

About a century ago it was pointed out that there were two types of *Quercus robur* in England and on the Continent: the *pedunculata*, with long acorn stems and short leaves, and the *sessiliflora*, with short stems and long leaves. A writer in the *Quarterly Review* claimed that the rapid decay of some English oak in the ships of war was due to the ignorance of the purveyors in failing to distinguish between the two. The article, which created quite a stir in naval circles, described the sessile or durmast variety as an "impostor" from Germany injuring the good name of English oak. Subsequent experiments in the Navy, however, showed that, if grown on the same ground, there was little difference in the quality of the timber, but that the durmast was less particular in its choice of soils and spread to localities which naturally produced inferior trees.[3] This difference has not

---

[1] Garraud, *Études*, p. 24.
[2] Admiralty Library, Corbett MSS, Digest, *Naval Stores*, p. 85.
[3] *Quarterly Review*, xxxix, 22; *Parl. Papers*, 1849 (o.30), xx, 117; cf. Evelyn, *Sylva*, i, 76.

been regarded as important, and the term "English oak" will cover both varieties.

The distinctive characteristic of the oak of England was its unusual individuality in the matter of shape. Oaks on the Continent could be found growing by the thousands in extensive forests, with almost uniformly straight, slender trunks practically free from branches. The English oaks, on the other hand, often assumed a great variety of forms, especially the rugged oaks growing in hedgerows, which had ample room to develop the branches essential for compass timber. It was believed that English oaks acquired a toughness from constant buffeting with the winds, which gave them strange shapes while it strengthened their timber.[1] Liable as it was to many defects in growth, the English oak produced timber admirably adapted for naval purposes. Its chief drawback was the slowness of growth, which required a century of foresight in matters of forest policy; but that very slowness of growth is very often an element of strength in timber.

The exalted position of English oak cannot be realized by a prosaic investigation of its technical timber qualities alone. Affection for their oak and an unswerving faith in its "preheminence as most meet for building and the navie" was part of the creed of nearly every Englishman. Admiral Stirling's declaration in 1827, that "the British Oak, however great its name, is not the best timber in the world," would have been considered little short of heresy a century earlier.[2] There was a quality peculiarly English in this "unwedgeable and gnarled oak," with its massive solidity, its defiant individuality in appearance, and its suggestion of enduring power — a tree rugged rather than graceful, and exceedingly dependable. As one of the essential elements of sea power, it received an added claim to patriotic admiration. Thousands of verses, good and bad, have extolled the "heart of oak" and its place in the "wooden walls." Prose, too, has rendered tribute since the time of Holinshed. Introductory to a logical explanation of why the oak of England, growing in isolation and exposed to the elements, was superior to other oaks, Charnock wrote in 1804:

[1] Charnock, *History of Marine Architecture*, iii, 172.
[2] Stirling, *Letters on Professional Topics*, p. 88.

It is a striking, but well-known fact, that oak the growth of other countries, though lying under precisely the same latitude with Britain, has been invariably found less serviceable in a degree almost incredible, than that of the latter, as though Nature itself, if it were possible to indulge so romantic an idea, had forbad that the national character of a British ship should be suffered to undergo a species of degradation by being built of materials which were [not] indigenous to it.[1]

More than by the works of poet or author, the loyalty of the English to their oak was shown by the universal use of it in their dockyards when price and supply would permit; and most of the great achievements of the English at sea took place in ships of the oak of Sussex and the neighboring timber counties. During a large part of the sailing-ship era, the average ship of the line contained some 3200 loads of English oak, with a little oak planking from the Baltic, some elm or beech below the waterline, and a little fir timber where less strength was required. These other timbers amounted ordinarily to scarcely 400 loads, and would have probably been dispensed with entirely if the supply of native oak had been sufficient. With the nineteenth century, the more broadminded Englishmen recognized certain tropical timbers as equal, if not superior, to the English oak, and one derided it as "a local idea, a Cockney idea," to "suppose that no other wood is equal to English wood." [2] Yet as late as the middle of the century there was more than one loyal "die-hard" who would declare that, "if we could get English oak I believe that it would be used in preference to anything else." [3]

This affection of the English for their oak, backed by the natural high quality of the timber, has an important bearing on the problem, for it delayed the use of foreign woods and hastened the depletion of England's forests. If these forests had been able to furnish an adequate supply, it is highly improbable that any other timber would ever have been considered for the hulls of the King's ships. As it was, the diminishing capacity of the native woodlands, by increasing the price and even cutting off the supply of their favorite timber, forced the English into a reluctant use of foreign woods.

---

[1] Charnock, *op. cit.*, iii, 171.
[2] *Parl. Papers*, 1847–88 (51), vol. xx, pt. 2, p. 666.
[3] *Ibid.* (o.48), vol. xxi, pt. 1, p. 346.

The first obvious substitute for English oak was the same *Quercus robur* of northern and central Europe, arriving by various rivers from the Rhine to the Düna at ports of the North Sea and Baltic.[1] Charnock has explained, in a passage already referred to, why the oaks grown in great, sombre forests, protected from the elements, are of a speedier, straighter, and weaker growth than the tough, gnarled oak of England.[2] The continental oak, therefore, produced less compass timber, and even if it had grown more crooked, compass timber occupied so much space in a vessel's hold that it was very expensive to import. Consequently, the Baltic forests did little to relieve the serious shortage of crooked timbers, and their oak was not usually considered strong enough for great timbers. The straight-grained, porous, brownish Baltic oak was used in the Royal Navy chiefly for planking, for which its pliability and its superior length and breadth made it valuable. The careful sorting into "crown" and "brack" grades by officials at the Baltic ports ensured its quality. It was natural that the English should turn to the Baltic when a timber substitute was required, for the timber trade was better organized in those parts than anywhere else in the world, with the consequence that business operations were simpler and the product more reliable.

Opinions on the value of Baltic oak varied widely. It was well known to English shipwrights before the Restoration when Hollond wrote: "I know the wood is poorish and 'frow' [brittle] as they phrase it, and it's probable (and I believe it) in that regard not so lasting as English oak, but I know withal, that they are generally gallant long plank." [3] The introduction of Baltic plank on a large scale was necessitated by the construction of thirty ships of the line in 1677, which found the English forests inadequate.[4] On April 17, 1686, the Navy Board held a conference with a group of shipwrights at Whitehall on the question of introducing Baltic plank into the Navy as a regular policy. Many favorable arguments, drawn from experience with merchant

[1] See Chap. IV. [2] Charnock, *op. cit.*, iii, 172.
[3] N. R. S., *Hollond's Discourses of the Navy*, p. 226.
[4] See pp. 225–229.

ships, were advanced. The Committee reported as their unanimous opinion that "large Plank, well chosen of the Forreign growth before-mentioned, is in its service at least as durable, in its cost less chargeable, and the use of it (through the scarcity of the English) become at this day indispensable."[1] An Order in Council authorized the contracting for such plank, and the naval building contracts, which had hitherto called for "good substantial English Oaken 'Timber and Plank," hereafter omitted the word "English" in regard to plank.

That meeting in Whitehall is a landmark in the history of England's timber problem. For the first time, the Navy officially recognized its dependence on foreign lands for timber in addition to masts. From that time on, nearly every English warship had part of its planking below the waterline from the Baltic.[2] While the Baltic oak was satisfactory for planking, its use for the heavy timbers of a ship was regarded less favorably. The Navy imported a large quantity of oak timber from Stettin and other Baltic ports between 1771 and 1775 because of the alarming scarcity of English oak. As will be seen, this experience confirmed the poor opinion that Englishmen already held in regard to Baltic oak, for they saw the ships in which it was used rot with alarming rapidity.[3] The fault lay more in the lack of seasoning and the mixture with English oak than in the inherent weakness of the imported timber, but the dissatisfaction was so strong, that as soon as the supply of English oak would permit, the Baltic timber was dispensed with. Meanwhile, admirals were wont to damn the German oak whenever a ship leaked.

The further experience with German oak timber from Dort and Holstein in 1802 and 1804 confirmed this unfavorable attitude, and once more "by reason of the softness of its texture" and the shaky, rotten condition of the sticks, it was regarded as an inferior substitute, to be used only in case of necessity.[4] The Eng-

---

[1] Pepys, *Memoires relating to the State of the Royal Navy of England*, pp. 35, 36, 44, 45.

[2] Derrick, *Memoirs of the Royal Navy*, p. 104; see R. O., N. B., *Contracts, passim*.

[3] See p. 161.

[4] *Parl. Paper*, s1805 (152) i, 45; R. O., Adm. Digest, 4853, *N.B. to Adm.*, Sept. 10, 1802; *Ibid.*, Sept. 30, 1802. (Letters to the Lords of Admiralty were addressed

lish view on Baltic oak, then, amounted to a consistent toleration of it for planking and an equally consistent low opinion of its value for other shipbuilding purposes. Baltic oak, the first substitute to be considered, consequently did little to relieve the most serious shortage, that of great and compass timber.

American oak met a more summary fate at the hands of the Navy Board. America had an oak undoubtedly superior to English oak in the *Quercus virens* or *Virginiana*, the live oak. This tree follows our southern coast in a strip never over twenty miles wide from Norfolk to beyond the Mississippi, with the best trees on islands off the coast of Georgia and Florida. A low, heavily branched tree of very rapid growth, it has a heavy, compact, fine-grained wood, producing splendid knees and short timbers.[1] Much of it lay in Spanish territory, but the English colonists used it for shipbuilding as early as 1750.[2] One of the early acts of the United States government was the purchase of two Georgia islands, to ensure a supply of live oak for the Navy.[3] Though it was later recognized by the English shipwrights themselves as superior to English oak, the Royal Navy, strangely enough, used very little of this timber, which was prized so highly by the Americans and was not unknown to the Navy Board.[4]

The answer seems to indicate chiefly a matter of business enterprise. To the northward grew the white oak, a tree producing timber almost equal to the English oak before those disadvantages of the transatlantic passage and the use in the repairs of old ships had detracted from its original strength. It was a tree decidedly inferior to the live oak. The New Englanders, however, had little to offer Europe except lumber and fish, and therefore aggressively forced their inferior oak on any possible purchasers, while the Southerners found other staples more agreeable

to the Secretary, — Burchett, Stephens, Nepean, Marsden, etc., — but for clearness, the recipient will be designated as "Adm.")

[1] Michaux, *North American Sylva*, i, 52–55; Sargent, *Silva of North America*, viii, 99, 100. See same works for other American timbers.

[2] Bishop, *History of Manufactures in the U. S.*, i, 85.

[3] See p. 358.

[4] R. O., N. B., In Letters, 1626; *Scott to N. B.*, Aug. 18, 1812; *Parl. Papers*, 1821 (186), vi, 17; *H. C. J.*, *1792*, p. 294.

than timber as a basis for their commerce. Consequently, England judged American oak by the cargoes from the North.

The terms of the botanist and the forester do not always coincide with those of the timber merchant, who groups under the single name "white oak" not only the *Quercus alba,* but a dozen similar oaks of varying quality. The *Quercus alba* resembles the *robur* of Europe in general, having the same pale reddish color, but it is often lighter, less compact, and more elastic. The bracketing of several different trees under the same timber name, and the further confusion with the even less valuable red oaks, allowed a wide range of opinion on the worth of American white oak.[1]

There was no wide range of opinion in the Navy Board, however. The dockyard officials inspecting a trial cargo at Deptford in 1696 reported that "the wood in general is of very tender and 'frow' substance mingled with red veins and subject to many worm holes with signs of decay."[2] The harsh, uncompromising tone of the whole report leads one to agree with Lord Bellomont, the governor of New York at that time, that "there was all the contrivance that could be by the officers of the yard . . . to disparage it and discourage any further undertaking of that kind."[3] The curse remained on American oak and the Navy Board, already prejudiced, hindered every attempt of the persistent colonists to introduce their oak into the dockyards.[4] The prejudice extended to the ships built in America for the Navy and for the English merchants, and it is worthy of note that the colonists often used white oak in most ships which they built for sale, and sent south for live oak for many of their own best vessels. The white oak of Canada was under the same stigma as that of New England; and though the acute shortage of the Napoleonic era necessitated heavy importations of it, the scorn of the Navy Board was consistent throughout. It was denounced as only

[1] Anderson, *Canada,* p. 170; Elliott, *Important Timber Trees of the U. S.,* pp. 230–232.
[2] *Cal. S. P., A. & W. I., 1696–97,* p. 10.
[3] *Ibid., 1700,* 682, 683.
[4] Adm. Lib., Corbett MSS, Digest, *Naval Stores,* f. 79; R. O., N. B. Out Letters, 2178, *N. B. to Adm.,* March 23, 1739; *Ibid.,* 2182, Sept. 19, 1746.

half as durable as English oak and inferior even to that of the Baltic.[1] Later English opinion was more tolerant.

Under their handicaps, the Baltic and American oaks could scarcely have been expected to compete with the English on its own ground, but the quality of these timbers justified a far more extensive use of them than was actually the case. The prejudice of the Navy Board prevented those forests from relieving the increasing scarcity in England and in so doing hastened the crisis which came in 1804. This prejudice of the Navy Board is less to be condemned than its inertia. In Europe and America, the best oak grew in the south, but it was the men of the north who organized a timber trade. By sending to Genoa instead of Dantzig, or to Savannah instead of Portsmouth, an ample supply of oak undoubtedly superior to the English could have been obtained.[2] That, however, meant the arduous and uncertain development of a timber trade where none existed on an efficient basis. The Navy Board followed the line of least resistance, haughtily passed judgment on the northern oaks, took a little plank from Dantzig, and continued to cut down most of the remaining trees in Sussex.

Of the four kinds of timber used in the hulls of the King's ships before 1804, oak was so predominant that the others are almost insignificant in comparison and they can be described quickly. Elm was used quite consistently in most of the ships built during the period, but the nature of the wood limited its availability to portions of the hull below the waterline, near the keel. Only the strongest oak could withstand intermittent exposure to moisture and air, but in places where air was excluded, elm could remain well preserved. The tough, cross-grained wood of the *Ulmus campestris* and the *Ulmus montana*, England's two species of elm, served in a satisfactory manner in the nethermost parts of the ship, both for planking and for large timber. The size attained by the tree allowed it to relieve the scarcity of great oak timber by use in the keel. Nearly all ships also had elm planking in the strips nearest the keel, known as the "garbord strakes," just

---

[1] R. O., N. B. Out Letters, 2231, *N. B. to John Sullivan*, Feb. 23, 1803; In Letters, *Surveyor of Navy to N. B.*, March 3, 1807; Adm. Digest 4871, *N. B. to Adm.*, July 21, 1806; *Ibid.*, 4901, March 11, 1811.

[2] See *H. C. J.*, *1792*, p. 343.

below the Baltic oak plank. Elm sometimes became even scarcer than oak. It grew in many parts of England, but it grew singly rather than in groves, and the constant naval demand tended to eliminate these lone trees. Consequently, the somewhat inferior American elm was occasionally imported to supply the deficiency.

Beech, the third of the principal timbers, was even more limited in its adaptability for naval construction. Like elm, it could be used for planking only below the waterline, but, unlike elm, it was not strong enough for use in the keel. Elm was ordinarily employed without question for the lowest planking, but beech, though it was used over a long period, was generally regarded as an inferior substitute. The most famous example of longevity among English wooden warships, the *Royal William*, had "beech" planking which remained sound for more than fifty years.[1] Throughout the eighteenth century the royal forests furnished the dockyards with a hundred or two hundred beeches annually, but very little of this timber was purchased outside that source.[2] In 1757, the dockyards received 20,000 loads of oak, 3800 loads of elm, and only 274 loads of beech, a typical proportion for the century.[3] When oak cost £4 5s. a load in 1771, elm cost £3 and beech £2 16s.[4] Later, a reaction set in against beech, and in 1812, when a merchant builder requested permission to use beech planking to complete his gun brig because elm was not available, the Navy Board forbade the use of beech, stating that "that plank has been found by experience to injure the copper fastenings."[5] Elm and beech, therefore, derived their slight importance only from the frequency of their use, rather than from the amount employed.

The last of the four principal timbers was the *Pinus sylvestris*, the Scotch pine, or, as it was more generally called, the fir. This chief timber tree of Europe was most versatile in its applicability to naval construction, for an entire ship from keel to topmasts

---

[1] *Commons Reports*, iii, 18, 19.
[2] *Cal. Treas. Papers, 1731-34*, p. 114; *H. C. J., 1792*, p. 350.
[3] R. O., N. B. Out Letters, 2191, *N. B. to Adm.*, Jan. 15, 1759.
[4] *Commons Reports*, iii, 18, 19.
[5] R. O., N. B. In Letters, 1561, *E. Larkin to N. B.*, May 31, 1812 (marginal answer).

could be built of fir. This tree will come up shortly for full consideration in connection with its very important function of furnishing masts. As a material for hulls, it was used only occasionally by the Navy in times of emergency or shortage. Fir had several advantages over oak as a ship timber. It was capable of rapid application, for it contained resin instead of sap, and required less time for seasoning. It was a softer wood, and could be more easily converted into form. Fir vessels were lighter and consequently faster. The reason for building the original fir frigates in 1757 is said to have been the desire to match the superior speed of the French frigates.[1]

These advantages were more than offset by certain defects which prevented the regular use of fir for ship timber. It was far less durable, and the general opinion was that it splintered much more freely in battle.[2] Deck "deals" of Baltic fir were used throughout the period. Fir was sometimes used for the construction of entire ships, usually frigates, and occasionally it was introduced to save oak in the case of beams and inner works, or for repairs. It was, however, an admittedly inferior substitute for English, if not for Baltic oak.[3] The first heavy importation of fir was made early in the Seven Years' War, and considerable amounts were brought from the Baltic until the American Revolution. It will be seen that 15,000 loads of Baltic fir rushed from Dantzig were of great importance in making possible the repairs necessary before Trafalgar.[4] Fir played a more interesting rôle than elm or beech, but the use of none of those three was more than incidental, compared with oak.

Masts and spars, "those Jewells that so highly concern the safety and service of the State," presented a problem entirely independent of the hull timbers just described.[5] The considera-

[1] B. M., *Add. MSS, 37275*, f. 292; *Parl. Papers* 1805 (152), p. 41; Charnock, *History of Marine Architecture*, iii, 204; Matthew, *On Naval Timber*, p. 61.

[2] Charnock, *op. cit.*, ii, 298.

[3] B. M., *Add. MSS, 37275*, f. 292.   [4] See p. 382.

[5] On masts in general, see esp. Fincham, *On Masting Ships*; Forfait, *Traité élémentaire de la Mâture*; Kipping, *Rudimentary Treatise on Masting, Mast-Making and Rigging of Ships*; [Steele], *The Art of Making Masts, Yards . . . as practised in the Royal Navy*; and works on shipbuilding.

tion of unusual size was as important in connection with masts as it was in the case of great timber. There was no counterpart of compass timber, though shape was a factor in the exact tapering proportions required of every stick. The diameter of a mast was its most important feature, and the difference of a few inches in diameter had a profound effect on the whole mast situation. There were twenty-three masts, yards, and spars in a ship, varying in size in a first rate from the mainmast, forty yards long and forty inches in diameter, and weighing over eighteen tons, to the foretopgallant yard, a slender stick seven yards long, four inches in diameter, and weighing only seventy-five pounds. All these various sticks will be included under the general heading of "masts" unless specific reference is made to a particular form. The situation in several subsequent passages will be more clearly understood if the requirements of size for various masts in various classes of ships are understood. In the lower masts, the proportion usually called for an inch of diameter to a yard of length. Bowsprits were thicker in proportion to length, and yards more slender. The dimensions at the close of the Napoleonic period for typical masts and spars in three important classes of ships, arranged in order of size were: [1]

	First Rate 120 guns		Third Rate 74 guns		Frigate 28 guns	
	Diameter Inches	Length Yards	Diameter Inches	Length Yards	Diameter Inches	Length Yards
Mainmast..............	40	40	36	36	20	24
Bowsprit..............	37	25	34	22	21	14
Foremast..............	37	37	31	33	19	22
Main yard.............	25	35	23	33	14	21
Mizzenmast............	24	27	22	25	16	18
Maintopmast..........	21	23	19	22	13	14
Maintopsail yard.......	15	25	14	23	6	9
Jib boom..............	15	17	14	16	9	11
Maintopgallant mast....	12	11	11	11	7	7

The chief difficulty lay with the fore and main masts and bowsprits of the ships of the line. As there were few virgin forests in

[1] Adapted from R. O., N. B., Misc.; and Edye, *Calculations relating to the Equipment of Ships*, pp. 36, 93, 97, 107.

the regions supplying the Baltic ports, it was difficult to find single sticks over twenty-seven inches in diameter, thick enough to serve alone for these capital ships. Consequently, as early as the *Harry Grace à Dieu*, of 1514, there were composite or "made masts," in which several trees were formed around a central spindle, or arranged in quarters to secure the required dimension. After 1652, the Navy Board began to draw on the forests of New England for great masts as large as forty yards long and forty inches in diameter, sufficient to form "single stick" masts even for a first rate. These one-piece masts of American pine were used in the Navy until after 1775, when the Revolution cut off the supply and the composite masts of Riga fir were employed again.[1]

In the largest sizes, an additional inch of diameter made a tremendous difference in price. Lower masts of the proper proportion measured a yard in length to an inch of diameter. In 1770, a single stick of 36 inches and yards cost £110; of 35, £88; of 34, £72; and of 33, only £56, while a bowsprit 38 inches in diameter but only 25 yards long cost only £48.[2] These were exorbitant prices, but the mainmast of a ship of the line came from a tree in ten thousand. The slightest defect might cause its rejection after it had been transported across the Atlantic.[3] Garraud tells of the discovery of a single tiny rotten knot which reduced the value of a great mast from 2000 to 1200 francs.[4] Contractors, therefore, often bored out the rotten knots, filling the holes with plugs. Such masts often passed the purveyors and their defects were not discovered until they treacherously snapped in a gale. A slight error in felling could render a single stick, potentially worth £100 as a mast, unfit for anything but £15 worth of timber. There was always a problem of large masts, therefore, but it was less serious than that of great timber, for there could always be recourse to "made masts."

The choice of the Navy Board in the matter of trees for masts

[1] See pp. 221, 234, 286, 288.
[2] R. O., *Adm., Acct. Gen., Accts. Misc., Var.,* 124, *Contracts,* 1770.
[3] *Cal. S. P. Dom., A. & W. I., 1701,* p. 180.
[4] Garraud, *Études sur les Bois de Construction,* p. 75.

was even more restricted than in the case of woods for the hull. Up to 1804, only three kinds of trees were used for masts in the Navy — fir, pine, and spruce. Diameter was the principal factor in determining which of those three trees should be used, but considerations of texture settled which countries should be drawn upon for trees.

This was particularly noticeable in the case of the *Pinus sylvestris* already referred to in connection with ship timber. Less fastidious than the oak as to climate and soil, the fir ranges from the barrens of Lapland to the heights of Mount Aetna. It is at its best in Northern Germany and Russia, between 53 and 65 degrees north latitude, east of the Oder, where it is the predominant tree. South of that zone it is a tree of the mountains, while its growth is slower and more stunted on nearing the Arctic Circle. An excellent variety of this tree grew in New England and Canada as the *Pinus rubia* or red pine, and was often used by the Navy for the same purposes as the Riga fir. If the fir could adapt itself to a wider range of climate and soil than the oak, the quality of the timber, nevertheless, remained largely dependent on those two factors. A fir was a fir whether it grew in Poland or in Scotland, but that did not mean that the latter was equal to the Polish for naval purposes. Neither in England nor in Scotland could the fir attain a quality equal to that of the southern Baltic shore. The even, humid climate which produced splendid oak was not suited to the *Pinus sylvestris*, which needs short, hot summers and very cold winters to form sound timber of slow growth. It was because of this that England had to look beyond the seas for masts long before the oak shortage was even noticeable. Scotch masts were used only on occasions of severe necessity, and were always regarded as inferior.

The qualities sought in a mast were cylindrical straightness, suppleness, elasticity, strength, durability, and the proper proportion of length to girth. Unlike deciduous trees, conifers secrete a resin which ensures resiliency and durability as long as it remains in the tree. In the masts from Riga, the resin remained long after cutting, while the trees of the far north secreted too little originally, and the coarse-grained firs grown to the southward lost their resinous preservative soon after felling, because of their rapid maturity. The rate of growth in Scotland was often double that of Russia. In the shipyards of France and Spain as well as of England, Riga masts were preferred above all others for their quality. The shavings could be twisted between the fingers without breaking, a sure sign of the proper resinous texture.

The chief rival of the *Pinus sylvestris* for "masting" was the *Pinus strobus*, or white pine, of North America. Its wood was soft and white, inferior in strength and durability to the fir of Riga, but against that superior quality of texture, the American pines could offer a size which made possible the use of single sticks for the masts of the largest ships, with the added advantage that they were lighter in weight by one fourth. There was a time when European forests had been able to produce fir masts over fifty inches in diameter,[1] but a timber trade of long standing seldom permitted the firs to approach the size of the great pines which the colonists found in the virgin forests of America. Sticks of the maximum sizes were shipped almost annually from Portsmouth, Falmouth, and, later, New Brunswick. The New Englanders did not have to force their masts on England as they did the oak — the Navy and the merchants were eager to get them, and after 1652, there was a regular supply, for both naval and general purposes. The tree was sometimes known as the Weymouth pine, from the efforts of Lord Weymouth to relieve the need of an overseas supply by planting it in England in 1705. The attempt failed because of the English climate.

The third mast tree in use before 1804 was the spruce. The *Abies excelsa* in Europe and the *Abies nigra* in America furnished good topmasts and spars. The older trees lost their youthful toughness, and were so coarse grained in comparison to the firs that spruce was disqualified for use as great masts. The little spruce sticks came chiefly from Norway throughout the two centuries, but there was opposition to the great masts of Norway at an early date. Milton, to be sure, in describing Satan's spear, compared it with

[1] *L. & P., Henry VIII*, vol. xxi, pt. 1 (1546), p. 606.

> . . . the tallest pine
> Hewn on Norwegian hills to be the mast
> Of some great ammiral, —

but the English Navy was not using many such pines for its flagships even at that time. "Of all masts, these being Norway masts, are the worst," reported an irate dockyard official in 1637.[1]

The conventional woods for masts, then, were American pine for lower masts and bowsprits of ships of the line, over twenty-seven inches in diameter; Riga fir for "middling" masts, between fifteen and twenty-seven inches; and Norway spruce for "spars" — the smaller topmasts and yards.

That restricted list of oak, elm, beech, fir, pine, and spruce for hulls and masts of warships was insufficient to meet the growing needs of the Navy. By the close of the eighteenth century it became evident that substitutes were necessary, particularly for the various forms of oak, which, as we have seen, caught the brunt of the naval demands.

On the eve of the long wars with Revolutionary France, the Commissioners of the Land Revenue faced the fact that the supply of English oak was rapidly approaching exhaustion and that none of the other trees common in England were adequate substitutes. In their great investigation of 1792, the most comprehensive official study of this subject, they sought the most eligible tree which would grow in England to produce an adequate supply of ship timber as soon as possible. Their choice fell on the larch, or *Larix*. Originally an Alpine tree, it was first introduced into Britain as a hothouse plant; but its practical value was shown in the large plantations made by the Duke of Athol at Dunkeld and Blair. While an oak requires nearly a hundred and twenty-five years to reach maturity, and the fir nearly a hundred, the larch attains its full growth in fifty or sixty years. In spite of its rapid growth, the timber is durable, tough, strong, and comparatively light. It could resist the attack of the worm, would not corrode iron, and, unlike the oak, would thrive in the poorest soils.[2]

[1] *Cal. S. P., Dom., 1637*, p. 296; see *Ibid., 1581–90*, p. 701.
[2] *H. C. J., 1792*, pp. 280, 281, 313, 314.

It was the best conifer that could be grown in England or in all Britain, and since the demands of the Navy could not await the slow growth of the oak, it was obviously the tree for the occasion. "We do not mean to recommend that the larch timber should be used in building ships of war in this country while oak can be had," declared the commissioners, who went on to say that "larch is the best substitute for oak we have heard of," equal perhaps to any oak in northern Europe.[1] Larches by the million were planted partly as a result of this report, and in 1820 a very satisfactory frigate, aptly named the *Athol*, was built entirely of larch. The value of the timber justified the expectations of 1792. The Navy also experimented between 1789 and 1805 with ash, chestnut, and "abele" or poplar, in the construction of frigates, but they were found to be unfit for the purpose.[2]

Throughout the first century and a half of the timber problem, the choice of woods, as has been indicated, was comparatively simple. Limited by commercial conditions and their own inertia, the Navy Board had passed judgment on the oaks, firs, and pines of England, Europe, and America, grudgingly admitting only a few of them into the construction of the King's ships. After 1804, however, the timber problem changed, broadening its scope to include dozens of timbers coming from every continent. The dwindling supply of English oak was threatened by a "Timber Trust." Attempts to secure timber from a dozen European countries were thwarted by the advance of Napoleon's armies and diplomacy. The supply from the United States was uncertain because of Jefferson's peaceful coercion policy and impending war. Canada remained the only reliable source, and Canadian oak was unsatisfactory. Many of the traditional sources of ship timber, therefore, were no longer adequate.[3]

All these circumstances made it absolutely necessary to enlarge the field of activity to meet the unusually heavy shipbuilding program. Admirals and captains on every station, diplomats and consuls at every post, were urged to coöperate in relieving the

[1] *H. C. J.*, *1792*, p. 281.

[2] *Ibid.*, pp. 312, 313, 366; R. O., N. B. In Letters, 1559, *Larking to N. B.*, June 4, Oct. 10, 1795; 1560, March 31, 1805.

[3] See Chaps. VIII, IX.

situation. Samples of timber by the dozen were submitted, and glowing accounts of forests growing to the water's edge, sufficient to supply the dockyards to the end of time, came in from every quarter. Forced out of its old prejudices and apathy by the exigencies of the time, the Navy experimented with these woods, some of which were to cost the oak of England its long supremacy. During the remaining half century of the sailing-ship era many of these exotic timbers were used constantly to piece out the avowedly inadequate supply of native timber.

Of all these new timbers, the one most extensively used during the Napoleonic period was the longleaf pine from the southern coasts of the United States. The Navy Board had consistently neglected the excellent timber possibilities of that region, not only in the case of longleaf pine and the live oak already mentioned, but it had also failed to utilize the equally valuable cypress for masts and red cedar for hulls, though the Americans used them in the construction of their own best ships. The attention of the Navy had been attracted to all those timbers, but, as was said, the inhabitants took little initiative in developing a timber trade.[1]

In 1804, the Navy Board awoke to the value of the longleaf pine. The *Pinus palustris*, or *australis*, has some twenty-eight names as a tree and as a timber. "Pitch pine," "Georgia pine," "yellow pine," and "southern pine" are among the commonest of them, but botanists and foresters prefer to call it the "longleaf pine." The timber term "pitch pine," by which the English knew it, is liable to confusion with the inferior "shortleaf pine." It grew in a strip along the southern coast of the United States, similar to the range of the live oak but about a hundred miles deep. It produced timber of moderate size, tough, straight-grained, resinous, and durable, suitable both for masts and for ship timber. It differed considerably from the conventional fir and pine already described. It was highly prized by the colonial shipbuilders, but did not arouse the interest of the Navy Board until 1804.

[1] Magdalene College, Cambridge, *Pepysian MSS*, iii, 1674; Adm. Lib. MSS Digest, *Naval Stores*, p. 86; R. O. Adm., In Letters from Governors, 3820, *Wentworth to Adm.*, Nov. 11, 1772.

During the following decade it was imported in large quantities when political conditions would permit. Several ships later sent against the Americans were built of this American timber.[1] Among new trees drawn from Europe were the Italian and Adriatic oak and the Polish larch.

The other timbers introduced after 1804 to relieve the dock-yard shortage had many qualities in common.[2] Nearly all of them were tropical, and lacked the tannic acid of the oak which was so destructive to iron. For the most part, they were hard, strong, and durable, and were much less subject to dry rot than the northern timbers previously used. There were drawbacks, however. Most of the trees were liable to "shakes," those longi-tudinal cracks imperceptible in standing timber. Moreover, in contrast to the Baltic, with its highly organized timber trade, the remote regions presented innumerable difficulties in felling, conversion, and transportation of timber. Freight from India was £6 a ton when it was £1 6s. from America. The freight from Sierra Leone was not prohibitive, but the freight from Australia and New Zealand was so high, unless transports returning empty to England could be used, that not much timber was imported from the South Seas.

Of all these timbers, by far the most important was the *Tectona grandis*, the teak of India. This deciduous tree resem-bled the oak in size, shape, weight, texture, and rate of growth. In place of the tannic acid which corroded iron, the teak con-tained a preservative oil, so that the Indian shipwrights could use iron spikes instead of treenails. Ships built of teak were famous for their durability and safety. The old convict ship, *Success*, built at Moulmein in 1790, crossed the Atlantic under her own sail a few years ago, and is still afloat. These teak ships could stand the cruising on a southern station, which was so destructive to ships of oak. Such a timber threatened to shift British shipbuilding to Bombay, according to the alarmed Thames shipbuilders, who opposed the admission of Indian ships to Brit-

---

[1] R. O., N. B., In Letters, 1560, *N. B. to Adm.*, Dec. 19, 1809; see Chap. X.

[2] For detailed descriptions of the individual timbers, with special reference to their use for naval purposes, see Laslett, *op. cit.*, and Garraud, *op. cit.*, *passim*.

ish registry.[1] Almost the only argument which they could bring against the teak ships was that the weight of the wood made them slow, and even this was refuted. The tree was distributed widely throughout India, and, like most trees, the quality varied with the region. The teak of Moulmein in Burma was generally considered the most valuable. Teak was used extensively by the Navy. Some teak was imported in timber form, and many warships were built of this timber in India.[2] It has since come to be recognized as the most valuable of all timbers for ship building.

A similar tree was the *Oldfieldia africana* of Sierra Leone, known as African teak or African oak. First introduced in 1812, it had an advantage over the other tropical timbers in its comparative nearness to England, so that much use was made of it for plank. The attempt to secure stinkwood from the Cape of Good Hope in 1812 failed partly because of the "shaky" nature of the wood. The masts of "yellow wood" from the same source likewise received adverse criticism from naval officers.

More satisfactory mast material was found in the poon of India and the kauri of New Zealand, which were stronger than the pine or fir in common use, but the distance was great for transporting masts and there was more urgent need of timber than of masts. The morung saul of India, somewhat inferior to teak, was imported occasionally, as was the Australian jarrah.

The regions around the Caribbean offered many valuable timbers which were utilized by the Spanish marine far more than by the English. These "*maderas incomparables, precios . . . tambien incomparables*" had given the Spanish warships built at Havana twice the durability of ships built in Europe.[3] Raleigh had repaired his ships with mahogany on one of his early voyages, and the durability of the old mahogany-built *Gibraltar* captured from the Spaniards was tangible proof of its value. Good mahogany was too expensive for general naval use, and some types of Honduras mahogany were so porous as to be worthless. There

---

[1] *Parl. Papers*, 1813–14 (115), vol. vii, pt. i, *Report of Committee on East India Ships*, esp. pp. 9, 10, 597–599.

[2] See pp. 365–368.   [3] Artiñano, *Arquitectura Naval Española (En Madera)*, p. 78.

were frequent naval contracts for mahogany during the Napoleonic era. The sabicu of Cuba, morra of Trinidad, and greenheart of Guiana were all hard, heavy valuable timbers of the tropical type, and were also imported during this period, together with certain similar woods of Brazil.

The cosmopolitan origin of a ship's timbers by the end of the Napoleonic period can be imagined. In contrast to the limited range prior to 1804, consisting of oak, elm, beech, and fir for the ship's hull, stands the list of about seventy-five woods allowed for shipbuilding to-day, by *Lloyd's Register*. It is perhaps the most adequate commentary on the hidebound opinions of the Navy Board with its predilection for English oak. The list is detailed for each part of the hull, and indicates the number of years for which a ship built of each timber may retain the highest rating. It is interesting not only for the final estimate on the trees that were known to the Navy Board at the time, but also for the strange names, which indicate how widespread has been the quest for ship timber.

According to Lloyd's ratings, East India teak stands at the head, at sixteen years. This is a long lead over the second group, rated at twelve years, consisting of English, African, Adriatic, Italian, Spanish, Portuguese, French, and live oaks, morung saul, greenheart, morra, iron bark, and white bark. Just below these, rated at ten years, are Cuba sabicu, pencil cedar, angelly, vanatica, jarrah, karri, blue gum, red gum, box, thingam, pubutukawa, molave, dungon, yacal, mangachapuy, betis, ipil, guijo, narra, batitinan, and palomaria de la playa.

All these timbers can be used in any part of the ship's hull. The inferior woods can be used only in certain specified parts or with different relative ratings. In Lloyd's fourth group are second-hand timbers of the first two groups. In the fifth group, with an average of about seven years, are stringy bark, red cedar, banaba, and Philippine Island cedar; and next to them, continental white oak (the Baltic oak of this study), mahogany of hard texture, Spanish chestnut, flooded gum, spotted gum, grey gum, turpentine, black butt, tulip wood, tallowwood, and mulberry. North American white oak stands alone, rated one year below the Baltic oak and four years below the English. In that particular case, the opinion of the Navy Board is confirmed.

The lower orders in Lloyd's list are filled chiefly with conifers, the leaders being pitch pine, Oregon pine, Huron pine, cowdie or kauri pine, larch (hackmatack or tamarack), and juniper. Below these in descending order by small groups come Dantzig, Memel, Riga, and American red pine (fir); English ash; foreign ash and rock maple; American rock elm and hickory; European and American grey elm; black birch and walnut; spruce, Swedish and Norwegian red pine, and Scotch fir; beech; and, at the foot of the list, with only four or five years allowance and a limited applicability, yellow or white pine, so excellent for great masts, but too soft for the body of the ship.[1]

The list of the Bureau Veritas, the international marine register, is very similar, though English oak is rated relatively still lower in the scale.[2] There may still be an element of prejudice in these lists but they are radically inclusive compared with the Navy Board opinions of the eighteenth century, and it is not difficult to realize that those opinions of the Navy Board had a decided effect on the problem of securing ship timber.

Each nation had its favorite timbers. Those of the French closely resembled the English. The Americans, with great forests at their disposal, gave the *Constitution* a keel of white oak from New Jersey, timbers of live oak and red cedar from Georgia, and masts of white pine from Maine. At times a ship of the line might contain timbers from all six continents; but whatever the botanists, foresters, and Lloyd's may say, oak will always be remembered as the great ship timber.

[1] Lloyd's Register of Shipping, *Rules and Regulations for the Construction and Classification of Wood Vessels, 1920*, Table A.

[2] Bureau Veritas, *Rules and Regulations for the Building and Classification of Wooden Vessels*, 1911.

CHAPTER II

CONTRACTS, CONSERVATISM, AND CORRUPTION

CONSERVATISM and corruption marked the system by which the Navy received and used its timber. Those qualities were in large measure responsible for the perversion of the well-devised contract system, which should have kept the Navy constantly supplied with plenty of good timber. They also hampered the efficient utilization of that timber in the building of the King's ships. This description of the workings of the civil branch of the Royal Navy must include more than a study of those two characteristics, but they were the outstanding features of that business which was conducted in a manner so unbusinesslike.

Practically all of the timber was procured by contract — the method still used by most governments in obtaining much of their materials. The Navy Board prepared each year estimates of the amount of timber and masts necessary to keep the dockyard stores at the proper level. These were included as a separate item in the general naval estimates, which were voted by Parliament after sometimes being revised. The Navy Board then publicly advertised for bids upon the different items of English oak in its various forms, and for the foreign supplies of timber, plank, and masts. Contracts, of course, were to be awarded to the lowest bidder who could meet the requirements in a satisfactory manner.

The contracts were drawn up on printed forms, with terms which should have effectively guaranteed the quality, quantity, and punctuality of the deliveries. Detailed specifications were made in regard to quality, and the right to reject any or all of the timber submitted was intended to act as a powerful check upon the contractor. The Navy demanded the best, and paid accordingly. An effort was made to secure a proper proportion of the different forms of timber and masts, lest the dockyards should become glutted with the easily obtainable pieces while their work was held up for want of those more difficult to secure. In the case of English oak, for example, it was usually specified that in every thousand loads of straight timber of ordinary size, there should be a certain amount of particular pieces of great and compass timber.

The term of the contract was ordinarily one year, but this was often extended to three or more, especially in situations where it was necessary to invest considerable capital in developing a new region. The contract insisted that deliveries be made by a certain date each year, indicating the distribution among the different dockyards. Rigid penalties were inflicted for delay or non-delivery, exceptions being made in the case of the usual acts of God, foreign princes, and other influences beyond the control of the contractor. War prices were on a higher scale than those in times of peace, and the government usually agreed to furnish armed convoys.[1]

Upon arrival at the dockyard the quality and quantity of the timber were to be subjected to a rigid inspection in the presence of the civil officials of the yard. The English oak would have already undergone a preliminary examination by the royal purveyor on the spot where it grew. This official numbered each log after stamping the broad arrow on the butt. These numbers were to be checked off at the dockyard inspection. If the deliveries were of satisfactory quality and tallied with the amount due, the contractor was given a certificate to that effect. He then received a Navy "imprest" bill, which he could discount at a rate that depended upon the current credit of the Navy treasury.

There were few exceptions to the contract system. Occasionally an agent was sent to Riga to secure an immediate consignment of masts in case of emergency or to prevent their falling into the hands of enemies. The Navy was bound to accept all material so secured, whatever its quality, and the agent received a commission of about five per cent on the purchase price, without risking any of his own capital. In the days of the Stuarts, timber was sometimes commandeered and purchased at the King's

<hr/>

[1] See typical contract, *H. C. J.*, *1792*, pp. 347–349.

price without the formality of contract. At times, royal purveyors and shipwrights cruised the country bargaining for individual lots of timber, and individuals might tender private lots
to the Navy Board. Trees from the royal forests were at times
secured through the regular contract method, but more often
the dealings were with the Treasury, which supervised the forests, and contracts were merely for the transportation. All these
cases were exceptional, however, and probably nine logs out of
ten that reached the dockyards during the sailing-ship era after
1700 were secured by contract.[1]

Theoretically, the contract system was ideal from the standpoint of the Navy. It provided for the proper amount of the
proper kind of timber, delivered at the proper time, and the
whole responsibility lay with the contractor. The public adver-
tising of bids should have guaranteed the low prices secured by
competition. If the system had worked properly at every stage
of the process just described, the timber problem would have
troubled the Navy but little. It failed to function perfectly for
four principal reasons. These perversions of the system, which
will be considered in order, were: first, an indolent, ignorant, or
injudicious management of the timber policy; second, the venal-
ity of the civil branch of the Navy; third, the growth of a contract monopoly; and, finally, the unstable credit of the Navy.
These four shortcomings were the chief causes of timber crises,
for it was largely through a miscarriage of the regular contract
system that danger arose from the depletion of the English woodlands or from the precarious nature of Baltic commerce.

The formulation of a timber policy, and, in fact, the supervision of the entire timber supply, rested with a group, from six
to ten in number, known as the Commissioners of the Navy, the
Principal Officers of the Navy, or, more commonly, the Navy
Board.[2] In their daily meetings at the Navy Office at Crutched

---

[1] *Oeconomy of the Navy Office, passim; Parl. Papers,* 1806 (1), v. 4, *12th Report of
the Commissioners of Naval Inquiry, on Timber Contracts.*

[2] For a general description of the Navy Board and the civil administration, see
Oeconomy of the Navy Office; Hamilton, *Naval Administration;* Duckett, *Naval
Commissioners;* Dupin, *Voyages dans la Grande Bretagne,* pt. 3, *passim;* and N. R. S.,
Barham Papers, ii, 207–208, 235–250, 300–304, 337–345.

Friars on Seething Lane, or later at Somerset House, this permanent civil board framed policies, discussed contracts, read and answered communications from their fellow commissioners stationed at each dockyard, and conducted most of the civil routine of the Navy not delegated to the subordinate boards of victualling, ordnance, and transport. Their most important charge was the building, repair, and care of the ships, and it was in this connection that the timber problem came within their province.

Being Englishmen, in official position, and quite permanent position at that, the Commissioners of the Navy were by nature conservative. Those who came from the sea service were ordinarily among the less ambitious of the captains. They lost caste among the officers of the line by abandoning the faint prospect of an admiral's flag in some distant future, in order to secure a life position at the same salary which a rear-admiral received. To the civil commissioners, on the other hand, admission to the Navy Board meant promotion. Their background, however, was scarcely one which promised a radical point of view, for they usually came to the board after rising in the dockyard hierarchy to the rank of master shipwright or resident commissioner, after twenty or thirty years of building ships — building them in the days of Napoleon in the same time-honored fashion which the Petts had developed under the Stuart kings. Such a group was usually endowed with much practical sense and a wealth of experience, but with them, new ideas generally fell on stony ground.

At the head of the board was the Comptroller of the Navy, who had more influence on the problem of timber supply than any other official. Under an energetic comptroller, the board generally reflected the opinions of their chief in matters of policy. Such men were Sir Charles Middleton, later Lord Barham, who became comptroller in 1778, and Sir Andrew Snape Hamond, who held office during most of the struggle with Revolutionary and Napoleonic France. In cases where the comptroller was a weakling like "that doating fool," Sir John Mennes, for whom Pepys expresses such contempt, other members exercised the control.

The Navy Board had complete responsibility in its field, but its authority was less complete than its responsibility. All transactions at the Navy Office had to be submitted in almost daily reports to Whitehall, where they were reviewed by the Lords of the Admiralty, who were charged with complete control of naval interests afloat and ashore. During a few short periods, there was a single Lord High Admiral instead of the commission which usually exercised the functions of that office. The Navy Board was not a body that inspired respect. "One can call the Navy Commissioners rogues and it will cost him only £10," it was once declared;[1] but the Lords of Admiralty, with their First Lord some eminent admiral or statesman sitting on the Treasury Bench, enjoyed far more prestige. This is reflected in the correspondence between the two boards, for the letters from Whitehall occasionally contained terms verging on insult in their reversal or modification of policies advanced by the Navy Board.

There were a number of conflicts of this nature over the timber policy. The lower board was in each case overruled, but in nearly every instance, there was a reversion to the *status quo ante* when a cabinet change brought in a new Admiralty Board. The most important disagreements in connection with the timber problem were occasioned by the Navy Board's objection to building warships in New England in 1747, by the institution of a stricter dockyard inspection of timber in 1801, and by Lord St. Vincent's cancelling of the timber contracts in 1802.[2] In such disputes the Admiralty view was often less conservative; but it was apt to be less practical, and at times the Navy Board was left to struggle with the workings of an impracticable policy of which they heartily disapproved.

The chief consideration in a timber policy was the "establishment" or quantity to be maintained in reserve at the dockyards. The value of an adequate reserve was generally recognized and generally neglected. The most fitting inscription for the door of the Navy Office would have been those remorseful words of Ovid: "*Video meliora proboque sed peiora sequor.*" The hand-to-mouth supply that was maintained throughout a large part of

[1] *Cal. S. P., Dom., 1663–64*, p. 176.   [2] See pp. 245, 319–324.

the two centuries was not only uneconomical — it was positively dangerous. Oak timber required nearly three years to season properly, but very little could be spared from the meager stocks to undergo such protracted drying. Naturally, the durability of ships was cut in half by the speedy decay of green timbers, and the timber demand was doubled in consequence. An added needless charge came in times of emergency at the outbreak of a war, when it was necessary to replenish the stocks at the cruel prices of contractors who seldom failed to profit by the situation.

Any organization conducted on business principles would have maintained an adequate reserve as a matter of economy; but the Navy Board was faced by an even more urgent reason. The outbreak of a war might cripple or even cut off completely the supply of masts, yards, plank, and naval stores which came from beyond the seas, and a crushing defeat at sea might leave the nation without means of replenishing the stores necessary to fit a fleet to regain the lost control. The Navy suffered from this situation on several occasions, especially when the Dutch and Danes seized the Eastland ships in 1652, and when the American mast supply was cut off in 1775 and not replenished before war broke out with France three years later.

A three years' establishment was the ideal that the Navy attempted to maintain at spasmodic intervals. Colbert had ordered that the French yards keep a ten years' supply of masts on hand, and enough timber in each yard to construct thirty or forty ships; [1] but the English Navy would have been well off if it could have maintained a sufficient reserve for three or four years. The task would not have been difficult, for once the extra effort was made to bring the stores up to the reserve level, the regular annual supply which was essential under any circumstances, would have been enough to keep it there.

During the seventeenth century, money was so scarce for regular naval expenditures that it was almost out of the question to find a year in which the extra amount could have been pur-

---

[1] Colbert, *Lettres, Instructions et Mémoires*, vol. 3, pt. 1, pp. 122, 128, 129; pt. 2, pp. 713, 715; see N. R. S., *Hollond's Discourses of the Navy*, pp. 207, 208.

chased, great as the economy would have been in the end. That excuse had less validity after the accession of George I, yet the dockyard surveys at the end of each year indicated barely enough material on hand to carry the Navy through the ensuing twelve months. Those annual reports in themselves give little indication of the amount expended during the year, but they at least show a consistently inadequate establishment.

The Seven Years' War depleted the timber supply to such a serious extent that the Admiralty was finally moved in 1771 to order that thereafter a three years' supply was to be maintained at all times. The average annual consumption of the preceding twenty years was shown to be 22,000 loads of oak timber, and an establishment of 66,000 loads was set as the conventional amount to be kept in reserve.[1] There was considerable difficulty in putting this wise order into effect, for it was issued at a time when oak was unusually scarce. In only three out of the following thirty years did the stock on hand reach the prescribed level of 66,000 loads, and in the meantime, the annual consumption had increased to nearly 30,000 loads.[2] The amount of oak used in the private shipyards for naval construction raised the annual total to 50,000 loads.[3] There was a three years' mast supply on hand when the New England supply was cut off in 1775, but no attempt was made to develop a substitute supply by 1778, when the entrance of France into the conflict found the reserve almost completely exhausted. The very grave results of this failure to maintain a proper reserve will furnish material for a later chapter.

During the decade which separated the wars with Revolutionary America and Revolutionary France, Sir Charles Middleton exerted himself to bring the timber and mast reserve up to the proper level. He never tired of boasting that he had found the dockyard stores worth scarcely £500,000 when he came into office in 1778 and left them worth over two millions in 1790. He outlined all the needs of a proper establishment and put his views into effect. The timber reserve rose to 88,000 loads, and

---

[1] R. O., Adm. Digest 4807, *Adm. to N. B.*, Sept. 2, 1773; *Adm. Acct. Gen., Accts, Misc., Var.*, 124, 1770.
[2] B. M., *Add. MSS*, 37275, f. 288.
[3] *H. C. J.*, 1788-89, p. 571; 1792, p. 273.

there were masts enough for several years' consumption. Middleton incurred the hostility of Lord Howe, then First Lord of the Admiralty, on grounds of extravagance, and withdrew from office. There was practically no timber problem during the fighting from 1793 to 1802, and the ample reserves which Middleton had collected during the years of peace well justified the value of an adequate establishment.[1]

A blunder in the policy of the timber reserve was largely responsible for the crisis during the two years preceding Trafalgar in 1805. Lord St. Vincent probably believed that the Peace of Amiens would amount to more than a temporary truce, and in the interests of economy had ordered the cancellation of most of the timber contracts, in spite of the protests of the Navy Board. The renewal of war with Napoleon in 1803 found the dockyard stores nearly empty, and insufficient to meet the demands for repairing the fleet, to say nothing of building new ships. Nelson and the other admirals were forced to keep the sea with crazy ships, nearly wracked out of shape for want of repairs, and it was only by extraordinary efforts that sufficient timber was finally secured to fit enough ships for sea to secure the victory at Trafalgar.[2]

To these definite crises, attributable to a faulty timber policy, can be added the inroads of dry rot, which raised havoc with the durability of English warships throughout the period — another direct consequence of the failure to maintain the piles of timber and plank at their proper level. The excuse of penury cannot justify this error to any extent — negligence and stupidity were the direct causes.

Aside from the amount of timber to be maintained on hand, the timber policy of the Navy Board also involved the question where such timber was to be obtained. Mention has already been made of the error of the board in following the line of least resistance, and through their innate conservatism, drawing upon the conventional sources of timber supply instead of utilizing the

[1] N. R. S., *Barham Papers*, ii, 186–189, 194–205, 293, 294; iii, 19, 20, 112, 113. N. R. S., *Journals and Letters of Sir T. Byam Martin*, iii, 379–384.

[2] See Chaps. VIII, X.

many alternative forests which were quite available with a little extra effort.[1] More will be said on that subject, for it played its part in bringing on the crises.[2]

Credit for the most rational and practical conception of a naval timber policy must go to a French statesman rather than to any English naval official. Colbert, the great minister of marine of Louis XIV, declared that France would perish for want of timber, and evolved an elaborate system to postpone that day. His policy was rewarded with success during his lifetime.[3] The nearest approach to Colbert's sound and comprehensive policy in England was that of Middleton, and, as has just been mentioned, the excellent general condition of the Royal Navy during the war with Revolutionary France proved its worth. On the whole, however, the usual practice fell wofully below the standard of those excellent programs. "The real timber problem of the Royal Navy was the trouble with the wooden heads which guided its policies," remarked a British naval official, "and England didn't have to import *that* kind of timber!" he added.

Indolence and ignorance are by no means creditable qualities, but they are at least more honorable shortcomings than the second charge to be brought against the civil service of the Navy for its failure in the timber problem. Among the officers at sea, a generally high code of honor prevailed, but ashore, corruption often permeated the entire service, from the treasurers of the Navy, who held large sums of the Navy funds for years on interest to their own profit, down to the dockyard workmen, who sawed up good timber into three-foot lengths to be carried away as their perquisite of "chips." An example of this "graft" can be found in the dealings of Hawkins under Elizabeth, and it continued, practically unabated, for two centuries.

An attempt was made to excuse these transactions. Government funds were generally considered "fair game" in that day — the Navy was not alone in feeling free to plunder the public treasury. Men who were comparatively honest in their private dealings had a different standard of financial morality in their

---

[1] See pp. 20, 25, 33.   [2] See pp. 75, 115, 243–245.
[3] Colbert, *Lettres, Instructions et Mémoires*, vol. iii, pt. 2, pp. 711–718, and *passim*.

official capacity. The English Navy had no counterpart of the bitter feud between the *Plume* and the *Épée* in the French marine, but there was a distinct difference in spirit between the civil and the fighting branches. The officers at sea had an opportunity for recompense in prize money and in lasting glory. The business men of the Navy, who sometimes deserved equal credit for the success of an action through their efforts in furnishing the fighters with weapons, took their rewards in a form more sordid but more immediately negotiable than glory. There is a revealing passage on this point in the diary of Samuel Pepys, where he quotes the remarks of his cousin, the first Earl of Sandwich, who had just secured for him the position of Clerk of the Acts or Secretary of the Navy Board:

> This morning My Lord . . . carried me by coach to Mr. Crew's (in the way talking how good he did hope my place would be to me, and in general speaking that it was not the salary of any place that did make a man rich, but the opportunity of getting money while he is in the place).[1]

At the risk of maligning many conscientious officials who doubtless served the King with an eye single to the Navy's good and lived on their salaries alone, those words can be said to sum up the spirit of the civil service in the old Navy.

Corruption affected the timber problem through the perversion of the contract system. It defeated the provision for fair open competition, where contracts would go to the lowest bidder, and it paralyzed the dockyard inspection, which should have ensured the quality and quantity of the timber delivered. In a less direct fashion it gave the contractors a decided advantage over the board which should have controlled and checked them. Partly because of this influence, the Navy Board was reluctant to shift to new sources of supply of which the contractors disapproved. The opening up of a new region usually meant the receipt of timber on a commission basis, in which there was no profit for the board. The Navy Board finally became tools of the timber magnates to such an extent that the commissioners defended the corrupt practices of the contractors against Admiralty investigation.

[1] Pepys, *Diary*, Aug. 16, 1660.

Charges of corruption are hard to substantiate, particularly when most of the records come from the men under suspicion. The Navy Board was in a particularly sheltered position, escaping the muck-raking which disclosed corruption in the highest and lowest reaches of the naval administration. The opposition in Commons might bring charges against the First Lord of Admiralty or the Treasurer of the Navy for political reasons,[1] but there was little political value in attacking the permanent civil board. Numerous investigations give a wealth of detail on corrupt practices in the dockyards, but the curtain was usually drawn before the searchings exposed the men higher up, at Crutched Friars or Somerset House.

Thanks to one outspoken source, it is possible to obtain an authoritative inside view of the relations of the Navy Board to the contractors without relying on innuendoes or the prejudiced charges of the disgruntled. The events which Samuel Pepys confided to the cipher of his famous diary from 1660 to 1669 may fairly be regarded as typical throughout a large portion of the period, even though little other definite proof is left by any other man. The results at other periods, however, were similar.

Pepys became Clerk of the Acts, or Secretary of the Navy Board, in 1660 and held that position for thirteen years, when he was promoted to secretary of the newly formed Admiralty Board. He made the most of the former office, arrogating to himself many of the important duties and privileges, especially in the dealings with contractors. Pepys was the foremost authority of the Restoration on naval matters in general, and was acknowledged to know more about naval timber and masts than any other official. An able student of the Restoration Navy calls him "one of the best officials England ever had."[2] His close connection with the timber supply gives to his diary revelations particular importance, especially as he enjoyed a reputation for integrity at a period when English official as well as private morality was at a low ebb.

---

[1] *E.g., Parl. Hist.*, xix, 728–730, 984; *Parl. Debates*, iii, 1147–1212.

[2] N. R. S., *Catalogue of Pepysian MSS*, i, 248.

In 1663, he secured the award of a £3,000 mast contract to Sir William Warren, and in discussing the affair, he wrote:

> But good God! to see what a man might do, were I a knave, the whole business from beginning to end being done by me out of the office, and signed by them [the Navy Board] upon the once reading of it to them, without the least care or consultation either of quality, price, number, or need of them; only in general that it was good to have a store. But I hope my pains was such, as the King has the best bargain of masts that has been bought these 27 years in this office.[1]

No official would be ashamed of such a record, — similar virtuous, self-congratulatory passages on successful contracts can be found throughout the *Barham Papers*, — but Middleton has almost nothing to say regarding the background of the contracts which Pepys frankly describes in detail. Sir William Warren, "a miracle of cunning and forecast in his business," had perceived that friendship with the Clerk of the Acts would be to their mutual advantage, and proceeded to gain the good-will of the diarist. There were frequent dinners at the Dolphin, the Sun, and the Pope's Head. There were visits to Warren's yard at Wapping, where Pepys saw the deal ships from Norway and learned the difference between Dram and Swinsound deals; there were long, long talks well into the night at their homes or at the Navy Office.[2] But the relationship did not stop with that innocent intercourse. Seven months before the mast contract referred to, Sir William left at the home of Pepys a letter and a box and went his way. The box contained a pair of gloves for Mrs. Pepys and "a fair state dish of silver, and cup, with my arms ready cut upon them, worth, I believe, about £18, which is a very noble present and the best I ever had yet."[3] During the summer, Pepys had procured for Warren a contract for Swinsound deals, amounting to about £1500, and later the £3,000 mast contract.[4]

A year after the present of the silver plate, Pepys hurried home from a long talk with Warren at the Sun Tavern, with a package which he found to contain another pair of gloves for his wife, and in them forty pieces of gold, "which did so cheer my heart

---

[1] Pepys, *Diary*, Sept. 10, 1663.   [2] *Ibid.*, June 23, July 4, 1662.
[3] *Ibid.*, Feb. 10, 1663.   [4] *Ibid.*, July 16, Sept. 10, 1663.

that I could eat no victuals almost for dinner for joy to think how God do bless us in every day more and more, and more yet I hope he will upon the increase of my duties and endeavours." [1] That summer Pepys made a contract with Warren for nearly a thousand Gottenburg masts, "the biggest that ever was made in the Navy and wholly of my compassing and a good one I hope it is for the King." Two weeks later Warren told Pepys that he was his debtor for £100 "for service and friendship in the last great contract," and remarking that "everybody must live by their places," suggested that Pepys "go shares with him in anything he deals in." That same week, Pepys was riding a very pretty mare sent him by the contractor.[2]

Shortly afterwards, at the Sun, Warren brought £100 in a bag, told Pepys it was his, and asked for no receipt. A month after that came "a very great contract with Sir William Warren for 3,000 loade of timber," the final terms being drawn up by Pepys, against those of the opposition.[3] Finally, early in 1665, the two had a four-hour talk until very late one night, and Pepys "concluded a firm league with him in all just ways to serve him and myself all I can, and I think he will be a most usefull and thankfull man to me." From that time on their *rapprochement* increased Pepys' income liberally, and probably amounted to more than his £350 salary.[4]

The alliance between Warren and Pepys did not pass unchallenged at the Navy Office. The commissioners soon lost that early indifference to signing contracts, and there were many contests on the subject. Pepys' bitterest opponent was Sir William Batten. It would seem that Batten also accepted bribes from contractors and was angry that he could not render service in return. This was especially true in the case of Justice William Wood, the chief rival of Warren in the mast business. Pepys relates time and again his own harsh treatment of Wood, both at the Navy Office and at the inspection of his masts; and when Wood's modified contract finally passed, Pepys takes great credit

[1] *Diary*, Feb. 2, 1664.
[2] *Ibid.*, March 3, July 21, Aug. 2, Aug. 5, 1664.
[3] *Ibid.*, Aug. 12, Sept. 14, Sept. 16, Oct. 18, Oct. 25, 1664.
[4] *Ibid.*, Feb. 6, 1665.

for having taken such great pains for no reward. Christopher Pett and other dockyard officials complained of the quality of Warren's timber, but Pepys silenced them with the observation that it was their duty to reject all unsatisfactory goods, and their fault if any poor timber was received.[1]

Pepys was very particular as to the form in which the influence should come. Warren had a nice sense of delicacy in the matter, at the outset at least, for his first presents were nominally pairs of gloves for Mrs. Pepys. When Edward Deering sent an intermediary to offer Pepys £50 for his influence toward a contract for Baltic deals, with a prospect of £200 more, the diarist wrote:

> I was glad to hear both of these, but answered him no further than that I would not by anything be bribed to be unjust in my dealings, so I was not so squeamish as not to take people's acknowledgment where I had the good fortune by my pains to do them just and good offices.[2]

And a week later:

> Up and to the office where we sat all the morning and I labored hard at Deering's business of his deals more than I would if I did not think to get something, though I do really believe that I did what is to the King's advantage in it, and yet, God knows, the expectation of profit will have its force and make a man the more earnest.[3]

Those two statements seem to sum up Pepys' attitude toward bribery. If the severe Evelyn could comment on Pepys' "great integrity," it is easy to imagine how less scrupulous men in the same position would have acted, and probably did act, time and again.[4]

The veil of secrecy which enshrouds the relations of the Navy Board with the contractors was partly lifted more than a century later, to reveal that these Pepysian practices had changed but little. In 1786, commissioners were appointed to inquire into what were euphemistically termed the "fees, gratuities, perquisites and emoluments" which were being received in the various public offices, and the Navy Office did not escape their scrutiny.[5]

[1] *Diary*, Oct. 17, 1662; Oct. 6, Nov. 14, Dec. 14, Dec. 31, 1663; Jan. 6, Jan. 7, Jan. 29, Feb. 16, Feb. 18, Mar. 9, April 2, April 14, April 27, May 3, 1664. *Cal. S. P., Dom., 1660–61*, p. 310; *1663–64*, p. 270.

[2] Pepys, *Diary*, Dec. 12, 1663.

[3] *Ibid.*, Dec. 19, 1663.   [4] Evelyn, *Diary*, May 26, 1703.

[5] 25 Geo. III, c. 19; 26 Geo. III, c. 66.

Sir Charles Middleton was later accused by St. Vincent of having grown rich in his office of Comptroller, but he testified under oath before these commissioners that he never did nor never would receive any gratuity or emolument, with certain specified conventional exceptions, "although upon his first coming into office several presents were offered which he constantly rejected, as well as recommendations in behalf of persons who were candidates for Navy contracts."[1] Middleton's head clerk, Thomas Davies, however, was either less scrupulous or more candid, for he testified that in 1781 he had managed to piece out his regular salary of £100 less tax, or £92 10s., with fees and gratuities amounting to £2,510 6s. 6d.! These gifts, he said, came from the proprietors of bills made out for stores supplied and services rendered to the Navy. They were purely voluntary, he went on to say, for as there was no positive authority for receiving them, they were accepted according to what he found to be the established custom when he came into the office, the conventional rate being one guinea for a bill of about a thousand pounds. It was never intimated to the contractor or his agent, however, that the fee was too small, nor had Davies ever attempted to increase the rate of the fees, he declared.[2]

Ten years later, the findings of these commissioners bore fruit in an Order in Council which gave force to their recommendations. Specific regulations were drawn up for the Navy Office, although it was by no means alone among the government bureaus in the acceptance of gifts. Every officer and clerk in the Navy Office was to enter a bond amounting to three times his annual salary, that he would receive nothing but his established salary, that he would not act as agent to any person having business with the government, and that he would not "be interested in any stores, wares, merchandize or provisions purchased or supplied for the use of the Navy." The penalty for default was forfeiture of the bond and dismissal. A few conventional fees were authorized, but they were not to be pocketed by individuals, and contracts of every kind, except for the secret services, were to be made by the entire Navy Board. To offset the loss of their "extras" to

[1] *Parl. Papers*, 1806 (309) vii, p. 191.　　[2] *Ibid.*, p. 207.

some extent, the officers and clerks were to be granted an increase in salary; but it is doubtful if Mr. Thomas Davies and his colleagues appreciated the raise under the circumstances.[1] The government could well afford the increase of pay, for, as was often pointed out, the contractors had naturally raised their prices to include the extra gifts. In 1803, another Order in Council established a separate and distinct department in the Navy Office "for the better execution of the duties appertaining to Navy contracts," to be headed by a clerk of "integrity, experience and ability" at £300 a year.[2] If the acceptance of gifts had survived the earlier rulings, the number of presents would at least be reduced. An effort had also been made during the American Revolution to prohibit members of Parliament from contracting for the public services.[3]

It is doubtful if all this regulating eradicated the old practices. St. Vincent levelled charges on these grounds against Sir Andrew Snape Hamond, who presided at the Navy Office while he was First Lord of the Admiralty. Among the products of the bitter relations between St. Vincent and Hamond are the eleventh and twelfth reports of the Committee of Naval Enquiry in 1805 and 1806. Hamond and the Navy Board were investigated in connection with irregularities in connection with the payment of navy bills and the contracts for hemp, masts, and fir timber from Russia.[4] The latter charge seems to have been much ado about nothing, but there seem to be ample grounds for the Admiralty's suspicions of the Navy Board's relations with the "Timber Trust" in 1804.[5] Unfortunately for our purpose, there was no Pepys among these later officials, to reveal the inner workings of the contract relations, and the charges must rest on these secondhand sources. Similar relations have not been at all uncommon among officials in many lands and ages, and the interests of the

[1] *Commons Reports*, xii, 331.

[2] *Ibid.*, xiii, 836, 837.

[3] *Parl. Hist.*, xx, 124–129; xxii, 1211, 1333–1336, 1356–1382.

[4] *Parl. Papers*, 1805 (47), vol. ii; 1806 (1), vol. iv; see *Parl. Debates*, 1st ser., v, 90. N. R. S., *Barham Papers*, ii, 247, 248; N. R. S., *Letters of Admiral Markham*, pp. 37, 38; N. R. S., *Letters of Lord St. Vincent*, vol. ii (in preparation), *passim*.

[5] See p. 320.

Navy and the efficiency of the contract system were bound to suffer.

The question of corruption leads directly into the third defect in the workings of the contract system — the development of a timber monopoly. It was partly through corrupting the Navy Board that the monopoly developed, and once formed, it could be an even more powerful instrument for "influencing" the officials.

The gradual evolution of the timber monopoly covers two centuries. The state papers of the seventeenth century contain the records of dozens of small, shrewd bargains made each year by the naval purveyors and dockyard commissioners for the fellings from individual woodlands or for the cargoes of individual mast and deal ships. During most of the eighteenth century, the conventional awarding of contracts by the Navy Board was in general vogue. Contractors assembled at the Navy Office in response to public advertisements, and bid against each other to furnish the whole supply of a particular commodity, or at least enough ordinarily to supply one dockyard for a year. There was competition for the contract, but the contracts themselves were large.[1] During the first half of the nineteenth century, this free competition had given way to a "Timber Trust" controlled by one or two magnates who were in a position to bully the Navy into a system of contracts for long terms, at secret prices, to the exclusion of all competition, through a successful cornering of the entire timber supply.

The tendency to monopoly showed itself first in the Baltic and New England trade rather than in the supply of English oak. Small dealers could not well afford to contract for foreign masts or deals. The foreign trade tied up considerable capital for a protracted period and involved risks of war, weather, and a dozen other phases of uncertainty, where a single miscarriage might ruin the man of small capital. Single cargoes arriving in the Thames might be purchased by the Navy Board, but the official contracts are associated with a few men of capital.

As early as Tudor days there was a "King's Merchant for Dan-

[1] R. O., *Adm.*, *Acct. Gen.*, *Misc.*, *Var.*, *Contracts;* N. B. *Minutes, passim.*

sike," or a "King's agent in the East parts," who had purchased
a royal patent of monopoly.   In that capacity William Watson,
Thomas Allen, Francis Cherry, and others in succession furnished
the bulk of the Baltic naval materials.   The office was still extant in 1660, but the King's merchant was beginning to be overshadowed by the first of the real timber magnates — Pepys'
friend and ally, Sir William Warren.[1]   At Wapping, just below
London, Warren had a great timber yard, where he conducted
an extensive general trade in imported and domestic wood of all
kinds.   His capital, experience, connections, and the opportunity
to dispose of surplus stock placed him in an excellent position to
take over a large part of the naval contracts.   With the assistance
of Pepys already described, he furnished most of the masts from
Norway, Gottenburg, and New England, together with Norway
deals and many forms of English oak.   He was usually able to
underbid his rivals in the mast trade, so that Wood, Shorter, and
Taylor finally combined with him as junior partners.

By the end of the century, John Taylor had succeeded him in
the monopoly of most of the Baltic and New England mast contracts, and used his position to exert a strong influence on the
Navy Board policy to his own advantage at that critical period.[2]
Between his death and the outbreak of the American Revolution,
most of the New England mast contracts were held by William
Gulston, John Henniker, and the firm of Durand and Bacon.
Their influential mast agents in the colonies, Waldo, Westbrook,
and the Wentworths, were able to maintain the contract monopoly at Portsmouth and Falmouth against the attempts of other
colonies to divert the trade.   In the Baltic trade, a few powerful
houses, such as the Normans in Norway, the Sollys at Dantzig,
and the Thorntons at Riga, met with similar success.[3]

There was less excuse for the rise of monopoly in English oak,
yet it was in this field that the most powerful and dangerous combination of all finally developed.   Dozens of small cuttings were
made in the country every year, and no large amount of capital

---

[1] *L. & P., Henry VIII*, vol. xix, pt. 1, 1544, p. 598; pt. 2, p. 332; *Cal. S. P., Dom.*,
1581–90, pp. 24, 613, 701; *Addenda, 1580–1625*, p. 423; *1603–10*, pp. 119, 189;
1625–26, p. 205; *1660–61*, p. 212.

[2] R. O., N. B. In Letters, 562, *Taylor to N. B.*, Sept. 20, 1702.

[3] See pp. 147, 148, 235, 240.

was necessary to cover the short carriage to the dockyards. In nearly every county there were small dealers, who bought up the local fellings, and occasionally the landowner tendered his trees directly to the Navy.

During the Restoration, it was customary for the naval purveyors to examine these small lots of timber and utilize their authority, or that of the dockyard commissioners, to make contracts on the spot. "I repaired to Reading and Newbury, chose the timber for the new ship at Woolwich, and proffered £4 a load; but they refuse to sell and deliver it under £4/5," wrote Robert Mayors, the principal purveyor in 1670, to the Navy Commissioners, who instructed him to make the best bargain he could.[1] Three weeks later Jonas Shish, master shipwright at Deptford, wrote: "I cannot proceed with the works on the decks, for want of the knees formerly demanded. I acquainted the purveyor where three or four loads might be had, and if you will give an order to agree for the price, they may be sent down."[2] Those letters are only random specimens, typical of dozens to be found in every volume of the Calendars of State Papers of the early Restoration period. In six months of 1673, Mayors listed some forty different bargains for small lots of timber which he made with twenty different individuals,[3] and the complete lists of tenders of timber and contracts at varying prices made by the Navy Board themselves give an adequate conception of the absence of monopoly in the nature of the bargaining at that period.[4]

Gradually that system underwent a great alteration. The purveyors lost their powers of bargaining and became mere inspectors attached to each dockyard, charged with the examination of trees felled on contract. In their place we find the development of a class of middlemen or timber brokers whose agents replaced the royal purveyors in treating for the small lots of timber. With a large portion of the oak supply thus concentrated in their hands, these middlemen were in a position to contract with the Navy Board to furnish a large portion of the entire

---

[1] Cal. S. P., Dom., 1670, p. 2.   [2] Ibid., p. 27.
[3] Ibid., 1672–73, p. 379.
[4] Ibid., 1664–65, pp. 132–137; 1665–66, pp. 129–135; 1667–68, pp. 122, 123; 1668–69, p. 126. See, however, ibid., pp. 26, 171, 338.

amount required in the dockyards. Instead of the wide range
of prices resulting from the numerous bargains of the earlier
period, there was a single flat rate, unchanged through several
decades, for each item of the timber supply.[1] The profits from
the individual bargains with landowners and small county dealers went to the middleman instead of to the Navy, and the contractor received a handsome profit for rendering to the Navy no
further service than its own officials had formerly performed.
The Navy Board favored the middleman because the new system
meant a relief from much labor and responsibility. The general
interests of the Navy, however, suffered from more than the increased charges alone. In their strategic position, the timber
magnates could dictate in matters of policy, could prevent a
rigorous examination of the quality and quantity of their deliveries and avoid penalties for shortcomings, and at times they
even created shortages in the dockyards as arguments for an
increase in price.

At the close of the Seven Years' War, the timber combination
had assumed such proportions that the Admiralty found it necessary to break up the monopoly in 1771, through the use of foreign
oak, and for a while there was free bidding again.[2] The ledgers
of the Treasurer of the Navy show that in 1771 English timber
was furnished by twenty-eight different contractors.[3] The dealers realized, as others have in later ages, that greater profits lay
in combination than in competition. By the close of the century
English timber was in the hands of a "trust," more powerful
than any which had yet existed. The leaders were John Larking
and William Bowsher, who finally concentrated practically the
entire timber output in their hands and worked together in perfect harmony in their relations with the Navy Board.

The rise of this "Timber Trust" is worthy of attention because in 1803 and 1804 it precipitated one of the gravest crises
in the history of the timber problem. A later chapter will describe in detail the success of the timber magnates in opposing
the wise measure of Lord St. Vincent in creating the new office of

---

[1] *H. C. J.*, *1792*, p. 289.   [2] *Parl. Hist.*, xix, 828.
[3] R. O., *Adm.*, *Acct. Gen.*, *Accts.*, 278–84, *Treasurer's Ledgers*, *passim*.

timber master to put an end to the abuses of timber receipt at the dockyards. In order to bring the Admiralty to terms, the "trust" nearly brought disaster on the nation by cutting off the entire supply of English timber at a time when Napoleon seriously threatened England with invasion. During this contest, the Navy Board often upheld the contractors against the Admiralty, who not without justice charged the civil officers of the Navy with being paid agents of the monopoly.[1] It is not unlikely that John Larking utilized the same methods which had been so successful in Sir William Warren's relations with Pepys.

That victory over the Admiralty placed the timber magnates in an impregnable position, and during the remainder of the war the Navy was at their mercy. Larking and Bowsher secured constant increases in price, and even persuaded the Navy to advance funds to capitalize their business. At a time when their timber contracts sometimes amounted to £450,000 in a single year, the loss in interest alone from this practice was excessive.[2] Competition was entirely abolished. One Thomas Watkins offered the Admiralty a parcel of timber at less than half the contract price, charging Larking and Bowsher with tremendous profits; but he was soon informed that owing to the terms of the contract the Navy could not buy his oak.[3] The board which had been making separate deals a century and a half before for four or five loads of knee timber would now entertain no bids for less than the entire annual consumption, which averaged over 50,000 loads during that period.

The monopoly did not end with the close of the Napoleonic wars. In 1817, the influence of Larking and Bowsher became concentrated in one man, John Morris or Morrice, who had served as an agent and later as a junior partner of Larking. For thirty years, Morris continued to supply the entire naval demands for

---

[1] See pp. 320–324.

[2] R. O., N. B. In Letters, 1559, *Larking to N. B.*, July 17, 1804; *N. B. to Larking*, July 20, 1804; 1561, *Larking to N. B.*, Nov. 23, 1813; *Larking and Bowsher to N. B.*, May 31, 1814.

[3] R. O., Adm. Digest, 4916, *Watkins to Adm.*, Mar. 4, 1813; see also *Ibid.*, 4901, *N. B. to Adm.*, Dec. 24, 1810; *Parl. Papers*, 1813–14 (115), vol. vii, pt. 1, pp. 149–171.

English oak except for the small amounts received from the royal forests. There were secret contracts for three-year periods, without even the form of public advertisement. In 1832, when the Navy Board was abolished and an Admiralty committee took over the timber problem, an attempt was made to break the monopoly, and the contracts were open to competition. Morris, who had received an average of £7 16s. 9d. for timber in 1830, lowered his bid to £6 9s. 7d. to meet the occasion. One firm offered to supply a single dockyard, but Morris would supply all or nothing. As no one else dared to bid, the Navy was forced to return to the magnate for the entire supply. Morris punished them for the attempt by a sharp increase in price.[1] Finally, in 1848, the Parliamentary Committee on Navy, Army, and Ordnance Estimates reported:

> Your Committee are inclined to think that, by judicious arrangements, and a firm determination on the part of the Admiralty, the monopoly which has so long existed might be broken through, and they believe that at a time when there is no immediate pressure for additional ships, a good opportunity is afforded for putting an end to a system which is disadvantageous to the public and unfair towards the merchants whose competition it would be a wise policy to encourage.[2]

This resolution did not kill the monopoly. Morris had just died, but his brother carried on the business. As in 1771, an effort was made to break the "trust" by the use of foreign timber, and the proportion of English oak dwindled to one fourth of the whole by the end of the next decade. Yet in 1860, in the very last days of the timber problem, the Admiralty spokesman in the Commons had to admit that the contracts were still in the hands of two or three great magnates, who were able to dictate their own terms to the Navy.[3]

In other times and in other lands, an effective weapon could have been brought to bear against the power of such a combination. In France, Spain, or Russia, or in England under the Tudors and early Stuarts, timber could have been seized for naval

[1] *Ibid.*, p. 172; 1847–48 (51), vol. xx, pt. 2, p. 571; (555), vol. xxi, pt. 1, pp. 392, 596, 597; 1848–49 (0.48), vol. xxi, p. 117.

[2] *Ibid.*, 1847–48 (555), vol. xxi, pt. 1, pp. lxiii, lxiv.

[3] *Parl. Debates*, clvii, 2030.

use on the principle of royal prerogative or eminent domain. The Czars set aside most of the oaks in Russia for naval use and forbade the export of that timber. Spain, too, gave her navy the right of preëmption over private as well as public forests.[1] France had the elaborate system of *martelage*, or maritime conscription of trees, whereby naval shipwrights could stamp their hammers on the trunk of any tree in the land desirable for naval purposes and compel its sale at a fair price. Colbert developed this system in his great forest ordinance of 1668,[2] and incidentally had a monopolist guilty of abuses in cornering the supply of naval timber thrown into the Bastille, where he died.[3] *Martelage* fell somewhat into disuse in the eighteenth century, but was revived with full force under the Convention and Napoleon.[4]

Prior to the Civil War, a similar right had been exercised in England. "The king may take . . . timber for his ships, castles or houses in the wood of any man, and this is for public benefit," declared Baron Clarke, one of the judges of James I, during the Bates case on impositions in 1606.[5] The right of commandeering timber by purveyance was maintained throughout the Tudor and early Stuart period. It was only occasionally, however, that royal purveyors insisted that reluctant landowners sell at the King's price the oaks on which the broad arrow had been stamped, or irate Hanse captains complained of "the King's officers who take away wood of all sorts, and when spoken to about payment, allege a new and unwonted price which impudently they call the King's price." The Privy Council of Henry VIII once ordered certain oak and elm prepared and taken to the waterside, "sparing no man's woods as this is for a special purpose."[6]

---

[1] Spain, *Real Ordenanza para el Gobierno de los Montes y Arbolados de la Jurisdiccion de la Marina, passim;* Artiñano, *Arquitectura Naval Española (En Madera),* p. 163; *Naval Chronicle,* i, 77; Fernow, *History of Forestry,* 223.

[2] Colbert, *Lettres, Instructions et Mémoires,* vol. iii, pt. 2, pp. 714–716; Brown, *French Forest Ordinance of 1668,* p. 127.

[3] Colbert, *op. cit.,* vol. iii, pt. 1, p. 212 n.

[4] Lambert de Saint-Croix, *Administration de la Marine de France,* pp. 234–236; Levy-Schneider, *Le Conventionnel Jeanbon Saint-André,* i, 451, 452.

[5] Prothero, *Statutes and Constitutional Documents, 1559–1625,* p. 340.

[6] *L. & P., Henry VIII,* vol. xvi (1541–42), p. 200; vol. xvii (1542), p. 672; vol. xx, pt. 2, (1545), p. 170; *Cal. S. P., Dom., 1581–90,* p. 283.

In the decade preceding the outbreak of the Civil War, considerable timber was taken in this manner for building the Ship Money Fleet, and the Earl of Southampton protested vigorously against the seizure of some two thousand of his oaks at Lichfield.[1] Purveyance was subjected to such constant criticism by the Parliamentary party at this time that the King was forced to modify it.[2] During the Protectorate, it was abolished,[3] though Parliament seized thousands of oaks on the estates of delinquents. A commission authorizing a royal officer in 1661 to press men, timber, and other naval necessities, arresting all who objected, indicates an intention to return to the practice.[4] Pepys incurred the wrath of Lord Clarendon in 1664 when the Navy Board sent Anthony Deane to mark certain oaks for the Navy in Clarendon Park, which had formerly been royal property. Only the great influence of the Lord Chancellor saved the trees. Purveyance never returned, however, with its original force. Landowners sometimes flatly refused to sell their timber to the King, during the Restoration, and naval officials sighed in vain for power to force the sale.[5]

Seizure of timber for government purposes became popularly associated with tyranny and absolute government. Referring to the practice of *martelage* under Napoleon, Captain Brenton wrote that "though the expedient was incompatible with a free government, it answered the purpose of a despot, and gave him that immediate power which a British monarch and a British parliament could not attain." [6]

A Parliamentary committee, considering the project of government control over the private woodlands for naval purposes, reported in 1788 that "the interference of government farther than in the protection of property, is always submitted to with reluctance, often evaded and seldom productive of any benefit

---

[1] *Ibid.*, *1634–35*, pp. 231, 359, 362, 363, 585.

[2] *Ibid.*, *1637–38*, p. 368.

[3] *Acts and Ordinances of the Interregnum*, ii, 1057.

[4] *Cal. S. P., Dom.*, *1661–62*, p. 521.

[5] Magdalene College, *Pepysian MSS*, 2265, p. 122; Pepys, *Diary*, July 14, 18, 20, 23, 1664; *Cal. S. P., Dom.*, *1664–65*, p. 421; *1668–69*, p. 338.

[6] Brenton, *Naval History of Great Britain*, ii, 112.

to the public." [1]   In 1804, when the "Timber Trust" was shutting off the whole English timber supply, it was proposed to the First Lord of the Treasury that an act be passed whereby "all saleable oak and elm timber shall be at the preëmption of the Navy Board at the prices individuals had agreed to give for it." [2] Such an act could have broken the hold of the monopoly, but nothing came of it.

The reluctance of Parliament to commandeer timber did not arise entirely from a laudable respect for private property in general. In this instance it was due primarily to a respect for the particular private property of the members of Parliament, most of whom owned oak on their estates.[3] Government seizure might have meant a curtailing of an important source of income. The Parliament which refused, in the name of property rights, to seize timber at a time when the dockyards were in crying need of it, did not hesitate to permit press gangs to tear men from their homes and occupations to serve in the King's ships. Parliament, so tender of its own oaks, had not hesitated to commandeer the pines of the American colonists, with only the most flimsy legal fiction to differentiate the process from Tudor purveyance or French *martelage*, while the oaks of Ireland met a similar treatment.[4] It remained for a more democratic Parliament, during the recent world conflict, to pass a Defense of the Realm Act which freed the Navy from such complete dependence on a small private group for its essential materials.

Three of the chief defects in the workings of the contract system — faulty policy, corruption, and the monopoly — have been discussed. There remains the final factor — the instability of naval credit — to consider. A navy often represented the heaviest single source of drain on the finances of a maritime power.[5] It required all that was expensive in an army, — pay, food, and ordnance, — and in addition it required the very costly item of ships. Most of an army could be disbanded in time of peace,

---

[1] *H. C. J.*, *1787–88*, p. 560.
[2] R. O., Adm. Digest, 4865, *N. B. to Adm.*, May 2, 1804.
[3] See *Parl. Hist.*, xx, 126.
[4] See pp. 255–259.
[5] See Playfair, *Commercial and Political Atlas*, Plate 23, opp. p. 91.

but a navy continued to "eat its head off" even when little was required of it. A certain amount of patrolling and convoy duty was essential at all times. Even if new ships were not built, the old ones were in constant need of repair, for which dockyards had to be maintained, and it was necessary to have a permanent corps of officials. The condition of a navy usually reflected the state of the treasury.

During periods of scanty or irregular revenue this constant charge was a serious problem. The second half of the seventeenth century saw that problem at its worst. Charles I had had his trouble with Ship Money, but had little occasion to use the fleet so raised. Cromwell had to finance England's first real naval war, in which the state owned rather than hired most of its ships. The cost was tremendous for that day. In 1652–53, the first year of the war, Cromwell spent on the Navy £1,400,000 out of a total revenue of £2,600,000. During the last years of the Protectorate, the total revenue fell off much faster than the naval expenses. In the fiscal year 1656–57, £809,000 out of a total of £1,050,000 went to the Navy; a year later, it was £624,000 out of £951,000, and in 1658–59, £848,000 from the entire revenue of £1,517,000. Even with three heavy grants, the navy accounts were woefully in arrears, and an increasing debt hung over from year to year. The Restoration made little change in the situation. The naval stores were so low that Charles II devoted £432,000 out of Parliament's grant of £1,200,000 to that item alone, and for a brief period at the end of 1663, the Navy was out of debt. The Second Dutch War, beginning in 1665, meant heavy arrears once more, and early in 1666, the Navy had only £1,500,000 to meet debts and current expenses of £2,300,000.[1] Subsidies from Louis XIV could not fully offset the coolness of Parliament and if the government lacked money, contractors could not long furnish timber on promises alone.

Contractors received in return for their goods imprest bills payable in "the course of the Navy." This meant that, when the Treasurer of the Navy lacked sufficient funds for immediate pay-

---

[1] *Cal. S. P., Dom., 1661–62*, p. 464; Pepys, *Diary, passim;* N. R. S., *Catalogue of Pepysian MSS*, i, 98–116; Clowes, *Royal Navy*, ii, 106.

ment, the bills were filed in order of issuance, to await their turn for payment at some distant future. The course of the Navy was frequently several years in arrears, and the bills were subjected to a discount on exchange so heavy that they became almost worthless at times. Some contractors were driven to the wall because they could not keep their small capital tied up during the long period of delayed payment, nor could they afford to stand the loss by discounting. They refused to serve the Navy except for "ready money." The more powerful contractors, like Warren, raised their prices to cover the probable loss by discount, with a good margin of safety. There was a wide divergence between the cash and credit prices — at one time deals obtainable for £8 a hundred in ready money cost £12 on credit.[1]

The Navy frequently lacked ready money, and the majority of contractors would not furnish more timber until their heavy arrears were paid. Typical of dozens of letters received at the Navy Office each year was the appeal of Christopher Coles, the leading timber merchant of Hampshire, in 1656:

I cannot deliver any more timber or contract for a supply of treenails unless I receive £600 on account of the £1600 already due for timber sent to Portsmouth, Plymouth, Deptford and Chatham 12 months since, when Mr. Shish promised me a bill of imprest for £500. The Commissioners also promised me a bill of imprest for £600, but I only had one for £400, the remaining £200 was promised at Portsmouth but I never received it, and the bill for £400 has hitherto done me no more good than an old almanac, I never having received a penny upon it. I hope you will consider the words of Solomon, that oppression makes even a wise man mad; I am at my wit's end for want of money.[2]

Coles's plight was not as desperate as that of many others who suffered from the low credit of the Navy. The wounded seamen and the wives and widows of the men in the fleet could bring no great pressure to bear on the Navy Office for the amounts due them. Unpaid sailors could mutiny, and dockyard workers, so destitute that they had "to buy and eat the offal formerly given

[1] See esp. *Cal. S. P., Dom., 1654*, p. 388; *1655*, pp. 382, 401; *1655–56*, pp. 425, 550, 569; *1656–57*, pp. 7, 121, 122; *1658–59*, pp. 86–87, 408, 411; *1659–60*, p. 457; *1661–62*, pp. 62, 135, 464; *1664–65*, pp. 376, 421; *1665–66*, p. 32; *1668–69*, p. 338; *1672–73*, p. 223; N. R. S., *Hollond's Discourses of the Navy*, pp. 208, 209.

[2] *Cal. S. P., Dom.*, 1655–56, p. 165.

to the dogs," could strike, but they could be subjected to severe
discipline.[1] The timber of the contractors was a vital necessity,
and they had to be kept in humor as far as possible. Twelve
years after Coles wrote that appeal for payment, he was in a position to get his own terms when his rivals were forced out of business for want of capital.[2] The contractors could scarcely be
blamed for refusing the Navy their timber on credit under such
conditions, and it was because of this state of affairs that the
dockyard stores were dangerously empty during the period of
the Dutch wars.

The situation did not improve until after the accession of
George I, in 1715. The course of the Navy was badly in arrears
during the wars against Louis XIV from 1689 to 1697 and from
1701 to 1713, and there was the same story of refusals from contractors. One group of them, known as "the old creditors of the
Navy," had gone unpaid for nearly fifteen years by the end of the
century. The papers of that day bristle with the complaints of
contractors, dockyard officers, and the Navy Board for want of
credit.[3] An old Admiralty digest on naval stores contains the
following picture of a situation which could apply at almost any
time during that period:

> In 1711, the credit of the Navy was so sunk, from the long arrears of their
> bills, and the uncertainty of their payment, that the Commissioners could
> get nobody to contract with them for Naval Stores, and some few, who had
> entered into agreement with the Board, refused afterwards to come and
> sign their contracts. When the Navy Board are under such like difficulties,
> it has been usual for the Lords of the Treasury to send for the merchants and
> discourse with them.[4]

Until about 1720, it was difficult to do more than live from hand
to mouth in the matter of timber and masts, for want of credit,
and the Navy was exposed to the constant dangers arising from
such shortage.

During the remainder of the century, naval credit was well
established in the years of peace. As the nation grew more

---

[1] Pepys, *Diary*, June 15, July 10, 1666, Aug. 27, 1667.

[2] *Cal. S. P., Dom.*, 1668–69, pp. 26, 171.

[3] *Cal. Treas. Papers, passim;* R. O., N. B. In Letters, p. 562, *Taylor to N. B.*,
Mar. 14, 1702; *Adm., Acct. Gen., Accts. Misc., Var.*, 123.

[4] Adm. Library MSS. — *Digest,* "Naval Stores," p. 4.

wealthy and the political situation more settled, adequate funds began to be taken for granted, and the menace of inadequate reserves tended to diminish. The unusual demands of the Seven Years' War, however, impaired the credit to such an extent that in 1762, contractors raised their prices sharply, "alleging that this is occasioned by the great discount on Navy Bills (which is now risen to 12 per cent) and the risque, from the uncertainty of their being unpaid with the same punctuality as formerly, of the discount being still higher."[1] The entrance of France into the American Revolution in 1778 caused a demand for stores so heavy that navy credit again succumbed and the Navy Board was obliged "to make bargains at the ruinous discount of 22 per cent."[2] It is significant that the timber supply was in a critical state at each of the periods of low credit. By 1789, provisions were inserted in the contracts to offset the discount on navy bills.[3]

The other three defects in the contract system continued throughout the period. The timber policy was bungled to the end, corruption survived even the reforms of 1801, and the monopoly constantly increased in power. The credit of the Navy, however, was firmly established throughout the wars with Revolutionary and Napoleonic France. Time and again, the Baltic merchants, who placed profit above national interest, rejected the offers of the French because of lack of faith in their credit, while English navy bills were practically as good as gold. Shortly after the close of the Napoleonic wars, Dupin, a Frenchman, wrote:

De tous les consommateurs de l'Europe, l'administration de la marine anglaise est le plus riche, le plus sûr, le plus equitable. C'est donc à lui qu'on vend de préférence; c'est pour lui qu'on reserve les munitions navales les plus parfaites. J'ai vu, dans plusieurs contrées, des munitions de ce genre, remarquables par leur beauté; j'ai demandé pour qui elles étaient destinées: "C'est pour la marine anglaise," me répondait-on avec emphase. Nonseulement cette marine est parfaitement servie; elle l'est à plus bas prix que toute autre, parce qu'elle achète plus en grand, et surtout qu'elle inspire plus de confiance.[4]

[1] R. O., N. B. Out Letters, *N. B. to Adm.*, Jan. 22, 1762.
[2] N. R. S., *Barham Papers*, ii, 185, 293, 294. See *Parl. Hist.*, xxiv, 1273–1290.
[3] *H. C. J.*, *1792*, p. 349; see Eleventh Report of Commissioners of Naval Enquiry, *Parl. Debates*, iv, appendix, i–xxxv.
[4] Dupin, *Voyages dans la Grande-Bretagne*, vol. ii, pt. 3, p. 104.

A far cry indeed, from the situation in 1669, when the Commissioner at Portsmouth had to furnish £20 in ready money to the purveyor that he might hasten to New Forest to find beams for the completion of a ship! [1]

Thus far, the working, or failure to work, of the machinery of the timber supply has been considered from the standpoint of the Navy Office, where the policies were formed and the contracts made. A survey of the civil service of the Navy in its connection with the timber problem must also take into consideration the dockyards, or navy yards as they are called on this side of the Atlantic. It was at the dockyards that the timber was received from the contractors, at the dockyards it was stored, and there it was used for construction and repairs. Through waste and corruption a sound timber policy of the Navy Board could be perverted at the dockyards, just as a faulty Navy Board policy could hamper the ablest dockyard administration.

During the era of wooden ships there were six principal dockyards in England, arranged in three pairs.[2] On opposite banks of the Thames just below London were the original yards of Deptford and Woolwich. At the mouth of the Thames on the Medway in Kent were Chatham and Sheerness. On the south coast, in Hampshire and Devon respectively, were Portsmouth and Plymouth. From time to time lesser temporary yards were established in various parts of the British Isles, especially at Harwich, Deal, and Milford in England, Leith in Scotland, Pembroke in Wales, and Kinsale or Haulbowline Island in Ireland. As the empire expanded, "foreign" dockyards developed, among them Gibraltar, Port Mahon on Minorca, and later Malta, in the Mediterranean; Halifax and New York in America, Antigua and Jamaica in the West Indies, Cape Town, and Trincomalee in Ceylon. The main interest here will center on the six great dockyards in England.

A dockyard served several purposes. It was a strategic naval base for the fleet, ships were built and repaired there, and it housed the various stores required for naval purposes. The diversity of these functions led to a differentiation in the rôles of

[1] *Cal. S. P., Dom., 1668-69*, p. 264.   [2] See map, opp. p. 108.

the six yards. The original yards of Deptford and Woolwich were too far up the Thames to have any value as naval bases. Eventually they became primarily shipbuilding centers, and contained the reserve stores of masts and timber. As long as Holland was the principal enemy, Chatham was the strategic base, for the fleet could quickly slip to sea from its nearby anchorage at the Buoy of the Nore. To relieve the strain on Chatham, Sheerness was established during the Dutch wars, even nearer the sea, and Harwich enjoyed a temporary importance. When France replaced Holland as the great maritime rival of England late in the seventeenth century, the primacy passed to the pair of dockyards on the south coast, where Plymouth, the present Devonport, was established in 1691, a hundred miles west of the older yard at Portsmouth. From that time on, the principal rendezvous of the high fleet was at Spithead or St. Helens off Portsmouth, or at Hamoaze or Cawsand Bay at Plymouth. There the ships were in a position to get a quick start for the Atlantic or for the French coast without the delay entailed in coming around from the Thames. The function of repairing was associated with that of the naval base, especially the speedy repairs required by ships damaged in battle, or other ships on active service. During the American Revolution a custom long in practice was crystallized in an order that Portsmouth and Plymouth should reserve their energies for repairing ships of the line on active service, while smaller ships would repair at Chatham and Sheerness.[1] Its particularly strategic location eventually made Portsmouth the greatest naval arsenal in the world, surpassing Brest and Toulon in France, Corunna, Cadiz, and Ferrol in Spain, and Cronstadt in Russia.

The six great dockyards were similar in their general appearance.[2] Over a spacious area were scattered dwellings, storehouses, and ropewalks, with dry and wet docks and several building slips along the waterfront. The provisions for timber are of most interest in the present study. Most of the oak tim-

---

[1] Derrick, *Memoirs of the Royal Navy*, p. 233; R. O., N. B. Out Letters, 2207, *N. B. to Adm.*, Sept. 6, 1779; N. R. S., *Barham Papers*, ii, 293.

[2] See Bentham, *Life of Sir Samuel Bentham*, p. 141.

ber was usually deposited in great piles of logs "in the rough" and left in the open to season in sun, wind, and rain. In well-ordered yards, the different sizes of logs were kept separate, with distinct piles for great timbers and the crooked compass pieces. Under more careless management, there was liable to be an indiscriminate heap, where workmen were apt to take whatever logs came most conveniently to hand, sometimes sawing up valuable pieces of great timber in preference to moving the heavy pile to find a piece nearer the required size. Logs at the bottom of a pile might rot untouched for years, while the upper, greener pieces were constantly being removed because of this laziness. Planks and deals were piled in a manner similar to that employed in lumber yards to-day, usually with small sticks between each two layers, to allow the air to penetrate. Sometimes these piles were covered with open sheds; more often not. The piles usually rested on cinders to prevent the bottom layers from rotting in the mud. Near the piles of timber and plank were the sawpits, where two sawyers, one on the ground and one in the pit, would pull a four- or five-foot saw slowly through the log or plank. Occasionally a raised platform took the place of the pit. Some of the pieces of irregular shape were converted with the adze. Conservatism kept sawmills out of the dockyards until the end of the eighteenth century, and even in 1860 half the timber was converted by hand. Planks were originally rendered pliable by "stoving" in hot sand, but eventually the dockyard had a steam house, where the planks were softened to fit the curves of the ship.[1]

The storage of masts presented a problem entirely different from that of oak timber. It will be remembered that oak is rendered durable by exposure to open air which dries up the sap. Masts, on the other hand, needed a total exclusion of air in order to retain the resin which kept them sound and resilient. They were originally buried in the mud, but all well-appointed dockyards eventually had mast ponds, where the great sticks were floated in at various stages of the tide, to be fastened into posi-

[1] Jane, *British Battle Fleet*, pp. 70–72; see Colbert, *Lettres, Instructions et Mémoires*, vol. iii, pt. 2, pp. 715, 716.

tion at either end between two heavy horizontal timbers. These were arranged in tiers, so that a mast pond could hold several hundred sizeable masts. Locks kept the water at the level of high tide. Nearby were the long mast houses, where the mast-makers converted the sticks, which had arrived barkless and hewed into "sixteen sides," into the proper proportions for the particular demand. A few masts were usually kept on hand already converted for use in case of emergency. Each yard had at least one hulk equipped with apparatus for installing and re-moving masts.[1]

The titular head of the dockyard was a port admiral, a regular line admiral on shore duty, who represented the Admiralty and was in command of the dockyard as a naval base. We have little to do with that official in connection with the timber problem, interest centering rather on the civil hierarchy entrusted with the shipbuilding, repairing, and the stores. The chief civil officer was the resident commissioner, a nominal member of the Navy Board and the representative of that body in the dockyard. At the head of the actual working of the yard was the master shipwright, who had specific charge of the shipbuilding and repairing. The other principal officers of the yard were the storekeeper, two masters attendant, the clerk of the cheque, and the clerk of the survey. Each yard had several hundred workmen, generally referred to as "artificers," who fell into the various classes of ship-wrights, caulkers, mast-makers, and ordinary laborers. The port admiral seldom interfered with the civil work of the yard, but disputes between commissioner and master shipwright were more common.[2]

The final scene in the progress of a timber contract was enacted in the dockyard, where definite rules were laid down to defend the King's interest. All deliveries of timber and masts, as well as other stores, were to be made in the presence of at least two of the principal officers. Inspectors known as "timber tasters" were to examine the timber thoroughly for such flaws as knot-

[1] N. R. S., *Barham Papers*, ii, 192, 193; Fincham, *On Masting Ships, passim;* Bentham, *Life of Sir Samuel Bentham*, p. 151.
[2] *Oeconomy of the Navy Office, passim; Parl. Papers*, 1803–04 (83), iii, 3, 4.

holes in masts and "shakes" or cracks in the timber. They were also to measure it accurately, and timber measurement in itself was an intricate art. Pepys devoted a great deal of industry to mastering this process, "whereby the king is much abused," and was able to expose the ignorance of the measurers and other officers. The serial numbers which the purveyors had stamped on the timber in the forest were to be compared with this list, and the quantity and dimensions of the timber checked against the terms of the contract. The logs were then to be marked with the initials of the officer on duty for that week, and his initials were also set against the item in the storekeeper's record. Any faulty timber was to be rejected on the spot, and any discrepancies between contract, purveyor's list, and the deliveries were to be reported to the Surveyor at the Navy Office.[1]

The precautions of this intricate system were frequently nullified by the contractors' gold. The timber inspection became a farce, and subordinate clerks marked the initials of officers who were never present. A third of the timber paid for by the Navy never reached the yards, it was estimated in 1609.[2] That proportion is perhaps too severe for the whole period, but discrepancies were constant and large. Quality was no more carefully checked, for rotten and knotty masts and rotten, split, and cross-grained timber were received into the King's stores.

The causes of this carelessness, which had a most unfortunate influence on the problem of timber supply, are not hard to find. The air of sleepy indifference which characterized so many government institutions pervaded the routine atmosphere of the dockyards. The "spirit of the civil service" did not always steel men against the constant financial temptation. Many dockyard officials and clerks received larger incomes from the contractors than from the Navy. A clerk did not hesitate to accept a bribe when he knew, or well suspected, that the master shipwright was even more deeply involved in the same procedure, and the officials in turn felt safe because of the example set by their superiors at

[1] *Oeconomy of the Navy Office*, pp. 62–90; *Parl. Papers*, 1805 (1), ii, 9, 10; also in *Parl. Debates*, iii, 1125, 1129.

[2] Adm. Library MSS, 141, p. 15; see N. R. S., *Hollond's Discourses of the Navy*, pp. 221, 222, 226.

the Navy Office. Occasionally the officials dealt in timber them-selves, in spite of an order from the Duke of York forbidding this much-abused practice.   Peter Pett, master shipwright at Chat-ham, was continually recommending the purchase of timber, at a good price, from a certain Moorcock.   When it was found that Moorcock was really a dummy contractor, the selling agent for Pett's own timber, that son of the famous Phineas was suspended from his office.[1] Late in the eighteenth century, clerks at Ply-mouth yard received from the contractors a regular "honorarium" of two guineas on every £1000 for passing timber and bills.   In 1798, they were successful in the request for an increase, and an assistant clerk, who had formerly been receiving £80 to £85 a year from this source, testified that his income jumped to £276.[2] A whole chapter, or even a whole book could be written on this subject of dockyard "graft," for there is a wealth of interesting and edifying source material, showing that the above instances are only typical of a condition which existed throughout the period.[3]

From time to time, reform waves swept over the civil admin-istration of the Navy, attempting to eradicate those glaring abuses.   In 1608 and 1618, there were detailed investigations, in which dozens of witnesses testified even to their own pecula-tions.   In 1661, the Duke of York drew up stringent regulations for better administration.   It meant little that commissioners from the Navy Board inspected the yards at intervals, for their own practices were evident; but the occasional Admiralty tours of investigation were somewhat more severe.   Lord Anson, in 1746, again revealed the widespread inefficiency and corruption. After each of those exposures, however, matters slipped back into the lazy corruption.   Even the self-confessed offenders usually escaped with impunity.   The dockyard towns returned members to Parliament, and the men came to know that "a proper vote would cover a corrupt practice." [4]   The suspension of Peter Pett

[1] *Cal. S. P., Dom., 1667–68*, p. 501; 1671–72, pp. 112–114.
[2] *Parl. Papers*, 1805 (1) ii, 53, 54.
[3] See esp. *Parl. Papers*, Reports of Commissioners of Naval Enquiry, 1802–06; also, without appendices, in *Parl. Debates*, pp. 865–1211.
[4] Adm. Lib. MSS, 141; Charnock, *Hist. of Marine Architecture*, ii, 200 ff.; *Oeconomy of the Naval Office, passim*.

had been due less to the nature of his corruption than to the general animosity of the Navy Board, for he was a troublesome individual, and they needed a scapegoat for the Dutch invasion of the Medway in 1667.

The creation of the office of timber master in 1801 was the most radical step toward eliminating these abuses. One of these officials was appointed for each yard, given complete authority and complete responsibility in the receipt, storage, and use of all timber, and paid a salary sufficiently high to make him less susceptible to bribery. The establishing of this new office was one of the chief factors in the famous St. Vincent reforms which will be described more fully later.[1] The coercion of the timber contractors in 1803 and 1804, already alluded to, was directed against these new timber masters. The victory of Larking and Bowsher meant that, while the office remained, the well-conceived system of individual responsibility was rendered practically nugatory and corruption returned, to remain with the timber problem during its last half century.

So much for the receipt of timber at the yards — a system which did much to prevent an adequate stock of good timber. The question naturally arises, "What was done with the timber collected at such trouble and expense?" About two thirds of it went into the building of new ships and the rest into repairs. Construction of its own ships was the orthodox method of building up the Navy. Most of the larger warships during the two centuries, except those captured from the enemy, were built for the Navy either in the royal dockyards or in private yards. There were several alternative methods of gathering a fleet. Ships could be built outside of England, either in the colonies or in foreign nations, and merchantmen could be converted into ships of war.

There was a constant prejudice against building ships for the Navy in other lands. It was true that they could be built in foreign or colonial ports, where timber was plentiful and labor cheap, for a fraction of the high cost of construction in the English shipyards. To many men it seemed folly to exhaust the pre-

[1] See p. 319.

cious English oak, or to bring timber from forests thousands of miles distant to be set up in English yards, when that foreign timber could be put together and sailed to England as a ship all ready for service. Until the time of Elizabeth, the Navy occasionally purchased great ships built in the Baltic, but a strong reaction to this policy gradually set in.[1]

The authorities argued that it was better to pay the additional cost of English construction, thereby developing a large number of shipyards with thousands of trained native shipwrights, than to become dependent on a foreign country for ships of war and commerce. It was considered serious enough to have to depend on regions overseas for masts and other naval materials, without accentuating such dependence.[2] The Navigation Acts, with their insistence on ships of English or colonial construction, applied that principle to the merchant marine, and only a small proportion of foreign-built ships, captured in war, crept into British registry. With warships, the principle was adhered to in an even more rigorous manner. By 1670, when Colbert was buying up warships in Baltic countries where the cost of construction was about half of that in the home yards, England had long renounced the policy of building a navy in any foreign country.

The colonies presented a slightly different problem, for they were under stricter control. Spain built many of her finest warships at Havana all through the eighteenth century, and the English recognized the unusual durability of the mahogany and other West Indian timbers in the ships captured from the Spaniards. Colbert inaugurated the construction of warships in New France. Many ships were built for the French Navy at Quebec and elsewhere until the loss of Canada in 1763.[3] A few small warships were built in New England for the Royal Navy, in spite of constant opposition from the Navy Board.[4] Not until the extreme pressure of the timber scarcity during the Napoleonic

[1] L. & P., Henry VIII, vol. x, pt. 2, 1544, p. 369; vol. xxi, pt. 1, p. 96; Macpherson, Annals, ii, 140; Oppenheim, Administration of the Royal Navy, pp. 38, 39, 67.

[2] Brewster, Essays on Trade and Navigation, p. 86.

[3] Artiñano, Arquitectura Naval Española (En Madera), pp. 78, 153; Colbert, Lettres, Instructions et Mémoires, vol. iii, pt. 2, passim.

[4] See pp. 244, 245.

wars did the Navy depart from its usual policy. After an attempt
to build warships in Russia, it constructed a considerable number
in Bermuda and India.[1]

The first fleets of England were composed largely of ships hired
for the occasion, serving around a small nucleus of royal ships.
The Tudors even granted subsidies for the construction of merchantmen which could be used in war.[2] The English had nearly
two hundred ships of various sizes to oppose the Armada in 1588,
yet there were only thirty-four of the Queen's ships in the Royal
Navy at the time. The remainder were hired or volunteer merchantmen or the private warships of such adventurers as Drake
and Hawkins. In the First Dutch War, ninety-two merchantmen
were hired to serve as warships in 1653, and in the Second Dutch
War, forty-one were added to the fighting ships in this way.[3]
There was such a lack of men-of-war in 1692, that an Order in
Council called for the impressing and taking up of twenty-one
merchant ships fit for fourth and fifth rates.[4] Often the ships
were arbitrarily seized for naval service, and the outbreak of war
usually meant an embargo on all merchantmen until the Navy
Board had taken its pick. This hiring of merchant ships relieved
an impecunious navy from maintaining a large standing force in
times of peace, but the system had obvious disadvantages. The
ships were generally of too light a construction to stand up well
in battle, and the merchant-marine captains, who usually commanded their own ships in the naval service, were often too tender
of them in action.

About 1715, the divorce between ships of war and commerce
was quite complete.[5] After that, most of the ships of the line and
frigates were built specifically for that purpose, while merchantmen were hired only to serve as bomb vessels, fireships, small
cruisers, and transports.[6] The chief exception to this was in the
case of the great East Indiamen, which were built and armed

---

[1] See pp. 365-368.   [2] *V. C. H., Dorset*, ii, 202; see *Ibid.*, pp. 154, 155.

[3] Magdalene College, Cambridge, *Pepysian MSS* 2265, f. 19.

[4] Adm. Lib. MSS, *Digest*, "Shipbuilding."

[5] Artiñano, *op. cit.*, p. 144.

[6] R. O., N. B. Out Letters, 2179, *N. B. to Adm.*, Dec. 23, 1741; N. R. S., *Barham Papers*, iii, 106, 109.

practically like small ships of the line and were often utilized for purposes of war. In 1786, Gabriel Snodgrass, master builder for the East India Company, proposed that the Navy construct ships of the line "that would answer equally well in times of peace" and could be rented to the East India Company. He urged that this would not only save an immense amount of oak timber, for the East India Company was the chief rival of the Navy in securing the larger timber, but it would also prevent the ships from rotting idly in harbor in times of peace and relieve the Navy of expense of repairs.[1] This wise suggestion, adopted a century later by England and Germany in subsidizing the construction of fast liners which could serve as auxiliary cruisers, was neglected at the time.

The rejection of those alternative methods of developing a navy threw the burden of construction on the royal dockyards. It was chiefly for this purpose that timber had been gathered by the Navy in such quantities. The dockyards had adequate facilities for the average peace-time construction. Most of them had five slips sufficient for ships of the line or frigates. On those inclined slips, the pieces of the keel were laid on blocks, and on that foundation, the other pieces of the ship's frame were hoisted into place and fastened. Once the keel, stern, sternpost, and the ribs were in place, the ship's skeleton might stand in frame to season. Then, while some shipwrights were fastening on the lower planking and thickstuff of elm, beech, or Baltic oak, others were fashioning the lower deck beams, and fitting them into their resting place with knees. While the planking was rising to the topsides, there was further activity inside the ship, where the upper deck beams were laid and the decks covered with deals. The lower masts were usually "stepped" before launching, but even after the ship took to the water, there was much work still to be done by riggers and fitters.[2]

The English dockyards worked slowly. A ship of the line ordinarily required at least three years for completion, and some-

---

[1] Snodgrass, *Letter to Dundas*, p. 10.
[2] See Colbert, *Lettres, Instructions et Mémoires*, vol. iii, pt. 2, for detailed description of the building of an English warship.

times this extended to ten years.   The private yards had built
third rates in seventeen months late in the seventeenth century.
Similar ships had been rushed to completion in two years during
the Seven Years War, and one was built in fourteen months during the American Revolution, but three years was quick work
for the dockyards.   Frigates could often be completed in eight
months or a year, and smaller vessels could be turned out in a
few months.[1]   Other nations built with far greater speed.   The
Americans could build a seventy-four in a year and a frigate in
sixty days.   The French had built a seventy-four in ninety-five
days and a three-decker in fourteen months during the Seven
Years' War, and, with guillotines in the dockyards, a frigate was
completed in six weeks in 1794.   Colbert once sent orders to
Toulon for the construction of a ship of the line from the laying
of the keel to the launching in the ten days during which Louis
XIV was to be present.[2]   The English dockyards could not always
claim greater thoroughness to compensate for their slowness, for
laziness and a lack of timber were often responsible.   Referring
to the slow construction of ships of the line in the dockyards, the
younger Pitt declared in Parliament that "the great augmenta-
tion of our Navy does not arise from ships begun in a period of
war, but from ships which have been laid upon the stocks several
years antecedent."[3]

England's shipwrights deserve no great credit for the success
of the Royal Navy, during the eighteenth century at least.   English ships of war were usually admittedly inferior to the French
and, later, to the American.   Many of the improvements in the
building of English warships came from the copying of captured
foreign vessels.   The fault lay in the fact that the English Surveyors of the Navy and the master shipwrights could scarcely be
called naval architects.   Building by rule of thumb, they scorned
those elaborate treatises of the French on stability and resistance,

[1] Adm. Lib. MSS, *Naval Instructions; Ibid., Abstracts of Progress, passim;* R. O.,
Adm. Digest, 4871, *N. B. to Adm.,* Jan. 31, 1805; *Parl. Hist.,* xxii, p. 930.

[2] Colbert, *op. cit.,* vol. iii, pt. I, p. 327; N. R. S., *Barham Papers,* ii, 401; *Port-
Folio,* Jan. 1814, p. 74; Adams, *Annals of Portsmouth,* p. 262.

[3] *Parl. Debates,* 1st ser., i, 879.

supported by pages of mathematical calculations and intricate diagrams. Moreover, with their ignorance and conservatism, they lacked imagination and adaptability. Tied down by rule and tradition, they produced ships which may have been well put together, but which were a constant handicap to the men who sailed and fought in them. It was very well to say that their "rule-of-thumb" ships generally captured the products of French science, but it is the fighting men who deserve all the more credit for that. It was notorious that the fastest and most satisfactory ships in the Royal Navy were often French prizes.

In the seventeenth and early nineteenth centuries there were a few exceptions to those general low standards. The greatest of the builders of wooden ships for the Navy was Phineas Pett, the most illustrious member of a distinguished dynasty of ship-wrights. His *Sovereign of the Seas*, launched in 1637, marked a new era in the building of capital ships, and Pett's influence was felt for more than a century in many navies. Next to him in that early period was Sir Anthony Deane, who boasted that he could copy to the minutest detail any ship after examining it for an hour. He had inventive genius as well, and was of tremendous service to the Navy during the Dutch wars.[1]

Pepys has left a vivid description of the men available to re-place Deane in 1684 — Lawrence, master shipwright at Wool-wich, "has never built a ship in his life but the *Little Victory*, which he rebuilt at great charge, and when done was found fit for nothing but a fire-ship. A low-spirited, slow and gouty man . . . illiterate and supine to the last degree." John Shish, "illiterate . . . low-spirited, of little appearance or authority." Furzer, "always bred under his father, working little" — and so on, with similar not unbiased condemnations of the other leading shipwrights.[2] Those men were characteristic of the century of stagnation then setting in, and the light which went out with the passing of Deane was not rekindled until the days of the Napole-onic struggle when Sir Samuel Bentham and Sir Robert Seppings began to apply originality to the building of ships once more. A long-needed school for naval architects was started at Ports-

[1] See pp. 219–222.　　[2] N. R. S., *Catalogue of Pepysian MSS*, i, 77.

mouth at that time.[1] Meanwhile, the duller shipwrights, tied down by the rigid building rules of 1719, were responsible for a century without progress.

The resultant poor sailing qualities are beside the point in this study, but in several ways that stagnation of the eighteenth century bears directly on the timber problem. The French did more than draw intricate parabolas to illustrate the theory of resistance: they adapted their designs and building methods to the exigencies of their own timber problem. Englishmen were not wanting with similar suggestions, but the wise plans of timber economy in construction advanced by Gabriel Snodgrass, Samuel Bentham, and a host of others, were lost on the stiff-necked conservatives who built the King's ships. The fact that the size of oaks limited the size of ships did not prevent abundant development within those limits; but the Surveyors of the Navy and the master shipwrights were not of the stamp to achieve such development. The Navy let the East India Company, the merchant marine, and foreign navies experiment successfully for decades with innovations before they would change their time-honored course. Even worthy precedents were allowed to lapse if they involved over-exertion. A few instances of the failure to conserve timber stand out sharply.

Phineas Pett had travelled up the coast to Chopwell Woods near Durham with his timber molds, to select and convert on the spot the trees suitable to form timbers for the famous *Sovereign of the Seas*. When the timbers were carted out of the forest, they were ready to be assembled into the ship's frame at Woolwich.[2] The system was practical and economical, and Pett's name should have carried the authority of precedent in later days, but "molding in the woods" died out after the Restoration. Instead, contractors delivered at the dockyards the entire logs, with certain general proportions of great and compass timber. The latter system represented an increase of fully one fourth in the timber bill of the Navy, for from one third to three fifths of a log was wasted

[1] N. R. S., *Journals and Letters of Sir T. Byam Martin*, iii, 392, 393.

[2] N. R. S., *Autobiography of Phineas Pett*, pp. 157–160.

in conversion.[1] The carting and shipping of English oak often equalled or exceeded the original value of the timber, and almost half of this transportation charge was for wood destined to become sawdust, chips, and other waste. Moreover, the shipwright in the woods could pick a tree of nearly the requisite girth and curvature, while those dependent upon what was at hand in the dockyard often complained of having to cut down high-priced pieces of large size where smaller and less valuable timber would have served even better. Unsound wood could have been detected on the spot in the woods, and many of the evils of the dockyard receipt of timber could have been avoided. The only opposing argument was the disputed theory that timber seasoned better in the log.[2] Inertia, however, was the real cause for the decline of conversion in the woods — it was easier to direct the sawyers and axemen from one's front dooryard.

Connected with this process was an even more thorough-going suggestion — the standardization of each class of ships in the Navy so that parts could be interchangeable. Instead of having seventy-fours under construction simultaneously, on three different plans, at Chatham, Deptford, and Plymouth, and instead of having, as Nelson did, a half-dozen different designs of seventy-fours under his command, so that one could not lend a spare topmast to another, it was suggested that a competent board select the best possible model for each rate and build along those lines until a definite change was advisable. Standardized knees, keel pieces, beams, and other pieces for seventy-fours, thirty-twos, and every other class, could be cut in the woods and kept on hand at every yard ready for any demand. When ships were broken up, some parts of the frame were usually sound. These were often made over to use again; but with standardization the convenience would have been even greater.[3] If naval architecture had been constantly progressing, this uniformity would have had a

---

[1] Adm. Lib. MSS, *Naval Instructions; Parl. Papers*, 1803–04 (83) iii, 281; Bentham, *Life of Sir Samuel Bentham*, p. 144; Sutherland, *Shipbuilder's Assistant*, p. 57.

[2] See *H, C. J.*. 1792, p. 363.

[3] *Quarterly Review*, viii, 31, 48, 49.

stiffening effect, but in those days of stagnation, it would have been of very great value.

It will be remembered that the Navy made several spasmodic efforts to combat dry rot.[1] Ever since the sixteenth century, it was known in England that the Venetians covered their building slips with roofs which protected the ships' frames from the elements, yet admitted enough air to season them. The French and Swedes adopted these roofs, but their use in England was slight. Snow and rain frequently entered cracks in the frame timbers, caused by the sun's rays, and so rotted the timber that it had to be replaced even before the ship was planked over. In spite of the weight of testimony on the superior durability of oak felled in the winter when free from sap, the shipwrights showed little interest in the various attempts to introduce it, beyond a few trials. Lack of ventilation during construction caused premature rotting of timbers, and in the entire fight against dry rot, the official navy constructors showed a want of initiative. Many of the suggestions to remedy the situation were the impracticable products of cranks, but sound advice was discarded with the rest.[2]

Finally, there was generally a faulty building policy, which caused a tremendous waste of timber, in addition to the unfortunate policy of the timber reserve. Blame for this rested with the Admiralty and the Navy Board rather than with the shipbuilders who had faults enough already. The most sensible policy was the building of a few ships each year, thus permitting a regular supply of seasoned timber which would represent a uniform demand on the forests. The older ships were to be kept in reasonable repair so that they could be patched up for emergency service.[3]

Instead of this, the close of a war usually meant a slackening or suspension of building, a wholesale discharge of dockyard workers, and a neglect of the stores. Many of the ships were removed from "sea pay" or active service, and placed "in ordinary" or reserve at the dockyards, where they remained stag-

[1] See p. 14.   [2] See *H. C. J.*, 1792, pp. 310, 311, 363, 373, 374.
[3] *Ibid.*, pp. 360, 363.

nating and unventilated in "Rotten Row." The beginning of the next war — and in those days the periods of war and peace were almost equal — meant that, when the toadstools and other filth were shovelled from the ships "in ordinary," many of them were found utterly unserviceable. The huge amount of timber which they contained was almost a total loss, and the reserve fleet, which had looked formidable on paper, melted into insignificance. Then there was the hurry to call a new fleet into being. This combined with the inadequate timber reserve to cause building at exorbitant rates. Oaks were slashed prematurely under the influence of the high prices, and ships constructed of green wood were rushed to sea, where they rotted with notorious speed.[1]

The construction of new ships consumed about two thirds of the timber collected at the dockyards. The use of the other third now deserves attention. Repairs fell into two classes. A wooden warship was never finished: the *status quo* could never be maintained for long; some timber or plank was constantly rotting or cracking, and the ship came back to the dockyard time and again to be overhauled, ripped open, and have the defective pieces replaced. Such was the regular repair duty of the yards — a constant burden in war and peace. Far more exciting were the extraordinary repairs necessary when a fleet put into port with masts and hulls shattered in action, calling for immediate attention so that the ships could be at sea again ahead of the enemy.

Both of these demands — the constant, prosaic repairs as well as the infrequent, spectacular ones — are associated with the timber problem, for the former represented a steady drain on timber, while it was in the emergencies that the timber problem most distinctly affected the action of the Navy. The regular repairs fell into four general groups, ranging from the "triennial trimming" through small and middling repairs to great repairs.[2] At least once in three years a ship was supposed to go into dock for examination. With repairs, it was a matter of "a stitch in time saves nine." A rotten or cracked knee could be replaced with little delay, expense, or waste of timber; but let that go

---

[1] See *Parl. Hist.*, xix, 729, 893; xx, 185, 431; N. R. S., *Barham Papers*, ii, *passim*.
[2] *Ibid.*, ii, 360–364; *Parl. Hist.*, xix, 986.

unremedied for a few months, and the dry rot would spread to much sound timber, while the whole ship would be wracked out of shape in heavy seas. A later chapter will tell how Nelson experienced this in his blockade of Toulon in 1803 and 1804. A few small repairs, he said, could easily save some of the finest ships in the Navy, but for want of timber at home, no ships could be sent to relieve the squadron on its stormy blockade duty. The *Kent* 74, a comparatively new ship, was so twisted out of shape that, after a dangerously leaky passage to England, her repairs came to £28,544; and those of the *Gibraltar* 74, at the same time, cost £30,643, fully half their original cost.[1] The expense in money was not the serious part, for England was rich; but about half of every repair bill stands for timber, and England could ill afford oak at that time. The same held true of the ships in "Rotten Row" — a knee or a plank now and then could save a thousand loads of oak later.

Inferior timber was often used in repairs, it will be recalled. On several occasions where foreign substitutes were introduced, it was ordered that they first be employed in repairing old ships. Different kinds of timber — even different kinds of oak — did not go well together in the same ship. A vessel originally built of English oak, which came in for a small repair and received a dozen knees of Canadian oak, some upper planks of Baltic oak, and a new beam or two of Riga fir, with a few pieces of green inferior English or Irish oak in other parts of her anatomy, was almost bound to decay quickly.

There was a close relation between durability, great repairs, and consumption of timber. It is irony that wooden warships, which would still be "in style" a century after their launching, decayed quickly, whereas durable warships of steel now become obsolete while still perfectly sound. The "life" or duration of a ship was reckoned from the date of her launching to the time when her condition necessitated repairs as costly as the construction of a new ship. The outstanding example of real longevity was the *Royal William* 90, built in 1719, which participated in a campaign in 1780 and lasted altogether nearly a century without ex-

[1] Adm. Lib., *Abstracts of Progress, passim;* see *Parl. Hist.*, xix, 729.

tensive repairs. A famous antithesis was the *Queen Charlotte* 110, which was almost completely rotted within two years after her launching in 1810, before she ever put to sea.[1] The average duration for the whole period was between ten and twenty years. It was estimated at twenty-five or thirty years in the seventeenth century, about thirteen years in 1771, twelve in 1792, and around eight during the Napoleonic period. The ravages of dry rot were so severe by 1815 that one naval official exclaimed, "There is no duration!"[2] Fifteen years was perhaps the average duration for the two centuries. Often a ship was broken up when she reached the stage where repairs would equal new construction, but occasionally it was considered desirable to rebuild her in spite of the cost. A "great repair" was practically equivalent to a complete rebuilding, so that very little of the original ship remained. The last part of a ship to decay, however, was usually the portion of the frame which contained the great and compass timbers most difficult to procure, and that served as an inducement to rebuild around them. Moreover, it was often held desirable to maintain the "personality" of a famous or successful ship, as in the case of Nelson's *Victory* or our own *Constitution*. While those ships to-day contain scarcely a stick of their original timbers, they are regarded as the same vessels that won the glory. Finally, the master shipwrights even complained that great repairs, more difficult than new constructions, were undertaken to deprive them of the silver plate given at the launching of a new ship. A late admiral of the days of wooden ships told a story of the United States Navy, which has close parallels in the Royal Navy. Congress refused for a long period to appropriate for new construction, whereupon an old ship was broken up at Norfolk and a cabin window sent overland to Philadelphia, where a complete new ship was "built up around the window" and the whole charged as great repair.

Some of the older ships in a fleet represented the expenditure

[1] See p. 395.

[2] Charnock, *History of Marine Architecture*, ii, 108, 109; Petty, *Treatise of Naval Philosophy*, p. 132; Layman, *Pioneer*, p. 81; Pering, *Premature Decay of our Wooden Bulwarks*, p. 11; Oppenheim, *Administration of the Royal Navy*, pp. 110, 253; *Quarterly Review*, viii, 32, 33.

of enough oak to build several counterparts. Nelson's famous flagship at Trafalgar, the *Victory* 100 (later, 104), was commenced at Chatham in 1759 and launched on May 7, 1765, having cost £63,174, of which £54,748 represented hull, masts, and yards, while the remainder went for rigging and stores. Before she went o sea in 1778 as Keppel's flagship in the Channel, her repairs had cost £13,297, and when she fought at Trafalgar in 1805, forty years old, her total cost to the Navy had been £251, 981. At the close of the war, ten years later, after her service as the flagship of Saumarez in the Baltic, the total had risen to £371,922. She had undergone three great repairs, in 1787, 1800, and 1814, costing £36,782, £70,922, and £79,772 respectively, in addition to various small repairs and triennial trimmings. She had outlasted four ordinary ships, at about six times her original cost. Probably enough timber had gone into her to build five other first rates.[1] Sentiment and frequent repairs still preserve her at Portsmouth, and her cost has been well over a half-million pounds. The *Victory* is an exceptional case, but there were many ships, built during the Napoleonic wars, which were rebuilt with a heavy expense of timber, within six or eight years.

There was little excitement connected with the patching up of the regular wear and tear. It was usually a leisurely process, often taking several months for a small repair and two or three years for a middling or great repair. It was the emergencies which put the dockyard to the real test. Chatham, Sheerness, and Harwich caught the brunt of these in the Dutch wars; Portsmouth and Plymouth in the later contests with the French. The principal demand was for masts and yards, but there was also a demand for plank and deals. Even if the mast ponds were well stocked and the plank piles high, there was work enough in taking out the broken masts and shattered planks to replace them with sound timber. The critical instances arose when thirty or forty "lame ships" descended on a yard, to find a shortage of masts and other essentials. The shipwrights exhausted their scanty stores on the ships of officers who were most influential or disagreeable, and "fished" or patched with braces the other

[1] Adm. Lib., *Abstracts of Progress, passim.*

masts while admirals, impatient to be at sea again to regain control of the Channel, cursed the Navy Board in general and the local officials in particular. The outstanding examples of this will be related later in more detail.[1] The dockyards also had to be ready at any time to repair cracked masts and bad leaks of ships on duty. So much depended on numerical strength at times, that the protracted absence of a single ship could be serious.

Before leaving the relation of the dockyards to the timber problem, it is necessary to mention one final unnecessary cause of timber consumption — the perennial question of "chips." It was a traditional perquisite of the shipwrights to have all chips which fell from the axe, for firewood. Under lax supervision this came to mean all waste pieces of wood under three feet in length, and on certain days, women were allowed to come into the yard to gather this "offal timber" in their aprons. The system was open to constant abuse. When ships were being repaired, the artificers purposely smashed the planking with their axes, so that one commissioner at Chatham expressed the fear that two whole ships under repair would be carried away by the women in their laps. The shipwrights even began to stop work an hour early, in order to saw up large pieces of sound and valuable timber into three-foot lengths. Samuel Bentham, who went to Portsmouth to investigate abuses in 1798, reported that he had purchased some of these "chips" for firewood and found that they pieced together into fine long planks; that many of the houses in the town were built of three-foot wood; and that an officer who tried to stop the process was put in danger of his life by the angry artificers. Admiral Warren estimated, doubtless in exaggeration, that the daily loss of timber from this source was nearly enough to build a sloop of war. Time and again the Navy compounded for this perquisite by an increase of wages, but the workmen soon returned to it as a right. In addition, there was frequent embezzlement of larger timber. The abuse of "chips" has been recorded in great detail, and it certainly represented an excessive waste; but artificers were the lowest members of the civil service, and

[1] See pp. 208–210, 215, 219–222, 304, 309–312.

their superiors, who pointed out this petty larceny, caused an even greater waste of timber through their own corruption and faulty policies.[1]

The royal dockyards were not equal to the entire task of building and repairing for the Navy. Especially in time of war, it was customary to allot by contract to private shipyards much of the building and part of the repairing. The insistence of the Navigation Acts upon British-built ships was justified by these reserve yards with their thousands of trained shipwrights, capable of supplementing the regular facilities for construction. The greatest of these were in the Thames. They were accustomed to building great ships for the East India Company, and could easily turn their hands to the construction of ships of the line. The principal Thames yard at Blackwall, conducted in the seventeenth century by Sir Henry Johnson, later by Wells and Company, and in the Napoleonic period by Wigram and Green, was more extensive than the neighboring royal dockyards at Deptford and Woolwich.[2] The yards of Pitcher and Sons at Northfleet, Barnard and Roberts at Deptford and Rotherhithe, and Brent and Sons at Rotherhithe were almost on a par with the King's yards. Smaller warships such as frigates, sloops, and brigs were often constructed in various little "outports" by men who often risked their all in the building of a single ship.[3]

Much ink has been wasted on the relative merits of ships from the royal yards and the merchant yards.[4] The contract ships were certainly cheaper and were built more quickly. Even when the builder took a profit of 15 per cent, his prices were usually

---

[1] R. O., N. B. Out Letters, 2188, *N. B. to Adm.*, June 18, 1756; *Commons Reports*, xiii, 499; *H. C. J.*, 1792, p. 372; Lott, *Account of Proposals for H. M. Naval Service*, pp. 10–29; Bentham, *Life of Sir Samuel Bentham*, pp. 142, 143; Warren, *A View of the Naval Force of Great Britain*, p. 15.

[2] Green and Wigram, *Chronicles of Blackwall Yard, passim*.

[3] *Parl. Papers*, 1813–14 (115), vol. vii, pt. 1, pp. 2–7, 19, 343; *V. C. H., Sussex*, ii, pp. 164–167; for typical contract, see Knowles, *Naval Architecture*, pp. lix–lxvii.

[4] See esp. *H C. J.*, 1792, pp. 309, 310, 365; *Parl. Debates*, 1st ser., i, 920; v, 72–110; *Quarterly Review*, x, 20 ff.; Maydman, *Naval Speculations*, p. 72; *Brief Enquiry into the Present Condition of the Navy of Great Britain*, p. 22; Oppenheim, *Administration of the Royal Navy*, p. 339.

that much below the cost of constructing a similar ship in the King's yards. Usually the ships could be finished much more quickly by the merchant yards. On the other hand, the Navy insisted that its own ships received a much more thorough construction and better timber. The dockyard officials were charged with undue discrimination against ships built in private yards which came to them for repairs, while they generally upheld the superiority of their own creations. This professional pride may have been warranted at times, but the real answer seems to be that the private yards were run on a business basis while the King's yards were not. The contractor, whose profits depended on efficiency and to whom delay meant penalties, had more reason for fast, efficient, economical work than the master shipwright, comfortable in his permanent position, with all bills paid by the public. The contractor's work was subject to constant supervision by the Surveyors of the Navy, and he could not afford to allow the lax introduction of rotten timber prevalent in the dockyards.

Building in private yards had several of the faults already described in connection with timber contracts. There was the same influence exerted at the Navy Board in securing contracts, and the surveyors occasionally found it profitable to be a little blind in their inspections. The great Thames builders joined in an *entente cordiale*, not unlike the relations of Larking and Bowsher, and were at times in a position to dictate to the Navy.[1]

The supply of timber for the private yards was badly managed by the Navy. When the forty fir frigates were built in merchant yards in 1812 and 1813, the timber was furnished from the dockyard supply, but that was exceptional. Ordinarily, the private builders bid against the Navy for the available supply of English oak. They were in a position to outbid the Navy timber contractors, and then to raise their own contract price to meet the added charges.[2] Thus the Navy lost all around. The unneces-

---

[1] R. O., Adm. Digest, 4871, *Perry, Wells, Green to Adm.*, Nov. 2, 1805; 4916, *Adm. to N. B.*, July 17, 1813; *Parl. Papers*, 1813–14 (115) vol. vii, pt. 1, p. 354; *Parl. Hist.*, xxii, 930; *Parl. Debates*, 1st ser., i, 902.

[2] R. O., N. B. In Letters, 1559, *Larking to N. B.*, Dec. 26, 1794; *Parl. Papers, ibid.*, 172, 173.

sary competition increased the price of its own timber, and it had
to pay the money used to defeat itself. The private builders,
able to pay the higher price, could secure the best timber. If the
Navy had acted consistently on that policy of 1812, purchasing
all the available timber and issuing it to the merchant yards, it
would have saved millions. Colbert had learned that a century
and a half before.

Whatever the relative merits of the royal and private yards,
the latter were essential to the Navy. In most of the later wars,
many of the capital ships and nearly all of the smaller ones were
built by contract, while the fleets which won several of the greatest victories contained a majority of ships of the line built in the
merchant yards.

In concluding this survey of the machinery of timber supply
and consumption, the cost of timber and shipbuilding deserves
attention. It is almost impossible to give a systematic account
of the gradual rise of the price of timber. A table of prices at
different dates would be next to useless, and quite dangerous for
any purposes of drawing conclusions. Price lists can be found by
the dozen in every period, often valuable for comparison within
the range of years they cover, but almost worthless alongside
lists for the succeeding periods. The trouble lies in the lack of a
common basic standard.

The rise and fall of the price of a quarter of wheat or a gallon
of beer can be traced fairly accurately through the decades and
centuries. The load of timber, on the other hand, had too many
different values at the same time. The load, as was said, represented fifty cubic feet, but the value of that load depended on
the size of the timber in question. Instances of this variance have
already been mentioned in connection with the question of great
and compass timber. The more elaborate price lists give the
different prices per load according to "meetings" depending on
the girth of the logs and representing the number of cubic feet
in a log forty feet long. Some lists take the "average" price
of straight timber on the basis of sixty-foot meetings, others on
a hundred. Between those two standards alone, there was a difference of about twenty per cent, and other meetings ran far

above and below those. The "average" price could mean either
or neither of these two. In compass timber and in plank the difference was even more marked, while the prices of masts, varying with every inch of diameter and yard of length and measured
sometimes in inches, sometimes in palms or hands, utterly defy
comparison. The unsteady credit of the Navy makes another
element of uncertainty, with wide differences between prices
based on ready money and on regular contract. Only the general
outlines of the increase can be given with any pretence to accuracy
— relative changes are evident, but absolute comparisons are
unsafe.

In the early days of Henry VIII, the Navy could purchase oak
at 12d. to 18d. a load. During his reign the increase was rapid with
the growing demands for building and the marine, and at his
death in 1547, ten shillings may be considered an average price.
By the time of the Armada, a load of timber cost the Navy about
a pound. By 1618, it was about £1 5s. and rose gradually to
about £1 13s. in 1655 and £2 at the Restoration. Between 1660
and 1670, the average price of a load, in those hundreds of separate transactions, was about £2 6s. There was another period
of very gradual rise until it stood at about £3 6s. in 1740. From
1752 to 1792, Navy contract prices did not change, standing at
an average of £4 5s. Between 1792 and 1804, prices increased
rapidly in an irregular fashion, to over £7. By 1813, the "Timber Trust" was charging the Navy about £13, though timber
on the general market was only about £9. During the last half
century of the problem, the price varied between £5 and £8.[1]
The general scale of living had risen during that time, but the
purchasing power of the pound sterling had not diminished as fast
as the cost of oak increased. The difference is an indication of
the increasing scarcity of timber. With straight oak of average
size as a mean, the prices of other forms of timber can be roughly

---

[1] *Commons Reports*, iii, 39; *Parl. Papers*, 1849 (0.30), xx, 120; *H. C. J., 1792*,
pp. 289, 307, 365; *L. & P., Henry VIII; Cal. S. P., Dom.;* R. O., *Adm., Acct.
Gen., Misc., Var., Contracts, passim;* Fisher, *Heart of Oak*, p. 62; Fincham, *History of Naval Architecture*, p. 216; Oppenheim, *Administration of the Royal Navy*,
p. 371; Rogers, *History of Agriculture and Prices*, iii, 401, 417; iv, 444–449; v,
518–530; vi, 494–506, 678–679; vol. vii, pt. 1, pp. 412–420.

estimated, adding twenty to twenty-five per cent for average oak plank and compass timber, and deducting a similar amount for elm and beech. Baltic oak timber and plank would average in the long run about the same as the English in cost, while the American oak was somewhat cheaper. Fir and pine timber cost about twenty-five per cent less than oak, on the whole. Prussian or "sprucia" deals cost more than the Norwegian, which, in turn, were more than American boards.

The cost of shipbuilding reflected the price of timber, for timber was the chief item of expense. Like timber costs, the varying prices of building ships cannot be plotted accurately for want of a common basis of comparisons. Some figures include the hull alone; others, hull masts, and yards; and still others, the ship all rigged, stored, and ready for sea except for her armament. Often the statistics do not show which of these three stages is meant. Figures were usually given in the cost per ton. This varied with each rate. A "ton of seventy-four" cost more than a ton of frigate partly because the larger timbers were proportionately more expensive. Finally there was the difference in cost between construction in the private and the royal yards. A table of prices per ton of shipping for 1675 from the *Pepysian Manuscripts* at Magdalene, Cambridge, will illustrate the last two points:[1]

Rate		Contract	King's Yards
1	....	..	£15 0
2	....	..	14 0
3	....	£9 0	10 0
4	....	8 0	8 10s
5	....	7 10s	7 15s
6	....	7 0	7 5s
Fireships	....	6 10s	6 10s

That general proportion held throughout the two centuries, though the divergence of cost between the different rates and between contract and royal building tended to grow wider.

The cost per ton of a third rate (usually a seventy-four in the eighteenth century), built in a merchant yard, including hull, masts, and yards, but not rigging or stores, can be traced through

[1] Magdalene College, Cambridge, *Pepysian MSS*, 2265.

two centuries and a half, making allowances for the uncertain basis of comparison. The general rise corresponds quite closely to the increasing cost of timber. The cost per ton is equivalent to four or five times the average cost quoted for a load of timber; for a ship of the line consumed a great deal of large timber far above the average in cost. In 1600, it was about £5 10s. and in 1675, as quoted above, it was £9. By 1693, it had risen to about £11 5s. Between 1719 and 1741, the cost gradually rose from £12 to £13. During the Seven Years' War, it was £16 or £17. This increased to over £20 in the American Revolution and between 1793 and 1802, £20 or £21 was the usual cost. This rose to £34 10s. in 1803, and the timber crisis of the following year brought the maximum price of £36 in 1805. During the remainder of the war, the rates hovered between £33 and £36. By 1836, it had dropped back to £26. After that, new forms of steam warships caused too radical a divergence from the old third-rate tonnage to be accurate for comparison.[1]

Many causes contributed to the rise of timber and ship-building costs. Chief among them was the failure of the English forests, but by no means the least was the spirit in which Samuel Pepys accepted the silver service from Sir William Warren.

In 1676, a third rate measuring 1000 tons consumed 1000 loads of timber, and cost, by contract, £9,000. A seventy-four of the Napoleonic period varied between 1600 and 1900 tons, so that the total cost of hull, masts, and yards was about £60,000. Of that amount, over £35,000 represented timber, of which some 3,000 loads were required. The masts and yards cost £3,000 or £4,000 more, while the remainder went for other materials and for labor. Rigging and stores would bring the total to nearly £70,000 and the guns would mean another heavy item of expense.[2] Farington remarks in his diary that in the eighteenth century it was customary to estimate the cost of a ship at £1,000

[1] Adm. Lib. MSS, *Digests*, "Shipbuilding" and "Naval Instructions"; R. O., *Adm., Acct. Gen., Misc., Var., Contracts, passim; Commons Reports*, iii, 22; *Parl. Papers*, 1813–14 (134), xi, 2–6; (115), vol. vii, pt. 1, pp. 354, 554; *H. C. J.*, 1792, p. 365; Farington, *Diary*, i, 18, 92, 206; Clowes, *Royal Navy*, iii, 10.

[2] Adm. Lib., *Abstracts of Progress, passim;* Barnaby, *Naval Development in the Century*, p. 46.

a gun; but that probably included the ordnance.[1] With half
the cost of a completed ship representing wood, the influence of
a rise in timber prices on the building policy can be imagined,
especially in the earlier decades, when naval funds were low.

With all its faults and shortcomings, with all its unnecessary
expense and inefficiency, the system by which the Navy gathered
its timber and built its ships accomplished its main purpose. The
admirals were furnished with ships. The ships may have been
poorly designed, and they may not have lasted as long as they
should, but most of them were good tough ships of Sussex or
Hampshire oak, and there were usually enough of them. Some
of the admirals knew how to use them well, and that was enough
to give England her control of the seas.

[1] Farington, *Diary*, i, 18.

CHAPTER III

ENGLAND'S DIMINISHING WOODLANDS

THE universally high regard felt by Englishmen for their native oak as the choicest of ship timbers led them to depend upon their own woodlands for a constant supply with which to build hulls for the King's ships. The forests that had once covered England dwindled into groves unequal to that constant demand, for the Navy had many rivals in its quest for oak and an adequate national forest policy was lacking. The want of a consistent forest policy arose largely from the unusual amount of foresight required, for the men who planted oaks would not live to see their maturity a century hence. Most of England's wooden fleets came from those groves, but the supply was often threatened, and at one of the most critical periods in English naval history, when Napoleon was threatening invasion, it failed, and did not recover again before the end of the era of wooden ships.

This failure of the woodlands had not come on unexpectedly. For more than two centuries before that struggle with Napoleon, men had come to believe that when England's forests could no longer supply ship timber, her sea power was threatened. Old Admiral Sir William Monson well summed up that feeling in his interesting Naval Tracts, written just before our period opens:

All kinds of wood that belongs to the building of ships or other works that have relation to timber, we do and shall find, in a little time, a great want of. For wood is now utterly decayed in England, and begins to be no less in Ireland. . . . If money, or wealth, decay in a kingdom there may be means of trade to recover it again; if seamen die so long as there are ships and navigation they will soon increase and make their deaths forgotten; but if our timber be consumed and spent it will require the age of three or four generations before it can grow again for use.[1]

Those words are typical of dozens of opinions expressed through nearly three centuries. There was concern in the days of the Armada and there was concern in the very last year of wooden

[1] N. R. S., *Naval Tracts of Sir William Monson*, v, 268.

warships. Time and again attention was called to the alarming inroads of the choppers; time and again measures were taken which would have been adequate to relieve the situation permanently if properly carried out; yet the supply of naval timber steadily diminished.

That constant worry over the prospect of a timber shortage was doubtless overdone at times. Just before the Second Dutch War, the American Revolution, and the war with Revolutionary France, investigators reported almost complete exhaustion of the native oak supply, yet the Navy sustained all those contests without suffering the extreme consequences predicted in such black colors. In 1849, a naval timber inspector denied the whole bugbear of the timber shortage:

Generally speaking, whatever supply we wanted, that we always got, whether there were railways or whether there were not. The prediction that our dockyards must be shut up on account of the scarcity of timber, is of very ancient date, and is periodically repeated by some very excellent and by others very interested people.[1]

He understated the situation just as the alarmists exaggerated it. The latter were wrong in assuming that a failure of the English groves meant maritime ruin, for if masts could be imported, oak could be, also. It was not true, on the other hand, that the Navy had always got all the oak it wanted. There were several periods when the work of the dockyards and the condition of the Navy were seriously affected for want of an adequate supply of native timber. On one occasion, the failure of the forests was positively dangerous. Even if the chronic alarm of the Navy and the nation was based on an exaggerated supposition, it is a real factor to be reckoned with, for a false creed seriously believed has influence.

In view of those facts, the record of the causes of the oak shortage has a decided value in connection with the timber question. This account will commence with a description of England's woodlands and the problems incident upon cutting and transporting the oaks. It will then turn to various economic factors which worked against an adequate supply of naval timber. Finally, it

---

[1] *Parl. Papers*, 1849 (o.30), xx, 123. See *H. C. J.*, *1787–88*, pp. 559, 560.

will trace the history of the English forest policy and its relation to the oak supply.

The timber problem was first realized in the sixteenth century. It became acute during the Restoration. A century later, after the Seven Years' War, the scarcity of oak caused very general alarm, and during the remaining hundred years of wooden ship-building the groves of England became less and less capable of meeting the increasing demands of the Navy. In order to understand why England's woodlands had almost failed in their function of supplying naval timber by 1660, it will be necessary to anticipate the period covered by this study and go back into the reign of Henry VIII to analyze the causes, political and economic, which really created the timber problem.

The very nature of the English groves accounts in part for their inadequate rôle in the naval timber supply. These woodlands could scarcely be called forests. That term was used in England to denote the royal hunting preserves, whether wooded or not. Yet even if the word "forest" had not been preëmpted for that special purpose, it could scarcely be applied to the English groves. Unlike the foreign regions from whose vast expanses of virgin forest she later drew timber, England was not a heavily wooded region during the period under consideration.

Great forests had covered most of England when the Romans first came to Britain; but these were largely cleared away to make possible the settlement of the land. It was estimated at the end of the seventeenth century that about one eighth of England was wooded, and even the principal timber counties had less than one half of their area covered by woods.[1] Many districts in what Ruskin terms the "woody or green country" — a mixture of park, pasture, and variegated forest — had a distinctly sylvan aspect, but single woodland tracts more than twenty miles square were rare. It was from hundreds of groves smaller than this that the Navy drew its supply of timber.

[1] Rogers, *History of Agriculture and Prices*, v, 92; see *Agricultural Returns for Great Britain*, 1901, giving acreage and percentage of woodlands by counties, quoted in Schwappach, *Forestry*, p. 17; also 1895 figures quoted in Forbes, *English Estate Forestry*, p. 21.

The great oak region lay in the southeast corner of England, extending from the Thames southward to the sea. The Andred Weald, the greatest of the original forests, had once covered much of this region. Sussex led all the counties in the quality and quantity of its oak, but the neighboring counties of Surrey, Hampshire, and Kent were not far behind.[1] The oak belt gradually diminished as it extended westward to Gloucestershire. Most of the Midland counties were well wooded, but oak was scarce in the north with its great expanses of barren moor, and the oak of the north was considered inferior in quality.

The other parts of the British Isles were relatively unimportant in the matter of naval timber. The Tweed serves not only as a rough frontier for England and Scotland, but also for the oak and fir which characterize the woodlands of those two countries. It was not an absolute frontier in those days, for a strip of fir extended down into the high country of north-central England, while the oak penetrated into parts of the Lowlands of Scotland; but on the whole, England was a land of oak and Scotland of fir. Scotch fir was held in low esteem by the naval authorities and was used by the Navy for masts and timber only in cases of emergency.[2] Wales grew good oak of small dimensions; but much of it was inaccessible, and the Navy did not utilize it to any extent until after the Seven Years' War. Ireland was well wooded in the earlier part of our period, but the forests were rapidly wasted. Irish oak was occasionally used in the dockyards, but Irish fir was held beneath contempt.[3] The oak groves of England, and of the southern counties of England in particular, deserve most attention.

Unlike the Baltic and American regions, England had no virgin forests in the accessible districts. Most of the groves had been cut over and replanted time and again. The fact that the trees

---

[1] Fraser, *Bellerophon*, p. 5; *Victoria County History, Surrey*, ii, 562; *Sussex*, ii, 291, 299, 313.

[2] Macpherson, *Annals*, ii, 726; *Description and History of Vegetable Substances*, ii, 37, 38; Nairne, *Notes on Highland Woods, passim*.

[3] R. O., N. B. In Letters, 1561, *Larking to N. B.*, Sept. 3, 1811; *Cal. S. P., Dom., 1636–67*, xxvii, 523; *Cal. Treas. Papers, 1557–1696*, p. 542; *Hist. MSS Com., Finch Papers*, ii, 469.

were planted as an investment covering about a century partly explains the high price of English oak.

There were two principal forms of grove. They might be "high woods" composed of great oaks growing old together. This more picturesque form was particularly characteristic of parks and estates where oaks were grown primarily for ornamental purposes. More common on the estates where oaks were grown for profit was the "copse" or "coppice with standards." This was a sort of two-storied grove, with a few high trees towering above the younger oaks of the underwood. The latter were cut every twenty years or so for firewood and tanbark. At these fellings a few trees were spared to grow to full size. About fifty of these great "standards" could be raised on an acre. This system provided for a regular succession of large and small wood, as great oaks from successive plantings would be reaching maturity at least every twenty years. Woodlands well conducted on that basis could yield a good income. Compass timber came chiefly from oaks growing alone in the hedgerows between fields, where exposure to the elements gave them the desired irregularity of form.[1]

The time for felling the great oaks was one of the chief problems of the timber grower. There was a "psychological moment" for cutting, when the tree would yield a greater profit than at any other time. Oaks, it will be remembered, grow very slowly. The period of maturity is reached between the ages of eighty and a hundred and twenty years, when the tree attains a diameter of fifteen or eighteen inches. Up to that time it was not profitable to cut oaks for ship timber because of the additional value of a large-sized tree. Beyond that period of maturity, the risk of decay was great. Therein lay one of the principal problems of the naval supply of oak, already suggested in connection with the great pieces of timber needed for ships of the line. Many of those large pieces had to come from trees of more than twenty inches in diameter, at least 150 years old. The exceptionally

---

[1] For general description, see esp. Brown, *Forester;* Maw, *Practice of Forestry;* Evelyn, *Sylva;* Forbes, *English Estate Forestry;* and Nisbet, *Our Forests and Woodlands, passim.*

high value of such pieces scarcely compensated for the risk of delay in cutting; for the results of a century of patience might be wasted in attempting to grow great stern-posts or beams. The tree might live on for centuries as a picturesque, staghorned old giant, sound outside, but rotted away at the heart and quite worthless for timber.

The judging of standing timber was a fine art. There was much truth in Evelyn's dictum, "A tree is a merchant adventurer; you shall never know what he is worth until he is dead." The forester could form some estimate of the value of timber on the stump by viewing the dead branches, knot-holes, and the nature of the soil, and after striking the tree with a hammer, he could listen for the hollow sound which would denote decay. Such an examination, however, was only superficial and left much to chance.

Felled timber could be judged more accurately. Smell, sight, and sound were all employed in the examination. Good oak timber had a clean, strong odor of tannic acid. Absence of odor indicated *bois passé*, which had lost its vitality, while a disagreeable smell betrayed some disease rotting the interior. English oak at its best had a fresh, bright, reddish appearance, in healthy contrast to various colors which were symptoms of serious diseases. The butt was examined for signs of "shakes," those longitudinal cracks caused by heavy winds, frosts, or uneven growth; and the annular rings were inspected to judge the regularity of its growth. Again, after it had been felled, the log was struck with a hammer to test its soundness. Garraud, the French authority on naval timber, lists twenty-seven of the most common defects in standing timber, with thirty-eight more to be found after felling, indicating in each case whether the wood should be accepted, rejected, or used with caution. The trees destined for naval purposes ordinarily underwent three examinations. A naval purveyor inspected them while standing and again after felling, while the dockyard officials were supposed to give them the final and most searching test upon their arrival at the yard. The Navy paid for the best quality of timber, and unless the inspectors were subject to the corruption already described, only the choicest oaks found their way into naval construction.[1]

The proper season for felling timber was a subject for controversy throughout the two centuries. Most of the oak was cut in the spring, for at that time the sap in the tree permitted the removal of the bark, which was valuable for tanning leather. In discussing dry rot, attention was called to the fact that winter-felled timber was supposed to be more immune from that decay. The long-lived *Royal William* was built of oak cut in the winter. The Navy Board at times offered an extra price for such timber, to compensate for the loss of bark, but only spasmodically were attempts made to secure much of it.

Several ships were built to experiment on the relative value of winter and summer-felled oak. The *Montague* 74, and the *Achilles* 60, built in 1774 of winter-felled oak, each gave good service without requiring any large repairs for over twenty years. The sloop *Hawke*, built at Deptford in 1795, with one side of winter-felled and the other of summer-felled oak, was badly decayed at the end of ten years, when both sides were found in bad condition. The experiment was ordered again in 1815, but the apparent advantage of cutting the wood when free from sap was not utilized to any extent.[2] The arguments in favor of winter felling ranged from scientific discourses in the Royal Society to pertinent doggerel, but they were ineffectual against tradition and inertia, so that spring continued to be the busy season for the woodchoppers. There was even a widespread superstition that timber cut during the waning moon was less subject to dry rot.[3]

[1] Laslett, *Timber and Timber Trees*, p. 39; Garraud, *Études sur les Bois de Construction*, pp. 100–113; Stevenson, *Wood*, pp. 51–67; Betts, *Timber*, p. 77; Romme, *L'Art de la Marine*, p. 208. For an admirable series of colored illustrations of chief defects, see France, Ministère de la Marine, *Instructions sur les Bois de Marine*, Plates 45–58.

[2] R. O., Adm. Digest, 4809, *N. B. to Adm.*, Dec. 9, 1790; 4916, *Adm. to Treas.*, Apr. 4, 1813; *Adm. to N. B.*, Dec. 22, 1814; *N. B. to Adm.*, Aug. 23, 1815; *H.C.J.*, *1792*, pp. 277, 278, 365-371; Derrick, *Memoirs of the Royal Navy*, pp. 286–288; Knowles, *Dry Rot*, pp. 16–22; Garraud, *op. cit.*, pp. 31–34, 39, 40.

[3] *Quarterly Review*, xxx, 220; Garraud, *op. cit.*, pp. 38, 39; *Philosophical Transactions*, no. 192, p. 455; no. 213, p. 244; *Parl. Papers*, 1847–48 (o.48), vol. xxi, pt. 1, p. 362.

The felling of English timber was an orderly, almost incidental process, conducted on a very small scale compared with the extensive lumbering operations in the Baltic or American forests, where little colonies of woodchoppers migrated into the wilderness for the whole winter. Except for occasional fellings of the entire stand of timber on some estate, English cutting was a process of felling individual oaks in a manner that would injure the surrounding trees as little as possible. It required no regular lumbering population, for there were always ordinary laborers at hand to assist the "fellmonger" in his occasional work. In certain counties, saws were used for felling the trees, in order to leave a flat stump for the new shoots, but axes were in far more general use. Those who have felled trees to any extent will realize the labor involved in cutting through a great oak. It is not a simple task as in the case of pine, where great soft chips fall out with every blow. The axe bounds back with a sharp ring from the tough oak, and blows resound far through the woods for some time before the great crash indicates that the chopper has finally hacked his way through the century-old trunk. Branches were usually lopped off beforehand, to preserve them from splintering. In the royal forests, the officials enjoyed as perquisites these trimmings of "top and lop," which contained much good wood. The tree was stripped of its bark soon after felling, and the glistening whiteness of the exposed wood of the trunk soon changed to a reddish brown through contact with the air.[1]

Those great reddish-brown logs were usually carried intact to the dockyards, for the inert, conservative shipwrights did not follow the example of Phineas Pett in converting the oaks into ship timber where they grew. The only oaks not carried entire to the yards were the taller, thinner trees intended for planks, which were sawn out by hand in the forest. Sawmills had developed in Europe before the seventeenth century and were used extensively during that century by the Dutch, the French, and the Baltic peoples, as well as by the colonists in New England, where a sawmill followed close upon the establishment of nearly

---

[1] See esp. Gilpin, *Forest Scenery*, ii, 192–194; *V. C. H., Surrey*, ii, 572, 573; Brown, *Forester*; Schlich, *Manual of Forestry, passim*.

every town. Yet England consistently refused to employ them. A Dutchman set one up in England in 1633, but was forced to abandon the venture on account of the violence of the hand-sawyers, who feared unemployment as a result of the innovation. A similar experience occurred as late as 1761, and it was not until nearly the end of that century that sawmills gained a footing in England. In the meantime, sawpits similar to those described in the dockyards were dug in the woods, and hand-sawyers slowly pulled their long saws through the logs to make plank. Very few deals or boards were cut in England because of the expense of this primitive process. It was cheaper to import deals and plank from Dantzig, where the oaks were sawn by windmills.[1]

The principal single item in the cost of timber was usually transportation, because of the extreme bulk of wood in comparison with its value. The cost of Baltic timber delivered in the dockyards was twenty times the value of the tree on the stump. With English timber, the ratio was more variable, but transportation charges often equalled the value of the standing timber.

Transportation of English timber was divided into land carriage and water carriage. The former was far more expensive and important in its results. When the period of shortage came, there was still plenty of good oak in England, but much of it was inaccessible. Twenty miles was ordinarily considered a maximum haul. Beyond that distance land carriage added heavily to the cost of timber, so that in the more remote localities many great oaks which would have made splendid ship timber were cut up for ordinary carpenter's purposes. The strips of woodland within fifteen or twenty miles of the coast or navigable rivers were the first places to be exploited for timber.

Timber was usually hauled in "tuggs," or wagons drawn by several pairs of horses or oxen, relieved in frequent relays. The ordinary timber wagon could carry a good-sized log, weighing somewhat over a ton. The term "load," which became the standard of timber measurement, arose from this source.[2] Oc-

[1] Macpherson, *Annals*, ii, 377; Wood, *History of the Royal Society of Arts*, p. 247; Knowles, *Naval Architecture*, p. 434.

[2] Gilpin, *op. cit.*, i, 205.

casionally, extra effort was needed for logs of exceptional size such as the great keelson of the *Sovereign of the Seas*, described in 1637: "One great piece of timber, which made the kelson, was so great and weighty that twenty-eight oxen and four horses with much difficulty drew it from the place where it grew, and from whence it was cut, down unto the water side." [1] A century or two later, the Navy would gladly have made twice that effort if such logs had been available.

A dry summer was essential for land carriage, unlike the Baltic and American forests, where a hard winter with a heavy fall of snow was necessary for hauling the logs to the river. Land carriage was especially difficult in the region of the old Andred Weald in Sussex and its vicinity, where the choicest oak grew, for many of its best groves were remote from navigable water. Sussex did not receive snow enough to make sledding possible, and the winter meant rains which turned the clayey soil into an impassable sea of mud. There were few good roads in that oak country, and logs were sometimes held up for over a year before the ground was dry enough to allow the tuggs to resume their work. Even under ordinary conditions, their progress was slow.

Land carriage provoked one situation so interesting that it tempts a fuller treatment than proportion will permit in this study. Under Charles I it amounted to a *corvée*, or an extra, unparliamentary tax closely related to the famous imposition of Ship Money, which it resembled. The King used only sparingly his claim to the right of commandeering timber itself by purveyance, but regularly insisted in the purveyance of timber carriage by the counties in which the oak was cut. Justices of the peace in those counties were instructed to requisition this transportation at the King's price of fivepence a mile, but the actual cost of the hauling was often four times that amount. If timber carriages were not forthcoming at the reduced royal rate, the counties had to compound in cash for the heavy difference. The State Papers are full of protests against this unparliamentary levy. As long as the burden fell upon the counties where the timber grew, the King

---

[1] Heywood, *A True Description of His Majesty's Royal Ship built this Year*, 1637, etc., quoted in Charnock, *History of Marine Architecture*, ii, 283.

was within his technical right; but the practice was extended as in the case of Ship Money. Hampshire, for instance, would complain that it was overburdened by the constant demands for carriage of timber from its many woodlands. When the protests grew defiant in tone, Dorset and other neighboring counties would be ordered to share the expense. The justices of Dorset would claim with right that such an order was illegal, as the timber was not grown in their county and was not even carted through its territory. The objections of the southern timber counties finally grew so menacing that the King decided to cut most of the timber in the north, where royal authority was more secure, even if the timber was of inferior quality. It was principally for that reason that Phineas Pett cut the timbers of the *Sovereign of the Seas* in Durham, where he received every assistance in the matter of land carriage from the bishop, while Yorkshire helped to pay the cost of that transportation. The requisitioning of land carriage lasted until after 1688, though the King's price was somewhat raised and the injustice was mitigated.[1]

After 1695, the Navy had to pay full price for land carriage. As the woods near navigable water became depleted, the Navy Board finally increased the allowances for land carriage in order to open up new regions. When the cost of land carriage on a load of timber exceeded thirty-eight shillings, the contractors were allowed a bonus of a shilling for each extra mile and some timber was brought in which had been carried twenty miles extra. The development of canals and turnpikes late in the eighteenth century and railways in the early nineteenth opened up woodland tracts which hitherto had not been available.[2]

The final stage in transportation was the water carriage. This was simpler and cheaper than land carriage, but it was more expensive in England than in other countries. Oak alone is so heavy that it floats with difficulty, but in America and the Baltic

[1] See esp. *Cal.S.P.,Dom.*, *1581–90*, p. 283; *1631–33*, pp. 308, 372, 381, 405, 436, 449, 553, 578; *1633–34*, pp. 238, 239; *1634–35*, p. 1; *1635*, pp. 156, 308, 338, 339; *1636–37*, pp. 9, 32, 33; *1637*, pp. 138, 451, 469; *1637–38*, pp. 480, 550; *1638–39*, pp. 121, 382, 393; *1639*, pp. 401, 406; *1644*, p. 556; Adm. Library, *Digest*, "Shipbuilding," p. 14; see Colbert, *Lettres, Instructions et Mémoires*, vol. iii, pt. 2, p. 378.
[2] *Commons Reports*, iii, 16; H. C. J., 1792, pp. 296, 297, 321, 323, 393.

regions it could be joined with the lighter fir or pine logs and rafted down the rivers. In England those fir and pine logs were lacking, so the river trip was usually made in open lighters or in "hoys" — low sloops with great dull-red sails. The latter were also used in carrying timber along the coast. That coasting service was more adventurous than it sounds, for the timber hoys were exposed to enemy raiders. The Turks captured timber cargoes bound from Dean Forest to Plymouth during the reign of Charles I, while the French and Dutch occasionally seized shipments of oak off the Cornish coast or the Isle of Wight in later times. It was often necessary to detail naval convoys for this service. Unless the sea carriage was too dangerous or the land carriage very muddy, English timber ordinarily reached the dockyards still green, within a few months after it was cut.[1]

That general description of the woodlands and the exploitation of timber applies to all the English groves, whether in royal forests or on private estates. The royal forests are of interest here not for what they did to help the Navy, but for what they might have done. They have already received attention far out of proportion to their importance as sources of timber. They represent a wasted opportunity, for the Navy could have secured an ample supply from its own reserves if plans, well conceived on several occasions, had been followed out. As it was, years were rare when more than a tenth of the Navy's supply of oak came from the royal forests. The parks and woodlands of the nobility and landed gentry furnished the remainder.

The term "forest" used in this connection has only an incidental relation to woodlands, it will be remembered. It denotes a region "afforested" by English kings as far back as Saxon days, in the interest of hunting.[2] They enacted savage laws in order that there should be no interference with their chasing of deer and

[1] See *Cal. S. P., Dom., 1636-37*, pp. 87, 104; *1664-65*, p. 378; *1667*, p. 329; R. O., N. B. Out Letters, 2179, *N. B. to Adm.*, Aug. 8, 1742; 2189, Jan. 18, 1757; 2191, Mar. 27, 1759; 2208, May 9, 1780; N. R. S., *Barham Papers*, ii, 2.

[2] See *Seventeen Reports of the Commissioners of the Land Revenue, 1787-93*, also in *H. C. J.*; Manwood, *Forest Laws;* Selden Society, *Select Pleas of the Forest;* Petit-Dutallis, *Studies*, vol. ii; Brown, *Forests of England;* Cox, *Royal Forests of England, passim.*

other game. In the afforested regions, this harsh legislation, of which the thirteenth-century "Carta de Foresta" is an example, supplanted the customary law of England. The hunt determined the course of English forest policy centuries before naval timber was a consideration, but the original forest laws indirectly provided for the later maritime need. The severity with which the kings protected their game preserves had incidentally saved the trees from the prevalent destruction involved in clearing the land for agriculture. There were dozens of afforested tracts scattered throughout England. Many of them had fewer trees than the moderate park of some country squire. It was written of Exmoor Forest in 1622, for instance: "There were noe woods in the said Forest except one oak called Kite Oak."[1] Some of the others, however, were well wooded.

Prior to the Civil War, many of these forests in various parts of the country were drawn upon by the Navy for timber. Much oak for the dockyards was felled during the early Stuart period in Sherwood, Shotover, Stow, Chopwell, and other royal forests of the north; but after that heavy cutting and the wholesale alienation of crown lands by James I and his son, those northern forests practically dropped from view so far as the Navy was concerned. At the Restoration there were still sixty-eight royal forests, together with many royal chases and parks, but only three of these are intimately associated with the supply of ship timber — Dean, New, and Alice Holt forests. Occasionally one of the others might be drawn upon. Hainault Forest, in Essex, furnished oak to build the "fighting *Téméraire*," which Turner has pictured, and a little naval timber was cut from time to time in Bere, Whittlewood, Salcey, Rockingham, Windsor, and Bushy Park; but the interest of the Navy centered upon its main reserves in Dean, New, and Alice Holt.[2]

The Forest of Dean was the most famous of these nurseries of naval timber. It was located in the southwestern corner of

---

[1] *V. C. H., Somerset*, ii, 566.

[2] *Cal. Treas. Papers, 1702–07*, pp. 400, 498, and *passim; H. C. J., 1792*, p. 350; see detailed maps of royal forests in *Parl. Papers*, 1849 (513), vol. xx, and general location of mediaeval forests in *Royal Historical Society Transactions*, 4th series, iv, 140.

Gloucestershire, at the western extremity of the oak belt which began in Sussex and Kent. On the high lands between the Severn and Wye, the forest contained some 16,000 acres of oak of excellent quality.[1] Dean was famous for its oak and iron even in the days of the Roman occupation, and its reputation spread abroad. The story goes that in a ship of the Armada wrecked on the south coast, orders were found for the destruction of the oaks in Dean as a blow to England's sea power.[2] It has been called the "largest and most valuable oak-growing tract within the kingdom."[3] That honor could be contested by the privately owned Ashdown Forest in Sussex, the largest single remnant of the old Andred Weald, which furnished a great amount of oak to the Navy from its 18,000 acres.[4] The name of Dean, however, was more closely associated with naval timber than that of any other woodland in England, and it furnished a more constant supply of oak than any of the other crown forests. Most of its naval timber was sent around Land's End to the dockyard of the west at Plymouth, but at one time, the Navy built frigates of Dean oak at Lydney on the edge of the forest.

Next to Dean in importance was New Forest, which stretched westward from Southampton Water in Hampshire. It had been formed by William the Conqueror, who wiped out more than thirty towns to make a great hunting preserve. In later centuries, only about a third of its 66,000 acres were wooded. Its timber was inferior to that of Dean in quality, because of the nature of the soil; but for more than two centuries an intermittent supply of oak was cut at Bolderwood, Castlemalwood, Eyeworth, Gadshill, Lady Cross, and other places in the forest, to be shipped from Redbridge, Beaulieu, and Lymington to the nearby dockyard at Portsmouth.[5]

The third important timber-producing forest was Alice Holt or Aylesholt, also in Hampshire, some thirty miles northeast of

[1] *H. C. J.*, *1787–88*, pp. 563–632; *E. H. R.*, xxi, 440 ff.

[2] *V. C. H.*, *Gloucestershire*, ii, 271, 272.

[3] *Ibid.*, 263.

[4] *Ibid.*, *Sussex*, ii, 313.

[5] *H. C. J.*, *1788–89*, pp. 522–639; *V. C. H.*, *Hampshire*, ii, 409, 442, 464; R. O., *Adm.*, *Acct. Gen.*, *Misc.*, *Var.*, 121, pp. 50, 156; *Parl. Papers*, 1847–68 (0.48), vol. xxi, pt. 1, p. 365.

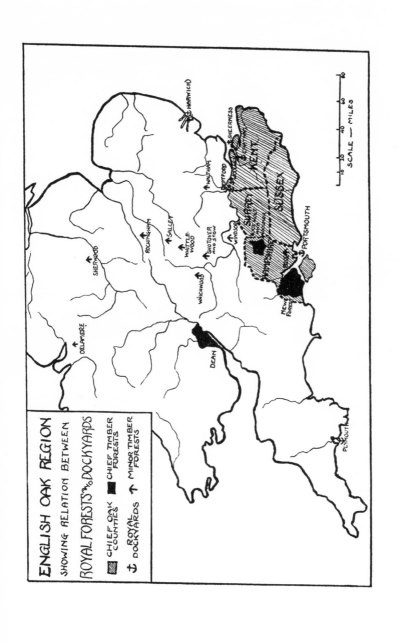

ENGLISH OAK REGION
SHOWING RELATION BETWEEN
ROYAL FORESTS & DOCKYARDS

CHIEF OAK COUNTIES
CHIEF TIMBER FORESTS
ROYAL DOCKYARDS
MINOR TIMBER FORESTS

SCALE — MILES
10 20 40 60 80

HARWICH
SHEERNESS
WALTHAM
DARTFORD
KENT
SURREY
SUSSEX
WINDSOR
PORTSMOUTH
ROCKINGHAM
SALCEY
WHITTLE-WOOD
SHOTOVER AND STOW
SHERWOOD
WHICHWOOD
NEW FOREST
DELAMERE
DEAN
PLYMOUTH

Portsmouth. With the neighboring forest of Woolmer, it covered less than 6,000 acres, only half of which was wooded. Its timber was ordinarily carried overland to Godaling in Surrey and thence down the Thames to Deptford.[1]

The administration of these forests reflected the sleepy, remote atmosphere which pervaded them all. There was a strongly medieval air about the verderers, regarders, bowbearers, and other officials, who not only bore thirteenth-century titles but even performed certain rituals of Plantagenet days on state occasions.[2] From the little lodges scattered among the great oaks, they exercised the royal authority with extremely doubtful effectiveness. The chief of each forest was the Lord Warden, who administered the forest law in the woodmote and swanimote courts, with the assistance of the other officials. For the actual preservation of the oaks there were regarders and woodwards, who were supposed to guard the woods against depredations by the lawless elements of the population which gradually settled within the forest limits, and particularly by the turbulent miners, who disturbed the somnolence of Dean and wrought havoc among its oaks. Such police duty was ineffectively performed, for most of the offices declined into nominal positions, often without pay and with a consequent neglect of duty. They were accepted primarily for the perquisites of venison and of the "top and lop" of trees felled in the forest, together with the more considerable revenue from the illicit sale of timber.[3] Some of these custodians of the King's woods actually became timber contractors on their own account. Under their neglect, young trees were chewed up by browsing deer and cattle while the great oaks were allowed to pass their prime and become decayed, staghorned "dotards." Surveys of the forests always showed an inexcusable number of decaying trees which would have made the choicest naval timber if cut in time. Those picturesque, useless anachronisms in the local forest administration continued to the last years of the wooden-ship era, and help to explain the failure of the crown reserves.

---

[1] *H. C. J.*, *1790*, pp. 120–180. [2] *Ibid.*, *1787–88*, pp. 561, 562.
[3] *Ibid.*, pp. 570–572.

The first step taken to centralize the administration of the various royal forests with regard to the timber supply was the appointment of John Mynne as Master of the Woods in 1542.[1] The only previous coördination of the forest administration had existed in the Justices in Eyre, who administered the forest law. The office of Master of the Woods became that of Surveyor-General of Her Majesty's Woods and Forests during the reign of Mary, and as such it lasted with slight changes for three centuries, until the last years of the era of wooden ships. It was originally under the Court of the Exchequer, so the forests came to be part of the Treasury jurisdiction. The Surveyor-Generalship was usually regarded as a sinecure, and the inactivity of most of the incumbents reflected that view.[2] It was less important in England than in America, where it was introduced in 1685 with much more extensive powers and responsibilities. The difference between the original Surveyor-Generalship and its colonial counterpart is shown by the correspondence from the two sources during the eighteenth century. While the officers in America were writing of their earnest efforts to preserve the woods, most of the letters from the Surveyors-General in England dealt with matters of perquisites, even though there was almost as great a need for strenuous measures to prevent illicit cutting in the English forests as there was in the colonial timberlands.[3]

The inefficiency and neglect which permeated the administration of the royal forests was enough to prevent an effective supply of naval timber, but that supply was further subject to the evils of divided authority. The Treasury administered the woods but the Navy used the timber. The coöperation between the two branches of the government in this matter was clumsy and sometimes inharmonious. When the master shipwright at Portsmouth needed oak logs from the adjacent New Forest, for instance, the application for a specified number of trees or loads had to pass through the offices of the Navy Board, Admiralty, Treasury and

[1] 33 Henry VIII, c. 39; *L. & P., Henry VIII*, vol. xiii, pt. 1 (1538), p. 582; vol. xvii (1542), p. 211; vol. xviii, pt. 1 (1543), pp. 65, 84.

[2] *H. C. J., 1787–88*, pp. 562, 600; *1792–93*, pp. 566–575.

[3] *Cal. Treas. Papers, 1720–28*, pp. 49, 86, 135, 143; *H. C. J., 1792*, p. 339. See *infra*, chapter VI.

Surveyor-General before it reached the local authorities in the forest. There was a naval purveyor attached to each of the principal forests, and it was he, rather than the regular forest officials, who marked the trees with a broad arrow — the sign of naval authority — and inspected them for quality, while he resisted the rapacity of the forest officials in their claims of "top and lop." The Navy made a much more consistent effort than the Treasury to check waste in the royal forests. At times, the Treasury disregarded naval interests to such an extent that it threw the forest timber on the open market, where the Navy had to take its chance for whatever oak it needed.[1] Such lack of harmony between two great branches of the government, together with the chaotic state of tenant rights within the forests, led the Commissioners of the Land Revenue in 1788 to denounce the whole forest system as "a perpetual struggle of jarring interests."[2]

Under such circumstances, it is not difficult to understand why the royal forests provided the Navy with only 77,256 loads of oak and 16,056 loads of beech timber between 1730 and 1787, a period when the dockyards were using nearly 30,000 loads a year. The average annual supply from this source during the crisis of the Napoleonic era was only about 4,000 loads a year, scarcely a tenth of the total naval consumption of English oak. Between 1833 and 1848, the Navy received no timber at all from the crown reserves. As nurseries for naval oak they had been a miserable failure.[3]

Timber from the private estates, then, had to be the mainstay of the naval supply. Nearly every nobleman and landed gentleman had oak growing on his estates. In Sussex, in the great timber region of the old Andred Weald, there were the extensive woodlands of the Duke of Norfolk, Duke of Richmond, Duke of Dorset, Lord Egremont, and several commoners, who could supply from their estates more timber than the Navy ordinarily received from Dean or New forests. In Kent, there were the great "Church Woods" belonging to Canterbury, extending nearly to

---

[1] *Cal. S. P., Dom., 1629–31*, p. 105; *1634–35*, pp. 237, 592, 593; *1635*, p. 238; R. O., N. B. Out Letters, 2199; *N. B. to Adm.*, Jan. 5, 1770; *H. C. J., 1792–93*, p. 568; N. R. S., *Barham Papers*, ii, 149.

[2] *H. C. J., 1787–88*, p. 561.

[3] *Ibid.*, *1792*, p. 350; *Parl. Papers*, 1849 (0.30), xx, 14, 123, 160.

the sea and capable of furnishing enough to build several ships
each year. All through the wooded region, conditions were
similar. Timber merchants cruised the country, bargaining with
the stewards of these estates for oak to be sold to the Navy. Some
well-managed woodlands like those of the Earl of Carnarvon in
Hampshire could produce regular fellings worth about £3,000 a
year, while in other cases, great sales of timber worth £100,000
might be made.[1]

The Navy could not place entire reliance upon the supply from
private estates, because three factors prevented an adequate
supply of great timber. Some landowners refused to cut their
oaks at all, others slashed them before they reached maturity,
and even on the well-managed estates, where oaks were allowed
to reach their prime, it was not considered profitable to raise
great timber. These shortcomings, arising from the natural conflict between private and public interest, are more excusable than
the failure of the royal forests, which should have been able to
furnish the Navy with all the timber it needed.

The oaks that the owners refused to cut at all were usually
the trees grown for ornamental purposes. Many landed proprietors felt a positive affection for a park of staghorned old oaks,
not only because of their rugged beauty, but also on account of
the dignity and age which they represented. Thousands of
splendid oaks in the parks, therefore, went untouched through the
stage where they would have been of greatest service for stern-
posts. Sentiment spared them and they passed into a picturesque,
decaying old age, in spite of the entreaties of naval purveyors and
timber merchants.

The premature felling of oaks was as detrimental to naval interests as that refusal to fell at all. An oak cut when forty or sixty
years of age was practically worthless for naval purposes, and its
felling prevented the normal supply of mature timber that should
have been expected.[2] It required a large amount of patience and
self-restraint to wait the hundred years, more or less, required for

---

[1] *Parl. Papers*, 1813–14 (115), vol. vii, pt. i, pp. 174, 185, 259–264, 301–304,
518–524, 583.

[2] *Cal. S. P., Dom., 1591–9*, p. 289; *H. C. J., 1792*, p. 4275.

an oak to reach its prime; and a grove of full-grown oaks represented the English spirit of family continuity at its best. It meant that the great-grandson of the man who planted the oaks was usually the one to gain the full benefit of their sale, which represented an average rental of about five per cent on the value of the land for each year of the century. It meant also that the intervening generations had abstained from a chance to gain £20,000 or £50,000 in order that their descendant might receive £100,000 for the full-grown trees, for the greatest increase in the value of oaks came in the decades just preceding maturity. To the credit of the landowners, it must be said that the majority of them had sufficient family feeling, self-restraint, patriotism, and ready money to allow their oaks to grow to their proper size.

The interest here centers on the minority who were impatient in cutting their timber. Sir William Monson complained of this practice and, as an official of the Navy, felt the need to

restrain the felling of timber in England, which is too common by the liberty that is given to widows to fell and sell without impeachment or waste, and to young heirs after they come to possess their father's lands. For the readiest monies they can think on (towards their wasteful expenses) is a sale of timber, and whilst this is suffered and no provision for preserving or planting of trees, as the law provides for in that case, what can be imagined will befall England hereafter in succeeding times? [1]

Widows and young heirs were not the only offenders. Too many land-owners believed with a certain Restoration peer that wood was "an excrescence of the earth provided by God for the payment of debts." [2] In the days of entailed estates, when lands could not be alienated, the sale of timber represented the easiest means of raising ready money. A change in the status of the land or an unusual financial demand was the usual cause of the untimely cutting. Lands were sometimes bought with the view of meeting a part of the purchase price by an immediate sale of timber; and in some shrewd bargains, the whole estate was soon paid for in that way. In cases where the title to the land was insecure, the man on the spot was apt to make the most of his provisional possession by turning the oaks into cash. Forfeited estates were

[1] N. R. S., *Naval Tracts of Sir William Monson*, v, 268.
[2] Pepys, *Diary*, May 5, 1667.

sometimes found stripped of timber when their new owners arrived. The government sometimes intervened to preserve timber for the Navy. In one instance a "simple" old gentleman who was recklessly slashing oaks to provide marriage portions for his three daughters was checked by the government; the remaining oaks were saved and the dowries were paid from the national treasury. About that same time, the Master and Fellows of Queen's College, Cambridge, were severely reprimanded for felling a large part of their timber to raise funds for the erection of a brewhouse.[1]

Such a practice prevented the private woodlands from functioning in a regular, rational manner, but only the flagrant cases were dealt with. Strict legislation could scarcely be expected from the oak-owning Parliament, whose members were often offenders themselves. Nelson suggested that if a gentleman found himself forced to sell his half-grown oaks, the government should purchase them from him at the time and allow them to continue to maturity; but his suggestion was never adopted, and these premature inroads on the nation's stock of oak continued to the end.[2]

Those exceptional cases would not have been serious if the regular fellings on the majority of estates had satisfied the Navy's demands, but even the most efficiently conducted woodlands fell short in the matter of great timber. They could usually furnish plenty of timber of average dimensions, but because of the risk of decay already mentioned, owners did not usually find it profitable to allow their trees to grow to the extra size. Landowners could adjust their corn crops to meet an increasing demand, but the slow-growing oak was too inelastic for that. It will be seen that the Commissioners of the Land Revenue, in 1792, decided that the Navy could not safely rely upon the private supply, for these reasons.[3]

[1] *L. & P., Henry VIII*, vol. xiii, pt. 1 (1538), p. 175; pt. 2, pp. 123, 278; *Cal. S. P., Dom., 1547–80*, pp. 643, 664, 667; *1631–33*, pp. 173, 174; *Acts. P. C., 1578–80*, p. 438; *1580–81*, p. 122.

[2] R. O., N. B. In Letters, 1560, *Larking to N. B.*, Nov. 9, 1805; *English Forests and Forest Trees*, p. 303.

[3] *H. C. J., 1792*, p. 265; *Parl. Papers*, 1849 (o. 30), xx, 263.

If the woodlands of England had been called upon for nothing except naval timber, they could have met the demands of the dockyards with comparative ease. As it was, the needs of the Navy were opposed at every step by rival economic demands for oak. The national importance of naval timber gave it a primacy among these demands, but the others cut heavily into the supply of oak which might otherwise have gone to build warships.

Even in the matter of ship timber the Navy had a close rival in the merchant marine, which annually consumed about three times as much oak as the dockyards. For instance, in 1790, as a typical year of peace, when the Navy had about 300 ships with a total tonnage of 391,450, there were over 15,000 merchantmen in British registry, with an aggregate tonnage of 1,460,823. That year, when the Navy spent about 25,000 loads of timber in building a few large ships and repairing the others, 620 new merchantmen were constructed, with a total tonnage of 57,566. It was estimated that a "ton of warship" required about a load and a half or two loads of timber, whereas a ton of merchant shipping represented about a load. Repairs consumed about half as much timber as new construction each year, so that the merchant marine in 1790 required somewhat more than 80,000 loads.[1]

The provisions of the Navigation Acts and their modifications had increased the demands on English oak by requiring that British merchantmen should be built in Great Britain or her colonies. Of the 15,111 ships in British registry in 1790, 717 were prizes taken from the enemy, and only 94 others of foreign build had wormed their way into British registry. All the rest had been built within the British dominions, and of these, 9,594 were English. Prior to the American Revolution, nearly a third of the ships in British registry were built in the colonies; but American ships were rigidly excluded thereafter, so that the drain on English oak was greatly increased.[2]

---

[1] B. M., *Stowe MSS*, 435, ff. 7-12, 37; *Add. MSS*, 11255; *H. C. J., 1792*, pp. 353-325; *Parl. Papers*, 1813-14 (115), vol. vii, pt. 1, p. 76; Fincham, *History of Naval Architecture*, p. 213.

[2] B. M., *Stowe MSS*, *Ibid.*; *H. C. J., 1792*, pp. 356-357; *Lloyd's Register*, 1775; Macpherson, *Annals*, iv, 11.

Fortunately for the Navy, much of the timber required for
these ships of commerce was of a size much smaller than the
great pieces required for ships of the line, which averaged nearly
2,000 tons. The merchantmen averaged only about 100 tons.
Nearly half of them were fishing boats and other small craft of
fifty tons or less, while only 201 of the 15,000 in 1790 measured
over 400 tons. Most of England's commerce to the West Indies,
the Baltic, and the Mediterranean was carried on in tubby little
vessels about 300 tons in size. Even if these required oak of small
scantling, the cutting of trees for that purpose prevented their
growth to the size fit for naval purposes. The builders of private
ships were under the influence of the prestige of English oak,
but for reasons of economy, they began to utilize foreign timber
long before the Navy.[1]

There was a certain type of merchantman, however, which
competed with the Navy for the best and largest English oak.
In times of peace, the great private yards of the Thames were
chiefly occupied in building ships for the East India Company.
These were veritable warships, very solid, and often equal to a
small ship of the line in size. Expense was not an important
consideration in their construction, and the builders often outbid
the Navy for the choicest timber. On several occasions, the East
India Company was ordered to reduce the size of timber used in
its ships, and in 1771, it was ordered to suspend construction
until its tonnage was reduced to a specified level; yet the naval
supply constantly suffered from that rivalry.[2]

Naval oak had even more powerful rival forces in iron and corn.
Iron was intimately associated with the Navy's timber problem.
It was instrumental in creating the problem, and even more so
in dispelling it, for the introduction of iron ships definitely put
an end to the Navy's timber troubles. Before the introduction
of coal, charcoal was necessary for the smelting of iron, and oaks
by the million were burned to make the charcoal. Iron was de-

[1] B. M., *loc. cit.*; Kirkaldy, *British Shipping*, pp. 21–24.
[2] *Common Reports*, iii, 16; *H. C. J., 1792*, p. 312; *Parl. Papers*, 1813–14 (115),
vol. vii, pt. 1, pp. 16, 78–80, 362, 639; Snodgrass, *Letter to the Rt. Hon. Henry
Dundas, passim.*

posited under a large part of England, but it was natural that smelting should develop in regions of the best oaks. By the thirteenth century, the great oak forest of the Andred Weald was being felled to feed the numerous forges which sprang up within its limits, particularly in Sussex. Dean also became the scene of a considerable iron industry during the Middle Ages. For several centuries the felling of oaks to make charcoal went on practically unrestrained, and the forges and furnaces "devoured many famous woods." [1]

The Andred Weald was well devoured before the needs of the Elizabethan maritime expansion drew attention to the danger. During the reigns of Elizabeth and James I, and even more so under Charles I, there was a growing alarm over the situation, so that the iron industry was curbed in the interests of the Navy. In the first years of Elizabeth's reign, iron workers were prohibited from taking trees more than a foot in diameter within fourteen miles of the sea; but this did little to check the "great waste of oak timber in the county of Sussex fit for the building of ships." [2] In the decade preceding the Civil War, the situation became so serious that stricter measures were taken. It was estimated that the 300 iron works in the country were consuming 300,000 loads of timber a year, and to restrain the waste of naval timber, a Surveyor of Iron Works was appointed.[3] When Sir John Wintour was given permission to establish ironworks in the Forest of Dean, he was instructed to use only the superannuated "dotards" to make charcoal; but the Dean miners constantly violated this provision, sometimes boring holes in good trees to kill them quickly.[4] In the middle of the seventeenth century, the shortage of wood led several men to attempt to use coal in smelting. Coal had been brought from Newcastle for centuries for use as fuel, but these early efforts to use it in the iron industry were failures.

[1] Pearson, *Historical Maps of England*, p. 50; Scrivenor, *History of the Iron Trade, passim; E. H. R.*, xiv, 514.

[2] 1 Eliz., c. 15; *Cal. S. P., Dom., 1547–80*, pp. 438, 474.

[3] *Ibid., 1635–36*, p. 400; *1636–37*, p. 162.

[4] *Cal. S. P., Dom., 1633*, p. 191; *1637–38*, p. 168; *E. H. R.*, xxi, 450; *V. C. H., Gloucestershire*, ii, 273; R. O., N. B. Out Letters, 2199, *N. B. to Adm.*, May 30, 1769; *H. C. J., 1787–88*, pp. 574, 575.

The experiments of the inventor Darby were more successful in 1713, and by the last of the century, less than a quarter of England's iron output was made from charcoal. The center of the industry had moved from the oak groves of the south to the coal fields of the north. The general introduction of coal had been hastened by the scarcity of naval timber.[1]

Iron had consumed grown oaks — corn prevented their growth. Agriculture pressed hard on the woodlands from the beginning. At first, the process was necessary, for in nearly every country in northern latitudes, forests had to be cut down and their trunks grubbed out in order to make arable or pasture land. As in the case of iron, there was a reaction to this destruction of wood in the middle of the sixteenth century. In 1544, Parliament declared that "the turning woodland into tillage is prohibited."[2] This was quite ineffectual against the enclosure movement, however, and the enclosures were particularly destructive to the crooked oaks growing in the hedgerows thrown down to unite the little fields.

There were several reasons for preferring to grow corn instead of oaks. The two contended for the best lands in England. There were vast tracts of barren moor which might have been given over to forest, but the fastidious oaks scorned them. "The oak, to become great timber, requires the strongest and deepest soil, which being also the most profitable for agriculture, is the least likely to be employed by individuals in raising timber," reported the Commissioners of the Land Revenue in 1788.[3]

In this contest for the best soil there was a psychological consideration in favor of corn. Even if the ultimate profit from raising oaks would be as great, — and that was often doubtful, — the immediate returns from a grain crop were more appealing to the landowner than the remote prospect of a timber felling by one of his descendants a century later. The country, moreover, was in need of corn during a long period, and there seemed to be as much justification for meeting that immediate need as for

---

[1] Scrivenor, *op. cit.*, pp. 37-56, 87; *Cal. S. P., Dom., 1627-28*, pp. 347, 348; *1635*, p. 76; *1635-36*, p. 465; *H. C. J., 1792*, pp. 328-330.

[2] 35 Henry VIII, c. 17.   [3] *H. C. J., 1787-88*, p. 560.

providing for a navy in a distant future. During periods when corn was scarce, there were frequent protests against holding the oak groves in "maritime mortmain." This view was vigorously expressed in 1791 by Dr. Thomas Preston, a former county official of Suffolk, who wrote:

> England possessed in the past Age a great Plenty of Oak. Why? Because Cultivation was in a barbarous State. It is the Improvement of the Kingdom, a Thousand Times more valuable than any Timber can ever be, that has wrought the very good and proper Diminution of Oak; and it is to be hoped the Diminution will continue, for if it does not, the Improvement of our Soil will not advance. While we are forced to feed our People with foreign Wheat, and our Horses with foreign Oats, can raising Oak be an Object? The Average Oak of Suffolk, of 100 Years Growth, is worth £5; and let it grow in a Hedge, Wood, or Field, it has at that Age done Ten Pounds worth of Mischief. There are soils . . . singularly favorable to the Growth of Oak, and yet yielding not more than 8s to 10s an Acre. On such, Oak would pay, but the Crop to be Timber only, and no Cattle ever admitted. But where is the Owner who will sow a Crop of 100 Years? Vanity does something; it does at present more than it ought to do, by planting Soils not of the right Sort.
>
> The Scarcity of Timber ought never to be regretted, for it is a certain proof of National Improvement; and for Royal Navies, Countries yet barbarous are the right and only proper Nurseries. Buy Oak, as you buy Fir to build your Houses.[1]

With such opinions prevalent at the time of the enclosure movement, it is not surprising that for every enclosure made for the growth of oak, there were dozens intended for agriculture. These latter involved the destruction of hedgerow oaks, and sometimes whole groves were grubbed up. Land once lost for timber purposes was seldom recovered.[2]

The extra-naval demands on oak did not stop with iron and corn. Houses and other buildings consumed a tremendous amount in their construction. Oak timber came into very general use with the large amount thrown on the market by the suppression of the monasteries after 1535, but the government finally began to curtail such use of oak in the interest of fire protection and timber economy. The half-timber buildings gradually gave

[1] *H. C. J.*, *1792*, p. 343.
[2] *Ibid.*, pp. 266, 295, 298, 301, 304; *Commons Reports*, iii, 20; *V. C. H.*, *Oxford*, ii, 299.

way to more substantial structures of stone, but even these required beams, rafters, floors, and other forms of wood. For rebuilding London after the great fire of 1666, Parliament required the use of oak in certain portions of the new buildings, but there was such a scarcity of oak in the country that a large amount of fir had to be brought from Norway and the Baltic. During the eighteenth century, the cheaper imported timber came more and more to replace oak.[1] Brewers took many of the best and largest oaks to make staves for their casks, as they claimed that foreign timber was too coarse-grained to withstand the working of the beer. The production of glass and lead required charcoal in the same manner that iron did. The Ordnance Board constantly bid against the Navy for large oak, as fortifications required a considerable amount of timber. Bridges and docks ate heavily into the oak supply. The canals, it was noticed, opened up new oak regions, but they almost offset this by their consumption of timber in locks, canal boats, and the like. The early forms of machinery developed during the Industrial Revolution required many very large pieces of timber. Thousands of good oaks were unnecessarily sacrificed for park palings, but the naval supply was not cut into heavily for firewood. "Dotards" and coppice wood could be burned, and "sea coales" from Newcastle were used in large quantities. A good oak tree was valued too highly in England to be used for such a purpose.[2] In the earlier part of the period, there was an extensive illicit export of ship timber to Holland and elsewhere from England and Ireland, but this was eventually stopped.[3] Many of these extra demands consumed as much oak as the Navy, and they certainly hastened the depletion of the forests. Most of this consumption was justifiable from an economic standpoint, but when men thought of the diminishing woodlands, the need of naval timber transcended all other considerations.

[1] *H. C. J., 1792*, pp. 271, 272; 19 Chas. II, c. 3.
[2] R. O., N. B. In Letters, 1561; *Larking to N. B.*, Nov. 23, 1813; *H. C. J., 1792*, pp. 272, 292, 325–328; *Parl. Papers*, 1813–14 (115), vol. vii, pt. i, pp. 44–46; *Quarterly Review*, viii, 47; *Naval Chronicles*, vii, 146.
[3] N. R. S., *Naval Tracts of Sir William Monson*, v, 269; Charnock, *History of Marine Architecture*, ii, 298.

Those economic motives help to explain why men desired to cut oaks for purposes other than naval timber. The English forest policy from the middle of the sixteenth to the middle of the nineteenth century was primarily an effort to curb these extra-naval demands in the interest of the dockyard supply. Naval needs had definitely supplanted the chase as the prime motive for the official preservation of timber during that period, but the policy was spasmodic and irresponsible. The government policy had destructive as well as constructive phases, and the oak supply was sensitive to political conditions. Some kings were more guilty of wasting oaks than any private landowner, and Parliament was reluctant to enact any severe measures of preservation. The review of the official treatment of the forests will record more sins of omission and commission than instances of constructive policy; and that story should make clear that the final failure of the woodlands was the result of constant neglect and abuse.[1]

If any arbitrary date can be set for the beginning of the timber problem, it is 1535, when Henry VIII commenced his suppression of the monasteries through Thomas Cromwell. Up to that time, the cutting of oak had served a good purpose, on the whole, in clearing land for habitation. It had brought together the peoples originally separated by the extensive forests. "The axe of the woodman clearing away the forests . . . gradually transformed England into one land inhabited by one people."[2] Only the most meagre form of forest legislation had been necessary, for timber was of little value.[3] Even when Henry VIII came to the throne, England had an ample supply of wood. As one versifier wrote:

> No lack of timber then was felt or fear'd
> In Albion's happy isle.[4]

The blows of Thomas Cromwell, the *malleus monachorum*, can

---

[1] For general review of English forest policy, see *H. C. J.*, *1787–88*, pp. 560–562; *1792*, pp. 262–271; *V. C. H.*, *Hampshire*, ii, 426–433; Brown, *Forests of England*, pp. 227–236; Stebbing, *Commercial Forestry in Great Britain*, pp. 13–32.

[2] Pearson, *Historical Maps of England*, p. 6.

[3] *Quarterly Review*, v, 9, 47.   [4] Quoted in Knowles, *Dry Rot*, p. 26.

well be taken as marking the end of that period of plenty.   Revenue for the crown was no unimportant consideration in the abolition of the monasteries and the seizure of their lands.   Most of
the religious houses owned woodlands, and the oaks were one of
the most readily negotiable parts of the confiscated property.
For the first time England saw a wholesale felling of trees for
timber purposes.   Oaks which the abbots and priors had not
already cut when they realized their impending fate were liable
to fall under the axes of royal agents who often made the most of
the lands before disposing of them.   The trees which survived
those two perils were usually cut by the new proprietors who were
thus able to regain a part of the purchase price.   There was a rising demand for oak in domestic architecture and in the new Navy
and merchant marine, so that most of the timber found a ready
market.[1]   By 1538, a surveyorship of woods of suppressed monasteries was created, and the real purpose of appointing John
Mynne as Master of the Woods four years later may be judged
from his alternate title of "Master of the King's Wood Sales." [2]
Lord Lisle, who was later the notorious Duke of Northumberland,
deserves to go on record as the first great wholesale timber merchant in England, for he traded heavily in the oak from abbey
lands.   Confiscations of private estates following the Rising of the
North at that time increased the slashing of oak.   The last twelve
years of Henry's reign saw more oaks cut than in an ordinary
half-century hitherto.[3]

   Destructive and constructive phases of the timber policy went
almost hand in hand; for during that wholesale destruction cf
oak, Parliament passed the first important timber preservation
act, one provision of which was that, wherever woods were cut
down, at least twelve young trees must be left on every acre.[4]
During the reign of Edward VI, there were attempts to check

[1] Rogers, *History of Agriculture and Prices*, iv, 445–447.

[2] *L. & P., Henry VIII*, vol. xiii, pt. 1 (1538), pp. 125, 175, 499, 582; pt. 2, p.
179; vol. xvii (1542), p. 484; vol. xx, pt. 2 (1545), pp. 552–553.

[3] *Ibid.*, vol. xii, pt. 2 (1537), pp. 421, 430; vol. xiii, pt. 1 (1538), pp. 76, 101, 117,
131, 202; pt. 2, pp. 123, 278, 388, 478; vol. xiv, pt. 2 (1539), pp. 15, 28, 56, 356,
370, 559.

[4] 35 Henry VIII, c. 17.

the felling of oaks and to preserve naval timber on the Thames to supply Deptford Yard.[1]

Elizabeth's first Parliament passed an act to preserve ship timber near the coast, and the Queen checked up reckless timber cutting in various parts of the kingdom.[2] This early enthusiasm for conservation soon passed, and it was more than offset by Elizabeth's prodigal grants of cutting rights. Destruction of timber was heavy during her reign. In Duffield Forest, the 59,412 large oaks and 32,820 small ones standing in 1560 were reduced to 2,864 large and 3,032 small trees in 1587. This may have been an exceptional case, but there was also St. Leonard's Forest in Sussex, where over a million cubic feet of timber were cut on royal licenses in twenty years. This reckless cutting was prevalent throughout the land, and in spite of the large amount of timber offered for sale, prices more than doubled during the period.[3]

The first real alarm over the timber situation was expressed in the middle of Elizabeth's reign. Harrison's article in Holinshed referred to "the great sales yearlie made of wood, whereby an infinit quantitie hath bin destroied within these few years." The danger to naval timber was not urged, but fears were expressed that London might be driven to the use of "seacole" for fuel.[4] These fears found expression in an act of Parliament in 1570, which strengthened the timber conservation provisions of the act of 1543.[5] Burleigh began in earnest in 1580 to check the inordinate felling of oaks. He checked up all the bishops, and pounced upon the most flagrant secular offenders.[6] That same year he ordered thirteen acres of Cranbourne Walk in Windsor Park to be sown with acorns. This is credited as the "oldest regular and authenticated plantation that can be shown," and

[1] *Acts P. C.* 1550–52, p. 49; *Cal. S. P. Dom.*, 1547–80, p. 34.

[2] *Ibid.*, p. 140; 1 Eliz., c. 15.

[3] *V. C. H., Sussex*, ii, 309; *Cal. S. P. Dom.*, 1547–80, *passim*; H. C. J., 1792, pp. 340, 341.

[4] Holinshed, *Descriptions of England*, i, 357, 358.

[5] 13 Eliz., c. 25; also 43 Eliz., c. 7.

[6] *Cal. S. P. Dom.*, 1547–80, pp. 645–654; 1591–94, p. 216; B. M., *Lansdowne MSS*, 103, 89, f. 65.

fifty years later it had developed into "a wood of some thousands of tall young trees." [1]

The naval struggle with Spain turned attention to the problem of ship timber. The commander of the fleet which defeated the Armada, Lord Howard of Effingham, protested to Elizabeth against her further grants to cut timber, saying that he was "grieved to think of the state her woods are now in, and what want there is for building and repairing her ships which are the jewels of her kingdom." [2] When men began to write in that vein, the menace of the Navy's timber problem was coming to be appreciated. The net result of Elizabeth's reign was a serious depletion of the woods, partly by royal sanction, which the acts of Parliament and the personal exertions of Burleigh could not wholly offset.

In the reigns of the first two Stuarts this situation was accentuated. Elizabeth had sold licenses to cut in the royal woods — James I and his son not only extended that practice, but actually disafforested a considerable portion of the crown lands, some of which were well wooded, while their feeble attempts to check the cutting were quite ineffectual. [3] The forest policy of these impecunious kings affords an interesting illustration of their attempts to utilize extra-parliamentary sources of revenue and the opposition which such a step aroused, though it has more significance in this study as one of the important causes for the subsequent failure of the English timber supply. There is ample material for a more extended study of this situation than space will here permit.

The policy of James I at the outset was to extend the Elizabethan timber grants and to farm the woodlands without actually alienating them. Before he had been on the throne three years, James received an offer to rent the royal woods for the exploitation of their timber at £10,000 a year more than he was then receiving. By 1607, the offer was doubled and the King was seri-

[1] *V. C. H., Berkshire*, ii, 349; *E. H. R.*, xxi, 447, 448; *Cal. S. P. Dom.*, 1627–28, p. 245.

[2] *Ibid.*, 1591–94, p. 289.

[3] *Ibid.*, 1603–10, pp. 92, 133, 491; 1611–18, p. 420; 1634–35, p. 380; 1636–37, p. 162; 1638–39, p. 7.

ously considering the project in spite of the protests of Nottingham, the Lord High Admiral, who feared for the naval supply of
oak.[1] James wished to learn how large a portion of the crown
forests could be disposed of without endangering that naval supply, and in 1608 he ordered a thorough survey of the oak in all
the royal woods except Dean. The detailed findings of this survey showed a total of 784,748 "Tymber Trees" and 682,058
"Decaying Trees," worth altogether nearly £900,000, in addition to the land on which they stood.[2]

The next step was the actual sale of some of those groves that
offered such a tempting revenue independent of Parliament.
James was contemplating the step by 1613, and three years later,
the Council submitted to the Treasurer "Propositions for the increase of the King's revenue by composition for homage, and by
disafforesting distant forests and chases, etc." Early in 1617, the
King granted a patent to Sir Giles Mompesson for raising
£100,000 in a year from the sale of the King's woods. Ellsmere,
the Lord Chancellor, refused to set the seal to the patent, but
James sealed it himself.[3] Mompesson's monopoly of timber sales
was associated with his more famous monopoly of inn-licensing,
for which he was impeached by Parliament shortly afterward.
The projected sales of crown woods provoked such opposition
that the agents dared not press them at the outset. James, who
had borrowed heavily against this expected revenue, found the
treasury embarrassed by the failure of the wood sales in 1617.
They increased by the following year, and the squandering of
England's forest reserves continued throughout the reign.[4]

After the accession of Charles I in 1625, the sales of woods
showed a decided increase. Two royal forests were sold to provide
funds to pay the fleet on its return from its expedition to the Isle
of Rhé to relieve the Huguenots in La Rochelle.[5] Early in 1627,
the commissioners of the wood sales received advice which indicated the popular disapproval of the measure: "The first sale

[1] Cal. S. P. Dom., 1603–10, p. 388.
[2] Ibid., p. 484; H. C. J., 1792, pp. 283–289 (detailed report).
[3] Cal. S. P. Dom., 1611–18, pp. 199, 377, 439, 441, 449.
[4] Ibid., pp. 475, 485–486; 1619–23, pp. 371, 374.
[5] Ibid., 1627–28, pp. 113, 232, 242, 290, 372.

is fittest to be made in the south parts only, as well to lessen the popular scandal that will ensue from a general devastation, as also because the trial is more safe where woods are more saleable and the people more conformable, and more able to buy." [1]

One woodland after another was alienated as the financial necessity of the King increased. Permission was given to convert woodlands into farmland in defiance of old statutes, and the need of money was so great that grants were even made of all the roots and stumps of trees felled in the King's forests. [2] The Forest of Dean itself did not remain inviolate. James had omitted it from the survey of 1608, but up to 1633, fourteen grants of timber and lands had been made in the forest and the inhabitants armed to oppose the intrusion. There was a plan to dispose of the forest piecemeal to avoid the scandal of a single grant, but the Lords of the Treasury flatly opposed such a project. Finally, in a last desperate effort to raise funds, in 1640, Charles granted the great timber forest to Sir John Wintour three weeks before the Short Parliament met. This was the gravest of the timber alienations, but it was too outrageous to last, and Parliament repealed it in 1657. [3]

The Navy had already begun to suffer from the scarcity of timber. In 1618, the extensive building of ships strained the supply to the limit, and during the subsequent campaigns against France, the shortage was at times acute. [4] Because of the lack of timber, a shipwright declared that he would as soon build ships in hell as in Deptford Yard. [5] Some of the royal forests that were not sold were entirely stripped of timber to build ships for the Navy, as in the case of Chopwell Woods, where Pett cut oak for the Ship Money Fleet. [6] One naval purveyor declared that pop-

---

[1] *Cal. S. P. Dom.*, 1627–28, p. 202.

[2] *Ibid.*, 1628–29, pp. 239, 354, 422, 502.

[3] *Ibid.*, 1631–33, pp. 87, 90; 1633–34, p. 381; 1634–35, p. 607; 1639–40, pp. 39, 567; 1641–43, pp. 285, 349, 455; *Acts and Ordinances of the Interregnum*, ii, 1114, 1115; *H. C. J.*, 1787–88, pp. 563, 564; *E. H. R.*, xxi, 449–457.

[4] *Adm. Library MSS*, 141; Charnock, *History of Marine Architecture*, ii, 248; *Cal. S. P. Dom.*, 1628–29, pp. 376, 492; 1631–33, pp. 51, 111.

[5] *Ibid.*, p. 408.

[6] *Ibid.*, pp. 199, 308, 331, 390; 1633–34, pp. 51, 53, 551; 1634–35, pp. 367, 499, 502, 512; *V. C. H., Durham*, ii, 380, 381.

ular resistance to this cutting was so strong that he was in danger of his life.[1] The Navy became constantly more alarmed at the growing scarcity, and in 1638 the Lord High Admiral secured an Order in Council for the general preservation of timber for ship-building.[2]

The first two Stuarts greatly hastened the danger of an oak shortage by extending the exploitation of forests commenced by the Tudors. That practice of deriving revenue at the expense of the future oak supply must stand as the real forest policy of England from 1535 to 1660. The Civil Wars and the Interregnum were to give the *coup de grâce* to England's forest plenty. The forces let loose during those twenty years destroyed whatever surplus was left after the previous royal exploitation and failure to check waste.

The "Act for the Limitation of Forests," in 1640, was the signal for the beginning of widespread destruction of timber.[3] While Charles I had been disposing of some of the royal forests, he had used shadowy mediaeval claims to extend the boundaries of others, profiting by the consequent suits for trespass. In doing away with that evil, the act practically put an end to the old forest courts with their harsh laws, but "indirectly it also gave fresh impetus to the transformation of woodland tracts into arable and pasture lands, while wholesale clearance and sale of timber turned many wooded parts of England into stretches of barren moor and heathy waste." [4] Enclosures were thrown down, trees were slashed wholesale and sold for a few pence, and all authority that could check such measures was for the time removed. The military campaigns increased the damage to the woodlands. Parliamentary troops even injured the woods of their own leaders until restrained, and the destruction of cavalier groves went on unchecked, much of the damage being "for the mere sake of spoiling." [5]

---

[1] *Cal. S. P. Dom.*, 1629–31, p. 425; see 1603–10, p. 508.

[2] *Ibid.*, 1638–39, p. 7.

[3] 16 Chas. I, c. 16.

[4] *V. C. H., Hampshire*, ii, 429.

[5] *Cal. S. P. Dom.*, 1641–43, pp. 441, 442; 1644, p. 321; *Quarterly Review*, ix, 48; Cox, *Royal Forests of England*, pp. 130, 281, 299.

The official forest policy of the Interregnum proved as destructive as that of the first Stuarts. Numerous acts and ordinances led to an abnormal felling of timber on private estates and in the crown forests. These measures more than offset the provisions which reserved timber fit for the Navy, since they at least mortgaged the future supply. The groves of the royalist sympathizers suffered severely at the hands of the Parliamentary government. The Cavaliers were heavily fined and frequently their estates were sequestered. In the case of fines, the delinquents themselves often had to fell their oaks to meet the unusual penalties; and when an estate was sequestered, the government was unsparing of the woods. A committee of sequestrators would be given orders to fell and dispose of timber on the condemned estates, and Parliament had control of the funds so raised. An individual creditor of the nation might receive an order against the timber on a particular estate in settlement of his claim. By 1644, the Earl of Thanet alone had lost from his estates timber to the value of £20,000 — enough to build at least ten ships of the line. Only one of the eight parks of the Duke of Newcastle escaped destruction; and dozens of Cavaliers returned at the Restoration to find their woodlands ruined as a result of the three-fold attack incidental to military campaigns, lawlessness, and official sequestration.[1] Such private groves, it will be remembered, were the mainstay of the naval timber supply.

The royal forests also suffered from governmental measures during the Interregnum. By 1644, the Navy was authorized to make heavy fellings of timber in several of the crown reserves. This was extended in 1649, when the naval authorities were granted permission to take whatever oak they needed from the royal forests, parks and chases during the next eight years.[2] This free timber carried the Navy through the demands of the first Dutch War and the heavy shipbuilding program that followed it; but

---

[1] *Acts and Ordinances*, i, 422–424, 457; ii, 332, 340, 341, 645, 1121; *Cal. of the Committee for Advance of Money*, pt. 1, pp. 68, 273, 404, 528; pt. 3, p. 1478; *Cal. of the Committee for Compounding*, pt. 2, pp. 839, 901; *Cal. S. P. Dom.*, 1644, p. 556; *V. C. H., Nottinghamshire*, i, 378, 379; *Sussex*, ii, 305, 318; *Buckinghamshire*, ii, 143.

[2] *Acts and Ordinances*, i, 422, 423; ii, 189, 341, 342, 502.

the stimulus to cut all the available oak within the limited term left the forests completely stripped. In 1653, an act "for the deafforestation, sale and improvement" of most of the crown lands continued the policy of James I and Charles I. It provided that "all Timber Trees . . . shall be valued . . . and sold for the benefit of the Commonwealth as the rest of the premises by this act are appointed to be sold."[1] Dean, New, and five other forests were specifically excluded from this measure; but a year later, an act authorized the sale of four of these other forests, to satisfy the arrears due to the officers and soldiers.[2]

The steps taken for the preservation of timber proved quite feeble in comparison with the destructive influence of these acts. In 1646, crooked timber was reserved for the Navy. Two years later, an ordinance called for the preservation of timber in the Forest of Dean, and all timber growing on crown lands within fifteen miles of navigable rivers was reserved in 1649. In that same year, with the beginning of the Commonwealth, a "Committee for the Preservation of Timber" was formed to check the depredations of the "looser and disordered sort of people"; but the reports of that committee were so full of complaints of constant waste of timber that the preservation cannot have been very effective.[3] Included in the act of 1653 was the clause that "forasmuch as there is absolute necessity of preserving a competent quantity of Timber, Fitting for the use of the Navy," surveyors were appointed "to take especial notice of all thriving Timber of Oak or Elm" which was to be reserved for the government and deducted from the sales, while a further attempt was made to check the "great Spoils, Wastes and Incroachments" in the forests.[4] More far-reaching but equally futile was the act in 1657 which permitted the Lord Protector and his successors to encoppice and enclose not more than a third of the waste and demesne land in the Forest of Dean "for and toward the raising and pre-

[1] *Acts and Ordinances*, ii, 785. [2] *Ibid.*, pp. 811, 993, 994.
[3] *Ibid.*, i, 846, 1125; ii, 189, 341, 502, 503, 575, 947, 948, 1121, 1281, 1410; *Cal. S. P. Dom.*, 1651–52, p. 230; 1652–53, pp. 32, 111; 1653–54, pp. 153, 185, 241, 278, 376; 1660–61, p. 295; 1661–62, p. 280.
[4] *Acts and Ordinances*, ii, 788.

serving of Wood and Timber."[1] It was ten years more before an effective planting act was passed.

The Forest of Dean suffered heavily from actual fighting and from the depredations of its lawless population between 1640 and 1660. Young and old trees were burned and cut, while even the timber prepared for building frigates in the forest was carried away. After struggling against this anarchy for seven years, Major Wade, in charge of the forest, wrote to the Admiralty in 1660: "It eats my very heart and mind to see the barbarous dealings that are done in this forlorn, disowned piece of ground, so much talked of and so little cared for in reality."[2] Like many other oak tracts in England, Dean came out of those twenty years with only a fraction of its former woods.

When Thomas Cromwell began the attack on the monasteries in 1535, England had scarcely a thought of the future scarcity of timber. When Richard Cromwell abdicated, a century and a quarter later, that splendid heritage of oak had been wasted. England was faced with a very real naval timber problem, and for the two remaining centuries of the era of wooden ships, the possibility of a complete failure of the forests frequently haunted the Navy.

The woodlands of England never fully recovered from that low condition at the Restoration. During the next century and a half, England was engaged nearly half the time in naval wars. As the size of the Navy and the size of the ships gradually increased, the groves became less able to supply the dockyard needs. The forest policy after 1660 was a combination of Parliamentary acts carried out in a half-hearted manner, and private propaganda for planting oaks, which was much more successful. The policy of deriving profit from the crown woods, which had been practised consistently since the days of Henry VIII, had to go because the royal forests were at last unequal to the naval demands. Instead of granting permits to cut, the government had to plant.

The first outstanding feature of the Restoration treatment of the timber problem was a classic work of planting propaganda by John Evelyn, the diarist. The Navy Board in their alarm

Acts and Ordinances, ii, 1115.   [2] *Cal. S. P. Dom.*, 1659–60, p. 413.

over the timber shortage appealed to the Royal Society for advice on possible methods of relief. The task was assigned to Evelyn who delivered to the society in 1662 his *Sylva; a Discourse of Forest Trees, and the Propagation of Timber in his Majesty's Dominions.*[1] This massive work, full of classical allusions and sound arboricultural advice, was an appeal to the landed nobility and gentry to plant oaks to relieve "the impolitic diminution of our timber" which arose not only from the increasing demands of shipping and glass and iron works,

but from the disproportionate spreading of tillage, caused through that prodigious havoc made by such as lately professing themselves against root and branch (either to be reimbursed for their holy purchases or for some other sordid respect) were tempted not only to fell and cut down, but utterly to extirpate, demolish and raze as it were, all those many goodly woods and forests, which our ancestors left standing for the ornament and service of their country.[2]

This great planting tract was published in 1664, and passed through several editions on other occasions of timber shortage. Evelyn boasted in the preface of the 1679 edition that several million timber trees were planted as a result of his book alone. Shortly after the Napoleonic Wars, the elder Disraeli wrote, "Inquire at the Admiralty how the fleets of Nelson have been constructed, and they can tell you that it was with the oaks which the genius of Evelyn planted."[3] Later opinion underestimates this effect. Forbes, for instance, expresses a doubt "if Evelyn did more than record the prevailing practice of arboriculture in his day."[4]

Whether or not the *Sylva* actually caused the planting of "millions of timber trees," it is certain that the Restoration plantings matured in time to carry the Navy through the wars of the later eighteenth century. Other authors of planting propaganda before and after Evelyn wisely directed their attention, as he did, to the class which could best respond to their appeals —

[1] Evelyn, *Diary*, Oct. 15, Nov. 5, 1662, Nov. 5, Nov. 26, 1663.
[2] Evelyn, *Sylva*, i, 1, 2.
[3] *Quarterly Review*, xix, 47.
Forbes, *English Estate Forestry*, p. 12; see Wood, *History of the Royal Society of Arts*, p. 144.

the landed proprietors.[1] The *Sylva*, however, stands out as the classic in the field, and it gave Evelyn his reputation before the Diary appeared.

The planting example set by private individuals was soon followed by the government. Charles II displayed considerable interest in Evelyn's work and in the naval timber problem in general. He granted some New Forest oaks to one of the maids of honor, but that was amply compensated by the plantations of oak in Dean.[2] That forest stood in need of such treatment, for Sir John Wintour, who had purchased it from Charles I in 1640, lost it by act of Parliament in 1657, and received grants again in 1660, had 500 axes at work among the oaks. Between 1660 and 1667, his men felled over 30,000 trees to feed the iron furnaces.[3] The Corporation of Shipwrights had proposed to the King shortly after the Restoration that lands be enclosed for the growth of ship timber. In 1668, Parliament passed "An Act for the Increase and Preservation of Timber within the Forest of Dean." This was the first real official plantation made by the government, for Burleigh's example in 1580 had not been followed. The act provided that 11,000 acres of waste land were to be enclosed at once and planted with oak. The enclosures were to remain until the trees were safe from browsing cattle and deer, when new sections were to be enclosed. Other provisions of the act attempted to protect the forest from the former spoliation.[4] Over 8,000 acres were enclosed and planted at once, and the remaining 3000 somewhat later. Then the plan "evaporated." [5]

In 1698, a similar act called for plantations in New Forest, where 2,000 acres were to be set out with young oaks at once, and 200 acres a year for twenty years.[6] Only 1,022 acres were

[1] See esp. Standish, *New Directions of Experiences, for the encreasing of Timber and Fire-Wood* (1615); Cook, *Ordering and Improving Forest Trees* (1721); Langley, *Landed Gentleman's Useful Companion* (1741); Pontey, *The Forest Pruner, or the Timber Owner's Assistant* (1805).

[2] *V. C. H., Hampshire*, ii, 450.

[3] *H. C. J.*, 1787–88, p. 565.

[4] 19 & 20 Chas. II, c. 8; *H. C. J.*, 1787–88, pp. 565–566; Evelyn, *Diary*, Nov. 5, 1662.

[5] *H. C. J.*, 1787–88, pp. 567, 568, 577, 581, 582; *E. H. R.*, xxi, 450, 451.

[6] 9 & 10 William III, c. 36.

planted as a result of this act. Before 1725, the enclosure policy in Dean and New Forests had fallen into neglect and very general destruction of wood was reported in all the forests.[1] The policy embodied in those two acts was sound and well conceived. If it had been carried out consistently, England would have had plenty of naval timber from its government reserves, where the trees could have grown to the proper age without the uncertainty incidental to the private supply. The government, however, seemed to lack all *esprit de suite* in the forest policy and there were few further plantations in the royal forests for a century.[2]

The naval supply of oak during the Restoration was dangerously low. It will be seen that the Navy suffered for want of timber between 1660 and 1675 because it could not pay for the available oak. By 1677, the drain occasioned by the Dutch wars and the fire of London actually hampered the building policy of the Navy in the matter of capital ships. Great timber and plank were especially scarce and Baltic oak had to be introduced in place of English.[3] During the first half of the eighteenth century, the timber problem was dormant in the English forests. The oaks that had been young enough to escape destruction prior to 1660 were gradually coming to maturity, and the Restoration plantings provided for a regular succession for some time to come. Secure for the immediate future, men neglected to plant for more distant decades when the need was bound to be acute.

The Seven Years' War from 1756 to 1763 brought the timber shortage back to where it had been just a century before. Dozens of new ships were added to the Navy, and many large woodlands were cut off under the influence of the high price of oak. The end of the war left England almost stripped of woods capable of furnishing naval timber. Many of the counties had only a quarter, or even a tenth, of the woods they had possessed forty years before, according to answers to a questionnaire published by Roger

---

[1] *Cal. Treas. Papers*, 1702–07, pp. 474, 475; 1729–30, p. 26; 1731–34, pp. 228, 249, 295; *Cal. Treas. Books and Papers*, 1735–38, pp. 185, 545; *V. C. H., Hampshire*, ii, 451, 452.

[2] For a general survey of official planting, see *Parl. Papers*, 1849 (0.30), xx, 237, 238.

[3] See *infra*, Chapter V.

Fisher in his *Heart of Oak, the British Bulwark*, in 1763. The timber dealers and shipwrights who gave those opinions also stated that there had been very little planting.[1]

The situation was so unmistakably acute that immediate action was necessary. As usual, private initiative preceded the government measures. In 1759, the Royal Society of Arts determined to encourage proprietors to plant timber trees by offering gold and silver medals for the largest plantations of each kind of tree every year. These awards were continued throughout the century, and millions of trees, by actual count, were planted before the century was over.[2] This step, like Evelyn's, helped to provide for the future, but it could not relieve the serious present necessity.

In 1768, the Navy Board sent the Admiralty a long account of their extreme difficulty in procuring timber since 1756, and they desired that some step be taken to relieve the shortage. The dockyard timber stores at times were equal to only six months' consumption and it was necessary to import much foreign oak.[3] In 1771, a Parliamentary committee considered the naval timber situation at length, and its findings revealed a dangerous lack of oak. Almost no great timber or compass pieces were to be obtained in the country, even at high prices, and the royal forests were almost worthless as far as naval timber was concerned.[4] No change in the national forest policy resulted from the report of that committee. John Pitt, the Surveyor-General, had a few trees planted in the royal forests but sustained effort seemed impossible, and the plantations were soon neglected.[5]

The Admiralty, having a more vital interest in the matter, adopted four very wise measures. They curtailed the principal rivalry for large ship timber already mentioned by restricting the tonnage of the East India Company's shipping; they ordered that

---

[1] Fisher, *Heart of Oak*, esp. p. 56, and *passim; Commons Reports*, iii, 23; *An earnest Address to the People of England, containing an Enquiry into the Cause of the great Scarcity of Timber*, etc. (1766).

[2] Wood, *History of the Royal Society of Arts*, pp. 148 ff.; *Transactions of the Royal Society of Arts, passim.*

[3] R. O., N. B. Out Letters, 2199, *N. B. to Adm.*, Aug. 9, 1768; also May 30, 1769.

[4] *Commons Reports*, vol. iii, *passim.*   [5] *H. C. J.*, 1792–93, p. 581.

a three years' supply of timber be maintained at all times in the yards; they broke up the timber monopoly which was interfering with the supply; and they accomplished the last two measures by importing a large amount of oak from the Baltic.[1] The temporary application of that fourfold program served as a palliative which gave relief from the shortage for a few years.

There was oak enough to maintain the Navy in weakened condition during the American Revolution; but the loss of the colonial merchant marine threw a new burden on the woodlands of England, and shortly after 1783 the scarcity of timber was again acute. The need was felt for a very thorough study of the entire forest policy. Accordingly, Commissioners of the Land Revenue were appointed in 1787 to investigate the condition of the royal forests and other crown lands. The commission was headed by Sir Charles Middleton, who had handled the timber situation in a very able manner as Comptroller of the Navy. The work of the commission was thorough and able, and their seventeen reports are excellent sources for the history of England's forest policy.[2] These reports make it evident that the preservation of naval timber was the guiding influence in that forest policy. There was a prevalent opinion that it would be well to sell the royal forests and convert the land into cornfields. In 1792, the commissioners made an exhaustive investigation of the naval timber problem, to determine whether or not it would be safe to dispose of the forests, and these investigations formed the eleventh report.[3]

That eleventh report is the most comprehensive study of the problem that can be found, for Middleton was thoroughly conversant with the subject and approached it from every angle. Questionnaires were sent to every county, and to the naval purveyors and timber merchants, to determine the causes and extent of the oak shortage. Eminent shipwrights were called upon for

---

[1] 12 Geo. III, c. 54; *Parl. Hist.*, xix, 827, 828; xx, 444, 445; R. O., Adm. Digest, 4807, *Adm. to N. B.*, Apr. 1, 1771; *N. B. to Adm.*, Feb. 14, 1771, Nov. 5, Nov. 8, 1775.

[2] *Seventeen Reports of the Commissioners of the Land Revenue.* See bibliography for list of individual reports and references in *H. C. J.*

[3] *H. C. J.*, 1792, pp. 264–374.

suggestions on methods of economizing in the use of naval timber through improved construction and the prevention of dry rot. These different authorities, with many others, were asked for general opinions upon the most practicable methods to relieve the shortage. Learned works were frequently quoted throughout the report and many official documents were reproduced to throw light on different phases of the subject.

The testimony from dozens of such sources all indicated that the woods of England were approaching very general exhaustion. The situation was apparently more grave than it had been directly after the Seven Years' War. Great timber was hardly to be had, and compass timber was equally scarce, owing to the widespread demolition of the hedgerows. Corn was crowding out oak all over the kingdom, and private landowners were more reluctant than ever to raise timber of a size adequate for ships of the line.

The King's woods had fallen into a notoriously low condition during the century, and, as indicated before, there had been practically no planting. In fifty-seven years they had supplied the Navy with the equivalent of only four years' consumption.[1] When the trees of the Restoration planting were gone, there was no succession provided for, and the number of available timber trees was low. A survey of the oaks in the royal forests in 1783 showed an alarming contrast with the figures for 1608:

	1608	1783
New Forest	123,927	32,611
Alice Holt	13,031	9,136
Whittlewood	51,046	5,211
Salcey	15,274	2,918
East Bere	5,363	256
Sherwood	23,370	(1789) 1,368 [2]

The Dean figures had not been taken in 1608, but the relative decrease had been much the same. The earlier reports of the Commissioners, especially the third report, had revealed the shameful instances of mismanagement and neglect which produced such results.

The Commissioners reported that, if the private woodlands could be relied upon for a supply of naval timber, it would be to

[1] *H. C. J.*, 1792, p. 350.   [2] *Ibid.*, p. 351.

the public advantage to dispose of the royal forests and buy naval timber in the open market. The alarming shortage of oak throughout England, however, demonstrated that the private groves were not dependable. It was therefore recommended that the government plant 70,000 acres in the royal forests.[1]

Not until 1808, sixteen years after that report, were the recommendations put into effect. The exhausted forests had sustained a few years of the naval war with Revolutionary France, but after 1803 they were admittedly inadequate for the task. Private landowners had been far more responsive to the Navy's needs. Many followed the example of Admiral Collingwood, who carried a pocketful of acorns to drop at intervals during his infrequent weeks ashore. The medals of the Royal Society of Arts were scarcely necessary to encourage the private planting of millions of trees in groves often named after admirals to indicate the purpose of their planting.[2]

When the government finally adopted an official planting policy in 1808, the timber situation was in a very acute stage, for English oak was not to be had in quantity and the foreign supply was precarious.[3] The old planting acts of 1668 and 1698 had become invalid through disuse, and a new declaratory act was necessary to revive them. It was planned to enclose and plant about 100,000 acres, which would produce about 65,000 loads of timber a year when the oaks matured a century hence.[4] Several old timber tracts, such as Chopwell in Durham, were revived as naval nurseries, and others were purchased. By 1816, the planting program was well under way.[5] The oaks so planted matured too late to be of service to the Navy, for the era of wooden ships ended before they were half grown.

That remaining half-century of the timber problem saw the

---

[1] *H. C. J.*, 1792, pp. 264–269.

[2] Collingwood, *Correspondence of Lord Collingwood*, p. 100; *V. C. H., Sussex*, pp. 299–300; *Nottingham*, i, 378; *Durham*, ii, 381; *Transactions of the Royal Society of Arts, passim.*

[3] See Chapters VIII, X.

[4] 48 Geo. III, c. 72. See *Parl. Debates*, 1st series, ii, 1068.

[5] 1 *C. L. R.*, 2d series (1812), pp. 18–23; 2 *C. L. R.*, 2d series (1816), p. 22; *Parl. Papers*, 1849 (0.30), xx, 237–261; *V. C. H., Durham*, ii, 381.

royal forests relapse once more.   From 1833 to 1848, the Navy
received no timber at all from them, and Parliamentary investigations in 1848 and 1849 showed such a general neglect and corruption in their administration that a radical change was made in
1851.   A large felling of oaks in Dean two years later ended the
sorry rôle of the crown timber reserves in their relation to the
Navy.   The general supply of English oak never recovered from
the drain of the Napoleonic Wars and the Navy looked more and
more to foreign lands for her ship timber.   It will be seen in a
later chapter that during the last years of the period, barely a
quarter of the timber used in the yards was English oak, and
naval construction was frequently retarded for want of great
stern-posts.[1]

Culpable neglect was responsible for that condition.   The
entire eighteenth century had passed without any effective
official planting, and the forest policy of England had failed in
its main purpose — a sufficient supply of native ship timber.   The
failure was inexcusable, for the remedy was evident, and was
exceedingly simple to apply.   The alarmists had been wrong in
predicting that the stripping of England's woodlands would put
an end to maritime supremacy.   They were right, however, in
perceiving some connection between forests and sea power, for
time and again the Navy suffered from the failure of the groves.
To have continued the 1668 plan would have furnished the Navy
with plenty of oak, but, as Melville wrote in 1810, "It would
seem as if the successive governments of this country had invariably become disheartened and had therefore abandoned all
attempts to place this important branch of our naval resources
upon a permanent basis, because the members of it could not
hope to live to see the success of their own measures." [2]

---

[1] See Chapter X.
[2] Melville, *Letter to the Rt. Hon. Spencer Perceval on Naval Timber* (1810), p.
25.   See also 1 *C. L. R.*, 2d series (1812), p. 137.

CHAPTER IV

BALTIC TIMBER AND FOREIGN POLICY

THE earliest and most important relief to England's timber shortage came from the forests of northern and central Europe. The great fir forests of the Baltic shores and the oak belt which lay farther to the south and west were tapped by the rivers flowing into the Baltic and the North Sea. In the ports which grew up at the mouths of these rivers, a thriving timber trade developed even in the medieval days of the Hanse. The whole forest region of northern Europe was generally known to the men of a few centuries ago as the Eastland or the East Country, for the Baltic was the "East Sea" of the Germans. At times these terms referred only to the coast of Prussia and the Baltic Provinces, but it will be convenient here to follow the English custom of extending the terms "Baltic," "Eastland" and "East Country" to include Norway and similar regions which lie outside the Baltic proper.

The economic development of the northern forest regions of Europe and America was influenced by the paucity of articles available for export. The earliest trade was usually in furs or other forest products of little bulk, but this alone was insufficient to support the increasing population. The next step in economic progress was usually the exploitation of the forests themselves. Not only was timber cut for any market which would use it, but minor extractive products from the trees, such as pot-ashes, tar, and pitch were utilized. This gave an immediate staple to exchange for the products of the south, and served to clear the land to make possible the third step in economic development — the introduction of agriculture on a scale sufficient to allow a surplus of grain for export. It was only very slowly that the forest countries made the final step to manufacturing. During the period covered by this study, the countries of the north were in various stages of this process, though even the most advanced nations continued the trade in wood and grain. Sweden, Russia, and Germany passed through the corn stage before the end of the period, while Norway remained almost entirely dependent on its forests. In all of them, the timber trade played an important part in their economy.

The Baltic had vast quantities of wood available, though it was not always of the best quality. In oak, at least, the timber of southern Europe was far superior. The men of the Mediterranean, however, had so many more attractive outlets for commercial activity that the timber trade was left to the North, where a large quantity of any material of such economic value was bound to be important. Consequently, many men in the Baltic region devoted their entire activity to timber, and when England began to feel the need of supplementing her own forest supply, she found in the Baltic many traders who were ready to go fully half way in pushing their wares.

Such a trade soon involved political considerations because of its mutual value to both the exporting and importing nations. For building and rigging ships of commerce and war, France, Spain, and Holland, as well as England, became dependent on timber and naval stores from the Baltic. The northern nations were equally interested in maintaining this trade, which formed one of their principal sources of revenue. This reciprocal feature became a leading factor in the relation of the great powers with the "Northern Crowns." England's Baltic policy was one of keeping that sea open in order to secure the materials so essential to her naval supremacy, while closing it to her rivals. Russia and her neighbors could not afford to alienate such influential customers. Consequently, timber became a matter for diplomats as well as traders, and a cargo of masts was an acceptable gift for a king. Before relating the history of this trade and the international complications which it produced, it is best to consider the details of the trade itself.

It was usually associated with the names of the ports of shipment, though the timber often came from a thousand miles in the interior of the continent, down the great rivers which penetrated the chief forest regions. One of the earliest important centers of the timber trade was Dantzig, the old Hanse town at the mouth of

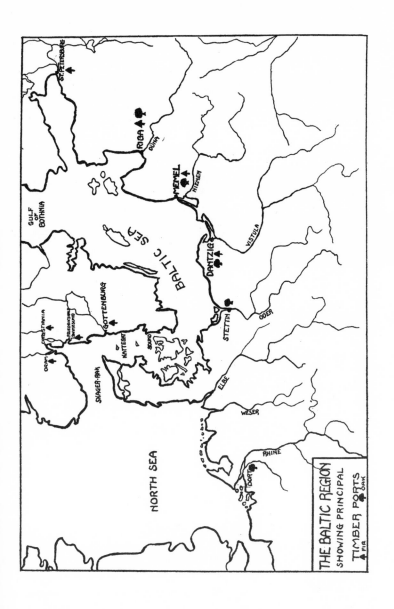

THE BALTIC REGION
SHOWING PRINCIPAL
TIMBER PORTS

FIR
OAK

NORTH SEA

BALTIC SEA

GULF OF BOTHNIA

SKAGER-RAK

KATTEGAT

SOUND

ST PETERSBURG

RIGA

DUNA

MEMEL

NIEMEN

DANTZIG

VISTULA

STETTIN

ODER

GOTTENBURG

FRIEDRICHSHAVN SWINEMUND

CHRISTIANIA

DRAM

ELBE

WESER

RHINE

DORT

the Vistula. This great river of Poland, with its tributaries, brought fir from the eastward in northern and central Poland, while its upper reaches penetrated the oak regions even into Galicia, so that oak and fir were almost equally important as Dantzig exports. Farther east lay Riga, which had the reputation of exporting the best masts in the world. These came at first from Livonia and the other Baltic provinces, but as these sources were exhausted, other fir forests on the upper Düna as far as the government of Vitebsk were drawn upon. Canals made it possible to penetrate into Volhynia and the Ukraine on the Dnieper even beyond Kiev, not only for masts and fir timber but also for the oak which became famous as "Riga Wainscot." Some of the best timber of European commerce floated down the Düna to Riga.

In the middle of the eighteenth century a new timber port sprang into prominence when Prince Radziwill began to send the timber from his great forests down the Niemen to Memel. This easternmost port of Prussia drew on the region lying between the Dantzig and Riga zones just described. By the Niemen came fir from the sandy plains of the Baltic provinces and farther south, where the 55th parallel forms a rough frontier between the fir and oak. From still farther to the southward, Memel received oak from Volhynia and Podolia. Though it was a Prussian port, practically all its timber came from Russian forests.

These three ports, which furnished England with the bulk of its naval timber and masts, exported both fir and oak. St. Petersburg, on the other hand, exported fir almost exclusively, while most of the timber shipped from Stettin was oak. The Russian capital developed an extensive timber trade after Peter the Great shifted as much business as possible from Archangel to his new "window into the west" in 1715. Whatever oak might reach St. Petersburg by the long passage from Kazan was monopolized by the Russian Navy. The Oder, on the contrary, tapped the hardwood forests of central Germany even into Silesia, so that, except for a little fir coming through canals from the Vistula, the timber exports of Stettin were chiefly oak.

The timber trade of the southern Baltic shore centered at these five ports. There were three other sources of timber not within the Baltic, which presented a problem so similar that they have often been included in that term for convenience. The Elbe and the Rhine, like the Oder, brought to Hamburg and Dort the oak of Germany, while masts from Switzerland also occasionally came by the Rhine. The timber carried by the Weser to Bremen was considered of inferior value in England. Even the Rhine and the Elbe never played the part of the Baltic rivers in supplying the English Navy, for their timber was laid under a commercial ban shortly after the Navigation Acts were passed. This was partially lifted in 1780, but was not fully removed until the extreme scarcity in 1799 forced such a measure, and by 1804, Napoleon had cut off such trade.[1]

The third timber region, lying just outside the Baltic, was one of the most important of all. The western slope of the Scandinavian peninsula was covered with dense forests of fir and spruce which could be floated down the Norwegian mountain torrents to Longsound, Dram, Friedrikstad, and a dozen other ports which developed a timber trade at an early date. Spruce spars and fir timber were the chief exports of Norway to England, for the early oak shipments ceased when Denmark reserved that timber for its own ships. Norway's commercial existence was almost entirely dependent on this timber trade, so that events such as a war or the fire of London might mean great prosperity, while an unfavorable tariff could bring ruin. The nearness to England, combined with the strategic advantage of its lying outside the Sound, caused Englishmen and Scotsmen to turn to Norway early in the sixteenth century for masts and timber. Strange to say, Sweden supplied little timber for the English Navy after 1700. There were ample forests that could furnish good masts and timber, and at the time of the Restoration, mast fleets came annually from Gottenburg (or Gothenburg), which was one of the chief staple towns of Sweden lying outside the Sound near the frontier of Norway. The protectionist policy inaugurated by Charles XII did much to check this trade, and Sweden on the whole did less than the other northern countries to encourage timber exports. The Swedish ports on the Baltic and the Gulf of Bothnia sent

[1] 13 & 14 Chas. II, c. 11, sect. 23; 20 Geo. III, c. 75; 39 Geo. III, c. 111.

some building timber to England, but practically none for naval purposes.

This Baltic timber trade, was not a matter which affected Dantzig, Riga, Longsound, and the other timber *ports* alone. Extending even into Bohemia, Galicia, and the Ukraine, it afforded employment to men living hundreds of miles in the interior. This is more clearly indicated when the trade is analyzed into its various processes from the decision to cut the trees until the arrival of the timber at Deptford or Portsmouth. The details of the trade changed little during the entire period, and varied only slightly from country to country, so that, with a few alterations, a general description will fit any region at any time from 1650 to 1860.

Jews managed the internal timber trade in central Europe — Soltan, Kalezkis, Bontschewsky, Simonowite, Fazezes, Szewillowik, Dernalowitz, Chariza, and Smuylowitz are among the names of those who gathered one mast shipment from Riga.[1] Prussia excluded them from the business in 1761 on the ground that they were wasting the forests, but in Poland and Russia it was chiefly in their hands.[2] The first step in the process was the advancing of money to the merchant by a Dantzig, Riga, or Warsaw bank in the autumn. He would then negotiate with the owners of the forests.[3] In Poland, the timberlands were for the most part owned by great nobles, chief among whom were the Radziwills and Czartorinskys. In Russia, part of the land was so held, some of the remainder being owned by the crown, while communal forests were occasionally held by a village.

The merchant contracted for the stumpage on a given area, paying a specific amount per tree, with the stipulation that the timber must be removed within a certain time. If the trees should prove unsound, that was the contractor's misfortune, but naturally the business was a profitable one on the whole. Occasion-

[1] *Parl. Papers*, 1806 (1), iv, 230.
[2] Fernow, *History of Forestry*, p. 50.
[3] For a general description of the process, see *Parl. Papers*, 1835 (519), xix, 79, 104, 107; Krünitz, *Oekonomische Encyklopädie*, xxiv, 593 ff.; Brown, *Forests and Forestry in Poland, etc.*, pp. 194–196, 241, 247; Brown, *Forestry of North Russia*, pp. 110, 111.

ally the proprietor would undertake to convey the timber all the way to the Baltic, but ordinarily he furnished serfs to cut the wood and carry it to the bank of the nearest stream. Sometimes the agreement was made with the elder or council of the village *mir*, and the peasants would undertake the operation on their own responsibility. This method became more common after the abolition of serfdom. At least a portion of the payment was made in advance to the cutters, and was often in the form of provisions. Lumbering played a prominent part in the economic life of these peasants, who could have little else for occupation during the winter. Except for the Jews and serfs, the arrangements in Norway were similar to this.[1] In the German oak forests, the process more often resembled the English.

The season for lumbering, if that American term may be applied to the operations in Europe, started about November, when sometimes two or three hundred peasants, comprising practically the entire male population of a village, each with a pony or two, moved into the forest and erected their huts. For cutting, the axe was in far more general use than the saw.[2]

The cutting was usually on a selective plan, with little of the reckless slashing so notorious in the virgin forests of America. The timber of proper size was culled out and removed with the least possible damage to the younger trees. The forests in the basins of the Vistula and Düna had been cut over for centuries and remained quite productive, though trees could seldom grow to the size requisite for great masts. It was scarcely necessary to replant, for nature ordinarily reseeded the ground and, in the coniferous region especially, succession took care of itself.

Germany commenced forest conservation early in the Middle Ages, and some forests on the upper Rhine have been profitable for six hundred years of continuous cutting.[3] Toward the end of the eighteenth century, however, the effects of the increased de-

[1] *Parl. Papers*, 1835 (519), xix, 48, 54; Broch, *Le Royaume de Norvège*, pp. 111–114; Amneus, *La Ville de Kristiania*, pp. 56, 57.

[2] Krünitz, *op. cit.*, xxiv, 607. See *Ibid.*, plates 5 and 6, for 18th-century saws and axes.

[3] Fernow, *op. cit.*, pp. 42–70; Gee, *Trade and Navigation of England Considered*, p. 96; Pepys, *Diary*, Dec. 11, 1663.

mand for timber began to be noticeable. In Russia it was especially evident between 1790 and 1800, and the old sources of
supply grew inadequate. It became necessary to go farther and
farther up the rivers and deeper into the woods away from the
rivers in order to find suitable trees, which naturally increased
the price of timber, and was one cause for the Russian timber embargo of 1798. Even the rivers grew shallower as a result. This
was laid at the door of the Jews.[1]

Transporting the logs to the river was the most difficult portion
of the whole process. A mild winter meant timber scarcity. The
logs were hauled on sleds or axles by horses or oxen, and a heavy
snowfall was essential to success. A mild winter or a sudden
thaw made the clayey or swampy ground so miry that transportation was out of the question, and logs might remain in the woods
for several seasons before a winter came sufficiently cold for the
operation. Just as in England, it was not ordinarily profitable to
carry timber by land for more than twenty miles, so that the
available forest area was really a strip forty miles wide along the
streams large enough to float logs. Only in the later days of increasing scarcity did high timber prices make it worth while for
lumbermen to go farther into the woods, at times even thirty or
forty miles, for choice trees. Delivery on timber contracts was
often made subject to proper winter weather for lumbering, and
the mast supply was sometimes held up at a crucial time because
of a light winter, while prices at the ports tended to fluctuate with
the amount of snowfall.[2]

Floating the logs to the Baltic was a simpler though more
lengthy process. In the smaller streams the logs, which had been
drawn to the water's edge, were often thrown in singly, to be collected at a strategic point and assembled into a great raft for the
long trip down the river to the sea. This voyage occupied several
months, and in the case of masts from the Dnieper or oak from
Kazan and Bohemia, sometimes two years. These rafts, often
formed of over a thousand logs, and sufficient to load several tim-

---

[1] Schleiden, *Für Baum und Wald*, pp. 105–120; DeRaymond, *Tableau de l'Empire,
de Russie* i, 245, 368; Brown, *Forests in Poland*, etc., p. 54.
[2] Brown, *Forests in Poland*, p. 251; Pepys, *Diary*, June 23, 1662.

ber ships, were veritable floating islands, sometimes carrying several families with their huts, cattle, horses, poultry, and wagons. On the Dnieper it was necessary to make the trip upstream to connect with the Düna for Riga; but usually the rafts sluggishly drifted downstream, steered by huge sweeps and often accelerated by oars or sails. On reaching the sea, the rafts were broken up for timber, the crew returning by land either on foot or in the wagons which they had brought. On the Rhine, rafts often eight hundred feet long and sixty feet wide, propelled by several hundred rowers, were formed at Andernach for the trip to Dort. In Norway the logs were ordinarily sent singly upon the shorter trip down the turbulent mountain streams.[1]

The most important stages in the progress of the log from the forest to the dockyard took place at the Baltic ports. Here the timber which had come down the rivers was floated into the "mast ponds," formed by booms in the river, and sorted for the various forms of timber needed for exportation. The choicest fir sticks were used as masts because of their greatly increased value for that purpose. The others were sent to the sawmills for conversion into the forms most in demand. Dantzig in the later days could furnish barely enough masts for its own shipping, and its chief exports of fir were in the form of "timber" over eight inches square; plank between two and eight inches thick; "deals" or boards; and "battens" or smaller, narrower boards. The pieces of "timber" were often referred to as "baulks," an adaptation of the German word, just as "spruce" developed from "Sprucia," the old English term for Prussia. Masts, in their turn, were ordinarily divided into "great," "middling," and "small," measured by "palms" of circumference, equivalent to about an inch and a third, so that Baltic masts were often known in England as "hand masts." The smaller spars, usually of spruce, were referred to as "boom," "cant," and "barling," according to size. Baltic masts were often shipped with the bark on, unlike those from America, which were hewn into "sixteen sides." The term

[1] Johnston, *Travels through part of the Russian Empire and the Country of Poland,* p. 75; *Description and History of Vegetable Substances,* i, 45–47; Peuchet, *Dictionnaire Universel de la Géographie Commerçante,* iv, 172; *Parl. Papers,* 1835 (519), xix, 24, 78.

"wainscot" applied to oak referred originally to the form in which the logs were shipped from Dantzig and Riga, with two sides of the log hewn flat to take up less room in the ship's hold. Attention has been called to the fact that England was more inclined to use Baltic plank and deals because they could be sawn so much more cheaply in the Baltic by the windmills, which conservatism kept out of England. Every port had its sawmills, often dozens of them, but the greatest collection of these mills was at Zaandam and Dort, where the Dutch sawed not only the Rhine timber but that which they had brought from Norway and the Baltic.

In these gray Baltic towns there was the same general busy dreariness which stamps the seaport living by trade alone. Save for a few old monuments of Hanse splendor, there was little of the picturesque in Dantzig, Riga, Memel, and Stettin, whose streams and warehouses were crowded with timber and corn, and whose inhabitants lived almost entirely in a world of contracts, discounts, and demurrages. "Heaven protect the traveller who arrives in this city without a commercial commission!" wrote an Englishman at Dantzig in 1804.[1]

England gained its eventual predominance in the Baltic trade partly through its "factors" living in the Eastland ports. Even in Tudor days, agents of the King or Queen had occasionally resided at Dantzig, where resident English merchants soon formed a "factory" or "college" with certain privileges. At St. Petersburg, a similar college, supported by a British consul-general, was influential in molding the Russian commercial policy in favor of England. Most of the factors living in these outposts of English commerce carried on a general business in the commodities of the port, ordinarily on a commission basis of about three per cent. Gradually, great English houses, rivalling in importance such native houses as that of Blankenhagen at Riga, began to engross much of the trade in timber and naval stores. The names of Thornton, Pierson, and Morison at Riga, Solly at Dantzig, Moir at Memel, Tooke at St. Petersburg, and Norman in Norway are inseparably connected with the Navy's timber supply from the Baltic during the latter part of the period. Carrying on the same

[1] Carr, *A Northern Summer*, p. 285. See *ibid.*, pp. 277, 278, 284–286.

business for generations, and having powerful commercial connections in England, these Baltic Britons concentrated the timber trade in their hands to such an extent that the French grew alarmed. During the American Revolution, the French awoke to the fact that they had to purchase most of their masts and naval stores from these Englishmen, who often informed the British cruisers, so that the capture of the masts for France was almost certain. It was a profitable and sometimes anomalous patriotism, but on the whole they served England well.[1]

These merchants contracted with the Navy Board for timber, masts, and naval stores, and were responsible for the wood during the major part of its trip from the forest to the dockyard. They would buy up timber enough for their contract quota from a number of Jews whose timber had arrived by raft from the interior, and after sorting it, would float the logs to their own timber ponds and saw them in their own mills. Because of the added responsibility which a contract entailed, their profits often amounted to several times the three per cent gained in the general commission business.

To ensure the quality of the timber exported, nearly every Baltic port had official "brackers," or inspectors, who sorted the timber into three qualities and stamped each piece with the appropriate symbol. At Dantzig, for instance, a 'K" was hammered on the "crown" or first quality timber; a "B," or later a "W," on the second quality; and "BB," or later "WW," on the "brack" or third-rate pieces. At Riga, where the bracking system was highly developed, masts were also inspected on the stump in the forest at the bracker's own responsibility. The status and duties of these officials varied from port to port. Occasionally they were royal officials, but more often they were chosen by the municipality as a relic of the virtual Hanseatic independence. They acted under oath and their word was final. The bracking system was most effectively organized at Dantzig and Riga. At Memel and Stettin it was more carelessly executed, while at St. Peters-

---

[1] Marbault, *Essai sur le Commerce de Russie*, pp. 138–144; Peuchet, *Dictionnaire Universel de la Géographie Commerçante*, v, 364, 466; Hist. MSS Com., *Marquess of Lothian MSS*, pp. 222–234.

burg a bureaucracy imposed so many conditions on export that the timber merchants much preferred Riga. Bracking obviated much of the risk in practically guaranteeing a uniform quality of timber, and the term "Danzig Crown" meant as much in timber circles as Lloyd's A 1 signifies to shipowners. The British Navy demanded crown timber, and the bracking system was one consideration which influenced the preference of the Navy Board for Baltic timber.[1]

Once his timber was properly converted for the English market, the next task of the merchant was to secure shipping. Under the terms of the Navigation Act either English ships or those of the exporting nation could be used, the choice depending on availability and freight rates, modified by certain constant advantages of Baltic shipping. Because of the sandy bars at most of the Baltic ports, the ships in the timber trade were comparatively small, ranging ordinarily from 250 to 400 tons; for the larger ships had to receive their cargoes from lighters while anchored in an exposed roadstead, which was a process not only expensive but often dangerous.

The average timber ship could carry a cargo of about three hundred loads of timber, reckoning on about one load for one ton of displacement. The loads were usually mixed, for the weight of oak usually limited that wood to about a hundred loads in a cargo, the remainder being the lighter fir, while masts required fir timber equivalent to about a third of the cargo to facilitate stowage. Mast ships had specially constructed ports in the stern for the difficult process of loading, and the average cargo of great masts was about fifty. A mast cargo stiffened and strained a ship considerably. "Our old vessel shipped many seas," wrote a sailor in 1785; "being bound up with long spars was not nearly as lively as with another cargo."[2]

The Baltic timber ships were ordinarily preferable to the English. Devoted entirely to the timber and grain trade, their holds

[1] Oddy, *European Commerce*, pp. 195, 255, 271; Peuchet, *op. cit.*, v, 498; *Commons Reports*, iii, 22; *Parl. Papers*, 1805, (1) iv, 59.

[2] Richardson, *A Mariner of England*, p. 25. For typical cargoes see *Parl. Papers*, 1805 (1), ii, 254; 1835 (519), xix, 395; 1839 (0.91), ix, 13, 45.

were not blackened with Newcastle coal, while the low cost of shipbuilding in the Baltic, together with the meager wages of the Eastland crews, ordinarily enabled them, of course, to offer lower freight rates. Their captains, too, the Peter Ipsens, Klaes Hansens, and the rest, represented the cream of a maritime race, for this trade was practically the only career open to their talents. Finally, the Baltic ships could load during the winter and be ready to sail as soon as the ice broke up, though the English ships had a similar advantage as winter came on.[1]

The English ships were usually worn-out veterans of the West Indian or Mediterranean trade, timber carrying usually being their last employment before they sank or were broken up. Struggling under heavy deckloads of timber, many of these old ships succumbed to autumn gales in Kattegat and Skagerrak. The masters were like their ships, an illiterate lot, the dregs of a commerce which could offer such prizes as those of the East India and Levant trades. These timber ships were the "tramps" of that age, picking up a freight of any nature that might be trusted to them, anywhere in the world. Such a ship was the old *Forrester*, a craft so crazy that the crew once deserted her on the eve of a Baltic voyage on discovering the rottenness of her planking. Richardson gives her itinerary from 1783 to 1786, going in ballast to Finland for timber, after which she took Newcastle coal to St. Petersburg, returning with naval stores, iron, and tallow. After a year in the coal trade between Newcastle and London, she took a cargo of salt from Cadiz to Pillau, going over to Memel to load "spars as long as the hold of the ship" for Corunna. Cargoes into the Baltic were often hard to secure, for one shipload of manufactures or colonial wares might pay for some seventy cargoes of timber. Such were the ships which brought much of the naval timber from the East Country to England.[2]

Norway had an advantage over the regions within the Baltic, not only because of the greater security of the trade in time of war, but because of the nearness to England as well. With a fair

---

[1] See *Cal. S. P. Dom.*, 1664–65, p. 152.

[2] Richardson, *A Mariner of England*, pp. 15–26; Klaer, "Development of Scandinavian Shipping," *Journal of Political Economy*, i, 393; Lindsay, *Merchant Shipping*, iii, 141, 142; *Parl. Papers*, 1820 (269), iii, 16, 21, 45; 1835 (519), xix, 76, 81, 110.

wind, ships could sometimes make the 350 miles to Fredrikstad in three days, and the trip was often accomplished in a week; while the voyage of 1000 to 1500 miles to Stettin, Dantzig, Memel, Riga, and St. Petersburg was seldom completed inside of a month and was much slower than that in times of war, when hundreds of merchantmen sailed in convoy. This naturally affected freight rates, and at a time when it cost 12s. a load to bring timber from Norway, the Memel rate was 20s., Riga, 23s., and St. Petersburg, 25s. The more distant ports, like those of the Bothnic Gulf, had to sell their timber at a lower rate in order to compete on equal terms in England.[1]

The voyage was ordinarily without incident in time of peace, beyond paying the Sound dues at Elsinore. Captains were sometimes offered a third of the dues they could save by navigating the Great or Little Belt in defiance of the Danish frigates. In war, a few old warships were told off to serve as convoy for the Baltic merchant fleet, which often numbered over six hundred ships; for to navigate alone would be suicidal. Privateers of every flag swarmed in those northern waters, and occasionally were powerful enough to interfere with the Navy's timber supply. In 1702, the naval contractor complained that his mast ships were held up for several months in Norway "for fear of the Sieur Lombi." [2]

The final stage in the progress of the timber that started in the Russian or German forests was its reception at the dockyards. After paying the customs, for even the King's timber had to pay the King's duties, it was inspected by the master shipwright and other dockyard officials, and if found satisfactory, was checked to the credit of the contractor.

A striking feature of the timber trade was the unusual proportion of labor and transportation to the original cost of the timber on the stump. A tree that could be purchased for five shillings as it stood in the forests of Poland was worth £1 5s. as a load of timber at Dantzig, and cost the Navy, when delivered at the dockyard, £5 5s. On account of the bulky nature of the commodity, the original value was less than five per cent, while transporta-

[1] *Parl. Papers*, 1820 (269), iii, 45; 821 (186), vi, 43.
[2] R. O., N.B. In Letters, 512, *Taylor to N. B.* July, 17. 1702.

tion, with its incidental charges of insurance and the dues at the Sound and the ports, amounted to very nearly two thirds of its final value. During most of the period under consideration, the duties were about twenty per cent *ad valorem*, and the profit of the contractor ordinarily ranged between five and ten per cent. These cannot be absolute estimates, for considerations of war or peace, masts or deals, and monopoly or free competition, all affected the relative importance of the different items; but those figures represent the usual proportion.

In the case of American timber, the original value of the wood was relatively even lower, for transatlantic freights were about three times as high as those to the Baltic, and the removal of duties on American timber could scarcely rectify this until the abnormally high Baltic duties were imposed, in 1809. From these figures it can also be understood why England was so anxious to secure the freight for its own ships, since freight alone usually represented more than half of the final value of the timber.[1]

With this description of the Baltic timber trade as a background, the history of the development of that trade and the international complications which it produced can be interpreted more clearly. Considerations of this timber trade, and others which will be treated later, fall into two distinct phases so far as this work is concerned. Interest naturally centers upon the timber supply of the Navy itself, but that was only a small part of the general timber imports of England. The close relations between the two make the latter worthy of attention. As in the case of many other commodities, timber of varying quality was produced, and as the Navy would use only the best, the business could not be conducted efficiently and profitably unless there was a certain market for the inferior grades. Moreover, the shortage of oak in England created the policy of reserving the English oak as far as possible for the Navy, so that the nation became dependent on other countries for timber of many different varieties. The general trade included a much wider range than the naval

---

[1] *Parl. Papers*, 1806 (1), iv, 232; 1820 (269), iii, 101; 1835 (519), xix, 33; Oddy, *European Commerce*, p. 78.

supply. At a time when the Navy was limiting its Baltic imports to masts, spars, and a few deck deals, England was importing wainscot, plank, coopers' timber, and other forms of wood for general purposes too numerous to describe in detail. There was also an important distinction between the forms of timber for which the Navy was entirely dependent on the Baltic, and those being imported as a matter of convenience or economy to relieve the demands on English forests. England was at all times dependent on a foreign supply of good masts and spars, as well as hemp, sailcloth, tar, and pitch. As a matter of expediency, the Navy secured its deck deals from the Baltic throughout most of the sailing ship era, and a large part of the planking used below the waterline in the King's ships came from Dantzig after 1677. From about 1760 to 1780, Baltic oak was used quite extensively for the large timbers of the warships; but this supply was dispensed with as soon as the condition of the English forests would permit. Fir plank and timber were often imported for inferior portions of the construction, and repairs. After 1804, there was actual need for Baltic timber whenever it could be secured. The political significance of the Baltic timber supply of the Navy centered on the masts, spars, and naval stores of which the Baltic had a monopoly until an auxiliary supply from America could be developed.

Even in the medieval days when the Hanse was at its height, England imported timber from the Baltic. The term "Rygholt," occasionally met in the records of Henry III, has been taken to denote timber and boards from Riga, and the Subsidy Rolls of Henry IV about 1400 indicate a large importation from the Baltic. There was probably little naval timber among the "wainscots, clapholtz, tonholtz, bowstaves, righoltz, bords and delles," which the Hanseatics brought to the Steelyard, though even in the early fifteenth century there were imports of masts and "spars de firr." [1]

A regular importation of masts began with the Tudor period, for the "oaken masts" which had served for the earlier ships were

[1] Brown, *Forests of England*, p. 68 n.; Howard, *Timbers of the World*, pp. 197, 198; Stevenson, *Wood*, pp. 84, 85; Rogers, *History of Agriculture and Prices in England*, iv, 446–449.

inadequate for the Navy which came into being with Henry VII and his son. In 1498, the first Tudor made a treaty with the arch prefect, proconsuls, and consuls of Riga, and Henry VIII made frequent treaties with the "Proconsul ac Consules regiae Civitatis Gedanen," and with other Baltic towns beside Dantzig.[1] These treaties show a growing interest in the masts, naval stores, and grain which England was beginning to require in large quantities from the Eastland.

To build the *Great Michael* in 1512, James IV of Scotland wasted all the woods of Fife "besides all the timber that was gotten out of Norway,"[2] and there were foreign masts in the *Harry Grace à Dieu* built for the English Navy two years later. William Watson, "King's merchant for Dansike," was importing great masts for the Navy, to be delivered at Deptford Stronde, by 1540, he and his successors often residing in the Baltic for that purpose. Henry VIII occasionally granted permission to foreigners to import masts and other articles into England, on the condition that they were to "be brought to the King before sale, that he may have first choice of them."[3] An agent of the Emperor Charles V made the Navy an offer of Swiss masts, some with the extraordinary diameter of over fifty inches, in 1546, for the Emperor "taketh up all the money he can get."[4] Such great masts, twice as large as the later Baltic maximum, and larger even than the great white pines from America, were extremely rare, and "made masts" composed of several smaller sticks were in use by 1514.

Under Elizabeth the demands on Norway and the Baltic for masts and naval stores increased, with an effect on foreign policy that will be noticed later. The Chancellor Expedition to the White Sea in 1553 and 1556 opened a new supply of masts around Archangel, but the agents of the Merchant Adventurers to Russia received these instructions on the subject: "As for Masts, Tarre,

[1] *L. & P., Henry VIII*, vol. xxi, pt. 1 (1546), pp. 107, 135; Oddy, *European Commerce*, p. 138.

[2] Macpherson, *Annals*, ii, 42.

[3] *L. & P., Henry VIII*, vol. xiv, pt. 1 (1539), p. 419; pt. 2, p. 18; vol. xv (1540), pp. 126, 127; vol. xxi, pt. 1 (1546), p. 660.

[4] *Ibid.*, vol. xxi, pt. 1 (1546), 606.

Hempe Feathers or any such like, they would not bear the charges to have any considering our deere fraight." [1] The trade in masts and timber from Onega and the White Sea fell to the Dutch, who began to take masts from there in 1610, bringing some of them to England.

The proximity of the Baltic gave that region most of the English trade in masts and naval stores. "The entrance of English merchants into this neighboring and natural domain of trade was, after the middle of the sixteenth century, inevitable," says Cheyney.[2] Traders went there in increasing numbers, and in 1579 the "Fellowship of Eastland Merchants" was formed, with a monopoly of the trade into the East Country. For nearly a century most of the masts, timber, and naval stores were brought to England by this Eastland Company. This was a regulated company, not a joint stock organization like the East India Company. Its general effect of cramping, rather than stimulating, trade cost it the monopoly of the corn trade in 1629. The final blow came in 1672, when its privileges were abrogated, and membership was opened to all upon a payment of forty shillings.[3] The French had a similar "Compagnie du Nord," and Colbert attempted to secure materials for his navy through its coöperation around 1670.[4]

The Eastland Company had been established partly to combat the Hanse, but it found a more vigorous rival in the Dutch, who had an Eastland Company of their own. Driven to the sea for a living, and able to build and navigate ships more cheaply than the English, the Dutch pursued every kind of trade with untiring efficiency. By 1600, the English realized that the trade in the naval essentials, as in many other branches of commerce, had fallen into the hands of these "Sea Beggars." Their hold on the timber trade was especially secure.

---

[1] Lindsay, *Merchant Shipping*, ii, 556.

[2] Cheyney, *History of England from the Defeat of the Armada to the Death of Elizabeth*, i, 343; Camden Society, *Acts and Ordinances of the Eastland Company*, ed. Sellers, *passim;* Cawston and Keane, *The Early Chartered Companies*, pp. 60–66.

[3] Cheyney, *op. cit.*, i, 343–347; Macpherson, *Annals*, ii, 149, 164, 361, 362, 563, 564.

[4] Colbert, *Lettres, Instructions, et Mémoires*, ii, 488, 530, 631; iii, 133.

> The exceeding great groves of woods are in the east countries, chiefly
> within the Baltic; but the large piles of wainscot, clapboard, fir, deal, masts,
> and other timber are in the Low Countries, where none grows, wherewith
> they serve themselves and other parts, and this kingdom; and they have
> 500 or 600 great long ships continually using that trade, and we none at all,

wrote Raleigh.[1] The Dutch had relieved Norway from the
strangle hold of the Hanse about 1550 and then began to carry
oak and fir in great quantities to the sawmills of Zaandam.[2] Their
enterprise in the Archangel timber trade has already been mentioned. They secured a reduction of the Sound tolls from Denmark, and encroached on the almost monopolistic favor which
England had enjoyed at the court of Muscovy. With their ships
built at a third of the cost of the English and with a low rate of
interest to capitalize their ventures, the Dutch almost drove
England to the wall in commercial competition in the Baltic.
They undermined the English trade with the Eastland, whereby
English woolens were exchanged for Baltic timber; and England
became in large measure dependent on her great rival for the essentials of naval construction. The Dutch set high value upon
this Baltic trade.

> This trade of the East Sea is one of their greatest mysteries in trade, they
> venting there what they bring out of the east, south and west; and again,
> supplying other countries with commodities of that sea . . . and although
> their Spanish, and East-Indy and Spanish trade, be richer, yet the destroy-
> ing of this trade is also the destroying of those other,

wrote the English envoy to the Hague in 1658.[3]

The general importance of the Baltic trade and the particular
relation of the Eastland naval materials to sea power were influential in bringing on the Navigation Acts, by which the English
made a bid "to wrest the northern trade out of the hands of the
Dutch and take possession of it themselves."[4] The principal
Navigation Acts, passed in 1651 and 1660, stipulated primarily
that all English imports must be brought either in English ships
with English crews or in ships of the country producing the im-

---

[1] Macpherson, *op. cit.*, ii, 236; slightly different version in Raleigh, *Remains*,
p. 180.

[2] Klaer, "Development of Scandinavian Shipping," *Journal of Political Economy*,
i, 330–332.

[3] Thurloe, *State Papers*, vii, 525.   [4] Pearson, *Timber Trade*, p. 19.

ported articles. As the Tsar had practically no merchant marine at that day, the acts meant that most of the Russian naval materials were to be carried in English ships. Much timber had been brought down the Rhine to Dort, and to prevent the excuse for any Dutch ship to bring timber to England, the importation of this timber was absolutely prohibited. Timber from Hamburg and other German ports was included in the original ban, but this was raised to permit importation in British ships long before necessity caused the Rhine timber from the Dutch port of Dort to be released from the prohibition.[1]

The commercial history of the Baltic timber trade will be carried on for another century before considering the international complications which arose from this source in plenty after the passage of the first Navigation Act. The immediate effect of the acts upon the timber situation were less than had been anticipated. Exceptions were necessary during the Dutch wars, and further liberal concessions of Charles II to the Hanse towns almost gave over the Baltic trade to the ships of the East Country. The fire of London in 1666 created an unusual demand for timber to rebuild the city, and the Norwegians "warmed themselves well at the fire." In the following year, the King granted liberty "to import Norway timber and deals in any foreign ship whatsoever"; but in 1668, the Council of Trade refused to continue this, favoring instead the purchase of sixty foreign timber ships.[2] Foreign ships, even Dutch, were allowed to bring timber and stores for the Navy in later wars, but the general timber trade was seldom so favored.[3]

Sir Josiah Child, in his famous mercantilist work the *Discourse on Trade*, declared that by 1669 the Navigation Acts had by no means achieved their end in giving England control of its trade. He considered them excellent in principle, however, and felt that they should be enforced to the limit. He devoted several pages to the timber trade, showing that, whereas there were two hundred Eastland ships coming to England, not one English ship had

[1] 6 Geo. I, c. 15.
[2] *Cal. S. P. Dom.*, 1667–68, pp. 295, 296; 1668–69, pp. 167, 290–292; Papillon, *Life of Thomas Papillon of London, Merchant*, pp. 66–60.
[3] *Cal. Treas. Papers, passim.*

been built for the Baltic trade between 1651 and 1668. The
Danes, Swedes, Holsteiners, and all Easterlings, he complained,
had increased their shipping engaged in the timber trade by at
least two thirds during that period, while the English shipping
had proportionately declined. He advocated a 50 per cent duty
on all Baltic timber not brought in English ships, and even advised the limitations of the timber trade to English ships alone.[1]
The chief interest of the English in securing this trade for their
own bottoms was less the consideration of security in the supply
of naval stores than the freight, which was often several times the
value of the timber. As one Englishman later expressed it,
"Freight is the most important raw material which we possess." [2]
England failed to gain this trade at once, as Pearson explains in
very elaborate detail.[3] The Dutch were driven from it before the
end of the century. So far the Navigation Act was a success.

The period around 1700 is one of the most important in the
history of the timber problem. After the conclusion of the Peace
of Ryswick in 1697, Englishmen suddenly turned their attention
to the Baltic trade in all its details. During the eight years of
war, the French had made great depredations on English shipping,
over four thousand vessels having been lost by 1694. Bounties
were offered for building new ships, with a consequent heavy
demand for naval materials from the north and east.

Trade conditions were growing more unfavorable in that region.
In the first place, the Eastland trade was a pernicious one in the
eyes of the mercantilist economists of the day, who disapproved
of an excess of imports over exports. Practically every branch
of Baltic commerce had an unfavorable balance of trade, as Gee
wrote:

[1] Child, *Discourse on Trade*, pp. 89, 90, 128.
[2] *Parl. Papers*, 1847–48 (7), vol. xx, pt. 1, p. 131.
[3] Pearson, *Timber Trade*, pp. 22, 37, 38, 44, 48. For varying views on Baltic
trade and timber situation, see Coke, *Reason of the Increase of the Dutch Trade*, p.
115; Mun, *England's Treasure by Foreign Trade, passim;* (Pettyt), *Brittania Lan-
guens*, p. 184; (Pollexfen), *Discourse of the Trade, Coyne and Paper Credit*, p. 84;
Brewster, *Essays of Trade and Navigation*, pp. 87–89; Gee, *Trade and Navigation of
England Considered*, pp. 45, 46, 94, 100; Defoe, *Plan of English Commerce*, pp. 348–
368; (King) *British Merchant*, i, 3, 24, 25; Cary, *Discourse on Trade*, pp. 76, 77.

Norway and Denmark take from England guineas, crowns pieces and bullion, a little tobacco, and a few coarse woolens of small value.

England takes from Norway and Denmark vast quantities of deal boards, timber, spars and iron; we pay them a very great balance which is greatly increased by the late establishment of ships in the navigation and freight of their timber.[1]

Conditions in other parts of the region were equally unfavorable from the mercantilist point of view. From 1697 to 1700, the average balance against England in the trade with Norway and Denmark was £36,672; with the East Country, £154,539; and with Russia, £53,368.[2] By 1714, these conditions showed little improvement.[3] Only half of this entire trade was carried in English bottoms, and, in the case of Norway, "from Michaelmas 1691 to Mich'as 1696, there were entered on the Customs House at London 1070 foreign ships from those parts and but 39 English."[4] Such a loss of freight accentuated the already disadvantageous balance. Later writers could appreciate the value of this trade in spite of the excess of imports over exports, but it met almost universal condemnation at the time. The Board of Trade made an exhaustive inquiry into the situation in 1697, recommending that England become less dependent on the Baltic by turning to Ireland and New England, and that an attempt be made to remove the hindrances under which English merchants labored in the Baltic.

The unfavorable balance of trade was only a part of England's discontent with the Baltic trade. English merchants were faced by an increasing hostility on the part of Sweden, where Charles XII was fighting England with her own protectionist weapon in an attempt to build up the nascent industries. About 1680, a duty of over 50 per cent had been laid on English woolens, and by 1700, English merchants had been virtually forced out of the Swedish dominions by a series of harsh discriminations.[5] Except for Gottenburg, Sweden proper played only a minor rôle in the

---

[1] Gee, *op. cit.*, p. 45. See Brewster, *op. cit.*, p. 102.

[2] Macpherson, *Annals*, ii, 719. See Hist. MSS Com., *House of Lords MSS*, 1697–1702, pp. 430–436, 455–457.

[3] Chance, *George I and the Northern War*, pp. 6–8.

[4] *Ibid.*, p. 7; see Wentworth, *Works of Davenant*, i, 396 ff.

[5] *E. H. R.*, xvi, 680–684; see Postlethwayt, *Dictionary*, "Sweden."

timber problem, but in 1700 the whole Baltic was practically a Swedish lake. The authority of Charles XII extended around a large portion of that sea, so as to include Riga and Stettin. The Swedish attitude, therefore, seriously affected the trade in naval supplies, and this came to a climax in 1703, when the Swedish tar monopoly refused supplies to England except in Swedish ships, only in such quantities as they saw fit, and at their own price.[1] Dr. Robinson, the envoy at Stockholm, informed London of this, warning the government "that they might see how much it was in the power of the King of Sweden either to forward the fitting out of the Royal Navy or to keep it in harbour." [2] Denmark had offered to take Sweden's place, but could not supply the deficiency; so England made an attempt to encourage Russian trade.[3]

England needed a strong fleet to face France in the War of the Spanish Succession, and was suddenly brought to realize how precarious was her supply of naval necessities from the north. In 1697, it had been a matter of traders grumbling at an unfavorable balance; in 1703 it was a question of sea power which was threatened. At the earlier date, England had begun to play with the idea of naval stores from America; in 1703, the movement gained momentum, resulting in acts encouraging the production of these stores. The participation of an English fleet in the Great Northern War, in order to keep the Baltic open, will be treated in its place under foreign policy, and the question of the balance of trade and Baltic dependence will rise again in considering American commerce,[4] but it was over a century before the timber imports from America exceeded those from northern Europe. The crisis around 1700 is to be remembered chiefly for the stimulus which it gave to the colonial supply.

All through the eighteenth century, the Navy drew an ever-increasing supply of naval materials from the Baltic, but except for the armed intervention, which will be discussed shortly, the

[1] Macpherson, ii, 724.   [2] Postlethwayt, *Dictionary*, "Naval Stores."
[3] R. O., C. O., Index 8303, Trade, Foreign, Aug. 3, 1696; Hist. MSS Com., *House of Lords MSS*, 1699–1702, pp. 83–85.
    See Chapter VI.

use of Stettin oak was the only outstanding event in the monot-
onous chronicles of that important trade. It will be remembered
that the Seven Years War left England's woodlands so exhausted
that they were unable to furnish the Navy with the requisite
large timber, and that the Admiralty determined to import Baltic
oak in order to build up an immediate reserve, to break the timber
monopoly, and to give the English groves time to recuperate.[1]
This was the first occasion where the Navy made extensive use
of large foreign oak timber. It had been using Baltic plank for a
century, and during the Seven Years' War, it had begun to utilize
fir timber from Dantzig. During the seven years preceding 1770,
the dockyards had used 16,776 loads of English oak plank, and
9,778 loads of Baltic oak plank. With large timber it was a different story, for the 155,188 loads of English oak timber were supplemented by only 11,720 loads of fir and 724 loads of Baltic oak
timber.[2] Between 1771 and 1775, the negligible amount of that
last item showed a tremendous increase. The Navy Board sent to
Stettin, Bremen, and Rostock for dozens of cargoes of German
oak. Most of it had floated down the Oder to Stettin, and the
name of that port became associated with all the important timber. The association was not complimentary, for the German
timber received widespread disapproval and condemnation. A
few ships were built entirely of this foreign oak, but it was used
more extensively for the great repairs of the ships hastily constructed during the late war, which had soon rotted.[3] In connection with the decayed English oak, the Stettin timber rotted even
more rapidly, the most notorious example being the *Mars*, 74.[4]
The importation of the timber had been necessary under the circumstances, but Stettin oak became the scapegoat for the generally low condition of the fleet. Members of Parliament became
familiar with its supposedly deleterious effects during the attacks
of the Whigs against the notoriously corrupt and inefficient naval
administration of Lord Sandwich. "It is this foreign timber

[1] See pp. 133–135.
[2] R. O., N. B., 3406, *Deptford Letter Book; Commons Reports*, iii, *passim*.
[3] R. O., Adm. Digest, 4807, *Adm. to N. B.*, Apr. 1, 1771; *N. B. to Adm.*, Feb. 14,
1771, Nov. 5, 1773, Nov. 8, 1775.
[4] *Parl. Hist.*, xix, 449, 729, 825, 882, 883.

which has, I fear, entailed rottenness on your fleet; and if the last
fire in your dockyards had made a providential sweep of all your
oak from Stettin, I believe it would have more than compensated
for its destruction of other truly valuable articles," declared
Temple Luttrell in 1778.[1] The administration defended the
maligned timber, though Captain Walsingham must have been
more amusing than convincing when he declared that Stettin oak,
like Lord Sandwich's heart, was sound and incorrupt, notwithstanding all the misrepresentations that had gone forth in the
country.[2] The importation of Stettin timber soon ceased. The
supply on hand was consumed by 1785, and it was not until
1802 that necessity once more forced the use of large German
oak.[3]

The balance of trade in the Baltic trade was unfavorable to
England throughout the century except from about 1762 to 1768.
The excess of imports over exports was at its height between 1780
and 1790. Unlike Child, Mun, and other seventeenth-century
writers, however, some men came to believe that it was advantageous to England to import the Baltic commodities more
cheaply than she could produce them at home, provided she had
a reserve supply in the colonies in case of need.[4]

The political status of the ports showed a change during the
century. Peter the Great shifted much of the Archangel trade to
his new capital on the Baltic about 1715. St. Petersburg thus
became one of the leading ports for timber, masts, and naval
stores. He captured all the Baltic Provinces from Charles XII,
so that Riga became a Russian port. Dantzig was separated from
Poland in 1772, a preparatory step to its annexation by Prussia
in 1793, after Frederick the Great had encroached on the old
Hanseatic freedom of the city and crippled its trade.[5]

There was a gradual increase of trade during the century at
these ports. About 250 ships a year were sailing from Riga at the
beginning of the century. This had doubled by 1750 and doubled

[1] *Parl. Hist.*, 728.   [2] *Ibid.*, xx, 406.
[3] B. M., *Add. MSS, 37275*, f. 303.
[4] Playfair, *Commercial and Political Atlas*, chart, xiv, 57.
[5] *Commons Reports*, iii, 21; Macpherson, *Annals*, iii, 530; Damus, *Die Stadt Danzig*, pp. 75-77.

again by 1800.[1] Dantzig loaded a thousand ships a year about 1750, and this had risen to nearly 1300 when Frederick's influence cut the trade in half. Not until the end of the century did the annual clearances reach a thousand again.[2] Memel came into prominence as a timber port about 1765, when the Radziwill forests were opened to lumbermen. Thereupon the cargoes exported annually jumped from 133 in 1762 to 784 by 1788, which was about the average for the rest of the century. The Stettin trade amounted to about a thousand ships a year.[3] The Russian trade showed the greatest increase during the century, with the Prussian next, and the Swedish remaining nearly stationary.

Only a minor portion of the exports of St. Petersburg and Hamburg was of timber, while at Dantzig, about two cargoes of grain were shipped to one of wood. At Riga, timber represented about half the exports, while it nearly monopolized the export trade of Memel, Stettin, and Norway. England had found a good market for her woolens in the cold regions, centuries before, and as her commerce developed, other manufactures, together with the "colonial wares," — sugar, coffee, tea, tobacco and the like, — were sent in exchange for naval materials and grain.

The English trade was relatively much more important to the Baltic countries than theirs to England. At the end of the century, the commodities which England drew from the Baltic represented about two thirds of the exports of these Northern Crowns but only a fifth of the British imports, being about equal to the India and China trade. The relative importance of timber in the Baltic trade depends on whether one considers its bulk or its value. In 1789, timber represented only about one twelfth of the value of England's Baltic imports, and only a fifth of the value of the grain from that region. Timber and naval stores together amounted to only a quarter of the total imports from the East Country. So far as the number of timber ships was concerned, it was a different story. Out of a total of 4388 ships leaving the principal ports of the Baltic in 1789, over 1300 carried timber, 210 cargoes of which were ship timber. The aggregate

---

[1] Oddy, *European Commerce*, p. 142.
[2] *Ibid.*, p. 258.   [3] *Ibid.*, pp. 223, 267.

cargoes of naval materials amounted to nearly half of the total number.[1]

Those cargoes of timber and naval stores, amounting to barely one twentieth of England's total imports, were more significant than their commercial value would indicate. The fitting out of a navy and a merchant marine long depended upon these shipments from the East Country, making them what oil, coal, and iron have become to-day — an influence in foreign policy, urgent and continual, though usually inconspicuous. The influence of timber and naval stores on England's Baltic policy was tremendous. Leaving the commercial history of the Eastland supply, which will be concluded later with a study of Continental System,[2] the story will now deal with the inception of that Baltic policy and its later application.

One of the cardinal factors in the English Baltic policy was the control of the Sound, for, like the Black Sea and the Mediterranean, the Baltic had a narrow entrance of great strategic value. The other entrances, the Great and Little Belts, were shallow, rocky, and dangerous to navigate, so that shipping for the most part passed "as through a turnstile" at Elsinore, where the King of Denmark collected his Sound dues. These had originated about 1430, when each ship passing the Sound paid a nominal sum for the maintenance of lights and buoys.[3] Later, they had become a recognized prerogative of the King, who in 1639 raised them to "what the traffic would bear," a level rate of about one per cent.[4] With the guns of Kronberg Castle and of Danish frigates in the Sound, these dues were collected by force if necessary. Holding the province of Scania, the southern tip of the Scandinavian peninsula, the King of Denmark controlled both sides of the Sound.

With the increasing dependence of a growing navy on the

[1] Oddy, *European Commerce*, tables, pp. 394, 396, 399, 464.

[2] See pp. 335–344.

[3] For a thorough study of the Sound dues, see Hill, "The Sound Dues" (unpublished thesis, Harvard).

[4] Marien, *Tableau des Droits et Usages de Commerce Relatif au Passage du Sund*, p. 16; Bernhardt, *Handbook of Treaties*, p. 266.

masts, timber, and naval stores from the Baltic, it became a definite part of English policy to keep the Sound open for the Baltic trade in these essential articles. Such a policy was passive and consequently not prominent in the history of British foreign relations. England thought little of the matter so long as the annual fleets of merchantmen from the East Country brought their cargoes of masts, hemp, timber, and tar unmolested. But whenever there seemed any danger of closing the Sound, or when any power seemed likely to make the "East Sea" into a private lake, England acted promptly and with force. Diplomats were ordinarily called upon for this purpose, but on several occasions the diplomats were admirals, sent in the spirit of Nelson's remark to Lady Hamilton: "I hate your pen-and-ink men; a fleet of British ships of war are the best negotiators in Europe." [1] On nearly twenty occasions between 1658 and 1814, England sent fleets to the Sound on this mission, and more than once they severely punished the Danes before the supply of naval materials was deemed secure. So long as her trade was maintained unharmed, England showed little interest in the frequent half-forgotten wars of the Baltic powers, with their dogged, bloody battles, or in the tangled diplomacy of those "Northern Crowns," which sometimes involved all Europe. It was to England's interest to have a weak nation like Denmark at the Sound, just as she wished a weak Turkey at the Bosphorus. The trouble arose when those guardians of the strategic waterways fell under the influence of England's rivals, as when Denmark acted with the Dutch during the Commonwealth and Protectorate, and with Napoleon in 1801 and 1807. To maintain a balance of power at the Sound, England ordinarily backed Denmark's more powerful neighbor and rival, Sweden; but this support ceased when Sweden threatened to become too strong, and on several occasions English fleets were actually sent against the ambitious Charles XII.

This policy of maintaining the freedom of the Sound and division of the *dominium maris Baltici* was Cromwellian in its conception, and the first ships sent to enforce it sailed for the Sound five days before Oliver's funeral. There had been considerable com-

[1] Pettigrew, *Letters of Lord Nelson*, i, 444.

mercial diplomacy since early Tudor days in regard to the Baltic. Elizabeth persuaded the Sultan in 1590 to abandon a projected invasion of Poland on the ground that it would interfere with her supply of naval materials from Dantzig.[1] The definite policy of armed intervention, however, was formed during the rule of Cromwell.

The creation of this policy deserves particular consideration, for, once formed, it became a definite part of British foreign policy and fleets were despatched to the Sound without the slightest hesitation whenever there seemed to be danger that the Baltic might be closed. The sending of some of those later fleets has been fully described by many historians. It is of more import here to understand why Oliver saw the necessity of intervention and why his son risked a war with the Dutch at a time when England was divided and uncertain, in order to keep the sea open. Writing of the policy at this period, Seeley says: "In those days, and after those days for more than a century, it was a matter of life and death for England that no Power, whether Denmark or Sweden or Russia, should acquire the power of shutting the Baltic. On this principle our Baltic policy almost exclusively rested." [2]

The Baltic situation in the decade following the execution of Charles I called for decisive action on England's part. At the very time that England was passing her first Navigation Act, in 1651, Denmark was making a treaty with Holland whereby the Dutch were to farm the Sound dues for £35,000 a year, and the Danes were to close the Sound to English ships in case of war. This they did during the First Dutch War of 1652–54. Timber ships bound for England, even under neutral flags, were seized in the Sound, so that the supply of masts and naval supplies in the dockyards was threatened. That episode gave England a concrete example of what the closing of the Baltic meant. A squadron was sent to the Sound to convoy the English merchantmen, and its commander was instructed to remonstrate politely with the King of Denmark.

---

[1] *Cal. S. P., Venetian*, 1581–91, pp. 494, 495; Lodge, *Illustrations of British History*, ii, 414.

[2] Seeley, *Growth of British Policy*, ii, 40; see also Kirchoff, *Seemacht in der Ostsee*, ii, 15.

Storms dispersed this force, and Captain Ball, the commander, returned without accomplishing his mission.[1] It was six years more before the first real fleet was sent to intervene at the Sound.

Sweden had already been seeking an English alliance, with mutual concessions,[2] and in 1654, Cromwell sent Bulstrode Whitelocke to Stockholm to take the initiative in relieving the dangerous situation at Elsinore. Before leaving on the mission the envoy asked Cromwell: "If I find the queen willing to join with you, for the gaining of the Sound, and against the Dutch and Danes, and that heartily and hopefully, shall I put that business to the utmost and are you willing to enter into such a conjunction?"

The Protector showed no hesitation in his reply: "If you find them inclinable to it, put it on as far as you can, and let us hear from you what you judge best to be done in it. No business can be of greater consequence to us and our trade, wherein the Dutch will endeavor to overreach us and it were good to prevent them and the Danes and first to secure our own interests."[3] Cromwell's last words to Whitelocke were: "Bring us back a Protestant alliance"; but he had taken care to impress upon him to arrange for the freedom of the Sound, "that it may not depend upon the will of the King of Denmark or the United Provinces of the Netherlands."[4] The Protector was anxious to promote the Protestant cause, but a great commercial struggle was on, and the Sound was a vital element in it.

Whitelocke found Queen Christina inclined to favor the idea of English intervention, but Oxenstierna, her aged minister, opposed the measure. The end of the Dutch War relieved the immediate need, and Whitelocke's mission ended in a simple commercial treaty. Shortly after that, England secured "most favored nation" terms at the Sound from Denmark, for the Dutch farming of the dues had ended.[5]

---

[1] *Cal. S. P., Dom.*, 1651–52, pp. 291, 385, 386, 442, 448, 452, 453, 479, 491; see chapter V.

[2] Jones, *Diplomatic Relations of Cromwell and Charles X*, pp. 12–14.

[3] Whitelocke, *Swedish Embassy*, i, 94.

[4] *Ibid.*, ii, 119.

[5] Gardiner, *History of the Commonwealth and Protectorate*, iii, 73–76.

The Baltic situation did not rest long in that peaceful condition. Soon after Whitelocke's departure from Stockholm, Christina abdicated in favor of her mother's nephew, Gustavus, who became Charles X. This ambitious young king was overrunning Poland with his armies within a year, and Dantzig was saved from Sweden by a Dutch fleet. In 1657, England was drawn into the Baltic question again. Knowing that Russian and Imperial forces were on their way to expel Charles X from Poland, Frederick of Denmark suddenly declared war on Sweden. Cromwell saw that, if Sweden should be crushed by the powerful coalition against her, Denmark would become too powerfully intrenched at the Sound. Therefore, when Charles asked for an English fleet in the Baltic, the Protector issued a warrant for the equipment of twenty ships in order to offset the Dutch, who were arming in favor of Denmark; but when the Dutch decided to keep their fleet at home, the English ships also remained in port.[1]

Meanwhile, Charles X had created an embarrassing situation, and England's attitude showed her real interest in the Baltic. Abandoning the doubtful contest in Poland, the Swedish king led his army westward to Denmark. After conquering the mainland, he made a remarkable passage of the Great and Little Belts over the ice, and placed the Danish capital at his mercy. In the subsequent peace negotiations at Roeskilde early in 1658, Charles X desired to take from Denmark not only Scania, the tip of the Scandinavian peninsula, but all of Norway as well. Sir Philip Meadowe, the envoy who was acting as mediator, stated the English view in these words:

Thus the power over that narrow entry into the Baltic being balanced between two emulous crowns will be an effectual preventive of any new exactions or usurpations in the Sound. . . . It was moved that the whole kingdom of Norway should be cut from Denmark and united to Sweden with which it lay contiguous; this entrenched upon England as giving the Swede the sole and entire possession of the chief materials, as masts, deal, pitch, copper, iron, etc., needful for the apparel and equipment of our ships, too great a treasure to be entrusted to one hand.[2]

[1] Thurloe, *State Papers*, vi, 582.
[2] Meadowe, *Narrative of the Principal Actions Occurring in the Wars between Sweden and Denmark*, pp. 58, 59.

Meadowe was influential in modifying the Swedish demands so that Denmark lost only Scania and two provinces in Norway, and agreed to close the Sound against ships hostile to Sweden.[1]

This Roeskilde solution, so favorable to England, was not an end to the trouble. Claiming that certain provisions of the treaty had not been fulfilled, Charles X attacked Denmark a few months later, in August, 1658, taking Kronberg Castle and again threatening Copenhagen. This aroused the Dutch, who were alarmed over the safety of their Baltic trade. Downing, who had been sent to the Hague in the previous year to arrange joint mediation in the war of the north, wrote that many Dutchman thought that the purpose of Charles X was "to make himself absolute master of the Baltique Sea and thereby make himself formidable to all that have to doe at sea."[2]

The Baltic trade was all-important to the Dutch. Not only did they declare it to be the basis of their whole commerce, but they were more dependent than England on timber imports from the East Country, for they had practically no trees at all and needed naval stores and more masts than came down the Rhine. Thus the Dutch and English were vitally interested in keeping the Sound open for themselves, though each was ready enough to have its northern ally close the Baltic against the other. To protect her trade, Holland sent Lord Admiral de Wassenaer, Lord Opdam, to the Sound with a fleet on September 14, 1658, and six weeks later he defeated the Swedes in a stubborn and sanguinary battle.[3]

Roeskilde had produced a balance of power at the Sound somewhat in favor of the English. Opdam's intervention threw the balance to the other side, and events of the past decade showed what Dutch control might mean. It was obviously to England's interest to back Sweden in the present crisis. Cromwell's death on September 3 had thrown the government somewhat into confusion, but his policy clearly ruled the situation. In one of his last speeches to Parliament, a few months before his death, he

---

[1] Firth, *Last Years of the Protectorate*, ii, 227–229; *E. H. R.*, vii, 720–742.
[2] Thurloe, *State Papers*, vii, 338.
[3] *Ibid.*, vii, 370.

had sounded a warning against Dutch interference with the
sources of naval materials:

> If they can shut us out of the Baltic Sea and make themselves masters of
> that, where is your trade? Where are the materials to preserve your ship-
> ping? Where will you be able to challenge any right by sea or justify your-
> selves against a foreign invasion on your own soil? Think upon it, this is in
> design! [1]

This policy governed the action of his son. English regiments
were already forming for Swedish service, and Admiral Ayscue,
with several captains, was preparing to leave for the Swedish
fleet. On October 25, Richard Cromwell and the Council "satt
again in private debate touching the Swedish affaires," [2] and on
the following day the Admiralty received orders to take on additional workingmen and to refit all frigates in harbor, "that they
may be put to sea in any emergency." Three weeks later twenty
ships of the winter guard were ready. [3]

The problem of timber and naval stores, in the interest of which
England was arming, was in a more critical state than at almost
any other time during the two centuries when that problem
troubled England. [4] Navy finances were badly in arrears, in spite
of the constant pleadings of the Admiralty for funds. This shortage was felt acutely in the matter of oak from the English forests
and in masts, deals, tar, and hemp from the Baltic. Letters came
in constantly from the dockyards complaining that there was not
a plank or mast on hand, or that the entire stock of timber was
dangerously low. [5] The effect was shown in the condition of the
ships at sea, which had to turn back from service with masts and
yards gone, or knees and beams cracked, and leaking dangerously,
only to find no materials to repair them when they arrived at the
dockyards. [6] Had the Baltic been closed during such a crisis, the
result to the Navy would have been disastrous. This was a con-

[1] Carlyle, *Letters of Cromwell*, Speech to the Two Houses, Jan. 25, 1658.

[2] Camden Soc., *Clarke papers*, iii, 118, 143, 166.

[3] *Cal. S. P., Dom.*, 1658–59, pp. 182, 186, 187, 461, 470.

[4] See pp. 211–213.

[5] *Cal. S. P., Dom.*, 1658–59, pp. 86, 87, 280, 408, 411, 552, 556; 1659–60, pp. 476,
479, 486, 490, 496.

[6] *Ibid.*, 1658–59, pp. 231, 246, 470, 476, 496, 497; 1659–60, p. 470; Bodleian
Library, *Carte MSS*, 74, 234.

sideration in sending the fleets to the Baltic, though the sending of the fleets exhausted the stores completely.

Two months after the death of Oliver Cromwell and five days before his funeral, England sent its first fleet to keep the Baltic safe for shipbuilders. It sailed in a storm of snow and hail. Vice Admiral Goodson protested against sending a fleet to the Sound in such weather, for until a century later, warships usually kept safely in port during the winter months, and November 18 was considered too late to start a winter cruise. Goodson never reached the Sound. The gales forced some of the craziest ships back to port immediately. The storms and ice dismasted and racked still more of the fleet, compelling it to turn back at the Skaw on December 15. By the 29th, Goodson had been thrown back on the Suffolk coast.[1] Yet this winter cruise had been successful as a show of force. "However, the sending of the fleet thus farre hath not been without effect, for it hath such influence upon the Dutch that it hath hindered them from sending their new supplies of 4000 foote and shippes of warre," wrote Thurloe to Monk.[2] The Dutch had been given the impression that Goodson was going to intercept the Spanish plate fleet from Havana, and their surprise and anger were great when they learned the truth.[3]

The early months of 1659 nearly precipitated a war with the Dutch. Feeling on the Sound question ran equally high in The Hague and in London. There was a general realization that the First Dutch War of 1652–54 had left the great question of trade rivalry unsettled and that a further struggle was necessary for mastery of the seas. Downing wrote that the Dutch said "that they shall never bee well till they have a little brought downe the courage of the English."[4] They were laying in a vast stock of timber for building a fleet for the "business of the Sound" which "they of Amsterdam say plainely they will [go] through with, although it cost them the half of their estates."[5]

It is not difficult to understand the enthusiasm of the Dutch

[1] *Cal. S. P., Dom.*, 1658–59, pp. 199, 231, 240.
[2] *Clarke Papers*, iii, 172.
[3] *Ibid.*, iii, 171; Thurloe, *State Papers*, vii, 533.
[4] *Clarke Papers*, iii, 170.
[5] *Ibid.*, iii, 175–177.

for war at this juncture. Affairs in the East Indies and Montagu's seizure of their ships with contraband were immediate irritants almost unnecessary to add to the gravity of the Sound situation.[1] A war at this time would have found the Dutch at a great advantage. The government of Richard Cromwell was growing daily more precarious and there was possibility of chaos ahead. The finances were in a desperate condition, especially evident in the army and navy arrears. It was fortunate for England that the Second Dutch War was deferred five years, but it is evidence of the boldness of the men of 1659 and their realization of the vital importance of the naval stores from the Baltic to England's existence that they risked a war with the Dutch. There was an element of "bluff" in their actions, but both sides realized that in sending ships to the Sound, nominally to mediate between the Danes and the Swedes, the contest of the peacemakers was more important than that of the belligerents.[2]

It was practically taken for granted that both nations would send stronger fleets to the Sound as soon as the ice should go out. On February 21 and 23, debates on the subject took place in Parliament, and the speeches give as good an enunciation as can be found of the Baltic policy which England was then forming, and which she followed consistently thereafter.[3] Secretary Thurloe reviewed the situation, and announced the five points of the Protector's policy:

1. The continuance of the war in these parts would infinitely hinder our trade and be of very great prejudice to this nation; many of our manufactures being transported and vended thither, many of our materials for shipping and navigation being carried from thence hither.

2. Considering what the issue of this war might be, that the Sound was likely to be put into the hands of those that would exclude the English or put us in such condition, as we should be as bad as excluded; the consequences of which would be the ruin of our shipping; hemp, pitch, tar, cordage and masts, coming all from thence and an obstruction there would endanger our safety. We had experience of this in our war with the Dutch, when the Dane did prohibit our access thither, which put us to great distress, having none of those commodities but what came from our enemies at double rates.[4]

[1] Harris, *Life of Edward Montagu*, i, 121.
[2] Manley, *History of the Late Warres in Denmark*, p. 58.
[3] Burton, *Diary*, iii, 376–403, 437–447, 450–493; *Clarke Papers*, iii, 183, 184.
[4] Burton, *op. cit.*, iii, 380, 381.

The minor considerations were that the Emperor might get control of the Baltic and Flanders, and, finally, that the Protestant cause was in danger of being overthrown. In view of the Dutch preparations, the Protector was equipping a fleet to aid the mediation between Sweden and Denmark, knowing "that unless he hath considerable fleets as well as the Dutch," his bare interposition for peace will signify little or nothing. "*Altum silentium* for a good while" followed this speech.[1]

In the debate which followed, many of the most prominent men of the Interregnum took part, and the decision was almost unanimously in favor of intervention, even if it should involve war. The side issues were cleared away, religion being dismissed on the ground that Holland, Denmark, and Brandenburg were all Protestant nations as well as Sweden, and the menace of the Emperor was not considered great. There was some question as to whether Sweden might not be more dangerous than Denmark in control of the Sound. "The King of Denmark hath but the door into the Sound. But what if we should help put it into the hands of Sweden that hath both the door and the house too?" asked Neville. "If we put the Sound into the Swede's hand, we must, forever after, trade but at his courtesy."[2] "If the Swede hath it he cannot keep it without us," answered Raleigh.[3] Lambert hit on a keynote of the whole Sound policy — "It is best in his hands that, it seems, is least able to keep it."[4] There was a question as to whether Sweden might not be in the wrong in her second attack on Denmark. "Never let us sound into the justice of the quarrel, but find a necessity to provide a good navy," said Onslow.[5] Such a blunt statement is interesting from one of those men accused of cant.

The real question was the Dutch rivalry, — all the speakers came back to that, — Dutch rivalry that threatened the security of the naval stores. "If we had to do only with the Dane and Swede, the thing were not very considerable, but the Dutch are most in our eye, and we most in theirs," said General Kelsey.[6]

[1] Burton, *Diary*, iii, 382.
[2] *Ibid.*, pp. 388, 391.
[3] *Ibid.*, p. 399.
[4] *Ibid.*, p. 400.
[5] *Ibid.*, p. 444n.
[6] *Ibid.*, p. 440.

"Contending for that trade, we are like two rivals that go awooing to one woman," remarked Neville.[1] The dangers of such a war were considered. "If you engage suddenly in a war with Holland, I think all England will be lost. When our forces are gone to the Sound, an army may be landed here, and Charles Stuart to head them," warned Haselrigg.[2] The need of striking at once, before the Dutch once secured control of the Sound, outweighed such opinion. "The Sound, that is now at stake, is the gate of your trade, and will you see it cast out and given away, and not look about you, till it is too late?" asked Colonel Burch. "If you give them this opportunity of getting the Sound, they will be too strong for you. Yourselves will be the next morsel. Let them get this step, and they get all."[3] This consideration prevailed and, after a discussion on financing the expedition, and disputing as to where the authority should lie, Parliament voted, on February 23, "that a very considerable navy should be provided and put to sea, for the safety of this commonwealth, and for the preservation of the trade and commerce thereof."[4]

The details of the intervention are of less importance in this connection than the decision to intervene. England's Baltic policy, commenced by Oliver Cromwell, had been definitely founded in that winter of 1658–59, and it was thereafter sufficient for powers to know that a threat to close the Sound meant intervention on England's part. In March, General Edward Montagu, later Earl of Sandwich, was sent to the Sound with sixty ships, instructed to mediate between the kings of Sweden and Denmark. The English arrived before the Dutch, and Goodson was ordered to fight Opdam rather than let him attempt to relieve Copenhagen.[5] The Scandinavian kings rather resented the authoritative tones of the allies who came without urging to their assistance. "Je vous reçois comme mediateurs, non pas comme arbitres," Charles told the English. Opdam was reinforced by De Ruyter, so that the Dutch fleet outnumbered the English about two to one, but there were no hostilities during the period of suspicious coöperation.[6]

[1] Burton, *Diary*, iii, 388.

[2] *Ibid.*, p. 396.

[3] *Ibid.*, p. 398.

[4] Thurloe, *State Papers*, vii, 620.

[5] Harris, *Life of Edward Montagu*, i, 124.

[6] *Clarke Papers*, iv, 29, 30.

Instead, England, France, and Holland, irritated at the reluctance of both Baltic kings to accept terms, held three conferences at The Hague, on May 21, July 24, and August 4, at which it was determined to impose a modification of the terms of Roeskilde on the combatants, through the English and Dutch fleets. France had long backed Sweden, and Mazarin's support strengthened England's hand. After the fall of Richard Cromwell on April 23, Parliament sent Algernon Sydney, Robert Honeywood, and Thomas Boone as commissioners to coöperate with Montagu, but the admiral considered Sydney a spy upon his actions. The unsettled political conditions in England led Montagu to feel that it was better to have the fleet at home, ready for the part which he was finally to play in the Stuart restoration. In spite of orders to leave fifteen ships to coöperate with the Dutch, Montagu brought back the entire fleet in September, leaving Sydney in charge of the negotiations. The affair dragged on for another year.[1] Finally the Dutch became "very weary of the troubles in the east"[2] and withdrew their support from the stubborn Frederick III, who made peace at Copenhagen. The terms were similar to those of Roeskilde, except that two Norwegian territories were restored to Denmark, and the Danish king was no longer obliged to close the Sound to enemies of Sweden. England's intervention had been successful, for the Sound remained open, and her ally, Sweden, held one shore of it. Had Richard Cromwell and Parliament been less bold, Holland might have firmly established control of that vital "turnstile of trade."

The closing of the Sound was not seriously threatened again during the century. Denmark continued its alliance with Holland, and the Swedish king was on good terms with both France and England during most of the period. He entered the Triple Alliance, but sent presents of masts to Louis XIV in return for subsidies.[3] England remained dependent on the annual fleets from the Baltic for naval stores, so that danger to the "Freedom of the Sound" would have doubtless resulted in sending diplo-

---

[1] *Sydney Papers, passim.*

[2] Thurloe, *State Papers,* vii, 864, 868, 874.

[3] Colbert, *Lettres, Instructions et Mémoires,* vol. iii, pt. 1, p. 76.

mats and fleets to the scene. Though the policy remains inconspicuous throughout most of the period, Admiral Rooke intervened with Holland and Sweden against Denmark in 1700. The
casus belli lay in the Schleswig-Holstein dispute, and William III
desired to keep allies in line to fight Louis XIV. Rooke's instructions scarcely mention commerce.[1]

The second episode of intervention in behalf of the timber supply came during the Great Northern War, when Charles XII,
after imposing the commercial restrictions on England and her
trade already described, threatened to make himself master of the
Baltic. Again, as in 1659, the "hand-to-mouth" supply of Eastland naval stores was running dangerously low. Townshend
wrote in 1715 that, if the Baltic convoy miscarried, "such a scarcity of naval stores must ensue as would disable His Majesty from
fitting out a fleet next Spring upon any event";[2] and a year later:

> It is our misfortune at this juncture, by the knavery of the Muscovites in
> imposing on our merchants last year, to have our magazines so ill provided
> with stores, particularly with hemp, that if the fleet of merchant ships now
> loading in the Baltick should by any accident miscarry, it will be impossible
> for His Majesty to fitt out any ships of war for the next year, by which
> means the whole navy will be rendered perfectly useless.[3]

English merchantmen in the Baltic had suffered at the hands
of various northern powers during the war; but in 1714 the depredations of the Swedish privateers exceeded anything hitherto,
endangering the supply of "naval materials" and causing an out-
cry of the merchants. This time, the Navy's supply was threatened, not by the danger of closing the Sound, but by attempts on
the Baltic trade, which were practically as serious and resulted in
the decision to send Admiral Archibald Hamilton to the Baltic
with a small squadron to convoy the trading fleet. "The clamours
of the merchants, and the increasing scarcity of naval stores,
forced the queen's hands," writes Chance, whose exhaustive study
of the intricate diplomatic relations of George I to the Northern

---

[1] N. R. S., *Journal of Sir George Rooke*, p. 9.

[2] B. M., *Add. MSS, 28154*, f. 248.

[3] Coxe, *Memoirs of the Life and Administration of Sir Robert Walpole*, ii, 86.
Similar dependence indicated in R. O., Adm., Acct. Gen., Misc., Var. 123, *N. B. to
Adm.*, 1710.

War leaves little further to be said on the subject.[1] Hamilton was ordered to return rather than fight a powerful Swedish fleet which had orders from Charles XII "to sink by their sides" sooner than allow England's or any other nation's ships to reach his Baltic ports. After a hostile demonstration by the Swedes, Hamilton returned to England with his mission unfulfilled. The expedition had received its orders from the ministers of Anne, and this intervention was the work of the Tories.

The accession of George I immediately afterward complicated the situation. That original intervention in the Baltic had been purely commercial and with a view to protecting the naval stores. The English fleets which went into the Baltic in subsequent expeditions were sent not only to ensure masts and hemp for the dockyards, but to secure Bremen and Verden for the Elector of Hanover. Chance reiterates the fact that the original intervention was determined upon to protect the supply of naval materials before England had the slightest interest in Bremen or Verden.

Early in 1715, Charles XII threatened to annihilate unprotected English commerce in the Baltic through a savage ordinance to privateers. During the spring, Hanover joined Prussia and Denmark in a league against Sweden,[2] and in May, Admiral Norris sailed with a powerful fleet to convoy hundreds of merchantmen.[3] Diplomacy in the northern courts became more and more intricate, though the protection of trade and Sweden's relations with the Pretender were weighty reasons for English intervention. Norris sailed to the Baltic again in 1716, convoying the traders, and Byng took an even stronger fleet in 1717, with no convoy. Again, in 1718, Norris went as a sailor diplomat with a fleet to back his arguments. These measures against Sweden "only lacked the name of war," writes Chance.[4] Then Charles XII was killed.

The immediate *volte-face* in England's Baltic policy indicates her desire to divide the *dominium maris Baltici* in the interest of

[1] Chance, *George I and the Northern War*, p. 46.

[2] *Ibid.*, pp. 58–68.

[3] B. M., *Add. MSS, 28, 128, Journals and Letter Books of Admiral Norris;* Hist. MSS. Com., *Lord Polwarth MSS*, vols. i and ii, *passim;* Boyer, *Political State of England*, xii, 315.   [4] Chance, p. 209.

her trade and dockyard supplies. After the death of Charles, it
seemed that a Russian instead of a Swedish lake was threatened.
Carteret went to Stockholm with private instructions to the effect
that, if the security of trade was threatened, England would help
Sweden to bring the Czar to reason.[1] Consistently with the policy
of balance of power, the ships of Norris which had gone three times
against Charles XII backed the harassed Swedes against Peter
the Great in 1719. A year later, Norris was in actual conflict with
the Russians and, in 1721, hurried again to the Baltic in a vain
attempt to influence the Peace of Nystadt, which was a crushing
blow to Sweden and unfavorable to English interests.[2] Though
Peter died in 1725, Sir Charles Wager took a fleet to watch the
Russians off Reval in 1726; and in 1727, for the tenth time in
fourteen years, a British fleet went to the Baltic to maintain the
balance of power, when Norris blockaded the Russians in their
ports to aid Denmark and Sweden.[3]

This was the last intervention until 1801. England's chief aim
had been to maintain its supply of stores for the Navy. Denmark,
Sweden, and Russia had been alternately aided and opposed by
her fleets in this mission. As in 1659, England's own interest was
paramount, and aid or opposition to any particular northern
crown was quite incidental to this. England's attitude was ordinarily the very "Armed Neutrality" which those Baltic powers
turned against her in 1780 and 1801.[4]

The most famous instances of the Baltic intervention policy
were the attacks on Copenhagen by British fleets in 1801 and
1807. The story of those two sudden and successful descents upon
the nominally neutral Danes has been related time and again in
great detail. There are certain factors in connection with the
supply of naval materials which have been generally overlooked.
In 1798, the Tsar Paul issued a ukase forbidding all timber exports. This step was taken, so it was said, at the instigation of a
powerful group of iron manufacturers who were alarmed at the
manner in which the recent heavy demand for timber in western

---

[1] Chance, *op. cit.*, p. 334.   [3] *Naval Chronicle*, 1801, v, 269.
[2] *Ibid.*, pp. 486–488.   [4] See pp. 193–196.

Europe was stripping Russia of its woodlands.[1] The Russian dockyard stores, too, were almost empty, and this furnished an added excuse for forbidding the export of timber which Russia herself needed.[2] The English dockyards had been well filled in prospect of such an event,[3] but the Foreign Office took no chances on a protracted timber embargo. Lord Grenville instructed Whitworth, the minister at St. Petersburg, to represent England's concern over the consequences of an edict "of so serious and embarrassing a nature," and at the same time to play on Russia's commercial interest by hinting that England would regret to have to shift its trade in timber and naval stores elsewhere.[4] Thomas Grenville criticized his brother's instructions:

> I know that this necessity is very great, but I cannot think that it is either prudent or decorous that an English Minister should represent at Petersburg that it depends upon them "that the English fleet should not be stopped in all its enterprises, paralysed in the middle of all of its great efforts, and rendered incapable of pursuing and annoying its naval enemies." [5]

He foresaw that a powerful instrument of coercion was being placed in Russia's hands, and that the Tsar was soon to utilize it.

For the immediate present, Whitworth secured the Tsar's permission to relax his edict enough to permit the exportation of masts and fir timber for the Royal Navy only.[6] Though English commerce in general still suffered, and the merchant ships had to get masts from the royal dockyards, Whitworth consoled himself with the fact that France would be cut off more securely than ever from Baltic masts and timber.[7]

In 1800, the Russian supply received a more serious blow when Paul ordered the seizure of all British ships in his ports upon the renewal of the Armed Neutrality. For a year England was cut off from all naval stores as well as timber, though Whitworth had

[1] R. O., F. O., Russia, 42, *Whitworth to Grenville*, Apr. 30, 1799.

[2] *Ibid.*, *Consul Shairp to F. O.*, Oct. 1, 1800; *Quarterly Review*, xxxix, 22.

[3] Derrick, *Memoirs of the Royal Navy*, p. 216 n.

[4] R. O., F. O., Russia, 42, *Instructions to Whitworth*, Feb. 5, 1799.

[5] Hist. MSS. Com., *Report on MSS of J. B. Fortescue, preserved at Dropmore*, v, 166, 167.

[6] R. O., F. O., *Whitworth to Grenville*, Apr. 30, 1799.

[7] R. O., Adm. Digest, 4847, *Adm. to N. B.*, Dec. 12, 1801.

bought naval timber "to the limit" when he foresaw the trend of
affairs.[1] Baltic fir had already been introduced as a substitute for
oak in repairs and the building of frigates, and now it was necessary to use the inferior native beech in place of this imported fir,
while a project to make tar from seaweed was entertained.[2] The
Navy was feeling the pinch of the curtailing of Russian naval
materials in 1801, when news came that the proposed active co-
operation of Denmark in the second Armed Neutrality threatened
to cut off the entire Baltic supply, through the closing of the
Sound. England acted at once in accord with the old Cromwellian policy. Nelson crushed the Danes at Copenhagen and
entered the Baltic. The assassination of the mad Tsar Paul
ended the crisis.

When friendly relations were resumed with Russia later in 1801,
Lord Hawkesbury tried to counteract the unfortunate impression
of the Navy's dependence on Russian stores which Lord Grenville
had given two years before. He instructed Lord St. Helens to
point out at St. Petersburg that England could draw on reserve
supplies from Canada and other parts of the world, while Russian
economic prosperity would suffer greatly if the English market
were lost.[3] That argument was a persuasive one, and was seconded
by many nobles whose firs were their fortune, for they knew that
interference with the English naval supply would cut off one of
their principal sources of income. At the same time, the vital importance of their timber and naval stores to the British Navy
frequently tempted the Baltic nations to use it as a weapon, and
Napoleon was not slow to suggest such a procedure. The two
arguments almost counterbalanced each other, and a later chapter
on the Continental System will describe in detail how the "Northern Crowns" occasionally started to strike a blow at British sea
power by cutting off such exports, only to relax the process when
their own trade suffered more severely than did the British Navy.[4]

[1] R. O., F. O., Russia, 428, *Whitworth to Grenville*, May 19, 1800; N. R. S.,
Spencer Papers, iv, 273, 274.
[2] R. O., Adm., In Letters from Inspector General, 3526, *Bentham to Adm.*, July
10, 1801, May 5, 1802.
[3] R. O., F. O., *Hawkesbury to St. Helens*, July 18, 1801.
[4] See Chapter VIII.

Only the bare outline of that story will be anticipated here, to round out the account of the Baltic intervention policy.

For five years after 1801, the Baltic trade in naval materials progressed on a larger scale than ever before, but in 1806 a change was evident. The first intimation of it came when the Tsar refused to allow the English to proceed with their building of warships in Russia. The extension of Napoleon's power to the Prussian timber ports on the Baltic was a further warning to England of the danger to her naval supplies. Possibly Alexander had the British admission of naval dependence on Baltic stores in mind at Tilsit in 1807, when he and Napoleon drew up plans for the exclusion of England from the Baltic with the coöperation of Denmark. Canning certainly considered that naval supply as soon as he heard of the transactions at Tilsit. Admiral Gambier was at once despatched to the Sound, with instructions to defend the Baltic commerce and the supply of naval stores.[1] He attacked the Danes at Copenhagen as Nelson had done six years earlier, and after applying the intervention policy more ruthlessly than any of his predecessors, he brought back to England all of the Danish fleet that he had not destroyed.

England retained the advantage of that bold stroke to keep the Baltic open by maintaining a fleet in that sea during the remainder of the Napoleonic wars. Admiral Saumarez was sent to the Baltic with a fleet in 1808 and remained there intermittently until 1813, when he was relieved by a smaller force under Admiral Hope.[2] He was instructed to consider the protection of trade his principal object.[3] That course involved minor hostilities with Russia and help for Sweden. The rôle of Saumarez in the Baltic was very similar to that of Norris a century earlier. Saumarez was an able and tactful diplomat, backed by the support of a powerful fleet. He was able to keep Sweden favorable to an irregular trade in naval materials, even when it was nominally at war with England, and his conciliatory policy was of value when the Russians became constantly more desirous to sell their accumulating products

---

[1] N. R. S., *Barham Papers*, iii, 383.
[2] Ross, *Memoirs and Correspondence of Admiral Lord de Saumarez*, ii, 99, 297.
[3] *Ibid.*, ii, 135.

to England. As a result, England drew a certain amount of naval material from the Baltic even when Napoleonic influence was nominally paramount along the shores of the entire sea. Admiral Hope, the successor of Saumarez, remained in the Baltic until after Napoleon's fall. This was the final application of the policy of intervention, for the expedition of Napier to the Baltic in the Crimean War was little concerned with naval supplies.

In almost every instance of applying her Baltic policy, England had intervened as an armed neutral, ready to fight, if necessary, to keep the Baltic open. The spirit in which the nominally friendly state of Denmark was twice attacked recalls those words of Onslow in the 1659 debate on this question: "Never let us sound into the justice of the quarrel, but find a necessity to provide a good navy." The supply of naval stores from the Baltic was such a "matter of life and death" that a serious threat to cut it off seemed almost justification in itself. Whether moral at all times or not, England was successful in averting the day when masts should no longer be brought from Riga or planks from Dantzig.

Seeley overstated the case when he said that Britain's Baltic policy rested almost entirely upon this intervention to keep the sea open to ensure her own supply of naval materials.[1] If sailor-diplomats were sent to the Sound on a score of occasions with that end in view, even more numerous were the frigate squadrons sent to Kattegat and Skagerrak in every war, to keep the Baltic closed to England's rivals so that their shipyards might suffer for want of stores. This second half of the policy, also occasioned by masts and timber, had its important historical consequences, as well as the first. If one led to the two attacks on Copenhagen, the other occasioned important developments in international law, culminating in the Armed Neutrality of 1780, and it also helped to complete the demoralization of the navy of Revolutionary France by cutting off Baltic masts and other naval necessities.

England was not alone in her timber problem. Her principal maritime rivals, France, Spain, and Holland, were also partially

[1] See p. 166.

dependent on the Baltic for the masts, timber, and naval stores essential to the construction of a navy. Colbert had attempted to avoid dependence on the Baltic by making France self-sufficient in the matter of naval materials. In 1670, he wrote to Louis XIV:

Ce qui sert à la construction des vaisseaux est à présent estably dans le royaume en telle sorte que Vostre Majesté se peut passer des estrangers pour la marine, et mesme que, dans peu de temps, elle leur en pourra fournir et tirer leur argent par ce moyen.[1]

His ambitious plans, more far-reaching than any attempt England ever made to relieve the timber problem, were neglected after his death. The pines of the Pyrenees, upon which he counted so strongly, were of too coarse a nature to make good masts; the *martelage* by which he attempted to conscript all suitable trees in the land fell into misuse and disuse; hemp was not grown or tar extracted on the scale which he had anticipated; and the supplies of masts and other naval materials from New France grew constantly less dependable. Consequently, instead of being able to sell naval stores to other nations, as he had predicted, France found within a few decades after his death that the construction and repairs at Brest and Toulon were almost entirely dependent on the masts, planks, hemp, and tar from Gottenburg, Hamburg, Dantzig, and Riga. In the case of masts, France was in a worse situation than England, for the neglect of the American pines forced the French mastmakers to pin together composite sticks of Riga fir. Like the constant dread of a timber shortage in England, Colbert's warning that "La France perira faute des bois" caused grave concern among the French ministers of marine.

Spain at first had fir and oak enough to supply her dockyards at Cadiz, Ferrol, and Corunna; but lumbering evidently became distasteful to the proud and indolent Spaniards. As early as the time of the Armada, Spain was sending its silver from America into the Baltic for masts, timber, and naval stores.[2] Holland, practically treeless, was able to draw some of the necessary masts and timber from the Rhine, but it had to rely upon the Baltic for some of the materials for her shipyards.[3]

---

[1] Colbert, *Lettres, Instructions et Mémoires*, vii, 243.
[2] Artiñano, *Arquitectura Naval Española* (En Madera), pp. 371, 392.
[3] *H. C. J.*, 1787–88, p. 560.

These needs of her rivals were not lost upon England. It did not take her long to perceive that she could secure a double advantage by waylaying the Baltic stores on their way to enemy ports. By utilizing her control of the seas, she could cut off from her rivals the very materials with which they might threaten that control, and at the same time, though this was a secondary consideration, she could augment the stock of those materials always needed in her own dockyards. Lord Burleigh realized the possibilities of such a course at the time of the Armada when he wrote:

> Without having of masts, boordes, cables, cordage, pitch, tar, copar out of Estland, all Spayn is not liable to mak a navy redy to carry the meanest army that can be imagined, and if his money brought out of the Indies should not tempt the Hanzes to bring these provisions, Spayn would not offer to mak war by sea with England.[1]

These thoughts were expressed in action, for dozens of ships of the "Hanzes" were soon being searched for naval materials in English ports.[2] Even as early as 1545, three "tall ships . . . laden with masts" bound for French ports had been brought into Dover, beginning a practice which was to last for nearly three centuries.[3]

The story of the seizures was much the same, whether they took place at the time of the Armada, the Dutch wars, the Seven Years' War, or the contest with Napoleon. To start with, there was usually a little Baltic merchantman of some two or three hundred tons. Below decks, under a protective covering of grain or fir boards, she might have a dozen masts or so, a hundred loads of oak plank, and the remainder of her hold filled with lasts of tar, bales of hemp, or bolts of sailcloth, ordered at Dantzig or Riga for the French or Spanish navy. At her masthead would be flying some neutral flag, and in her captain's cabin there would be carefully prepared papers indicating a neutral port as her destination, with some neutral merchant as owner of the cargo and some equally disinterested person as consignee. The chances were good that a shot across the bow from an English frigate would

---

[1] B. M., *Lansdowne MSS*, civ, f. 71.

[2] Cheyney, *History of England from the Defeat of the Armada to the Death of Elizabeth*, i, 477–497; see *Cal. S. P. Dom.*, 1591–94, p. 172; 1595–97, pp. 219; 1601–03, p. 101; 1628–29, pp. 253, 278, 370, 377, 383, 455.

[3] *L. & P., Henry VIII*, vol. xx, pt. 1 (1545), p. 480.

check this cargo of subterfuges and naval stores almost before it issued from the Baltic. Then the right of search would be carried out in arrogant fashion, by an officer probably already forewarned of the real nature of the cargo by the efficient secret service which England maintained through consuls, merchants, and special agents in the Baltic ports. Even without such previous information, the frigate captain would be skeptical of a cargo of dockyard necessities coming from the Baltic in time of war, in spite of the most ingeniously innocent appearance of the ship's papers and the loudest protestations of the detained skipper. The next scene would be laid in an English port, where the burden was shifted from the frigate captains to the Admiralty judges. There was as little chance of escaping the verdicts of Sir Leoline Jenkins, Sir William Marriott, or Lord Stowell as there had been of evading the men-of-war off Denmark. Lucky were the owners who escaped with a mere preëmption of the naval materials at the King's price. Frequently, the masts and stores were condemned as contraband, with the proceeds going to the captors, and at times, the ship itself did not escape condemnation. Some of these little Baltic cargo carriers, such as the *Vryheid* and the *Jonge Margaretha*, have become famous in the history of international law because of the decisions which their cases drew from the Admiralty bench.[1]

These seizures gave rise to two questions in international law: "How much protection should a neutral flag afford?" and "Are naval materials contraband of war?" Neutral flags were quite essential to England's enemies in their wartime commerce. It would have been suicidal for a merchantman to attempt to traverse the North Sea bearing the flag of France or Spain during most of the wars. Consequently, their trade had to assume a "protective coloring." The neutral flags might be divided into three classes. Most legitimate were those of nations such as Russia and Sweden, which exported their own products in their own ships. Then there were regular neutral nations, like the United States, which frequently made great profits by carrying the wares of others in time of war. Finally, there was a farcial prostitution of neutrality afforded by little cities such as Knyp-

---

[1] See Robinson, *Admiralty Reports, passim.*

hausen and Pappenburg. Their tiny normal merchant marines
were sometimes expanded a hundredfold overnight in time of war
by wholesale registration of belligerent ships. A French brig
might secure shelter behind the sacred palladium of neutrality by
a mere scratch of the pen and a liberal cash consideration. The
Admiralty judges often differentiated between these varying degrees of neutrality and based their decisions accordingly. England, however, had to take a stand on the matter of neutrality as
a whole. If the doctrine of "free ships, free goods" were allowed,
the whole advantage which the command of the seas gave her in
cutting off enemy supplies would be nullified. Consequently,
though she herself sometimes used all three types of neutral flags
for her own commerce, her policy entailed a general lack of respect for neutral flags. Her justification for the harsh measures
against neutrals has been well expressed by a present-day authority:

> Interference with neutral trade is justified whenever the premise on which
> the neutral claim rests — unconcern with war — is negatived by the facts.
> When the neutral has established relations with the enemy, his claim of
> absolute right is vitiated. [1]

Pitt expressed a similar view before the Commons in 1801,
referring directly to the seizure of naval materials:

> The question is, whether we are to permit the navy of our enemy to be
> supplied and recruited — whether we are to suffer blockaded ports to be
> furnished with warlike stores and provisions — whether we are to suffer
> neutral nations, by hoisting a flag upon a sloop, or a fishing boat, to convey
> the treasures of South America to the harbours of Spain or the naval stores
> of the Baltic to Brest or Toulon. [2]

Many of the disputes over neutral status arose from the Baltic
trade in naval materials. England's twofold policy of cutting off
the supplies of her enemies while she defended her own was of
vital interest to the Northern Crowns. They desired to exploit
the political value of their control of the source of these stores,
and at the same time they wanted to protect this important
branch of their commerce in a manner consistent with national

---

[1] Piggott, *The Freedom of the Seas Historically Treated*, p. 3.
[2] *Parl. Hist.*, xxxv, 916; see Sheffield, *Strictures on the Necessity of Inviolably
maintaining the Navigation and Colonial Systems of Great Britain*, p. 112.

dignity as well as profit. Russia and Sweden naturally resented England's search and seizure of their vessels at sea, yet they could not afford to alienate their best customer, who might fall back on a colonial supply.

The situation was naturally one which would produce friction, and this was aggravated by the doubtful status of masts, ship timber, and naval stores as contraband of war. The most brazen neutral would scarcely question the inclusion of arms and ammunition in the lists of contraband; while England's attempt to starve France in 1793 by declaring foodstuffs contraband, found scant support in international law. Naval materials lay between these two, constituting a most perplexing case of "conditional contraband," with strong arguments on both sides.

The nations affected by England's seizures contended that timber could be used for many purposes other than shipbuilding, and that even ship timber, masts, and naval stores were as applicable to merchantmen as to ships of war. England answered that since the term contraband implied materials which could be used in carrying on war, the component parts of such instruments of war as frigates and ships of the line, if bound to an enemy port, were certainly of warlike nature and liable to seizure as contraband. "If one Dutch ship carries masts, another anchors, another sails, another a ship's frame," declared Sir William Marriott, "a whole fleet may go by detail from Holland to the King of France's service." [1]

The impression commonly associated with the Armed Neutrality of 1780 is that England constantly maintained this contraband view of naval materials in the face of a strong conviction to the contrary on the part of the rest of the world. Such an impression is dispelled by a review of the official opinions of the maritime nations on the contraband status of timber during the sailing-ship era. The closely debatable nature of the problem and the varying interests of the different countries at different periods resulted in the fact that practically every maritime nation declared itself on each side of the question. The mass of treaties,

---

[1] *Vryheid* case, quoted in Piggott, "Ship Timber and Contraband," *Quarterly Review*, ccxxxvi, 110.

edicts, orders in council, and court decisions which refer to this subject reveal clearly that the abstract merits of the case meant little alongside the immediate interest of the nation.[1]

Some amusing inconsistencies illustrate this situation. England and Holland, for instance, each upheld both sides of the question between 1660 and 1680. The United States agreed with England, in the Jay Treaty of 1794, that naval stores and all timber except pine plank should be regarded as contraband; yet this stand was made in the midst of several treaties of the United States with France, Spain, Holland, Sweden, and Prussia between 1778 and 1800, which excluded naval materials from the list of contraband.[2] If such shifting was possible during two decades, it is easy to imagine the changes of face in the course of three centuries.

England first specifically declared masts and naval materials to be contraband at the time of the Armada, according to Cheyney.[3] From then until the end of the era of wooden ships, she held quite consistently to this contraband view. When the injured nations sought refuge behind a "Law of Nations," quoting Grotius, Bynkershoek, Vattel, Pufendorf, and other contemporary publicists, England countered with a more hoary authority, the old *Consolato del Mare*, which had once regulated the trade of the nations. It is true that England gave lip service to the opposite view in the treaties of Nimwegen and Utrecht, in the commercial treaties with Russia in 1766 and 1797, and in the Convention of 1801.[4] These diplomatic divergences, however, seem to have had little effect upon the scores of Baltic cargoes brought into English ports in every war. Except for Sweden, Prussia, and Spain, which quite steadily opposed the contraband view, the other maritime nations revealed inconsistencies in their attitude. Holland took the contraband stand in no uncertain terms during the days of

[1] See esp. Wiegner, *Die Kriegskonterbande*, pp. 68–104, 228–232; Hautefeuille, *Droits des Nations Neutres*, ii, 136–146; Atherly-Jones, *Commerce in War*, pp. 54, 55.

[2] Martens, *Recueil des Principaux Traités*, ii, 598, 599; iii, 451, 569; v, 674; vi, 158, 678–680.

[3] Cheyney, *History of England from the Defeat of the Armada to the Death of Elizabeth*, i, 494.

[4] Du Mont, *Corps Universel Diplomatique*, vol. vii, pt. 1, pp. 337–349; viii, 345, 377; Martens, *op. cit.*, i, 395, 396; vi, 362; vii, 262, 263.

her greatest sea power, but shifted to the other side late in the seventeenth century. Denmark also changed to the "free ships" side quite late in the period, after long declaring naval materials to be contraband. France and Russia were generally opposed to the contraband position, but when it suited their interests, they changed to the other side more than once.[1]

All of these maritime rivals of England, whatever their previous opinions had been, adhered to the declaration of neutral rights in the Armed Neutrality of 1780. That important landmark in international law was occasioned principally by the severity and thoroughness with which England enforced her policy of cutting off French stores from the Baltic during the American Revolution. Upon the outbreak of war with France in 1778, England declared a blockade of French ports which she was entirely unable to maintain. In the instructions to naval commanders and to privateers, the government ordered, among other things, the seizure of neutral ships carrying timber and naval stores to France. In August it was reported that Dutch ships were loading naval stores for France at St. Petersburg, and by September the English cruisers were bringing victims into English ports. Late in the month, the Russian and Dutch envoys protested against these seizures.[2] On October 7, orders were given to release all detained ships "except such as have Naval or warlike stores on board destined for French ports or for the use of the Rebellious Subjects in North America," and to take no more ships unless loaded with such stores. Two weeks later, the Navy Board was instructed "to purchase all Naval stores laden on neutral ships fit for His Majesty's service, that are or may be considered as prizes." [3]

A conflict immediately arose between the Navy Board and the Admiralty courts, in which the Lords of Admiralty under Sandwich were inclined to favor the latter. Though the British Navy was in need of masts and hemp, the detention of the neutrals and

[1] For an excellent detailed treatment of this subject, see Wiegner, *Die Kriegskonterbande*, pp. 228–232.

[2] R. O., Adm. Digest, 4808, *Earl of Suffolk to Adm.*, Aug. 20, 1778; *Lieut. Trollope to Adm.*, Sept. 2, 1778; *Adm. Buckle to Adm.*, Sept. 15, 1778; *Russian Minister to Adm.*, Sept. 23, 1778.

[3] *Ibid., Adm. to Adm. Buckle*, Oct. 7, 1778; *Adm. to N. B.*, Oct. 22, 1778.

the purchase of their cargoes was inaugurated less to help England than to hurt France. Sir Charles Middleton, who headed the
Navy Board, did not or would not accept the order in this light.
He proposed that a list of all the stores fit for the Royal Navy on
board the detained ships be made as soon as they were brought
into port, and submitted to the Navy Board to ascertain whether
such articles could be used in the dockyards. Middleton afterwards wrote to Pitt that if such a plan had been carried out, the
Armed Neutrality would never have been declared.[1] Constant
protests went from the Navy Office to the Admiralty at Whitehall
on this issue. The Navy Board claimed that the Admiralty judges
were over-zealous in their condemnations because of the fees
involved, feeling, perhaps, that any one else who gained extra
income from naval timber was poaching on their own preserves.
The Navy, according to Middleton, was forced to pay dearly for
a vast quantity of inferior material. The Admiralty, knowing that
the policy was intended primarily to injure the French dockyards
rather than to help the English, continued to insist on the purchase of all naval materials. The French yards, they maintained,
were less discriminating than the English in the matter of materials. Consequently, the timber, hemp, and tar of poor quality
which the Navy Board scorned for its own use might nullify the
whole value of the seizure policy if allowed to proceed to Brest.
By January 19, 1779, more than a hundred ships with naval materials were being detained, and four months later, the Navy
Board had paid more than £220,000, "notwithstanding the officers' valuation of them amounts to no more than £135,000."
Middleton protested that these stores were "neither useful to us
nor to the enemy," but the policy was rigidly maintained. Unfortunately for the Royal Navy, the detained cargoes contained
few of the great masts which were needed so sorely in England.[2]

One of the principal grievances of the neutrals was the long
detention of their ships at a time when freights were high. Orders
had been given to the dockyards to hire extra laborers to expedite

---

[1] N. R. S., *Barham Papers*, ii, 220–223.
[2] R. O., N. B. Out Letters, 2206, *N. B. to Adm.*, Jan. 19, 1779; 2207, May 29,
1779, Oct. 5, 1779.

the unloading, in order to reduce demurrage charges for delay; but in December, 1779, Lord Stormont, who directed the policy of cutting off the French stores, complained that the Navy Board had caused great inconvenience by its loose interpretation of the order. He requested the Admiralty to require a stricter compliance. The Navy Board retorted that they had done everything possible for the convenience of the neutrals, allowing a ten per cent profit and even buying materials which they afterwards sold at a loss; but in spite of this, complaints and demurrage increased.[1] Stormont clung to his plans of withholding all Baltic stores from the French. He ordered that resistance to search on the part of armed convoys should be met with force. The Admiralty constantly tightened its net on neutral commerce, then largely in the hands of the Dutch, while Sir William Marriott gave splendid support as judge in the Admiralty courts.

Then came the Armed Neutrality, which wrecked the Admiralty scheme. Even though its promulgation may have been a whim of Catherine, representing the victory of Panin over Potemkin in a court intrigue, it had an important effect on the immediate situation as well as on future theory. It stood for the views of Frederick the Great and other Baltic neutrals on England's interference in the supply of naval materials. Timber is referred to in two of the cardinal points of the Russian declaration of February 28, 1780, which sets down the principles that (a) all neutral vessels may navigate freely from port to port and on the coasts of nations at war; (b) goods belonging to the subjects of belligerent powers shall be free in neutral vessels, except contraband goods; (c) Russia holds the definition of contraband made in the treaty of commerce with Great Britain in 1766, extending these obligations to all powers at war; and (d) a blockaded port must be so closely guarded that there is an evident danger in attempting to enter it.[2] The Anglo-Russian Treaty of 1766 had not included naval materials in the list of contraband,[3] and the Russian decla-

---

[1] R. O., N. B. Out Letters, 2206, Dec. 19, 1778, Apr. 29, 1779; 2207, Dec. 12, 1779; *N. B. Standing Orders to Dockyards*, 2508, Dec. 21, 1778, Feb. 11, 25, 1779; Adm. Digest, 4809, *Lord Stormont to Adm.*, Dec. 15, 1779; *Procurator Gen. of Adm. to Adm.*, Dec. 16, 1779.

[2] Scott, *Armed Neutralities of 1780 and 1800*, p. 275.

[3] *Ibid.*, pp. 342, 343.

ration clearly aimed at restoring free trade in naval stores and timber in opposition to the English seizures. Nearly every civilized nation except England subscribed to the principles of the Armed Neutrality within the next few years.

England was in no position to oppose this doctrine openly. France and Spain were threatening her naval supremacy, the American War still dragged on, and she could scarcely hope for success in facing the fleets which the Northern Crowns were gathering to enforce their protest. With New England masts cut off and the New Brunswick supply still undeveloped, the Navy was in desperate need of Riga masts.[1] At the same time, English pride and interests would not permit an acceptance of the doctrine of "free ships, free goods"; so that England avoided the issue as far as possible until the crisis was over, making a few concessions to Russia, the most threatening member of the coalition.

One result of the Armed Neutrality was the replenishing of the French dockyards, which had already begun to feel the pinch. Had the English plan been carried out with the original rigor, Brest and Toulon might have been emptied of their timber, tar, and hemp; but the relaxation of seizures of Russian ships permitted plenty of these stores to arrive from the Baltic. Within ten weeks of the Russian declaration, Harris, the English minister at St. Petersburg, wrote Stormont that French and Spanish houses were engaging Russian ships to carry home their commissions, and that imperial permission for this trade, which had been denied at his representation in the previous year, was now being granted.[2] Harris assured Panin that English cruisers would refrain from molesting Russian ships "on the solemn assurance of Her Imperial Majesty, that she will not allow her flag to protect and cover collusory trade, so injurious to Great Britain."[3] England conceded more than this by instructing the commanders of privateers concerning the terms of the Anglo-Russian commercial treaty of 1766, which did not include timber and naval stores in the list of contraband. Late in 1781, Harris tried to soothe Catherine's indignation over the fact that the Russian ships were searched at all, with the explanation that

[1] See p. 288.   [2] Malmesbury, *Diaries and Correspondence*, i, 258.
[3] *Ibid.*, i, 263 n.

ships carrying her flag were barely visited; and although they were laden universally with naval stores, all evidently destined for the service of our enemies, yet they were never taken notice of by our Courts of Admiralty, and the most profuse damages were paid, if their short detention had been attended with any detriment.[1]

England's concessions were only enough to avert Russian hostility. With the less influential adherents of the Armed Neutrality she was less conciliatory. On July 4, 1780, she amended the vague phrasing of her 1670 treaty with Denmark to include timber and naval stores definitely as contraband.[2] The seizure of cargoes under the flags of the smaller neutrals went on steadily, but evasions were plentiful. In the last days of 1780, Holland had been forced into the war. The number of ships under Dutch colors passing the Sound dropped in a single year from 2051 to nine, while the British ships increased from 1701 to 2001.[3] The flags of Prussia and the Empire were loaned to hundreds of Dutch ships, and several thousand masts and spars were taken from Riga by these improvised neutrals. At Emden, over 100,000 tons of Dutch shipping were transferred to Prussian registry while Ostend developed into a great neutral mart for Baltic naval materials.[4]

The futility of continuing to enforce the policy of cutting off these supplies from her enemies was recognized by England after the Armed Neutrality. From Riga alone, the exports of masts and spars from 1778 until the end of September, 1782, to the different nations amounted to:

	Masts	Spars
Holland	1855	1570
England	996	1743
France	868	1100
Spain	405	298
Portugal	297	494
Denmark	199	195
Genoa	29	72
	4649	5472 [5]

[1] Malmesbury, *op. cit.*, i, 410. [2] Martens, *Recueil des Principaux Traites*, iii, 177.

[3] Macpherson, *Annals*, iii, 705; see *ibid.*, pp. 565, 649.

[4] Malmesbury, *op. cit.*, i, 437; Mahan, *Influence of Sea Power on the French Revolution and Empire*, ii, 309.

[5] R. O., *Chatham Papers*, Bundle 111.

All of these were on the accounts of the different governments for their navies, except about 600 of the Dutch masts. The masts for Genoa were on the French account. Those for England were considerably larger and more valuable than the others. A large proportion of the later shipments escaped the English, and it is certain that the British Navy suffered more severely during the war from the mast shortage arising from its own negligence, than the French marine suffered from England's aggressive policy.

Russia's intervention in the name of neutral rights saved the French mast supply in 1780, but in the next war, Russian support enabled England at last to attain her cherished end — the emptying of the mast ponds at Brest and Toulon. Polish considerations prevented Catherine's active participation in the First Coalition against France in 1792–93, but she played her part against republicanism in another way. In order to cripple the French marine and starve the nation, Russia threw the "free ships, free goods" principles of 1780 to the winds, agreeing with England to a radical extension of the contraband definition. Not only masts and naval stores, but even foodstuffs bound to France, were considered liable to seizure. Denmark and Sweden, who had commenced a remarkably profitable trade with France in these products, protested loudly at this defection of Russia from the principles which she had championed in 1780, and in 1794 they prepared fleets to maintain an Armed Neutrality of their own. With Russian support, however, England was successful in intercepting most of the French grain and naval stores from the Baltic.[1] To starve France was considered even more important than to cripple her dockyards. The cargoes of grain which British cruisers were constantly bringing into port replaced timber as the center of interest in disputes over neutral rights. Nevertheless, France was not starved into submission, but the thoroughness with which England intercepted Baltic cargoes of naval materials did much to render the French fleets impotent for several years.

England was able to waylay most of these cargoes of French naval materials as they emerged from the Baltic, but in 1795 she

[1] R. O., Adm. Digest, 4816, *Consul Fenwick to Adm.*, Mar. 23, 1794; *Harris to Adm.*, May 5, 1794.

drew the net even tighter. Early in that year, Andrew Lindegren was sent to Riga with instructions to forestall all the hemp and great masts which French agents were purchasing for their navy. This was no novel procedure. Robert Savage, a Baltic mast contractor of Elizabethan days, had written in 1598:

Last year I disappointed the King of Spain's factors of 24 great masts that were in Dantzic, 18 of which I brought hither to Her Majesty but the rest are lying in Dantzic, to my loss and hindrance. I will undertake to cause all the great masts there and at Norway to be bought from the King of Spain or else give such advice that they shall be intercepted, as also any other provisions that shall come from thence.[1]

In 1782, Consul Durno at Memel had proposed to engross the Baltic naval materials in similar fashion.[2] Lindegren, who was to receive a commission of five per cent on all the supplies which he should secure from the French, was successful in his mission. Three months after his appointment, he wrote to Hamond, the Comptroller of the Navy:

It was really fact, that all the Masts of 20 inches and upwards at *and expected this year and next year at Riga, were bought up for France*, and I am convinced you will be pleased to hear that I have been so fortunate to deprive them of a large parcel on which they depended for this year's supply for their Fleet, and have got out of their Agent's hands a very great part they thought they had secured for next year.[3]

Lindegren found "Monsieur Chapeaurouge," as he termed the French agent, venal enough to part with some 500 "remarkable fine sticks" of the 1795 supply upon the spot, together with 2,300 more for which he had contracted, to be delivered in the following year. "It will be highly necessary that this transaction remain a profound secret as long as possible, that the enemy may not know too soon the loss that they have sustained," wrote Lindegren. By 1799, he had sent more than 4,000 masts, bowsprits, and spars, in addition to several thousand tons of hemp, to the British dockyards, which were already being supplied on a regular contract with Usburne in Russia. Lindegren's commission on these tranactions was enough to ensure a comfortable income for life, and "Monsieur Chapeaurouge" also profited well by the business.[4]

---

[1] *Cal. S. P., Dom.*, 1598–1601, p. 29.
[2] R. O., N. B. Out Letters, 2209, *N. B. to Adm.*, Jan. 28, 1782.
[3] *Parl. Papers*, 1806 (1), iv, 227.
[4] *Ibid.*, 1–63, 151–168, 215–232.

There is no more striking example of the disastrous effects of a lack of timber and naval material than is afforded by the condition of the French dockyards between 1793 and 1799. The timber stores in several of the arsenals were destroyed by fire and the British policy prevented a replenishing of these from the Baltic, while efforts to secure American naval materials were unsuccessful. The revolution had already demoralized the personnel of the marine and this loss in material was enough to complete the damaging effect upon French naval activity. France finally utilized less satisfactory trees from her own forests and those of the Mediterranean, incidentally finding the oak of Italy a most valuable substitute. The ready-made ships of Holland, Spain, and Venice also helped to make up the deficiency, while Jeanbon Saint-André accomplished wonders with inadequate supplies in the dockyards where he set up guillotines; but every French fleet which put to sea was handicapped by weak masts and crazy hulls.[1]

After 1801, it seemed that France might once more secure masts and naval stores from the Baltic. The renewal of the Armed Neutrality in the previous year led to England's agreement in the Convention of 1801 to strike timber and other naval materials from her list of contraband. This, however, did not affect her old course. In April, 1803, Bonaparte sent one Bergevin, principal commissioner of the marine, into the Baltic, to purchase a very large quantity of masts and naval stores for the encounter with England. Bonaparte may have heard of the dealings of "Monsieur Chapeaurouge" with Andrew Lindegren at Riga, for a treasury agent was sent with Bergevin "pour tenir les comptes des fondes."[2]

The artistic manner in which England defeated this attempt is one of the most interesting passages in the history of the Baltic mast supply. A month after Bergevin received his orders from Bonaparte, William Moir left London with secret instructions from the Admiralty and from Lord Hawkesbury, the Secretary of

[1] A more detailed study of this situation, which lies outside the real timber problem of the English Navy, will be found in the manuscript copy of this study in Harvard College Library, pp. 410–421. See esp. Levy-Schneider, *Le Conventionnel Jeanbon Saint-André, passim.*

[2] Levy-Schneider, *op. cit.*, i, 207.

State for Foreign Affairs. Moir had been engaged for years in the timber trade at Memel, where his brother James was still carrying on the business. Bergevin contracted with the neutral houses of Helmund and Blankenhagen at Riga for more than 1500 great masts and considerable hemp. His next step was to procure a nominal neutral ownership for the shipments. On August 6, 1803, Bergevin made a contract with Moir, who agreed to make the cargoes ostensibly neutral by becoming the nominal shipper, receiving a commission of two per cent for his services. The masts and hemp were to be sent in Russian, Prussian, or Swedish ships, as the property of Moir, and they were consigned to one Claas Tholen of Emden, who also lent his neutral name for a similar consideration. The apparent innocence of such cargoes, Bergevin thought, would be convincing to the most dubious frigate captain or admiralty judge. To allay French suspicion, the British allowed a few ships to slip through with their masts and hemp, but by September, 1804, twenty-six of the neutrals had been brought into English ports by warships which had received the necessary instructions from Moir. Moir made a protest against the seizures in the Admiralty Court as a matter of form. At the same time that he was receiving constant instructions from the Secretary of State and the Admiralty, Moir maintained a heavy correspondence with Bergevin and the Riga contractors, in order to secure damning evidence which would nullify the value of the neutral ships' papers in the Admiralty Court. Realizing the value of these papers as essential to condemnation, Moir would not relinquish them until he was promised thirty per cent of the value of the condemned cargoes, which he received in addition to his French commission. The affair was managed with such secrecy and skill that shortly after Trafalgar, Decrès, the imperial Minister of Marine, expressed his satisfaction with Moir's services to France.[1]

The principle of *post hoc ergo propter hoc* can be carried to unwarranted conclusions, but there is an evident relation between a letter from Moir in 1804 and one from Villeneuve a year later. The timber agent, reviewing his services, wrote:

[1] *Parl. Papers,* 1810 (187), xiv, 1–19; *Ibid.* (259–260), xiv, 1–24; R. O., Adm. In Letters, 4162, *Sec. of State to Adm.,* Apr. 2, 1803.

I succeeded beyond, perhaps, what any person in a similar situation ever did before; and as far as timely and particular information with a certainty of condemnation could go, I put into the powers of His Majesty's naval departments forty cargoes of the finest masts and hemp in Europe, worth per original invoices, £166,110. I betrayed no trust, I went at my own risk, for the express purpose of depriving the enemy of those masts.[1]

The effect of the cutting off of those masts is indicated in a letter from the French admiral on January 21, 1805, to Decrès:

I declare to you that vessels thus equipped, short-handed, encumbered with troops, with superannuated or bad materials, vessels which lose their masts or sails at every puff of wind, and which in fine weather are constantly engaged in repairing the damages caused by the wind, or the inexperience of their sailors, are not fit to undertake anything. I had a presentiment of this before I sailed. I have now only too painfully experienced it.[2]

Moir's letter was a demand for a reward, and Villeneuve's was an apology for inactivity which brought a sharp retort from Napoleon; but evidence from many other sources indicates a critical lack of stores in the French yards. The available masts of France and the Mediterranean were poor substitutes for those masts ordered from the Baltic which had found their way into Nelson's ships instead of the ships of Villeneuve.

England's policy of depriving her enemies of Baltic naval stores, practised since the days of the Tudors, never bore such fruit as it did in the twelve years preceding Trafalgar. France had poor sailors for the most part during that period, but the timber shortage was largely responsible for the occasions when she had weak ships. The combination formed a tremendous handicap. The controversy over ship timber lasted until the Declaration of Paris in 1856, in which England secured the inclusion of naval materials in the contraband list. Throughout the centuries during which she exercised it, England's seizure policy had resulted in dozens of contraband clauses in old commercial treaties and hundreds of rotten masts in the fleets of France and Spain.

The firs and oaks of the East Sea, then, were important silent factors in the maritime history of Europe. In the great sea fights of more than two centuries, the shots from each side shattered

---

[1] *Parl. Papers*, 1810 (259–260), xiv, 9.
[2] Thiers, *Consulate and Empire*, iii, 307; see *Ibid.*, pp. 379, 380 n.

spars of Riga fir and crashed through planking of Dantzig oak, for few ships were launched in any of the European dockyards which did not contain Baltic materials above and below decks. The trade in those materials stimulated the prosperity of the Baltic shore, and the control of that trade time and again called for the activities of diplomats and of admirals.

CHAPTER V

PENURY AND THE DUTCH WARS

THE timber supply had a direct bearing on the effectiveness of the Navy in several wars. However much the naval officials might be interested in the problems incident to the quality and sources of timber, their real concern lay in the relation of that supply to the fighting efficiency of the fleet. Where the supply was adequate, it attracted little attention, but it came into decided prominence on the occasions when it miscarried. Three of those periods of failure, arising from distinct causes, will be treated in this study — the Dutch wars, the American Revolution, and the contest with Napoleon.[1] The timber shortage first appeared prominently in the Dutch wars, and it was present in several of its most serious forms.

Poverty was an incubus which hampered the Navy throughout the three wars in which it checked the sea power of Holland. Blake, Monk, Sandwich, Rupert, and the other admirals all felt the pinch of inadequate naval finances at almost every stage of their fierce conflicts with Tromp, De Ruyter, Opdam, and De Witt. Readers of naval history are familiar with the stories of crews and shipwrights sullen and sometimes mutinous for want of pay, beer, and proper food. This story will deal with another result of the navy debts — the hand-to-mouth supply of timber and naval stores constantly at the mercy of accidents of war, which resulted in costly delays and weakened ships. The jingoes of two centuries later could sing: "We have the ships, we have the men, we have the money, too." The English Navy which fought the Dutch was woefully deficient in the last two items, and even the ships were very often defective.

There were three of those short, rough conflicts with an able foe who could maintain an almost equal fight in spite of handicaps

[1] See Chapters VII, X.

which outweighed the English lack of money. The First Dutch War, it will be remembered, lasted from July, 1652, to April, 1654, though the main fighting ended with the defeat and death of Tromp in July, 1653. The second contest began unofficially in 1664, but war was not declared until February, 1665. It ended with the Peace of Breda in July, 1667. During the last year of the war, the French were allied with the Dutch. The third and final war lasted from March, 1672, to February, 1674. France was allied with England, and while the Dutch were fighting at sea, they had to withstand the invading armies of Louis XIV. The naval participation of the French was half-hearted, both in the second war when they were enemies of England, and in the third when they were allied with her. The financial embarrassment of the English Navy was counterbalanced by a similar condition in Holland, whose revenues depended chiefly on the interrupted seaborne trade. The Dutch were still further handicapped by the danger of invasion by land and by the division of authority among their seven provinces. The English timber shortage made itself felt in the First Dutch War, it was more acute in the second, and in the third it was actually dangerous.

Certain considerations on the relation of the timber supply to naval operations are essential to a clear understanding of the situation during the Dutch wars, and the later conflicts. A scarcity of timber and masts could make itself felt in two ways. It was reflected in the general condition of the ships at sea, where leakiness or weak masts would retard the speed of a fleet or cause a cruiser to lose a prize. If the case were acute, the active strength of the Navy was lessened by the necessity of sending ships into port for repairs; and in some extreme instances rotten ships foundered at sea. In addition to this chronic condition resulting from a shortage of timber, there were the emergencies mentioned in connection with dockyard repairs, where fleets returned from battle shattered in masts and hulls, with their officers eager to put to sea again in the shortest possible time, to secure the results of a victory or to retrieve the consequences of a defeat.[1] It was this latter consideration especially which often cost admirals and

---

[1] See pp. 86, 87.

navy commissioners sleepless nights, wondering whether the mast ponds and timber piles at Chatham or Portsmouth would be equal to the occasion. Sometimes they were not, and the fleet either remained inactive or returned to sea with masts poorly patched and shot-holes inadequately plugged. The delay was not always caused by a want of timber. At times, the need of beer or seamen would seriously impair the fighting strength. The Navy suffered in either case.

A prevalence of such damages at sea, arising from gales rather than from injuries in action, reflected a bad condition of the timber stores. It was to be expected every year that a few ships would leak and lose masts, but there are periods when the records teem with accounts of such injuries incurred even during the summer months. These occasions synchronize with a shortage of stores arising from some evident cause. The damage usually arose from a want of timely repair. It was customary, one will remember, for ships to go into dock at least once in three years for a thorough "triennial trimming," when any unsound masts or weak timbers would be replaced. If masts and timber were scarce, however, these repairs were apt to be slighted and the decayed portions of the ship were left for the unequal contest with the elements. Chronic shortage and poor condition of the ships are evident from hundreds of sources, but the points of vital interest are the occasions when the fleets came in for repair after battle. Those instances were the real test of the timber and mast stores. In every case, the fleets were finally fitted out after some delay, but none of the English fleets, as will be pointed out, was really crushed in action. What would have happened to England after one real defeat with the stores in such condition can be imagined.

The conventional tactics of the day consisted chiefly in fighting in two parallel lines, with each ship ranged alongside a similar ship of the enemy. As the ships of the line of the principal naval powers differed little in size and armament, the numerical standard became one of the principal criteria of strength. Hannay, in discussing the Dutch wars, declares that the consideration of numbers "in every generation and in every kind of war is the least

valuable element of strength," [1] but it is certain that beyond a
certain point, disparity in numbers rendered victory impossible
for the weaker fleet, even in the Dutch wars. It was an English
tradition that thirty English ships of the line were equivalent to
forty of the French or Spanish, though the Dutch were esteemed
more highly. This might hold true under leaders like Blake,
Hawke, Rodney, and Howe, but there were dozens of more conventional and slow-witted admirals who required almost equal
numbers to have any chance of success. The skill of an admiral
or the valor of captains and crews might compensate for the lack
of a few ships, but if the difference were too great, even a Nelson
with the bravest, ablest men afloat could not secure victory. [2]
There came a time, therefore, when two or three ships of the line
possessed what the economists call a high marginal value, for the
outcome of the contest might depend on their participation.
Nelson, himself, appreciated this point, saying that a two-decker
alongside the enemy in battle was worth more than a three-decker
a great way off. [3]

With the presence of a ship of the line at such a premium, it is
surprising to find how little could put one out of commission.
Apart from damage sustained in battle, a mainmast cracked, a
bowsprit carried away in a gale, a few broken knees straining in
heavy seas, or rotten planks leaking could render such a ship unable to accompany the fleet. Every ship ordinarily carried in her
stores a few spare topmasts and yards and a few loads of plank
and deals. The ship's carpenter could usually rectify minor injuries, but naturally there was no room to carry extra mainmasts
or knees; and repairs below the waterline were difficult. If the
damaged mast was not too badly cracked, it might be "fished"
by binding a concave piece of timber to the injured portion; but
such patched masts often proved unequal to the necessary strain.
When an admiral needed every possible ship, a crippled or leaky
vessel presented a difficult problem. To keep her at sea would
retard his fleet, endanger the lives of the crew, and perhaps wrack

[1] Hannay, *Short History of the Royal Navy*, i, 333.
[2] See pp. 385, 386.
[3] N. R. S., *Barham Papers*, iii, 324.

the vessel beyond hope of repair. To send her into port, on the other hand, would dangerously weaken his fleet so that it could not function properly. The greatest damage was usually incurred during the autumn and winter months. The First Dutch War was distinctive in that two of the six important actions occurred in November and February. For a whole century after that, until Hawke made a winter blockade of Brest in the Seven Years' War, it was customary to keep the great ships in port usually from September to April.[1] In estimating the extent of damage by the account of repairs it has to be remembered that some officers could repair efficiently at sea, while others needed, as Collingwood said of one officer, supply ships to accompany them constantly if their ships were to remain in good condition. A broken topmast was often considered a good excuse to run into port for shore leave, and, finally, some officers pleaded the bad condition of their ships to provide an excuse in case of defeat or cause for greater glory in victory — it was a good reputation-insurance. In spite of those considerations, a prevalence of ships in bad condition reflected a poor supply of timber and masts — and the Dutch wars were certainly a period when that held true.

With those general considerations in mind, we can turn to the First Dutch War. The English Navy in 1652 began its first real war with a powerful nucleus of regular ships against a worthy rival. The Navy had gained experience and coördination during the previous three years in chasing Rupert's royalist squadron around the Mediterranean and into the West Indies; and in the Navy Commissioners appointed in 1649, England had its first really efficient naval administration. The principal actions of the Dutch wars occurred in the vicinity of the Channel, off the coasts of England and Holland. The campaigns in the Mediterranean and elsewhere are of little interest in this connection. The strategy was largely a matter of protecting one's own convoys of merchantmen and attacking those of the enemy. Control of the seas meant a severe crippling of the enemy's resources. Holland, with her immense commerce, was particularly on the defensive in this respect. There were seven principal actions in the main

---

[1] See *Letters of Horace Walpole*, ed. Toynbee, iv, 340.

theatre of operations during this First Dutch War, four in 1652 and three in 1653. It was one of England's shortest naval wars, but it was perhaps the fiercest of them all.

The timber problem did not seriously affect England until the last of 1652. Naval poverty was not as extreme during the First Dutch War as it was to prove in the other two, yet it was constantly troublesome. The Navy was quite liberally supplied with oak from the confiscated estates of delinquents, and that timber was not yet exhausted.[1] The stock of masts and naval stores, on the other hand, had not been sufficiently recruited to stand the drain of such a war. There was little trouble in repairing the fleet after the opening action on May 19, 1652, after the action between Ayscue and De Ruyter in August, or after the defeat of Tromp and De Ruyter in September. The Dutch themselves were suffering from bad ships and a want of timber.[2]

The second action revealed a characteristic of England's opponents which had a pronounced effect on the mast situation. An Englishman reported from Plymouth after the battle: "We shot altogether low at them, and they received many shots in their hulls. They shot high at us, aiming thereby to spoil our masts, sails, and tackles, in which most of our ships received the greatest loss, and yet our Admiral had many shot in her hull."[3] Superior English gunnery was able to accomplish the decisive result of sinking ships, while the English themselves suffered only temporary disability. The English ships, moreover, were much more heavily timbered than the Dutch. They were often slower on this account, but they were strong in battle. The French were to prove worse offenders than the Dutch in the matter of shooting high. In one war after another, it was remarked that most of the English damage was sustained aloft. Napoleon tried to rectify this habit and urged his gunners to fire at the hulls of the English; but wherever they aimed, the shots went high. It was a satisfaction to know that enemy ships were sunk or limped off with badly battered hulls, but this general advantage still left England with

[1] See p. 128.
[2] N. R. S., *First Dutch War*, ii, 138, 305, 308, 309, 313, 324, 329, 348; iii, 136, 137.
[3] *Ibid.*, ii, 116, 117.

a serious mast problem.[1] Almost every major action meant a heavy drain on those materials which had to be imported — masts, spars, tar, and hemp.

For this reason, it was a grave matter for England when the King of Denmark seized the English ships laden with Baltic masts, timber, and naval stores in the autumn of 1652. Ball's expedition, sent to the Sound to release them, was a failure, and they remained in Danish hands until the end of the war.[2] At the same time, the Dutch Baltic squadron was carrying on a similar process. More than a dozen neutral ships carrying cargoes of timber, masts, and naval stores, ostensibly bound for Lisbon and other neutral ports, were seized and brought into Dutch ports to prevent their reaching England. This was in accord with an official Dutch declaration of naval materials as contraband. Many of the English masts came from Norway and Gottenburg, outside the Sound, but the active Dutch cruisers and "capers," or privateers, intercepted several ships from that source.[3]

By December, the Dutch were congratulating themselves that the English were suffering from a great want of naval materials. Their satisfaction was not unwarranted, judging by an order from the Council of State to the Admiralty, "to take into consideration the condition of the State's stores, which as the Council is informed are at this time very empty, and to inform themselves where any pitch, tar, hemp, cordage, masts, and other commodities useful for the Navy may be had."[4] The defeat of Blake's inferior fleet off Dungeness in November had forced the English to retire for repairs. This imposed a heavy drain on the stores, and the English remained quite inactive, while, according to legend, Tromp cruised the Channel with the famous broom at his mast-head.[5] Fortunately, the Navy Commissioners were an extraordinarily able and energetic group of men, and they had already been considering alternative sources of supply. They

[1] *Corr. de Nap.*, vii, 111; see also *A Narrative of the Proceedings of His Majesty's Fleet in the Mediterranean* (1744), p. 94; Chevalier, *Histoire de la Marine Française sous la Première République*, p. 187.   [2] See p. 166.

[3] N. R. S., *First Dutch War*, iii, 12, 150, 170, 184, 190–195; iv, 143.

[4] *Ibid.*, iii, 291, 292.

[5] *Cal. S. P., Dom.*, 1652–53, p. 493.

turned to three sources — New England, Scotland, and neutral cargoes lying in port.[1]

Great masts from New England had already been brought into the dockyards from time to time, but there had been no regular supply.[2] The action of the Navy Commissioners in November, 1652, is a landmark in the timber problem. When they called in the New England agent and consulted with merchants about the feasibility of bringing masts thence in prize ships, they were beginning the regular supply of all the largest masts used by the Navy for nearly a century and a quarter. Major Nehemiah Bourne, one of the Navy Commissioners, — a soldier under Cromwell and at one time admiral at sea, — undertook to furnish three cargoes of American masts. Shipwreck and capture by the Dutch made this initial project a failure. It was a year later, in the last days of 1653, after the main fighting was over, that the first consignment from this source finally arrived.[3]

More immediate results were necessary, so the commissioners turned to Scotland. Scotch fir made inferior masts and was consistently scorned by the Navy. In this crisis, Scotland offered an immediate means of replenishing the scant supply remaining in the mast ponds. Early in January, 1653, the Navy made arrangements with Colonel Robert Lilburne, who forwarded a lengthy proposal of one Andrew Sandilands to furnish masts and tar from forests in the extreme northeast of Scotland near Cromarty. Scotland was still hostile to Cromwell, and it was another year before Monk quieted the turbulent Highlands. A regiment of Highlanders under one Munroe nearly broke up the masting project by force, but the Scotch masts proved a temporary relief. Unlike the simultaneous attempt to bring masts from New England, which developed into a very important permanent source of supply, Scotch masts were never used except as a last resort.[4]

[1] *Cal. S. P., Dom.*, 1653–54, pp. 162, 163.

[2] *Cal. S. P., A. & W. I.*, Addenda, 1574–1674, pp. 75, 76.

[3] *Ibid.*, pp. 87, 88; *Cal. S. P., Col.*, 1574–1660, pp. 392, 394, 396, 398, 399; *Cal. S. P., Dom.*, 1652–53, pp. 508, 522; 1653–54, pp. 375, 376, 485, 497, 523, 534; N. R. S., *First Dutch War*, iii, 50, 64, 65; Jameson, *Privateering and Piracy in the Colonial Period*, p. 25.

[4] *Cal. S. P.. Dom.*, 1651–52, pp. 103–105; 1652–53, p. 537; 1653–54, pp. 163, 375; N. R. S., *op. cit.*, iii, 369–371, 377, 378; iv, 105–107.

The third alternative — the use of neutral cargoes in port — was perhaps the most fruitful of the three for the period of the immediate crisis, spasmodic and unreliable as it was. Some Baltic stores were brought overland through Holstein from Lübeck to Hamburg, but masts were too bulky for that. Penn tells of securing seven Swedish ships loaded with masts and other stores, six of which came willingly and the other by coercion. There are also various instances of seizing upon cargoes at different ports.[1] From these sources, the Navy pieced out a supply, but events scarcely justify Gardiner's remark that the needs of the Navy were sufficiently met.[2] The English, to be sure, came out victorious, but the lack of stores proved a handicap at several points.

The action of the Dutch and Danes in cutting off masts and naval stores showed its effect when Blake brought his battered ships into Portsmouth after defeating Tromp in the Battle of Portland on February 18, 1653. The mast ponds and storehouses of Portsmouth yard were unequal to the demand. Commissioner Willoughby and Anthony Deane, the master shipwright, reported a "great want of masts and cordage for the fleet," and a week after the battle were still urging that stores be sent. A day later, they were glad to hear that a shipload of masts was being sent around from Deptford, while a hoy was dispatched to Scotland for great masts.[3]

These stores were slow in arriving, and not until three months after this battle were the English at sea in force again. The chronic lack of men contributed to the delay, and even when stores were on hand, it took time to pull out old masts and install the new. The shortage of stores, however, can be reckoned as causing an extra delay, which might amount to several weeks, in putting off the final struggle with the Dutch. It helped to postpone the establishing of the blockade, which was the principal factor in bringing Holland to submission. During that period of inaction, while the English and Dutch were both patching up their damaged warships, Dutch commerce came and

---

[1] N. R. S., *First Dutch War*, iii, 280, 281; iv, 379; v, 409.

[2] *Ibid.*, iii, 2; see *Ibid.*, iv, 202.

[3] *Cal. S. P., Dom.*, 1652–53, pp. 179, 186–188, 537; N. R. S., *First Dutch War*, iv, 202.

went with little obstruction. Although England had a potentially greater fleet, Tromp was able to escort a large convoy to the northward in May, and bring back another, unmolested.

Early in June, Tromp was defeated off the Gabbard Shoals in mid-channel by an English fleet numerically superior to his own. The English ships came off with comparatively slight damage. Blake and Monk sent a few "lame ships" home and ordered a supply of top-masts and "fishes" for repair at sea, while they pursued Tromp's defeated fleet to its own shores.[1] For nearly two months they maintained a close blockade of the Dutch coast, so effective that "grass grew in the streets of Amsterdam." The Zuyder Zee became a "forest of masts" of idle merchantmen, and business was near a standstill. That brought the war close home to every Dutchman and the nation was nearly ready for peace.

Finally, Tromp put to sea with all his available ships, in the forlorn hope of breaking the blockade. The English were again greatly superior in force, and on the last day of July, the great Dutch admiral was killed and his ships defeated by Monk off Scheveningen. That was the Trafalgar of the First Dutch War, and after that the Dutch did not appear again in force. If the blockade could have been resumed at once, Holland would probably have been speedily brought to her knees, but the lack of masts was partly responsible for prolonging the war another eight months.

Monk retired to England with his fleet badly mauled, for the Dutch had died hard. Gardiner laughs this off, saying that it is equivalent to remarking that the fleet which won Trafalgar was badly damaged.[2] There was a certain difference. In 1805, other English fleets remained to block the French coast, but during the first three weeks of August, 1653, almost the entire English force lay repairing in Southwold Bay or Solebay.

The little yard at Harwich caught the brunt of the refitting of the fleet, and like Portsmouth five months earlier, it was unprepared for the task. The English did not dare leave many masts in exposed ports where the Dutch could get them, so the reserve

[1] *Cal. S. P., Dom.*, 1652–53, pp. 384, 389, 399.
[2] Gardiner, *History of the Commonwealth and Protectorate*, iii, 57.

supply was kept at Deptford, some eighty miles from Harwich and half that distance from Chatham. That reserve was scarcely equal to the occasion. Upon his arrival in Solebay on August 4, Monk wrote that the first great need was for masts and yards, and urged that as many as possible be sent down at once.[1] Two days later, he informed the Admiralty that several ships were so shattered that they would have to be sent to Chatham, and in a postscript, he added: "Masts are much wanted and nothing can be done until they come." He proposed to send out a "party of frigates" to hold the seas for a while, and on August 8 he again wrote that there was especial need for masts for frigates "as for want of them nothing can be done."[2] Meanwhile, equally urgent demands for masts were reaching London from Nehemiah Bourne who, as commissioner at Harwich, was in charge of repairs. Two hoy loads of masts and yards were sent over from Chatham, while a large flyboat was bringing still more down the Thames from Deptford. The cargoes of masts, pitch, and tar in two large Swedish ships at Yarmouth were laid under contribution — but still there was a call for more masts.[3] More than two weeks after the battle, Bourne had forty-five ships on his hands, nearly all needing new masts and yards. He complained that these were not properly furnished, and as late as August 17 he was still charging the delay to lack of masts. At the same time, there was an urgent call for powder, shot, and beer, which may have even prolonged the delay. Not until August 21, over three weeks after the battle, could Lawson take forty-five ships to sea, Monk following a week later with the rest.[4]

Though decisively crushed in the last major action, the Dutch profited by those long repairs which detained the English at Harwich. The blockade was raised and De Witt took out a large convoy, returning safely with four hundred merchantmen from the Baltic. This made the Dutch less desirous of an immediate peace.

The mast shortage continued to make itself felt until the end

---

[1] *Cal. S. P., Dom.*, 1653–54, p. 74.   [2] *Ibid.*, pp. 77, 79.
[3] *Ibid.*, pp. 85, 475–481; N. R. S., *First Dutch War*, v, 409.
[4] *Cal. S. P., Dom.*, 1653–54, pp. 96, 108.

of the war in April, 1654. Bourne still called urgently for masts
to complete repairs at Harwich. The September equinoctial gales
cracked many masts, though the Dutch suffered more heavily,
for half of the four-score ships which De Witt had gathered were
dismasted in one of the "line" storms.[1] The active Navy Commissioners brought masts from Hamburg, and when a large vessel
took the horses and retinue of Bulstrode Whitelocke on his mission to the Swedish court, it was ordered to return with a cargo of
masts. In October, three ships were sent out to New England for
great masts, and it was during the last days of this year that the
first regular cargoes finally arrived from that source.[2]

The First Dutch War, then, had seen the timber problem in the
form of a shortage of masts and other imported naval materials.
Inadequate funds had resulted in an inadequate reserve. The
closing of the Baltic supply produced delays in repairs after
action, and these delays permitted a movement of Dutch commerce which tended to prolong the war though it did not affect
the outcome. It is probable that on the whole the Dutch suffered
more severely from a want of those materials than the English.

It was twelve years after Tromp's last battle before the English
were again engaged in general action with the Dutch, but Cromwell kept the Navy busy during the remaining years of his life.
Most of the work was on distant cruises against Spain and the
Barbary pirates, either in the Mediterranean or the West Indies.
Those expeditions are of little interest in this connection, but the
situation in the dockyards at home was bringing on a more acute
phase of the timber problem. As the national revenue fell off, the
navy charges became heavier in proportion and accounts fell seriously into arrears.[3] There was an active building policy which
added several fine new ships to the Navy, but increased the debt
and drew heavily on the timber supply. Lack of oak had not
troubled the Navy to any extent during the first war with the
Dutch, for there was still free timber from the sequestered lands
to be had for the cost of transportation. By the terms of the act
of 1649, this timber was all to be removed before 1657, and even

[1] *Cal. S. P., Dom.*, 1653–54, pp. 485, 490, 494–498.
[2] *Ibid.*, pp. 489, 494, 497, 523, 534.   [3] See p. 64.

before that most of it had been exhausted.[1] This left a dangerously low supply of oak in the dockyards, and for years letters
poured into the Navy Office — from Anthony Deane, Thomas
Middleton, Jonas Shish, Peter Pett and his brother Christopher,
Commissioners or Master Shipwrights, at the various yards — all
telling the same story — "emptiness of all the stores," "works
stayed for want of timber," "timber available but price too high,"
and so on by the dozen, every year.[2] In 1654, many ships needing
repairs were still in service and the stores were running very low.
A year later the report was made that "for want of timber the
navy stores are not furnished to carry on any considerable action
at sea, the late undertaking having exhausted them, nor can they
be recruited without money."[3] In 1656, it was the same, and
Daniel Furzer was instructed to build two frigates in the Forest of
Dean, for want of timber elsewhere.[4]

The scarcity of oak in the dockyards has been at times interpreted to mean that the Civil War, on top of Stuart waste, had
completely exhausted the available trees. It is true that oak was
growing scarcer, but in those years, most of the letters indicate
that there was oak to be had if the Navy could pay for it. Twenty
years later, oak was actually scarce — but the trouble from 1654
to about 1672 was chiefly a matter of credit. The letter of Christopher Coles, quoted in a previous chapter on navy credit, was
typical of the position of the timber contractors.[5] Some were
driven to the wall, others would deal only for ready money, and
the more powerful took advantage of the dangerously low condition of the stores. John Hollond, a Surveyor of the Navy under
the Commonwealth and at this time a timber contractor, wrote
that the purveyors would refuse the price of a lot of timber, only
to return a few months later in absolute need, to pay double the
price.[6]

---

[1] See p. 128.

[2] *Cal. S. P., Dom.*, 1654, pp. 388, 508, 550, 584; 1655, pp. 401, 493, 501; 1656–57,
p. 7.

[3] *Ibid.*, 1655, p. 382.

[4] *Ibid.*, 1656–57, pp. 15, 16.   [5] See p. 65.

[6] *Cal. S. P., Dom.*, 1655–56, pp. 165, 425, 550, 569; N. R. S., *Hollond's Discourses
of the Navy*, pp. 207, 208.

The stores of imported goods were in the same condition. During the latter part of 1654, Portsmouth was badly in need of masts and deals, and at one time there was not a single great mast in store; while at Chatham, they were having to saw up masts worth £20 in want of fir timber worth £8.[1] New England masts began to appear with greater regularity. Captain Hatsell, Commissioner at Plymouth, wrote, "I desire no more New England masts, having 4 of white pine which I am loth to use," displaying a stubborn prejudice against the innovation.[2] On the whole, however, they were received with enthusiasm, and some of the first to arrive in the regular supply from Piscataqua were installed in the great new *Naseby* which, renamed the *Royal Charles*, was the principal flagship in the Second Dutch War and was carried off in triumph by the Dutch from the Medway in 1667.[3] Welcome as the new masts were, there was often a shortage of them, and Gottenburg masts were even scarcer.[4] In 1658 and 1659 the stores were at their lowest ebb, when the death of Cromwell further deranged the national finances. The effect of that shortage on the fleet has already been described in connection with the expeditions to the Sound.[5] The Restoration brought only slight relief, and the efforts of Pepys and his fellow commissioners to provide an adequate store were hampered as usual by the state of navy credit. It was even proposed to purchase masts in Portugal with the Queen's dowry.[6]

Such conditions were bound to make themselves felt during the Second Dutch War, yet that war was of such a nature that the Navy was much less sensitive to a shortage than it had been twelve years before. The heroic atmosphere of the dogged, constant fighting had passed. Blake and Monk had taken their fleets to sea even in November and February, to crush Dutch commerce, and seven real fights were crowded into a brief period. The second

---

[1] *Cal. S. P., Dom.*, 1654, pp. 508, 584; 1655, p. 483; 1655–56, p. 207; 1656–57, pp. 38, 39, 404.
[2] *Ibid.*, 1655–56, pp. 207, 552.
[3] *Ibid.*, p. 502; 1656–57, p. 496.
[4] *Ibid* p. 464; 1657–58, p. 544.
[5] See pp. 170, 171.
[6] *Cal. S. P., Dom.*, 1661–62, p. 440.

war saw none of that — all the fighting was in the summer; three major battles, a raid on Bergen, and the disgraceful impotence against the Dutch raid on Chatham sum up the activities. It seemed at times as if the fleet went to fight, even in the summer, because a war demanded some fighting as a matter of form. The wholesome driving force which characterized the first struggle had given way to the spirit of Charles II.

Such a half-hearted war put less drain upon the stores. There were only two battles, exactly a year apart, which sent the whole fleet into port for heavy repairs. In each case the demands were met by exhausting the entire stock on hand. The mast ponds could not have supported the damages of a Blake campaign in 1665 and 1666. Middleton at Portsmouth described himself "at his wits end for want of masts and money."[1] He was, he said, "in terror at the want of masts," the sight of which would make him young again.[2] Deptford, Woolwich, and Chatham were in a similar state of emptiness, causing a complete stopping of work at times. The shortage of oak was felt in the building of new ships, which for want of plank or beams lay unfinished on the stocks for months, when they might have been on active service against the Dutch. Repairs were inadequate, and masts were patched where they should have been replaced. When Lord Ossory tried to take his ship out to the Four Days' Battle, he found the foremast and mainmast too weak to support sails.[3]

There were several reasons for a mast shortage. Pepys had gained a profit in securing the use of the frigate *Elias* for the New England mast contractor in 1664. The frigate had foundered on her return, with most of her crew and all of her masts. The loss of the latter was felt keenly. At the same time, the Dutch had captured one of the Gottenburg mast ships during the hostilities in 1664 which preceded the declaration of the war — an inadequate reprisal for the contemporary loss of New Amsterdam. Those accidents cut down the anticipated supply. There was further cause for apprehension, for France, which was soon to

---

[1] *Cal. S. P., Dom.*, 1665–66, p. 32.   [2] *Ibid.*, p. 23.
[3] *Ibid.*, 1664–65, pp., 71, 100, 188, 245, 289, 377, 403, 421, 429; 1665–66, pp. 23, 108, 111, 122.

come in on the Dutch side, was cornering Baltic plank, while the King of Denmark was sending cargoes of Norway masts as presents to Louis XIV. On top of that, news came in 1665 that the King and Council of Sweden had decreed that no more mast trees be cut for seven years. Warren gathered eight cargoes of the masts then available in Gottenburg, but their arrival in England was being delayed for want of a convoy.[1]

The first great demand for masts followed the action off Lowestoft on June 3, 1665. Historians still disagree as to which side deserves credit for victory, but both fleets were certainly badly smashed. Again, Harwich caught the brunt of the repairs. It was the story of 1653 repeated. The scanty stores on hand were soon consumed. Urgent messages finally brought a raft of masts from Deptford and more from Chatham, but those were not enough, and only after considerable delay was most of the fleet at sea again a month later.[2] The emergency was met, but as Peter Pett wrote, the great expense of masts at Harwich had "drained the stores so dry that further supply was impossible."[3] The Navy Commissioners knew that another such mauling from the Dutch that year would be perilous, and consequently bought frantically whatever masts could be found. These exigencies of the Navy were a source of profit to Sir Josiah Child, author of the well-known *Discourse on Trade*, who informed a friend that he was "to have the highest price in their books for masts served, this being the dearest time that ever was."[4]

It was exactly a year before the whole fleet came in again for new masts. The protracted struggle in the Channel early in June, 1666, known as the Four Days' Battle, resulted in somewhat of a victory for the Dutch. It left the English fleet severely damaged, and the high aim of the Dutch gunners again meant especial damage to the masts. There was an abnormally long delay at Chatham and Sheerness, where repairs were conducted under the

---

[1] *Cal. S. P., Dom.*, 1664–65, pp. 102, 152, 255, 292; 1665–66, p. 37; Pepys, *Diary*, Apr. 19, Nov. 14, 1664.

[2] *Cal. S. P., Dom.*, 1664–65, pp. 406, 407, 410–417, 428, 429, 433, 437, 443–445, 464.

[3] *Ibid.*, p. 421.

[4] *Ibid.*, p. 564.

supervision of Sir William Penn. Masts were slow in arriving and Pepys feared violence against the Navy Office if the true conditions were known — but the masts were all in and repairs completed long before the ships finally sailed.[1] Pepys was informed that "the fleet hath laine now near fourteen days without any demand for a farthing worth of anything of any kind, but only to get men."[2] After seven weeks in port, it finally put to sea and in two days defeated De Ruyter in the only real English victory of the war. The damages in this action were not heavy and the ships were able to raid the Dutch coast. That was the last major action of the war. There was a small fight in 1667 after the disgrace at Chatham, when the Dutch burned and carried away part of the English fleet.

This second heavy demand for masts emptied the stores as thoroughly as the first, and it was with great difficulty that repairs were made during the last year of the war.[3] Pepys, who was a better authority on the mast situation than any other man in England at the time, leaves two accounts which indicate the situation in December, 1666. "There is also the very good news come of four New England ships come home safe to Falmouth with masts for the King, which is a blessing mighty unexpected, and without which, if for nothing else, we must have failed the next year."[4] Three weeks later he wrote in a similar vein: "No newes yet of our Gottenburgh fleete; which makes [us] have some fears, it being of mighty concernment to have our supply of masts safe." His fears may well be taken at their face value. The Gottenburg ships finally did arrive, after encounters with storms and the Dutch. The shortage had had its effect on the Navy, according to the same authority, who speaks ruefully of "the greatest fleete that His Majesty had yet together, and that in as bad condition as the enemy or weather could make it."[5]

There is no indication that naval operations were curtailed

[1] Pepys, *Diary*, June 19, July 4, 20, 1666.
[2] *Ibid.*, July 23, 1666.
[3] *Cal., S. P., Dom.*, 1666–67, pp. 159, 184, 192, 233.
[4] Pepys, *Diary*, Dec. 3, 1666; see *Cal. S. P., Dom.*, 1666–67, p. 309.
[5] Pepys, *Diary*, Dec. 24, Dec. 29, 1666; *Cal. S. P., Dom.*, 1666–67, pp. 365, 366, 377.

during the Second Dutch War on account of the want of masts and timber alone, but the dockyard stores in their emptiness could not have supported the heavy repairs incident to a campaign as aggressive as that of the First Dutch War. There were many other considerations at Whitehall to explain the relative inactivity and meagre accomplishment of the Navy. The mast shortage was only one example of the general influence of the spirit of the Restoration.

The timber troubles of the Navy did not end with the peace in 1667. In the years immediately following the war, the lack of credit further reduced the timber stores, and once more there are frequent reports of "not one foot of elm timber left," "not one deal board in the yard," and the like. Ships three-quarters finished at Portsmouth had to be delayed another year for want of timber.[1] At such a time, the gift of two cargoes of great masts from the General Court of Massachusetts Bay to the King was particularly acceptable, for it had been necessary to resort to cheap Scotch masts again.[2] The scarcity arose principally from the lack of ready money, for most materials were reported to be plentiful. The low credit of the Navy hindered even the supply of free timber from the royal forests. "No money to be heard of," wrote Pepys in 1667, "no, not £100 upon the most pressing service that can be imagined of bringing in the King's timber from Whittlewood while we have the utmost want of it, and no credit to provide it elsewhere."[3]

In one form of timber, there was an actual scarcity. English oak plank was not to be found in any quantity, even for ready money. The fire of London in 1666 subjected the forests to an unusual demand, and in the following years little plank was available. Sawing by hand was so slow and expensive that men would not do it in the low state of navy credit, and the dockyard letters time and again complained of a lack of plank. The shortage drove the Navy Board to seek new sources. They contracted

[1] *Cal. S. P., Dom.*, 1667, pp. 269, 391, 452; 1667–68, pp. 29, 206, 243, 371, 439; 1670, p. 314.
[2] *Ibid.*, 1666–67, pp. 196, 225, 226, 258, 369; 1667–68, p. 508; 1668–69, pp. 7, 79; 1670, pp. 58, 59.
[3] Pepys, *Diary*, Aug. 20, 1667; *Cal. S. P., Dom.*, 1666–67, pp. 49, 190.

for Irish oak, and, what was more important, began the extensive importation of Baltic plank.[1] The new minister to Russia was instructed to buy hemp, tar, and timber.[2] There is a reference in the *Calendar of State Papers, Domestic*, to the importation of East Indian plank for the Navy in 1670, but the context indicates a misreading of the word "Eastland."[3] The unusual project of securing oak from Brittany was entertained by the Comptroller of the Navy in 1671.[4]

The Third Dutch War saw the timber problem at its worst during that whole period. The possibilities of disaster from want of masts had been grave enough in the previous contest, but that was looked back upon as a time of comparative plenty. On March 16, 1672, the day before war was declared, Commissioner Tippetts at Portsmouth reported that "timber, without which the works cannot go on, may be had for money," but that there was very little in store, and there were no masts in case the ships should put in after a battle.[5] On the following day, a letter from Phineas Pett, grandson of the famous shipwright, revealed a similar peril at Chatham. There was not one mast for a first-rate, "the stores of great masts being so very much exhausted that if any of the great ships come in disabled in their standing masts, yards and topmasts, I do not see how they can be supplied out of the stores we now have."[6] Pepys and Lord Clifford informed the King of this great danger, and Charles ordered a thorough investigation.

Early in May, Lord Shaftesbury, Lord Clifford, and others viewed the stores at Deptford and Woolwich. Conditions there were found to be little better than at Portsmouth and Chatham. At least four shiploads of New England masts were needed in addition to a considerable Baltic supply. A series of contracts for various forms of timber followed close upon this investigation, but there was no time to fill them before the great demand came.[7]

---

[1] *Cal. S. P., Dom.*, 1670, pp. 396, 397; 1671, pp. 76, 77.
[2] *Ibid.*, 1666–67, p. 300.
[3] *Ibid.*, 1670, p. 279; see *Ibid.*, pp. 76, 396, 397.
[4] *Ibid.*, 1671–72, p. 32.   [5] *Ibid.*, p. 209.
[6] *Ibid.*, p. 212.
[7] *Ibid.*, 1671–72, pp. 396, 422, 610; 1672, pp. 24, 32, 40, 54.

In the meantime Anthony Deane, who was to prove the hero of the situation, wrote a long letter to Lord Arlington suggesting the best means of meeting the crisis. The letter was sound and valuable in its advice, deserving more than the curt reply which it received from the future James II, then Lord High Admiral. Deane wrote of the reports of the large size of the Dutch fleet, which was constantly increasing.

Consequently the greater mischief likely to happen on our own parts as to those matters which our stores afford but a small number of for so great an action and therefore above all it's to be considered how to make the most of what we have and to aim at a second dispatch after the engagement, and to prevent the disorders I observed last war, when method seems to be at greatest distance as it is after a battle.

Some of the captains, he declared, were insistent on an entirely new outfit of masts and rigging, and failing to get these, complained vigorously of the dockyard authorities.

Without some remedy this may be as great an evil as possible, especially now, when masts, yards, cordage, sails, boats and many other things are not in store equal to the great occasion which may presently happen, nor, perhaps, to be had in the Kingdom, though money were at the greatest plenty. Therefore, I presume one hint, that in my observation last war, when stores were plentiful, more of all sorts were issued for the first battle than in the two latter, or, indeed could be had, and the necessity drove a seeming content of patching masts, at which I was no small botcher.[1]

The opening battle of the war came close upon this, and justified the predictions of the alarmists. The war was an unequal one, which threw immense credit upon the Dutch. De Ruyter and his followers fought with greater boldness and skill than ever before, against the French, who did little, and the English, who again fell below the standard set in the first war. Holland was being invaded by Louis XIV, and a few months after the outbreak of the war, the De Witts were murdered, to be replaced by William of Orange. The strategy of the naval war centered around De Ruyter's blocking of the attempt of the English and French fleet to land an army in Holland. In the only battle of 1672, he came over to England to break up the projected invasion before it crossed the Channel. In 1673, he was too weak to maintain the offensive

[1] *Cal. S. P., Dom.*, 1671–72, p. 563; see *Ibid.*, 1672, p. 142.

and was protecting his fleet behind the sandbars of the Dutch coast, darting out at favorable moments to engage the enemy in three different battles.

Badly mauled as usual after an encounter with the Dutch, the English fleet limped into Chatham and Sheerness during the last days of May, 1672. De Ruyter had won most of the honors in a sanguinary drawn battle against a superior force of the Allies on the 28th, in Southwold Bay or Solebay. The ships had headed first for the more convenient port of Harwich, but Harwich had scarcely been able to provide them with necessary masts and stores in last-minute demands before the battle.[1] "I have much more trouble without stores now than I had with them the last war," wrote Silas Taylor, the commissioner, in desperation from Harwich on the 29th, after a few ships had put in, to find nothing at all for repairs.[2] A day later, Sir Charles Lyttleton wrote: "It is a mighty unhappiness that there is nothing at Harwich to refit the disabled ships that come in. If there were, they might have been out again ere this."[3] A small vessel was stationed outside to send the rest of the "maimed" vessels on to Sheerness and Chatham.[4]

By the first of June, thirteen ships were at Chatham or the new, uncompleted yard at Sheerness, most of them disabled in masts and yards, some in their hulls as well. "If we want of stores, never was more frugality practiced, nor more need, or else a dearth of masts attends us, if the rest of the fleet prove as these do," wrote Anthony Deane, who was doing all that was humanly possible to accomplish something in face of the shameful lack of material.[5] More ships did come in and the officials stayed in constant attendance, "for if we keep in absence very little will be done." Orders were sent up the river to hurry down masts, spars, deals, plank, and cordage — "all that can be spared from Woolwich." Mastmakers, shipwrights, and caulkers were also needed immediately.[6] A large contract, which should have been attended to months before, was signed with Sir William Warren for masts

---

[1] *Cal. S. P., Dom.*, 1672, pp. 49, 77.   [2] *Ibid.*, p. 98.
[3] *Ibid.*, p. 104.   [4] *Ibid.*, p. 107.   [5] *Ibid.*, p. 136.
[6] *Ibid.*, pp. 107, 116, 117, 138, 139, 142.

and spars from Gottenburg, Norway, and Riga, two fifths of which were to be delivered in three months and all by the end of October.[1] That did not relieve the immediate necessity. Timber was purchased at £5 a load, an exorbitant rate; yet even at such prices, the supply was far short of the demand.[2]

A week after the ships arrived, Sir Thomas Allin, the Comptroller, sent to London a letter which further reflected the woeful lack of preparation. After the well-deserved tribute: "Mr. Deane is a great contriver, and preserver of many masts that would have been laid aside," he wrote:

Today we want nails, spikes, fishes and oak timber. . . . I entreated the Surveyor, who knew the state of all things at the dock, to write the Board for what he judged most wanting for refitting out this fleet. Great masts will be the chief, which I fear, are not to be had; so when this brunt is over, Mr. Tippetts and Mr. Deane must bethink themselves of making some after the French way, till your New England masts come. Plank is very scarce, and I judge it needful that some of all sorts be presently sent down to Sheerness. Masts are wanting here for the *Rupert, Dover* and *Greenwich*, also 60 shipwrights. I desire that they may be ordered down with all speed. . . . If you have any yards or topmasts made, pray send them down forthwith to furnish the fleet at the Buoy of the Nore.[3]

Two rafts of the small masts arrived three days later, but they were inexcusably in a rough condition, and several days were lost while the overworked mastmakers trimmed them into shape. The call went back for more — all that were available, and fishes, too, "ready split." On the 11th, there were no small masts or yards at Chatham or Sheerness, and so great was the need that a boat's crew rowed twelve miles to get a Dutch yard which had drifted in after the fight. "Your plank is not come," wrote Allin to his fellow commissioners, "which puts us to a standstill in all our business."[4] Small masts and spars continued to be the chief hindrance. "We have no masts from fourteen inches downwards, nor cant spars, nor small spars for any use and therefore pray for a good supply," Allin wrote on the 12th.[5] After similar declarations that there was not a single one of those sticks on hand, a report from Allin, Commissioner Middleton, and Pepys on the

---

[1] *Cal. S. P., Dom.,* 1672, pp. 139, 140, 509.
[2] *Ibid.,* p. 152.
[3] *Ibid.,* pp. 167, 168.
[4] *Ibid.,* pp. 187, 191, 208, 209.
[5] *Ibid.,* p. 216.

19th declared that they had not yet arrived, and that this non-arrival was one of the chief causes of delay.[1] It is unfortunate that Pepys's eyesight had forced him to abandon his diary in 1669 — his account of this glaring instance of the danger of an inadequate timber supply would have made excellent reading.

Five of the ships had sailed on the 15th, and it was nearly four weeks after the fight before they were all at sea again.[2] It had taken a month to refit on several other occasions, but this time there were fewer ships to repair and many of them went out patched and unfit for protracted service. It was due principally to the splendid work of Anthony Deane that the ships were able to put to sea, even in that condition. He was promoted from Master Shipwright to Commissioner of the Navy for his services, and was later knighted.[3] The Dutch had been at sea much earlier than the English, and De Ruyter had convoyed a large number of merchantmen in safety. A valuable summer month had been lost at the very time when the army of the French was most menacing to Holland and the De Witts were losing their power. The attempt to land troops in Holland was abandoned for the year.

The lack of timber made itself felt in other ways than in the disgraceful condition revealed by the action at Solebay. All through the remainder of 1672 and the spring of 1673 the dockyard clamors of emptiness continued. As usual, many forms of timber could have been had for money, but Robert Mayors, the purveyor, reviewing the timber supply available in the whole country, with all the possible fellings of oak, declared that plank was bound to be very scarce and that there were almost no small masts and spars at all.[4] A long and interesting report from Chatham told of having to waste good timber for want of cheap.[5] At times some of the yards were entirely out of deals, while elm, fir, and compass timber were all in demand. Phineas Pett at Woolwich stopped a vessel proceeding down the river and appropriated its timber cargo, while the other yards, for want of similar timber, had to suspend repairs or send the ships to sea inade-

[1] *Cal. S. P., Dom.*, 1672, pp. 221, 253.
[2] *Ibid.*, pp. 209, 231.
[3] *Ibid.*, pp. 254, 266.
[4] *Ibid.*, 1672–73, pp. 361, 362.
[5] *Ibid.*, p. 388.

quately refitted.[1] Ship after ship came into the yards with masts or bowsprits cracked or carried away. Many were too leaky to keep at sea, the *Diamond*, for instance, being "so very leaky that she can but just swim." For one ship, no new bowsprit could be found, and the only possible substitute at hand, a hoy mast, proved too small and rotten.[2]

Perils of the sea had cut off many of the masts expected from New England and the Baltic. A letter from Warren, the principal contractor, in March, 1673, explains easily why convoys were later considered necessary for this essential supply. Recounting his great losses during the past few months he told of

the *Young Blackcock* with New England masts taken by the Dutch 1 Feb. last; — the *Great Blackcock* with ditto masts taken by the Dutch 23 Jan. and retaken by the French 16 Feb. and carried into Dunkirk, — one of our Gottenburg ships taken, when laden, and carried into Holland: two other Gottenburg mast ships taken by the Scots, one already by them against all right and reason condemned, and the masts sold into private hands, and the other like to be sold in the same manner, so that, if you have any kindness from the consideration of our losses, let us serve you again. Another, the *William and John* which went out under your order for us to New England, is now retaken on her return of which news came two or three days since.[3]

Once more, in May, 1673, came the alarmist tones of Anthony Deane, who wrote as he had written a year earlier:

I believe you have laid the barrenness of the stores of the other yards as well as ours where it concerned you, but, if they be not supplied for a second fitting out the fleet which may soon be called for, let me beg for the King's safety, the nation's good and our own security that the state of the stores be pressed home and that money may be procured to provide what can be had before so pressing occasion happens, as will unavoidably fall out if the fleets engage, and ours returns very much shattered.[4]

This was not idle speculation: Deane knew that Portsmouth yard was bare and unable to sustain the burden of such repairs and that the other yards were little better off. He had suffered from the general want of preparedness a year before, and tried to avert its repetition.

[1] *Cal. S. P., Dom.*, 1672, p. 605; 1672–73, pp. 223, 254, 395, 452, 516; 1673, pp. 9, 83, 114, 125, 128, 166, 215–217, 239, 290, 291.

[2] *Ibid.*, 1672–73, pp. 39, 103, 122, 150, 188, 209, 221, 276, 356, 357.

[3] *Ibid.*, p. 21; see pp. 152, 153.

[4] *Ibid.*, p. 218; see p. 217.

It is worth recalling that, if an English fleet had been really crushed at sea in either of the wars, it is extremely doubtful if the stores on hand could have provided for a new force to regain the seas from the Dutch. That was the real menace of the timber problem, and the mast problem in particular. Deane's warnings may seem rather overdone in the light of what happened, but in none of the battles with the Dutch was an English fleet overwhelmed. The action at Lowestoft, the Four Days Battle, and Solebay had been practically drawn battles. So were the two actions off Schoneveldt on the Dutch coast, which occurred on May 28 and June 4, 1673, shortly after Deane's warning. If the difficulty of refitting was so great after a nominal victory or a draw, the peril in case of a defeat can be imagined.

The first action at Schoneveldt resulted in only a few "lame ships," [1] but the second, a week later, brought twenty-nine crippled ships into Chatham and Sheerness. It was the story of the year before repeated, with all the delays, inadequate mast supplies, and patchings.[2] It was hoped when the fleet arrived that it could sail again in eight or ten days. Masts, men, and beer detained Prince Rupert, then in command, for six weeks, while Dutch ships paraded with impunity off the immediate vicinity of the overburdened dockyards.[3]

The closing battle of the war, and the last major action in the Dutch wars, was an unsatisfactory encounter in the Texel, from which the allies came off with a little damage and less glory. Rupert came back to "see our lame geese in," but materials were inadequate even for the refitting of those few ships. The repairs went slowly, and it was necessary to strip the worst ships in order to allow the others to proceed to sea.[4]

The Treaty of Westminster in 1674 relieved the Navy of the mast shortage, only to leave it facing the most critical oak shortage of the century. The alliance of Charles II and Louis XIV was

---

[1] *Cal. S. P., Dom.*, 1672–73, pp. 308–310, 329, 330.

[2] *Ibid.*, pp. 349, 351, 360, 366, 367, 385.

[3] *Ibid.*, pp. 356, 398, 415, 416, 432, 442.

[4] *Ibid.*, pp. 494, 498, 503, 509, 510; N. R. S., *Catalogue of Pepysian MSS*, ii, 36, 45.

so unpopular in England that most of the English crews in the Third Dutch War would probably have preferred to ally themselves with the Dutch, whom they respected as Protestants and fighters, against the French, who were hated as Catholics and laggards at sea. This spirit found expression in 1677 in Parliament's appropriation of £600,000 to build thirty new ships. This measure was aimed against the French marine which was increasing rapidly under Colbert's care.[1]

The English Navy was left in a wretched condition at the close of the final war with the Dutch. In 1675, many of the largest ships were rotting, with the shot holes received at Solebay still unrepaired. They had not been in dock for five years, for there had been no money to repair all the damages sustained in the late war.[2] During the first year of peace the French had built nineteen great ships, and in 1676 had seven or eight more under construction, while the Dutch dockyards were also busy. In 1677, only twenty-three of England's seventy-five ships of the line were at sea or preparing for sea, and not one of them was a first- or second-rate, while about thirty ships, including eight of the two largest rates, were greatly out of repair and in need of "much time and charge to fitt them for sea service." The situation called for a radical increase of the Navy, especially in the matter of the three-decked first- and second-rates. These had not been needed so much against the Dutch, whose ships had to be small enough to manoeuvre on their shallow coast, but they were essential against the great ships which Louis XIV and Colbert were preparing at Brest and Toulon.[3]

The construction of those great three-deckers was curtailed by the lack of large timber, and even the two-decked third-rates, prototypes of the seventy-four, presented a serious timber problem. The increasing scarcity of oak had been noticed several years earlier — now it was a reality, which faced the naval authorities and influenced their program. In this address prepared for a

---

[1] N. R. S., *Catalogue of Pepysian MSS*, i, 43–48.
[2] *Parl. Hist.*, iv, 774.
[3] N. R. S., *Catalogue of Pepysian MSS*, pp. 48, 49; Pepys, *Memoires relating to the State of the Royal Navy of England*, p. 10.

Parliament not reluctant to appropriate money to fight the French, Pepys declared:

It is Sir Anthony Deane's judgment all the king's forests, and private men's timber within twenty miles of his Majesty's yards and river of Thames, will not afford compass timber, knees, standards, breast hooks, &c., to build two first-rates and six second-rates in four years; for straight timber it may be had to do it in two years, if private persons will let it be felled when occasion [requires]; besides the first and second-rates above mentioned I conceive it very difficult, if not impossible, to find compass timber, knees, standards, stems, harpins, &c, to build twenty third-rates in four years, stripping all the forests and gentlemen's timber within twenty miles of any land or water carriage or navigable place of England; for straight timber, if the gentlemen will fell, I suppose there may be as much got in four years as to complete the said work.[1]

It was in that same vein that Pepys had written the words quoted in the introduction: "But God knows where materials can be had for so many first and 2d rates however wee shall thinke fitt to propose the building of them." [2] The result was that the thirty ships were divided into one first-rate of 1460 tons, nine second-rates of 1300 tons, and twenty third-rates of 970 tons. A century later the tonnage of those rates was about double, so that the scarcity in 1677 appears even more extreme, in comparison with later building.

Securing the timber was more difficult than securing the appropriation. Early in 1678, Pepys outlined the many ways in which the whole country had been ransacked for available oak, "to evidence that we have used all means to buy goods and forward ye new ships." They are worth quoting to indicate what an active naval administration could do in face of great difficulties. They were, in Pepys's outline,

Publique invitations in the Gazette and on ye Exchange to merchants to [tender] Goods.

Several Country Gentlemen written to so soon as ye act was past whom we were informed had timber to ye number of about 30 in Norfolk, Suffolk, Essex, Hampshire, Devon, Somersetshire, Kent, Sussex and Berkshire inviting them to sell their timber.

Members of the Board and Purveyors sent abroad into all ye country where Timber was likely to be had, even as farre as Yorkshire.

---

[1] N. R. S., *Catalogue of Pepysian MSS*, pp. 49, 50.
[2] Magdalene College, Cambridge, *Pepysian MSS*, 2265, f. 113.

Shipwrights of ye Kings Yards alsoe sent abroad to seek for timber.

Borrowed Timber out of Kings Yard for ye new ships (in merchant yards) that the workes might goe forward till we could procure Timber elsewhere.

Contracted for a whole frame of a 3d [rate] ship to be hewed in Sussex; and workmen and moulds sent thither for it, which is now all come into Woolwich Yard.

Ordered ye working of foreyne East country planke under water without board to save English planke for the Decks & ye Works within board. . . .

Bought great parcells of Timber in ye woods and many Trees standing and sent workmen to convert ye same & bring it into ye Kings Yards.[1]

The use of German oak timber as well as the building of ships at Bristol and in Ireland were considered as relief measures, but the Admiralty flatly refused to use beech from the Forest of Dean.[2]

The journal of Phineas Pett, the grandson of the builder of the *Sovereign of the Seas*, gives an intimate picture of his experiences in Norfolk and Suffolk, where he and Sir Anthony Deane went around the countryside bargaining for small lots of timber. Many of the dealings were for only twenty or thirty trees, and seldom more than a hundred. "Called on the widow Gulledge and marked out several pieces of compass timber which we bought of her," wrote Pett, describing one of these petty transactions. It took hundreds of these little purchases to collect the thirty thousand trees required in the dockyards. Haggling was necessary in nearly every case, for there were no fixed prices.

Pepys had said that the timber might be secured "if the gentlemen will fell," but Pett and Deane were rebuffed by one who was a landowner, if not a real gentleman. The journal records: "There was one Haykins, in Stephen's parish, who had £300 worth set out at Witing-hall, but was not willing to sell it to the king, and would not speak with us." Forty years earlier, they could have set the Broad Arrow on that wood and seized it, but Parliament was paying the bills now, and its members wanted more than the "King's price" for their own trees.[3]

Eventually the timber was gathered, with the greatest diffi-

---

[1] Magdalene College, Cambridge, *Pepysian MSS*, 2265, f. 58; compare with N. R. S., *Catalogue of Pepysian MSS*, iv, 419.

[2] *Ibid.*, pp. 440, 471, 472, 475.

[3] Charnock, *History of Marine Architecture*, ii, 281. See N. R. S., *Catalogue of Pepysian MSS*, iv, 586.

culty arising more from actual shortage than poor credit. The timber collected for those thirty ships really stripped the English forests of practically all their available oak, and it was long before they recovered from the drain. The smaller trees were taken for ordinary timber, leaving little to provide for great timber in future wars.

The tragic element in this exhausting of the wood lay in the utter waste of that oak. Seven years later, most of it was hopelessly rotten and the Navy was in no better condition than it had been in 1677. The fault lay chiefly in the undue haste to get a fleet into being to oppose the French. It violated all the cardinal points of a good timber and building policy. The thirty-odd ships which lay rotting and unrepaired in 1677 could probably have been put in condition with a third of the timber required to build the thirty new ships. "We have been too busy in attempting too much at a time," wrote Pepys early in 1678; "Woolwich, Chatham and Portsmouth have more than enough of ye new works to ye hindrance of Repairds." [1] Consequently, while thirty new ships were being built at an expense of some 35,000 loads of timber, the other thirty were becoming hopelessly decayed when 10,000 loads might have made them ready for sea. The fault would seem to lie not entirely with the Admiralty policy, for the repairs had been planned. It developed, however, that the money voted by Parliament could be used only for the new ships, and the Lord Treasurer informed the Admiralty that there were no funds available for repairs.[2]

Moreover, the timber for the new ships was not allowed sufficient time to season and was bound to bring on decay. A sane policy under the circumstances would have called for the building of four or five ships each year and the repair of an equal number. The demand on the woods would have been less, timber would have been cheaper, the timber could have seasoned, and there would have been a navy in being all the time.

Instead of that, the new ships were neglected between 1679 and

[1] Magdalene College, *Pepysian MSS*, 2265, f. 122.
[2] *Adm. Library MSS, Digest*, "Shipbuilding," pp. 2, 3; N. R. S., *Catalogue of Pepysian MSS*, iv, 419, 425, 623.

1684, which was one of the lowest periods of English naval administration. Pepys, who was not in office during those years,
draws a striking but not disinterested picture of the decline which
took place. On his "melancholy visit" to Chatham, in 1684, he
found some of the new ships ready to sink at the moorings, timbers rotted everywhere, and the holes patched over as if they had
just returned from battle, though many had never even gone to
sea. He even gathered "toadstools as big as my fist" from the
decaying timbers.[1] Angry incriminations arose over the cause of
the decay. The green timber was undoubtedly largely responsible,
but English pride in its own oak shifted the blame to the Baltic
plank.[2] Pepys, since he had been very influential in building the
fleet, defended the construction of the ships in general and the
Eastland plank in particular, saying that only a very small proportion had been used. He placed the responsibility where part of
it certainly belonged, on the careless maintenance of the ships
which had lain in port unventilated and unrepaired.[3] That did not
relieve the Admiralty officials of 1677 of all blame, however. They
had exhausted the English forests to build of green timber a great
fleet which seven years later was almost a total loss. After all the
expense of gold and oak, England was without a navy.

A whole century elapses before we shall resume the story of the
effect of the timber problem on the Navy itself—a dull century
of stagnation and conservatism. The period just reviewed showed
the mast peril at almost its worst in the repairs after Solebay, and
the oak problem in an equally striking state in the building of the
1677 fleet. It was exactly a hundred years after Pett and Deane
were hunting for timber in the eastern counties that the lack of
masts from revolutionary New England made itself felt in the
fleets of the Royal Navy.

The effect of the timber problem in the intervening years can be
passed over quickly. The two long wars with Louis XIV, from
1689 to 1697 and from 1701 to 1713, saw a similar timber situation
to that which existed during the Dutch Wars, and repetition

[1] Pepys, *Memoires Relating to the State of the Royal Navy of England*, pp. 82–87.
[2] N. R. S., *Catalogue of Pepysian MSS*, i, 64.
[3] Pepys, *op. cit.*, pp. 86–90.

would be tedious. There was the same constant lack of navy credit, causing the same chronic shortage in the yards. For want of an adequate reserve, there was the same hand-to-mouth supply of masts, with constant anxiety over the arrival of the New England and Baltic ships. The "War of Jenkins's Ear" against Spain, begun in 1739, merging into the War of the Austrian Succession when France joined Spain at sea in 1744, revealed a scarcity of oak which lasted until the close of the war in 1748. Finances were on a stable footing by that time and the timber supply caused no real trouble. The same was true of the Seven Years' War, from 1756 to 1763. Oak and masts came regularly and the Navy was not affected in its operations, though the demand for oak was so heavy that serious results came immediately after the close of the war. The English woodlands were so nearly exhausted that the consequent effect of rotten ships was felt during the American Revolution. During that stagnant century, events of far more interest were going on in the pine forests of New England, where royal officers were enforcing the policy of the "Broad Arrow" in order to ensure a supply of masts for the Royal Navy.

CHAPTER VI

THE BROAD ARROW IN THE COLONIES

EVEN before the days of the Armada, England saw in the New World an opportunity for relief from dependence on the Baltic for masts and naval stores. Though many Elizabethan voyagers approached America with minds full of prospects of sudden wealth from gold, they recognized the needs of England's shipping as an argument for establishing colonies. "If we may injoy any large Territorie of apt soyle, we might so use the matter, as we should not depend on Estlande for flax, pitch, tarre, mastes, etc.," wrote a gentleman interested in Virginia, about 1580.[1] The same idea is expressed in the writings of Gilbert, Raleigh, John Smith, and of nearly every other Englishman who described his American impressions at the time.[2]

The earliest remarks center chiefly on masts and naval stores, for which England had long depended on a precarious Baltic supply. In the last years of Elizabeth's reign, the timber phase of the problem also came into prominence, for the depletion of England's forests had begun to alarm the Navy, and men saw that America could furnish substitutes for English oak as well as for Baltic masts. To relieve "the great and pitiful waste of our English woods . . . we may help ourselves out of Virginia and Sommer Islands," suggested a writer in 1615.[3] Seven years earlier, the political value of such a supply as a cause for establishing Virginia was suggested in the words of one Strachey:

Nor lett any man suppose that materialls of so good a navie as may be there framed for planckes, masts, pitch, and tarre . . . are of no value, or not worthy the exposure of a colonie for politique endes to be established there,

---

[1] Hakluyt Society; Hakluyt, *Divers Voyages touching the Discovery of America*, p. 136; see *Ibid.*, p. 18.

[2] See Hakluyt; *Force Tracts*; Capt. John Smith, *Works*; Lord, *Industrial Experiments in the British Colonies of North America*, chapter I; and Wertenbaker, *Planters of Colonial Virginia*, chapter I, *passim*.

[3] "Britain's Buss," in Andrew Lang, *Social England Illustrated*, p. 303.

since Muscovia and Polonia doe yearlie receive manie thowsandes for pitch, tarre, soap ashes, resin, flax cordage, sturgeon, masts, yardes, waynscot, firrs, glasse, and such like.[1]

It is small wonder that the forests of America roused these considerations in Englishmen who saw their country totally dependent on foreigners for many of the essentials of sea power. The entire Atlantic coast from the Straits of Bellisle to the Rio de la Plata presented an almost unbroken forest, sometimes a thousand miles deep. In North America, the Atlantic forest offered timber of every kind. The white pine belt reached the sea from Nova Scotia to New Hampshire and stretched westward across the upper Connecticut and Hudson and along the St. Lawrence, a forest tract which was to furnish the King's ships with great masts for two centuries. The oaks of the central hardwood belt were to find less favor with the Navy, but were indirectly to relieve the drain on English oak. The southern coast offered the choicest timber of all, with its live oaks, longleaf pine, red cedar, and cypress; but the indifference of the southern colonists made these woods only a minor factor in the relief of England's timber problem. Of all these trees, the white pines of the north were to play by far the greatest part in the timber problem of the Navy, for not only did England become largely dependent upon them, but in attempting to preserve them for the King's ships, England aroused at an early date an antagonism which foreshadowed the spirit of the Revolution.

A timber trade offered mutual advantage to the colonies and to the mother country. In England's need for forest products, the settlers found a commercial outlet for their most available material of commercial value. "To the settler the forest became an enemy to be fought and conquered before a higher civilization could be established." [2] Unlike the men of England, who grew oaks for profit, the colonist had to remove the trees anyway. If, instead of spending a year in clearing four acres with "log-rolling" and burning the trees, he could find a market for that wood, it

---

[1] Hakluyt Society; Strachey, *Historie of Travaile into Virginia Britannia*, p. 115.

[2] Defebaugh, *History of the Lumber Industry in America*, i, 274, 294; see Marsh, *Earth Modified by Human Action*, pp. 344 ff.

was an additional advantage. The timber trade soon developed lumbering for its own sake, and it was a decided factor in helping to clear land for agriculture.

It is not surprising, then, that timber shipments began almost as soon as the colonies were founded. Probably the first cargo of masts, if not of timber of any kind, from the colonies was a cargo of "fower score" masts from Virginia in 1609 in "a ship of three-hundred tonne burthen called the Starre (sent thither . . . upon purpose fitted, and prepared with scupper holes to take in masts.)"[1] The English commented on the size of the masts, which were so large that they had to be cut down to fit the vessel's hold. In 1623, the ship *Anne* took a cargo of clapboards from Plymouth, and three years later the Dutch were sending timber from New Amsterdam.[2]

The first sawmill in America is supposed to have been built near York, Maine, in 1623.[3] After that, these mills — which conservatism kept out of England for another century and a half — followed closely the frontiers of settlement. Scarcely was a hamlet settled before a sawmill was established.[4] The earliest mills had a single vertical saw, the progress of which through the logs of pine or oak was so noisy that its screaming could often be heard two miles away, and so slow that the sawyer could frequently sit on the log and eat his lunch while the stick was being sawn.[5] Numerous mills of this type, run by river, tide, or wind, followed the line of settlement in most of the colonies. It was in New Hampshire and Maine, however, that the lumber industry became most important, forming the backbone of the economic existence and the chief motive for new settlements, because, like Norway, these regions had little else save fish to offer. It has been said that the commerce of the Puritans smelled as strongly of fish as their theology smelled of brimstone. It is equally true of that commerce that it rested on a solid foundation of pine and oak.

[1] Strachey, *Historie of Travaile into Virginia Britannia*, p. 130; *Documents relating to the Colonial History of New York*, i, 38.

[2] *Ibid.*, i, 26.

[3] For a review of this disputed subject, see Defebaugh, *op. cit.*, ii, 6.

[4] *Ibid.*, ii, 8, 9, 307.

[5] *Ibid.*, i, 157; ii, 7, 154; *Cal. S. P., A. & W. I.*, 1701, p. 7.

This general lumber industry is of interest in connection with the Navy's timber problem in two ways. Together with colonial shipbuilding, the exports of pine and oak relieved to some extent the consumption of English oak. Masts, moreover, could not be furnished efficiently or economically except as a part of a general timber trade which would warrant effective organization of cutting and transport. Consequently, it was of interest to the Navy to stimulate lumbering in general even though it had no use for most of the American timber.

Attention naturally centers on the mast trade, for in this the Navy had a vital interest. In 1634, Emanuel Downing wrote Secretary Coke that the first mast cargo had arrived from New England. Foreseeing the importance of this trade, he advocated that in order to keep it out of the hands of the Dutch, the colonists be persuaded "to accept a new patent and thereby be bound to transport no masts &c for cordage and shipping but into Old England." [1] This was a forecast of the legislation which was to develop during the coming century, restricting the freedom of the colonists in the interests of the naval mast supply. For the time being, however, the settlers were left quite free to trade in timber and masts at will, and the value of the great sticks of white pine was soon appreciated by English shipwrights.

These huge trees, it will be recalled, were sometimes fully a yard in diameter, and could serve alone for the lower masts of even a first-rate ship of the line. This gave them a decided advantage over the smaller sticks of Riga fir, which had to be pieced together to form a "made mast." [2] During the First Dutch War, it was seen that the closing of the Sound by the Danes influenced the Navy's determination to send ships to America for these masts in 1652. [3] The arrival of the first cargoes a year later marked the beginning of this important supply which lasted a century and a quarter. The size of the New England masts attracted frequent attention as they began to take their place as a part of the regular dockyard establishment. [4] The legislators of Massachusetts Bay

[1] *Cal. S. P., A. & W. I.*, Addenda, 1574–1674, pp. 75, 76; also in *Massachusetts Historical Society, Proceedings*, xxviii, 383–385.
[2] See pp. 29, 31.   [3] See pp. 207, 213.   [4] Evelyn, *Sylva, passim.*

made a most appropriate present to the King in 1666 and 1667. They had to excuse their failure to comply with the mandates of the royal commissioners by refusing to undertake an overland campaign against the French in Canada. The effect of their diplomatic response was strengthened by the gift of a valuable cargo of masts "as a testimony of loyalty and affection."[1] They were anxious that the full value of the present be appreciated in England, and it has been seen that the gift arrived at a most opportune time.[2]

The mast trade centered at Portsmouth from the outset, and until the Revolution this early capital of New Hampshire at the mouth of the Piscataqua, known often as "Pascataway" or "Strawberry Bank," furnished most of the great masts for the Navy.[3] The traveller from Boston to Portland even today will recognize how the little strip of New Hampshire seacoast marks the frontier between the oaks of Massachusetts and the pines of Maine. Portsmouth, therefore, was the first available port in the pine region as the settlements pushed up the coast from Boston.

American masts were furnished to the Navy by the usual contract system.[4] The four great contractors during the colonial period, Warren, Taylor, Gulston, and Henniker, resided in England and contracted with the Navy Board for masts and naval stores from the Baltic as well as from New England. The contracts called for masts to supply the dockyards at Jamaica and Antigua in the West Indies as well as the great yards in England. The contractors had resident mast agents in New England, chief among them Samuel Waldo, Thomas Westbrook, and, above all, Mark Hunking Wentworth, all of whom managed the colonial end of the business on a very profitable basis. These agents, in turn, contracted with colonists who arranged the actual cutting and floating to the ports.

---

[1] *Records of the Colony of Massachusetts Bay*, vol. iv, pt. 2, pp. 316–318; no evident authority for interpretation in Peuchet, *Dictionnaire Universel de la Géographie Commerçante*, iv, 17.

[2] *Cal. S. P., A. & W. I.*, 1661–68, p. 590; Weeden, *Economic and Social History of New England*, i, 243.

[3] *Cal. S. P., A. & W. I.*, 1661–68, pp. 347, 363, 428, 429; 1700, p. 191; *Mass. Hist. Soc., Proc.*, xxvii, 233, 234.   [4] See pp. 39, 40, 55, 56.

Lumbering operations in the pine forests of New England varied little during the century. In many ways, they resembled the Baltic lumbering and were even more similar to the Norwegian.[1] Great masts were frequently worth more than £100, but many elements of risk and difficulty made such prices necessary. The cutting usually took place in the winter after a preliminary survey. Good mast trees were rare and appearances were often deceptive.

This Season the Mast Cutters for His Majesty's Contract found in one District a fine Growth of large and uncommonly fair trees, but on cutting them, one hundred and two out of one hundred and six proved rotten in the heart & not worth a shilling,

wrote Sir John Wentworth, the greatest of the Surveyors General of His Majesty's Woods.[2] Elaborate preparations were necessary for this felling. A roadway to the nearest stream had to be cleared and a bed of smaller trees cut to break the fall of the great stick. The felling was a delicate operation, for a slight error on the part of the axemen might ruin the tree.

Hauling or "balking" the huge stick to the river was a task of equal difficulty and art for the "mastmen." Anywhere from eight to twenty yoke of oxen were necessary for the great log, and as in the Baltic, either sleds or three pairs of axles were used. Descending a hill was particularly dangerous, for even though a snub line was used to hold the load in check, oxen were often choked or crushed at the bottom.

At the spring thaw, the logs were "twitched" into the river for a trip much shorter and less formal than on the Niemen or Vistula. The logs went singly instead of in rafts, and many fine sticks were shattered in going over the falls so as to be fit only for bowsprits or boards. At the mouths of the rivers were great mast houses where "mastwrights" hewed the sticks into "sixteen sides." The masts for Portsmouth first came from the Piscataqua, but later they were floated down other rivers and ferried along the

[1] See pp. 144–146.
[2] R. O., Treas., i, 195, *Wentworth to Commis. of Treas.*, Dec. 4, 1771; see *Cal. S. P., A. & W. I.*, 1710–11, p. 40.

coast. As early as 1683, an inspection similar to Baltic bracking was introduced.[1]

During the colonial wars, the French and Indians were a constant menace to the mast trade, for operations were conducted to the very frontier. In 1692, John Taylor, the mast contractor, requested permission to raise a company to cut or fight, and later Bridger, the Surveyor General of the Woods at the time, required an armed guard for his timber cruising.[2] The cutters were often organized in semi-military fashion. In 1706, Captain Cutting and his company, while "masting," were ambushed by Indians who inflicted heavy casualties. Four years later, Colonel Winthrop Hilton, who had gone fourteen miles into the woods from Portsmouth, was also ambushed and killed with two of his men while "the rest fled precipitately."[3] At times during those wars, it was true that "so generall a fear of the Indians has fallen upon the people that they will not for any gaine venture abroad in the woods."[4] Portsmouth was in constant dread of a French foray, and the contractors, by pointing out the danger to the Navy's supply, were influential in securing a fort and garrison there, while the frigates on that station had instructions to protect and aid the mast supply.[5] As late as 1744, the Portsmouth mast ships were considered in danger from the swarms of Cape Breton privateers "who may cut them out or burn them and all their cargoes even for next year."[6]

The unusual size of the American masts required specially constructed "mast ships," often built in the colonies. Usually of four or five hundred tons, and sometimes a thousand, they had a capacity ranging from forty to a hundred great masts with many yards and spars. These mast ships, unlike the little old Baltic

[1] Chapman, "Mast Industry of Old Falmouth," in *Maine Historical Society Collections*, 2d series, vii, 390–405; Redlon, *Saco Valley Settlements*, pp. 190–218.

[2] *Cal. S. P., A. & W. I.*, 1693–96, pp. 241, 522; 1702–03, p. 880; 1706–08, pp. 344, 354; 1708–09, p. 278; 1710–11, p. 13.

[3] Adams, *Annals of Portsmouth*, pp. 124, 125.

[4] Prince Society Publications, *Randolph Papers*, vii, 410.

[5] *Acts P. C. (Col.)*, 1680–1720, pp. 313, 515; 1720–45, p. 184; *Cal. S. P., A. & W. I.*, 1701, pp. 105, 576; Hist. MSS Com., *House of Lords MSS*, 1702–04, p. 319; 1704–06, p. 96.

[6] R. O., N. B. Out Letters, 2180, *N. B. to Adm.*, May 18, 1744.

"tramps," were the regular "liners" of New England, bringing passengers, troops, mail, and later, tea. The arrival of the "mast fleet" was an event of note in colonial journals.[1] After several of the first New England mast ships had been captured during the Dutch wars, a frigate was usually detailed as convoy in time of war.[2] Occasionally, great lumber rafts, shaped like a ship, were sent across the Atlantic. By 1670, Portsmouth was sending ten mast cargoes a year to England, two or three of which were for the Navy.

Up to 1688, the colonists developed their lumber industry with little interference from England, save for temporary encouragement during the Baltic crisis in 1652–53.[3] After the accession of William and Mary, the period of attention and regulation commenced. There were two reasons for this. The long struggle with the French which commenced almost immediately taxed the English shipyards heavily in turning out a navy and new merchantmen to replace the losses, while the supply of naval stores from the Baltic was being threatened by the hostile attitude of Sweden.[1] Referring to the interrupted importation of tar, Dr. Robinson, the envoy at Stockholm, wrote in 1703:

> What difficulties there are in making and bringing it from New England, I am not acquainted with, but take it for granted, England had better give one-third more from thence than have it at such uncertainties and in so precarious a manner from other countries.[4]

Economic considerations also turned England's attention to a colonial supply of naval materials. Such a supply would fit two cardinal points of the mercantilist theory of colonies then in vogue. It would obviate the unfavorable balance of trade with the Baltic and it would also divert the colonists from manufacturing woolens, it was hoped, by giving them valuable materials to exchange for English products. The state papers and the writings of the economists at this time bristle with arguments for the encouragement of this production of naval materials which seemed

---

[1] *Boston News Letter*, Oct. 21–28, 1706, and *passim;* see *Historical Digest of the Provincial Press, passim.*

[2] See *Cal. S. P., Dom.*, 1672–73, p. 252.

[3] *Cal. S. P., A. & W. I.*, Addenda, 1574–1674, p. 87.

[4] See pp. 158–160.

so obviously to favor both England and America.[1] The proposed
industry would give New England a more fitting place in the old
colonial system with its aim of relative imperial self-sufficiency.
The sugar colonies and the tobacco colonies helped to round out
England's needs, but New England was threatening to rival the
mother country with its fisheries and its shipbuilding. If masts,
tar, and pitch could be produced instead, "it would make New
England, of the most useless and unprofitable plantation of the
Nation, the best and most advantageous," wrote Brewster in
1695.[2] The encouragement of these articles also aimed at the in-
cipient colonial woolen industry. New England had "consumption of more woolen manufactures than all our Forreign Plantations," Brewster went on to say, "it being a Cold Climate and
Men with hard Labour wear out much Cloaths."[3] John Bridger,
while attempting to stimulate the New England supply of naval
materials as agent of the Navy Board, declared that "my saying
that by making tar, etc., they get money enough to buy 2 coats
in the time they are carding, spinning, etc., to make one, they
will not believe unless they see it tryed before their faces."[4] It
was England's purpose to make this trial and drag New England
into a helpful rôle in the colonial system. The attempts to grow
hemp and to manufacture tar do not fall within the province of
this work, but as far as masts and timber are concerned, the movement is important. The English were only doing what Colbert
had inaugurated in New France thirty years earlier with elaborate
detail. He wrote in 1666: "Vous voyez bien qu'il est ridicule que
nous allons chercher chez les estrangers ce que nous avons chez
nous avec abondance."[5]

This proposed colonial development was encouraged by the
economists and by the Lords of Trade and Plantations who were
reorganized in 1697 with instructions, *inter alia*, to encourage the

[1] Postlethwayt, *Dictionary*, article "Naval Stores"; see *Cal. S. P., A. & W. I.*,
1710–11, p. 19.

[2] Brewster, *Essays on Trade and Navigation*, p. 88.

[3] *Ibid.*, p. 88; see Defoe, *A Plan of English Commerce*, pp. 348–368.

[4] R. O., C. O., 5, 864, 244, *Bridger to B. of T.*

[5] Colbert, *Lettres, Instructions et Mémoires*, vol. iii, pt. 1, p. 86; see also *Ibid.*,
vol. iii, pt. 2, pp. 396, 447, 560, 715.

colonial supply of naval materials.[1] The measure met opposition from the group in whose interest it was ostensibly being advanced. The Navy Board showed a consistent antipathy to the colonial supply. "If stores cannot be imported from the Plantations not only as good, but also as cheap [as] from other countrys, premiums, etc., included, it will be a burthen to the Navy, and not a service," they wrote to the Lords of Trade.[2] They wanted an adequate supply of New England masts, but there their interest ceased.[3]

Compared to the Baltic, America was at a disadvantage in several respects. The American ports were three thousand miles from England, nearly three times the distance to Riga and five times as far as Norway. Therefore, the average rate for a ton of freight at this time was six to eight pounds from the colonies against 40s to 50s from the Baltic. Colonial labor was some six times as high as in many parts of Europe. The highly organized timber trade of Dantzig or Riga, moreover, could not be matched in the colonies at the time. John Taylor, who imported masts from both regions and favored America only as a reserve in case of necessity, wrote:

'T is not in New England as in Sweden and Denmark, where masts are brought to markett to supply Europe in general, whereas in New England non are provided but what are bespoke, & those for the King's service in particular, which makes the hazard in this trade incomparably greater than any other, for if any accident by the Indians or otherwise should obstruct the lading . . . the ship must certainly come back dead freight.[4]

Moreover, the naval authorities conceived a dislike for the colonial timber traders at an early period, judging by Hollond's remarks:

I would also encourage . . . the transporting of knees or knee timber from New England, they being scarce commodities here and very useful for the State's service; only I could wish that men of religion that bring them hither

---

[1] *Cal. S. P., A. & W. I.*, 1696–97, p. 542.

[2] *Ibid.*, 1706–08, p. 331; see also *Ibid.*, 1702–03, pp. 290, 693; 1710–11, p. 340.

[3] *Ibid.*, 1700, p. 178; 1702–03, pp. 499, 586; *Cal. Treas. Papers*, 1702–07, pp. 483, 524; Hist. MSS Com., *House of Lords MSS*, 1702–04, pp. 329, 330; 1704–06, 93–95.

[4] R. O., N. B. In Letters, 562, *Taylor to N. B.*, Sept. 20, 1702; see Gee, *Trade and Navigation of England Considered*, p. 156; *Cal. S. P., A. & W. I.*, 1702, p. 2.

would not (when brought) cull or garble them by selling the best to private men, and when the refuse will not off, then to sell the remainder as a great service to the State at an excessive rate.[1]

Yet in spite of the apathy, if not antipathy, of the naval authorities, England began to apply a twofold policy of encouragement and of restriction in the matter of these naval necessities. The encouragement took the form of "imperial" propaganda and the more tangible argument of bounties. The restrictions aimed at the preservation of the mast pines from wanton waste by commissioning surveyors to cut the "Broad Arrow" — the old sign of naval property, shaped like a crow's track and made with three blows of a marking hatchet — on the trees to be reserved by law for the Navy. After several preliminary acts, these two features were incorporated in the Act of 1729. The "Broad Arrow" enforcement is the chief source of interest thereafter; but before that final enactment, it is essential to describe the events in the colonies which led to its passage.

To men who had been stimulated to recklessness by the apparently inexhaustible capacity of the virgin forests, the idea of restrictions on cutting seemed almost incongruous. Yet this attempt to preserve the great pines for masting the King's ships was justified from the standpoint of maintaining the Navy's supply. The chief value of the American masts lay in their great size, and they had reached this size because they had had centuries in which to grow, unmolested by axemen. While the forests seemed limitless in extent, pines suitable for great masts were few and far between. The difficulties of land carriage limited the choice to those near the rivers, and the largest trees were marked victims from the outset. In a region where lumbering was the chief and almost sole occupation, masts were not the only end which trees could serve, in the eyes of the colonial woodsmen. Capable of furnishing fine smooth boards a yard wide, many potential mast pines were cut to pieces in the frontier sawmills. Consequently it was not groundless alarm which prompted the complaints of "great spoyles" in the woods of New Hampshire and Maine — complaints which increased in frequency and ur-

[1] N. R. S., *Hollond's Discourses of the Navy*, p. 227.

gency as the seventeenth century approached its close.[1] If the Navy was to depend on New England for its masts in the future, strong measures were necessary to protect the remaining pines in the regions already settled and the great trees in the lands to eastward, where lumber interests were bound to penetrate.

England's first official step of any consequence in the formation of a colonial forest policy was the appointment of Edward Randolph as Surveyor of Pines and Timber in Maine in 1685.[2] The office of Surveyor of His Majesty's Woods and Forests, it will be recalled, had existed in some form in England for a century and a half with a jurisdiction limited to the royal forests, parks, and chases.[3] The disputed royal claims to authority over the woods in the colonies were to give the surveyors in America far more extensive powers than the English office implied. The guardianship of the King's woods in America did not develop into an important office, however, for another thirty years. The £50 salary was apparently given to Randolph to piece out the income of an active, unpopular, and often unscrupulous supporter of royal authority, who had been instrumental in doing away with the Massachusetts charter. To the end it was a "part-time job," at first connected with the customs and later with the governorship of New Hampshire — the only exception to this being John Bridger. Randolph made an official survey in 1688, going into Maine as far as the "Sheeps gutt River" and Penobscot Bay. He reported that he had been successful in checking the devastation which had already commenced in that region.[4] In 1691, he became Surveyor General, and was succeeded in Maine and New Hampshire by Jahleel Brenton, an absentee represented by a deputy, Ichabod Plaisted. Plaisted was interested in the lumber business himself and was scarcely a fit guardian. Lord Bellomont, the governor of New York around 1700, complained that neither Randolph nor Plaisted had done a sixpenny-worth of work in the position.

---

[1] See *Cal. S. P., A. & W. I.*, 1669-74, p. 448, and *passim.* Frequent references in every volume.

[2] Prince Society Publications, *Randolph Papers*, i, 266; *Cal. Treas. Papers*, 1557-1696, p. 203. Date often erroneously given as 1656.

[3] See p. 110.

[4] *Randolph Papers*, v, 71-74; vii, 410, 479-486.

In 1696, at the instigation of the New England agents, the Navy Board sent John Bridger and three others as commissioners to investigate the possibilities of a supply of ship timber and to instruct the colonists in the making of tar and pitch.[1] Bridger alone of the four commissioners rendered valuable service to the Navy. For nine years he upheld royal authority in the New England woods on the strength of his Navy Board commission, and in 1705 he became the first real Surveyor General. He had to face not only the hostility of the colonists, but also the indifference of the Navy Board, which resulted in his final removal for political reasons after twenty-five years of faithful service. Actuated by the interest of the Navy, which he had previously served as a ship-wright, he did more than any other man to inaugurate the Broad Arrow policy.

Bridger believed that the American colonies could relieve the Navy's whole problem of timber and naval stores. Everything that the Navy imported from the Baltic, he declared, could be produced in America; for in addition to the mast pines, there was the possibility of raising hemp and extracting tar and pitch. Moreover, the serious shortage in the English woodlands could be offset by sending the American oak to England, either as ship timber or already built into warships. The question of hemp, pitch, and tar lies outside the province of this study, though frequent references will have to be made to that supply, so closely is it related to the timber problem. It is enough here to state that the government encouraged the colonial production of those naval stores, but the Navy Board rejected them for its own use because of their alleged inferior quality. The same held true of oak timber and the colonial construction of warships. The sequence of events will be anticipated slightly to show how little these projected sources of relief to the timber problem were utilized.

American oak had been used in the dockyards from time to time during the Dutch wars, but had attracted little attention.[2]

---

[1] Adm. Lib. MSS Digest, "Naval Stores," pp. 78–88; *Cal. S. P., A. & W. I.*, 1698, p. 537; *Acts P. C. (Col.)*, 1680–1720, p. 303; *Cal. Treas. Papers*, 1697–1701/02, p. 59. For full details on period to 1729, with references to Board of Trade papers, see Lord, *Industrial Experiments in the British Colonies of North America, passim.*

[2] *Cal. S. P., Dom.*, 1673, p. 166; N. R. S., *Hollond's Discourses of the Navy*, p. 227.

One of Bridger's first acts in 1696 was the gathering of a cargo of the various types of ship timber which New England could offer. Several colonists financed this as a business venture, and it was a keen disappointment to New England when the Deptford officers made the unfavorable report upon the quality of the colonial oak already referred to.[1] Another consignment in 1700 met the same fate. During the shortage of English oak around 1740, occasioned by the "War of Jenkins's Ear," a few shipments of New England oak were sent to relieve the situation, but they met with similar condemnation. Except for some small importations of Casco Bay oak after the Seven Years' War, the Navy made no further use of the colonial ship timber.[2]

The effort to introduce American oak into the dockyards in 1696 was accompanied by an agitation for the construction of warships in the colonies where timber was plentiful. The *Falkland*, 54, was built at Portsmouth in 1696, followed by the *Bedford Galley* a year later. Both ships served for a while on the American station, but they were soon laid up in English dockyards for repairs and before long were broken up. They were not very durable, but they lasted as long as many similar ships built of English oak during that period of hasty construction to make up for the heavy losses at the hands of the French.[3] The English dockyard officials reported unfavorably upon them, as they had upon the colonial oak, but it was well known that dockyard shipwrights were unfair to other ships which they themselves had not built.[4]

The Navy Board seemed determined to disparage the quality of colonial warships, and treated the policy exactly as it treated the importation of New England oak. No more were built until the shortage during the "War of Jenkins's Ear" made relief of the

[1] *Cal. S. P., A. & W. I.*, 1693–96, pp. 355, 357; *Cal. Treas. Papers*, 1557–1696, p. 517; see p. 24.

[2] R. O., N. B. Out Letters, 2182, *N. B. to Adm.*, Sept. 19, 1746; *Commons Reports*, vol. iii, *passim; Connecticut Historical Society*, vol. xix, *Pitkin Papers*, pp. 101, 102.

[3] R. O., *Adm., Acct. Gen., Misc., Var.*, 123; N.B. *Memorandum*, Feb. 25, 1722; *Cal. S. P., A. & W. I.*, 1700, pp. 564–566; 1704–05, p. 156; 1708–09, p. 236; Preble, "Vessels of War built at Portsmouth, N. H., 1690–1868," in *New England Historical and Genealogical Register*, xxii, 393–403.

[4] Maydman, *Naval Speculations and Maritime Politicks*, p. 73.

English timber situation desirable. The Admiralty instructed the Navy Board in 1747 to construct four frigates in New England, partly on account of the crying need of the admirals for more cruisers immediately, and partly to reward the colonists for their services under Pepperell in the capture of Louisburg. The Navy Board sharply opposed the project, arguing the poor quality of the first two ships, the need of sending all the ships' fittings from England, and the folly of rewarding the colonists at the expense of the Navy. After an acrimonious correspondence, the Admiralty won out, and contracts were awarded for four frigates to be built in New England. The *America*, 44, built near Portsmouth by Pepperell, was soon condemned for speedy decay and the policy was abandoned.[1] Another *America*, a seventy-four built at Portsmouth during the American Revolution and given to France to replace a ship of the line lost on the coast, was condemned almost as rapidly by the French, which tends to corroborate the English opinion.[2]

Poor timber was not the only cause for opposing the building of warships in America, because England, it will be recalled, was generally opposed to the policy of building for the Navy outside of the country.[3] The fear was expressed as early as 1664, in the writings of Sir Josiah Childs, that New England threatened to become the "most prejudicial" of the colonies because of its growing maritime strength; and this feeling, repeated frequently as the Revolution approached, prevented England from trusting its naval construction to the "prejudicial" New Englanders.[4] If Portsmouth in New Hampshire had been building as many warships for England as Havana was building for Spain in 1775, the Navy would have suffered a blow more severe than the loss of New England masts alone. From that standpoint, the Navy Board was wise in preferring to build at Portsmouth in old Hampshire.

[1] Preble, *op. cit.*, pp. 396, 397; R. O., N. B. Out Letters, 2182, *N. B. to Adm.*, Sept. 1, Sept. 19, Oct. 10, 1746; Aug. 6, 1747; Adm. Library MSS, *Abstracts of Progress, passim.*

[2] *U. S. Naval Institute, Proceedings*, vol. xxiv, no. 2.   [3] See pp. 74, 75.

[4] Child, *Discourse on Trade*, p. 135; Fisher, *Heart of Oak*, p. 74; Postlethwayt, *Dictionary*, article on "Naval Stores."

Colonial ships, like colonial oak, then, were rejected by the Navy, but they were both of considerable indirect service to the Navy in relieving the demand on English oak through their extensive use in the merchant marine. Shipbuilding became one of the chief industries in the American colonies, especially in New England, where ships were launched within a few years after the first settlement. By 1700, the colonial merchant marine amounted to a thousand ships, and these enjoyed the privilege of English registry, which was an important consideration under the Navigation Acts. Not only did the colonists build for their own triangular trade, but every year they constructed many ships to order for British merchants. The latter soon acquired a bad reputation for speedy decay. It must be said, however, in defence of American timber at the expense of colonial business morality, that the ships built to order were often thrown together in a few months with any kind of green timber, while the colonists used better wood and built more carefully for themselves.[1] The importance of this colonial shipbuilding in saving English timber can be judged from the fact that at the outbreak of the Revolution America was building a hundred ships a year and the colonial ships, numbering 2343, amounted to a third of the total British registry.[2] The antagonistic spirit after the Revolution, which found a powerful spokesman in Lord Sheffield, was responsible for the exclusion of United States ships from British registry. It was argued that, if England admitted them, she would finally have to send to America whenever she needed a frigate.[3]

The failure of the attempt to relieve the timber problem by American oak and ships concentrated the attention of Bridger and the Navy in general on the pines suitable for masts. Bridger had an enthusiastic ally in Richard Coote, Earl of Bellomont, who was governor of New York, and had nominal authority over all the northern colonies from 1698 to 1701. With instructions from the Lords of Trade to encourage the colonial supply of naval

---

[1] R. O., N. B. Out Letters, 2183, *N. B. to Adm.*, May 15, 1747; *Observations on the Importance of the Northern Colonies*, p. 13; Adams, *Annals of Portsmouth*, p. 258.

[2] *Lloyd's Register*, 1775–76; Macpherson, *Annals*, iii, 570.

[3] Sheffield, *Observations on the Commerce of the American States;* Coxe, *A Brief Examination of Lord Sheffield's Considerations, passim.*

stores, Bellomont went into that business with such eagerness that the Navy Board became annoyed at his measures. Declaring that the colony could furnish great masts for £38 10s, where Bridger charged £82, and Taylor, the regular contractor, £152, he pledged his own small fortune and the contents of the colony's treasury in an attempt to bring masts from the upper Hudson. There were many obstacles in the way of this venture. He dared not carry out the plan to use soldiers as lumbermen for fear of mutiny, some of the great sticks were shattered by the falls at Cohoes, and "certain wicked persons" at Albany tried to thwart his efforts to buy mast rights from the Mohawks by telling the Indians that every great stick was worth fifty beaver skins. He also arranged with one De Peyster to cut oak ship timber, with "beams large enough for a first-rate," from the lower Hudson. Bellomont's zeal might have developed this semi-official mode of supply from New York, even in face of the opposition of the Navy Board, who argued in favor of the contract system as ensuring good quality. Incidentally there was more profit for themselves in allotting valuable contracts to Taylor than in dealing with a zealous governor. The ambitious scheme collapsed, however, with Bellomont's untimely death in 1701 in the midst of the venture, which left his widow penniless and the New York treasury so empty that the troops could not be paid. Bellomont's successor, Lord Cornbury, shipped the masts to England in 1702, but recommended adherence to the contract system thereafter.[1] New Hampshire's hold on the mast trade was strong enough to thwart this attempt to divert it to New York, just as Connecticut was also to be checked in a like manner a half century later.

Bellomont's interest was not confined to masts from the Hudson. He constantly complained of the devastation among the pines of New Hampshire.[2] The particular target of his attacks was Richard Partridge, one of Bridger's fellow commissioners, who had become lieutenant governor of New Hampshire, and was

---

[1] *Cal. S. P., A. & W. I.*, 1697–98, p. 119; 1700, pp. 358, 359, 370, 563–567, 607, 671, 672, 690; 1701, pp. 7, 108, 109, 180, 199; 1702, 626, 627; many of the same also in *Documents relating to the Colonial History of New York*, vol. iv; Hist. MSS Com., *House of Lords MSS*, 1689–1702, pp. 439, 440.

[2] See esp. *Cal. S. P., A. & W. I.*, 1700, p. 563.

shipping masts and pine lumber in large quantities to Spain, Portugal, and Algiers. "To set a carpenter to preserve woods is like setting a wolf to keep sheep," Bellomont wrote in his successful effort to secure the removal of Partridge, while his denunciation of the inefficiency of Randolph and Brenton as surveyors was likewise severe.[1]

These complaints were not without effect. In 1705, Bridger, up to that time only an agent of the Navy Board, was made Surveyor General of Her Majesty's Woods and Forests in America, with a salary of £200 (equivalent to the value of two great masts), and was granted much more extensive powers than he had hitherto held. He was to encourage and instruct the colonists in the making of naval stores. What is more important, he was to restrain the people from taking liberties with the Queen's woods and he was directed to secure the coöperation of the governors for the passing of acts favorable to this preservation.

The original authority for the interference in the abuses committed against the royal pines was the last clause of the charter granted to Massachusetts in 1691 which supplanted the original charter withdrawn through Randolph's activity in 1684. The new charter reserved to the crown "all trees of the diameter of twenty-four inches and upwards at twelve inches from the ground," growing in the province on ground not before granted to any private person. These trees were not to be destroyed without license from the crown, under a penalty of £100 for every tree cut. Those terms, practically unchanged, not only served as the basis of the mast laws throughout the colonial period, but passed on later into Canada, and were even enacted, *mutatis mutandis*, by Massachusetts after the Revolution.[2]

This measure, together with an Order in Council of 1699 to the same point, was not enough to awe the cutters, especially in New Hampshire, where a separate government had recently been set up. After meeting constant defiance in the woods, Bridger was able to secure in 1708 from the reluctant New Hampshire legis-

---

[1] *Cal. S. P., A. & W. I.*, 1699, p. 537; 1700, pp. 563, 564, 682; 1702–03, pp. 135, 385, 386.

[2] *Acts and Resolves of the Province of Massachusetts Bay*, i, 20; compare *Laws of the Commonwealth of Massachusetts*, 1780–1800, i, 108.

lature an act couched in terms similar to those of the Massachusetts charter.[1] The Massachusetts legislators were less compliant. In spite of pressure from the governor, they refused to pass a bill proposed by Bridger, repeating the provisions of the charter of 1691, whereupon Bridger drew up a rough draft for an act of Parliament.[2] The result was "An Act for the Preservation of White and other Pine trees growing in Her Majesty's Colonies ... for the masting of Her Majesty's Navy," passed in 1711; for England was trying to strengthen Bridger's hand while he was arguing with the lumbermen.[3] The new act declared that the mast reservations of the Massachusetts charter were to be effective in the colonies from Maine to New Jersey. It was more to the point than the act of 1705, which forbade the cutting of small "Pitch Pine and Tar Trees, not being within any Fence or actual Inclosure, under the growth of twelve inches Diameter."[4] The earlier act was occasioned by the interest in colonial naval stores, while the 1711 measure directly concerned potential masts for the Navy.

This latter act proved little more effective than the charter clause or the colonial enactment. Ten years later, it was declared inadequate, and events in the New England forests had certainly proved it so. The more stringent terms of the act of 1721 declared that,

no Person or Persons whatsoever ... do or shall presume to cut, fell or destroy any white Pine Trees, not growing within any Township or the Bounds or Limits thereof, in any of the said Colonies or Plantations, without His Majesty's Royal License for so doing had first been obtained,

and the measure was extended to include Nova Scotia.[5] This act, forbidding the cutting of *any* pine, was more severe than the former twenty-four-inch limit, and was designed to guard the forest succession for the future. These terms were reënacted in the final blanket act of 1729, which provided better machinery

---

[1] *Cal. S. P., A. & W. I.*, 1706–08, p. 755; see *Ibid.*, pp. 697–700; 1701, p. 671; 1702, pp. 482, 483; 1702–03, p. 386; R. O., C. O. Index, 8303, *Orders in Council*, p. 18.

[2] *Cal. S. P., A. & W. I.*, 1708–09, pp. 19, 31, 32, 197, 442, 560; 1710–11, p. 10.

[3] 9 Anne, c. 17.

[4] 3 & 4 Anne, c. 10, sec. 6.

[5] 8 Geo. I, c. 12.

for the enforcement of the regulations.[1] This act of 1729 was in effect until the Revolution.

Mast reservations were not the only provisions of that act of 1729. It modified and recapitulated several previous acts passed to stimulate the supply of naval stores, chiefly by means of bounties.[2] In 1704, when Charles XII was enforcing his most obnoxious commercial restrictions against the English, the growing discontent with the unfavorable Baltic balance of trade and the precarious dependence on the Northern Crowns found expression in "An Act for encouraging the Importation of Naval Stores from America." The preamble of the act reviewed admirably the reasons which impelled England to turn to the colonies.[3] In this statement of the mercantilist doctrine of commerce and colonies, the American plantations, "still maintained and protected at a great expense," could furnish in "a more certain and beneficial Manner" those articles of such vital importance to the Navy, "now being brought in mostly from foreign Parts, in foreign Shipping, at exorbitant and arbitrary rates." Bounties of £4 per ton for tar and pitch, £3 per ton for "Rozin or Turpentine," £6 per ton for hemp, and £1 per ton for masts, yards, and bowsprits, were offered, and the Navy was to have the preëmption of all such articles within twenty days of their arrival in England. In return, these articles were included in the "enumerated" list, with sugar, tobacco, indigo, cotton, and dye-woods, which were to be sent to no country except England.

There is a close relation between these acts and the Baltic situation, which grew more tense as Charles XII added maritime depredations to commercial restrictions.[4] In 1721, when Charles XII was dead and the British fleet under Norris was cruising the Baltic to prevent the preponderance of Russian influence, Parliament again took up the question, analyzing a weighty array of petitions, memorials, and reports on the subject.[5] As usual, the

---

[1] 2 Geo. II, c. 35.

[2] Raynal, *Philosophical and Political History of Settlements and Trade*, vii, 396–399; see *Cal. S. P., A. & W. I.*, 1700, pp. 563–567; 1710–11, pp. 46–49.

[3] 3 & 4 Anne, c. 10; see text of preamble in Appendix A.

[4] See pp. 176, 177.

[5] Hist. MSS Com., *House of Lords MSS, passim.*

THE BROAD ARROW IN THE COLONIES   251

Lords of Trade advocated the bounties, in spite of the Navy
Board's rejection of American tar as dirty and of "too hot a nature." The colonial output had responded to the stimulus, and
the mast exports from America had trebled, though even in that
period of Baltic trouble, the largest number of masts shipped in
any year was 261 in 1713, when 1981 came from Europe.[1] The
act of 1721 maintained these bounties and removed the duties on
all forms of American "lumber" (this American word being first
officially recognized, in a cautious manner), but lumber was added
to the list of enumerated articles. The provisions were extended
to Scotland to stimulate the production of masts and tar in the
fir forests there. In the blanket act of 1729, the bounties, which
had expired in 1725, were renewed in modified form. The bounties on masts and hemp were kept the same, but those on tar,
pitch, and turpentine were lowered to £2 4s and £1 10s per ton,
respectively.[2] These remained in force until 1777, showing a
steady increase from a total average of about £16,000 a year in
1730–40 to about £35,000 in the decade preceding the Revolution.
The total cost to the Navy, which reluctantly paid the bounties
ostensibly created in its interest, came to £1,471,719 from 1706
to 1776.[3] More than half of this went to the southern colonies
for naval stores, but the figures indicate the development of the
mast trade as well.

The act of 1729 was bound to draw violent protests from the
colonists, whose agents petitioned in vain against its passage.[4]
The mast reservations were entirely contrary to their interests,
and even the "encouragement of naval stores" benefitted England more than it did America. The bounties helped to develop
the great naval stores industry of the south, but the Navy itself
scorned American tar and pitch. In the central and northern
colonies the mast bounties and the removal of the lumber duties
were more than offset by the sweeping restrictions on all pines
and the threat to cut off the lumber trade to southern Europe and
to the foreign colonies in the West Indies, which was an important

[1] Lord, *Industrial Experiments*, Appendix.   [2] 2 Geo. II, c. 35.
[3] R. O., N. B. Out Letters, 2204, *N. B. to Adm.*, Apr. 17, 1777 — with amount of
bounties each year. See Appendix B.   [4] *H. C. J.* 1727–32, p. 344.

part of New England's commerce. With some of the other
enumerated articles, America had the compensating advantage
that it enjoyed a monopoly of the English market, but in the case
of masts and timber there was only a twenty-per-cent duty to
protect it against Baltic products. The colonial opposition,
however, centered on the Broad Arrow policy.

After this display of interest in the colonies, unusual at that
period, Parliament lapsed into the general apathy regarding
America which characterized the first half of the eighteenth century. This nearly coincided with the withdrawal of English fleets
from the Baltic, where Charles XII and Peter had been partly
responsible for the brief attention to the colonies. The burden of
carrying out this policy fell upon the Surveyors General of His
Majesty's Woods and Forests in America, and their deputies.
They had to meet the continuous opposition of the colonists in
their legislatures, courts, sawmills, and forests — an opposition
ranging from discussion over the title to private property to such
direct action as throwing a deputy into a pond.

The men who held this office were a varied lot. John Bridger,
who had been in the struggle to save the pines since he came over
in 1696 as an agent of the Navy Board, devoted his entire energies
to the contest, while Surveyor General from 1705 to 1718. His
fate was that of the official who rigorously enforces an unpopular
law which affects the interests of those in influence, and he was
frequently charged with peculation.[1] Lacking political connections himself, he learned in 1718 that, while no fault was to be
found with his work, he was removed in favor of Charles Burniston.[2] This new incumbent never appeared on the scene, but depu-
tized the office to Robert Armstrong, an inefficient, unpopular
customs officer at Portsmouth.[3] Bridger offered to stay on as a
deputy, and, unpaid for two years, carried on some of his severest
conflicts until 1720. "'T is very hard," he wrote, "to serve the
King all my life and at last to want bread and do the Duty."[4]

---

[1] *Cal. S. P., A. & W. I.*, 1704–05, pp. 84, 87, 476; 1710–11, p. 152; *Cal. Treas.
Papers*, 1708–14, pp. 18, 19, 307, 311, 398, 530.

[2] *Ibid.*, 1714–19, pp. 187, 190, 242, 243.

[3] *Ibid.*, pp. 465, 466; 1720–28, pp. 28, 86.

[4] Lord, *Industrial Experiments*, p. 97; *Cal. Treas. Papers*, 1720–28, p. 104.

Armstrong received the same charges of bribery and extortion that had been levelled against Bridger.[1] In 1728 the surveyorship fell to a second-rate Irish soldier of fortune, David Dunbar, an arrogant, indigent reduced colonel who also secured the lieutenant governorship of New Hampshire. His spy system, his high-handed seizures, and the rich feathering of his nest in the Sagadahoc region drew unusual antipathy from the colonists.[2]

In 1743 the position was secured by the Wentworth family, where it was held for seventy years by two members. The elder John Wentworth had tried to obtain the appointment in 1723. Benning Wentworth finally paid Dunbar £2000 for the office. The new governor of New Hampshire, in paying such a price for the guardianship of the woods, was interested in more than the salary, now £800, from which he was to support four deputies. The Wentworth clan were virtual rulers of New Hampshire, and the basis of the fortune which enabled them to live in such princely style was the lumber trade. Benning himself had been extremely interested in this, and Mark Hunking Wentworth grew wealthy as agent for the royal masts at Portsmouth. Family control of the surveyorship, to further their own business and to check rivals, was quite evidently desirable under the circumstances. Less history was made in the Broad Arrow controversy in this administration than any other, for the King's interest in the pines did not weigh heavily on Benning Wentworth during most of the twenty-three years in which he was their rather neglectful custodian.[3]

John Wentworth, later Sir John, succeeded to the governorship and the surveyorship, which his uncle, Benning, abdicated in 1766. With all of Bridger's zeal and interest in the office, he possessed political and social prestige and tact, which the other lacked. He prosecuted the offenders with vigor, but with his conciliatory spirit and his reasonable interpretation of the

---

[1] *Cal. Treas. Papers*, 1720–28, pp. 135, 533; 1729–30, p. 55; *Journal of the Commissioners for Trade and Plantations*, 1718–22, pp. 391–393.

[2] *Cal. Treas. Papers*, 1720–28, p. 516; 1731–34, pp. 417, 418; Williamson, *History of Maine*, ii, 165, 173, 178; *Maine Historical Society, Collections*, 1st ser., ix, 80.

[3] *Cal. Treas. Papers*, 1720–28, pp. 222, 253; *Cal. Treas. Books and Papers*, 1742–43, pp. 336, 428, 438; Mayo, *John Wentworth, passim*.

King's interest, he irritated the colonists less than most of his predecessors had done. He saw the necessary modifications of the policy with the clearness of a statesman. When the Revolution drove the Broad Arrow policy, along with Sir John, from New England, he carried it to Canada. There it received its justification from the naval point of view in offering an unfailing supply of masts during the long wars with Revolutionary and Napoleonic France.[1]

As far as this study is concerned, that saving of the Navy during those twenty years is the chief point of interest. The more immediate effect of the Broad Arrow, in offering one of the earliest and most contniuous outlets of colonial hostility to English dominion, is very important, however, because of the bearing which it had in paving the way for the Revolution, which temporarily cut off that mast supply. One cannot subscribe fully to Sewall's statement: "The great issue began in the forests of Maine in the contests of her lumbermen with the King's Surveyor, as to the right to cut, and the property in white pine trees";[2] but as an instance of chronic irritation and defiance, more local perhaps, but as continuous as even the constitutional or commercial opposition, it is a factor to be considered in connection with the causes of the Revolution.

The basis of this opposition of the colonists to the reservation of pines was their questioning of the right of Parliament to encroach on what they considered private property. It was a general characteristic of the spirit of the Revolution at the outset that the Americans were trying to preserve the rights they already enjoyed rather than to gain new freedom. From the very first years of settlement they had cut timber freely on lands to which they thought they had clear title. The new laws struck at the root of this. A question of the justice of the royal claims began with the first restrictive acts and lasted until the Revolution. Strengthened by this theory, the colonists justified their evasions of the laws. "Lett Acts never soe strong made, and strictt, if Act putt in execution, will never obtain judgmt. for the Crown, because Crown never had rightt: soil being in the natives,

[1] See Chapter IX. [2] Sewall, *Ancient Dominions of Maine*, p. 328.

as judges of Courtt have declared, and all persons as judges agtt. Queen's right," wrote the lieutenant governor of New Hampshire in 1710.[1]

The question of the government's right to ship timber has already been considered. France had its *martelage*, instituted by Colbert in 1668, whereby naval purveyors could mark and cut any tree in the kingdom fit for ship timber, and this policy had been extended to the French settlements in Canada. A similar prerogative had been claimed by the English kings until the Civil War, together with the right of preëmption of all naval materials offered for sale. A Parliament, whose members nearly all owned oak groves, denied this right to the Navy after the Restoration, when some Englishmen, it will be recalled, refused to sell the trees which the Navy desired.[2]

The act of 1729 practically imposed on the English colonies the very situation from which Parliament had freed itself at home. All timber, masts, and naval stores were to be sent solely to England, where for twenty days the naval authorities had the right of preëmption. More than this, the laws approached the provisions of the French *martelage* in selecting naval trees on private property. The different acts had expressly excluded trees on private property, but a long dispute arose as to what that term implied.

The royal interpretation of "private property" practically rendered that term nugatory, so that, in spite of appearances, the pines were virtually being commandeered for the Navy. The colonists had considered that they held a clear and unreserved title to their lands, because no mention had been made of pines in the original patents. The officials answered that the abrogation of the Massachusetts charter by a Chancery writ in 1684 had wiped the slate clean, justifying the portion of the new charter in 1691 which reserved the great pines except on private property settled at that time.[3]

In an attempt to evade this, there had been a rapid creation of "paper townships" — grants of large tracts of practically unsettled wild lands being given to prominent citizens who were to

---

[1] *Cal. S. P., A. & W. I.*, 1710–11, pp. 280, 281.   [2] See pp. 62, 63, 227.
[3] See *Cal. S. P., A. & W. I.*, 1710–11, pp. 82, 83, 99, 123.

act as absentee proprietors until the townships should be popu-
lated.[1] To check this wholesale extension of "private property"
for lumbering purposes, the act of 1729 declared that the trees in
"any townships laid out or to be laid out hereafter" in any of the
colonies were subject to the Broad Arrow, while in the province
of Massachusetts Bay no pines over twenty-four inches in diameter, "not growing within some soil or tract of land the said
province granted before October 7, 1690," were to be cut without
license. So far as Massachusetts proper was concerned, the Crown
had a good case, but pines were of less importance there than in
many other regions. In Connecticut even the townships established before 1686 were not exempt.[2]

It was in Maine that the hypocrisy of the "private property"
clause was most evident, for Maine was rapidly becoming the
center of the mast and lumber industry. Under the provisions of
1729, very little land at all was under private ownership in the
eyes of the Crown, for the settlers who had penetrated into those
eastern forests before 1690 had been killed or driven out by the
French and Indians. It mattered little if property were respected
in Boston or on Cape Cod where there were few white pines; the
men who had been established for a dozen years or more at Casco
Bay or on the Kennebec, where the great mast trees grew, were
liable to visits of the Surveyor General.

These rights over the pines to eastward created a lively stir in
the provincial government at Boston about 1720, for at that time
and for another century Maine was a part of Massachusetts.
Governor Shute and his Council strongly supported Bridger in
his activities; but the House of Representatives of the General
Court threw itself decidedly into opposition to the Broad Arrow
policy, "for upon no other subject than the timber was the House
more sensitive." Elisha Cooke, one of the prominent colonial
politicians, led the attack on Bridger and his pretensions. The
ingenious argument that the purchase of the original patents to
Mason and Gorges made Maine the "private property" of Massachusetts was overthrown by the King's Advocate, and the legis-

[1] *Cal. Treas. Papers*, 1720–28, pp. 54, 533; *Acts. P. C. (Col.)*, Unbound Papers,
pp. 164, 165, 194–196.
[2] Conn. Historical Society, *Wolcott Papers*, p. 309.

lature grudgingly recognized the King's right to reserve the pines for the Navy. A resolution was passed, however, declaring that the great number of pines which had been cut into twenty-foot logs in Maine might once have been fit for masts but were no longer, and "although the cutting them should be allowed to be an infringement of His Majesty's rights reserved in the charter," yet in their present condition the King's rights had ceased, and it was the duty of the colony to seize them and convert them for their own use. A committee was appointed for that purpose.[1] This virtual sanction on the part of their own legislature emboldened the lumbermen in their attacks upon the pines, and in the next election the party of Cooke won several new seats in the General Court.

This colonial legislature was to be reckoned among the opponents of the Surveyor General from that time on. In 1730, in 1736, and again in 1743, the feeling in regard to property rights in the woods was still strong, and the legislature refused to pass new laws against trespass, declaring that the present ones were adequate if properly executed.[2] Even the governors' councils at times opposed the Broad Arrow, except the New Hampshire Council which was packed with Wentworths.[3] Though the commission of the Surveyor General enjoined the aid and assistance of "all our Governors, Lieutenant Governors, Justices of the Peace, constables, and all other civil officers" under threats, this support could not always be relied upon, with New Hampshire, where governor and surveyor general were usually one, again an exception. The governors of Massachusetts often gave hearty support, and usually maintained the appearance of it, although Governor Belcher had a sharp dispute with Dunbar over mast rights, while Governor Roger Wolcott upheld the colonial view of private property in Connecticut.[4]

---

[1] *Journal of the House of Representatives of Massachusetts*, i, 171, 181; ii, 109, 363–366, 381, 386; *Acts P. C. (Col.)*, 1720–45, pp. 93, 94; Hutchinson, *History of Massachusetts*, ii, 228; Williamson, *History of Maine*, ii, 96.

[2] *Ibid.*, ii, 188, 213; *Cal. Treas. Papers*, 1731–34, 418.

[3] *Mass. Hist. Soc. Coll.*, 5th series, vi, 207.

[4] Conn. Hist. Soc., *Wolcott Papers*, pp. 235, 309, 310; *Journal of the House of Representatives of Massachusetts*, i, 130; ii, 173; iii, 4.

The act of 1729 had restricted "private property" to lands actually settled and enclosed, and outside of Massachusetts even the 1690 date did not apply. There were immediate protests that enclosing the land, which might perhaps be feasible in England, was out of the question in the pine forests of America, where the expense would destroy any possible profit and the fences would use those very trees which they were intended to protect.[1]

In the dispute over the status in Maine in 1720, Cooke's party had to grant the validity of the royal claims to the mast pines. They suggested, however, that the fairest thing to the landowners and the surest way to prevent the destruction of great pines was to grant compensation equal to the lumber value of the tree for every pine taken for a royal mast, which would be worth ten times as much as the lumber.[2] Fifty years later, the Proprietors of the Kennebec Purchase, declining Wentworth's offer to submit the question of property rights to the courts, respectfully suggested once more that such a compensation be given. Wentworth forwarded this to the Treasury, saying that the proposal might be worthy of consideration "not as a matter of right, but as a Gratuity for the Timber being found well preserved upon their Land."[3]

The "private property" issue was not dead, therefore, in 1771, for Wentworth's proposal of compensation was a compromise in a case where the royal claim was none too sure. The petitioners — James Bowdoin, James Pitts, Sylvester Gardiner, and Benjamin Hallowell — presented a patent of purchase from New Plymouth in 1649, though the region was not definitely settled until a century later. They avoided litigation, they claimed in their petition to the Admiralty, as a "Lawsuit would appear like a refusal to supply Masts for His Majesty's service"; but they stated that they would accept reasonable compensation.[4] Went-

[1] *Pennsylvania Gazette*, May 17, 1729.
[2] Hutchinson, *History of Mass.*, ii, 229.
[3] R. O., Treas., I, 495, f. 119, *Wentworth to Commissioners of the Treasury*, Dec. 4, 1771.
[4] *Ibid. ff.* 123, 124, *Petition of Proprietors of Kennebec Purchase to Adm.*, Dec. 18, 1771; Treas., I, 471, ff. 149, 150, *Wentworth to Committee of Kennebec Purchase*, Oct. 19, 1769, June 29, 1770.

worth, in his later proposals for reforming the Broad Arrow administration, included compensation, which, if introduced earlier, might have been an effective means of saving the great trees.

The authorities were not all as conciliatory as Sir John, and the review of the theoretical dispute over naval interests and private property may well close with an order of Armstrong's in 1734, in Nova Scotia, which reads like a preëmption claim of Henry VIII or Colbert:

> An immediate demand in the King's navy of timber of specific dimensions. Certain inhabitants assert that they have no such timber on their own grounds. This authorizes them [the contractors] to cut and sell the requisite timber wherever it may be found on either side of this river unless the inhabitants on whose ground it is found are willing to cut and sell it at a fair price.[1]

This exchange of theories not only showed the contrast between Parliament's attitude toward oaks in England and pines in America, but it salved the New England conscience in its timber operations in defiance of the law. The law was almost impossible to execute to the letter. No surveyor with a few deputies could mark all the eligible trees, and the colonists, who depended on lumbering for a living, were not going to wait for the chopping of the Broad Arrow in woods where only a few pines in a thousand might be suitable for masts.

From the imposing of the first restrictions in 1690 to the outbreak of the Revolution, the pine laws were violated constantly.[2] Armstrong probably did not exaggerate when he wrote Burniston in 1721 that, during the previous twenty years, where one mast had been sent to England on contract for the Navy, five hundred pines suitable for masts had been cut or destroyed for other purposes.[3] "To the eastward at York, Wells, Keinbank, Saco, Scarborough, Cascobay, Keinbeck, and Pemquid they cut and saw at pleasure and send them where they please," came a complaint from Portsmouth in 1747.[4] "Shingle and Clapboard makers are

---

[1] Nova Scotia Archives, *Commission Book*, 1720–41, p. 199.

[2] *Cal. S. P., A. & W. I., passim; Cal. Treas. Papers*, 1708–14, pp. 18, 19; 1714–19, p. 152.

[3] *Ibid.*, 1720–28, p. 87.

[4] R. O., N. B. Out Letters, 2183, *N. B. to Adm.*, May 15, 1747.

the greatest destroyers of the White Pines," wrote Scammell in
1772 from Falmouth, for, "extremely delicate in their choice,"
they chopped into great trees to see if they split well, continuing
"this illegal practice until they find such as are suitable. The
trees thus wounded, soon perish, to the great detriment of His
Majesty's Navy." [1] The large quantities, not only of shingles and
clapboards, but of all sorts of lumber, even to ready-made frames
for houses, that were sawn out in the frontier sawmills, came
chiefly from contraband pines.

The mast agents, who secured from the contractors royal
licenses to cut pines for the naval contracts, were themselves

great destroyers of the woods under the colour of masting . . . for all or most
of them are concerned in Saw Mills & they take contracts to have greater
liberty to log & sell masts to private persons as cut off private property. It
may seem a paradox that men employed to get masts for the king should cut
them into boards that wont sell for half the price. [2]

The privilege had been abused even in the days of Bridger, who
made particular complaint of the "illegal" cutting of John
Plaisted, an influential provincial judge who served as agent for
John Taylor, the naval mast contractor. Plaisted flaunted a
royal license in defiance of Bridger's commission and, as the latter
wrote, "the more I spoke, the more he cutt." [3] The settlers strenuously objected to these intruders, who often had no particular
interest in the region and slashed far more than was necessary to
fulfil the mast contracts. [4] The men who cut for the contractors
were also New Englanders, but the settlers felt the injustice of the
abuse of these official privileges denied to themselves. With such
an example, it was not unnatural that everyone joined in the illicit
chopping.

On the whole, it was more profitable to cut lumber than masts.
The latter, for one thing, were too bulky to be smuggled out
easily. It was pointed out that four or five logs could be cut out
of a large tree, carried to the river-bank for fifty or sixty shillings,
and after free floatage to the mills, an additional thirty or forty

[1] R. O., Treas., 1, 496, f. 62, *Scammell to Wentworth*, July 20, 1772.
[2] R. O., N. B. Out Letters, 2183, *N. B. to Adm.*, May 15, 1747.
[3] *Cal. S. P., A. & W. I.*, 1706–08, p. 697.
[4] *Ibid.*, 1710–11, pp. 34, 39; *Maine Hist. Soc., Coll.*, 2nd ser., vii, 398.

shillings would pay for the conversion into boards or joists worth fifteen pounds. In the case of a mast, on the other hand,

the Hawling to the Falls, hewing (in which they often prove defective) and rafting down the river costs near as much as the price they are to have by contract, and often when they come to be survey'd and deliver'd have 4 or 5 lost in their year's work and then they are considerable losers.[1]

The illicit cutting was carried on in a region so extensive and so wild that it was impossible for the most energetic and conscientious Surveyor General, with his small staff, to do more than make occasional examples of the offenders.[2] The deputies had orders to seize any pines over twenty-four inches in diameter in Massachusetts and Maine, and of any size in the other colonies. They were to mark them with the Broad Arrow and sell this confiscated timber. Part of the proceeds of the sale was to go to the informer, part to the deputies and anyone helping them make the seizure, and the rest to defray the expenses of trial.[3] The deputies visited the woods to surprise the cutters and haulers at work, and they searched the sawmills and finally the shipping ports for illicit timber. They found that some cutters even marked pines with the Broad Arrow themselves, to scare away rivals. Armstrong, in a single survey in 1700, found 25,000 logs, two thirds of which exceeded the two-foot limit.[4] The methods of evasion were ingenious. Timber seized in the woods was thrown into the rivers, and later sawed to avoid identification, while that confiscated at the mills was also converted into planks and boards as soon as the officials' backs were turned. This task was assigned to the most impecunious sawyer, who would be unable to pay any fines imposed upon him. Knowing that a board over two feet wide would be *prima facie* evidence of illegal cutting, the mills turned them out just within the limit. The inner side of the roofs of old houses of the colonial period will reveal many splendid pine boards, now a rich golden brown with age, twenty-two and twenty-three inches wide, but almost never the damning twenty-four. Even if the

---

[1] R. O., N. B. Out Letters, 2183, *N. B. to Adm.*, May 15, 1747.

[2] See esp. *Cal. S. P., A. & W. I.*, 1706–08, pp. 697–700; *Cal. Treas. Papers*, 1708–14, p. 165; 1720–28, p. 87; 1729–30, p. 55.

[3] Conn. Hist. Soc., *Wolcott Papers*, pp. 232, 310.

[4] *Cal. S. P., A. & W. I.*, 1708–09, p. 19; *Cal. Treas. Paper*, 1720–28, pp. 87, 406.

condemned timber were offered for sale by the deputies, no one would purchase it. This evasion was not confined to any particular period of the Broad Arrow régime — Bridger was complaining of it in 1700 and John Wentworth was still trying to check it in 1774.

The attempt to enforce the regulations was met not only by protests in the legislature but often by a direct application of ruder methods called "swamp law" as well. Royal prestige was rather diluted by the time it had penetrated to the upper Piscataqua or Androscoggin. This was more true in the case of the earlier surveyors than of the Wentworths, but even the pomp and power of those Portsmouth magnates did not always shield their deputies from harm. Bridger's tireless activity in seizing logs and prosecuting offenders drew bitter hostility and calumny upon his head. Armstrong complained of "the barbarous treatment officers meet with that do their duty," and declared that he was often in danger o his life.[1] The opposition to the h'gh-handed Dunbar was even more violent. The best that can be said for him is that he was active and energetic; but his methods were unfortunate. In 1730, several settlers living near the Sheepscot River complained to the General Court that Dunbar "came with an armed force, turned them from their lands, seized their timber, burned and destroyed their houses," and "even threatened to throw them into confinement."[2] He made free use of the spy system, and the seizures of this arrogant Irishman, "plumed with a brief authority," galled the colonists.[3] At Exeter in 1634 they did more than protest. When Dunbar sent a company under a deputy to remove in a boat some lumber which he had seized, the people, dressed in "Boston Tea Party" fashion, gathered while the agents were drinking at the tavern and scuttled the boat, so that it nearly sank on the return trip to Portsmouth. At Dover, Dunbar's life was menaced when he made a threat against anyone who prevented his carrying away a boat load of confiscated timber.[4]

---

[1] *Cal. Treas. Papers*, 1720–28, pp. 406, 407.

[2] Williamson, *History of Maine*, ii, 170; R. O., N. B. Out Letters, 2183, *N. B. to Adm.*, May 15, 1747.

[3] Belknap, *History of New Hampshire*, ii, 90.   [4] *Ibid.*

In 1759, Benning Wentworth complained to Governor Wolcott of Connecticut that Daniel Blake, his deputy, had been seized at Middletown by one Whittemore 'and thrown into a Millpond whereby he was in great danger of being drowned." [1] A few years later, the settlers on the upper Connecticut above Northampton entered the camp of the men who were cutting masts for the Navy on Ingersoll's contract and removed all the fodder, so that the remaining mast sticks could not be taken out of the woods. [2] There were similar episodes in the Maine forests, where the settlers and Indians purposely led Scammell astray in his survey of 1772. Terrorizing royal officials in quest of naval timber was not unprecedented, for the royal purveyor in Shotover Forest in England had reported himself in danger of his life in 1630, and men whom Colbert sent into the Pyrenees to cut masts for the French navy in 1669 were fired upon by the mountaineers. [3]

No one ever actually laid violent hands upon a Wentworth, for Benning seldom acted in person, and if Sir John's execution of the law was vigorous, it was usually in good form. He was especially active along the Maine coast. On one occasion he appeared in person at Brunswick where, though unarmed, he influenced some trespassers to give up their illicit timber. [4] He also kept a careful eye upon the questionable exports from Falmouth. Hearing of operations in the eastern part of the state in 1772, he secured a boat from Captain Mowatt of the *Canceaux* and had his deputy make a sudden descent and seizure "of about 200 tons of timber and 70 thousand feet of Deals cut from the King's woods." "Although the value of the seizure is not considerable yet the unexpected manner in which it was effected has been of great use in restraining Trespasses as people find their Remote Situation does not save them," he wrote in requesting a regular patrol schooner. Wentworth claimed that he had reduced the illegal cutting of the colonists to a hundredth of its former extent, and in Tory spirit, wrote in 1773 that it was confined to "only the

[1] Conn. Hist. Soc., *Trumbull Papers*, i, 67; Gipson, *Jared Ingersoll*, p. 86.

[2] *Ibid.*, p. 101.

[3] *Cal. S. P., Dom.*, 1629–31, p. 425; Colbert, *Lettres, Instructions et Mémoires*, vol. iii, pt. 1, p. 386 n.; pt. 2, p. 447.

[4] Mayo, *John Wentworth*, p. 52.

very lowest and abandon'd among them, who will ever revile and calumniate every Law and its officer that prevents their enormities vainly hoping that thereby they shall overcome all government."[1] A royal governor could apply that description to many, two years before Lexington, and his estimate of his own efficiency was written, of course, for official eyes.

The lumbermen were not the only New Englanders who defied these acts of Parliament. From Portsmouth and Falmouth there was a constant illicit export of masts and lumber to the French and Spanish West Indies and to Spain and Portugal. Many New England fortunes grew from England's laxity in enforcing the Navigation Acts, and so far as lumber in general was concerned, the fact that it was listed among the enumerated commodities in 1729 meant next to nothing. Lumber and fish were what New England sent on the first leg of the prosperous triangular trade to the West Indies and across the Atlantic. If the customs authorities winked at the export of lumber in general to foreign countries, the Surveyor General often checked them up on the sending of masts, spars, and bowsprits, which had been "enumerated" twenty-five years earlier. Around 1700, Partridge, the lieutenant governor of New Hampshire, had been making fourfold profits in his extensive trade in masts and ship timber with Lisbon and Cadiz, and the information sent to the Lords of Trade by Bellomont and Bridger was partly responsible for the "enumeration" which stipulated that these articles should be sent only to England. Far more than ordinary lumber, the export of such naval necessities to a potential maritime enemy had an important political significance.[2]

The illicit trade continued in spite of the enumeration, and even Benning Wentworth himself was contracting with the Spanish court for naval timber in 1739, on the eve of the long "War of Jenkins's Ear" against Spain and just five years before he became custodian of the forests. During that naval war, the Spanish were reported to have sent commissioners to Portsmouth, where they

---

[1] Mayo, *John Wentworth*, p. 52.

[2] R. O., C. O., Index 8303, Orders in Council, May 5 and 23, 1700; *Cal. S. P., A. & W. I.*, 1699, p. 539; 1700, pp. 557, 682; *Cal. Treas. Papers*, 1714–19, p. 152; *Journal, House of Rep. of Mass.*, ii, 173, 174.

purchased masts for the warships which were building at Havana, while French privateers were supplied from the same source.[1] The law required that a bond be given that the masts were to go to England or to English colonies, but this was evaded, with the connivance of the customs officers, who entered as "baulks" or logs the masts from which a strip three or four inches wide had been chopped on four sides, and later cancelled the bond. Joshua Gee defended such a trade except in time of war. He said that the Spaniards had plenty of fine large oaks and pines, "but their indolent temper is such that if they can purchase what they want with money, they care not to stretch out a hand to help themselves (and I should be sorry that we should stir them up to becoming industrious),"[2] for the Dutch would take this lucrative trade if it were denied to New England. The Surveyors General saw it in a different light, and were interested in the source as well as the destination of mast cargoes. In 1767, John Wentworth wanted Governor Temple's "recommendation to the Custom House at Casco-bay to be vigilant and careful in requiring affidavits of the property and place where all Masts, Yards, & Bowsprits above sixteen inches diam. were cut and hal'd, and to verify the identity of the entry for exportation."[3]

The various elements of colonial society thus seemed inclined to violate the pine laws — legislatures, lumbermen, and merchants were against them, and even the royal governors were divided. The most damaging opposition of all came from the fact that the courts joined the others in defiance of the Broad Arrow. The charter of 1691 had specified a penalty of £100 for each violation, and Bridger secured definite evidence in dozens of cases. The remoteness of the courts, the prejudices of the judges and of any colonial jury, the intimidation of witnesses, and the fact that the costs fell upon the slender salary of the Surveyor General, all combined to render convictions next to impossible.[4] In order to facilitate prosecution, the act of 1729 provided that violations of

[1] R. O., N. B. Out Letters, 2183, *N. B. to Adm.*, May 15, 1747.

[2] Gee, *Trade and Navigation of England Considered*, p. 97.

[3] Mass. Hist. Soc. MSS, *Bowdoin-Temple Papers*, Wentworth to Temple, Sept. 3, 1767.

[4] *Cal. S. P., A. & W. I.*, 1708–09, p. 259; 1710–11, p. 524.

the mast laws were under the jurisdiction of the Vice-Admiralty courts at Boston and New York, where a royal judge with large authority, unhampered by a jury, would be more apt to render a decision against the trespassers.[1] Even this was insufficient. The distance of this court from the timberlands increased the difficulty and cost of prosecution, and the Admiralty judges themselves were not to be depended upon. Dunbar charged the elderly Judge Byfield with encouraging offenders and generally clearing them by his decrees;[2] and in 1773 Wentworth proposed one Parker for the position in order to ensure prosecution.[3]

The colonists, too, stole a march on the Surveyors General by making prosecutions themselves. Charges of trespass were brought in the colonial courts against loggers cutting masts on contract; and as the Charter of 1691 allowed appeal to England only in cases involving £300 or more, damages were set just below that figure. The most outstanding case of judicial defiance of royal authority in this connection was that of Frost *v.* Leighton. In 1734, Samuel Waldo, the mast agent in Boston, employed William Leighton of Kittery to superintend the cutting of masts on the license of William Gulston of London, the leading mast contractor. Leighton cut pines, already surveyed by Dunbar, on the land of John Frost of Berwick, claiming that the right was reserved to the crown because the land had not been granted by 1691. Frost won a trespass suit for £120 in the Court of Common Pleas of York County, in the April session of 1734. That court had already acquitted other colonists of charges brought by the Surveyors General.[4] Leighton appealed to the Superior Court of Massachusetts Bay, which sustained the decision. Gulston brought some of the weightiest influence in England to bear on the case. The almost omnipotent Newcastle wrote Belcher, but the governor was hostile to Dunbar and practically washed his hands of the matter. In spite of the provision of the Charter that cases under £300 were not subject to appeal, the Privy Council reversed the decision, authorizing Leighton to collect

---

[1] Gipson, *Jared Ingersoll*, pp. 80–84; *Acts P. C. (Col.)*, Unbound Papers, p. 194.

[2] R. O., N. B. Out Letters 2183, *N. B. to Adm.*, May 15, 1747.

[3] R. O., Adm. In Letters from Governors, 3820, *Wentworth to Adm.*, Jan. 13, 1773.

[4] *Cal. Treas. Papers*, 1720–28, p. 135; see *Ibid.*, 1731–34, p. 209.

from Frost. The Superior Court ignored the royal order to this effect in 1737, and also a second order of March 22, 1739, declaring on the second occasion that "the Justices of this Court now present see no reasons to depart from that opinion." [1] In the midst of this case in 1735, the Privy Council agreed with the Board of Trade that a New Hampshire act removing certain sessions of the court from Portsmouth to Exeter, Hampton, and Dover should be revoked as it was "very difficult, if not impracticable," to find a jury in those lumber towns who would give an impartial verdict in mast offenses. [2]

In 1769, Wentworth secured the conviction of several colonists in upper New York for illegal cutting, but the affair was practically nullified by the action of a colonial judge.

> The Whole Cost of the Prosecutions amounting to £162.19.4¾d ster'g . . . fall upon the Crown; For though the Trespassers were without Difficulty convicted, yet they escaped punishment by the unworthy Interposition of Judge Wells in becoming a Trustee in a fictitious conveyance of their Goods and Chattels, which alone were liable,

complained Wentworth. [3] Shortly afterwards the Proprietors of the Kennebec Grant finally instituted lawsuits similar to that of Frost in 1734, so that the naval supply of masts was hampered. [4] These instances are typical of scores of lawsuits which resulted from the Broad Arrow enforcement during the century. The colonists enjoyed the double advantage of virtual immunity from the suits brought against them by the Surveyors General, even in the Vice-Admiralty courts, while they were able to take the offensive against the mast cutters with equal prospects of success. The threats of Wentworth to appeal to the High Court of Admiralty or to the Privy Council were of little avail. When the courts arrayed themselves with the other colonial interests against the Broad Arrow, the policy was bound to fail since the only effective "teeth" for enforcement were removed.

[1] *Acts. P. C. (Col.)*, 1720–45, pp. 461–470; *Colonial Society of Massachusetts Publications*, iii, 246–264; *American Historical Review*, ii, 229–240.

[2] *Acts P. C. (Col.)*, 1720–45, pp. 453, 454.

[3] R. O., Treas. 1, 495, f. 133, *Wentworth to Commissioners of the Treasury*, Dec. 4, 1771; Mayo, *Wentworth*, pp. 56, 57.

[4] See p. 258.

The futility of enforcing the laws on the 1729 basis was recognized by Wentworth himself, who wrote to Lord George Germain during the Revolution:

> The acts of Parliament relative to the preservation of pine timber in America, being merely penal and too general, operated so much against the convenience and even necessities of the inhabitants that, had, or could they have been strictly executed, they would have prevented cultivation, and soon put an end to the lumber trade, both to the West Indies and England, though the latter was an object of parliamentary bounty. Hence it became almost a general interest of the country to frustrate laws which comprehend nearly an unlimited reservation.

The greatest part of the pines, he went on to say, were utterly unfit for masts, yards, or bowsprits and would remain so until they perished, while they had to be removed to clear the land and would make good lumber, "but the whole being equally reserved, it naturally rendered the real object disagreeable to the people, and therefore of course too often defeated the proper effect."[1]

In that period, it will be remembered, forest policy in nearly all the maritime countries was governed chiefly by naval interests. As forest policy, the Broad Arrow laws on the 1729 basis were a decided failure. The Navy had received a regular supply of great masts, it is true; but in a day when men could not foresee the radical changes of 1860 in naval architecture, a forest policy for naval purposes had to reckon on the supply a century or two into the future. Judged by such a standard, the 1729 laws would have failed the Navy. As early as 1736, an unsuccessful attempt was made to modify the laws in Parliament, and a further agitation took place in 1758 with no result.[2] Shortly after John Wentworth's appointment as Surveyor General, he received the support of Lord Hillsborough for a modification of the policy.[3] Instead of the blanket reservation so impossible to enforce, Wentworth suggested that definite tracts of choice pine lands be set aside for naval purposes, and strictly guarded, leaving the rest free for general lumbering. Some wholesale reservations on this plan had

---

[1] R. O., C. O., 5, 175, f. 81, *Wentworth to Germain*, Oct. 12, 1778.

[2] *Ibid.*, 391, 65, *B. of T. Journal*, Oct. 26, Nov. 1, 1758; C. O., 324, 16, ff. 143–158, *B. of T. to King's Attorney and Solicitor General.*

[3] *Acts P. C. (Col.)*, 1766–83, 22, 23; *N. H. Province Papers*, vii, 343.

been made as early as 1730, and Benning Wentworth was instructed in 1743 to make pine reservations of not less than 200,000 acres "free from any contests that may be occasioned by intermixture of private properties," but they were too sweeping in extent.[1] The new policy guided John Wentworth's extensive surveys in 1772, but the Revolution was too close at hand for effective application, and Wentworth's installation of this revised Broad Arrow policy in Canada will be dealt with later. In view of the widespread opposition to these laws, it seems strange that the Massachusetts legislature passed an act with almost the same provisions in 1783. So far as the Broad Arrow in New England is concerned, it had not been successful in its main purpose — the preservation of the great pines for the Navy.

Though the Broad Arrow laws and their enforcement are the outstanding feature of the naval supply of masts from New England, other aspects of that supply deserve consideration. The pine forests were not as inexhaustible as they had appeared to the original settlers. By 1700, it was necessary to go twenty miles into the woods on the Piscataqua for a good mast.[2] A half century later the Portsmouth supply was noticeably affected.

The mast men are obliged to go a mile or two farther into the country every year, being almost got to the foot of the ridge of mountains, it will be difficult (if not impossible) to get the masts over these mountains, therefore the necessity for applying a speedy remedy,

came a report from there in 1747, and the old sources of great masts in general showed indications of reaching the limit.[3]

The solution of the scarcity lay in going farther eastward. The quest for lumber colonized Maine. Even more than for fishing, the original settlers went to hew out a living or a fortune in the pine forests. The first sawmill in America was built in Maine, and a considerable part of the lumber and masts shipped from Portsmouth, which is situated on the boundary, came from the western part of the province. By 1639, the settlers had reached Cape Elizabeth and had shipped a cargo of lumber to England.[4] During

[1] *Cal. Treas. Books and Papers*, 1742–45, p. 336.
[2] *Cal. S. P., A. & W. I.*, 1700, p. 564.
[3] R. O., N. B. Out Letters, 2183, *N. B. to Adm.*, May 15, 1747; *Cal. Treas. Papers*, 1729–30, p. 55.
[4] *Mass. Hist. Soc. Proc.*, iii, 183.

that century, the choppers extended their settlements even farther to the eastward, encouraged by the government, which considered Maine an inexhaustible magazine of masts.[1] The French and Indians, however, wiped out most of this activity during King William's and Queen Anne's wars and threw the mast supply back to the Piscataqua.

After the peace of Utrecht in 1713, there was a new extension of the timber quest into Maine. By 1727, Falmouth on Casco Bay, the present Portland, was established as a regular shipping port for the King's masts. Colonel Thomas Westbrook, as agent for Samuel Waldo, had built a large lumber camp at Scarboro nearby, had hired a large crew of men, and had secured more than a hundred oxen to bring the masts to the shore. A massacre down the coast at Kennebunk temporarily checked the business, for the workers fled in panic, and would not return until the Massachusetts legislature had established a guard of nine soldiers to protect the cutters. Gulston, the contractor, urged the building of a fort at Falmouth to protect the new industry. Westbrook and his successor, Tate, not only furnished naval masts but also developed a thriving private lumber business. The masts came at first from the little Stroudwater River and then from the Presumpscot nearby, but as these limited sources became exhausted, masts from farther afield were floated down the streams and brought along the coast to Falmouth for shipment.[2] As early as 1734, Falmouth built a mast ship of its own, and its general lumber trade gradually gained on Portsmouth; but Wentworth influence kept the larger part of the naval contract business at the old mast port, which shipped five cargoes of masts to the Navy while Falmouth sent but one.[3]

In 1762, a great fire, starting in New Hampshire, swept eastward for some fifty miles, until it burned itself out on the shores

[1] See esp. *Cal. S. P., A. & W. I.*, 1700, p. 564; 1702–03, p. 692; *Cal. Treas. Papers*, 1702–07, p. 182.

[2] *Ibid.*, 1729–30, p. 55; *Acts P. C. (Col.)*, 1720–45, p. 184; *Journal of the House of Rep. Mass.*, vii, 130, 140; *Maine Hist. Soc. Coll.*, ser. 1, ii, 157–166; ser. 2, vii, 390–405; Willis, *History of Portland*, p. 454; Gould, *Portland in the Past*, pp. 198, 199; *New England Weekly Journal*, May 8, 1727.

[3] R. O., N. B. Out Letters, 2180, *N. B. to Adm.*, May 5, 1744; Smith, *Journal*, Oct. 14, 1734.

of Casco Bay after destroying many of the finest pine tracts upon which Portsmouth and Falmouth had been drawing. As a result, the inhabitants whose homes had been ruined moved into eastern Maine. New lumbering settlements immediately sprang up as far to the eastward as Machias, where a sawmill was set up in 1764, with four others by 1770. There was a similar rapid development at Mount Desert and other points along the coast, as well as up the Kennebec and Penobscot Rivers. Georgetown, the present Bath, on the Kennebec, became a port of shipment for naval masts before the Revolution.[1]

This called for activity on the part of John Wentworth and his deputies to protect the new regions and discover where the best pines lay. There had been a fair amount of surveying all through the century, and Bridger alone had marked over 6,000 trees. Wentworth conducted the surveying on a more extensive scale than any of his predecessors. After some preliminary timber ranging, he planned a triple survey in 1771 which would cover the pine regions where settlers were most likely to penetrate. Wentworth himself, with Timothy Ruggles, was to cover north central New England; Adolphus Benzel, Lake Champlain and the St. Lawrence; while Thomas Scammell was to survey eastern Maine. There are detailed accounts of all the surveys, sent in to the authorities of the Treasury and the Admiralty, for the Surveyors were under the authority of the former and were paid by the latter.

Wentworth reported in 1773 that he had in person

traversed the Woods from Winnipisioket to White River Falls on the Connecticut River, thence up the said River to the 45th degree of Latitude, & thence by another direction thro' the pathless wilderness down to the sea coast.

He was evolving the principle of definite localized reservations, and he marked out special pine regions on the upper Connecticut, of which he went on to say:

I informed the nearest, & indeed all the Settlers Hunters and Indians that they must be preserved for His Majesty under the severest penalty of the

---

[1] Defebaugh, *History of the Lumber Industry*, ii, 50, 79-86.

Law & they have all promised me to obey and notify others, that I believe they will be safe.[1]

Benzel discovered splendid mast material along Lake Champlain, though there were signs of considerable devastation already. After stamping the Broad Arrow freely, he drew up one of the first good maps of the locality. He recommended the use of the splendid white oak of the region and the erection of a mast depot at Sorel.[2]

Scammell's survey had more of the police element in it, for he was carrying the Broad Arrow into the region where the fire of 1762 had driven the lumbermen. He found extensive violation of the pine laws, and cruised in a small schooner from port to port and river to river, examining the output of the new mills. Going inland, he put to flight some trespassers on the upper Androscoggin and proceeded then to his survey proper — on the upper Kennebec and Sebasticook and into the region east of the Penobscot. He came to the conclusion "that the Pines were more numerous in the interior Parts, than near the Sea," and remarked the discovery of a pine of old growth with a circumference of over seventeen feet.[3]

Those Maine settlers had more than the royal surveyors to worry them. The predominance of white pine in the settlements of northeastern New England produced a poorly balanced economic life. Absorbed in lumbering, the pioneers neglected agriculture to such an extent that, when grain cargoes failed to arrive from southward, they were sometimes on the point of real starvation. As early as 1631, the Privy Council had to send grain to Portsmouth to keep the lumbermen alive,[4] and the neglect of farming was a problem that affected New Brunswick two centuries later. "The ships and other vessels loading here are a wonderful benefit to us. They take off vast quantities of timber, masts, oar-rafters, &c.," wrote old Parson Smith of Falmouth.[5]

[1] R. O., Adm. In Letters from Governors, 3820, *Wentworth to Adm.*, Jan. 13, 1773.

[2] *Ibid.*, enclosing 16-page report of *Benzel to Wentworth*, Nov. 11, 1772.

[3] R. O., Treas., 1, 496, ff. 62, 63, *Scammell to Wentworth*, July 20, 1772.

[4] *Acts P. C. (Col.)*, 1613–80, p. 160; *Cal. S. P., Col.*, 1574–1660, p. 184.

[5] Smith, *Journal*, Jan. 22, 1765.

His diary, however, is full of passages showing that men could not live by wood alone. "The vessels are sailed to-day. They have left us quite bare and nothing of the country's produce left, only three bushels of corn and some small things," he recorded in 1732.[1] A few years later he wrote, "All the talk is, no corn and no hay, and there is not a peck of potatoes in all the eastern country." [2] Even the taxes were payable in lumber. As in Norway, the situation on the coast in the lumber settlements became desperate when their trade was cut off. In 1779, Timothy Parsons of Pownalborough, a little lumbering settlement on the coast, was pleading for a bushel or two of seed barley for the town, at any price in silver, paper, or lumber. Over half the people, he said, had been without bread for a month, deriving a slight sustenance from clams and small fish. Some had already died of hunger, some were helpless, and there was a general stupor.[3] When the corn ships returned empty to such a town, it seemed as if the end certainly had come.[4]

At the price of this ill-balanced economic life, Maine was the only region to share New Hampshire's original monopoly of the trade in masts for the Royal Navy. The attempt of Connecticut to attract at least part of the mast contracts during the Seven Years' War was no more successful than Lord Bellomont's efforts to draw the trade to New York in 1700. Like the Hudson, the Connecticut River tapped the great pine belt; and when the shortage in New Hampshire became apparent in the middle of the century, Jared Ingersoll, the energetic colonial agent, tried to interest the Navy Board in this fresh supply. The mast pines did not grow in Connecticut itself, whose exports were chiefly of oak, but came from the river above Northampton where Benning Wentworth was granting lands freely on a very doubtful claim to New Hampshire settlers. Ingersoll interested Henniker, the contractor, and secured a mast contract of his own in 1760, but the Wentworth interest, which was powerful in London as well as in

[1] Smith, *Journal*, Aug. 2, 1732.
[2] *Ibid.*, Apr. 8, 1737; see also *Ibid.*, Jan. 3, 1737, May 15, 1741; Adams, *Annals of Portsmouth*, p. 259.
[3] *Mass. Hist. Soc. Proc.*, xliv, 84.
[4] Raymond, *The River St. John*, p. 302.

the colonial forests and ports, prevented the development of a Connecticut supply. Even the settlers from "Deerfield to the Cowhees," where the masts were cut on Ingersoll's contract, were jealous of this activity, which would enrich New Haven, and they actually obstructed the cutters. Consequently, just as the single cargo of masts sent in the *Benjamin* in 1702 was the only direct result of Bellomont's activity, the masts which the *Prince Henry* took to England in 1764 represented Connecticut's sole official contribution to the Navy.[1]

From the commercial standpoint, the mast trade thus concentrated in New Hampshire and Maine was only a small part of the general timber trade of the American colonies. The unprecedented activity of the customs officials in America in the decade preceding the Revolution produced detailed statistics from which it is possible to judge the volume and distribution of the colonial exports of wood. So far as the Navy was concerned, masts were the only object of direct interest, and these represented only one tenth of the total timber export, which in turn was one twentieth of the total export of all materials from the colonies.

Leaving masts for more detailed consideration, the lumber output as a whole deserves attention on account of its relieving the drain on English timber and its developing of an industry essential to a mast supply which would be reliable and not too expensive. Nearly half of the volume of the total timber export in 1770 — £78,121 out of £164,066 — was in oak for cooperage, formed into hogshead or "pipe" staves, headings, and hoops. The exacting requirements of the coopers had converted some of the best oaks in England into barrels for beer and pork, when they might have formed ribs and stern-posts, and the substitution of the somewhat inferior colonial oak relieved this demand.

At £3 a load, American oak was cheaper than English or even Baltic oak, while the soft boards of American white pine sold at a lower price than Baltic or Norway deals. Consequently, colonial

---

[1] *Conn. Hist. Soc. Collections*, vol. xviii, *Fitch Papers*, p. 69; *Ibid.*, vol. xix, *Pitkin Papers*, pp. 99, 242, 243; *New Haven Colony Historical Society Papers*, ix, 255–267; Gipson, *Jared Ingersoll*, pp. 89–109; Weeden, *Economic and Social History of New England*, ii, 578.

oak and pine were used extensively in England for houses and other general building purposes. The shipbuilders, who had to consider economy in the construction of merchantmen, imported American oak in large quantities.[1] The Navy itself used only seventy-one loads of colonial oak during seven years when it was using thousands of loads from Dantzig and Stettin, but the extra-naval use of American oak was so general that New England alone furnished England with more oak timber and plank than the Baltic during most of the period just before the Revolution. The "enumeration" of American lumber never hampered colonial trade to any extent, and Parliament recognized an accomplished fact in 1765, when it permitted the export of lumber, except masts, to Ireland and southern Europe. A further stimulus to the lumber trade was a bounty on American oak for cooperage in 1771, when Parliament was attempting to relieve all unnecessary exhaustion of the forests in the interest of the Navy.[2]

Overshadowed by tobacco and other southern staples, timber represented only a twentieth part of the total exports of the colonies, but this gives no indication of its importance in New England, where it was often the chief output. Ports like Portsmouth and Falmouth depended almost entirely upon it. The trade was widespread, oak being sent from all the colonies north of Carolina, and especially from the region between the James River and Rhode Island. Pine came from the more northern portion of the colonies, Portsmouth alone shipping over 14,000,000 board feet in 1772, more than the combined exports of all the other ports. Great Britain and Ireland received most of the large timber, over a third of the coopers' oak, and one seventh of the boards. Five sixths of the boards went to the West Indies, together with more than half of the staves. Southern Europe and Africa received the small remainder.[3]

Maine had taken from New Hampshire its old primacy in the mast trade by 1772. The mast exports to Europe from the three customs districts of the pine region in that year were:

---

[1] Macpherson, *Annals*, iii, 573.

[2] 5 Geo. III, c. 45; 11 Geo. III, c. 50.

[3] R. O., Customs, 16, 1, *Exports and Imports, American Colonies*, 1768–73; Macpherson, *loc. cit.*

	Falmouth	Portsmouth	Nova Scotia
Masts	382	329	189
Bowsprits	69	80	25
Yards	451	12	283
Spars	476	1086	... [1]

These figures do not include the large number of masts shipped along the coast to other ports in the American colonies. The first three items comprised the large and valuable sticks of pine, while the spars were small spruce sticks of comparatively slight value. The Portsmouth customs district was practically limited to the port of Portsmouth alone, while the Falmouth district included Georgetown and other eastern ports in Maine in addition to Falmouth itself. The mast trade which had developed even farther to the eastward in Nova Scotia will be considered more fully in the next chapter. A number of masts came from some of the other colonies, especially Pennsylvania, which developed a considerable trade just before the Revolution, but the entire naval supply of American masts, together with most of the large masts for the merchant marine, were shipped from Portsmouth and Falmouth. With lumber and fish, they virtually monopolized the export trade of those two ports. Such was the wooden foundation of northern New England's economic structure, erected at the frequent risk of starvation.

As royal authority had come into contact with the settlers of Maine and New Hampshire chiefly in dispute over the Broad Arrow, it was natural that the outbreak of the Revolution reacted in a violent and spectacular manner against the King's masts and those who procured them. The first Continental Congress, in 1774, had adopted the "Association," an agreement to import nothing from England after December 1, 1774, and to export nothing to any British port after September 10, 1775. The armed encounters at Lexington and Concord on April 19, 1775, led to immediate enforcement of the latter provision in the case of masts for the Navy. Spars and other naval materials on Noddle Island in Boston Harbor were burned by the Americans, and the Navy feared a raid which might destroy the stores in the

---

[1] R. O., Customs, *loc. cit.*

dockyard at Halifax.[1] More important was the interruption of the mast supply at Georgetown, Portsmouth, and Falmouth, the regular ports of shipment.

In the Massachusetts Provincial Congress at Concord, eight days before the historic action there, it was reported,

that Col. Thompson be desired immediately to repair to Brunswick, Casco Bay, Woolwich, Georgetown, and other places, and take the most effectual measures to acquaint the people that one Mr. Perry is in the eastern part of the country, endeavoring to supply our enemies with masts, spars and timber, and to make use of all proper and effective measures to prevent their aiding him in procuring the said articles.[2]

The mast procurer referred to was Edward Parry, a Londoner, who was acting as agent for the naval mast contractor. The first trouble arose at Georgetown, where Parry had a crew of mastwrights at King's Dock hewing the great pines which had been brought down the Kennebec by the spring freshets, while ships lay in the stream ready to carry them to the British dockyards. The county committee of safety determined that these royal masts should not be removed or fitted for use and secured Parry's agreement to that effect. Colonel Thompson, however, brought the Georgetown mast supply to a more exciting close. As soon as the news of Lexington and Concord reached the town, some thirty inhabitants hastily armed themselves and hurried to King's Dock. Their leader commanded the mastwrights in the name of the people of Massachusetts Bay to stop work. Leaving Parry and the masts in the hands of the men of Georgetown, the startled mastwrights threw down their adzes, took to their boats, and rowed to the empty mast ships, which dropped down the river. The colonists later made a further seizure of masts at Brunswick. Parry was forced to give a £2000 bond, narrowly escaped hanging, and was imprisoned for a year, while the masts never reached England.[3]

---

[1] R. O., Adm. 1, 485, *Graves to Adm.*, June 7, June 16, 1775; *Barkley to Graves*, May 19, 1775.

[2] *Journals of each Provincial Congress of Massachusetts*, p. 139.

[3] *Ibid.*, 214 n.; R. O., Adm. 1, 485, *Mowatt to Graves*, May 4, 1775; *Maine Hist. Soc. Coll.*, 1st ser., ii, 215, 216; 3rd ser., i, 433–435, 451; Reed, *History of Bath and Environs*, pp. 50–53.

Neither did the masts seized at Portsmouth three weeks later. The Wentworth clan there had divided. John, as governor, remained loyal to the Crown, while Hunking became chairman of the local committee on the colonial side. On May 17, Hunking informed the New Hampshire Provincial Congress that two ships were in port intending to load cargoes of masts, and he asked the opinion of the Congress on the propriety of such a step.[1] Portsmouth did not wait for the decision. Two days later, the local newspaper declared: "A Mast-Ship and the Canso Man of War have arrived here from Casco Bay — Our *Sons* are now in *Motion*, to hold a Conference about Shipping *Masts*, and it 's thought they will vote in the Negative." [2] Captain Barkley of H. M. S. *Scarborough*, then in port, tells the rest of the story in his report to Admiral Graves on May 19:

> Yesterday Governor Wentworth sent me a message by his Secretary acquainting me there was about three hundred Men had assembled to carry away a Quantity of Masts, that were in a Pond near the Town, I asked the Secretary if the Governor desired that I might send my Boats to prevent their so doing, he said no, by no means, for if such a thing was attempted they would immediately cut them to pieces. I ask'd him what they intended to do with them, he replied they were going to carry them higher up the River for their better Security, I asked him where could they be so well secured or safe as under the Protection of a King's Ship and told him if Governor Wentworth, or whoever was the proprietor of these Masts would apply to me, it was in my power to have protected them, as they were made up in Floats to be carried up the River, he said he had no such request to make, about an hour after he was gone I received a Letter from Governor Wentworth . . . by which you may see, that they intend they never shall be made use of for the King or his Service.[3]

It must have been a trying situation for the governor, who had spent years of hard work as Surveyor General in advancing the Navy's supply of masts; but Wentworth was a wise enough man to know the temper of the town. Within two years, three cargoes of the masts gathered for the British Navy at Portsmouth had reached France.[4]

---

[1] *New Hampshire Province Papers*, vii, 471; see *Ibid.*, p. 409.

[2] *New Hampshire Gazette and Historical Chronicle*, May 19, 1775.

[3] R. O., Adm. 1, 485, *Barkley to Graves*, May 19, 1775.

[4] R. O., C. O. 5, 175, f. 67, *Wentworth to Germain*, Jan. 6, 1777; *N. H. Gaz. and Hist. Chron.*, Aug. 1, Sept. 12, 1775.

The most dramatic episode in cutting off the naval mast supply occurred at Falmouth. Thomas Coulson, an outspoken Tory merchant residing there, had just launched the *Minerva*, an unusually large mast ship of about a thousand tons. He had also collected the masts which she was expected to take to England. In violation of the American non-importation agreement, Coulson had brought rigging and stores for the *Minerva* in another of his ships, but the exasperated colonists would not allow him to unload them.

The Navy, however, had a definite interest in the threatened mast supply, and early in May, Captain Mowatt appeared at Falmouth in H.M.S. *Canceaux*. Under her guns, Coulson was able to transfer the fittings to his new mast ship. Mowatt was kidnapped on shore by the rash Colonel Thompson, but was released after a short detention. He sailed away on May 16, accompanied by Coulson in the *Minerva*. The Tory merchant had been prevented from loading the masts which he had collected at Falmouth, and it has just been seen that he was equally unsuccessful in his efforts to secure a similar cargo at Portsmouth.[1]

Three weeks later, Coulson was back at Falmouth in the *Minerva*, accompanied by a small warship, the sloop *Senegal*, 14. At the approach of these vessels, the men of Falmouth towed Coulson's masts several miles from the harbor to the mouth of the Presumpscot River, and they seized the boat, men, and guns sent after them. Unable to secure the masts, the *Minerva* and the *Senegal* sailed for Boston early in July.[2]

Meanwhile, Captain Mowatt, desiring revenge for his kidnapping, reported the affair to Admiral Graves, then commanding on the station. The Admiralty had just sent orders for the naval commanders to secure any possible masts, by force if necessary. According to the story of a Casco Bay skipper who had been detained by Graves, the admiral told him that, if the men of Falmouth did not permit Coulson to load his masts, he would "send

[1] *N. H. Gaz. and Hist. Chron.*, Mar. 10, May 26, 1775; *Journals of each Provincial Congress of Massachusetts*, pp. 217–219, 237, 238; *Maine Hist. Soc. Coll.*, 2nd ser., viii, 91–95; 3rd ser., pp. 437–448.

[2] R. O., Adm. 1, 485, *Barkley to Graves*, May 19, 1775; *Graves to Adm.*, July 16, 1775.

a ship or ships, and beat the town down about their ears." [1] On
the strength of this mast situation, Mowatt, "by his most earnest
solicitation," received an order from Graves to punish the colonists. He appeared before Falmouth on October 17 with a small
flotilla and, after a long bombardment, laid most of the town in
ashes. The masts, however, like those at Georgetown and Portsmouth, never reached England, and it is said that a half century
later they still lay rotting in Portland Harbor.[2]

For a century and a quarter, the Navy had been able to depend
on its cargoes of masts from New England each year. At times
there had been difficulty in convoying, for Dutch "capers" or
French privateers would pick off an occasional luckless ship; but
there had nearly always been an adequate supply of the great
sticks, not only at Piscataqua and Falmouth, but at Deptford
and old Portsmouth as well, and the ships of Russell, Norris,
Benbow, Anson, and Hawke had their masts from the King's
woods in New England. In that respect the Navy had been justified in depending on the colonies.

The Broad Arrow policy, on the other hand, had been a failure
in New England, and the old sources could not have supplied
masts forever, with violations so widespread. A few mast ships
had slipped out early in the spring of 1775, and this was the last
supply of the great American sticks which the Navy was to have
in seven years. The loss of those American masts made itself felt
in the naval operations between 1778 and 1782 in a most striking
manner, as the next chapter will explain. The dwindling stock in
the dockyard ponds could not replace the rotten and shattered
masts most urgently needed, so that more than one fleet failed to
accomplish its purpose, as a result of encountering moderate
storms which ordinary masts could have easily withstood. The
news of Lexington had put an end to the supply that had started
in the days of Cromwell, and the colonists in Georgetown, Portsmouth, and Falmouth provided a dramatic close to the long
struggle against England's attempt to commandeer their choicest
trees.

[1] Goold, *Portland in the Past*, p. 342.
[2] R. O., Adm. Digest, 4807, *Adm. to Graves*, Sept. 14, 1775; Williamson, *History
of Maine*, ii, 417–435.

CHAPTER VII

MASTS AND AMERICAN INDEPENDENCE

BLAMING the weather is a time-honored excuse. The Chinese told Marco Polo that only an easterly gale prevented their conquest of Japan. The Spaniards cursed the gales that helped to save England by shattering their Armada. More to the point here, there were Englishmen after the Revolution who claimed that America owed its independence to the winds.

This excuse was especially popular in naval circles. The Royal Navy had not achieved its usual success during the American Revolution. Men speculated on what might have been the outcome of the contest if British blockading squadrons could have kept the French cooped up at Brest and Toulon while the Americans fought alone. The situation called for explanation, and with this end in view, a naval officer wrote in 1788: "Indeed, it appeared as if the elements had joined our foes, for storms and hurricanes assisted them to destroy our navy, which by their own strength they were unable to shake." [1]

The anonymous apologist was partly right. The winds certainly had made sport of the King's ships in an unusual manner. Time and again throughout the war came the tale of squadrons scattered and great ships rendered useless as spars crashed to the deck while worn-out masts split open and tumbled into the sea. The plans of admirals miscarried more than once at critical stages of the conflict when the rotting pine aloft gave way in the stress of the winds.

Those winds, however, were not entirely responsible for the relative weakness of the Navy. With the exception of one wicked hurricane in 1780, the winds of the Revolution probably blew no harder than at any other time. There were the usual fierce September gales in the North Atlantic, the regular hurricanes in the

---

[1] *A Short Account of the Naval Actions of the Last War, by an Officer*, p. 122; see Brenton, *Naval History of Great Britain*, i, 33.

West Indies, and the customary nasty weather in the Channel.
Yet British fleets in other wars had met similar winds with only
the occasional loss of minor spars. Even in the American Revolution, the breezes that shattered the masts of King George's
ships blew also upon the fleets of Louis XVI with no particularly
damaging effect.

The real cause of this wholesale loss of masts has been overlooked by our naval apologist and by subsequent writers. It was
the work of the Americans themselves, for, as will be recalled, the
colonists of the New England ports put an end to the supply of
great masts upon which the Navy had depended since the days of
Oliver Cromwell. A lax naval administration neglected to replenish the stock from other sources while there was time, and the
Navy suffered keenly from the lack of great pines.

The empty mast ponds were only one reflection of the maladministration of the Earl of Sandwich, that lord of misrule in
charge of the Admiralty. By neglecting the material condition
of the ships and by alienating the Whig admirals, Sandwich probably did more damage to the Navy entrusted to his care than any
hostile French admiral had ever done. In addition to this, England was in the difficult strategic position of having to defend her
own shores and commerce while she supported a distant war in
America. "For the first time in her history," writes Fiennes,
"she fought at a serious disadvantage in geographical position."[1]

It is futile, of course, to stress a single factor as the sole cause
for victory or defeat in a contest so complex as the American
Revolution, but certainly the lack of masts deserves more of a
place than it has yet received among the various reasons for England's temporary decline in sea power. The experiences in the
Dutch wars showed that the condition of the ships could have an
influence on naval success. Granting the truth of Mahan's statement that "good men in poor ships are better than poor men in
good ships," it must be recognized that the ships must not be too
poor, especially if the men were not particularly good. There
were a few men of outstanding ability among the British admirals
in the American Revolution, but they were in a minority, and the

---

[1] Fiennes, *Sea Power and Freedom*, p. 186.

ships with which most of the admirals fought were in a state of decrepitude. Some of the causes of that weakness can be discovered if the mast supply, just now observed in the American forests and ports of shipment, is regarded from the standpoint of the dockyards.

At the beginning of 1775, the Navy was well provided with masts. The ponds at Portsmouth, Plymouth, Deptford, and the other yards contained enough for about three years' consumption, the reserve which the Admiralty was trying to maintain regularly. The total number of each kind of masts on hand on January 1, 1775, was:

NEW ENGLAND

Over 30 in.	75
29½–27 in.	322
27 –25 in.	188
24½–20 in.	49
19½ in. and under	39

ST. PETERSBURG AND RIGA

27 –25 in.	17
24½–20 in.	1075
19½–14 in.	883
13½ in. and under	58

NORWAY

27 –20 in.	408
19½–14 in.	695
9 –13½ in.	1262 [1]

The first two items of the New England list were of particular importance, for, with the exception of a few shipments early in 1775, they represented the last masts of that size which the Navy was to have for several years. It was the exhaustion of the stock of masts over twenty-seven inches in diameter, amounting to barely 400, that caused the crisis three years later. In addition to these, there were 23 New England bowsprits between 33 and 39½ inches, with 408 more over 26 inches, and 142 New England yards larger than any in store from Riga. Throughout this study, the bowsprits and large yards will be included in general considerations of "masts" unless the latter are definitely specified. Most

[1] R.O., *Adm., Acct. Gen., Misc., Var.,* 124.

of these larger sticks were at Portsmouth and Plymouth, where the fleets were fitted and repaired.[1] The stock was ample for usual peace demands, but in three years it was drained, and no sticks of adequate size had been brought in for replacement.

There was an almost normal supply of masts from America in the early months of 1775. It was customary for mast ships to sail from the colonial ports early in the spring so that they could take a second cargo later in the year; and it will be recalled that there was no interference with the mast exportation until late in April, after the news of Lexington and Concord reached the ports of New Hampshire and Maine. The total imports of "great masts" into Great Britain during 1775 from America and the Baltic were:

Nova Scotia	87	Russia	561
New England	239	"East Country"	106
New York	73	Denmark-Norway	31
Pennsylvania	295	Sweden	0
Virginia-Maryland	28		—
Carolina	2	Total, Baltic	698[2]
	—		
Total, America	724		

Those shipments were not as valuable a supplement to the naval supply as the figures would indicate. They include the general importations for the merchant marine as well as for the Navy. The latter, it will be remembered, had the right of preëmpting any cargoes of colonial masts within twenty days after their arrival, but the naval authorities did not avail themselves of this right in the spring of 1775, for they underestimated the seriousness of the situation in America. Consequently, most of the colonial masts went to the builders of merchantmen. Another reason for discounting the appearance of those figures is the loose use of the term "great masts." In the customs accounts, all masts over twenty inches in diameter were included under that designation. The particular value of the New England pines, of course, lay in their ability to furnish sticks more than thirty inches in diameter, and it is probable that none of the Baltic masts and few of the large number from the newly developed Pennsylvania supply

[1] R. O., *Adm. Acct. Gen., Misc., Var.*, 124.
[2] R. O., Customs, 3, 75, *Imports and Exports*, 1775.

were of that exceptional diameter requisite for ships of the line. There were a few of those choice pine sticks in the shipments from New England, but they made no material addition to the stock of great masts in the dockyards at the beginning of the year.

The last cargo of American masts reached England shortly after the news of Bunker Hill. The arrival of this shipment on July 31, 1775, marked the definite end of England's regular receipt of masts from the thirteen colonies, though tar and pitch from the southern colonies continued to arrive for another year.[1]

More than two weeks before that last mast cargo arrived, Henniker, the principal contractor for American masts, wrote to the Navy Board, suggesting that the supply cut off by the colonists be replaced through extra efforts to secure masts from the Baltic. As soon as he had heard the news from Georgetown, Portsmouth, and Falmouth, he wrote:

> As the unhappy state of affairs in America may render it difficult to procure masts from thence, and may considerably raise the price, if not cause great alterations at Riga, I thought it my duty to inform your Honours, that my agent, Hancock, is now at Riga (on his own affairs) and might be of great use in providing masts for any future occasion.[2]

The Navy Board deserves censure for not immediately developing this alternate supply. They "desired Mr. Henniker to write to his agent to procure a cargo of Riga masts of the largest sizes to be delivered in this year," but there all worry over the matter seems to have ceased.[3] The Baltic forests at their best could not produce adequate substitutes for the largest New England pines. The Riga market normally produced few masts over twenty-seven inches in diameter. Special exertion might secure sticks of thirty inches or over, but almost never more than thirty-two. The value of an extra inch in the diameter of a great mast made itself felt to the utmost during the American Revolution, but the Navy Board was not sufficiently insistent that Henniker try to get the largest sizes. The contractor saved himself from loss by transferring his American contracts to the Baltic, but the 716 masts and 91 bowsprits which he had sent from Riga by the end

---

[1] R. O., *Adm. Acct. Gen.*, 274, *Treasurer's Ledgers*, 1775–76.

[2] R. O., N. B. In Letters, 1228, *Henniker to N. B.*, July 14, 1775.

[3] *Ibid.*, marginal note.

of 1777 did little to relieve the need for lower masts for ships of
the line.[1]

Even if the largest Baltic masts had been available, they could
not have fully met that need, and the Navy Board was also culpable in not ordering the construction of "made masts." It will
be remembered that the French, who were almost entirely dependent on the Baltic supply, constructed composite masts for
their largest ships out of several pieces of Riga fir, just as the
English had done before New England masts began to arrive
regularly in 1653. The piecing together of those "made masts"
had soon become a lost art in the English dockyards, and no attempt was made to revive it before 1778.[2]

In the meantime, the mast ponds of Portsmouth, Plymouth,
and the other yards, which had been amply stocked in 1775, were
being drained month by month of their great New England masts
and bowsprits. Thinking, perhaps, that the New England supply
would be speedily resumed with the crushing of the colonial revolt, or possibly neglecting the situation entirely, Lord Sandwich
at the Admiralty and Nelson's uncle, Maurice Suckling, at the
Navy Board adopted none of those measures which could have
relieved the drain. There was only a normal demand for naval
materials, for the rôle of the Navy in the first three years of the
American Revolution was principally one of vexatious police
duty along the coasts of the revolted colonies, enlivened by occasional encounters with the diminutive American navy and the
active privateers. Small vessels like the *Canceaux*, which had
bombarded Falmouth, were adequate for much of that service,
and the Navy had very few ships of the line at sea on any station.
The hasty shipbuilding during the Seven Years War and the
severe shortage of English oak after that contest had resulted in
general decay, and the introduction of Stettin oak had not improved the situation. Most of England's ships of the line lay in
reserve in the dockyards, with their hulls and masts disin-
tegrating.

[1] R. O., N. B. In Letters, 1228, *Henniker to N. B.*, Aug. 30, Nov. 15, Dec. 18,
1775; *Adm., Acct. Gen.*, pp. 278–280, *Treasurer's Ledgers*, 1776–78, *passim*.

[2] *Cal. S. P., Dom.*, 1671–72, pp. 167, 168.

France joined the American cause early in 1778 and the Royal Navy was rudely stirred out of that torpor. It had been a comparatively easy task to bully the American seaboard and armed vessels, but it was an entirely different matter when a first-rate power entered the contest with a navy which had been put in excellent condition by Choiseul after the French naval failures in the Seven Years' War. The British paid heavily for the negligence of their naval administration during the preceding three years. The able Sir Charles Middleton replaced Suckling as Comptroller of the Navy in 1778, but his untiring efforts could not offset the protracted neglect.[1]

This was particularly noticeable in the matter of masts. The three years' reserve on hand at the beginning of 1775 lasted the normal time expected of it; but late in 1777, the Navy Board informed the Admiralty that "Although His Majesty's magazines are at present well supplied with masts, there are but few large masts due upon contract, and the present contractor apprehended difficulty in procuring further supplies."[2] Deptford still had some New England masts in stock, but the other yards had few left. Sandwich lied outright when he gave Parliament the impression of such a surplus of stores that the dockyards could not accommodate them. Middleton never tired of calling attention to the empty condition in which he found the stores.[3] The Admiralty gave instructions to send proper persons to Russia, with power to purchase whatever large masts could be had immediately and to contract for an adequate future supply. Butt, an officer of Deptford yard, and Scammell, who had cruised the Maine woods six years earlier on Wentworth's survey, went on this mission.[4] They secured some masts at St. Petersburg larger than any which Henniker had provided, with a few almost equalling the largest New England masts. By March, 1778, they had purchased on commission forty-one masts over thirty inches in diameter, with many more between twenty-three and twenty-

[1] N. R. S., *Barham Papers*, ii, 2–30, 207–209, 217.
[2] R. O., Adm. Digest, 4809, *N. B. to Adm.*, Nov. 11, 1777; see N. B., *Deptford Letter-Book, passim.*
[3] *Parl. Hist.*, xx, 444; *Barham Papers*, iii, 15, and *passim.*
[4] R. O., Adm. Digest, 4809, *Adm. to N. B.*, Nov. 11, Nov. 25, 1777.

nine inches. In June they returned to England, and at Butt's suggestion, a contract was made with Wales, Pierson, & Company of Riga to furnish a supply of great masts.[1]

Most of these masts which Butt and Scammell secured could not replace the New England pines as single sticks. Too late, the mastwrights began to study the forgotten art of making great masts out of small firs. The difficulty did not lie in actually constructing the masts, for it was comparatively simple to pin the sticks together in quarters or around a central spindle, but to proportion the weight and strength of the masts to the sailing requirements of each size of ship involved intricate mathematical calculations. A slight error might diminish the speed perceptibly, and if the sticks were too heavy or too light, they were liable to be broken in a strong wind.[2] Riga fir was heavier than New England pine by one third, and the first composite masts were as unsuccessful as the decaying American ones which they replaced. It was fully a year before the art was well developed.[3] As soon as peace came in 1783, orders were given to discontinue the use of composite masts.[4]

The Riga supply from Wales, Pierson, & Company was maintained, with occasional difficulties, throughout the war.[5] In 1780, the Navy Board was still apprehensive about the supply, for Russia's attitude in the Armed Neutrality was threatening. Instructions were sent to the officers at sea to exercise all possible care of masts and cordage in view of the precarious state of the Russian supply.[6] Though a dockyard was occasionally worried about where to store a temporary supply, it was not until 1782 that the storehouses and mast ponds were filled in a satisfactory manner.[7] From 1778 to 1782, England imported 996 masts over

---

[1] R. O., N. B. Out Letters, 2204, *N. B. to Adm.*, Mar. 10, Mar. 23, Mar. 28, June 17, 1778.

[2] See esp. Fincham, *On Masting Ships*, and Forfait, *Traité de la Mâture, passim.*

[3] R. O., N. B., *Standing Orders to Dockyards*, 2508, Jan. 6, 1779.

[4] *Ibid.*, Jan. 27, 1783.

[5] R. O., N. B. Out Letters, 2209, *N. B. to Sec. of Treas.*, Nov. 6, 1781, Apr. 30, May 24, 1782.

[6] *Ibid.*, *N. B. to Adm.*, Dec. 8, 1780, Mar. 3, 1781.

[7] *Ibid.*, Feb. 2, 1779, Jan. 28, Feb. 20, 1782; *Deptford Letter Book*, Oct. 15, 1778, May 4, 1786.

twenty-one inches in diameter from Russia.[1] These were almost the only large masts which the Navy received during the war.

These Riga masts eventually relieved the mast situation in the English dockyards to some extent, but there were not enough to spare for the little yards in the West Indies and America, which were called upon to repair the damages incurred in the important and almost constant campaigning in those waters. The dockyards at Jamaica and Antigua, cut off from the usual New England supply, had to subsist on inadequate doles from England, which amounted to almost nothing. The Halifax yard, located near extensive virgin pine forests under British control, was able to provide masts for itself during most of the war, though at the outset, warships had to send their own crews into the woods to cut the necessary sticks.[2] There were other forests full of great pines not far from the provisional yards at Newport and New York, but the trees were inaccessible to the British and those little yards suffered extremely for want of masts.

It is surprising that in America, of all places, there should have been a lack of masts. The British ships on that station, with their patched masts liable to tumble over the side in any strong wind, often sailed within sight of Maine forests capable of furnishing them, and a hundred other fleets, with the masts so sorely needed. New England, however, kept a close hand on its pines. The Massachusetts legislature passed an act early in 1779 forbidding the export of masts or spars of fifteen inches diameter or more, "to prevent the enemy, as far as may be, from obtaining a supply of masts and spars, which there is reason to suppose they are at this time in great want of." [3] This was a counter to the Admiralty's instructions to secure any available masts in New England, by force if necessary.[4] Great masts were too clumsy to be smuggled out of a hostile country, and there seems to have been no attempt to land a force to cover cutting operations. In 1778, the

---

[1] R. O., Chatham MSS, Bundle 111, *Middleton to Pitt*, Oct. 26, 1786; N. R. S., *Barham Papers*, ii, 220; see p. 193.

[2] N. R. S., *Journal of Rear-Admiral Bartholomew James*, pp. 24, 25.

[3] *Acts and Resolves of the Province of Massachusetts Bay*, v, 930, 931.

[4] R. O., Adm. Digest, 4807, *Adm. to Graves*, Sept. 14, 1775; Adm., 1, 310, *Young to Adm.*, Mar. 13, 1778.

British seized a ship loading masts for Nantes in the Sheepscot River in Maine. They had tried to carry away a similar cargo in the same place the year before, but were able only to destroy the cargo to keep it from reaching France. Other mast shipments intended for France were occasionally intercepted during the war, but such a supply was trifling and undependable.[1] The French, moreover, were much more successful in securing masts intended for the British Navy. It has been mentioned that three cargoes of masts gathered at Portsmouth by the British naval contractor had reached France by 1777; and when the British evacuated Boston, early in 1776, some of the great pine sticks which they left behind them went later to refit the French fleet at Boston.[2] In 1778, the French minister, with the approval of the Continental Congress, offered a reward for the capture or destruction of "any vessel of the enemy loaded with masts and spars, and destined to the ports of Halifax, Newport or New York."[3] The American privateers scarcely needed such encouragement.

The naval administration should have shifted its mast contracts to Nova Scotia or some of the other extensive pine regions still under British control, as soon as their supply was cut off at Falmouth and Portsmouth in 1775. An ample stock of the largest American sticks could have been secured within a year; but the authorities toyed with the idea so long that masts from the new source did not reach the English dockyards until the fighting was over, in 1782. At first, it was felt that pines could be secured from the Penobscot territory in eastern Maine. Sir John Wentworth drew up proposed regulations for the administration of the forests there in 1777, and there were strong arguments for retaining it at the close of the war as a source of masts. On second thought, however, the Navy preferred a region more likely to remain permanently in British control.[4]

---

[1] R. O., Adm., 1, 488, Howe to Adm., Nov. 23, 1777, Sept. 28, 1778; Adm., Acct. Gen., Accts., 280, Oct. 31, 1778; N. R. S., Letters of Sir Samuel Hood, p. 159.

[2] R. O., Adm. Digest, 4809, Greenwood to N. B., Mar. 18, 1781.

[3] Weeden, Economic and Social History of New England, ii, 784.

[4] R. O., C. O. 5, 175, f. 67, Wentworth to Germain, Jan. 6, 1777; Parl. Hist., xxii, 640, 641; Colonial Policy of Great Britain Considered, p. 79; (Hollingsworth), Present State of Nova Scotia, p. 12.

Their choice fell upon the virgin pine tracts of the St. John River in New Brunswick, then still a part of Nova Scotia. It was no new experience for Nova Scotia to furnish naval masts. Colbert had loaded Frontenac and the other governors with orders and exhortations to aid his great plan of supplying the French marine with masts, timber, and even ships, from the forests of New France. Though his successors failed to develop the supply to the full extent of Colbert's projects, it was reported about 1700 that "Acadie can furnish four cargoes of masts a year," and French frigates occasionally carried back masts to Brest or Toulon.[1]

The British had begun to cut masts there as soon as they captured Port Royal, in 1710; and when Acadia fell to them at Utrecht three years later, to be renamed Nova Scotia, one of the first acts of the new governor was an inquiry into the "masting" possibilities of the province. The Broad Arrow jurisdiction was extended to include Nova Scotia in 1721, and by 1730 Dunbar's deputies were busy making reservations in its woods.[2] Considerable lumbering was carried on in Nova Scotia proper prior to the Revolution, and in 1772, its exports of masts amounted to about half the output of Portsmouth or Falmouth, while there was an extensive general lumber trade.[3]

The early Nova Scotia lumbermen did little damage to the great pine forests of the New Brunswick region, which was practically a wilderness when England began to grant land there during the war to the Loyalist exiles from the revolted colonies. The St. John River was marked to succeed Portsmouth as the source of American masts for the Navy. The pioneer in New Brunswick's masting was William Davidson, who began to cut on the upper St. John in the winter of 1779, after an agreement with the dockyard authorities at Halifax. The initiative came from Captain Andrew Snape Hamond, commissioner at Halifax, who

---

[1] Ontario, *Report of the Minister of Lands, Forests and Mines, 1907*, pp. 148–154; Colbert, *Lettres, Instructions et Mémoires, passim;* Murdock, *History of Nova Scotia*, i, 204, 260.

[2] *Cal. S. P., A. & W. I.*, 1708–09, pp. 407, 408; 1710–11, pp. 245, 551, 552; *Acts P. C. (Col.),.Unbound Papers*, p. 164; *Nova Scotia Archives*, ii, 24, 176.

[3] See p. 276.

handled the whole timber problem as Comptroller of the Navy during the next war. Davidson's cutters worked under the protection of the little garrison at Fort Howe. This was necessary because of the activity of the Americans at Machias, who attempted to incite the Passamaquoddy Indians against the lumbermen cutting for the Navy.[1] These Indians were finally bought off by a boat-load of presents from Colonel Michael Franklin who wrote to the chief:

> Brethren — King George wants masts for his ships and has employed people to provide them on your river, depending on you to protect the workmen in cutting them and conveying them to Fort Howe. The Governor sends you some presents which Major Shuldholme will deliver to you. They are intended to bind fast your promise that you will protect the mast cutters.[2]

The first cargo of masts that the Navy received from this new source arrived in November, 1780, at Halifax dockyard, where they were applied to the ships on the American station repairing there. A second load from St. John followed shortly, and by 1782, Davidson and his rival, Peabody, whose lumbermen were almost fighting with each other to gain possession of the best trees, had several hundred large masts cut and ready to float. At first, there had been enough masts for the Halifax yard alone, but by 1782, there was a surplus for the dockyards in England.[3]

This shift from New England to New Brunswick was of little value to the Navy during the war, but it is worthy of note here as an added example of the opportunities wasted by the Navy. It is even more important as the initial step in the New Brunswick supply which, as will be seen, kept the dockyards well furnished with great masts until 1804, when there was a further shift to the St. Lawrence.[4]

The blunders and dilatory conduct of the Navy Board were felt keenly in the fleets. The Russian masts which Butt and Scammell procured in Riga did not arrive in time to be of service

[1] Raymond, *The River St. John*, pp. 478–480.   [2] *Ibid.*, p. 481.

[3] R. O., Adm. Digest, 4809, *Adm. to Arbuthnot*, May 18, 1781; *Hamond to Adm.*, May 22, 1782; Naval Hist. Soc., *Graves Papers*, p. 95; *Winslow Papers*, pp. 354, 360; Murdock, *op. cit.*, ii, 611; Raymond, *op. cit.*, pp. 486–490.

[4] See pp. 348, 353, 356.

in fitting out the ships in 1778, when the effects of the mast shortage were seen at their worst. By 1780, the English dockyards had
pieced together enough masts out of the Russian firs to meet their
most urgent needs. It will be seen that the inadequate stock of
masts in the little American and West Indian yards was the
source of most of the trouble in the later years of the war.

It is surprising that the very evident relation of the loss of New
England masts to the failure of several naval campaigns in this
war has hitherto attracted so little attention. In most of those
campaigns, bad masts were only one of several causes for failure,
but in one outstanding instance, the best squadron that England
could send to sea for a very important service was dismasted and
entirely dispersed by summer gales, and its failure produced a
decided effect on the course of the war in that year.

The correspondence of admirals on such subjects must be read
with caution, as has been said, for some of them were apt to at-
tribute the results of their own shortcomings to the condition of
their ships.[1] In this war, moreover, a certain political animus
must be discounted. Nearly all the highest naval officers at the
time of the Revolution owed their appointment and promotion
to previous Whig ministries. Many of them were opposed to the
war in America, and nearly all of them were even more bitterly
opposed to the notorious naval administration of the Tory
Sandwich. The minutely detailed accounts of the defects in the
ships under their command, therefore, might almost be regarded
as Whig tracts directed against the Admiralty. In the matter of
masts, however, Rodney and Palliser, favorite admirals of Sandwich, denounced the situation as openly as the Whigs Howe and
Keppel. In fact, all the correspondence from naval leaders, able
or slow-witted, Whig or Tory, pointed to the fact that the almost
empty mast-ponds of the dockyards had an unfortunate influence
on the efficiency of their ships. Constant leakiness from rotting
hulls, indirectly due to a shortage of English oak, was another
form in which the timber problem made itself felt during the war.
If France had possessed bolder admirals, England might have
suffered even more severely from that handicap.

[1] See p. 204.

Naval operations during this war were carried on in several distinct theatres of action. The major engagements took place in America and around the Channel. In America, the rival fleets usually spent the summer months in the north, often coöperating with the land forces; but as the autumn gales came on, the French and English admirals generally headed south, to spend the winter in seizing West Indian islands, returning again to the north in the spring to avoid the hurricanes. At the same time, England had to protect her shores against the menace of the powerful French fleet at Brest, which was reinforced by the Spanish in 1779. With a few exceptions in the case of operations around Gibraltar, Minorca, and the North Sea, interest centres in the American operations and in those of the "Western Squadron" formed to defend England. The contest of Hughes and Suffren in Indian waters was too remote for detailed consideration in this connection, though both fleets suffered for want of masts.[1] Chronology will occasionally have to be subordinated to locality in discussing the effects of the mast situation in America and Europe.

It was apparent in England that the Navy would probably be drawn into a severe contest, long before the Comte de Noailles formally announced that on February 6, 1778, France had signed a treaty of alliance with the United States. The situation called for the immediate preparation of two fleets or squadrons (these terms were often used indiscriminately) which could take the offensive and prevent France from threatening England or aiding America. At Brest, there was a force of about thirty ships of the line under D'Orvilliers, who should have been blockaded to prevent any menace in the Channel. It was also known as early as January that D'Estaing was gathering a fleet of about twelve ships of the line and a few frigates at Toulon for an expedition to America, which would transport some 4,000 French troops to aid the Americans.[2] This French naval force would heavily outnumber the English warships in America under Howe. An adequate English fleet, however, could easily intercept D'Estaing before he ever left the Mediterranean, and if the French could

[1] Mahan, *Influence of Sea Power on History*, pp. 429, 443, 444, 451.
[2] *Parl. Hist.*, xix, 1161, 1162.

not get to America in force, the alliance would mean little.[1] The needs of the situation were perceived even by the amateur Whig strategists in Parliament, but they were lost upon the Lords of Admiralty under Sandwich.[2]

The failure of the Admiralty to grasp the situation early in 1778 cost England the opportunity to assume the offensive; but even if Sandwich had realized the strategical advantages of such a course, there were no ships ready to enforce it. England maintained its Navy nominally on a "two-power basis," so that it could face the combined Bourbon fleets of France and Spain; but the strength which the Admiralty reported to Parliament was chiefly on paper. The figures represented more than a hundred ships of the line mostly rotting in reserve. Sandwich stated early in the year that he could send thirty-five ships of the line to sea at once and seven more within a fortnight; but when Admiral Augustus Keppel went to Portsmouth in March to take command of the "Western Squadron," he declared that he found only "six ships fit to meet a seaman's eye."[3]

The British, as has been seen, should have despatched fleets to Brest and Toulon by March at the latest, but it was not until June 9 that Byron finally left to intercept D'Estaing, and Keppel could not put to sea against the French Channel fleet under D'Orvilliers until June 12. The timber problem was prominent among the causes of that delay which helped the cause of American independence.

The lack of masts and naval stores was keenly felt during that spring of 1778, when the dockyards tried to patch up enough of the decayed ships from "Rotten Row" to form two fleets. Many of them had so succumbed to dry rot that it was necessary to shovel away the toadstools and filth from the rotting planks and timbers. That rot resulted from the timber shortage of the past decade. There was no alarming scarcity of oak in the yards in 1778, but there was no time to give the ships the thorough rebuilding which they needed. Throughout the war, as will be seen, they often

---

[1] Mahan, *Influence of Sea Power on History*, pp. 359 ff.
[2] *Parl. Hist.*, xix, 726–730, 818–834, 874–893, 980–996.
[3] *Ibid.*, xix, 479, 480; xx, 184.

leaked, and sometimes foundered, as a result. The mast situation
is the primary interest in this chapter, however. Many of the
ships had been in reserve since the close of the Seven Years' War,
fifteen years before. Masts were ordinarily supposed to last about
twelve years before their resin dried up and deprived them of
strength and resilience. Scores of masts, yards, and bowsprits,
therefore, should have been replaced before the ships were sent to
sea. There would have been time for this process, along with the
other repairs, if extra pieces had been available, for in an emergency the old masts could be removed and new ones stepped very
quickly. The store of large New England pine sticks was so low,
however, that the scant supply remaining in the mast-ponds was
kept to replace masts and other pieces actually shot away in
battle or broken off at sea. The ships were allowed to sail with
the old sticks, in the hope that they might possibly be able to
stand the strain. That possibility was lessened by the necessity
of using old second-hand rigging which could not hold them firmly
in place.[1]

Admiral Keppel was slowly gathering such a patched-up fleet
for the Channel service in April when Admiral John Byron,
grandfather of the poet, arrived at Portsmouth with orders which
gave him precedence in collecting ships to intercept D'Estaing.
The French admiral sailed from Toulon on April 15, and it would
still have been easy for an English fleet to stop him at Gibraltar,
for it was four weeks before he left the Mediterranean. The dockyards did their best to provide Byron with ships as soon as possible, even stripping some of those already prepared for Keppel,
but it was June 9 when Byron started out for America with thirteen ships of the line.[2] Leaving Keppel to gather another fleet
from the remaining ships, it will be best here to follow Byron to
America, for the experiences of those thirteen ships of the line
under "Foul Weather Jack," as the sailors called him, form the
most striking example of the influence of the timber problem on
English naval operations.

[1] *Parl. Hist.*, xx, 431.
[2] R. O., Adm., 1, 94, *Keppel to Adm.*, Apr. 28, 1778; 486, *Byron to Adm.*, May 5,
June 5, 1778; *Parl. Hist.*, xx, 431; Keppel, *Life of Viscount Keppel*, ii, 332; Fraser,
The Fighting Fame of the King's Ships, pp. 221, 222.

Late as Byron was in starting, he still had a possibility of thwarting the expedition of D'Estaing, which was crossing the Atlantic in a leisurely manner. Byron's ships of the line outnumbered the French fleet, but D'Estaing with his twelve sail of the line and five frigates was much stronger than Howe, whose strongest ship was a fourth-rate of 64 guns. The reinforcements under Byron were necessary to establish British control of American waters, if not to save Howe from destruction or impotence. The old masts, which should have been replaced, prevented Byron's squadron from playing its intended rôle. Poorly supported by the second-hand rigging, they succumbed to the strong southwest gales which struck the ships on July 3, in 49° 4′ north latitude and 26° 48′ west longitude, when they were less than a third of the way across the Atlantic. Byron's squadron was completely dispersed by that storm.[1] Some of his thirteen ships were forced back to Europe, and the remainder, alone or in groups of two or three, limped into various American ports a month later.[2]

When those gales struck the squadron, masts, yards, and bowsprits by the dozen, deprived of their original elasticity and in some cases reduced to nothing but punk at their hearts, "sprung" or cracked. If the injury was not so serious that the masts went by the board, the ships' carpenters "fished" them by binding anchor stocks or other available wood with rope or wire around the injured portion. Sometimes these repairs were inadequate and the sticks crashed to the deck or into the sea. Even if the masts remained in place, they were often so weak that the ships had to run before the wind with shortened sail.

Captain Evans of the *Invincible*, 74, gave a description of the effect of the gales on his masts which may be taken as typical of the damage to the whole squadron. He had parted company with the others in the July storm, the bowsprit being dangerously sprung in three places. On August 13, with the wind blowing hard,

the mainmast was sprung close to the gundeck, so much that it was expected to go with every roll. We cut it away on the quarter deck to prevent the

[1] R. O., Adm., 1, 486, *Byron to Adm.*, Aug. 27, 1778.
[2] Hist. MSS Com., *Var. Coll.*, vi, 317; *Naval Chronicle*, xxiv, 178.

upper deck from being torn up. [No sooner was this done] than the foremast went in three pieces, all of which fell on the forecastle and wounded several men but only one killed. The bowsprit being sprung some time before and now so bad, we had to cut part of that away.

After rigging up temporary or "jury" masts, the *Invincible* finally reached Halifax after running into D'Estaing's fleet and escaping by a narrow margin.[1]

The other ships had varying adventures. Byron's flagship, the *Princess Royal*, 90, arrived alone at New York in August, with her foremast sprung just above the upper deck. Seeing nothing of Howe's fleet and fearing to run into D'Estaing, Byron steered for Halifax. The master shipwright there advised him to have the mast replaced, for Halifax was the one dockyard where American masts were available; but Byron was impatient to join Howe and put to sea with the mast fished.[2] The *Cornwall*, 74, was the first ship to reach Howe, arriving on July 30 with her mainmast fished, her spars and yards in bad condition, and her hull badly wracked by the storm. This gave Howe his only seventy-four, and represented the sole aid which he received before his encounter with D'Estaing, where he was too weak to offer battle.[3] The arrival of the *Cornwall* demonstrated that Byron's whole squadron could probably have arrived in ample time to drive off D'Estaing if the ships had been in ordinary condition. By August 18, the *Monmouth*, 64, under Collingwood, joined Howe, with her mainmast badly sprung and with two maintopmasts carried away.[4] The *Culloden*, 74, had first put into St. John's, Newfoundland, badly damaged, with the *Russell*, 74, and the *Guadeloupe*, 74, and then proceeded to Halifax for repairs.[5] The *Albion*, 64, Byron's original flagship, reached America in October, after having been driven to Portugal, where she got new fore- and mainmasts and other repairs at Lisbon.[6] The remaining ships returned to England.

The loss of the expected reinforcements forced Howe into a

---

[1] R. O., Adm., 1, 488, *Capt. Evans to Howe*, Aug. 17, 1778.

[2] *Ibid.*, 486, *Byron to Adm.*, Aug. 27, 1778.

[3] *Ibid.*, 488, *Howe to Adm.*, Sept. 9, 1778.

[4] *Ibid.*, *Howe to Adm.*, Aug. 18, 1778.

[5] *Ibid.*, *Howe to Adm.*, Oct. 25, 1778; 486, *Byron to Adm.*, Aug. 27, 1778.

[6] *Ibid.*, *Byron to Adm.*, Oct. 24, 1778.

defensive position, but his bold and resourceful manipulation of the small force under his command prevented the French victory which might have resulted if D'Estaing had been equally bold. Barely in time, Howe transported the stores for Clinton's army across Delaware Bay late in June, and left for New York ten days before the French arrived off the Capes of the Delaware. Had D'Estaing shortened his slow voyage from ten weeks to eight, he could easily have prevented this movement of the military supplies. Howe retired to a strategic position at Sandy Hook, which D'Estaing, in spite of his superior force, dared not attack. The Frenchman then sailed to Rhode Island.[1]

Howe was joined by a few of his ships from Halifax, but had as his only third-rate the *Cornwall* of Byron's fleet, which left his force only two thirds as strong as the French. In spite of this, he saved Rhode Island for the British by following the French thither. Unable to assume the offensive, he was in a dangerous position when D'Estaing stood out to sea to meet him on August 9. Winds and cracked masts again affected the situation, but for almost the only time during the war, the winds blew for the British. Only a few isolated contests took place, for the French lost several masts and retired to Boston to refit. Howe's flagship and several of the other English ships were partially dismasted, but the French suffered more severely.[2]

In spite of this instance where the French masts gave way before a storm, France suffered far less than England, as a whole, from this source. D'Estaing had brought his entire fleet across the Atlantic with trifling damage, while the English force sent to intercept him was entirely dispersed because of poor masts. The French, moreover, could easily repair their losses at Boston, while the English were compelled to continue at sea with masts in crippled condition.

The provisional dockyards at Newport and New York, for reasons already described, were unable to keep the British ships

[1] R. O., Adm., I, 488, *Howe to Adm.*, Aug. 18, 1778; Mahan, *Influence of Sea Power*, pp. 360, 351.

[2] R. O., Adm., *Ibid.*; Mahan, pp. 362, 363; Barrows, *Life of Howe*, pp. 107-109; Hist. MSS Com., *Var. Coll.*, vi, 317.

in condition. New York received forty small masts from Philadelphia early in 1778, but great sticks were almost entirely wanting there and at Newport.[1] Some of Howe's ships had been on the
American station for three years or more without adequate repair, but his pleas for fresh ships to replace them brought no response until the Byron fiasco.[2] Some of the repairs to their hulls
required the facilities of dockyards less crude than Newport or
New York, but masts could have been replaced, had there been
any available. In the first week of 1778, Howe wrote:

> The *Lark* and the *Flora* losing their masts on their last cruise off of Boston,
> added to the many other accidents of the same kind which have happened
> last year, will render the scarcity in that article of the fitting stores a con-
> siderable inconvenience.[3]

Eight months later, when Byron's *Monmouth* crept in with a
sprung mainmast as the most serious of many injuries, Howe expressed the hope that the mast could be fixed without changing
it for the present, "but if more of the ships of the same squadron
should be in similar circumstances, I know not how to repair the
injury." [4]

Howe retained his command long enough to avert the crisis
which arose when Byron failed to intercept D'Estaing; but on
September 25, 1778, he turned over his fleet to Gambier. Influenced by Whig interests or by disgust at an Admiralty from which
he expected and received comparative neglect, Howe sailed back
to England, to lower his flag and participate in the Parliamentary
opposition to North and Sandwich. On the day he sailed from
New York, he drew up a detailed report of the condition of his
ninety-two ships. The desire to make political capital for the
opposition and to safeguard his professional reputation, which
was then under fire, doubtless accounted for such explicit details
as "one of the foretopsail bits sprung," "several rotten veins in
Bowsprit at partners and shot lodged in it," and "cheek on starboard side of knee of head rotten"; but Howe's name at least
ought to be an insurance of the accuracy of these minutiae. The

[1] R. O., Adm., I, 488, *Howe to Adm.*, Aug. 28, 1778.
[2] *Ibid.*, Sept. 27, Dec. 6, 1777; Jan. 5, Jan. 20, Feb. 4, May 9, 1778.
[3] *Ibid.*, Jan. 5, 1778.   [4] *Ibid.*, Aug. 18, 1778.

report gives indubitable evidence of a fleet in no condition to ful-
fill the services expected of it; a fleet to which few admirals would
care to trust their reputation or the national interests. Only one
of the thirteen ships of the line and seven of the thirty-nine frigates were reported as "fit for sea." Some of the ships were in as
battered condition as the *Amazon*, 32, which was still under jury-
masts and yards, with several beams, knees, and the starboard
cathead sprung, the rudder loose, the sails bad and not to be
trusted, and, like nearly every ship in the fleet, in need of cables
and anchors. The length of the list forbids further detail, but bad
masts, leaky topsides, and weak frames were found throughout
the fleet, from ships of the line like the *Somerset*, 64, which had
supported the attack on Bunker Hill, to the little fireship *Stromblo*,
whose hull was so rotten that water gained on the pumps an inch
an hour in a gale.[1]

Byron's ships gradually assembled from the various ports
where they had taken refuge, and their admiral soon replaced
Gambier in command on the American station. He had great
difficulty in securing masts and stores for repairs at New York,[2]
and when he led out his patched-up fleet in October to blockade
D'Estaing in Boston, another gale caught it, scattered it, and
drove the ships, with further damage to their masts, back into
Newport.[3] The loss of a few French masts in the August gale had
saved Howe and Rhode Island, but the October storm prevented
Byron, who now had superior numbers, from blocking D'Estaing's
escape to the West Indies. On November 4, 1778, the Frenchman
left Boston and sailed for Martinique. The story of the previous
summer was repeated. Byron, with a fleet superior in numbers,
was unable to hinder him on account of masts, and D'Estaing
was left free to fall upon a weaker English fleet under Barrington,
who nevertheless defended himself as ably as Howe had done at
Sandy Hook. The French were able to capture Grenada during
the winter. While D'Estaing was halfway to the West Indies,
Byron was trying to repair his ships at Newport,

---

[1] R. O., Adm., I, 488, *Howe to Adm.*, Sept. 25, 1778.
[2] *Ibid.*, 486, *Byron to Adm.*, Oct. 24, 1778.
[3] *Ibid.*, Nov. 11, 1778.

but most of them being crippled in their lower Masts and Yards, and all in the utmost want of Stores which could not be procured at this place, I found it a work of Great Labour and extreme Difficulty to get the Ships in condition to put to sea.[1]

Not until five weeks after D'Estaing had left Boston was Byron able to start from Newport for the Barbadoes. Once more masts and spars were lost, and one of his largest ships, thus disabled, was nearly driven ashore.

While the British were losing the advantage of superior numbers in America on account of bad masts, the mast situation was at the same time affecting the naval operations in the Channel. Admiral Augustus Keppel was too much of a Whig to serve against the Americans, but when war with France seemed inevitable, early in 1778, the King persuaded him to take command of the "Western Squadron," the fleet which was to defend England and hold the Brest fleet in check. Keppel was reluctant to trust his reputation to a fleet prepared by Sandwich, and stated in Parliament that he preferred a small fleet well fitted and completely manned to a large number of badly equipped ships.[2] He knew well that he would receive the latter. Even if the First Lord of the Admiralty had been benevolent, a sound fleet was not to be had.

Once more an effort was made to gather a fleet for Keppel, but again there was no opportunity to replace the worn-out masts. Keppel, as was seen, had gone to Portsmouth in March to take command of the Western Squadron, but had found only six ships in condition. The preparation of his ships had been retarded by the more urgent need to fit out the wretched squadron for Byron. Finally, on June 12, three days after Byron had finally left for America, Keppel sailed from Plymouth with twenty ships of the line, "well enough equipped, that is, neither the best nor the worst I had seen."[3] Two other ships had joined his fleet, when he learned from papers in the French frigate *Licorne*, whose capture was regarded as the opening act of the war with France, that

[1] R. O., Adm., I, 486, *Byron to Adm.*, Nov. 30, 1778; see *Rhode Island Historical Society, Collections*, vii, 299–325.

[2] *Parl. Hist.*, xix, 893.

[3] *Minutes of the Court Martial of Vice-Admiral Augustus Keppel, 1779*, p. 105.

D'Orvilliers had twenty-seven ships of the line ready for sea at Brest, with five more nearly fitted out. On receipt of this information, Keppel returned to England. The nation was stirred by the news of this retreat. Admiral Byng had been shot on his quarter deck in the previous war for a similar action.

Consideration of the complete lack of masts and naval stores in the dockyards was Keppel's defence when he was later charged with cowardice in this retreat. In a passage already quoted in part, he declared that the disparity of numbers rendered the English liable to a crushing defeat. In that event the supply of naval stores was so low, with the storehouses and mast-ponds practically empty, that a new fleet could not have been fitted out, and the French could have prevented the importation of any articles which England itself could not produce.[1]

A few more ships were patched up during the month, and on July 9 Keppel was at sea again with thirty ships of the line and six frigates. D'Orvilliers had sailed from Brest with a fleet outnumbering the British by two sail of the line and eight frigates. Within two weeks, Keppel encountered one of those short summer gales, ordinarily innocuous, but so disastrous to British masts and naval plans in 1778. Several of the ships sustained damage aloft. The *Thunderer*, 74, which suffered most severely, was stripped of her main-yard to replace a similar yard lost from the flagship, *Victory*, 100, and thus dismantled, was sent back to Plymouth.[2]

Keppel met the French in full force off Ushant on July 27. The running fight which ensued was a mere "feeble parade," for both admirals displayed more caution than boldness, and both were hampered by the failure of subordinate admirals to obey their orders. The affair attained a sordid prominence in England from the partisan wrangle and courts-martial of Keppel and Vice-Admiral Sir Hugh Palliser, a member of Sandwich's Tory Admiralty Board, who held a third of the British fleet inactive in not complying with Keppel's orders. D'Orvilliers suffered a similar lack of coöperation from the Duc de Chartres, later known as Philippe Egalité, who commanded the French van. There was

[1] *Minutes of the Court Martial of Vice-Admiral Augustus Keppel, 1779*, p. 106. See p. viii.
[2] R. O., Adm., 1, 94, *Keppel to Adm.*, July 16, July 21, 1778.

more of masts and politics than of brilliant strategy and tactics in this encounter. The Duke of Richmond, a Whig leader in the attacks on Sandwich, brought out some of the mast considerations in a letter to Keppel, shortly after the battle:

When *all our fleet* and our *first admiral* sail, Englishmen have been made to expect a capture of at least half the navy of France, and they had rather blame a commander, whose ships were so crippled that he could not pursue a flying enemy in a hard gale of wind on a lee shore, than a ministry for reducing the nation to such circumstances, as to be unable to send out a fleet equal to France.[1]

The masts of Keppel's fleet were in a terrible state after the action. A list drawn up in full detail by Keppel on his way home, showed that nearly every ship in the Western Squadron had "masts, yards and sails much cut and wounded." [2] French gunnery caused considerable damage of this nature even in well-appointed fleets, but there is good Tory evidence that the masts of the Western Squadron were especially vulnerable. In his own court-martial, Palliser excused his inaction partly on the ground that smoke obscured the signals flown from the *Victory*, and also that the foremast of his flagship, the *Formidable*, 90, would not permit him to join in the conflict. A shot had "discovered the Mast to be perfect Touchwood" and it was in danger of going over the side. The ship's carpenter produced some extremely decayed wood "taken out of the very heart of the mast," to substantiate the claim.[3]

The mast-ponds of Portsmouth and Plymouth proved inadequate to the demands of Keppel's fleet for repairs. The port admirals, commissioners, master shipwrights, and artificers won Keppel's gratitude for their untiring efforts to fit the ships for sea, but materials were lacking.[4] There were enough Norway and Riga sticks on hand to replace most of the injured topmasts and yards, and a few fore- and mizzen-masts could be supplied, but the mainmasts and bowsprits required sticks of New England size, and these were nearly gone. When Keppel was at last ready

---

[1] Letter of Aug. 21, 1778, quoted in Keppel, *Life of Viscount Keppel*, ii, 63.
[2] R. O., Adm., 1, 94, *Keppel to Adm.*, July 30, 1778.
[3] *Minutes of the Court Martial of Vice-Admiral Sir Hugh Palliser*, 1779, pp. 69–74.
[4] R. O., Adm., 1, 94, *Keppel to Adm.*, Aug. 16, Aug. 20, Aug. 26, 1778.

for sea again late in August, a week after D'Orvilliers had made his repairs and sailed, twelve of the thirty-three ships had main-masts which had been injured by shot and were only temporarily fished for want of substitutes. Six bowsprits were in the same condition. Sticks averaging a yard in diameter were necessary for those purposes, but Riga and Norway did not furnish that size. Nine other lower masts and seven of the largest yards were like-wise patched.[1]

If summer storms could damage masts in 1778, the autumn gales could not be expected to be more merciful. By the end of October, eight great masts and three bowsprits which had escaped injury at Ushant, in addition to many of those already patched, gave way before the winds.[2] One after another, ten ships had parted from the fleet during stormy October nights. Some of these were so crippled that they had dragged astern the fleet, and Keppel had had to detail stronger vessels to stand by them.[3] Not only were the masts in dangerous condition, but in most of the ships the upper works were leaky, and the rotting timber of the "sickly" ships which had lain in reserve contributed to the fevers which swept through their crews. The Tory Palliser reported the masts, hulls, and health in the ships of his division to be in as wretched a condition as those of Keppel's.[4] After cruising for some time, too weak to seek out the French and in danger if they should encounter them, Keppel and Palliser finally put into Portsmouth to face their courts-martial.

The naval situation in 1778 had been grave on both sides of the Atlantic. The condition of the fleets, with their shaky hulls and old masts, combined with the antagonism of Whig admirals and a Tory ministry, had prevented a repetition of the glorious exploits of Hawke and Boscawen in the previous war. Unable to assume a powerful offensive, the British Navy was reduced to a state where admirals more aggressive than D'Estaing and D'Orvilliers could have utilized the situation to great advantage.

The following year saw an event which marked the nadir of

[1] R. O., Adm, 1, 94, *Keppel to Adm.*, Oct. 27, 1778. [2] *Ibid.*

[3] *Ibid.*, Sept. 20, Sept. 27, Oct. 20, Oct. 22, Oct. 26, 1778.

[4] *Ibid.*, Oct. 27, 1778.

British sea power in the eighteenth century. Winter cruising is ordinarily done by frigates, which are able to weather almost any seas with impunity, but for lack of these cruisers, ships of the line were kept at sea, wracking their hulls and straining their masts, to protect commerce.[1] When Sir Charles Hardy was called from retirement in 1779 to assume command, the Western Squadron was thus in even worse shape than in the previous year. He sailed with thirty-five ships of the line on June 16, to protect commerce and cover the enemy. During July he had to send seven sail of the line back to Portsmouth or Plymouth because of sprung masts or leaky hulls, with orders to rejoin the fleet as soon as possible.[2] Reduced to a weaker condition than D'Orvilliers alone, he was entirely unable to oppose the added strength of the Spaniards, who entered the war in the summer. D'Orvilliers and the Spanish commander, old Don Luis de Cordoba, had an opportunity which Napoleon was to seek in vain twenty-five years later. This combined fleet of sixty-six ships of the line late in August drove Hardy's ships before them up the Channel, while Rochambeau was ready with over 50,000 men assembled at Havre and St. Malo. They had free run of the south coast as far as Plymouth, creating a panic at the dockyards and even in London. The "Armada" wasted its rare opportunity because of sickness, an east wind, and a lack of coördination; but so far as England's "first line of defence" was concerned, there was no effective opposition.

Complaints of bad masts in the Western Squadron continued for a long period. Hardy was unable to follow the Admiralty's instructions to send the *Isis*, 50, against the American, John Paul Jones, because her masts, which had been sprung in America, were still unrepaired.[3] Ross, despatched with a squadron to cruise off Brest, complained of similar defects.[4] In 1780 and 1781 Admiral Darby was sending in reports, which by that time must have had a familiar sound at Whitehall, of cracked masts and bowsprits, leaky hulls, defective rudders, broken knees, and of

---

[1] *Parl. Hist.*, xix, 825.

[2] R. O., Adm., I. 95, *Hardy to Adm.*, July 2, July 5, July 25, July 27, Aug. 3, 1779.

[3] *Ibid.*, Sept. 23, 1779.   [4] *Ibid.*, *Ross to Adm.*, Sept. 25, 1779.

injured ships towed astern, until finally detached for dockyard repairs, so that his fleet was unable to hold the seas against the Bourbon allies.[1] The Western Squadron was still losing masts in 1782. The dockyards had been better supplied by that time, but on one occasion, at least, there were no masts in store at Portsmouth to replace the loss.[2]

Meanwhile a naval war was in progress in the West Indies, where this account left Byron nursing his weakened fleet through winter storms in tardy pursuit of D'Estaing. From this time on, the effect of the mast problem is less marked than it had been in those first campaigns. The admirals, as was said, were absorbed chiefly in capturing and defending islands, and as the hurricane season approached in the late spring, they went north to coöperate with Clinton and Cornwallis, returning again each year when winter came. The outstanding feature of the mast problem in the West Indies was an almost total lack of great masts at the Antigua and Jamaica yards. Ships were constantly arriving with masts in bad condition, only to find nothing in store to substitute for those they had sprung or lost. The West Indian dockyards had been supplied from Portsmouth and Falmouth in New England all through the century, and the outbreak of the Revolution had left them with a peace-time establishment, naturally smaller than that of the home yards. When America became the main theatre of the war, the demands on these usually unimportant yards were greatly increased, and their mast stocks were subjected to a heavy drain. England, as was seen, could spare few masts from her own dwindling supply, and when a few were sent out to Jamaica from England in 1777, samples of the rotten wood were indignantly returned to the Navy Board.[3]

Admiral Gayton, commanding on that station, complained that the Jamaica yard was in need of masts and bowsprits at the very beginning of 1777, as those in store were entirely decayed.[4] Masts were so weak and hulls so foul that "the American privateers

---

[1] R. O., Adm., I. 95, *Darby to Adm.*, Oct. 9, Oct. 10, Oct. 11, Oct. 13, Dec. 1, 1780; Oct. 19, Oct. 21, 1781.

[2] *Ibid.*, Apr. 4, Apr. 25, 1782; *Capt. Brown to Barrington*, Nov. 17, 1782.

[3] R. O., Adm. Digest, 4809, *Jamaica Yard to N. B.*, Nov. 25, 1777.

[4] *Ibid.*, *Gayton to Adm.*, Jan. 3, 1777.

very much outsail our ships except the *Ariadne* and *Portland*,"
wrote Admiral Young, on the Leeward Islands station, later in the
year, explaining that they were "now in want of Naval Stores of
all kinds at the King's yard" at Antigua.[1]

Early in 1778, several of Howe's ships, blown off the northern
station, arrived at Antigua with masts lost or sprung. The repairs of those ships overtaxed the capacity of the dockyard, which
had scarcely been able to supply Young's little squadron.[2] Barrington, the Whig admiral, who was to follow Keppel and Howe
into retirement after successfully fighting D'Estaing's fleet with
his small squadron, replaced Young and continued to complain as
Young had complained.

> There appears to be a want of every kind of stores and of masts in par-
> ticular, there not being one fit for a frigate or any ship of a larger class, and
> those of the *Boreas* and the *Aurora* being at this time fished,

he wrote from Antigua in September, 1778, emphasizing the small
size and important duties of his squadron, and the need for every
ship.[3] Two months later, it had been necessary to fish the rotten
foremast and mainmast of his flagship, as there were still no substitutes, and he added:

> If a supply is not soon sent out, I shall be under the necessity of laying up
> some of the few ships I have, and if any ships arrive from America in the
> condition these did during the last winter, it will be attended with the
> greatest difficulty to fit them for service.[4]

Before the year was over the usual winter quota of ships began to
arrive. The frigate *Carysfort* had lost two of her masts and sprung
her bowsprit in a gale off Sandy Hook, and the hull was considerably damaged by the falling masts. She had also lost another set
of masts while cruising during the previous year. Other frigates
and some of Byron's ships of the line arrived with injuries of a like
nature.[5]

---

[1] R. O., Adm., 1, 310, *Young to Adm.*, Dec. 21, 1777.

[2] *Ibid.*, Mar. 13, 1778.

[3] *Ibid.*, *Barrington to Adm.*, Sept. 25, 1778.

[4] *Ibid.*, Nov. 19, 1778; N. B. In Letters, 1242, *Barrington to N. B.*, Nov. 24, 1778.

[5] *Ibid.*, *Capt. Fanshawe to Barrington*, Dec. 11, 1778; *Barrington to Adm.*, Jan. 7, 1779.

After 1778, summer casualties were rare, but the autumn gales continued to ruin many of the doubtful masts. The tremendous hurricane of October 13, 1780, dismantled dozens of ships in West Indian waters. The *Thunderer*, 74, was never heard from, eight other English warships foundered, and three were totally wrecked. French ships as well as English suffered in the hurricane.[1] The loss of masts was not to be wondered at, but the inability of the English to replace them was serious. Commissioner Laforey at Antigua, sending a list of injured ships, wrote to Middleton at the Navy Board: "What we shall do for masts, sails, and stores to repair all these damages we know of, and those we have yet to learn, I know not; if storeships are on the road to us it will be happy."[2] A month later the situation was unrelieved, and he told of the *Boreas* which "came in for what we had not—a mast."[3] One seventy-four was fitted out with masts intended for a sixty-four, and many other ships lay inactive at Antigua, waiting for masts.[4]

In the event which really ended the war, the lack of masts accentuated the incapacity of Admiral Graves in his bungling attempts to relieve Cornwallis at Yorktown. Seconded by the able but contemptuous Hood who had brought reinforcements from the West Indies, Graves lost an opportunity to force the entrance to Chesapeake Bay, in his unsuccessful action with the superior fleet of De Grasse on September 5, 1781. He had been far bolder in ordering the destruction of defenceless Falmouth for its refusal to supply masts, six years earlier.

Graves refused to renew the action, which might have been victorious, because his ships "had not speed enough in so mutilated a state to attack them."[5] There were sprung masts and leaky hulls in his ill-equipped squadron even before the action,[6]

---

[1] R. O., Adm., I, 310, *Hotham to Adm.*, Oct. 23, Nov. 5, 1780.

[2] N. R. S., *Barham Papers*, ii, 106.

[3] *Ibid.*, ii, 110.

[4] R. O., Adm., 1, 310, *Hotham to Adm.*, Oct. 23, 1780; Mundy, *Life and Correspondence of Admiral Lord Rodney*, iii, 414, 447–449, 454, 465, 472.

[5] Naval History Society, *Despatches of Thomas Graves*, 1781, p. 43.

[6] R. O., Adm., 1, 481, *Arbuthnot to Adm.*, Mar. 30, 1781; N. H. S., *Graves Despatches*, pp. 8, 9, 33, 34, 72.

and French gunnery had its usual damaging effect on the masts of the English. This impressed the cautious Graves so strongly that he withdrew his ships to New York, fearing the effect of the approaching equinoctial gales on the masts. While Washington, Lafayette, and Rochambeau were closing in on Cornwallis, Graves and Hood were struggling with the meagre mast-supply at New York. The *Carysfort* providentially brought a captured ship bound from New England to France with masts into port at this juncture, which, wrote Graves, "at this time of scarcity is a most valuable acquisition, there being hardly a spar left in the yard." [1] The captured masts were insufficient, and several of the ships had their masts patched up for want of proper materials. These masts were so weak that they could carry only a moderate sail to prevent them from tumbling over the side.

Clinton had 7,000 troops ready for the relief of Cornwallis, but repairs for the ships which were to convey them and force their entrance into Yorktown dragged on with painful slowness. Hood wrote to a friend in the Admiralty on October 14, five days before Yorktown fell:

Every moment, my dear Jackson, is prescious; and I flattered myself when we came in that we should ere this have been in the Chesapeake, but the repairs of the squadron have gone on unaccountably tedious, which has filled me with apprehension that we shall be too late to give relief to Lord Cornwallis. I pray God grant my fears be abortive! [2]

Two days later, Graves wrote in the same vein:

The excessive want of stores and provisions and the immense repairs wanted for a crazy and shatter'd Squadron, with many cross accidents which have interven'd has thrown back the equipment of the Squadron to a great distance. They are not quite ready. . . . I see no end to disappointments. [3]

On October 19, the day that Cornwallis surrendered, twenty-three ships, with Clinton's troops abroad, sailed out past Sandy Hook to his relief. Five days later, off the Virginia Capes, they learned that news which was to have such a significance in history, and returned in dejection to New York. Graves "did his best, but it was a fatally bad best," and he had held chief command on

---

[1] N. H. S., *Graves Despatches*, pp. 8, 9, 33, 34, 72, 119, 184.
[2] *Ibid.*, p. 117; N. R. S., *Letters of Sir Samuel Hood*, p. 37.
[3] N. H. S., *Graves Despatches*, p. 121.

the American station "just long enough to ruin his reputation as a naval officer." Under his command, it is questionable whether Cornwallis could have been saved even if the New York repairs had not caused such delay; but the mast situation had afforded an excuse at which such an over-cautious leader was wont to grasp. There were other admirals in the British navy who could probably have saved the situation in this striking instance of the influence of sea power on history.[1]

While Hood was nursing his damaged ships with their poorly fished masts on their return to the West Indies, a month later, he was worried over the state of the dockyards there. Remote from the centre of supplies, they still lacked the masts and stores which the English yards were by this time beginning to receive from Canada and the Baltic. They lacked, moreover, the appliances for replacing injured masts. Antigua had only eleven masts for ships of the line, the Jamaica yard at Port Royal was poorly provided, and there were only a few masts at St. Lucia, where a naval base had been established after its capture from the French in 1779.[2] There was not "a single lower mast for a 74-gun ship in this country," wrote Hood.[3] Many of the ships on the station already had masts in bad condition, and Hood foresaw the battles of the coming year which would cause heavy casualties in masts even if the British were victorious. He wrote the Admiralty that masts "*must* be supplied," just before his action with De Grasse at St. Kitts on January 26, 1782.[4]

Admiral Rodney's battle with De Grasse at Dominica on April 12, 1782, was regarded as England's chief victory in a war generally unsuccessful for her Navy. Rodney, however, was bitterly criticized by Hood at the time,[5] and has been blamed by later historians for allowing most of the French fleet to escape. Rodney considered it his first duty to take the bulk of his ships to Jamaica, to repair the heavy damage which their masts had sus-

---

[1] See N. H. S., *Graves Despatches*, pp. lxxii–lxxvi; Mahan, *Influence of Sea Power*, pp. 389–400.

[2] R. O., N. B. Out Letters, 2209, *N. B. to Adm.*, Feb. 22, 1782.

[3] N. R. S., *Letters of Sir Samuel Hood*, p. 49.   [4] *Ibid.*, pp. 59–62.

[5] *Ibid.*, pp. 104, 107, 132; Mundy, *Life and Correspondence of Admiral Lord Rodney*, ii, 285.

tained, while he left Hood to pursue the French with the few ships which remained comparatively sound.[1]

Rodney found the sleepy little dockyard at Port Royal in a shamefully run-down condition, for Antigua and St. Lucia had hitherto borne the onus of repairing the fleets. He had had the foresight to send his largest storeship to St. Lucia for masts before the battle, but these were not enough. "No one ship is perfect in her masts and yards, or without wants of various kinds," wrote Hood on April 30.[2] Rodney, anxious to intercept the French, mercilessly berated the dockyard officers, who seemed to him to have "not the least idea that the nation had the misfortune to be engaged in war."[3] Although he was the Tory favorite, he denounced in scathing terms the Sandwich naval administration, just fallen, which had allowed such a situation to develop.[4] When a dozen ships of the line were finally ready, he sent them out under Drake; but three soon returned "with their masts dangerously sprung," and before long the other nine were in the same condition.[5] That was one reason for the French escape.

The lack of masts at Jamaica produced another result, less important in its bearing on the war than the scattering of Byron's squadron, but fully as spectacular and far more tragic. Several of the English ships and a number of the French prizes had been so badly battered that Rodney considered it unwise to repair them at Port Royal, where the supply of masts and the facilities for repair were insufficient. Consequently he despatched nine of the injured ships of the line with several frigates under Graves, to act as a convoy for nearly a hundred merchantmen.[6] Rodney thought that the ships could stand a summer passage, but the September "line storm" struck them on the Grand Banks of Newfoundland. The *Canada*, 74, partially dismasted, was the only one of the

---

[1] R. O., Adm., 1, 314, *Rodney to Adm.*, Apr. 20, Apr. 26, 1782; Mundy, *op. cit.*, ii, 248–450.

[2] N. R. S., *Letters of Sir Samuel Hood*, p. 136.

[3] R. O., Adm., 1, 314, *Rodney to Adm.*, May 5, 1781; Mundy, *op. cit.*, ii, 272–276, 280, 281.

[4] R. O., Adm., *Ibid.*, May 18, 1782.

[5] *Ibid.*, June 26, July 9, 1782.

[6] *Ibid.*, May 5, 1782; Mundy, *op. cit.*, ii, 319.

nine ships of the line to reach England with part of the shattered convoy. The great *Ville de Paris*, 110, foundered with her entire crew of 800; the *Centaur*, 74, *Hector*, 74, and *Glorieux*, 74, also sank with most of the men on board; the flagship, *Ramilles*, 74, was abandoned and blown up at sea; and three sixty-fours captured from the French put into American ports with masts badly damaged and hulls leaking like sieves. The effect of the bad masts on Graves's flagship. the *Ramilles*, may be taken as an example. When the storm struck the squadron on September 16, the mainmast almost at once went by the board, the foretopmast fell over the starboard bow, and the fore-yard broke in the slings where it joined the mast. The wrecked masts which fell over the side tore much of the copper from the starboard side and exposed the seams so much that "the whole frame became at once exceedingly porous and leaky," while the rudder was nearly torn off. The ship was such a total wreck that she finally was blown up, after the admiral and crew had been fortunate enough to reach another ship. The total loss of life from that equinoctial gale off Newfoundland was more than 3,500 — exceeding the total number killed in action in the Navy during the whole war.[1]

There was no further fighting after that last contest in the West Indies, where England had finally retrieved some of its lost glory. The mast situation had been felt throughout the four years of war with the French. The most striking instances of it had been seen in the first squadron sent against the French and one of the last to return from the scene of action, while it was a constant drawback to the British during the intermediate campaigns.

The attendant problem of rotting oak in the hulls of the King's ships was also a serious matter throughout the war. As has been explained already, the decayed condition of the ships came not only from the general neglect of the Sandwich administration, but also from the building of ships with unseasoned timber during the Seven Years' War and in the decade following the close of the war, when the English groves were unable to furnish enough sea-

---

[1] N. R. S., *Journals and Letters of Sir T. Byam Martin*, iii, 379; *Mariner's Chronicle*, i, 200, ii, 293–302; Mundy, *op. cit.*, ii, 319 n.

soned oak to build sound warships. Credit must be given the
Sandwich administration for the wise measures taken to relieve
the shortage in 1771,[1] but they were soon neglected. The scores of
ships of the line which decayed prematurely were not ade-
quately replaced even when timber was available, and their rotting hulks did little but swell the brave paper total of naval
strength at the beginning of 1778.

The Navy was seriously handicapped by actual numerical disparity at the beginning of the war, and the utmost exertions could
not restore the lost "two-power" standard necessary to oppose
France and Spain, to say nothing of the Dutch and Americans.
The dockyard artificers worked by candlelight, "two days in
one," and orders were given to allow no time for seasoning timber. "Everything that could swim" was patched up to swell the
number of ships of the line — even the worst ships in "Rotten
Row" were temporarily repaired for home service. In spite of
all those efforts, however, the handicap from the earlier timber
shortage, the consequent dry rot, and the general Sandwich
neglect were so great that England was able to maintain barely a
hundred ships of the line at sea at a time when her opponents had
at least half as many more.[2]

While the influence of rotting oak on the effectiveness of campaigns is more difficult to recognize than the results of cracked
masts and lost bowsprits, there are evidences of a general prevalence of decay which must have diminished the efficiency of the
Navy. There was very frequent reference to leaky hulls and decayed timbers, with the accompanying story of water gaining in
the hold in spite of the constant work of crews at the pumps.
There were accounts of ships so rotten that it was necessary to
strap their hulls with cables to keep the planking in place —
ships so decayed that admirals would not trust them to cross the
Atlantic alone.[3] There was the *Vigilant* on the American station,
whose crew absolutely refused to trust their lives to her crazy hull
at sea.[4] There was the story of the *Bute*, an old East Indiaman

---

[1] See pp. 45, 58, 134.   [2] See Mundy, i, 381, for admission by Sandwich.

[3] R. O., Adm., 1, 310, *Hotham to Commissioner Laforey*, Aug. 8, 1780; *Ibid.*, 314,
Rodney to Adm., May 5, 1782.

[4] *Ibid.*, 486, *Arbuthnot to Adm.*, Apr. 10, 1780.

converted into a warship, so leaky on her return from the West
Indies that it was impossible to keep her afloat even in fair
weather; and when it was determined to scuttle her, one of the
sailors performed that task by clenching his fist and "driving it
without much pain to his knuckles, clear through her hull." [1]
Above all, there was the *Royal George*, 100, which went to the bottom with Admiral Kempenfeldt and several hundred of her crew
at Portsmouth in 1782, when her bottom fell out while she was
being "heeled over" in the ordinary fashion, for a slight repair
just below the waterline. The oak which had been worked into
her hull while still green, during the hasty building of the Seven
Years' War, was so far decayed that it could not hold the sheathing nails, and it was heard to split apart when the ship was subjected to the slight strain. [2] Similar conditions, accentuated by
the generally bad condition of the masts, were probably responsible for the loss of many of the sixty-six ships of the Royal Navy
which foundered during the war. [3]

The timber and mast supply was a weak spot in the constitution of the Navy. Interruptions to the regular supply were often
harmless under a sound administration; but when the Navy was
in a run-down condition, those interruptions resulted in dangerous
complications. Timely repairs of the ships rotting in reserve before the war would have helped to prevent the numerical disparity and the leaky hulls just described. An attempt has also
been made to show that the loss of the New England masts could
have been offset by several prompt measures; but under the administration which guided the Navy during the American Revolution, those steps were not taken. Consequently, storms and
hurricanes, playing on rotten pine and oak, helped to reduce the
British fleets to a condition where they could not prevent the
invaluable French assistance to American independence.

---

[1] *Parl. Hist.*, xix, 885.
[2] Fraser, *Londons of the British Fleet*, p. 264; see *Court-Martial Minutes, passim.*
[3] Snodgrass, *Letter to Dundas*, pp. 17–19.

CHAPTER VIII

TIMBER TRUST AND CONTINENTAL SYSTEM

SCARCELY had the Royal Navy definitely settled its mast problem after the troubles of the American Revolution, when the oak groves of England proved themselves unable to meet the heavy demands of the dockyards. That long-dreaded failure, more complete than on any previous occasion, materialized just at the time when Napoleon was threatening England with invasion. The native woodlands, exhausted by the decade of naval war with Revolutionary France, could supply scarcely half of the timber needed by the Navy, and even that amount was withheld for some time by the action of a powerful timber monopoly. As a result, shipwrights at Portsmouth and Plymouth clamored for oak which they could not obtain, while admirals on blockade duty were handicapped by battered ships which could not be repaired or replaced because of that same lack of oak. Unusual efforts to secure timber finally enabled the Navy to patch up enough ships to bring about the triumph at Trafalgar, but the lack of oak hampered it during the whole decade while Napoleon ruled as Emperor.

England turned to Europe for enough oak to make up the deficiency in her native supply, but she could obtain little from a continent which was rapidly coming under French control. By 1809, the spread of Napoleon's influence had checked every attempt of the British to secure timber from ports around the entire coast from the Baltic to the Black Sea. For clearness, the story of the domestic shortage and the thwarted quest for European oak will be carried through the decade, before turning to the partial relief which England received from the forests of her possessions overseas, and to the effect of the lack of oak upon the efficiency of her fleets.

Gloomy predictions of an immediate shortage of naval oak had been made by the Commissioners of the Land Revenue after an exhaustive study of the situation in 1792, on the eve of the long contest with France.[1] In spite of these forebodings, it was another ten years before the effects of a lack of oak were felt to any appreciable extent. During the first phase of the war with France, the dockyards experienced the benefits of the adequate stores piled up in reserve by Sir Charles Middleton during the years of peace. All the regular sources of timber supply had been available to the British, with only occasional interruptions, and the impotence of the French navy had somewhat lessened the necessity for dockyard exertions. When the naval war was renewed in May, 1803, however, the British timber stores were so low that they proved quite unequal to the task of properly repairing a navy to oppose Napoleon.

Certain episodes in the British politics and naval administration of the period help to explain that unfortunate depletion of the timber stores and the difficulty in replenishing them. Lord Spencer was replaced as First Lord of Admiralty by John Jervis, Earl of St. Vincent, in March, 1801, when Addington succeeded Pitt as Prime Minister. The three years during which St. Vincent served at the head of the Admiralty were marked by two steps in his general reform programme which had a pronounced effect on the timber situation. He reduced the timber stores to a dangerously low condition by cancelling many of the contracts, and he prevented the replenishing of the supply by alienating the timber contractors through a well-intentioned but untimely reform in the method of receiving timber in the dockyards.

Corruption was so prevalent in the civil branch of the Navy that St. Vincent commenced a campaign to straighten out the whole system as soon as he came into office. There had been an attempt at such reform directly after the American Revolution, sponsored by the Shelburne and Rockingham ministries. A commission of inquiry was finally appointed in 1786, and it has been seen that it attempted to do away with the wholesale taking of fees and gratuities in the Navy Office. The outbreak of the war with France, however, checked the reform movement before it

[1] See pp. 135–137.

accomplished much that was tangible.[1] Reform agitation was renewed about 1798 by one of the most interesting characters associated with the timber problem. Sir Samuel Bentham, younger brother of the famous Jeremy, was an adventurous and irascible genius with a penchant for naval architecture. After a sojourn in Russia, where he built a fleet for Catherine the Great on the Black Sea, Bentham returned to England. There influence and insistence secured for him the novel office of Inspector General of the Navy, which involved no specified duties or authority. Bentham applied his inventive talents to many improvements in naval construction, notably the building of warships without the use of the scarce large timber. More important, however, were the activities which won him the title of "Fault-Finder General." On the strength of his roving commission, Bentham pried into every corner of the corrupt civil administration of the Navy and threatened alarming exposures. Finally, in 1798, he drew up a series of proposals for putting the Navy on a basis of business efficiency. The hostility of the Navy Board and the dockyard officers was so great that nothing was done under the Spencer administration.[2] In 1801, Bentham found an enthusiastic champion for reform in St. Vincent, who was already inclined to drastic measures for cleaning out the corruption of which he had seen ample evidences while in command of the Channel fleet.[3]

Retrenchment of naval expenses was an important plank in St. Vincent's reform programme. Economy was made the watchword in the dockyards. Thinking, perhaps, that the cessation of hostilities in 1801 meant more than a short breathing-spell, St. Vincent had scores of dockyard workmen discharged. The building of new ships and the repairing of old ones were curtailed, and many of the smaller vessels were sold out of the service. The passion for economy extended even to the sale of surplus dockyard

---

[1] N. R. S., *Barham Papers*, ii, 71, 72, 176–178, 182, 192, 232, 320, 321, 337–345, 347–349; *Parl. Hist.*, xxxvi, 1139.

[2] *Commons Reports*, xiii, 494, 495, 499; Bentham, *Life of Sir Samuel Bentham*, pp. 135–142, 187–198; Sargent, *Essays of a British Manufacturer*, p. 266; R. O., Adm. In Letters from Inspector General, *passim*.

[3] Bentham, *op. cit.*, pp. 198–204; Anson, *Life of John Jervis, Earl of St. Vincent*, pp. 299–301.

stores of naval materials, and the Navy abandoned the attempts which it had recently made to secure timber from abroad.[1]

As a result of these measures, the timber supply was in a dangerously low condition when the two navies were at war again in 1803. While Bonaparte was collecting his armies and his flat-boats around Boulogne, England had less than a year's supply of timber on hand, and there was a total lack of certain necessary kinds of oak.[2] Most of the ships were badly in need of repair after their nine years of service in the previous contest, and there was a crying need for enough oak to patch up an adequate naval force. St. Vincent had reduced the naval expenses by some two millions in two years, but his measures proved to be false economy. After a dangerous delay, the stores were finally replenished at abnormally high prices and the premature rotting and wracking of the ships through want of proper oak offset these savings by a tremendous additional cost. There is no doubt that the old admiral meant well, and that the economy would have been of real value in time of real peace. Unless, however, St. Vincent felt that the contest with France had definitely ended, there is some ground for Middleton's condemnation of these actions as "madness and imbecility in the extreme."[3]

That unfortunate effort to reduce expenditure nearly emptied the dockyard stores — another reform of the St. Vincent administration prevented a rectification of the mistake. Bentham had been particularly impressed by the corruption and waste resulting from divided responsibility in the handling of the timber supply in the dockyards.[4] He was partly responsible for the creation of the office of "timber master" in 1801. These new officials were assigned to each yard, charged with the sole responsibility for the receipt, storage, and conversion of all timber.[5] This also was a

---

[1] R. O., Adm. Digest, 4853, *N. B. to Adm.*, Aug. 14, Sept. 30, Oct. 7, Oct. 29, Nov. 23, Dec. 4, 1802; 4865, Apr. 2, 1804; *Parl. Papers*, 1805 (152), ii, 45; Bentham, *Life of Samuel Bentham*, p. 205; Derrick, *Memoirs of the Rise and Progress of the Royal Navy*, p. 217; James, *Naval History*, iii, 212; Mahan, *Influence of Sea Power on the French Revolution and Empire*, ii, 122, 166.

[2] See pp. 377–381.   [3] N. R. S., *Barham Papers*, iii, 69.   [4] See pp. 71–73.

[5] R. O., Adm. Digest, 4853, *Bentham to Adm.*, Dec. 26, 1801; *Commons Reports*, xii, 833–836; *Parl. Papers*, 1803–04 (134), iii, 16–25; Bentham, *op. cit.*, pp. 206–209.

well-intended measure, but it nearly proved ruinous to the Navy through its application at this time.

The creation of these timber masters aroused the hostility of the powerful timber contractors who had obtained a virtual monopoly of the available supply of English oak. They argued that they had been able to supply timber at a comparatively low price because of the free and easy method of checking its amount and quality by the dockyard officials and clerks, who, it has been seen, received more pay from the contractors than they did from the government. The new timber masters, the dealers claimed, were too zealous in rejecting timber for trivial defects, knowing that they were held personally responsible for its quality. The contractors argued that the arbitrary exercise of power by these new officials threatened to wipe out all their profits. They were determined to do away with these obnoxious inspectors or at least to render them innocuous. To accomplish this end, they utilized the very powerful weapon which they had at their disposal in the threat to cut off the supply of English oak from the Navy.

The Navy was in a vulnerable position in this contest with the "Timber Trust." The dockyard timber piles contained less than a third of the amount necessary for a safe reserve. There was a certain scarcity of timber in the country, but the private ship-yards had little trouble in securing all they needed for the construction of East Indiamen. The contractors, however, showed no desire to furnish oak to the Navy as long as the timber masters were retained. The Navy Board tended to side with the contractors in this contest, urging a relaxation of the rigid dockyard inspection. St. Vincent, however, stood firmly behind the new reform measure and opposed all compromise. No love was lost between St. Vincent and Sir Andrew Snape Hamond, the Comptroller, and the Navy Board gave the Admiralty only half-hearted support against the timber magnates. Violent recriminations passed between the two boards. St. Vincent hinted that the relations of the Navy Board and the contractors were not above suspicions of bribery, while the Navy Board retorted that, if they had been free to carry out their own measures, there would be no shortage of oak in the dockyards. Certainly, the adequate supply of naval timber was the paramount consideration at the time.[1]

Early in 1802, the displeasure of the contractors was evident in the curtailed supply of English oak. Various plans were suggested for the relief of the situation by the use of foreign timber, and tentative plans were made to secure oak from Holland, Canada, the Baltic, the Adriatic, and the Black Sea, while the building of warships in India was proposed. The economy programme put a stop to most of these measures, and the contest narrowed to the supply of native oak. Hamond urged conciliation with the contractors. "I hold it to be next to impossible that 30,000 load of timber is to be procured but by timber dealers," he wrote in March, 1802.[2] St. Vincent would hear none of this and felt that the power of the monopoly could be broken by appealing to the country. Printed contracts were sent to scores of gentlemen who owned oak groves in various parts of the country and naval purveyors attempted to make individual bargains as they had done at the time of the Restoration. The response was disappointing, for only 1,450 loads were secured by this means.[3]

The contractors, in the meantime, were badly in arrears in deliveries on the contracts which they had already made. In February, 1803, the Navy Board reported that nearly 12,000 loads were due on old contracts, although the price had been raised fourteen per cent the previous year. Once more, Hamond attempted compromise, writing:

> We have had several meetings with the timber merchants, and after much discussion of the many objections which have been made by them from time to time with the mode of receipt at present pursued in the dockyards and of the points which might be conceded to them in regard to the service, and also taking into consideration the urgent [need] there is for procuring a large supply of timber with as little delay as possible, we have at length come to a final conclusion.

The Navy Board consented to a twenty-five per cent increase in price; but even at that, the principal merchants, Larking, Bow-

---

[1] See esp. B. M., Add. MSS, 37275, ff. 270, 289, 298. This collection of correspondence on the timber situation between 1801 and 1804 contains many papers which are duplicated in the Record Office archives.

[2] R. O., N. B. Out Letters, 2231, *N. B. to Adm.*, Mar. 23, 1802.

[3] *Ibid.*, Nov. 30, 1802, Feb. 2, 1803.

sher, Collins, and Adams, agreed to furnish only 16,800 loads, a
small part of the Navy's needs.[1]

That was the last concession on the part of the magnates, and
their refusal to make further contracts became serious when the
naval war was renewed three months after that agreement. St.
Vincent still tried to get along without them. The "Timber
Trust" was irritated by the fact that shortly after that February
conference, the Navy publicly advertised for timber in the county
papers. The appeal brought little response and served only to increase the price of oak. In spite of Navy Board protests, the
Admiralty ordered Sir William Rule, Deputy Surveyor of the
Navy, to make a tour of the country in an effort to procure oak,
but his mission brought only 2,000 loads into the dockyards.[2]
The royal forests should have proved valuable in such a crisis, but
the appeals of the Admiralty for heavy fellings in Dean and New
forests resulted in only another 2,000 loads, scarcely a month's
supply.[3] St. Vincent desired an act of Parliament which would
enable the Navy to commandeer whatever oak it needed, after
the manner of the French *martelage*, but such a measure could
scarcely be expected from a body of gentlemen who owned oak
groves themselves and profited by the prevailing high prices.[4]
These various attempts demonstrated the strength of the monopoly control of the oak supply, but the old First Lord of the Admiralty would not abandon his timber masters.

The contractors remained equally stubborn. The desperate
need for oak which followed the renewal of hostilities in 1803 led
the Navy Board to write to all the merchants in September, ask-
ing what they would have to offer. Not a single reply was received
before the end of the year, and when the contractors finally did
respond, most of them declared that "the rigid mode of receipt in
the dockyards" was their reason for not making offers. Some of
the most prominent contractors stated that they had withdrawn
altogether from contracting with the Navy because of the timber

---

[1] R. O., N. B., Out Letters, 2231, *N. B. to Adm.*, Feb. 22, 1803, Mar. 24, 1804.

[2] B. M., Add. MSS, 37275, f. 293 (N. B. Memorandum on Timber Supply).

[3] R. O., N. B. Out Letters, 2231, *N. B. to Adm.*, Nov. 11, 1802, Dec. 17, 1803;
Adm. Digest, 4858, *Adm. to Treasury*, Jan. 18, 1804.

[4] See p. 63.

masters. Reviewing this situation in their report to the Admiralty, on March 24, 1804, the Navy Board continued:

> The quantity offered to us at this season of the year has generally been considerable and as that is not the case at present, we deem it incumbent on us to apprize their Lordships of the uncertainty of obtaining the necessary supply of timber (beyond what will be received from His Majesty's forests) by the usual mode of contract, that no time may be lost before the felling season commences.[1]

Hamond declared that new measures must be adopted "rather than rely any longer on the old contractors many of whom have apparently ceased to have an interest in their relations with this board." [2] He scouted the Admiralty suggestion that Rule, the Deputy Surveyor, be sent on another quest for oak, arguing that such a step would call attention to the desperate needs of the Navy and would "induce a combination among the timber merchants with a view of buying up the whole stock of timber in the country and selling it at their own prices" — an amusing statement in view of the fact that the Navy had been fighting just such a combination for two years. Instead, he recommended the appointment of a Purveyor General, and the Navy Board nominee for that position was none other than John Larking, the ringleader of the monopolists.[3]

Relief from this deadlock was not far off. It could not come too soon, for, as will be seen, the shortage of oak in the dockyards was at its worst in these early months of 1804.[4] Pitt was already launching an attack against St. Vincent's shipbuilding policy, and the timber situation received ample publicity from its inclusion in the charges against the old admiral.[5] St. Vincent was replaced as First Lord of the Admiralty by Henry Dundas, Viscount Melville, when Pitt returned to power on May 10, 1804.

That date is important as a turning-point in the timber situation. The Navy Board abandoned its obstructionist tactics and

---

[1] R. O., N. B. Out Letters, 2231, *N. B. to Adm.*, Mar. 24, 1804.
[2] *Ibid.*
[3] *Ibid.*, Mar. 29, 1804.
[4] See pp. 377–381.
[5] See esp. *Parl. Debates*, 1st ser., v, 81–102; vii, 175–184; *Parl. Papers*, 1805 (152), vol. 1, *passim*.

coöperated wholeheartedly with the new Lords of Admiralty in a solution of the timber problem. During the year in which Melville served as head of the Admiralty, the timber piles were replenished so that it was possible to patch up enough ships for the successful completion of the Trafalgar campaign.

In order to accomplish that end, it was necessary to make peace with the "Timber Trust." It was a peace without victory for the Admiralty. Larking was appointed Purveyor General, and the Navy Board arranged for higher prices, together with a revision of the printed contracts whereby the timber masters were rendered innocuous.[1] The "Timber Trust," as has been seen, flourished for half a century after that victory, frequently dictating its own terms to the Navy.[2] Even with the coöperation of the merchants, however, the Navy found that the groves of England were inadequate to meet the increasing demands of the dockyards. The surrender to the monopolists brought considerable native oak into the yards, but it amounted to less than half of what the naval construction and repairs required.

Realizing that it would be necessary to secure timber from beyond the seas, the Navy Board made a thorough canvass of all apparently available sources of foreign relief for the domestic timber shortage, drawing up a comprehensive memorandum on the subject. This memorandum, evidently suggested by Middleton, outlined the chief points of the great quest which lasted more than ten years, a quest which met with constant checks when one proposed source after another was cut off, and which ended with the importation from remote parts of the earth of timbers which were absolutely unknown to the Navy Board in 1804.[3] The problem was almost entirely one of timber for the hulls of ships, for British North America could supply an immense number of excellent masts. The Navy would have been spared many of the worst effects of the timber crisis if it had not interrupted the search for foreign timber begun in 1802.

[1] B. M., Add. MSS, 37275, f. 292 (N. B. Memorandum on Timber Supply); N. B. In Letters, 1561, *Larking to N. B.*, Sept. 26, Dec. 12, 1804.

[2] See pp. 59–60.

[3] B. M., Add. MSS, 37275, ff. 292, 293. Compare with N. R. S., *Barham Papers*, iii, 34.

The first consideration of the Navy Board was "to import as much foreign oak timber as can be procured from all parts of the world, for the purpose of being used in repairs of all old ships, so as to reserve the English oak entirely for the building of ships or giving a slight repair to those in best condition." It was planned to secure 3,000 loads of oak from Upper Canada at once. The importation of Rhine oak from Dort, which had been started in 1802 and cancelled as a part of the economy programme, was to be renewed and efforts would be made to obtain oak from other parts of northeastern Europe. Even the forests bordering the Adriatic and the Black Seas were to be examined for a possible supply of oak. The high quality of Dantzig oak timber was recognized, but Solly, the contractor, demanded such a price for it that importations for the time being would be limited to the usual crown plank. Dantzig, however, could be of great service in another way. "With a further view of lessening the consumption of oak timber, we propose to repair ships' upper works with fir and to substitute fir for oak in such parts of new ships as it may be applied to without injury to their strength or durability," wrote the Navy Board.[1] At the suggestion of St. Vincent's Admiralty Board, the new administration had just ordered 15,000 loads of fir timber to be rushed from Dantzig, and it will be seen that this single step was of great value in enabling the dockyards to patch up a large number of ships as quickly as possible.[2]

The Navy had used only a very limited range of timbers prior to 1804, it may be remembered.[3] Oak, with a little elm, beech, and fir for the hull, and fir, pine, and spruce for masts, was the only wood used to any extent. An important landmark in the timber problem, indicative of the weakening of old prejudices under pressure of the situation, was the proposed importation of pitch pine from the southern United States, and East Country larch from Poland, with the remark that they had never been employed before. These were the forerunners of the new woods which broke down the old belief that oak was essential for the construction of a good warship.

[1] B. M., Add. MS., 37275, ff. 292, 293.
[2] R. O., N. B. Out Letters, 2231, *N. B. to Adm.*, Apr. 2, 1804. See p. 382.
[3] See pp. 15–33.

The Navy Board immediately began to arrange for a supply of these timbers. Leaving the project to import American timber for the next chapter, the story will deal next with the efforts to secure timber from Europe — those efforts blocked at every step by the extension of Napoleon's influence. The first and the boldest attempt was an effort to get French and other oak from Holland. This venture was entrusted to Larking, the timber magnate, who agreed to furnish foreign timber as Purveyor General. A timber monopoly had been broken up in 1771 by the use of foreign oak, but Larking prevented the repetition of such a process by gaining control of the foreign supply himself. The contract for Dutch timber which he and one Dorrien had made in 1802 had been cancelled in accordance with the fatal policy of economy.[1] It was now much more difficult to secure timber, for Napoleon was considering a large purchase of naval oak from the same region.[2] Through the medium of a Dutch house, Larking was able to collect some 5,000 pieces of timber, part of it valuable compass timber from the Saar valley. The timber was collected easily, but shipping it was a matter of extreme difficulty.[3] By means of "secret service money to French commissaries," nearly half of the logs were brought to England *via* Emden, where Prussian ships were secured; but the remainder, worth £27,000, was still rotting in Dort in 1814. In 1811, the Navy Board went so far as to authorize the sale of this ship timber to the French — an anomalous procedure which failed because the Dutch house had a low opinion of the credit of the French marine.[4]

After the failure of this impudent attempt to draw timber from a market under French control, where the French were buying timber for their own navy, Larking shifted his efforts to a region a little farther removed from Napoleon's influence. In the autumn of 1804, the Navy Board approved of Larking's suggestion that he investigate the timber offered by Viscount Borsthal in his forest of Borsthal in Holstein. In October, he visited the viscount

[1] R. O., Adm. Digest, 4853, *N. B. to Adm.*, Aug. 14, Sept. 30, Oct. 7, Nov. 23, 1802; *Parl. Papers*, 1805 (152), ii, 45.

[2] *Corr. de Nap.*, x, 18, 19.

[3] R. O., N. B. In Letters, 1559, *Larking to N. B.*, Feb. 14, Sept. 26, Nov. 26, 1804.

[4] *Ibid.*, 1560, Mar. 9, 1806, July 7, 1810, June 28, 1811; 1561, July 13, 1814.

at his château, and shortly afterward, contracted with the Navy for 50,000 loads of oak, an amount sufficient to have built half of Nelson's Trafalgar fleet. This timber was to be delivered during the next four or five years, at the same price as English oak, on the condition that the Navy Board advance Larking £30,000 to finance the operation.[1] It was not difficult to arrange for the purchase of timber, for European landowners were generally far from reluctant to cut their oaks at the high price which naval timber then commanded, and English gold outweighed French promises. As in Holland, the great difficulty lay in securing shipping. No part of Holstein is more than twenty miles from navigable waters, and the region abounded in semi-independent ports which thrived in those years when neutral flags still offered some protection. French control over the ports varied from month to month, and until the spring of 1806, Larking shipped dozens of cargoes from Lubec, Hamburg, Lauenburg, Tonningen, and finally Bremen.[2]

The French advance deprived Viscount Borsthal of more than half the projected revenue from his forest, for in April, 1806, Larking wrote:

> The Ports of the Elbe, the Weser and the Baltic from which I have to import the foreign timber that I have contracted for being shut against me, I have turned my thoughts to other channels. . . . The timber, together with the thickstuff, plank and knees that I propose to send, grows in the same countries from which Danzick is in great part supplied with plank, and of course the quality will be good.[3]

He agreed to supply it at the same price as the English and Holstein oak. The Navy Board offered no objection, and Larking, driven from Holland and then from Holstein, proceeded to fill the remainder of his contract from farther east in the Baltic, at Libau and Riga, until the agreements at Tilsit again thwarted him.[4]

From 1801 until 1807, England was able to draw timber from the eastern Baltic with almost no interruption. It was natural

---

[1] R. O., N. B., In Letters, 1559, *Larking to N. B.*, Sept. 26, Dec. 12, 1804; Adm. Digest, 4865, *N. B. to Adm.*, Dec. 14, 1804. See 39 Geo. III, c. 111.

[2] R. O., N. B., *Ibid.*, 1560, Apr. 11, 1805, Feb. 7, July 21, 1806.

[3] *Ibid.*, Apr. 9, 1806.

[4] *Ibid.*, 1625, *Solly to N. B.*, Apr. 19, 1806.

that the Navy Board should turn to the well-organized timber trade of the East Country in the crisis of 1804. The house of Solly at Dantzig had monopolized the naval timber contracts from that port for many years. It served the Navy well during the Napoleonic era, and profited well by it. The Navy Board had been unwilling to pay the £15 a load which Isaac Solly demanded for oak timber, and it was not until Larking was driven from the west that recourse was had to Polish and Russian oak; but Solly furnished fir, which the Navy urgently needed.[1]

England was also drawing on the Baltic for the usual masts and naval stores. Usborne and Lindegren were supplying masts from Riga, and the houses of Morison, Cummings, and Pierson there, as well as Thomas Tooke at St. Petersburg, offered their services, alarmed at the activities of Bergevin, the French naval commissioner.[2] They were not parties to the secret that Moir, the secret agent posing as a timber dealer, was luring those enemy cargoes into the clutches of English Admiralty courts.[3] Up to 1807, the Baltic timber trade was heavier than in times of peace, under the impulse of high prices caused by the heavy demand.

The situation in the Baltic was so favorable to England in 1805 that the Navy took an exceedingly unusual step for the relief of its timber shortage. When Samuel Bentham had been constructing warships in the Crimea for Catherine the Great, he had become acquainted with Admiral Tchichagoff, who suggested in 1805 that England might find a partial solution for her timber problem by constructing warships in Russia. It will be recalled that it was a cardinal principle in British policy to build all warships in English yards and even the construction of warships in New England had been frowned upon.[4] Bentham was sent to Russia in the summer of 1805, however, to take Tchichagoff's suggestion at its face value and build ten ships of the line and ten frigates at St. Petersburg and Archangel. Lord Barham, the

[1] *Parl. Papers*, 1835 (519), xix, 85.

[2] *Ibid.*, 1805 (1), iv, 328–333; Adm. Digest, 4858, *Sec. of State to Adm.*, June 16, 1803; *N. B. to Adm.*, Mar. 9, Aug. 17, 1803; *Adm. Warren to Adm.*, Apr. 4, 1803; *Cummings to Adm.*, Mar. 18, 1803; *Adm. to N. B.*, June 27, 1803; F. O., Russia, 66, Nov. 11, 1806; *Ibid.*, Consuls, 71, May 14, 1807.

[3] See pp. 196–198.   [4] See pp. 74–76, 244–245.

former Sir Charles Middleton, who had just been raised to a peerage, and to the head of the Admiralty in place of Melville, claimed that this step was taken to relieve the timber shortage which was so serious just before Trafalgar; but there is reason to believe that an added cause for the mission was the Navy's desire to be rid of Bentham, with his troublesome searchings into naval maladministration.[1]

In June, 1805, Bentham left for Russia, taking with him a group of shipwrights and two transports full of necessary copper and iron fastenings. He was well received by Admiral Tchicha-goff, then Minister of Marine, and proceeded to contract for timber enough, not only to build the ships, but to bring back in them a supply of masts and other naval timber. Whether the admiral's original remark had been unauthorized, or taken too seriously by Bentham, or whether the Tsar had a change of heart, considering the irregularity of the procedure, it soon became apparent that Bentham would not be permitted to build warships for England in Russian ports, though he received flattering inducements to apply his talents to building up the Tsar's marine. The representations of Stuart, the chargé d'affaires, were in vain, and Bentham's efforts to utilize the influence of friends powerful in the government also failed. By 1806, the project was given up as futile, and Bentham returned to England with some of the timber which he had collected.[2] The Baltic will be considered again, at a time when the unrestricted access of English commerce had given way to a necessity to smuggle timber out of the East Country.

While those events had been going on in the Baltic on the eve of Napoleon's campaign against Prussia and Russia, naval timber agents were busy in the south of Europe. Malta had just become England's chief naval base in the Mediterranean. After the loss of Minorca in 1782, there had been no dockyard east of Gibraltar.

[1] N. R. S., *Barham Papers*, iii, 101, 111; Bentham, *Life of Sir Samuel Bentham*, pp. 236, 237.

[2] R. O., Adm. In Letters from Inspector Gen., 3527, *Bentham to Adm.*, July 24, July 25, Aug. 8, Aug. 27, 1805; N. B. Out Letters, 2539, *N. B. to Bentham*, July 29, 1805, Sept. 11, Sept. 20, 1806, June 20, 1807; Adm. Digest, 4916, *N. B. to Adm.*, Oct. 2, 1813; F. O., Russia, 62; *Baron Budberg to Stuart*, July 14, 1806; *Stuart to Fox*, July 31, 1806; *Ibid.*, 63, *Instructions to Lord Gower*, May 24, 1806; *Ibid.*, 66, *Adm. to Fox*, May 11, 1806; *Bentham to Adm.*, Apr. 9, 1806; Bentham, *op. cit.*, pp. 238-240.

The naval situation demanded the presence of English ships in that region, and Nelson had realized the need of a centrally located port for refitting when he had to search the Archipelago for naval stores. England was therefore willing to incur the hostility of the Tsar, and to offer a cause for the renewal of war with Bonaparte, in her determination to keep this old stronghold of the Knights of St. John, which Keith captured from the French in 1800. Nelson was continually sending his ships to Malta to refit during his blockade of Toulon in 1803 and 1804.

The supply of naval materials at the foreign dockyards was important, but was liable to be neglected. British admirals had learned that to their cost when they took their battered ships to New York, Newport, Antigua, and Port Royal during the American Revolution. The foreign dockyard had to be ready not only to repair the sprung masts and leaky hulls resulting from high winds and heavy seas, but also to meet the urgent demands of refitting a fleet after an encounter with the enemy. With Nelson's force constantly blockading Toulon, it was possible that such an action might occur in the Mediterranean, and it was essential to keep the new yard at Malta well supplied. At the same time, there was such a crying need for timber at Portsmouth, Plymouth, and the other English yards, that oak from the usual sources could not well be spared for Malta.

It was, therefore, determined to follow the French example by utilizing the old Venetian supply of excellent oak which grew along the eastern shore of the Adriatic, and to provide Malta with a further supply of timber and masts from the Black Sea. For the former purpose the Navy Board, in 1803, sent "Mr. John Leard, a very intelligent officer who has been sometime resident in that country," to investigate the possibility of securing oak timber from the Hungarian forests of "Croatia and Sclavonia." Leard had been in the government service for over twenty years, and in 1802 had begun to supply the Navy with Adriatic hemp, cordage, and deals until his contract, along with so many others, fell victim to St. Vincent's retrenchment.[1]

[1] N. B. Out Letters, 2231, *N. B. to Adm.*, Mar. 23, 1803; In Letters, 1559, *Leard to N. B.*, Apr. 23, 1802, June 23, 1804; 1561, Mar. 31, 1813.

Leard reported that splendid timber could be procured, at a rather high price, from the oak forests which extended along the Save and Danube as far as the Turkish frontier. Some of these forests were the property of the Hungarian nobility, and others, divided into "regiments," belonged to the Emperor Francis I. The most convenient source of timber was the forest of the Szleiving Regiment near Carlstadt, on a tributary of the Save some seventy miles from Fiume. A merchant of Fiume, one Adamich, agreed to deliver this timber to British transports at Buccari and Fiume, bringing it by wagons over the military road which was then nearing completion. Five horses could draw two tons of timber over the seventy miles of road in a week. There was need of haste, Leard reported, for French and Spanish agents were swarming into the country in an effort to procure timber for their dockyards.[1]

The Navy Board authorized Leard, at a generous commission, to arrange with Adamich for 30,000 loads of oak in various forms of timber, plank, knees, and treenails. Through the assistance of Lord Harrowby, the British minister at Vienna, Adamich received permission to cut 1,570 trees at once, with provisions for subsequent cutting, and there were prospects that Malta and the English yards would soon be supplied with oak timber superior in quality to any from the Baltic and Canada.[2]

The battle of Austerlitz broke up these plans, for at the Peace of Pressburg which immediately followed, on December 26, 1805, Austria ceded the eastern Adriatic littoral to Napoleon's Kingdom of Italy, and French troops took possession at once. They seized a large amount of timber which Adamich had collected at Fiume and Buccari, and 3,000 logs which had been cut near Carlstadt were still lying in the forest in 1809, when Adamich hoped to renew operations.[3] The Wagram campaign dashed those hopes and it was not until late in 1813 that timber from Fiume was finally on its way to the Malta dockyard, though Adamich had

[1] *N. B. In Letters*, 1559, *Leard to N. B.*, June 2, 1804.
[2] *Ibid.*, Out Letters, 2232, *N. B. to Adm.*, July 26, 1804. Much of this correspondence also in B. M., Add. MSS, 37275, ff. 292–313.
[3] R. O., N. B. In Letters, 1560, *Leard to N. B.*, Mar. 1, 1809.

smuggled a little out of the country in spite of the French control.[1]
Leard, who had been dismissed in 1811 for suspicious handling of
the timber funds, was appointed consul at Fiume to carry on the
supply. England continued to use Fiume timber after the war.[2]

Driven from the northern Adriatic, the Navy turned to the oak
groves of Albania in 1809. Turkey was emerging from the French
influence which Sebastiani had exercised at Constantinople, and
Adair, the British minister, began to make representations to the
Sublime Porte in view of a supply of ship timber. Finding the
government in financial straits, he proposed to the Grand Vizier a
loan on the condition that Turkey permit the export of oak for the
Navy. A palace revolution checked his plans, but the consent was
finally secured.[3]

At the same time, England was negotiating with that picturesque viceroy of the Sultan, Ali Pasha of Janina, a resourceful brigand who had carved out a sizable domain in Albania which
he held in virtual independence of his suzerain. The French were
establishing an arsenal at Prevesa to utilize Albanian timber, and
Ali Pasha had a free choice between the two.[4] British gold decided the question, and Captain Leake reported that

His Highness Ali Pasha had no objection to a supply of construction timber
being furnished from his territories provided the contract be made in such
a manner as to have the appearance of a speculation of the merchants of that
country and not as supplied from His Highness to the British Government.[5]

It has been mentioned several times that an efficient timber
supply depends largely on a well-organized trade such as that in
the Baltic. Organized business scarcely existed in the wild domain of Ali Pasha, and the few merchants, declaring that "timber
was a poor and troublesome article," demanded an impossible

[1] R. O., Adm. Digest, 4910, *N. B. to Adm.*, Mar. 4, 1812; Hoste, *Memoirs and
Letters*, ii, 29, 137.

[2] R. O., Adm. Digest, 4809, *N. B. to Adm.*, June 6, 1811, *Sec. of State to Leard*,
July 14, 1811; N. B. In Letters, 1561, *Leard to Castlereagh*, Dec. 23, 1812. See *Adm.,
Acct. Gen., Misc., 135. Correspondence on Adriatic Timber, passim.*

[3] R. O., F. O., Turkey, 64, *Adair to Canning*, Sept. 24, Oct. 10, 1809; Adm. Digest,
4898, *Adair to Adm.*, Oct. 23, 1809.

[4] R. O., F. O., Turkey, 64, *Meyer to Adair*, Dec. 26, 1809; Adm. Digest, 4901, *Sec.
of State to Adm.*, Nov. 23, 1811.

[5] *Ibid.*, 4898, *Capt. Leake to Adm.*, May 12, 1810.

price. It was finally arranged that Ali Pasha's lieutenants, Cap-
lan Pasha and Ibrahim Bey, should bring the timber to the shore
at Durazzo, where boats under the protection of a British cruiser
would convey it to Corfu, whence it was to be carried in transports to Malta.[1] Thus the Mediterranean station was finally provided with an ample supply of good oak in the last years of the
timber crisis.

Ali Pasha was later rewarded for this service in a way which
reflects England's appreciation of the value of ship timber more
than any feeling for self-determination of peoples. Dreading the
savage rule of "The Lion of Janina," as Ali Pasha was styled, the
inhabitants of the port of Parga had placed themselves under
British protection. Ali Pasha coveted this port "as the dearest
object of his existence." In 1818, Sir Thomas Maitland agreed
to cede Parga to the Ottoman Porte, to come under Ali Pasha,
who was to indemnify all who wished to emigrate from Turkish
rule. The whole population of Pargiotes, abandoned by England,
determined to emigrate, and Maitland arranged that England pay
the £150,000 indemnity on condition that Ali Pasha furnish
50,000 loads of naval timber. As soon as the Albanian chief demonstrated sufficient activity in the oak forests, Parga was handed
over to him.[2]

When Leard was sent to investigate timber conditions in the
Adriatic in 1803, the Navy Board also sent William Eton to the
Black Sea on a similar mission.[3] Admiral Warren had urged the
exportation of timber and naval stores from the Crimea.[4] It will
be remembered that some of the best timber and masts exported
from Riga grew in the Ukraine and were carried on a slow two-
year passage up the Dnieper to be transferred by canal to the
Düna in order to reach the great timber port. It was much
cheaper and simpler to float the logs down the Dnieper to Cherson
or Glubocca, but there was scarcely a vestige of a timber trade
there. In 1802, Russia's exports of timber from the Black Sea

[1] R. O., Adm. Digest, 4893, *N. B. to Adm.*, May 26, 1809, Mar. 8, 1811; N. B.
In Letters, 1561, *Leard to N. B.*, Aug. 28, 1813, Nov. 21, 1814.

[2] R. O., Adm., Acct. Gen., Misc., 135, *Maitland to N. B.*, July 18, 1820.

[3] B. M., Add. MSS, 37275, ff. 277, 295.

[4] R. O., Adm. Digest, 4858, *Adm. Warren to Sec. of State*, Sept. 7, 1803.

ports amounted to only 420 rubles, the equivalent of one moderate-sized mast or about twenty loads of oak timber.[1] Admiral Warren, however, believed that Malta could be well supplied with masts, timber, and other stores from that source, and Eton's report was very sanguine.

He was accordingly given £20,000 by the Navy Board and an equal amount by the Victualling Board to purchase stores to be sent to Malta. Like Leard, Eton acted as an agent of the Navy, receiving a commission on the purchases, while the actual business was transacted by the houses of Yeams and Forester, and Baring, Moir and Company, already established in the Russian trade.[2]

Malta received more immediate benefit from the Black Sea than from the Adriatic. By 1806, transports had made several trips to Cherson and Glubocca, returning with masts, timber, grain, and hemp. They were convoyed in the Mediterranean by a frigate which could not pass the Bosphorus because of the prohibition of armed ships.[3] Admiral Warren had considered the £20,000 insufficient and in 1805 Eton returned to the Black Sea with more funds, with which the contracts were extended. Later in the year, Eton was required to give up his credentials because "his expectations are so extravagant, his charges so extraordinary and his plans so visionary." The supply which he had established was placed in the hands of the St. Petersburg houses on a regular contract basis.[4] Sir Samuel Bentham even urged the Navy to build warships at Caffa, near Cherson, and to send masts to England from Asia Minor where they were cheap and abundant.[5]

Napoleonic influence shortly fell upon this remote source of timber supply. In the sequestration of British property in Russia which followed Tilsit in 1807, the contractors lost a large amount of timber and stores which had been gathered at Glu-

---

[1] Oddy, *European Commerce*, p. 175.

[2] B. M., Add. MSS, 37275, p. 295; R. O., Adm. Digest, 4858, *Forester to Sec. of State*, Nov. 20, 1803; *Parl. Papers*, 1805 (47), iv, 509.

[3] R. O., Adm. Digest, 4865, *Nelson to Adm.*, Mar. 3, 1804; 4871, *N. B. to Adm.*, May 22, Dec. 30, 1806.

[4] *Ibid.*, *Adm. to N. B.*, July 22, Nov. 14, 1805.

[5] Bentham, *Life of Sir Samuel Bentham*, p. 240.

bocca and Caffa. They also lost the large Tartar bath which they used as a storehouse, and the funds on hand for further payments for timber. Baring, Moir and Company wanted an order on any Russian property in England to the amount of £60,000, as compensation. Eton advised the Russian government not to raise the sequestration until the Navy Board had satisfied his claims.[1] Further imports of timber from the Black Sea were out of the question for four years, and Turkish oak and masts were temporarily cut off, for Constantinople was under the control of Napoleon's general, Sebastiani. Unarmed transports certainly could not pass the Straits when Admiral Duckworth's fleet failed. An attempt to secure timber from Thasos and hemp from Cyprus for Malta was also unsuccessful.[2]

When Russia began to cool toward Napoleon in 1811, the Navy Board determined to send an agent to secure Black Sea timber and naval stores from Russia and Turkey. William Moir, who had secured the French mast cargoes from the unwitting Bergevin just before Trafalgar, went on this mission and was able to arrange for a few masts but no hemp. These were sent to Malta from Odessa, and later in the year arrangements were made with Prince Lubomirski for the purchase of ship timber from his estates near the Black Sea.[3] Between the Black Sea and the Albanian supply Malta was by this time well furnished with timber and masts.

The Dutch, Holstein, Adriatic, and Black Sea attempts were all broken off or interrupted by the rapid spread of French power. In the meantime, the Baltic, which had been trading quite freely with England in 1806, had come under the influence of Napoleon's Continental System, and every port in that sea was nominally closed to English ships by the workings of that effort of Napoleon to crush England by starving her commerce. The Continental System, together with the Continental Blockade which

---

[1] R. O., F. O., Russia, 75, *Baring, Moir & Co. to Spencer Perceval*, Apr. 5, 1809; N. B. In Letters, 1626, *Season to N. B.*, Dec. 27, 1812; Adm. Digest, 4916, *N. B. to Adm.*, Mar. 18, Dec. 8, 1813.

[2] *Ibid.*, 4910, Jan. 14, 1912.

[3] *Ibid.*, 4901, *Adm. to N. B.*, June 29, 1811; *Sec. of State to Adm.*, Aug. 17, 1811; *N. B. to Adm.*, Aug. 20, 1811.

England opposed to it, have been ably treated by many writers. There is room here only for a consideration of the result of those measures upon the supply of naval timber, for they were bound to affect the Navy through its dockyard oak supply. It was possible to get good masts from Canada, but there was a real need for Baltic oak.

By the end of 1807, the stage was fully set for the great commercial contest between Napoleon and England. Each had made sweeping and savage decrees, and in the Baltic each side backed its claims with force. Napoleon's Berlin Decree of November 21, 1806, it will be recalled, nominally closed the ports of his empire and its dependencies to all ships from Great Britain, made British goods liable to seizure, and declared Great Britain in a state of blockade. At Tilsit in July, 1807, he secured the adherence of Russia and Prussia to these principles, and Denmark also joined. Napoleon's Milan Decree of December 17, 1807, declared all neutral ships denationalized and liable to seizure if suspected of English trade.

England had countered with Orders in Council; the severest of these, issued on November 11, 1807, declared Napoleon's coasts in a state of blockade and practically required all neutrals to trade through British ports. Two months after Tilsit had theoretically excluded British commerce from the southern Baltic shore, Admiral Gambier prevented the complete closing of that sea by attacking Copenhagen and taking the Danish navy back to England. Early in 1808, Admiral Saumarez passed the Sound with a strong fleet, to remain for four years in full control of sea power in the Baltic, whatever Napoleon and his allies might be doing on land.[1]

The timber trade immediately felt the effects of these measures, for the chief timber ports were in the hands of Napoleon and his allies. Even in the summer of 1806, the Navy Board was extremely concerned over its supply of timber from Dantzig.[2] Davoust had begun to close in on that city late in 1806, and it fell, after a spirited resistance, on May 26, 1807. Not content with

---

[1] See pp. 181–182.

[2] Hist. MSS Com., *Fortescue Papers*, viii, 243; and see *Ibid.*, pp. 212, 234.

Prussia's promise to join the Continental System, Napoleon kept troops in Dantzig, and established a severe régime under Rapp. At Memel it was a similar story. Stettin and other western Baltic ports had already been closed. At Riga and St. Petersburg, Alexander showed his enthusiasm and earnestness by sequestering all English property, and for a while after 1808, timber shipments to England from those ports were practically out of the question. Denmark's coöperation with Napoleon meant the extension of the Continental System to Norway. Of the Baltic ports, those of Sweden alone remained open to ships from England. In 1805, 11,000 ships passed the Sound. Two years later the number had dropped to 6,000.[1]

Timber prices in England showed a tremendous increase, while the imports showed a decrease that was proportionately even greater. Freight rates were extremely sensitive to the Baltic situation and represented almost the entire amount of variation in prices, for the price of timber at the Baltic ports showed little change. Great piles of wood of all kinds began to rot for want of a market, so that any offer was acceptable, and the price at Dantzig or Riga remained practically stationary compared with fluctuating costs of transportation. The approach of Napoleon in the autumn of 1806 caused the price of Memel fir timber in England to jump from 15 shillings to over £7, increasing to £9 early in 1808 and £16 in 1809, when obtainable at all. The valuable Dantzig plank, costing £12 in 1806, could scarcely be procured at all by English merchants until 1809, when it cost £24. Freight from Riga was normally about 7s. 4d a load; at the close of 1807 it was 23s. 4d. In 1808 and 1810, a London timber merchant offered 42 shillings in vain, and was equally unsuccessful a year later in offering unlimited rates. Those prices are typical of other items later submitted in detail by timber dealers.[2] In 1807, Solly wrote the Navy Board announcing a raise in his prices, and these were gradually increased to such a height that he was dismissed in 1812, when no longer needed.[3]

---

[1] Kirchoff, *Seemacht in der Ostsee*, ii, 155, 156.
[2] *Parl. Papers*, 1835 (519), xix, 31, 352, 353.
[3] R. O., N. B. In Letters, 1625, *Solly to N. B.*, July 11, 1807, July 31, 1808; *N. B. to Solly*, Apr. 12, July 11, 1812.

The sudden falling off of the imports of timber into England was more striking than the twofold and sometimes fourfold increase of prices. In 1804, during the shipbuilding boom preceding Trafalgar, Prussia had sent more than 11,000 loads of oak plank to England. In 1806, this export had reverted to about 4,000, slightly below the normal. Napoleon's hold on Dantzig reduced it to only 27 in 1807, and it rose but slightly in 1808. Dantzig normally exported to England some 400 loads of heavy oak timber annually, but not a single load came in 1807 or 1808, and only 15 loads were received between 1807 and 1811. The other Baltic countries were sending practically no oak timber or plank at the time.

Memel masts reacted a little more slowly than Dantzig oak. Imports of great masts from Prussia, almost exclusively from Memel, amounted normally to nearly a thousand a year. This was cut in half in 1807, but in the next two years only 42, and in the five years following Tilsit only 204, Prussian masts reached England. The effect of Napoleon's influence was felt still more slowly in Russia, but in 1809 the same thoroughness already seen in Prussia was evident. Riga and St. Petersburg sent nearly 17,000 great masts, an abnormally high number, in 1807, making the most of the situation before the restrictions set in. This fell to about 4,500 in 1808, and the figures for the next two years total only 333.[1]

The British customs lists from which these items are drawn demonstrate, more concisely and more eloquently than any other records, the effect of Napoleon's influence on British imports of timber from the Baltic. Those simple rows of figures in the Appendix, diminishing perceptibly after 1807 and swelling again by 1812, indicate clearly how successful the British were in drawing a very essential commodity from a sea the ports of which were eventually all declared closed against her. Those statistics represent the total imports into England for all purposes, but for reasons which will be explained later, nearly all the great masts and oak timber went to the Navy. The figures cannot be accepted as absolute, for they vary slightly in different sources, but all are

[1] See Appendix D.

close enough to determine the effect of the system, country by country and year by year.[1] It matters relatively little whether England imported 4,156 or 4,168 loads of oak plank from Dantzig in 1806, but it is of real significance that in the following year the imports were insufficient to plank a frigate.

Considering the control which Napoleon and his allies exercised over the Baltic ports, it is not to be wondered at that England's timber imports from that region were curtailed so severely. The wonder is that England imported any Baltic timber at all. The customs figures tell in concise form how much timber was drawn from there. To understand how the English were able to secure it requires a more extensive search.

Either the Continental System or the Continental Blockade could have practically put an end to commerce in the Baltic if the original edicts had been enforced at their face value. Napoleon and his allies could have prevented any ships from leaving port and British warships could have done almost what they wished with the merchantmen once they sailed. Each party, however, wished to maintain its own trade while crippling that of the enemy. In so doing, they made leakage inevitable, and generally in favor of England.

Neutral flags were absolutely essential for that commerce which survived the edicts of 1806 and 1807. The English flag would be as vulnerable in a Baltic port as the French flag at sea. Out of this situation arose the license system of "trading by exception" through maritime indulgences. Both sides adopted this system of organized hypocrisy, which profited the English greatly, while in the end it virtually nullified Napoleon's attempt to crush them by crushing their commerce. Each party had to utilize neutrals, but each distrusted them. The United States, a legitimate neutral, profited, then suffered, and finally fought because of this system, while Knyphausen, Pappenburg, and Oldenburg shamelessly lent their flags to convert the ships of England and other belligerents into mock neutrals.[2]

---

[1] *Parl. Papers*, 1814–15 (115), vol. vii, pt. 1, p. 92; 1820 (269), iii, 92–98. R. O., Customs, 17, 29, 30; *Imports and Exports, passim*.

[2] Mahan, *Influence of Sea Power upon the French Revolution and Empire*, ii, 307, 313; Heckscher, *Continental System*, pp. 205–220.

England was chary of its licenses to real neutrals because of the constant claims of British shipowners. With the suspension of the Navigation Act to meet the situation, they saw their own ships by the dozen lying idle by the docks while neutrals grew rich from exorbitant freight rates, offset of course by the constant liability to capture. The Privy Council of Trade, which had charge of licensing, recognized the Navy's need of timber and stores and seldom refused to grant a license to a neutral vessel to bring these commodities from ports in the enemy's hands; but it was less generous outside the Baltic. It ordinarily refused licenses to contractors desiring to bring timber for the Navy from Canada in neutral ships. It allowed American ships to bring timber from Prussia, and shortly afterwards allowed Prussian ships to bring timber from the United States during non-intercourse.[1] Solly, who managed most of the Navy's timber importations from the Baltic during this period, employed ships flying the flags of the United States, Russia, Prussia, Denmark, Dantzig, and some of the little mock neutrals. It was a matter of taking what he could get, and at times the difficulty was considerable. In 1808, he was offering salt at a third of the market price, as an inducement.[2] While the Council preferred to give licenses for naval timber only as a return cargo for British manufactures or colonial wares, Solly at times brought wine from Bordeaux in ships which returned through the Sound with timber for the Navy.[3] Many of the ships which had English licenses usually had others to use on the enemy port officials, and their papers were arranged to satisfy inspection from either side.

There were other reasons than the licensing of neutrals which caused leakage in the Napoleonic System. The Navy Board depended chiefly on Isaac Solly because he was well situated at Dantzig, and remained unmolested there. When Napoleon had

[1] R. O., B. of T., 5, *Board of Trade Minutes*, May 25, 1811, and *passim; Council Register*, 173–194, esp. 173, June 28, 1807; 186, Apr. 4, 1810; 194, Nov. 28, 1812; Adm. Digest, 4883, Memorial, *Adm. to Council*, Oct. 10, 1807; 4901, *Lord Chetwynd to Adm.*, Sept. 20, 1811; *N. B. to Adm.*, Apr. 21, 1812; Hist. MSS Com., *Fortescue MSS*, viii, 212.

[2] R. O., N. B. In Letters, 1625, *Solly to N. B.*, June 27, 1808.

[3] *Ibid.*, 1626, June 30, 1812.

visited the city early in 1807, a group of merchants held an audience with him, and "in consequence of a considerable contribution submitted to by this city, English goods and debts will remain untouched."[1] This by no means meant anything like unrestricted trade.[2] It was still necessary to resort to the conventional disguises, but Solly was at least enabled to conduct business with the Navy, directing shipments from other ports when Dantzig itself was closed. Two years later, the French demanded another two millions, claiming that the merchants had made five millions by French indulgence.[3]

The situation of the British merchants in the Russian ports was quite different. A *Liquidation Contoir*, the office of a Russian alien-property custodian, had been set up to direct the operations of the sweeping sequestrations ordered by the Tsar on April 1, 1808 and May 7, 1809, "whereby British property to a large amount and stores for the use of His Majesty's Navy and paid for by the said British merchants are now under arrest and at the discretion and disposal of the Russian government."[4] The former contractors from Riga and St. Petersburg were thus unable to act as Solly did. Alexander was killing the goose where the father of the Continental System was gathering golden eggs. By 1809, Russian ports were sealed quite hermetically while the Prussian were becoming easier of access.

If Napoleon received huge bribes in favor of English trade, it is no wonder that his subordinates showed the same trait on a smaller scale. Drusina, the British secret service agent who operated under the name of Hahn, reported early in 1809:

Notwithstanding the many impediments laid in the way of Trade, several ships have cleared out from these ports [Königsberg and Memel] actually bound for Great Britain with cargoes of hemp, flax, linseed, bristles, timber, staves, etc. — The French Consul takes a fee of 1 % for himself and a douceur to his secretary for his certificate d'origine. Bonds are also given by the merchants for the return of the ships that do not go to British ports — this is of course pro forma.

---

[1] R. O., N. B., In Letters, 1625, *Solly to N. B.*, July 11, 1807.

[2] Damus, *Geschichte der Stadt Danzig*, p. 143.

[3] R. O., F. O., Prussia, Secret 80, *Drusina (Hahn) to Foreign Office*, Oct. 31, 1809.

[4] *Ibid.*, Russia, 75, *Memorial of Russia Co.*, Mar. 1, 1809; *Annual Register*, 1809, p. 698.

That autumn, it was the same story — "Papers continue to be found in proper order for a douceur of some hundred louis d'or to French consuls."[1]

Consuls may have been changed from time to time, or may have had pangs of conscience, for Solly often had to change his timber shipments from one port to another on short notice. The Navy Board had told him that it was a matter of indifference to them from what port he shipped his timber provided it was timber of Dantzig crown quality.[2] This was a necessary precaution on their part, for the concentration of interest on the great ports had stimulated a timber trade in smaller ports where it was poorly developed in normal times. Solly found it much easier to ship from Memel than from Dantzig, while Rapp's severe régime was in force. When surveillance at Memel grew too strict, however, recourse was had to Pillau, the port of Königsberg, where timber had been exported on a small scale, and also to Narva, in the Baltic Provinces, where the timber was too poor to compete in a normal market. Solly often asked for blank licenses that he might have more freedom in choice of ships and ports. He occasionally exported from Riga and St. Petersburg, but ships by the hundred were detained at Riga for months while papers were considered at St. Petersburg with exasperating Russian slowness; and even then many were refused the coveted permission to sail.[3] At times, naval materials were brought overland from Riga to Memel, and British goods were sent in return.[4]

Another element of advantage for England was the coöperation of Sweden, who remained outside of the Continental System until 1809, when she was really forced into it after an unsuccessful war with Russia in which she lost Finland. Swedish forests sent little timber to the Royal Navy, though general timber exports from

---

[1] R. O., F. O., Prussia, Secret 80, *Drusina to F. O.*, May 19, Sept. 26, 1809. For an instance of similar practice by a British official, see *Elijah Cobb, a Cape Cod Skipper*, p. 62.

[2] R. O., N. B. In Letters, 1625, *N. B. to Solly*, Dec. 22, 1807, marginal note.

[3] *Ibid.*, *Solly to N. B.*, June 27, 1808; 1626, Apr. 24, May 2, May 10, May 22, Aug. 3, 1811; *Parl. Papers*, 1835 (519), xix, 357.

[4] R. O., F. O., Prussia, Secret 80, *Drusina to F. O.*, June 17, Aug. 28, Oct. 5, 1809.

Sweden assumed unusual proportions as the regular timber ports were cut off. Sweden rendered England a valuable service by furnishing at Gottenburg and elsewhere *entrepôts* for naval timber and other Baltic products. By 1807, Solly was sending cargoes from Memel and Pillau to Gottenburg under neutral colors. Realizing that he was well known as a contractor for the British Navy, Solly had the timber sent on the account of Danzfeldt and Company of Copenhagen, "for by employing a foreign house we hope to avoid that risk which is so obvious." [1] This was all "pro forma" of course, and the subterfuges and hypocrisy of the situation, which the French officials could not help knowing, are amusing. Gottenburg, like Heligoland, developed a trade as lively as at any port in Europe. Even after Sweden joined the Continental System and had listened to Napoleon's anathemas against British commerce, the tactful Saumarez maintained amicable relations with the Swedish court, and the illicit trade was winked at. The Baltic convoys, often numbering six hundred merchantmen under a mongrel assortment of flags and each armed with a few carronades, came annually into the East Country escorted by British warships. They were dropped off in groups to take their chances at ports which had been reported by the secret service as most favorable. Several hundred of the 1810 convoy were seized, but in other years there was surprising impunity. [2]

Perhaps the most important reason for England's success in drawing even this small amount of naval timber from the Baltic was Napoleon's obsession that it was far more important to shut England's manufactures and colonial goods out of Europe than to shut off her imports of Baltic timber and grain. To him, imports represented a loss and exports a gain, and this consideration outweighed the fact that he might help to starve England and cripple her sea power by withholding the materials in his control. This was accentuated by the feelings of the Baltic peoples. They might grumble at the loss of tobacco and coffee, but it was a more severe

[1] R. O., N. B. In Letters, 1625, July 11, Dec. 22, 1807; 1626, Apr. 23, 1811. *Council Register*, p. 186, Apr. 3, 1810.

[2] R. O., Adm. 1, 11, *Saumarez to Adm.*, Nov. 16, 1810, Aug. 22, 1812; Mahan, *Influence of Sea Power on the French Revolution and Empire*, ii, 322–325; Macgregor, *Commercial Statistics*, ii, 571.

blow when timber from their forests and grain, flax, and hemp from their fields lay rotting at the ports.[1]

A concession was made to this feeling in 1811, when Napoleon's Hanseatic licenses permitted the export of grain to England and allowed the export of timber and naval stores to France in the same ships, for he recognized the futility of trying to secure timber direct from the Baltic, since neutrals were forced to touch at an English port. He was planning at this time to bring 4,000 great masts from Dantzig.[2] Montalivet, his Minister of the Interior, in vain pointed out the folly of expecting that England would allow any naval materials to leave her ports for France.[3] As soon as Solly heard of the Hanseatic licenses, he wrote the Navy Board:

> Under the pretext of dunnage for the wheat, we could get away some deals and wheat, and perhaps oak plank if our agent had blanck licenses with which he could assist the shippers of wheat, and we should take care that the wheat was well dunnaged.[4]

By the middle of 1811, England knew of the probability of Russia's defection from the Continental System. On July 3, Wellesley informed the Admiralty that it was the Prince Regent's pleasure to supply gunpowder and lead to the Russian government in return for naval stores.[5] Later in the year Alexander began to open his ports to the English. In 1812 the Admiralty advised the Navy Board to take advantage of the state of relations with Russia immediately "to procure the greatest possible supply of Riga spars and other naval stores." [6] Within six months the dockyard stores were well filled.[7]

The Baltic crisis was over, but it had been severe while it lasted. From 1807 until 1812, England was deprived of a normal store of Baltic timber and masts. In 1809, when Napoleon's system was most effective throughout Europe, the timber smuggled out of the

[1] Hoeniger, *Die Kontinentalsperre*, pp. 26, 27; Rose, "Napoleon and English Commerce," *E. H. R.*, viii, 724; Rose, *Life of Napoleon*, ii, 203–206.

[2] *Corr. de Nap.*, xxi, 259.

[3] Melvin, *Napoleon's Navigation System*, pp. 203–205, 242, 243.

[4] R. O., N. B. In Letters, 1625, *Solly to N. B.*, May 10, 1811.

[5] R. O., Adm. Digest, 4901, *Wellesley to Adm.*, July 3, 1811.

[6] R. O., Adm. Minutes, Aug. 3, 1812.

[7] R. O., Adm. Digest, 4916, *Adm. to N. B.*, Jan. 20, 1813.

hostile ports was hardly enough to keep a frigate squadron in repair. The timber supply during the Napoleonic wars demonstrated the theories advanced a century earlier during a similar timber crisis. It may be recalled that between 1700 and 1715, when Charles XII and Peter the Great were struggling for control of the Baltic, England determined, after lengthy debates, that it was unsafe to rely completely upon foreign countries for a supply of vital naval necessities. The result had been the development of the colonial supply. That supply had failed England badly during the American Revolution, but it proved its worth at this critical period. With practically every foreign port barred to her ships, England was able to maintain her Navy with timber and masts from her own Empire. When Europe closed her ports, British possessions in every other continent contributed their trees to maintain the Royal Navy.

CHAPTER IX

SEARCHING THE WORLD FOR TIMBER

NAPOLEON'S influence excluded England from practically every port in Europe which could furnish masts and ship timber, but the sea, and the forests beyond the sea, were still accessible to British ships. So far as the land power could exert its force, it had curtailed and almost stopped the export of those materials necessary to sustain sea power. Napoleon, however, could do nothing to prevent the use of timbers from the two Americas, and from Asia, Africa, and the South Seas. Of all the foreign nations of the time, Portugal alone offered its services throughout the period when the others were trying to crush trade with England, and Portugal at the time was almost in the position of a British dependency. The Navy was supported during the critical years by Britain's overseas possessions. Of these, Canada stood so far above the others that it can almost be said that Canadian pines and oaks sustained the Navy during its long struggle with the Napoleonic Empire.

The services of the Canadian forests justified the colonial timber policy evolved a hundred years before. The struggles of John Bridger, Sir John Wentworth, and the other surveyors general to preserve the "King's Woods" by their enforcement of the Broad Arrow policy seemed to have been in vain when the inhabitants of Falmouth, Portsmouth, and Georgetown cut off the mast supply and drove the forest officials out of the land. A sort of apostolic succession was maintained, however, when Sir John Wentworth transferred the Broad Arrow policy, with reasonable modifications, to the remaining British colonies in North America, which may be referred to collectively as Canada although that name was not officially extended to Nova Scotia, New Brunswick, and the other Maritime Provinces until long after this period.

The Navy had turned to this new region for its masts, it may be recalled, as a tardy measure during the American Revolution, when there had been such desperate need for the great pine sticks.

Lumbermen had begun to cut masts on the St. John River in 1779 to supply the Halifax dockyard, but it was not until 1782 that the English yards began to receive masts from New Brunswick, as it was soon to be called.[1] After the war, there were several considerations in favor of maintaining this New Brunswick supply instead of returning to New England. The new region contained even more of the great pines which had been one of the original reasons for developing the New Hampshire supply, and the government could naturally exercise its old Broad Arrow policy in its own lands in a manner which would not be possible in an independent country.

Above all, the New England supply was no longer dependable. One of the main causes for turning to that region originally had been the desire to have a secure supply free from foreign influence. New England had crippled the Navy severely when it withheld its masts in 1775, and its conduct after the war showed that it would rather supply the French navy with its stores. Calonne abolished all duties on American masts and timber in 1787 in order to encourage the trade, and Portland, as the old mast port of Falmouth was now called, began to send masts to France by 1790.[2] At the outbreak of war between England and France in 1793, the French consul general at Philadelphia wrote to the Minister of Marine:

Si les ressources que la Marine de la Republique tire ordinairement de la Baltique étoient derangées par les mesures de la Russie, nous aurions à regretter d'avoir differé longtemps les arrangements propres à nous procurer les goudrons de la Carolina du Nord, les mâtures du New Hampshire, de la Province de Main et la rivière de Connecticut, et les bois de construction de la Georgie et de l'état de New York. La department de la Marine a depuis longtemps des rapports sur ces objets. Quelque uns portent l'empreinte des préjugés du tems et surtout de la crainte des innovations. Je l'ai observé frequemment.[3]

In spite of the "préjugés du tems" and the "crainte des innovations," which sound so much like the Navy Board across the

---

[1] See pp. 291–292.

[2] *Cumberland Gazette* (Portland), Feb. 19, 1789; May 24, June 21, Aug. 2, Aug. 29, Oct. 11, 1790; Apr. 4, 1791.

[3] France, *Archives du Ministère de la Marine*, BB3, vol. 39, f. 394, *De la Forest to Minister of Marine*, Mar. 24, 1793.

Channel, the Baltic situation forced the French navy to turn to America. Late in 1793, the Committee of Public Safety sent commissioners, with five million francs in gold, to purchase "substances et matériel naval" in the United States, while a committee of Bordeaux merchants sent Citizens Lecomte and Gernon with an additional three millions.[1] While the French consuls were busy placing contracts, Hamilton, the British consul at Norfolk, was informing the Admiralty of the eagerness of the Americans to furnish masts, timber, and naval stores to the French at Norfolk, New London, and Casco Bay, while the British were supplied with these materials very grudgingly.[2] He was able, however, to send information to the naval commanders which led to the capture at sea of several of these cargoes of masts and naval stores. Even those that reached France evidently did little to relieve the desperate shortage at Brest and Toulon, for the biographer of Robespierre's minister of marine writes: "Le materiel acheté aux États-Unis depuis le départ de Van Stabel ne vaut rien; quand il arrive en France on s'aperçoit que les Américains ont trompé à plaisir le gouvernement français." [3]

At any rate, the Royal Navy was by that time free of further dependence on such an unreliable source of masts, and the old mast ports felt the change. The mast exports of Portsmouth, which averaged over three hundred annually before the Revolution, fell to about twenty. Maine and the Connecticut River, having fresher supplies upon which to draw, held on to the trade a little longer. As late as 1787, New England had shipped 297 masts to England, while New Brunswick sent 200 and Quebec only sixteen.[4] In the following year, however, the naval shift was completed when the firm of Hunter, Robertson, and Forsythe made a large contract with the Navy Board to furnish great masts for six

---

[1] France, *Archives du Ministère de la Marine*, BB 3 vol. 39, ff. 71–73, *Consul Letombe to Minister of Marine*, Apr. 23, 1793; *Actes du Comité de Salut Public*, viii, 473; 618, ix, 233, 234, 277, 301; Levy-Schneider, *Le Conventionnel Jeanbon Saint-André*, i, 634; ii, 884; N. R. S., *Barham Papers*, ii, 366.

[2] R. O., Adm. In Letters from Consuls, 3842, *Hamilton to Adm.*, Jan. 22, June 15, Nov. 5, 1795; Feb. 3, June 14, Dec. 21, 1796; *Eastern Herald* (Portland), Mar. 10, 1794.　　　　　[3] Levy-Schneider, *op. cit.*, ii, 976.

[4] R. O., Customs, 4–6, *Imports and Exports*, 1787; Weeden, *Social and Economic History of New England*, ii, 833; Belknap, *History of New Hampshire*, iii, 62.

years. This was renewed in 1795 with a contract on a larger scale, calling for thirty cargoes of masts in seven years. Four or five cargoes were to be sent each year, supplying Halifax, Antigua, and Jamaica as well as England.[1] Up to 1804, New Brunswick virtually monopolized the naval mast trade.

The Broad Arrow followed this shift of the mast supply to Canada. The proposal of the Treasury to discontinue the office of Surveyor General had met with strong opposition from the Navy Board, and in 1783, Sir John Wentworth was confirmed in that office when he became lieutenant governor of Nova Scotia.[2] The forest policy that Wentworth carried into Canada showed some modifications of the 1729 regulations, which had proved so unsuccessful in New England. Yet the modifications were not as extensive as Wentworth desired. In 1778, the proposals that he submitted to Lord George Germain for administering the Penobscot region showed the result of his experiences with the law in New England. In a document interesting in the study of forest policy, he reached a solution which reconciled the interests of the colonists and the Navy as closely as the circumstances would permit.[3]

Wentworth's plan provided for small reservations of pine woods for the Navy in every township that should be laid out. These reservations were to contain the most promising trees conveniently situated near streams, and their area was not to exceed six hundred acres in each township of six square miles. On these, all trees over four inches in diameter were to be reserved for the Navy. This would provide a succession of great pines for the future, which was an important consideration at a time when the radical changes of the nineteenth century in naval architecture were not foreseen, and provision for a hundred years or more seemed necessary. Such reservations would leave the remainder of the woods in each township to the colonists, and there would always be lumbermen at hand for the occasional cutting of naval masts. In place of the old penalty of £100 for every violation of

[1] R. O., *Adm., Acct. Gen., Misc., Var.*, cxxi, 114–119; cxxiv, 113 — *Contracts*.
[2] R. O., Adm. Digest, 4809, *N. B. to Adm.*, Apr. 4, 1783.
[3] R. O., C. O., 5,175, ff. 81–96, *Wentworth to Germain*, Oct. 12, 1778.

the law, which defeated its end by its severity, Wentworth would make the punishment fit the crime, with a scale graded to the size of the tree and the income of the trespasser. In land still ungranted, the old Broad Arrow reservations were to hold in full force, as well as in the regions which were definitely private property. In the former, *all* pines would be reserved, while legitimate private property would be respected. Wentworth would offer a bounty equivalent to the lumber value of the trees as an inducement to preserve them for the Navy. There were to be more rigid certificates of origin as a prerequisite for lumber shipment. Wentworth also advocated that the mast export bounties, which lapsed in 1777 and were later to be renewed, in 1782, should be limited to masts sent to the Navy.[1]

These suggestions of Wentworth were not followed in detail, but the policy of setting aside definite tracts, instead of a sweeping reservation of all pines, was included in instructions in 1783.[2] As already mentioned, this policy had been formulated in a rudimentary way, at Wentworth's suggestion, in 1769, but there was not time then for its adequate application in New England. Later American forest policy was based on this principle of definite reservations. The Canadian "Crown lands" developed from this naval source, and the United States adopted a similar arrangement, commencing with the reservations of live oak tracts for naval timber.[3] The old 1729 policy had been wrecked in its conflict with private property.

The reservations under the new Broad Arrow policy were larger than the little township reserves advocated by Sir John. In 1774, under his direction, extensive forest tracts in Nova Scotia, including the region of the upper St. John, had been set aside for the Navy.[4] Between 1783 and 1794, Wentworth spent several months of nearly every year in timber-ranging, although his

[1] R. O., C. O., 5, 175, ff. 81–96, *Wentworth to Germain*, Oct. 12, 1778.

[2] R. O., *Adm., Acct. Gen., Misc., Var.*, vol. viii; *Instructions from the Navy*, 1783. See Mayo, *John Wentworth, passim.*

[3] For review of Canadian Crown timber regulations, see Ontario, *Report of Minister of Lands, Forests and Mines*, 1907, pp. 148–262. See pp. 268–269.

[4] *Charles Morris to Gov. Legge*, May 21, 1774, quoted in Murdock, *History of Nova Scotia*, ii, 526.

health "was impaired by the unremitted fatigue and hardships incident to such unprovided situations." His reservations were made chiefly in New Brunswick, at first at "Pumkeit, Shediac and Cocagne" on the northern coast of the province, and especially at Miramichi, where, as he wrote, "there is the largest and best growth of true Mast Pine that I ever saw: exceeding any shipped from New England in forty years past." Later he went inland, setting off Crown lands on the Stewiac and La Have rivers, and still farther west on the upper St. John.[1]

Even this modified Broad Arrow policy aroused the opposition of the settlers, who constantly violated the laws preserving the pines. British North America presented four distinct problems to Wentworth. In Lower Canada, the original seignioral grants had been made with a reservation of timber and masts for the French navy, for Colbert's *martelage* resembled the English Broad Arrow policy in many ways. The English respected the seignioral titles when they took over New France, and adapted the old French naval stipulations to their own. In 1772, Benzel reported that the seigniors had no objection to the cutting of naval timber on their lands, but at the same time they used whatever trees they pleased for themselves.[2] There were few good mast pines on the lower St. Lawrence, however, so this region was of less importance than the others.

Nova Scotia had had the Broad Arrow since 1721, and had lumbered heavily in the best forests, so that little of value was left in Nova Scotia proper. In 1783 an Order in Council had repealed all grants prior to 1774, in order to give a free hand for naval reservations.[3] The two remaining regions, New Brunswick, set off from Nova Scotia in 1784, and Upper Canada, the present Ontario, presented similar problems. Both were virtual wildernesses when the influx of Loyalists gave them their first real population, about 1783, so that the Navy had an opportunity to make reservations unhampered by many "private property" claims

[1] R. O., *Adm.*, *Acct. Gen.*, *Misc.*, *Var.*, vol. viii, *Wentworth to Adm.*, Dec. 29, 1788, May 4, 1794.

[2] R. O., Adm. In Letters from Governors, 3820, *Benzel to Wentworth*, Nov. 11, 1772; Defebaugh, *History of the Lumber Industry*, i, 98-100.

[3] *Nova Scotia Archives*, ii, 124; Murdock, *op. cit.*, iii, 19.

arising from previous grants. In both provinces, extensive tracts of "Crown lands" were set off, with the understanding that licenses were to be given to cut any timber unfit for naval purposes. Reservation was also made of all great pines on lands already granted.[1]

The opposition to the Broad Arrow centred in New Brunswick, since it was the chief source of masts for twenty years and Wentworth was close at hand to enforce it. Though he was constantly exhorting the coöperation of the governors of the Canadas, the system was never so rigidly enforced there. In New Brunswick, it was the New England story repeated, with the more violent scenes omitted. The cutting of naval masts on private property was objected to, for many of the provincial grants had omitted mention of the pines. The first governor of New Brunswick openly opposed the policy; and when a later governor tried to support it, he met a powerful legislative attack surprisingly similar to that in Massachusetts Bay just a century earlier. Even the government reservations were objected to on the "maritime mortmain" grounds, as thwarting the expansion of the colonies.[2] The increased demand for timber which followed the Baltic difficulties led to wholesale inroads into the Crown lands. Wentworth quoted 8 Geo. I, c. 12 and 2 Geo. II, c. 35 in vain, for those Parliamentary acts for mast reservation meant little to the province, which was all against him.[3] One of his deputies wrote that seventeen twentieths of the male population of New Brunswick was engaged in this industry, which was so exceedingly profitable during the Napoleonic wars.[4]

The subsequent shift of interest to Upper Canada weakened Wentworth's hand in New Brunswick, although as late as 1810, nearly half a century after his original appointment as Surveyor General, he was in London prosecuting offences against the King's pines in New Brunswick. The Broad Arrow policy was relaxed

[1] Murdock, op. cit., ii, 556.

[2] R. O., *Adm., Acct. Gen., Misc., Var.*, vol. viii, *Wentworth to N. B.*, Nov. 13, 1790; Raymond, *The River St. John*, pp. 474–477; Hannay, *History of New Brunswick*, i, 224–226, 361–364.

[3] New Brunswick Historical Society, *Winslow Papers*, pp. 388–390, 634, 685.

[4] *Ibid.*, p. 654.

by the end of the Napoleonic era, and was merged into the general forest policy of Canada. The Crown lands were retained, licenses to cut being sold at low rates, with little attention to mast pines. There were disputes over Crown reserves even at the end of the century, and the original purpose of the grants remained as an anachronism; for in grants of land to veterans of the Boer War, great pines were reserved for masting the Royal Navy.[1] The policy had served its purpose well during the long struggle with France, for the Navy depended on Canada as its one reliable source of masts and many of these had been saved from the axes of a population dependent on lumbering by the quick work of the Surveyor General.

Up to 1804, Canada's contribution to the Navy consisted chiefly in three or four cargoes of masts annually from New Brunswick. That year saw a radical change in the Navy's demands. The need of a tremendous amount of foreign timber, as well as masts, led to an abrupt shifting of the entire trade from New Brunswick to Quebec, where masts and timber, floated down the St. Lawrence from Upper Canada, were shipped to England. In order to establish a new Dantzig in America, it was necessary to attract capital to develop sawmills and to support the extensive lumbering operations. Capital took advantage of the Navy's need to make attractive terms for itself. The powerful house of Scott, Idles and Company agreed to furnish the Navy with all necessary masts and timber, provided it could have a monopoly of the trade. They reminded the Navy Board of this in 1807, when their strongest rival, Usburne, attempted to break the monopoly of their naval contract.[2] New Brunswick was a victim to the pressing needs of the Navy, which dictated this contract, and after that province had furnished masts for over twenty years, the Navy Board suddenly lost all interest in it, "discovering" that New Brunswick masts were decidedly inferior to those of Upper Canada, on the same grounds on which Connecticut

[1] Ontario, *Report of Minister of Lands, Forests and Mines*, 1907, pp. 148–262; Defebaugh, *Lumber Industry*, i, 105, 159, 226; Fernow, *History of Forestry*, 361–363.

[2] B. M., Add. MSS, 37275, f. 293, *N. B. Memorandum*, 1804; R. O., Adm. Digest, 4858, *N. B. to Adm.*, Sept. 3, 1806; N. B. In Letters, 1625, *Scott, Idles & Co to N. B.*, Oct. 6, 1807.

masts were found inferior to those of New Hampshire fifty years earlier.[1]

After scorning American oak consistently since the days of Bridger, the Navy Board in 1804 was faced with the necessity of importing it in large quantities. The use of this oak was recognized as a *pis aller*, for the white oak was considered decidedly inferior to the English and even to the Baltic. Shipwrights and carpenters were sent over from the English dockyards, and oak from the Ottawa region was soon being incorporated into the King's ships.[2]

No efficient timber trade dependent on naval contracts alone could be developed, and in most instances where the Navy encouraged a new supply of masts or timber, a general lumber trade sprang up which often consumed the trees most fit for the dockyards. The same reasons which compelled the Navy Board to turn to Canada for timber created a tremendous demand for foreign lumber for general building purposes in England. For every ship which took masts and naval timber to the royal dockyards, dozens of cargoes of lumber left Quebec for Liverpool, Bristol, and London.

The pioneer in this new trade, which did so much to develop Upper Canada, was Philemon Wright, who emigrated from Massachusetts after the Revolution and sent his "historic" raft of oak and pine logs down the Ottawa and St. Lawrence in 1800.[3] There had been exports of Quebec oak for the French navy as early as 1667, and in the decade before the Revolution a large amount of oak had been cut in the Lake Champlain region, to be shipped down the River Richelieu and the St. Lawrence for the English market. Much of the Quebec oak which helped to relieve the Royal Navy during the Napoleonic period came from Vermont. Canals finally diverted this Champlain timber to the Hudson in 1830, but for some time Vermont furnished more oak than Upper Canada for the Quebec trade. The houses of Scott, Idles

[1] R. O., Adm. Digest, 4883, *N. B. to Adm.*, Mar. 24, 1807; Hist. MSS Com., *Var. Coll.*, vi, 229.

[2] R. O., N. B. In Letters, 1625, *Surveyors of Navy to N. B.*, Mar. 3, 1807.

[3] Defebaugh, *Lumber Industry*, i, 155–157.

and Company, Usburne, and Gilmour developed great establishments at Quebec, rivalling those at Dantzig and Riga in extent.
These concerns frequently sublet their contracts to Vermonters,
who managed the French Canadians who did much of the actual
cutting and rafting. Lumbering became one of the chief industries of Canada, as it was already of northern New England and
New Brunswick.[1]

The timber magnates were able to dictate to the government
terms even more advantageous than the monopoly which the
house of Scott, Idles had exacted in the naval contract.[2] They
pointed out that England was in absolute need of timber for every
purpose, and that Canada's forests held an unlimited supply. In
order to exploit these forests, however, it was necessary to develop
a timber trade on a scale equivalent to that of the Baltic. They
were not willing to jeopardize their capital to meet the temporary
demand if the end of the Napoleonic wars would mean a reversion
to the Baltic with its advantages of superior timber and cheaper
freight. The normal freight from Quebec was about £3 5s., three
times as high as the Baltic; and in 1810, the Quebec rate had
risen to £7 10s. a load.[3] Between 1809 and 1813, these arguments
were successful in securing the passage of an almost prohibitive
duty on Baltic timber amounting to several times the cost of the
wood at Dantzig or Riga.[4] This was the origin of the notorious
timber duties, — those silent partners of the Corn Laws, — which
were not entirely removed until 1860, after several struggles in
Parliament.

An idea of the rapid growth of the timber trade in the different
provinces, and the relative importance of the Canadian supply to
that of the Baltic can be gained from those same customs figures
of imports into England during the period from 1799 to 1815 already quoted in connection with the Baltic. While the naval sup-

---

[1] R. O., N. B. In Letters, 3315, *Deptford Officers to N. B.*, June 20, 1768; *Parl.
Papers*, 1821 (186), vi, 139; Lower, *History of the Canadian Wood Trade* (in preparation).

[2] R. O., C. O., 5, 18, B. of T. *Privy Council Minutes*, Apr. 15, 1809; *Parl. Papers*,
1833 (0.58), iii, 386.

[3] *Parl. Papers*, 1820 (269), iii, 65.

[4] 49 Geo. III, c. 98; 50 Geo. III, c. 77.

ply represented only a portion of this, the value of Canada in relieving the English timber crisis may be judged.[1]

In the case of masts over twelve inches in diameter, New Brunswick sent 763 in 1799, with eleven from Nova Scotia and only seven from Canada, where the mast industry was new, the total being less than a fifth of that from Russia and Prussia, though the proportion of great masts over two feet was considerably larger. New Brunswick retained its lead with an average annual export of eighteen hundred, except for one year, until 1807, when the newly developed Quebec industry began to gain on it. In 1807, the Russian and Prussian exports amounted to over 17,000, but the agreement at Tilsit reduced that to 4,600. To offset this, the exports from British North America jumped from 4,442 to 16,729 in a single year, so that Tilsit left England unaffected in 1808 so far as masts were concerned. Quebec alone rose from 2,753 in 1807 to 13,333 in 1808, and from that time on its lead over New Brunswick was secure. The Canadian mast exports reached their maximum in 1811, with 23,053, against 3,319 from Russia and Prussia. In that year, Quebec sent 19,025 masts, New Brunswick 3,131, Nova Scotia 842, and Cape Breton and Prince Edward Island 54.

In oak timber, Canada supplemented the Baltic shortage with almost equal rapidity, most of it coming from Vermont and the St. Lawrence *via* Quebec, with practically none from the Maritime Provinces. The American exports averaged only about a thousand loads up to 1804, while Prussia was sending ten times that amount of plank alone from Dantzig and Memel. The Prussian supply was cut off when Napoleon occupied those ports, and the Canadian exports mounted steadily. The stimulus of the timber duties was visible in 1810, with the sudden jump from about 6000 loads to over 17,000, and again to over 24,000 in 1811, when Prussia sent less than 2,500 and the rest of the Baltic scarcely 50. Like masts, this item of oak timber was of prime importance to the Navy, as most of it was imported for shipbuilding.

The third great item, pine or "fir" timber, outweighed the others in volume and commercial importance, although its in-

[1] Appendix D.

fluence on the Navy was less direct. Some of the red pine found its way into the King's ships, but the bulk of it replaced oak and Baltic fir for general building purposes. It became the chief item in the exports of maritime Canada. This was the only branch in which New Brunswick had a lead over Quebec as a whole, and occasionally Nova Scotia showed the heaviest exports of the three. Up to 1805, the Baltic exportation averaged over 150,000 loads a year, while Canadian exports rose from 914 in 1799 to nearly 10,000 in 1805. Norway prevented the almost total collapse that occurred in masts and oak, and in only three years — 1809, 1811, and 1812 — did the Canadian supply exceed the Baltic. The effect of the timber duties was again evident, the exportation of 48,254 loads in 1808 rising to 77,542 in 1809, 101,416 in 1810, and 144,902 in 1812.

The rapid development of Quebec in the three branches may be judged by comparing the exports of 1799 with those of 1811, the boom year for Canada. In 1799, Quebec sent seven masts, 1,069 loads of oak timber, and 29 loads of pine. In 1811, this had risen to 23,053 masts, 24,469 loads of oak, and 52,888 loads of pine — enough to fill 500 timber ships. The Baltic exports at the same time were in reverse proportion. Developing thus as a temporary expedient, the Canadian timber trade remained as a great industry.

The timber and masts from Canada at this period gave England an excellent example of the value of colonies in time of need. The timber supply from her former colonies to the southward during the Napoleonic wars was less dependable. Trade with the United States was affected by a situation similar to that in the Baltic at the same time, for Jefferson inaugurated a policy of "peaceful coercion," in reprisal for the British attitude toward neutral ships. As a result, trade with England was permitted for only ten months between 1807 and 1815. The Embargo Act of 1807, forbidding *all* trade, was followed by the Non-Intercourse Act in 1808, which prohibited trade with England. This was raised from May, 1810, to March, 1811, when it was renewed, to be followed by war between England and the United States from 1812 to the beginning of 1815. In spite of these measures, it will be seen that England was successful in bringing scores of shiploads of timber from the United States, and some of this wood was used to build frigates which returned to fight the Americans.

The British naval needs had an effect on the new nation's forest policy. In 1783, Massachusetts virtually enacted many features of the old Broad Arrow policy.[1] The first measure of the new national government in forest policy dealt with live oak, which they considered their best ship timber, five times as durable as white oak. Fearing that England might finally realize the value of this tree, Congress considered purchasing islands off the Georgia coast to furnish timber for the young American navy.

The probability is, that an article so important to maritime nations as live oak will be sought after with much avidity, and that the land which is clothed with it may pass into hands that may make its attainment hereafter more expensive, if not impracticable.

But whether it is right that the United States should be the purchaser of such land is a question which no doubt you have examined,[2]

wrote McHenry, the Secretary of War, to the Congressional Committee. In 1799, the government made its first forest reservation by purchasing Grover Island off the Georgia coast; and a year later, Blackbeard's Island also was secured.

England's constant neglect of the high value of the southern timber is one of the surprising features of her naval supply from America. Not until the great quest of 1804 was the attention of the Navy Board directed to this possibility. It was determined to contract for more than 40,000 loads of pitch pine for repairs and the construction of "fir frigates."[3] Within ten years, "Old Ironsides," of Georgia live oak, was shattering the flimsy hull of the *Levant*, built of Georgia pitch pine.

Contracts for a large amount of pitch pine were soon allotted to the firms of Logan, Lenox and Company, and Luscombe and Donaldson, and ships under many flags began to load at Wilmington, Charleston, Savannah, and St. Mary's for English dockyards. England had urgent need of this timber, which could be so

---

[1] *Laws of the Commonwealth of Massachusetts*, 1780–1800, i, 108.

[2] *U. S. State Papers, Naval Affairs*, i, 27, 38; U. S. Dept. of Agr., Hough, *Report upon Forestry*, 1878, pp. 9, 10.

[3] B. M., Add. MSS, 37,275, f. 295; R. O., Adm. Digest, 4871, *N. B. to Adm.*, May 15, 1805, Jan. 29, 1806, Nov. 17, 1806.

quickly converted into frigates, and it was superior in quality to most of the pine that Canada had to offer.

The Embargo suddenly shut down on this trade, and the Non-Intercourse Act, which followed it, left England still nominally excluded from the American trade. Thousands of loads of pitch pine, paid for by the naval contractors and ready for shipment at Wilmington and the other ports, waited for more than two years before they could be taken to Plymouth, Chatham, and other dockyards where they were sorely needed.

Nominally, England was cut off from this timber by Jefferson's measures of peaceful coercion as thoroughly as from Baltic "naval materials" by the contemporaneous Continental System. There was ample leakage in both places, however, for the measures were opposed in each case by a powerful element in the commercial population, and timber ships arrived at the dockyards from the Baltic and the United States even when both systems were supposedly most strictly enforced. The American measures were enforced, on the whole, in a milder manner than Napoleon's and Alexander's in the Baltic.

Violations of the American measures were most flagrant at the extreme north and south. Vermont lumbermen defied the customs vessel which the United States placed at the frontier, and floated their great armed rafts to Quebec, where they helped to supply the Royal Navy with timber. Skippers of Bath braved the guns of the Kennebec River forts to take timber cargoes to England. Eastport, and other towns near the St. Croix River, utilized the proximity of Canada for an extensive and very profitable illicit trade in timber.[1] At the opposite extremity of the American seaboard, the St. Mary's River offered similar facilities for evading the law. Although the town of St. Mary's was a port of Georgia, Spain owned the right bank of the river, together with Amelia Island just off the coast. These became flourishing *entrepôts* for illicit trading, which amounted sometimes to a million dollars annually during the period of the trade restrictions.[2]

---

[1] Lower, *History of the Canadian Wood Trade* (in preparation); Reed, *History of Bath*, p. 78; Defebaugh, *Lumber Industry*, ii, 317.

[2] *Niles's Weekly Register*, iii, 93, vii, 168, 206, 317; Adams, *History of the United States*, v, 165.

Logan, Lenox and Company, the principal contractors for pitch pine for the Royal Navy, played the Amelia Island game successfully, and in 1809 were securing licenses from the Supreme Junta of Spain to bring away the timber cut in Carolina and Georgia.[1]

During the ten months from May 1, 1810, to March 3, 1811, when the restrictions on English trade were lifted, the Navy Board tried to increase its imports of pitch pine. The Luscombes renewed their contract to supply the timber detained at Wilmington by the Embargo, but refused to contract for a supply from Georgia, for fear of the revival of Non-Intercourse. In ignorance or defiance of the renewal of the American restrictions, Logan, Lenox and Company made a new contract on July 17, 1811, for 10,000 loads of pitch pine at £12 a load, to be delivered before November, 1812. In spite of the Non-Intercourse laws, they delivered more than 6,000 loads before the war broke out. They shipped not only from St. Mary's and Amelia Island, but even from Savannah and Charleston, and then requested naval aid at St. Mary's to facilitate the loading of the remainder.[2]

Even after the war started, pitch pine continued to arrive in England from Amelia Island, although many other cargoes were seized in the ports. The contractors lost heavily in this venture. The Luscombes pleaded to the Navy Board to remit the penalty for non-fulfillment of contract, in order "to preserve the little remnant of those fortunes we have lost"; but this was denied in spite of their protest against "an act of the American Government novel in its kind and which we considered ourselves guarded against in our contract — 'restraints of rulers and states excepted.'"[3] Logan and Lenox suffered also, although they violated American measures more successfully. Fourteen of their ships, bearing Baltic names for the most part, foundered at sea because they were so heavily overloaded. More than 4,400 loads of pine, which had already been loaded at the ports when war broke out, fermented so quickly in the hot summer that timber and ships were rotted. Only the consideration of such losses can

[1] R. O., Adm. Digest, 4898, *N. B. to Adm.*, Dec. 21, 1809.

[2] R. O., N. B. In Letters, 1561, *Lenox to N. B.*, Dec. 19, 1809; *Logan to N. B.*, June 17, 1811, Jan. 25, 1812, Aug. 24, 1812.

[3] *Ibid.*, 1560, *Luscombe to N. B.*, June 11, 1810; 1561, Nov. 22, 1813.

justify the big profit the timber contracts often brought.[1] More than a score of "fir frigates" were built of this American pitch pine, which became one of the leading items of the naval timber supply during the decade after Trafalgar; but important as these smuggled cargoes from the southern ports were, that supply was decidedly secondary to the constant procession of timber ships from the Canadian ports of St. John, Miramichi, and Quebec.

In 1809, the supply of timber from the United States and the Baltic was almost at a standstill, and the Navy Board was alarmed for the future of the dockyard supply. They began to search remote corners of the whole world for trees which had not been considered, or even known in many cases, in the survey of 1804. The Canadian supply was increasing rapidly in magnitude, but except in the case of great masts, the quality of the timber left much to be desired. The Croatian and Black Sea timber being shut off and the Albanian supply not yet begun, there was an urgent need of good timber and small masts and spars. The assistance of admirals, captains, diplomats, and consuls everywhere was solicited, and reports came in from every side.

The sanguine accounts of great forests, adequate to supply the Navy with timber forever, were subjected to a heavy discount. The Baltic situation was serious because it deprived the Navy of the most efficiently organized timber trade in the world. It had been simple to send an order for Dantzig crown plank, with the confidence that a cargo of assured first quality would be at the dockyards within a few months. It was quite a different matter to draw timber from the distant virgin forests, described in such glowing terms. Skilled lumbermen were scarce, transportation was difficult and expensive, and after the trees were cut, and even after they were brought to England, the quality of the timber often required its rejection.

A final attempt was made to round up any available timber near home. Timber and spars of fir and larch were brought from Scotland, the oak of Ireland was employed though its fir was rejected, and the inhabitants of Jersey were encouraged to develop

---

[1] R. O., N. B., In Letters, 1561, *Logan, Lenox Co. to N. B.*, Aug. 19, 1812, Oct. 18, 1815.

a timber trade.[1] Portugal, the only available region on the Continent, offered some pine timber and masts from Setubal.[2]

The Portuguese government, recently transferred to Rio de Janeiro by the British Navy, gave an expression of its gratitude by offering Brazilian ship timber. Samples of dozens of the tough, heavy tropical woods of Brazil were sent to the dockyards and found satisfactory after dockyard experiments. A contract for a regular supply of this timber was granted, but lumbering and transportation facilities were so poor that this supply, which lasted until 1815, was never extensive.[3] Timber of similar quality was offered from Demerara in British Guiana, but the timber resources of Trinidad were not exploited to any extent. There was a contract for mahogany from Honduras, where good mahogany was expensive and cheap mahogany so porous as to be worthless.[4] A supply of lignum vitæ for blocks and tackles was developed in Jamaica, the usual supply from San Domingo being cut off.[5]

An elaborate but disappointing attempt was made to procure timber from African forests near the Cape of Good Hope, in 1811. Several naval officers on the Cape station had reported that the forests on the Kuirboom, which flows into Plettenberg Bay not far from Cape Town, offered an inexhaustible supply of excellent ship timber which the Dutch had used for many years.[6] The Navy Board sent A. J. Jones, a dockyard shipwright, to utilize these forests. He was to have the support of Commissioner Shields at the Cape Town dockyard, and transports were instructed to return with cargoes of this wood.

Jones found two kinds of trees suitable for ship timber. There was a sort of oak called stinkwood, the wood of which was tough and heavy but possessed little curvature suitable for compass

---

[1] R. O., N. B. Out Letters, 1560, *Livie to N. B.*, Sept. 24, 1809; Adm. Digest, 4898, *Grant to Adm.*, Nov. 11, 1809; 4910, *Duke of Athol to Adm.*, July 22, 1812.

[2] *Ibid.*, 4898, *Adm. Berkeley to Adm.*, Aug. 8, 1809.

[3] *Ibid.*, 4871, *Treas. to Adm.*, Oct. 4, 1806; 4893, *Adm. Smith to Adm.*, Jan. 24, 1809; *N. B. to Adm.*, Nov. 6, 1815; *Quarterly Review*, viii, 52.

[4] R. O., Adm., Digest, 4910, *Laforey to Adm.*, July 19, 1812; 4916, *N. B. to Adm.*, Feb. 1, Mar. 21, 1813; *Parl. Papers*, 1847–48 (o.48), vol. xxi, pt. 1, p. 601.

[5] R. O., Adm., Digest, 4858, *N. B. to Commissioner Stanley*, Dec. 7, 1803.

[6] *Ibid.*, 4888, *Adm. Bertie to Adm.*, May 15, 1808; *Lieut. Street to Adm.*, June 6, 1810; *N. B. to Adm.*, Dec. 21, 1808.

timber. There was also the yellow-wood, or *actinqua*, producing sticks available for masts and spars. Jones experienced the difficulties attendant upon developing lumbering operations in a wild country. He arranged with the Boers in the neighborhood to furnish slaves for cutting and hauling. Soon he reported that "the Hottentots who . . . hired themselves as woodcutters are now all gone to the school of Mr. Van der Kemp near Algoa Bay"; and shortly after that, his lumbermen were all called away to repel a Kaffir invasion, for he was operating near the passes ordinarily used by the Kaffirs in their raids. He had to contend with sharp dealing on the part of the Boers. They cornered all the available timber carts in the region, demanding high prices for their use, and they thwarted him in many other ways.

It was very difficult to find suitable trees near the rivers. "Where there is the best timber there is the least means of obtaining it, and where that most unfit for naval purposes, the best," wrote Jones. Tree after tree, apparently sound, was found to be badly cracked or shaken at the heart, and Jones began to wonder if he had "been misguided by evil disposed or interested persons." In spite of these difficulties, Jones got considerable timber down over the falls of the Kuirboom and through the heavy surf into Plettenberg Bay, where transports took several cargoes to England. The dockyard officers found that plank sawn from stink-wood was very liable to cracks, but there were portions of a ship's anatomy where the strength of the African timber was valuable. Yellow-wood spars were used extensively for repairs at the Cape Town dockyard, and were also substituted for Riga and Norway sticks at Portsmouth. The captain of the *President* condemned them as too brittle, but opinion gradually grew more favorable.[1]

The impediments and the expense involved in the exploitation of this Good Hope timber were considered too great, and the effort was given up in 1812. Timber possibilities in Madagascar were discussed, as the French had discussed them in 1793, but Admiral Stopford's remarks on the unhealthy climate caused the matter to be dropped.[2] In 1813, Captain Irby of the *Amelia* sent

[1] R. O., N. B., Misc. 3570, *Correspondence on Cape of Good Hope Timber*.
[2] R. O., Adm. Digest, 4910, *Adm. Stopford to Adm.*, Jan. 2, 1812.

the Navy Board a box with samples of a dozen varieties of woods growing near Sierra Leone. Experiments showed that the *Tectonia Oldfieldiana*, the African teak or oak, might be satisfactory. A contract was entered into with the firm of Clay and Company, engaged in the African trade, for a regular supply of this timber. By 1815, it was being used in the dockyards, and it continued to find its way into the construction of warships and merchantmen until the close of the wooden ship era.[1]

Captains in the South Seas were sending enthusiastic reports of the excellent woods growing in New Zealand and New South Wales. By 1804, masts of New Zealand kauri, or cowdie, and timber from the Australian jarrah were arriving by transports, which would otherwise have returned empty. In 1809, New Zealand cannibals devoured the crew of the *Boyd* as she was loading kauri spars for the Cape Town dockyard. The excessive freight rates precluded a commercial supply, but throughout the war, and for many years after, the Navy continued to draw masts and timber from those remote sources.

The Navy and Army secured masts and timber in many irregular ways, to supplement the inadequate channels of supply. Admirals and captains on many stations occasionally purchased masts on their own responsibility wherever they could be found, or sent their crews ashore to cut masts for their particular needs. Admiral Saumarez had the crews of many of his ships cutting Baltic firs for masts and timber during the period of inactivity in 1809. The Admiralty agreed to pay them for the time so spent but not for the value of the masts.[2] Admiral Gambier had the storehouses and timber piles at the Copenhagen dockyard ransacked to the last treenail, bringing the spoils back to England along with the Danish navy.[3] The Walcheren expedition in 1809 had instructions to seize all timber and naval stores which were public property and to purchase all that were found in private hands. Practically the only tangible result of that fiasco was the bringing home of the frame of a ship of the line taken to pieces

---

[1] R. O., Adm. Digest, 4916, *Commis. Gray to Adm.*, Apr. 8, 1813; *N. B. to Adm.*, Nov. 26, 1813; *Parl. Papers*, 1847–48 (555), vol. xxi, pt. 1, pp. 604, 605.

[2] R. O., Adm. Digest, 4893, *Saumarez to Adm.*, July 21, 1809.

[3] *Parl. Papers*, 1808 (236), i, 9, gives detailed list of spoils.

at Flushing and incorporated into a seventy-four, which was launched at Woolwich in 1812.[1] In 1814, Napoleon's dockyard at Genoa was stripped of its timber, which was taken to England and used in the building of the *Formidable*, 80. The Antwerp yard was treated in the same manner.[2]

England had departed from her traditional policy of building warships at home when Bentham was sent on his unsuccessful mission to Russia in 1805.[3] The extreme need for timber during the Napoleonic period led to several similar attempts to relieve the shortage by building ships in foreign or colonial ports. A dozen sloops of war were built in Halifax in 1808, but they proved far from durable.[4] Many small warships were constructed at Bermuda of pencil cedar, though James gives an unfavorable verdict on their quality.[5] The possibility of building warships in Brazil and Portugal was entertained for a time, but it never materialized.[6]

The most successful attempt to relieve the timber shortage by foreign shipbuilding came from the use of teak in India. It has already been mentioned that teak was finally recognized as the best ship timber in the world. It had long been valued highly in India. The Mahrattas and other Indian powers had navies of teak, and in the last days of the Bourbons, Hyder Ali built warships for the French navy. He also furnished France with masts of poon and ship timber of teak. England armed dozens of ships built in India for her expeditions against Ceylon, Java, Manila, and the Moluccas, and into the Red Sea, between 1795

[1] R. O., Adm. Digest, 4893, *Castlereagh to Adm.*, July 16, 1809; 4910, *N. B. to Adm.*, Jan. 23, 1812.

[2] *Ibid.*, 4922, *Exmouth to Adm.*, May 20, 1814; 4028, *Adm. to N. B.*, Apr. 4, 1815; N. R. S., *Journals and Letters of Sir T. Byam Martin*, iii, 15.

[3] See pp. 328–329.

[4] R. O., Adm. Digest, 4883, *Cochrane to Adm.*, Nov. 23, 1807, *Adm. to N. B.*, Jan. 4, 1807; Knowles, *Dry Rot*, p. 162; Rosa, *La Construction des Navires à Quebec*, *passim*.

[5] R. O., Adm. Digest, 4827, *Goodrich to Adm.*, June 26, 1795; 4883, June 4, 1807; 4871, *Adm. to N. B.*, Apr. 28, 1806; 4893, Feb. 13, 1809; James, *Naval History*, iii, 376.

[6] R. O., Adm. Digest, 4888, *De Sonza Contruho to Adm. Smith*, Dec. 2, 1808; 4901, *Adm. de Courcey to Adm.*, July 13, 1811.

and 1800. It was claimed that had it not been the use of these improvised warships, her control of Indian waters would have been doubtful.[1]

When Melville replaced St. Vincent as head of the Admiralty in 1804, his interest in India led him to promote the construction of warships there. Orders for a seventy-four and a frigate had already been sent to Bombay in 1803. Melville secured the co-operation of Wellesley, then head of the Indian government, and of the East India Company, which had already been persuaded to build its own ships in India and now agreed to superintend the building of warships for the Navy.[2]

The choicest timber lay in the southwestern part of India, in the region known as the Malabar Coast, but even in India a shortage of good naval timber was already felt. Tippoo Sahib, who had controlled a large portion of that country, had cut off much of the largest teak in the interests of the French. The shipbuilding of the Portuguese was a constant drain on the supply of ship timber. Melville was advised to urge the Portuguese to desist from shipbuilding in India during the war, and if that failed, to seize their ports in order to preserve the supply. The Dutch had held a portion of the Malabar region around Cochin. They had become identified with Tippoo, who represented French influence in that part of India, and after the defeat of the sultan at Seringapatam in 1799, the English had seized his lands and those of the Dutch. Sir George Buchanan urged that the Navy exploit the former Dutch forests to the limit, as it was likely that they would be restored to Holland at the end of the war, and England could thus maintain her own teak forests intact for a future supply. This policy was acted upon, but the Dutch never returned to the mainland of India.[3]

The site for shipbuilding operations presented a problem. Ships had been constructed for many years at Calcutta and Bombay, but they were remote from good timber supplies. After rejecting

---

[1] *Parl. Papers*, 1813–14 (115), vol. vii, pt. 1, pp. 580, 664–666.

[2] R. O., Adm. Digest, 4858, *Adm. Rainier to Adm.*, Dec. 10, 1803.

[3] B. M., Add. MSS, 37275, ff. 260–262, 306–380. All papers on India shipbuilding during Melville's term at the Admiralty, 1804–05; see *Quarterly Review*, viii, 42 ff.; x, 18 ff., 467 ff.; Pettigrew, *Memoirs of Lord Nelson*, ii, 667, 668.

Pegu in Rangoon, where there was plenty of timber but considerable danger from its isolated position across the Bay of Bengal, it was determined that a dockyard should be built at Prince of Wales Island on the Malabar Coast, near some of the best forests. The utter lack of facilities for the construction of large warships led to the abandoning of the yard after one frigate had been built, and the *Akbar*, 74, was left unfinished on the stocks. Most of the ships built for the Navy in India were constructed at Bombay by the very able Parsee shipwright, Jamsetjee Jeejeeboy. Since teak did not corrode iron as oak did, it was possible to simplify shipbuilding by the use of spikes instead of wooden treenails.[1]

The first product of the Bombay yard was a thirty-six gun frigate originally called the *Pitt*, but later known as the *Salsette*, which was turned out in 1805. She was followed three years later by the *Doris*, 36. The *Malacca*, 36, was produced at the Bombay yard in 1809. Before the end of the war, the Bombay dockyard facilities had attained a sufficient degree of development to launch the *Minden*, 74, in 1810, the *Cornwallis*, 74, in 1813, and the *Wellesley*, 74, in 1815, in addition to several smaller craft. The records of these ships were excellent on the whole, though the *Minden*, which cost £58,000 in 1810, had received repairs to the amount of £85,000 within fourteen years, and the sole product of Prince of Wales Island was taken to pieces in seven years. Most of the ships, however, outlasted their contemporaries built in England. The *Salsette* served well in the Baltic, and after her capture of a French frigate, Pellew wrote to Jamsetjee commending him on his work.[2]

If the enthusiasm of Melville for the building of warships in India had been shared by his successors, the forests and shipyards of India might have done more to relieve the timber problem at home. There were several drawbacks, however. The distance between England and India, the old policy of building all warships at home, and the occasional lack of coöperation of the East

---

[1] B. M., Add. MSS, 37275, ff, 260–262, 306–380; Money, *Observations on the Expediency of Shipbuilding at Bombay*, pp. 42 ff.

[2] R. O., Adm. Digest, 4883, *Pellew to Adm.*, Sept. 14, 1807; *Adm. to Grenville*, Sept. 17, 1807; *Adm. to East India Co.*, Oct. 10, 1809; Adm. Library, *Abstracts of Progress, passim*; *Parl. Papers*, 1813–14 (115), vol. vii, pt. 1, p. 237.

India Company, which occasionally diverted timber from the naval construction to the building of their own ships, all tended to prevent a further use of this possible source of relief. There was a strong opposition to Indian shipbuilding on the part of the Thames builders, who feared that the high quality of teak and the low cost of labor might ruin their business. A Parliamentary committee was appointed in 1813 to consider their petitions against the admission of merchantmen built in India to British registry, and this committee investigated the whole timber problem to consider whether such a step was warranted.[1]

Very little teak timber was sent to the English dockyards before 1812 because of the high freights on the return voyage from India. It was feasible to bring timber from the South Seas, because the transports would otherwise have returned empty; but in the Indian trade the profits were made on the return voyage. At first it was planned to diminish the cost of the warships built in India by bringing them home filled with tea; but the increasing scarcity of great and compass timber of English oak led to the practice of sending the new warships to England with the teak frame timbers for a similar ship to be built in the home yards. Up to 1812, only one cargo of teak had reached England, but the policy of bringing home the frame timbers was continued to the end of the era of wooden warships. The Navy continued to build ships in India until 1831, and the *Asia*, 84, Codrington's flagship at Navarino, was among the splendid products of Jamsetjee and his brothers. Even after armorclads were introduced, teak was used for the backing of the plates because of its non-corrosive quality. The success of the few ships which were built for the Navy in India justified Melville's inauguration of the policy, and the timber problem could have been relieved even more if the practice had been carried out more fully.[2]

The forests of her empire saved England from disastrous consequences to her Navy when the English woodlands and the regu-

---

[1] *Parl. Papers*, 1813–14 (115), vol. vii, pt. i., *passim;* R. O., Adm. Digest, 4901, *Commissioner Dundas to N. B.*, Sept. 20, 1811; *East India Co. to Adm.*, Nov. 8, 1811.

[2] See Low, *History of the Indian Navy*, p. 237, for complete list of warships built at Bombay; James, *Naval History*, vi, 396; R. O., Adm. Digest, 4901, *Adm. to N. B.*, Aug. 20, 1810.

lar foreign supply proved insufficient during the struggle with Napoleon. The experiences of that decade reflect the wisdom of the men a century earlier who attempted to make the empire self-sufficient in the matter of naval necessities even if the cost might be greater. Many of the attempts to secure timber in remote regions were more spectacular than productive, but Jamaica, British Guiana, Sierra Leone, and New Zealand did their bit, while the teak of India and, above all, the masts and oak of Canada played an important part in sustaining British sea power in the decade when Napoleon was Emperor of the French.

CHAPTER X

TRAFALGAR AND DRY ROT

ONLY one flaw marred the otherwise able conception and execution of the Trafalgar campaign, according to Admiral Mahan. That lone defect was the inadequate supply of timber and other naval materials inherited from the St. Vincent administration.[1] For want of oak, the admirals had to hold their stormy blockade stations with ships which were being wracked out of shape, for there were no materials in the dockyards to repair the reserve ships which should have relieved these battered craft. For two whole years, the British squadrons suffered from this incessant wear and tear. Time and again, their commanders reluctantly weakened themselves by releasing their most unseaworthy ships, while the enemy whom they were trying to hold in check was constantly adding to the forces within the blockaded ports. Unusual efforts to secure additional timber for patching up the reserve ships finally gave the British strength enough to bring about the glorious consummation at Trafalgar.

It may seem invidious to dwell upon this single defect in one of the most successful naval campaigns of history, but this "wooden interpretation" has been only partially explained by the writers who have dealt with those events at sea.[2] This oaken background to the more important considerations of strategy and tactics enhances the credit due to the admirals who held their posts in spite of leaky ships and to the administrators who grasped the means to rectify a dangerous situation. Chief among these latter was Sir Charles Middleton, who coördinated the tangled operations against Napoleon's naval forces with consummate skill during the five months preceding Trafalgar, after he had been called to the head of the Admiralty as Lord Barham. From this old man in his eighties, who had wrestled with the Navy's timber problem for

---

[1] Mahan, *Influence of Sea Power upon the French Revolution and Empire*, ii, 166.
[2] *Ibid.*, p. 122; James, *Naval History*, iii, 212.

more than a quarter of a century, came the most pertinent suggestions which enabled the Navy to escape the effects of its desperate shortage of oak.

Thanks to Middleton, the Navy had suffered little from want of oak during the war with Revolutionary France. The full storehouses and high timber piles which he had provided after the American Revolution met the demands of dockyard construction and repairs for several years, and the usual foreign sources of supply were available during most of the time. Toward the end of the first phase of the long struggle with France, however, the English groves began to feel the drain of Lord Spencer's ambitious building policy, for the construction of two hundred warships had eaten heavily into the nation's oaks. In the last years of the eighteenth century, occasional complaints of leaky ships began to reach Whitehall, prophetic of the chorus which was to arise a few years later.

When hostilities were renewed in 1803, St. Vincent showed sound strategy in the blockade which he clapped down upon the enemy naval bases. Cornwallis was given some twenty ships of the line, with the important mission of holding in check the principal French fleet across the Channel at Brest. Collingwood was near-by with a smaller squadron, blocking Rochefort. Keith watched the enemy coast from Dunkirk to the Texel, while Pellew was sent to cruise off Ferrol, where five French sail of the line had joined the Spaniards, whose neutrality was under suspicion. Finally, Nelson was sent to hold Latouche-Tréville in check at Toulon and to guard British interests in the Mediterranean. If a rigid blockade could be maintained on all these stations, British commerce would be protected from powerful raids and, what seemed even more important in the nation's state of alarm, Bonaparte would be unable to concentrate his scattered squadrons to clear the Channel for his proposed *descente en Angleterre*, with the army at Boulogne. Whether or not he seriously entertained such a project, the threat was sufficiently real to call out the utmost exertion on the part of the Royal Navy.

To maintain this blockade, England had fifty-five sail of the line opposing forty-two of the enemy, at the outset, and enjoyed

a slight numerical superiority on every station. This was practically necessary from the very nature of the work. The enemy
had all his ships together for use at any favorable moment, while
the forces outside were liable to be scattered by storms or diminished by the necessity to refit. The blockading squadron had
a negative mission requiring constant vigilance, and if it was to be
successful, it had to be strong enough to drive the enemy back
into port. It was because of this that the admirals were to plead
so strenuously for reinforcements to replace their ships weakened
and strained from want of repair, for the presence of a single ship
might possess a high "marginal value." The constant service on
blockade kept the crews well trained while the enemy lay inactive, but it was a gruelling test for unsound ships.

There were plenty of such unsound ships in the squadrons which
St. Vincent sent to the blockade stations in the spring of 1803.
At the cessation of hostilities in the fall of 1801, he had had on his
hands a navy worn out by steady service since 1793. Instead of
repairing these ships, it will be recalled that, under the influence
of his desire for economy, he had discharged dockyard workers,
sold off some of the smaller ships and sent the larger ones into
"ordinary," or reserve, where they continued to decay, while the
timber stores fell to less than the equivalent of one year's consumption instead of the prescribed three. Bonaparte had utilized
the breathing spell in a far different manner. While St. Vincent
was cancelling timber contracts and letting the battered warships
sink into further disrepair, Bonaparte was commandeering a
huge amount of oak in the French forests and elsewhere, which
was used not only for the construction of the hundreds of flat-
boats but also for building and refitting ships of the line to face
the Royal Navy. When the short peace ended, the dockyards
lacked the timber necessary to put the worn-out ships in proper
shape, and many of those which sailed off to their posts were in no
condition to withstand the strenuous work ahead of them.

Nelson began to complain in vigorous style of the state of his
ships as soon as he reached his station off Toulon. "The fleet here
upon paper are very formidable," he wrote to Cornwallis late in
July, 1803, "but in fact the *Victory, Bellisle & Donegal* are the

only ships fit to keep the sea; the rest are unfit for service until docked, altho amongst the finest and certainly best-manned ships in the service." [1] A month later, he reported that three of his ships were in immediate need of replacement and that four of the others were not in condition to stand the winter gales which averaged three days in seven in the Gulf of Lyons. These ships were in the state, he said, where small repairs could have saved them, but the storms would soon attack them in their weak spots and necessitate practically a total rebuilding. [2]

The winter gales justified these predictions, and no relief came to Nelson from St. Vincent's remark, "We can send you neither ships nor men, and with the resources of your mind, you will do without them very well." [3] In December, Nelson wrote to Davison:

My crazy Fleet are getting in a very indifferent state, and others will soon follow. The finest Ships in the Service will soon be destroyed. I know well enough that if I was to go into Malta, I should save the Ships during this bad season; but if I am to watch the French, I must be at sea, and if at sea, must have bad weather; and if the Ships are not fit to stand bad weather, they are useless. I do not say much; but I do not believe that Lord St. Vincent would have kept the sea with such Ships. [4]

On the same day, he wrote St. Vincent that he was sending the *Kent*, 74, to Malta, although the passage was difficult and he expected to be deprived of her services for six weeks or two months. The *Superb*, 74, was in a very weak state and the "*Triumph* and *Renown* complain a good deal." "However," he wrote in closing, "you may rely that all which can be done by Ships and men shall be done"; and he remained doggedly on his station. [5] These remarks may be tinged with a certain amount of the same political and personal animus contained in the despatches of the Whig admirals who complained of their masts during the American Revolution. [6]

The condition of the *Kent* and *Renown*, however, showed that Nelson was not exaggerating. They were comparatively new

---

[1] Hist. MSS Com., *Var. Coll.*, vi, 399.

[2] *Ibid.*, p. 412; Nelson, *Despatches* (ed. Nicolas), v, 174, 175, 179, 210, 211; Mahan, *French Revolution and Empire*, ii, 123–129.

[3] *Despatches*, v, 283. [4] *Ibid.*, p. 306. [5] *Ibid.*, p. 307. [6] See pp. 293, 300.

ships, having been launched in the Thames in 1798, and a timely repair would have saved them. As it was, the *Kent* was "nearly done for," being so weak that her lower deck guns had to be removed. When Nelson finally ordered her to England, he wrote that "fearful of any accident happening to her on the passage, I shall direct a transport to accompany her." Her condition was so serious that the repairs came to half her original cost, and took so long that Nelson was deprived of her services at Trafalgar, although he had counted upon her in his preliminary battle order. Other ships in bad condition also had to be released, and several which should have gone were kept in service by the sheer ability of their captains and crews. They were "absolutely going to ruin for want of a few weeks in dock." [1]

Nelson hoped for better things when Melville replaced St. Vincent in the spring of 1804, but he appreciated the difficulties under which the new administration labored, writing in July:

> *Kent, Renown* and *Gibraltar* are gone for any further use; *Superb* and *Triumph* must go. Several of the ships want to go into port to refit, and if I was to do as they do in the Channel, I have not by that mode of judging, four sail fit to keep the sea. I absolutely keep them out by management; but the time must come when we shall break up, unless the new Admiralty act very differently from the old, and send out six sail of the line and fifteen frigates and sloops, and I do not believe that the late Admiralty have left them one to send. But I must not indulge in these thoughts or I should say more, but I pay it off with thinking. [2]

Relief was slow in coming, and Nelson longed for a fight with Latouche-Tréville before more of the British ships succumbed to the gales. By winter, Nelson was outnumbered by the growing Toulon fleet alone, while the entrance of Spain into the war left a hostile squadron at Cartagena on his flank. [3] Latouche-Tréville, the ablest of Napoleon's admirals, had died, and his successor, Villeneuve, was able to escape from Toulon early in 1805. The lack of frigates, those "eyes of the fleet," left Nelson in doubt of his destination.

Complaints of unseaworthy ships were not confined to Nelson. Similar reports came from the squadron off Ferrol, where five

---

[1] *Despatches*, v, 309, 319, 334; vi, 81, 82, 84.
[2] Laughton, *Letters of Nelson*, p. 357.
[3] *Despatches*, vi, 134, 158.

French ships had taken refuge and where Spain was fitting out ships which would strengthen the French navy as soon as Spanish neutrality was thrown off. Pellew was sent to blockade Ferrol and Corunna while Spain was still neutral, and his nine ships were to prevent even the Spaniards from entering and leaving port. Pellew later defended the condition of the Navy in Parliament, declaring that it was "never better found," yet signs of weakness had begun to appear in the Ferrol squadron even before Pellew was relieved by Cochrane early in 1804.[1] By the summer of that year, nearly half the squadron was reported as unseaworthy.

The ship's carpenter of the *Ganges*, 74, drew up a report which shows in elaborate detail what even the moderate summer seas could do when a ship began to give way after long lack of repairs. He may have been ordered to overlook nothing, but he certainly found enough to mark the ship as unfit for further service. Three of her forecastle beams were broken and two knees under the quarterdeck were sprung. Some of the lower deck planking was quite decayed, one plank forward being so far gone that the magazine and storerooms could not be kept dry in bad weather. All the decks were leaky for want of caulking, and there was a leak on the starboard bow ten feet below the waterline, apparently caused by a rotten treenail. "The poop deck," said the report, was "so thin as not to bear caulking, as appeared by a survey held on it at Portsmouth in September last, when there was no deals to repair it." The bowsprit was sprung, and "the whole of the knees and beams of the lower deck appears to work much," because the fastenings had given way. Every one of the scuppers had been broken in the gale of the preceding December, and, though seven had been borrowed from other ships, several remained broken. The guard iron of the head had been broken in that same gale and the essential fittings of the head were washed away. Two of the lower deck pumps were useless and "the ship made so much water at times as to gain on the pumps."[2] The carpenters of several other ships in the squadron, later called in consultation, reported

---

[1] N. R. S., *Blockade of Brest*, i, 315; *Parl. Debates*, 1st ser., iv, 892.

[2] R. O., Adm. I, 126, Report of John Gore, Carpenter, in *Cochrane to Cornwallis*, July 25, 1804.

that "for the preservation of the ship, if the service would permit, it would be necessary for her to go to England before the winter, as her defects cannot be completed where she now is." [1]

The *Ganges* was not alone in her decrepitude. In Cochrane's little squadron, three other seventy-fours, the *Mars*, *Dragon*, and *Illustrious*, were in practically the same condition, and the *Spartiate* was only a little better.[2] There was no question that they needed dockyard attention, but, as Cochrane wrote in September,

I will delay sending the *Ganges* and *Illustrious* to Plymouth until I receive further orders — as I do not think the remaining ships will be safe after their departure should orders arrive from Madrid to send the Spanish squadron to sea — which they can do in 24 hours — should their object be an attack upon the squadron under my orders.[3]

A large quantity of ship timber had just been discovered after it had lain buried for years in the mud at Ferrol, and three Spanish sixty-fours were taking it aboard to carry to Cadiz. Cochrane had orders to stop all warships, so a contest seemed likely. The *Ganges*, however, was finally sent to Portsmouth, and Cochrane remained on patrol duty with his weakened squadron.[4]

The effects of rotting oak were less noticeable on the Brest blockade. The soundest ships had been told off for this most important function of blockading the principal French fleet at its base so near England. Moreover, when a ship began to show signs of weakness, it was possible to release her for the short trip across the Channel to Portsmouth. The Brest squadron fluctuated in its numbers, maintaining an average strength of about twenty sail of the line, and the absence of one ship, which could return quickly, would be felt less keenly than on the isolated stations off Toulon and Ferrol, where every ship was needed and where a trip to the dockyards would entail an absence of several weeks. Consequently, Cornwallis could repair his ships before they were as far gone as the *Kent*, *Renown*, *Ganges*, *Illustrious*, and those other battered hulks on the stations to the southward. Cornwallis himself remained on his stormy post for months on end, but Calder, who is said to have had a penchant for shore leave, took

---

[1] R. O., Adm. I, 126, *Cochrane to Adm.*, Sept. 4, 1804.

[2] *Ibid.*, July 24, Aug. (undated), Oct. 26, 1804.   [3] *Ibid.*, Sept. 19, 1804.

[4] *Ibid.*, Aug. 20, Sept. 3, Sept. 24, Oct. 21, 1804.

the *Prince of Wales* into Portsmouth with part of her head gone, while the crew were beginning "to fall down very fast" from constant work at the pumps.[1] Ship after ship was sent into Portsmouth, some of them leaking so badly that the water gained on the pumps, and in one case, a ship was in such a dangerous state that ten of her guns had to be thrown overboard to keep her afloat.[2] Keith had some converted East Indiamen and other ancient craft in his North Sea Squadron and criticized them as "not equal to cruize against the armed vessels of the enemy with effect." [3]

Collingwood, who had an unsurpassed reputation for quietly making repairs at sea and denying himself shore leave, had his troubles in the little squadron blockading Rochefort. During the first winter of the blockade, he reported that his flagship, the *Venerable*, was in a dangerous condition, with the crew "almost worked to death." Describing the examination of this ship, which was to sink in the following year, he wrote:

We began by discovering slight defects in the ship, and the farther we went in the examination, the more important they appeared, until at last it was discovered to be so completely rotten as to be unfit for sea. We have been sailing for the last six months with only a copper sheet between us and eternity.[4]

Meanwhile, in the timber piles at the dockyards lay the explanation and the final solution of this prevalence of decrepit ships. As long as those timber piles were low, Collingwood and his colleagues had to keep the sea in battered hulks, while the British were gradually losing their numerical superiority on most of the blockade stations. Once the piles began to be replenished, it was possible to patch up the ships waiting in reserve and to give England the force she needed for the final drive. The political opponents of Lord St. Vincent gathered from official sources the following statistics of timber supply and consumption during this period, as an indictment of his policy. The figures for the

---

[1] R. O., Adm., i, 125, *Calder to Cornwallis*, Sept. 1, Sept. 24, 1804.

[2] *Ibid., Young to Adm.*, Oct.17, 1804; N. R. S., *Blockade of Brest*, i, 224, 229, 237; ii, 118.

[3] R. O., Adm., i, 544, *Keith to Adm.*, Dec. 5, Dec. 8, Dec. 14, 1804.

[4] Collingwood, *Correspondence of Lord Collingwood*, p. 95.

amount of timber on hand were taken in May of three successive years, at the outbreak of hostilities in 1803, the fall of St. Vincent in 1804, and the fall of Melville in 1805, five months before Trafalgar. The statistics of consumption represent the calendar year. Though produced by political animus, these figures correspond closely with the regular records and show in concise form the gist of the timber situation at this time:

Timber on Hand	1803	1804	1805
English Oak Timber	30,602	30,829	38,927
English Oak Thickstuff	2,349	2,710	2,406
English Oak Plank	921	1,004	1,423
Foreign Oak Timber	2,267	261	480
Foreign Oak Plank	690	2,027	3,574
Total Oak	36,829	36,831	46,810
Total Fir Timber	7,942	7,605	14,640
Consumption			
English Oak	29,250	42,833	31,822
Foreign Oak	10,784	8,561	9,684
Total Oak	40,034	51,394	41,506

The figures for the expenditure of fir timber are missing.[1]

Granting the relative accuracy of these figures, certain conclusions are obvious. St. Vincent had found some 42,000 loads of oak on hand when he came into office shortly before the conclusion of hostilities in 1801. The Navy Board, it will be recalled, had recommended in 1771 that the dockyards always keep on hand enough timber for three years' consumption, the figure being set arbitrarily at 66,000 loads. Middleton had secured this amount in the period following the American Revolution, and it was deemed an important security measure in order to allow the oak to season and to have an adequate supply to meet the demands of war. During the interval of peace between 1801 and 1803, however, the stock on hand actually decreased, dropping from 42,000 loads to less than 37,000, and this latter figure was suspiciously similar a year later when St. Vincent retired from

---

[1] *Parl. Papers*, 1805 (152), i, 54; 1813–14 (115), vol. vii, pt. 1, pp. 392, 638. See also B. M., Add. MSS, 37,275, f. 264, *N. B. to Adm.*, Mar. 24, 1804; N. R. S., *Barham Papers*, iii, 20.

office. Instead of maintaining the prescribed three years' reserve, there was barely enough for nine months of the heavy demands of that period.

Yet it would seem that the Navy was at least able to hold its own in the matter of oak, if one did not recall that the figures for a total supply often give a misleading sense of sufficiency. It might be possible for the dockyards to contain a sufficient amount of oak for the needs of a year or more, and yet find it impossible to complete a single ship of the line. Certain items of great and compass timber, such as stern posts, catheads, wing transom knees, and the like, were very hard to secure, and the paper total might represent medium-sized straight timber which was relatively easy to obtain. That total, moreover, was distributed between six dockyards, and each one in turn might be delayed for the want of particular pieces.[1] In this case, there was a particularly serious shortage of plank and knees.

There are constant instances of this lack of definite kinds of timber in the dockyard reports during 1803 and 1804. As early as February, 1803, three months before hostilities were renewed, the officers at Plymouth declared that they could not continue repairs and construction more than six months longer at the present rate of timber supply. Their thickstuff, they said, was of inferior quality, short and defective, but even if it were good, "the whole store falls 160 load short of the probable consumption for the year." The plank was short and not applicable for necessary purposes, "therefore the whole of what is due we request to be hastened into store." During the past year, Plymouth had received 781 loads of oak timber, had used 3,125, and had sent 490 additional loads to the eastern yards. They needed 47,000 treenails to finish the *Hibernia*, 110, and to repair five other ships then in dock, and they were likewise very short of Dantzig plank and knees.[2]

Portsmouth, which shared with Plymouth the bulk of the repair work on the capital ships, was also handicapped for want of timber. The officers there reported that the last supplies of timber, knees, thickstuff, and plank were inadequate for repairing the

---

[1] See pp. 7, 39–40, 43–47.   [2] *Parl. Papers*, 1805 (152), i, 39, 40.

ships which they had on hand. One shipwright at Portsmouth later declared that the plank was of such poor quality at this time that he had been compelled to use "such shaky and defective ones . . . that . . . must have always leaked."[1] It will be recalled that in the survey of the battered *Ganges* off Ferrol, it was stated that there had been no deals with which to repair her decks when she was examined at Portsmouth in 1803. The yard at Sheerness ran almost entirely out of timber early in 1804, and the officers there were informed that Chatham and Plymouth could spare them no oak from their own meagre stocks. The officers at Chatham wrote that they had on hand little of the timber of the size requisite for the frigates which they had been ordered to build, while Deptford reported that it was absolutely necessary that timber for carrying on repairs "should be furnished with as little delay as possible."[2]

It was necessary to resort to substitutes for the missing English oak. Early in 1803, the Plymouth officers requested and received permission to use German oak for the riders, plank, and thickstuff of the *Warrior*, 74, which they were then repairing. The dockyards had 2,267 loads of foreign oak on hand, principally from Larking's first contract at Dort which St. Vincent had cancelled. Though the quality of this timber was criticized, it was used to such an extent that barely a tenth of it was left a year later. The Deptford officers were allowed to go a step lower in the timber scale by using fir timber when their German oak was gone. At Plymouth, it was necessary to use second-hand knees from captured Spanish ships to equip the new *Hibernia*, and when those ran short, the experiment of iron knees was tried. The Plymouth officers also received permission to tear obsolete ships to pieces, that their old plank might be used to repair three ships of the line waiting there.[3]

The following graphic picture of the extreme shortage at Portsmouth in the last month of St. Vincent's administration received wide publicity at the time:

[1] R. O., N. B. In Letters, 3570, *Jones to Shute*, Nov. 25, 1811.
[2] *Parl. Papers*, 1805 (152), i, 40, 41.
[3] *Ibid.*, 39, 41; R. O., N. B. Out Letters, 2231, *N. B. to Adm.*, Feb. 10, 1803; Collingwood, *Correspondence of Lord Collingwood*, p. 100.

It would scarcely be believed, if the artificers and other persons belonging to the dockyard at Portsmouth were not ready to attest the fact, that on the 4th of the present month [May] not a single four-inch plank was to be found in the yard. In proportion as scanty supplies of timber were obtained, it was instantly applied to the ships, and on the arrival of a load there was so much scrambling for it, more especially for the crooked timber, that disturbances were nearly excited among the workmen. In the case of a part of the crooked timber, the leaves were still green.[1]

Another writer, in the midst of numerous serious charges against the St. Vincent administration, stated that the repairs were "made with wet, unseasoned stuff: — I have seen the timber worked up, while the mud and seaweeds were yet wet upon it." [2]

A certain discount may be applied to these reports, both official and unofficial, for they were used as political capital against the old sea dog at the head of the Admiralty, who was considered responsible for the timber situation. St. Vincent's reforms had touched the pride and the pockets of the civil personnel of the Navy, all the way from the Navy Board with their contracts down to the dockyard workman with his chips, so that their reports may have been colored by this animosity. Even the despatches of the admirals were possibly influenced by hostility to the First Lord to some extent; but there is such evident coördination between the situation at sea and that on shore that the lack of timber certainly must have been acute during the St. Vincent administration and must have been in large part responsible for the condition of the blockading fleets.

Relief came after Melville replaced St. Vincent in the spring of 1804. Consulting frequently with Middleton, who was to be his successor in office, Melville immediately applied himself to the solution of the timber situation. It has already been seen that peace was made with the "Timber Trust," and that steps were taken to secure the greatest possible amount of timber in the shortest possible time from overseas forests as well as from English groves.[3]

---

[1] *A Brief Inquiry into the Present Condition of the Navy of Great Britain and its Resources*, quoted in *Naval Chronicle*, xii, 40.

[2] Blagdon (Aristides), *Naval Administration*, p. 21.   [3] See pp. 323–325.

Melville, shortly after his accession to office, reveiwed the necessary building programme and its relation to the timber supply. Obviously there was no time to wait for the building of new ships of the line, for that process ordinarily took at least three years. The evident pressing demand was for repairing the ships waiting in reserve and those sent into port worn out by blockading service;

but [wrote Melville] with regard to them and every other object of naval exertion, we must be limited by the deficiency which may exist in the amount of our naval stores. . . . With a view both to our present exigencies, and to be able to meet future contingencies, we must, for some years, live on expedients. We must take first in hand those ships that can be repaired in the shortest time after they are taken in hand. We must have recourse to every substitute in order to spare our best timber, and we must be contented with less permanent repairs than would satisfy us in less pressing moments.[1]

Drawing on his long experience, Middleton was able to suggest an expedient which temporarily increased England's battle strength with more than a score of ships of the line. In 1782, during the last months of the American Revolution, it had been necessary to press into service "every ship that could swim." Gabriel Snodgrass, the able chief constructor for the East India Company, had devised a method of patching up old ships for temporary service by adding new planking and installing a system of diagonal bracings to strengthen their old hulls.[2] There were many old ships lying idle at the dockyards which would ordinarily have required practically a complete rebuilding, and there was material at hand in the 15,000 loads of Polish fir which Isaac Solly had rushed from Dantzig. This fir was especially applicable under the circumstances, for it did not require seasoning and could be quickly worked into shape. Twenty-two ships of the line and five frigates were fitted out early in 1805 according to these Snodgrass specifications. A sailor on the *Caesar*, 80, one of the ships so treated, leaves the following description of the process:

---

[1] N. R. S., *Barham Papers*, iii, 44, 45.

[2] Snodgrass, *Letter to the Rt. Hon. Henry Dundas . . . on the mode of improving the Navy of Great Britain, passim; H. C. J.*, 1792, pp. 363–365 (with diagrams); N. R. S., *Barham Papers*, iii, 273.

In the evening of the day the *Caesar* came out of dock having got her top-sides doubled with thick fir plank and eight diagonal shores on each side in her hold, reaching from the kelson to the ends of her lower deck beams, by way of strengthening her topsides when rolling.[1]

After being fitted with lighter masts and guns than was ordinary for their ratings, these ships were sent to sea at a time when England needed every one of them. Most of these resurrected veterans were used for convoy duty or for service in the North Sea, where they could relieve better ships and still make a show of force. One of them, however, the little *Africa*, 64, took part at Trafalgar, where she played an important solitary rôle.[2]

These were not the only ships which Melville and Barham were able to repair and send to sea to restore the numerical strength of the Navy. The new stock of timber available after St. Vincent's fall made it possible to fit thirty-nine ships for sea during the seventeen months between Melville's accession to office and the battle of Trafalgar on October 21, 1805. This was equivalent to more than one third of England's total battle strength at the time. The importance of the repairs after May, 1804, is evident in the records of the twenty-seven ships of the line with which Nelson won one of the most decisive naval victories of history. The repair record of each of those ships has been appended to this study because of the light which it throws on the timber and repair situation before Trafalgar.[3] Of the twenty-seven ships, all but four had received dockyard repairs since the war was renewed in 1803. Seventeen of the twenty-three ships thus repaired left the dockyards for active service after the timber situation was relieved at Melville's accession in May, 1804. Three of them were hurriedly fitted out and sent to Nelson only a month before Trafalgar. Some of the repairs, of course, were mere refitting or re-coppering, which was not dependent on the timber supply, but many of the ships required plank and knees which had been missing hitherto. The difference between the dates of arriving at the yards and of sailing for service shows that several of the ships lay

---

[1] Richardson, *A Mariner of England*, p. 207.

[2] Barrow, *Autobiographical Memoirs*, pp. 263, 264; James, *Naval History*, iv, 87, 453.

[3] See Appendix C, compiled from Adm. Library, *Abstracts of Progress*.

idle at the yards for two or three years because of the lack of timber for repairs. The *Ajax*, 74, the *Orion*, 74, and three little old sixty-fours built during the American Revolution, the *Africa*, *Agamemnon*, and *Polyphemus*, are examples of this long delay. In contrast to this is the speed with which some of the ships were repaired in 1805, when there was more timber at hand. The coppering and other extensive repairs of the *Royal Sovereign*, 100, amounting to nearly her original cost, were begun three months before Trafalgar and were completed in eight weeks. Her presence was important, for in her Collingwood led his division in breaking the enemy line. These statistics of the Trafalgar fleet were compiled because of the particular significance of those twenty-seven ships. They represented only a quarter of the nominal strength of the Royal Navy, and in some of the other fleets and squadrons the proportion of old patched-up ships added to the fighting strength of the Navy would be even greater.[1]

Barrow, an Admiralty official, probably did not exaggerate greatly when he expressed the opinion that these eleventh-hour repairs contributed much to the success of the Trafalgar campaign.[2] Five months before the final battle, Lord Barham wrote, "The Admiralty as well as myself are alarmed at the want of ships."[3] They had some cause to be alarmed. At the outbreak of hostilities in 1803, the British blockading forces had enjoyed a numerical superiority on every station. By March, 1805, they were quite generally outnumbered and some of the enemy squadrons were able to escape. The wear and tear of constant sea service and the lack of timber to repair ships for replacement had kept the numbers of the blockaders practically stationary, while the French had been completing new ships in their own ports and had secured the active services of the Spanish navy. The following tables of the relative strength in ships of the line sum up the general blockade situation at these two dates, though the figures cannot be taken as absolute because of frequent changes which have led to differences among the authorites.

---

[1] Corbett, *Campaign of Trafalgar*, pp. 146, 199, 243.

[2] Barrow, *Autobiographical Memoirs*, p. 264.

[3] N. R. S., *Barham Papers*, iii, 84.

Station	1803 British	1803 Enemy	1805 British	1805 Enemy
Brest-Rochefort..................	20	18	17	24
Texel-Dunkirk	9	5	11	9
Toulon (Cartagena)	14	9	12	17
Ferrol	7	5	8	12
Cadiz	..	..	6	7
	50	37	54	69

The French also had five sail of the line in the West Indies at the latter date, while the British had nineteen in the East and West Indies, two en route to Toulon, and several more in home waters. Altogether, the Royal Navy had a paper strength of some one hundred and fifteen of the line, but about thirty of these were not yet in condition for sea service.[1]

Naval history, of course, cannot be interpreted by numbers alone. "In following the story of Trafalgar," says Mahan, "it must be remembered that the naval superiority of Great Britain lay not in the number of her ships, but in the wisdom, energy, and tenacity of her admirals and seamen."[2] Clowes, in the same vein, writes: "Mere numerical equality in ships and men under such circumstances, goes for very little. Indeed, where quality is deficient, mere quantity is often, in itself, a source of weakness." Yet he also says that "in fleet actions, victory inclines to the bigger battalions," and that England cannot always count on a Nelson whose presence is worth half a dozen battleships.[3] In the case of the comparative statistics of the Trafalgar campaign, a discount may be applied to the force of the enemy numbers, for most of their ships had untrained crews, and some of them, in the words of Corbett, were "mere floating barracks."[4] Gravina, the Spanish admiral, used this as an argument against attacking, just before Trafalgar, referring to the "inherent inferiority" of the Combined Squadron.[5] Moreover, the British had a larger num-

---

[1] Adapted from Clowes, *Royal Navy*, v, 85, 86, 95; Mahan, *Influence of Sea Power upon the French Revolution and Empire*, ii, 123–125, 147–149; Jane, *The British Battle Fleet*, pp. 117, 118; Wheeler and Broadley, *Napoleon and the Invasion of England*, ii, 153; James, *Naval History, passim.*

[2] Mahan, *op. cit.*, ii, 141.

[3] Clowes, *op. cit.*, vol. v, pp. ix, 86.

[4] Corbett, *Campaign of Trafalgar*, p. 253.

[5] *Ibid.*, p. 325.

ber of three-decked first and second rates, and Corbett argues
that one of these in battle was equivalent to two two-decked
seventy-fours.[1]

Granting the validity of those arguments, the fact remains that
the duties imposed upon the Royal Navy in the final months of
the Trafalgar campaign called for every available ship. Barham
realized this fully during those sleepless nights when he wrestled
with the latest reports of the enemy squadrons which were playing hide-and-seek around the North Atlantic. He had a good
grasp of the situation and he made his dispositions with ability,
but he was often forced to take long chances, and there were times
when he had to weigh relative values closely before detaching one
or two sail of the line from posts where they were stationed. A
military expedition had to be sent to the Mediterranean with a
very weak escort while the elusive squadron of Allemand was still
at large; commercial convoys ran similar risks, and there had to
be a reserve force at home upon which the British forces could
converge in case the enemy should break loose for a bold stroke.
These situations had to be provided for, and at the same time the
main fleets had to be kept in condition to deal with the enemy in
case they should come upon him. Under the circumstances, it is
not surprising that orders were sent to the dockyards "to get
everything to sea that would float." [2] Even the ancient fourth
rates, with their holds propped up to keep them seaworthy,
must have been a godsend at such a time.

The active work of the dockyards in turning out every available
ship left the Royal Navy much stronger in October, 1805, than
it had been in March at the end of a stormy winter of blockade
duty. Nelson expected more ships than he received for his final
work, and a list of the ships upon which he counted in his preliminary battle order eleven days before Trafalgar includes the
Kent, which was still receiving extensive repairs after her trying
experiences off Toulon.[3] As it was, Nelson had twenty-seven sail
of the line to the enemy's thirty-three in that "culminating hour
of sailing warfare," and his genius more than compensated for the
numerical discrepancy. Whether it could have offset a still

[1] Corbett, *Campaign of Trafalgar*, pp. 46–49.   [2] *Ibid.*, p. 254.
[3] *Ibid.*, pp. 290, 353.

greater lack of numbers is a matter for speculation. The Admiralty was using every available ship for some important purpose in the campaign, and the absence of several of the units of battle force which had been repaired at the last minute might have involved serious risks. The hastily assembled supply of timber, assembled chiefly after Melville replaced St. Vincent, made it possible to swell the total British strength in sail of the line by fully a third, while nearly two thirds of the Trafalgar fleet were fitted for sea during that period. Referring to this in a letter to the King and Council the following year, Barham wrote:

When it is considered that, in the period alluded to, only 5 new ships have been launched and added to the fleet, and of these, only three have been at sea, the great importance of this measure will be manifest, as without fresh ships to replace those worn out by the necessary wear and tear of an unremitting blockade, every movement of our naval force must be crippled in an imminent degree. Without having had recourse to these means, it would have been impracticable to have given that number of ships to Lord Nelson, which the important services he was entrusted with necessarily required.[1]

The function of the Royal Navy underwent a decided change after Trafalgar. Napoleon had rushed his Boulogne army across Europe, and was at Ulm even before Villeneuve met his great defeat. In turning definitely to conquest on land, Napoleon relieved the strain upon those British ships of the line which had performed their duties in such thorough fashion. It was now the turn of the smaller craft to take up the Navy's burden in enforcing the Continental Blockade with which Britain opposed Napoleon's Continental System. The Navy proceeded to give a remarkable demonstration of

the noiseless, steady, exhausting pressure with which sea power acts, cutting off the resources of the enemy while maintaining its own, supporting war in scenes where it does not appear itself or appears only in the background, and striking open blows only at rare intervals.[2]

Frigates and sloops by the hundred were necessary for the exercise of this pressure. Even the little gun brigs were needed, for their ten guns were enough to make a merchantman heave to and prove that its papers and cargo satisfied Britain's commercial regulations.

[1] N. R. S., *Barham Papers*, iii, 110–112.
[2] Mahan, *Influence of Sea Power on History*, p. 209.

This new rôle of the Navy was reflected in a change of the timber problem. Instead of the hasty patching up of great ships for participation in a vital campaign, the Navy had to maintain nearly a thousand ships of all classes at sea for a whole decade, building nearly four hundred new vessels in the eight years following Trafalgar. While the Navy was exerting its steady, exhausting pressure on Napoleonic Europe, that same Europe was partly responsible for the steady, exhausting pressure of the timber situation upon the King's ships. The constant demands for repair and replacement had to be met with timber piles depleted by the increasing shortage of native oak and the radically curtailed supply from Europe and the United States. Fir and Canadian oak proved inadequate substitutes for the choicer timbers, and the effect of these substitutes was seen in the flimsy frigates and rotting ships of the line.

Leaving the ravages of the dry rot in the great ships of the Navy for later consideration, we can see the effects of the timber situation in the lesser craft. Partly in response to Nelson's appeals from the Mediterranean for more cruisers, the construction of six frigates was begun in June, 1804, the month after Melville had replaced St. Vincent. Five of them were built of the fir which Solly sent from Dantzig, and in the other, American pitch pine was tried. One of these ships, the *Jason*, was completed in three months, and three others were ready by November.[1] The use of fir timber accelerated construction, but it also hastened decay. Like the previous fir frigates built during the Seven Years' War and in 1795, the average duration of these ships was only six or eight years, and it was also claimed that the fir splintered too freely in action.[2] For a while after Trafalgar, there was enough small oak to build frigates, sloops, and brigs of that timber, but the shortage grew more serious by 1808, when the demands of the Continental Blockade combined with the closing of the Baltic and American ports. While the Navy Board was giving orders that new ships of the line might be allowed to season in frame for a long period, there were constant orders to rush the construction

[1] *Parl. Papers*, 1821 (186), vi, 169.
[2] *Ibid.*, 1820 (269), iii, 58; 1821 (186), vi, 14, 169.

of the lesser craft until 1811.[1] Time and again, however, the contractors complained that they could not obtain timber enough to
complete the work in hand and launchings were often delayed for
months until sufficient wood could be found.[2]

By the end of 1810, the Navy was able to curtail its building
programme in order to relieve the heavy drain on the timber piles,
which were feeling the pinch of the curtailed foreign and native
supply. The various classes of ships were well filled, and it was
even possible to have more than fifty worn-out vessels broken up
or sold out of the service. Where thirty-one ships of all classes
were built in 1810, only fourteen were launched in the following
year, and the dockyard consumption of oak for those two years of
extreme shortage averaged less than 48,000 loads, in contrast to
more than 64,000 in 1809 and 74,000 in 1812.[3]

In spite of the timber shortage, Britain was in a very compla-
cent frame of mind in regard to its Navy. "Never were its services more important and indispensable than when nothing was
left for it to conquer — when it had driven from the ocean every
ship of every foe, and rode triumphant and alone," declared a
writer in the *Quarterly Review*.[4] This smug statement about
"every ship of every foe" was quite true when written; but just
before that issue of the review appeared, H. M. S. *Guerrière*, 38,
had struck her flag to the *Constitution*, 44, of the little United
States Navy. Though the American war was only a side-show
compared with the European conflict, the result of this frigate
action and others which followed cut deeply into the pride of
"the Mistress of the Seas." With this new contest, the timber
problem again came to the fore.

Six weeks before the United States had declared war, the Admiralty had ordered another consignment of six fir frigates. Un-
mindful of the size of the *Constitution* and her sister ships, they

[1] R. O., Adm. Digest, 4888, *Adm. to N. B.*, Feb. 22, Sept. 19, 23, 28, Oct. 14,
Nov. 28, 1808; 4893, May 2, 1809; 4901, June 22–Dec. 26, 1810 (ten letters).
[2] See esp. *Ibid.*, 4888, *Taylor to Adm.*, Mar. 17, 1808; *N. B. to Adm.*, Mar. 29,
1808; 4901, *Rowe to Adm.*, Jan. 10, 1810; N. B. In Letters, 1625, *Sutton to N. B.*,
Aug. 24, Sept. 13, Nov. 23, 1806.
[3] *Parl. Papers*, 1813–14 (115), vol. vii, pt. i, pp. 179–182, 480–488, 638, 661, 662.
[4] *Quarterly Review*, viii, 55, Sept. 1812.

ordered the new vessels to be copied after the *Leda*, 36.[1] Oak was
so very scarce and expensive that it was decided to utilize Canadian red pine and the pitch pine from the southern United States.
Fir was used to "husband or save up the English oak," declared
Sir Robert Seppings, the famous naval designer, who went on to
say that he did not believe that the Navy would have used an
inferior timber like fir if a sufficient quantity of oak had been
available.[2] The news from America led to an increase of the contracts, and finally forty frigates were ordered, about half of which
were built of American pine furnished to the contractors from the
dockyards. Once again, the construction was rapid, and so was
the decay. Two were launched in April, 1813, and by November
all but one of the others had slid into the Thames. These hastily
built frigates of the American armament were popularly known
as the "forty thieves." The previous flotillas of fir frigates had
lasted six or eight years but most of these were condemned in
three or four.[3]

The American shipwrights had caught the British napping.
None of these "forty thieves" was strong enough to cope with
the powerful forty-four gun frigates designed by Joshua Humphries. Full specifications of the size and armament of the *Constitution* and the others had appeared in the *Naval Chronicle* as
early as 1799, but when the war started, the Royal Navy had no
ships which could meet them on equal terms. The old fifty-gun
fifth rates had been discarded as useless in the line of battle, leaving a large gap between the heaviest frigates of the *Java* type and
the smallest ships of the line of sixty-four guns. The *Constitution*
demonstrated that she could sail away from any ship of the line
and could pound to pieces the strongest frigate.

Aroused by the losses in American waters, the Admiralty began to build ships in a feverish and, for the most part, foolish
manner. These extra demands came at a time when timber was
still scarce, for the Baltic was only beginning to emerge from the

---

[1] R. O., Adm. Digest, 4910, *Adm. to N. B.*, May 2, 1812.

[2] *Parl. Papers*, 1813–14 (115), vol. vii, pt. 1, pp. 336, 337, 450, 451, 651, 652.

[3] *Ibid.*, 559; 1820 (269), iii, 58; 1821 (186), vi, 14, 169; Adm. Library, *Abstracts
of Progress, passim;* Green and Wigram, *Chronicles of Blackwall Yard*, pp. 48, 49.

restrictions on its trade. It was possible to meet the size of the American frigates but not their strength of hull. Two super-frigates of 1500 tons and sixty guns were hastily built and sent to sea as the *Leander* and *Newcastle*, while five heavy frigates of fifty guns were also constructed in a hurry. These ships, however, were built of Georgia pitch pine and Canadian red pine. James, the naval historian, who tried to explain away the British defeats, declared that it was suicidal to send ships with thin sides of such weak timber against the American frigates, with their twenty-two inches of the tough live oak. This excellent ship timber, which the Royal Navy had consistently neglected, gave the American ships the practical value of armor plating. "Old Iron-sides" fought with comparative impunity against an adversary like the *Levant*, whose thirteen-inch sides of fir were quickly shattered. Even the British ships of oak were at a disadvantage in this respect, for the lack of timber had led the Navy Board to permit lighter scantling in their construction. The frigate actions of the War of 1812 were important principally for their moral effect, but they afford one more instance of the influence of the timber problem. At great exertion, the Navy had secured from the United States itself the pine which weakened the hulls of many of the ships sent against the Americans, when, from the very same region, they might have secured the precious live oak which helped to give "Old Ironsides" her sobriquet.[1]

So much for the frigates. The Royal Navy was also having its troubles with the ships of the line during the decade after Trafalgar. These capital ships had relatively little to do after 1805 beyond the bombardment of Copenhagen, the fiasco at the Dardanelles, a little fighting in the Baltic, and several minor actions incident to patrol duty. Britain, however, had to maintain a respectable number of them ready for service, to offset the spasmodic construction which Napoleon was carrying on in a dozen or more dockyards of his empire, from Holland to the Adriatic.[2]

[1] James, *An Inquiry into the Merits of the Principal Naval Actions between Great Britain and the United States*, pp. 34, 52–54, 58, 68, 94; *An Inquiry into the Present State of the British Navy*, p. 10; R. O., Adm. Digest, 4916, *Adm. to N. B.*, Apr. 4, May 7, May 30, Sept. 4, 1813.

[2] See *Corr. de Nap.*, xvii, 218–220; *Quarterly Review*, viii, 28, 55.

Melville had recognized that the patching up of old ships for the Trafalgar campaign, necessary and valuable as it was, could be only a temporary makeshift. The war was to last for ten years more, and the Navy had to build more than fifty new ships of the line during that period. These new ships were not called upon for such important services as the patched-up fleet which they replaced, but they revealed in a very striking manner the results of the timber shortage through the unusual and alarming prevalence of dry rot. The study of the naval timber problem during the Napoleonic wars could have been brought to a more dramatic close with the hasty gathering of enough timber to patch up a fleet at the last moment before Trafalgar, but the story of the problem in its effect on the Navy would not be complete without the dismal anti-climax of great ships hopelessly rotten before they had completed their maiden voyage.

The decay was caused by the quality of the vast amount of timber which the Navy had to use during these years. During the eighteenth century, it will be recalled, the average annual consumption of oak in the dockyards was estimated at 22,000 loads. The extent to which this had increased during the Napoleonic era can be judged from the following tables, which do not include the probably equal amount consumed in the private yards building warships on contract, or the huge quantity of fir and pine which was authorized for use in even the largest ships.

	English Oak	Foreign Oak (*Chiefly Canadian*)
1806	46,861 loads	12,371 loads
1807	34,233	11,597
1808	34,039	26,847
1809	44,358	20,111
1810	37,297	10,496
1811	30,927	17,252
1812	44,269	30,077 [1]

The Canadian oak, which was the principal substitute for the native timber, tended to justify the long-standing prejudice of the Navy Board against American oak because of its tendency to rot.

[1] *Parl. Papers*, 1813-14 (115), vol. vii, pt. 1, p. 638.

The English oak, however, was little better at this period. The native woodlands would not seem to have failed the Navy in this critical period of the timber supply if one judged by quantity alone. Their contributions, however, were woefully deficient in respect to the pieces of great and compass timber needed for ships of the line. For almost the first time since the days of Anthony Deane during the Restoration, inventive genius in the dockyards was applied to the problems created by the lack of this essential timber.[1] Sir Samuel Bentham had taken the first step in this direction in 1797, when he constructed several minor warships near the New Forest on a plan which obviated the use of much of the larger pieces of oak.[2] After Trafalgar, several radical changes were introduced. The warships of the eighteenth century had bulging sides, but there were no longer enough of those pieces of curved timber for the futtocks which gave the form to this "tumble home." As a result, the dockyards began to produce "wall-sided" ships, which could utilize the available straight timber. The hedgerow oaks which produced knee timbers had practically disappeared, so the Navy had to borrow the idea of iron knees from the French, who had used them since the days of Colbert.[3] Gabriel Snodgrass had applied iron knees to the ships of the East India Company at the time of the American Revolution, but not until the time of the Trafalgar campaign were they introduced into the royal dockyards by Peake and Roberts.[4] Robert Seppings, who was knighted for this work, made an even greater change in the anatomy of the ship of the line about 1812. In his plan, the beams were fastened between long riders instead of by knees, while the inner planking or ceiling was removed and the intervals between the frame timbers filled in with pieces of old timber so as to make one solid mass with no room for stagnant air. Finally, Seppings introduced great triangular braces, which were bolted to the inside of the ribs to strengthen the ship longi-

---

[1] See pp. 5–6, 78–80.

[2] Bentham, *Life of Sir Samuel Bentham*, pp. 106–109, 313, 314.

[3] Colbert, *Lettres, Mémoires et Instructions*, vol. iii, pt. 2, p. 323; Duhamel du Monceau, *Élémens de l'Architecture Navale*, p. 50.

[4] Snodgrass, *Letter to the Rt. Hon. Robert Dundas, passim; H. C. J.*, 1792, pp. 363–365; Wood, *History of the Royal Society of Arts*, pp. 254, 255.

tudinally.[1] Practically all the innovations in British naval architecture during this period were occasioned by the inadequate supply of timber.

The cleverest of the naval architects, however, could not obviate the need for great timber in certain parts of the ship's frame, and these huge pieces were a constant source of difficulty in the construction of ships of the line. The continual cutting of oaks during the long period of naval war left very few of the extra diameter requisite for sternposts and similar pieces. In order to secure the requisite dimensions, it became necessary to include the outer rim of *alburnum*, or sapwood, instead of using only the tough *duramen*, or "heart of oak." The latter, when properly seasoned, would last indefinitely, but the sapwood which was left on the logs to give them the requisite size decayed rapidly. In fact, very little of the English oak furnished during these years could last long, for the steady demands left no time for seasoning. Referring to the period after 1804, a writer in 1812 declared that

The axe was set to work, and trees which were one year growing in the forest, were, in the next, floating on the ocean: and the demand since that time has trodden so closely on the heels of supply, that few, if any, ships have been built, either in the royal or private yards, with timber duly seasoned.[2]

Enough has been said concerning dry rot already to make it evident that such green timber, especially when mixed with other kinds of wood in the hull of one ship, was almost bound to decay.[3]

It is not surprising, therefore, that the great ships rotted rapidly. Many ships of the line, built at a cost of more than £60,000 and with a consumption of more than 3,000 loads of timber, were useless in five years after launching, or even in less time. Spencer's heavy building programme during the war with Revolutionary France had drained the forests of their best timber, and the first of the defective ships date from a period several years earlier than Trafalgar. The *Spencer*, 74, built in 1800, was thoroughly rotten in a very short time, and it cost £124,186,

[1] Seppings, *On a New Principle of Constructing His Majesty's Ships of War;* reprint from *Philosophical Transactions.*
[2] *Quarterly Review*, viii, 35, 36.
[3] See pp. 11–15.

more than twice the initial expense, to put her in condition again. The *Albion*, 74, and the *Scepter*, 74, built in Thames yards in 1802 and 1803 respectively, were found to be entirely unserviceable in India by 1806. They were so weak and leaky that the bottoms had to be strapped with cables, and the admiral on the India station was criticized for risking the lives of the officers and crews in sending them to England in such condition. Once more, the repairs were equal to nearly double the original cost. The similar case of the *Kent*, 74, in Nelson's Toulon squadron has already been mentioned.[1]

After Trafalgar, the list increased. The *Blake*, 74, and the *Devonshire*, 74, rotted with unusual celerity. The *Rodney*, 74, launched in 1809, had scarcely put to sea when the shrinking and rotting of her unseasoned timbers worked all her fastenings loose, and in 1812 she was brought home from the Mediterranean to be put on the inactive list. The *Dublin*, 74, was sent on a cruise off Madeira shortly after her launching in 1812, but in a few months she was back at Plymouth in such a condition that she had to be paid off. These were not exceptional cases. Similar stories were told of the *Ajax, America, Foudroyant, La Hogue, Mulgrave, Ocean, Stirling Castle*, and other products of the royal and private yards during these years. It is true that seven ships of the line built between 1809 and 1813 were still in active service in 1860, but some of them had been rebuilt at tremendous expense.[2]

The most flagrant example of dry rot was the *Queen Charlotte*, 110, which was built at Deptford in 1810 and rotted so quickly that it was necessary to rebuild her completely before she could ever be commissioned for sea. Her keel had been laid in the month that Trafalgar was fought. She was launched on May 17, 1810, "and never was a ship launched with less trouble or in a grander style."[3] Her hull cost £67,029, while the masts and yards brought the total to £88,524, about fifty per cent more than the cost of a seventy-four.[4] A year after her launching, while she

---

[1] Adm. Library, *Abstracts of Progress; Parl. Papers*, 1813–14 (115), vol. vii, pt. 1, *passim*.

[2] Adm. Library, *Abstracts of Progress, passim; Quarterly Review*, viii, 33; x, 473, 474.

[3] *Naval Chronicle*, xxiv, 36.   [4] Adm. Library, *Abstracts of Progress*, vi, 7.

was still in reserve being fitted for sea, it was reported that "some of the Canada Oak, Pitch Pine, timber and Treenails are found in a state of rapid decay." [1] To accelerate seasoning, she had received unwise treatment: "as soon as the unfortunate ship was closed in, stoves strongly heated were placed in the various parts of her hold . . . an excellent hothouse was thus formed for the growth of fungus on the surface of the unseasoned timber and it did grow out luxuriantly." [2] Official inspection disclosed that above the waterline, the *Queen Charlotte* was almost completely rotten. Seasoned and unseasoned English oak, Canadian oak, pitch pine, and English fir had all been used in her construction, and several different kinds of *boletus* or dry-rot fungus had attacked these various timbers. It was necessary to remove all the decayed wood and, after ventilating the rest, to wash it with a chemical preparation. The repairs up to 1816 had cost £94,499 in addition to the original £88,254, before she was of any use as a warship. The total cost of repairs had mounted to £287,837 by 1859, when her name was changed to the *Excellent*.[3] The *Queen Charlotte* became synonymous for the new spread of dry rot in the King's ships, just as the *Royal William* represented the durability of the old days. Each was an extreme case, but the rotting of the *Queen Charlotte* represented the gradual trend by the end of the Napoleonic period.

Dry rot became the talk of the day. "In the early part of my professional life, the dry rot was not a subject of conversation on the quarter-deck," wrote Admiral Stirling, who went on to say that interest in the matter had shown an "increase of late years." [4] The *Quarterly Review* and the *Philosophical Review* devoted much space to this form of decay, which threatened to offset any attempt to build great ships. Treatises in great numbers were written on the subject after 1812, usually by inventors like Dodd, Pering, and Wade who proposed panaceas for the evil.[5] Captain

---

[1] R. O., Adm. Digest, 4901, *N. B. to Adm.*, Aug. 20, 1811.

[2] *Quarterly Review*, viii, 36; see xii, 232.

[3] *Abstracts of Progress*, *passim*; R. O., Adm. Digest, 4901, *N. B. to Adm.*, Sept. 27, 1811; N. B. In Letters, 1561, *Lukin to N. B.*, July 8, 1812.

[4] Stirling, *Letters on Professional Topics*, p. 8.

[5] See esp. Bowden, *A Treatise on Dry Rot;* Chapman, *Preservation of Timber from*

Layman, in his *Precursor to an Exposé* and his *Pioneer*, made sweeping but doubtless exaggerated statements on the rottenness of the entire Navy, listing each ship and her condition; while Dodd claimed that five out of six ships were affected by the dry rot.[1] James did nothing to ease the public mind on the subject when, in trying to explain away the defeats by the Americans, he told of the decayed state of the *Guerrière* and the *Cyane*.[2]

Official records tend to confirm many of these charges, but a search of the sources shows an obvious attempt to suppress some of the most damning evidence. The Committee of Naval Revision, in the course of their searching investigations into many branches of the Navy, made a thorough study of the timber situation. Most of their reports were published as "blue books," but the timber report, together with one on the projected naval base at Northfleet, was omitted from the published series. Lord Melville, who was interested in both of these suppressed subjects, brought up the matter in the House of Lords early in 1810. He was answered by Lord Mulgrave, who declared that he would never consent to the publication of the timber report, because a knowledge of its contents might reach the enemy. He went on to say that there was nothing to fear, for the British fleet enjoyed such growing prosperity "that if the whole of these Reports had been burnt, or torn to pieces, and lost to the country, he could assure their lordships the navy of the country would, in spite of every abuse, still prosper."[3] Melville's answer to this insolent bombast was an open letter to the Prime Minister, Spencer Perceval, in which he declared that the public should know the seriousness of the situation. The letter reviewed some of the main features of the shortage and its effects, but the charges were hardly

Premature Decay; Dodd, *Practical Observations on the Dry Rot in Timber,* etc.; Layman, *The Pioneer, or Strictures on Maritime Strength and Economy; Precursor to an Exposé on Forest Trees and Timber;* Pering, *A Brief Inquiry into the Causes of Premature Decay in our Wooden Bulwarks;* Wade, *A Treatise on the Dry Rot in Timber.*

[1] Layman, *Precursor,* pp. 48–50; Dodd, *op. cit.,* p. 59.

[2] James, *An Inquiry into the Merits of the Principal Naval Actions between Great Britain and the United States,* p. 52.

[3] *Parl. Debates,* 1st ser., xv, 366.

detailed enough to give aid or comfort to the enemy.[1] It is evident
that another timber report must have been "burnt, or torn to
pieces, and lost to the country," two years later, for in the summer of 1812, the Admiralty inquired of the Navy Board to what
extent the timber supply would affect the building programme for
the next three years. The reply was omitted from the volume of
Navy Board Out Letters, which ordinarily give every letter in
full. It was merely referred to as "Secret and important." The
digest of Admiralty In Letters made a similar reference, and did
not hint at the tone of the subject-matter.[2]

This extraordinary omission came just at the time when the war
with the United States was entailing the wholesale construction of
fir vessels for want of oak; when the scandalous condition of the
Queen Charlotte was becoming known to the public; and when the
"Timber Trust" was extorting the highest price paid for naval
oak during the whole two centuries of the timber problem. Sufficient proof of the seriousness of the timber situation was revealed in the report of the committee on East India ships a year
later to indicate that, if the whole truth had been made public
earlier, inconvenient political consequences might have resulted.[3]

The failure of the English woodlands and the cutting off of the
regular European sources of timber supply had resulted in
wracked and battered ships before Trafalgar and rotten ships
afterwards. The course of the war with Napoleon would have
been little changed if there had been a more ample supply of oak,
but the situation presented a grave menace in 1804, and it might
have gone badly with the Royal Navy ten years later if a naval
force stronger than that of the Americans had opposed the decaying British ships.

The era of wooden warships can be carried quickly to its close
a half century after the fall of Napoleon. The timber problem
haunted it to the end, but, strangely enough, it did little to hasten
that end. There was little real naval fighting to enliven this story,
though the Admiralty never knew when Palmerston's lively

[1] Melville, *A Letter from the Rt. Hon. Lord Viscount Melville to the Rt. Hon.
Spencer Perceval on Naval Timber.*

[2] R. O., N. B. Out Letters, 2259, Nov. 26, 1812; Adm. Digest, 4910.

[3] *Parl. Papers*, 1813–14 (115), vol. vii, pt. i.

foreign policy might suddenly call for the utmost exertions of their ships. The details of the coming of the ironclads can well be omitted from this account, for they have been related time and again. Interest here will center, rather, in the last days of those oaken men-of-war which slipped almost unnoticed from the seas which they had dominated for so long.

That last half-century of the timber supply did not differ greatly from the preceding centuries, though some of the old generalizations cease to apply. The Navy Board came to an end in 1832, when it was absorbed in a committee of the Admiralty. The old primacy, and almost supremacy, of English oak had been shattered during the Napoleonic wars and was never recovered. Strange new timbers from all corners of the earth were to be found regularly in the dockyard stores, and by many they were esteemed above the traditional *Quercus Robur*. Naval architecture, too, dormant since the days of Phineas Pett and Anthony Deane, had come to life again because of the stress of the timber shortage during the contest with Napoleon, and during the last years of wooden ships of war, it enjoyed a renaissance typified by the establishment of a school for naval architects at Portsmouth. The limitations which the size of trees imposed on the dimensions of ships were radically overcome by ingenious devices, and the introduction of steam in the eighteen-thirties accelerated this process. The old seventy-four ceased to be a type which remained in style for decades. Beginning with the eighteen-forties, the Royal Navy contained many mongrel craft which would have seemed strange to Nelson, yet even then the general form was almost static compared with the constant evolution since 1860.

Yet in spite of these changes, many phases of the old timber problems remained almost unaltered. There was still a need for masts and spars, for straight and compass timber, for deals and plank and the minor forms of wood used in earlier periods. There was the old concern over the diminishing oak supply of England, the same complaints of negligence in the royal forests, and the same drawing of great masts from America and the usual stores from the Baltic. As long as wooden shipbuilding lasted in the Navy, those general features characterized the timber supply.

Foremost among the rivals of the oak of England was the tough brown crooked oak of Italy. The French had exploited the forests of northern Italy early in the Revolution and the shipwrights of Toulon fully appreciated the value of this timber. It will be remembered that the English brought home the stores from Napoleon's dockyard at Genoa in 1814, and the builders of Portsmouth and Chatham were not slow in realizing the advantages of a further supply. The English groves had failed principally in furnishing compass timber, and most of the oak brought from Italy consisted of those valuable crooked pieces.[1]

The following decades witnessed a lively rivalry between France and England for this long-neglected oak of Italy, and the Italians saw with dismay many of their most beautiful wooded hills denuded to satisfy the demands of the two great maritime powers. Diplomatic negotiations were conducted at Turin to secure the oak of Sardinia, Tuscany sent thousands of its finest trees, and the Papal States stripped their forests to build warships for England and France. The timber was so expensive that purveyors were sent to Italy to inspect it on the spot. Other timber could be rejected at the dockyards, but the word of the purveyors in Italy was final. Shipwrights complained that the wood was so tough that it turned the edges of their tools, and in some cases refused to work it, but that very quality made it splendid ship timber. At the close of the timber era, nearly half of the oak on hand in the dockyards was from Italy.[2]

Other valuable woods made themselves at home in the English yards with equal facility. Teak was often imported, and to the very end, the custom of bringing teak frames from India was maintained. There were regular contracts for African teak from Sierra Leone, and frequent shipments of greenheart, morrah, mahogany, and other species of the tough Central and South American timbers reached the royal yards. Masts of kauri from New Zealand and jarrah timber from Australia were supplied

---

[1] R. O., Adm., Acct. Gen., Misc., 135, *Navy Board Memorandum*, July 3, 1818; Laslett, *Timber and Timber Trees*, p. 128.

[2] R. O., Adm. Digest, 4986, *Lieut. Forbes to Adm.*, Apr. 28, 1825; 5091, *Petition of Merchants to Adm.*, Jan. 9, 1837, *Balfour to Adm.*, June 7, 1837; *Parl. Papers*, 1847–48 (0.48), vol. xxi, pt. 1, p. 366; 1848–49 (0.48), xxi, 118.

quite regularly, for ships from the South Seas would otherwise have often returned with empty holds.[1] Larch, which had been recommended as an oak substitute by the Commissioners of the Land Revenue in 1792, was brought from Scotland and Poland, and larch plantations were advocated in the royal forests.[2]

There was a lively contest between Baltic and Canadian timber interests which filled whole volumes of Parliamentary "blue books." It continued until 1860, when Gladstone caused the abolition of the last of the duties laid against Baltic timber around 1809, when it had been necessary to develop a timber trade in Canada. The subject makes an exceedingly interesting study in tariff protection, for the timber duties were silent partners of the Corn Laws.[3] Canadian timber had previously suffered in its rivalry with the Baltic because of the excessive cost of freight. The timber duties of 1809 were high enough to offset the difference between Canadian and Baltic freight, leaving a margin in favor of the Canadian. Under this protection, British capital had been invested heavily in the Canadian lumber business, and it has been seen that the results saved England from the rigors of the Continental System. The timber duties had been well justified as a war measure, for Canadian timber undoubtedly pulled the Navy through the crisis of the Napoleonic wars.[4]

The trouble lay in the retention of the duties after 1815 through the influence of a powerful group of shipowners and timber merchants. This protection produced a tremendous boom in the Canadian timber trade, and undoubtedly hastened the settlement of the wild forest lands in Ontario and the Maritime Provinces; but it had three unfortunate effects. Men who had the economic future of Canada at heart regretted that lumbering detracted from agriculture and permanent settlement. The predominance of the timber trade attracted a wild type of lumberman instead of steady settlers, and the neglect of agriculture produced an eco-

[1] R. O., Adm. Digest, 4986, *Gov. of New South Wales to Adm.*, July 20, 1825, *Lenox to Adm.*, Sept. 2, 1825; 5091, *Adm. Minutes*, Dec. 18, 1837; *Colonial Office to Adm.*, Jan. 25, 1837; *Bartholemy to Adm.*, Sept. 12, 1837; *Parl. Papers*, 1847-48, (0.48), vol. xxi, pt. 1, pp. 600, 601, 604.

[2] *Ibid.*, 364; R. O., Adm. Digest, 5091, *Solly to Adm.*, Dec. 20, 1837.

[3] See Lower, *History of the Canadian Wood Trade* (in preparation).

[4] See pp. 353-355.

nomic dependence similar to that described on the Maine coast a century earlier. The excessive cost of freight from Canada, offset by the high duties, meant that old, decrepit ships unfit for any other service ended their days in bringing Canadian timber to England. Many of them ended their careers under tragic circumstances. The desire for profits extended to burdening the ships with heavy deckloads of timber; and when the owners tried to get three round trips a year out of their vessels, the casualties in winter seas were notoriously heavy.

The final evil effect of the timber duties was felt in the Baltic, where the old, established timber trade suffered in its inability to compete with the heavily protected Canadian timber. Several great Norwegian timber houses failed after the close of the war, and distress was felt at Dantzig and other Baltic ports. Friedrich List, the great German protectionist, wrote bitterly of the German feeling toward England's high barriers against her principal Baltic exports of corn and timber. England preferred Baltic timber to Canadian, and the duties produced the strange practice of shipping Dantzig or Memel timber to Quebec, and bringing it back across the Atlantic to English ports where it could enter duty free. It was cheaper to carry it six thousand miles than to bring it directly seven or eight hundred miles. These anomalies resulted in gradual reduction of duty in 1821 and subsequent years, after it was shown that all England suffered from high timber costs, while the practice benefitted only a few shipowners and timber magnates.[1]

The Navy was affected by the timber duties through the increased cost of the Baltic timber which it used, for it will be remembered that timber for the King's ships had to pay the King's duties. The Navy had used Canadian timber only in the crisis when the Baltic supply failed. The prejudice of the shipwrights against American oak and pine was so strong that the Navy began to import timber and plank from the Baltic again as soon

---

[1] See esp. *Parl. Papers*, 1820 (269), vol. iii; 1821 (186), vol. vi; 1835 (319), vol. xix; 1839 (333), vol. ix, *passim; Observations on the Reports of the Select Committees of Both Houses of Parliament on the Subjects of the Timber Trade and Commercial Restrictions; Observations on the Report of the Select Committee of the House of Lords relative to the Timber Trade*, by a British Merchant, *passim*.

as Napoleon's influence there had relaxed. The timber duties, therefore, added materially to the cost of every ship. Canadian masts, which were supplied to the Navy in ample quantity, were exempt from the duties.

The supply of English oak, it has been seen, was slow in recovering from the tremendous drain of the Napoleonic era. Large timber was scarce to the end of the period, as will be seen from the debates in 1860 and 1861. The plantings stimulated by the shortage around 1810 had not matured in time to be of service, when the period ended.[1] It will be recalled that the timber magnate, James Morris, had drawn the entire English oak supply into his hands during this period.[2] His monopoly grew so distasteful to the Admiralty that during the last decades of the wooden ship era they drew more and more upon foreign forests. This weakened the timber monopoly by lessening the demand for English oak, while the native wood was conserved in preparation for a crisis which never arose. The proportion of English oak to foreign timber and to other oak substitutes, such as larch, is indicated by the amount of each on hand at Deptford for five-year periods — figures which are typical of the situation in the other yards.

	English Oak	Foreign Oak or substitutes
1840	15916 loads	9366 loads
1845	1029	2196
1850	1259	3693
1855	1868	4596
1860	857	6977
1865	5490	14077 [3]

One of the most surprising features of the whole naval timber problem is the seriousness with which it was taken in 1860 and 1861, the very last years of wooden capital ships. The official attitude of the Admiralty and the views expressed in Parliamentary debates in those years lead one to question the accuracy of Sir William Laird Clowes's statement that "wood and sails went out, and steam and iron came in, in 1855." [4] It is true that

---

[1] *Parl. Papers*, 1847–48 (51), vol. xx, pt. 2, p. 569; (555), vol. xxi, pt. 1, pp. 359–364; 1849 (0.30), xx, 14, 120–123, 160, 407. See pp. 137–138.   [2] See pp. 59–60.

[3] Laslett, *Timber and Timber Trees*, Appendix.

[4] Clowes, *Royal Navy*, vi, 473.

armored ships had been under consideration ever since Paixhans had proposed the use of explosive shells and the iron casings which could check them. The Admiralty had made half-hearted experiments at the proving grounds, and the Crimean War had demonstrated the weakness of wooden ships against explosive shells. The French had sent armored batteries into action in that war, and had followed that by the construction of *La Gloire* in 1859, which Britain followed by the building of the *Warrior*, launched at the end of the following year.[1]

Yet the Admiralty was still unconvinced that the days of wood were over. The years 1860 and 1861 witnessed a powerful last stand by the protagonists of "wooden walls." In view of the events of the preceding six years, it was no marvel that iron came in — the wonder is that wooden warships still found such strong official support, which was not abandoned until the action of the *Merrimac* with the wooden *Congress* and *Cumberland* and the iron *Monitor* definitely put an end to the era of wooden warships, in 1862. In 1849, Captain Chads, head of the naval gunnery school, had declared: "I think iron very inferior to wood for warlike purposes. . . . There is no iron vessel that can be built that will resist shot, unless it be of such a weight that she will not float." [2] That statement was at least made before the Crimean War, and is consequently more excusable than the assertion of General Sir Howard Douglas, the influential Chief of Ordnance, who wrote in 1860: "*The days of timber ships, whether commercial or warlike, are not, nor ever will be over.*" [3] Even at that late date there were plenty who could say with a certain dockyard official: "Don't talk to me about ships of iron — it's contrary to nature." [4]

With so many loyal "die-hards" in high places, one can understand why great anxiety was expressed over the acute shortage of large timber and why the Navy made one of the greatest pur-

---

[1] See esp. Paixhans, *La Nouvelle Force Maritime;* Barry, *Dockyards and Private Shipyards of the Kingdom; Dockyard Economy and Naval Power;* Busk, *Navies of the World;* Reed, *Shipbuilding in Iron and Steel;* Russell, *The Fleet of the Future—Iron or Wood.*

[2] *Parl. Papers,* 1849 (o.63), xvii, 81; see also *Ibid.,* pp. 86–88.

[3] Douglas, *Postscript to the Section on Iron Defenses,* p. 52.

[4] Kirkaldy, *British Shipping,* p. 49.

chases of ship timber in the history of the era of wooden ships of war in the very year before that era was to end. The lengthy debate in the House of Commons on the naval estimates in May, 1860, included an argument concerning the timber reserve establishments in the dockyards and the shortage of great timber which sounds more appropriate for 1760 or 1810 than for the year in which England was building her first ironclad. The Admiralty asked for £722,758 for timber, masts, and deals. In the previous decade, the annual timber estimates had averaged only half that sum, but it was felt that the dockyard supply was running dangerously low. The aim was to maintain an establishment of 60,000 loads, enough for two years' ordinary consumption. During 1859, the abnormal construction programme consumed 64,000 loads, leaving only 59,000 at the beginning of 1860, which was not quite enough for even the proposed building of wooden ships in 1860. Impulse was given to the need for an adequate timber reserve by the report that the French dockyards had on hand 160,000 loads, "far above anything we have ever had in this country." The principal argument for an ample reserve of English oak had formerly been the two or three years necessary to season that timber properly. Now, three quarters of the naval timber came from beyond the seas. When it was pointed out that teak and the other tropical woods required practically no seasoning and that the hard Italian oak dried *en route*, it was answered that this dependence on foreign lands placed timber in the situation of masts and naval stores, so that war would greatly increase the danger of empty stores.[1]

Those considerations led up to the fact that the timber shortage was very acute even in those last days of the wooden ship era. Robert Dundas, Storekeeper General of the Navy, had reported in 1859:

I believe we got every load of timber which any amount of money could have got. If we had had more money we could not have got more timber of the requisite dimensions and quality. . . . We have contracts outstanding; we have money provided for timber which will not come because we cannot get it.[2]

---

[1] *Parl. Debates*, 3d ser., clv, 979; clvii, 2027–2029, 2035, 2036.
[2] *Ibid.*, clxiii, 32, 33.

This was the antithesis of the situation two centuries earlier, when timber was plentiful but money was lacking.[1] The shortage was felt most keenly in the matter of certain pieces of large English oak in parts of the frame where foreign timber could not be used. Stern-posts were a particular problem, for the increase in the size of ships of the line necessitated trees of larger diameter than ever before for that purpose. Consequently, there was a repetition of the old story of great trees cut down only to be found rotten at heart, and ships remaining uncompleted on the stocks while the woods were searched for the rare trees of suitable size and soundness.[2] When such trees were found, there was not time for seasoning, and much green oak had to be used. As a result of causes already considered, the woods of England were practically played out. They had not been equal to the increased demands of the naval building programme of 1859, and had failed to support the Navy to the end.[3]

Such a scarcity of timber would have induced the Admiralty to turn to iron as a welcome relief, one would naturally suppose. Far from it. In those debates where much was said on the introduction of iron and much was said on the shortage of oak, the two were almost never linked. The advocates of iron scarcely touched upon this argument, and there is no evidence that it influenced the Admiralty to any extent.[4] The contrast between England and France in respect to their timber supply and the introduction of iron presents a strange anomaly. France had about twice as much timber on hand as the English dockyards had ever contained at one time, and the French were in a position to add to their supply with far greater ease than the English, while France, moreover, was short of coal and iron. Yet a Frenchman had developed the weapon which necessitated armor for ships and had been one of the first to propose such armor. France had armored batteries fighting in the Black Sea, and after the Crimean War, France had practically abandoned unarmored wooden ships.

[1] See pp. 64–66, 212–213. [2] *Parl. Debates*, 3d ser., clvii, 2029.
[3] *Parl. Debates*, 3d ser., clvi, 979; clvii, 2017, 2018, 2027–2031. See Chap. III.
[4] See *Report of Chief Engineer J. W. King, United States Navy, on European Ships of War, etc.*, p. 162.

England, on the other hand, lacked oak, while she had coal and iron in abundance. The introduction of iron into the Navy was to prove of great value to England once she was freed from the timber problem; yet in these first years of the eighteen-sixties, when all signs pointed to iron as the coming material, the Admiralty still called for more timber and set its face against innovation.

It was ridiculous enough to buy £722,758 worth of timber in 1860, but the height of absurdity came a year later, when the item for timber in the naval estimates was £949,371; and even that was not all, for the Admiralty later took an additional £250,000 from that year's appropriation for armor plate, to purchase still more timber.[1] The original estimate was based on the purchase of nearly 75,000 loads for the fiscal year — an amount exceeding the purchases in any one year of the whole two centuries of the timber problem except the period around 1812. With the additional expenditure of that quarter million, the 1861 timber purchase is without doubt the maximum on record. Three weeks before the fiscal year covered by that appropriation had closed, the contest in Hampton Roads had definitely ended the Royal Navy's need of large timber forever. That wholesale purchase of ship timber in the very last year of wooden warships is the most outstanding piece of folly in the long record of foolish actions connected with the naval timber supply.

The estimate, it is true, did not go unchallenged. William S. Lindsay, one of the most active advocates of iron ships, moved that it be reduced by £300,000.[2] The debates on March 11 and May 23, 1861, showed that many still had faith in wooden ships. The favorable maiden voyage of *La Gloire* had nearly converted the Admiralty to the view that the largest ships should be armorclad, but "that these ships only should be built of iron." Wooden ships were still considered necessary for the smaller classes and for service on distant stations where the bottoms of iron ships would become foul.[3] Sir John Parkington declared:

---

[1] *Parl. Papers*, 1861 (o.14), xxxviii, 59; *Parl. Debates*, 3d ser., clxiii, 33–35.

[2] *Ibid.*, 30.

[3] *Ibid.*, clxi, 1736, 1737.

I certainly heard with pleasure that the Admiralty intend to ask for a much larger Vote to increase our stock of timber. I agree . . . that it is a visionary idea that iron will entirely supersede wood in the construction of ships; and, to build your ships properly, you ought not to allow your stock of timber to get so low as it has been during the past two or three years.[1]

Those were the words of a man who had recently been head of the Royal Navy and was soon to hold that position again.

Lord Palmerston, who often spoke with more bluster than intelligence on naval matters, voiced a similar belief:

The House must not suppose that iron ships will wholly supersede those of wood. We may depend on it that, in case of war, wooden line-of-battle ships will play their part, and that an important part.[2]

The motion of Lindsay to reduce the estimate failed to carry, even though it was pointed out that the wooden navy of England already outnumbered the combined wooden navies of the rest of the world, and that such an abnormal purchase of timber was absurd in the extreme. The Admiralty maintained that Parliament was in honor bound to pass the measure, in its full amount, since they had already contracted for the timber. Their excuse was that purchases of foreign timber required two- or three-year contracts in advance, and that it was necessary to appropriate not only nearly a million now, but also another half million in 1862, to meet their obligations. Protests against this overriding of Parliament's right to control expenditures were unavailing, and belief in the future of wooden ships, plus the security of support of a ministerial measure, allowed the preposterous estimate to pass.[3] Even in February, 1862, the value of wooden warships for certain duties was still argued, and the half million for timber was voted with little debate.[4]

A month later came the news from American waters which sounded the death-knell of wooden warships in the Royal Navy. In the action of Hampton Roads, two wooden ships, the *Congress* and the *Cumberland,* had put up a gallant resistance against the ironclad *Merrimac,* but the pathetic futility of such resistance was shown when one was blown up and the other rammed and

[1] *Parl. Debates,* 1755, 1756. [2] *Ibid.,* 1790.
[3] *Ibid.,* clxiii, 30–52. [4] *Ibid.,* clxv, 827–834.

sunk. The shells of the ironclad had made slaughter-houses of the wooden ships, while their own guns were quite innocuous against the new armor. The action with the *Monitor* on the following day showed that iron offered the only adequate resistance to iron. This news had immediate and decisive effect in England, and the conservative skepticism which had resisted the introduction of ironclads was at an end. The debates in Parliament three weeks after the battle reveal a far different tone from those recent discussions of the timber estimates. In the hall where a half million had been voted for timber less than two months before, one speaker now declared that "the great question of iron-plated ships against wooden vessels [has] been brought to an issue, and happily, without any action on our part."[1] Another called it "positive madness to send people out to fight in wooden vessels."[2] A third summed up the situation in the emphatic words:

> We have learnt what, if two months ago any man had asserted he would have been scouted as a lunatic; we have learnt that the boasted navy of Great Britain, when opposed to iron vessels, is useless as a fighting navy. There is no blinking the question. This is what we have learnt.[3]

There were those who argued against the great expense of an immediate radical revolution in naval construction. Some pointed out that the smallest vessels might still be constructed of wood, but no one denied that the usefulness of that great fleet of ships of the line, many of them fresh from the builders, was at an end.

The end of the era of wooden warships had come suddenly, but it was taken for granted thereafter. The full history of this transition period naturally cannot be found in the utterances of parliamentary smatterers, but their opinions are at least interesting in these last days of oak and teak. The Admiralty had launched its last wooden ship of the line, though the Duke of Somerset, then First Lord of the Admiralty, announced that for some time to come ironclads would be built by the cheap and speedy method of placing iron plates over wooden frames.[4] By 1866, that makeshift expedient was abandoned, and from that time on, iron was

---

[1] *Parl. Debates,* clxvi, 263.   [2] *Ibid.,* 268, 269.
[3] *Ibid.,* 601.   [4] *Ibid.,* 439.

the material for the backbone of the Navy — the capital ships. Timber was still needed in small amounts for the teak backing of armor plates and for deck planking, but even the masts were usually of iron. With the 112,000 loads of timber on hand at the time of the "naval revolution," there was little further need to purchase timber. The parliamentary appropriations for timber, masts, and deals during those last years show graphically how rapidly the timber problem dwindled away. The votes are in some cases lower than the estimates and include the period to March 31 of the following year:

1860	£722,758	1866	117,565
1861	949,731 (plus £250,000)	1867	71,625
1862	560,713	1868	78,831
1863	266,633	1869	23,929
1864	213,092	1870	15,650 [1]
1865	165,800		

The final explosion of the burning *Congress* in Hampton Roads may be regarded as the requiem of wooden battleships; but there was another scene, in the Royal Navy itself, which had a melancholy significance in the last act of the old oak fighters. Though two wooden corvettes, the *Sapphire* and *Diamond*, were built as late as 1874, the last unarmored ships of the line were launched by the Royal Navy during the spring and summer of 1861. The *Defiance* took the water in March; the *Albion*, *Bombay*, and *Prince Regent* within a single week in May, and, last of all, the *Collingwood* was launched on July thirteenth.[2] The last four were older ships which had just been refitted with steam, but the *Defiance* was a new sailing ship, England's last construction in the type which had changed relatively little since the days of the Stuarts.

There is a tinge of sadness in the story of these last great wooden ships, a story generally overlooked in the interest in the new era just dawning. They were splendid specimens of their type, all third rates, pierced for eighty-odd guns, counterparts of the famous old seventy-fours. Their frames of English and Italian oak, with their beams and planking of many exotic woods,

---

[1] *Parl. Papers*, 1860 (0.27), xlii, 55; 1861 (0.14), xxxviii, 59; 1863 (0.19), xxxv, 48, etc. — Naval Estimates.

[2] *Ibid.*, 1876 (297), xlv, 14-16.

were fashioned with all the skill of that final high development in the designing of wooden ships; but they were ships of the past, obsolete before they were ever ready for sea. The *Bombay* actually saw service as flagship in South American waters, where she was burned to the water's edge late in 1864. The others met a more prosaic fate. The *Defiance* eventually became a schoolship at Plymouth; but most of the great wooden ships of the line left on hand at the time of the "naval revolution" were either sold for little more than the price of firewood, to be broken up while still new, or passed into the reserve, to fall into decay as their obsolescence became more and more apparent. There are only a few veterans of those days of "wooden ships and iron men" still extant in the Royal Navy, preserved as curiosities and serving as receiving or training ships or as port flagships. In the Thames off Gravesend, there is a fine old third rate, and farther downstream, a tremendous, lumbering first rate is anchored just above Tilbury. Nelson's famous flagship, the *Victory*, is a treasured relic at Portsmouth. The others, for the most part, slipped unhonored and unsung out of the service, while their names have passed on to the great, gray steel fighters of today.

With the construction of the last great oaken men-of-war, the timber problem of the Royal Navy passed into history after having worried England for more than two centuries. The problem of masts had been the first to arise and the first to be solved, while the lack of oak had continued to the very end. Even in Tudor days, builders in the royal yards had been dependent upon masts from the Baltic ports for the completion of their ships. So important was this supply that England sent squadrons time and again to prevent its interruption, while she provoked doctrines of neutral rights by her constant waylaying of those same Baltic naval materials on their way to the dockyards of her rivals. Desiring a more certain supply of masts, the Navy turned to the New England colonies, which furnished great pines for more than a century. The laws by which Parliament guarded those trees, however, were one source of irritation leading to the revolt which crippled the Navy by cutting off the pines upon which it had become dependent. After the American Revolution, the remaining

American colonies relieved England of further concern over her mast supply.

In the meantime, the problem of timber for the hulls of the King's ships was growing more serious. The ample heritage of excellent native oak which England had possessed when Henry VIII came to the throne was wasted during the next century, partly by royal policy and partly by rival economic demands, until the groves were so depleted by the time of the Restoration that the Navy felt the effects during the Dutch wars. Wise measures were then drawn up to ensure an adequate supply from the royal forests, which might have met the entire oak demands of the Navy; but these were so neglected that the dockyards became dependent on the precarious contributions from private groves. The estates of the gentry were able to support the heavy shipbuilding occasioned by the constant naval wars of the eighteenth century, with only occasional lapses; but just as Napoleon started his great attack on British sea power, the native groves proved themselves equal to only a part of the heavy dockyard demands. Even that inadequate amount was withheld for a time by a powerful monopoly, while the blockading squadrons were hampered by leaky ships which could not be repaired or replaced for want of oak. Extraordinary eleventh-hour efforts relieved the timber shortage enough to ensure the crowning success at Trafalgar; but during the rest of the war, the closing of the European and United States ports prevented adequate replenishing of the insufficient supply of native oak. British possessions overseas, sending Canadian oak and Indian teak, saved the situation but could not prevent the alarming prevalence of dry rot which was pulverizing the whole Navy. The ridiculously large purchase of ship timber in the very last year of building wooden capital ships showed that the problem was vital to the end. England had "muddled through" and had won dominion of the seas in spite of the lack of oak and pine; but her bungling timber policy had entailed two centuries of anxiety and tens of millions of needless expense, while more than once the lack of essential timber had left the dockyards in a condition where a defeat at sea might have led to disaster.

Just outside the dockyard at Portsmouth, one can see at low tide a few oak logs once cut for ship timber. Slimy and neglected, they lie in the mud near the final resting place of the *Victory*. For all practical naval purposes, they are as useless as that glorious old first rate on which Nelson died at Trafalgar, and their passing will attract far less attention. At high tide, the logs are completely hidden from view, and the clatter of the riveters working on some new cruiser in the yard proclaims that the Royal Navy is finally free from the anxiety of the days when forests had a direct bearing on sea power.

APPENDICES

APPENDIX A

3 AND 4 ANNE, CAP. 10

An Act for encouraging the Importation of Naval Stores from Her Majesty's Plantations in America.

Whereas the Royal Navy, and the Navigation of England, wherein, under God, the Wealth, Safety and Strength of this Kingdom is so much concerned, depends on the due Supply of Stores necessary for the same, which being now brought in mostly from foreign Parts, in foreign Shipping, at exorbitant and arbitrary Rates, to the great Prejudice and Discouragement of the Trade and Navigation of this Kingdom, may be provided in a more certain and beneficial Manner from Her Majesty's own Dominions: And whereas Her Majesty's Colonies and Plantations in America were at first settled, and are still maintained and protected, at a great Expence of the Treasure of this Kingdom, with a Design to render them as useful as may be to England, and the Labour and Industry of the People there, profitable to themselves: And in Regard the said Colonies and Plantations, by the vast Tracts of Land therein, Lying near the Sea, and upon navigable Rivers, may commodiously afford great Quantities of all Sorts of Naval Stores, if due encouragement be given for carrying on so great and advantageous an Undertaking, which will likewise tend, not only to further Imployment and Increase of English Shipping and Seamen, but also to the enlarging, in a great Measure, the Trade and Vent of Woollen and other Manufactures and Commodities of this Kingdom, and of other Her Majesty's Dominions, in exchange for such Naval Stores, which are now purchased from foreign Countries with Money or Bullion: and for enabling Her Majesty's Subjects, in the said Colonies and Plantations, to continue to make due and sufficient Returns in the Course of their Trade; Be it therefore enacted," etc.

APPENDIX B

AMOUNT OF BOUNTIES PAID — AMERICAN NAVAL STORES, 1706–1776

From *R. O., N. B. Out Letters, 2204* (April 17, 1777).

(Shillings and Pence not given)

Year	Bounty	Year	Bounty	Year	Bounty
1706	£ 554	1730	£11,148	1754	£22,109
1707	4,410	1731	10,804	1755	23,587
1708	1,370	1732	16,868	1756	24,041
1709	5,840	1733	19,008	1757	14,059
1710	4,259	1734	28,459	1758	20,507
1711	3,170	1735	22,968	1759	21,402
1712	3,934	1736	14,612	1760	14,689
1713	5,783	1737	18,048	1761	19,961
1714	6,860	1738	19,199	1762	17,963
1715	10,135	1739	10,999	1763	18,753
1716	27,410	1740	15,097	1764	29,516
1717	40,354	1741	16,005	1765	35,579
1718	52,011	1742	21,560	1766	41,100
1719	43,743	1743	22,237	1767	38,909
1720	28,684	1744	21,094	1768	34,700
1721	23,539	1745	12,726	1769	30,119
1722	24,732	1746	11,199	1770	29,803
1723	36,317	1747	15,382	1771	34,702
1724	45,110	1748	12,059	1772	34,534
1725	36,974	1749	18,314	1773	35,203
1726	21,709	1750	20,325	1774	37,292
1727	234 [1]	1751	23,218	1775	45,866
1728	. . . .	1752	35,669	1776	8,574
1729	423 [1]	1753	32,609		

[1] On none except imports.

Rebate for stores exported, £6,532.
Total cost to Navy, £1,471,719.

APPENDIX C

REPAIRS OF THE TRAFALGAR FLEET

(SHOWING IMPORTANCE OF REPAIRS AFTER SUPPLY OF TIMBER WAS INCREASED IN 1804. GIVES REPAIRS AFTER PEACE OF AMIENS.)

From Admiralty Library, Abstracts of Progress, passim

Name	Guns	Year Built	Arrived for Repairs	Sailed after repairs	Cost of repairs
Victory............	104	1765	April 11, 1800	May 14, 1803	70,922
Britannia.........	100	1762	Feb. 19, 1805	March 18, 1805	...
Royal Sovereign.....	100	1787	July 16, 1805	Sept. 10, 1805	60,600
Dreadnought........	98	1798	July 5, 1802	March 1803	...
Neptune..........	98	1797	April 24, 1802	Oct. 29, 1802	5,728
			July 17, 1803	Aug. 18, 1803	...
Prince............	98	1788	Jan. 21, 1805	Feb. 23, 1805	5,691
Téméraire.........	98	1798	Sept. 28, 1802	Feb. 23, 1804	16,898
			Feb. 19, 1805	March 16, 1805	9,143
Tonnant..........	80 (Fr)	1795	July 17, 1799	Dec. 25, 1802	...
Achille............	74	1798	April 23, 1802	Nov. 15, 1803	50,524
Ajax..............	74	1798	April 8, 1802	Oct. 5, 1804	38,853
Bellerophon........	74	1786	Aug. 24, 1804	Nov. 1, 1804	11,914
Bellisle...........	74	1793	Aug. 24, 1805	Sept. 22, 1805	5,494
Colossus	74	1803	(No repairs)		
Conqueror.........	74	1800	....	April 8, 1803	...
Defense...........	74	1763	Oct. 3, 1804	Oct. 26, 1804	4,131
			April 19, 1805	June 1, 1805	5,681
			July 2, 1805	July 5, 1805	...
Defiance..........	74	1783	July 5, 1804	Aug. 22, 1804	5,076
Leviathan.........	74	1789	Oct. 24, 1803	Jan. 29, 1804	22,261
Mars.............	74	1794	Aug. 22, 1804	Oct. 5, 1804	...
Minotaur.........	74	1793	Jan. 21, 1805	Feb. 25, 1805	...
Orion.............	74	1787	June 28, 1802	July 24, 1805	...
Revenge...........	74	1805	(No repairs)		
Spartiate..........	74 (Fr)	1793	Dec. 10, 1804	Jan. 18, 1805	11,238
Swiftsure..........	74	1804	(No repairs)		
Thunderer.........	74	1783	Sept. 16, 1804	Oct. 5, 1804	...
			Feb. 6, 1805	April 3, 1805	...
Africa............	64	1781	Sept. 29, 1798	July 13, 1805	32,208
Agamemnon.......	64	1781	April 13, 1802	Sept. 20, 1804	...
			Sept. 6, 1805	Sept. 24, 1805	...
Polyphemus.......	64	1782	April 27, 1802	July 6, 1804	...

APPENDIX D [1]

IMPORTS INTO GREAT BRITAIN, 1799-1815

Oak Timber and Plank

Year	Russia	Prussia	Norway	Sweden	Canada	New Brunswick	Nova Scotia	Cape Breton	British North Am.	Europe	Total
1799	331	8,664	11	..	1,072	..	17	..	1,009	9,006	10,095
1800	360	8,046	11	..	876	..	64	..	940	8,417	9,357
1801	170	7,172	3	..	486	..	3	..	489	7,353	7,834
1802	111	6,144	4	32	387	..	33	..	420	6,291	6,711
1803	43	10,593	23	76	1,998	10	17	..	2,025	10,735	12,760
1804	138	10,912	246	6	1,954	119	138	..	2,211	11,302	13,513
1805	45	11,841	1,656	..	2,466	546	8	..	3,120	13,542	16,662
1806	297	5,941	1,412	..	3,688	736	35	..	4,459	7,650	12,109
1807	3	4,230	369	59	5,734	12	..	..	5,476	4,661	10,407
1808	19	27	69	26	8,832	..	8	..	8,840	141	8,981
1809	6	388	..	79	5,853	34	55	..	5,942	473	6,415
1810	11	2,413	15	74	17,234	2	12	16	17,264	2,513	19,777
1811	6	2,562	42	17	24,451	..	42	6	24,499	2,627	27,126
1812	2	2,248	11	3	18,231	6	56	31	18,324	2,264	20,588
1814	1 [2]	5,799	41	2	4,963	3	14	7	4,987	5,843	10,830
1815	1	16,240	42	..	3,393	..	4	11	3,408	16,283	19,691

[1] Adapted from *Parl. Papers*, 1820 (269), iii, 92-98. Figures represent loads.
[2] 1813 figures missing because of Custom House fire.

IMPORTS INTO GREAT BRITAIN, 1799–1815

Great and Middling Masts

(Over 12 inches diameter)

Year	Russia	Prussia	Norway	Sweden	Canada	New Brunswick	Nova Scotia	Cape Breton	British North Am.	Europe	Total
1799	3,098	1,304	*220*[1]	*499*[1]	7	763	11	..	781	*5,121*[1]	*5,902*[1]
1800	9,528	1,819	*268*	*18*	55	792	5	..	852	*11,633*	*12,485*
1801	17,049	2,137	*422*	*216*	25	1,922	689	..	2,636	*19,834*	*22,470*
1802	5,040	764	*137*	*77*	195	2,234	94	..	2,523	*6,018*	*8,541*
1803	4,664	1,478	*146*	*77*	165	2,161	103	..	2,429	*6,365*	*8,794*
1804	8,717	909	*99*	*90*	1,314	761	224	..	2,299	*9,815*	*12,114*
1805	12,748	921	*307*	*17*	535	1,426	43	1	2,004	*13,093*	*15,997*
1806	6,010	746	*97*	*35*	1,152	1,023	33	..	2,208	*6,888*	*9,096*
1807	16,988	459	*205*	*62*	2,753	1,616	31	42	4,442	*17,714*	*22,156*
1808	4,584	17	*15*	*418*	13,333	2,870	104	422	16,729	*5,034*	*21,763*
1809	180	25	*22*	*538*	8,333	523	513	160	9,529	*765*	*10,294*
1810	153	103	*267*	*740*	16,680	1,157	735	106	18,678	*1,253*	*19,931*
1811	3,260	59	*137*	*240*	19,025	3,151	842	54	23,082	*3,696*	*26,778*
1812	3,149	..	*175*	*11*	14,019	2,125	524	17	16,685	*3,335*	*20,020*
1814	2,368	867	*143*	*55*	668	221	44	27	960	*3,433*	*4,303*
1815	2,552	896	*583*	*194*	2,492	599	113	8	3,209	*4,225*	*7,434*

[1] Figures represent number of masts except for Norway and Sweden which represent loads. Masts of this size averaged a load apiece; so totals in italics are approximate.

IMPORTS INTO GREAT BRITAIN, 1799-1815

Fir or Pine Timber

Year	Russia	Prussia	Norway	Sweden	Canada	New Brunswick	Nova Scotia	Cape Breton	British North Am.	Europe	Total
1799	5,302[1]	103,135	31,224	382	29	278	607	..	914	140,043	140,957
1800	14,591	124,474	35,492	903	323	783	565	..	1,671	175,460	177,131
1801	12,903	103,157	30,028	844	267	991	1,349	..	2,607	146,932	149,539
1802	10,994	184,034	38,824	1,244	365	2,126	2,112	..	4,603	235,096	239,699
1803	11,964	196,889	46,640	1,718	1,350	3,022	5,414	..	9,786	257,211	266,997
1804	19,887	190,805	44,356	1,556	2,282	2,834	6,940	151	12,207	256,604	268,811
1805	13,098	171,531	42,140	474	1,263	2,146	5,680	328	9,417	227,243	236,660
1806	26,616	42,535	62,973	2,239	1,754	7,062	6,781	..	15,597	134,363	149,950
1807	22,250	119,953	45,593	9,951	2,700	13,938	9,475	1,189	27,302	197,747	225,049
1808	3,406	7,415	1,243	12,727	9,861	23,056	20,576	3,882	57,375	64,791	122,166
1809	40	12,988	6,522	32,457	17,353	35,572	26,777	10,356	90,058	51,987	141,945
1810	1,209	29,726	72,348	27,105	38,869	59,807	22,271	4,704	116,651	130,388	247,039
1811	10,539	33,872	58,437	17,647	52,888	75,870	17,419	5,800	151,977	120,495	272,472
1812	1,768	4,861	11,271	6,032	32,716	20,932	25,203	11,113	89,964	23,932	113,896
1814	18,751	52,666	16,867	22,659	8,349	71,245	10,742	3,403	93,793	110,943	204,682
1815	21,176	76,878	51,441	18,391	11,676	92,553	19,382	5,127	128,738	167,886	296,624

[1] Figures represent loads.

BIBLIOGRAPHY

BIBLIOGRAPHY

THIS study of the timber problem is based primarily upon the Navy Board papers and other naval archives preserved in the Public Record Office, many of which are probably being used for the first time in a historical work. Other manuscript sources in the Public Record Office, Admiralty Library, Pepysian Library, British Museum, French Archives de la Marine, and elsewhere have been of service, as well as several official and private collections of published original sources. It has been necessary to consult a very large number of secondary works, particularly for the descriptive and technical passages.

This bibliography will consist of a short critical sketch of the most important sources, followed by a list of the principal sources consulted. In each case, there will be a division into (a) bibliographical aids; (b) manuscript sources; (c) official published original sources; (d) semi-official and private published original sources, and (e) secondary works. The secondary works are of so variegated a nature, that it seems that a subdivision into several homogeneous subjects will result in lists which may be more useful than a general indiscriminate list of all the works utilized. The lists will contain very brief comments upon some of the more important works.

BIBLIOGRAPHICAL AIDS

No previous bibliography could be expected to cover more than a portion of the subject, as its various branches have not been co-ordinated heretofore. The greatest assistance came from the subject indices in the card catalogues of the Admiralty Library, Essex Institute, Harvard College Library, Princeton University Library, Boston Public Library, and, above all, the New York Public Library, with its James Owen Proudfit collection of naval history — probably the most complete collection on that subject in existence. The list of works consulted will indicate the regular and special bibliographical works which have been of service, as well as several helpful bibliographies attached to secondary works.

MANUSCRIPT SOURCES

The civil papers of the Royal Navy, which form the foundation of this work, have had a constant fight for existence. Those in the dockyards have been thrown away for want of room, while the "Destruction Committee" of the Public Record Office has disposed of many of the papers formerly deposited there, for the same reason. Further research in these sources should be made as soon as possible, for many of these manuscripts are not at all secure in their future. The dusty papers of the Navy Board, however, contain a wealth of unexploited material, and it is to be hoped that they may be preserved until more use can be made of them.

The correspondence of the Navy Board is divided, naturally, into "Out Letters" and "In Letters." The former consist chiefly of the almost daily letters to the Admiralty, interspersed with occasional messages to the Treasury. They are bound in quarto volumes, each covering about a year. The letters to the Admiralty review the daily actions of the Navy Board in handling the various problems which arose, and occasionally give long exhaustive surveys of particular aspects of the timber supply and dockyard construction. Usually they summarize the return correspondence of the superior board at Whitehall. It is necessary to discount the frequent hostility between the two boards, the corruption which often affected the relation of the Navy Board and the contractors, and the desire of the lower board to escape censure by minimizing the effects of its neglect or overstating its exertions. The correspondence with the Treasury deals chiefly with timber from the royal forests.

The promiscuous "In Letters" of the Navy Board present even more of a virgin field for research. They are arranged in bundles, each covering one or more letters of the alphabet for a number of years. A single bundle, for instance, might contain a hundred letters written between 1794 and 1799 by individuals whose surnames began with R and S. Most of the letters are inscribed with a summary of the reply of the Navy Board. Most valuable for this study were the letters from persons who held, or wished to hold, contracts for naval timber and the construction of ships. They throw much light on the relation of the Navy Board to the contract system, and frequently contain descriptions and discussions of the different fields of supply. The letters of Isaac Solly, for instance, have a general interest because of their pictures of Napoleon's Continental System at work in Dantzig. The letters of the regular contractors have to be used with caution, because they were always apt to exaggerate the difficulties of supply or danger of shortage in order to procure an advance in price or to excuse a failure in delivery. The correspondence of individuals who wished to contract and of cranks with panaceas for the whole timber problem are liable to an even heavier discount for exaggeration.

Unfortunately, one of the most useful sources of information about the timber problem has gone forever. The letters of the commissioners and master shipwrights at the dockyards gave an excellent view of the effect of the timber problem on construction and repair, especially in times of shortage. Such correspondence, prior to the forced retirement of the Duke of York as Lord High Admiral in 1673, is preserved in the *Calendars of State Papers, Domestic,* and makes possible a study of the dockyard situation during the Dutch wars which cannot be duplicated for later periods. A few of the dockyard letters relative to the timber shortage in 1803 and 1804 are preserved in a Parliamentary Paper, but these were culled by the enemies of St. Vincent to prove a point. As for the rest, the Navy Board "In Letters from the Dockyards" were preserved in the Public Record Office until 1905, when they were destroyed to make room for other papers. Duplicates of this correspondence existed at the dockyards in letter books which were quite generally preserved until the World War; but a thorough search in 1921 revealed that they had all been thrown away in order to utilize the space for more pressing needs. The only survivors of this regrettable destruction are the *Deptford Letter Books* for the latter part of the eighteenth century, a period when Deptford was probably the least active of the yards. Certain other Navy Board records in the miscellany, including scattered records of contracts and a collection of correspondence on timber from the Cape of Good Hope, were useful.

Though the Navy Board papers are included under the general classification of "Admiralty," they are distinct from the records of the Admiralty proper, for the two boards sat in different parts of London and each had its own secretary. The "In Letters of the Secretary of Admiralty" covered a much wider range than those of the lower board, as is indicated in the list of sources; but they dealt less directly with the timber problem. These letters were addressed to the secretary in person, — Burchett, Stephens, Marsden, Nepean, etc., — but in the references in this work, the recipient has been designated as "Adm." for the sake of clearness.

Most useful of all this variegated Admiralty correspondence for the purpose of this work have been the despatches of the admirals. These are arranged in quarto volumes for each station, such as the Channel, the Mediterranean, and North America, and contain indications of the effect of the timber situation on the condition of the ships in active service. These have been supplemented on occasion by the letters of subordinate officers and by the log-books of particular ships. Such sources are subject to the limitations mentioned in the text, for some officers may have used the bad condition of their ships as an excuse to secure their reputation, while others may have merely wanted shore leave, while there is a possible political animus in some of the reports. Scattered references to bad condition of masts or hulls are to be found in the reports of every year, but the prevalence of bad masts during the

American Revolution and bad hulls during the Trafalgar campaign stands out as unusual.

Other information concerning the timber problem lies scattered through these letters written to the Lords of Admiralty. The reports which Sir Samuel Bentham was required to write in his unique rôle as Inspector General of the Navy are full of valuable discussions of the timber problem, which was a special object of his attention. Correspondence with the Secretaries of State and the Foreign Office shows that ship timber had a peculiar international importance, for the diplomats were sometimes called upon for assistance in procuring foreign supplies. There was less harmony in the Admiralty's relations with the Treasury, which had control of the royal forests and the administration of the mast preservation in America. Differences of opinion were also frequent with the Board of Trade over the policy of encouraging the American supply of naval materials and over exemptions from the Navigation Acts in securing neutral ships for naval timber. Conflicts with the Privy Council and the Customs Office on similar questions throw light on certain aspects of the timber problem, while they reveal a surprising lack of coöperation between different branches of the government — the Admiralty even had to mediate between the Admiralty Courts and the Navy Board on the policy of condemnation. Colonial governors, and consuls in other countries, have left detailed descriptions of the timber situation in various regions, while there was also occasional mention of timber in the miscellaneous correspondence. Few of these Admiralty letters show the intimate acquaintance with the timber supply evident in the Navy Board papers, but they reveal the problem in a broader light.

Many of the original letters of that Admiralty correspondence have disappeared. The gist of all the letters has been preserved, however, in the exceedingly useful series of *Digests of Admiralty Correspondence.* The compilation goes back to 1756, and after the American Revolution there is at least one great folio volume for each year. There is a separate section in each volume devoted to timber and naval stores, together with sections on shipbuilding and other subjects relevant to the problem. There is a similar Index series, in which the same material is arranged on a general alphabetical plan, occasionally useful in checking up the names of certain men or ships. In addition to the Secretary's "In Letters," there were several other helpful sources in the Admiralty papers. Under the heading of *Admiralty, Accountant General* are the ledgers of the Treasurer of the Navy and a collection of papers entitled *Various* and *Miscellaneous, Various.* The ledgers give indications of the amounts paid to different contractors for materials of every kind as well as the details of payments for mast and naval stores bounties. The other more general title includes tables of contracts for short periods, but unfortunately no systematic record of the contracts. The minutes of neither the Admiralty nor the Navy Board were of any great value in this study.

The archives of the Public Record Office have also been drawn upon for source material from certain extra-naval sources. The Treasury papers were particularly useful in connection with the forest administration both in England and America for the Surveyors General on both sides of the Atlantic reported in considerable detail to the Lords of the Treasury. The colonial records of the Board of Trade and the Colonial Office contained much that was of value. Many of these papers, which show the workings of the Broad Arrow policy, have been copied for the Historical Society of Pennsylvania. The Customs records were valuable throughout the entire period, though they do not distinguish the timber imported for the Navy from the general supply. The diplomatic efforts to secure timber are revealed in certain Foreign Office papers which also include valuable reports from consuls and secret service agents, while the special collections of *Chatham Papers* and *Rodney Papers* have occasional material of value.

The manuscripts of the Admiralty Library at Whitehall come next to those of the Public Record Office in point of usefulness for this study. For reference purposes, the great volumes entitled *Abstracts of Progress* were of constant service. In these, the time, details, and cost of dockyard construction and repairs for every individual ship are given in full detail. The relative durability of ships built in periods of war and peace and in times of timber shortage or plenty can be deduced from these accounts. The *Abstracts* also indicate the condition of the fleets and the ability of the dockyards to handle repairs. The Admiralty Library also contains several old digests compiled around 1700 for the use of the board, containing a full survey of the problems of timber, naval stores and shipbuilding.

The Pepysian Library at Magdalene College, Cambridge, contains some of the regular Admiralty papers of the Restoration period, when Samuel Pepys was Secretary of Admiralty, together with a large general collection of manuscripts gathered for his proposed naval history. These have been summarized and calendared by J. R. Tanner for the Navy Records Society, but it was necessary to consult many of the originals at Cambridge for detailed information concerning the timber problem during the Restoration. A few papers from the same period were also consulted in the *Carte Papers* and *Rawlinson MSS* in the Bodleian Library at Oxford.

The *Additional MSS* of the British Museum contain a valuable collection of correspondence and memoranda concerning the timber situation between 1802 and 1804, sent to Marquess Wellesley by Lord Melville, who wished to secure his coöperation in the building of warships in India. Some of these papers are duplicates of the regular correspondence also found at the Record Office, but there are several memoranda and private letters which have been of great service. The British Museum MSS also contain other papers of occasional usefulness. Several letters were copied from the French marine archives relative to the French quest for timber and masts from the United States and the Baltic at the time of the Convention and Directory, while other incidental manuscript sources are referred to in the lists which follow.

Published Original Sources — Official

By far the most useful of the printed official sources was the *Eleventh Report of the Commissioners of the Land Revenue*, which contains the findings resulting from a thorough study of the naval timber problem in 1792. Enough has been said of this report in the text to indicate its high value. The other reports of the commissioners were also of service in the study of English forest policy. These reports were issued as a separate work, but as they are all included in the *House of Commons Journals*, references are given to that source. The second series of Land Revenue reports early in the next century is of less value.

Two other investigations dealt with the naval timber supply and contain a wealth of material on the subject. One of these was made in 1771 and is contained in the *Commons Reports*, while the other was made in connection with the proposed admission of India-built ships to British registry and is found in the *Parliamentary Papers* for 1813–14. Some of the reports of the Commissioners of Naval Inquiry and Naval Revision went deeply into the subject matter of this study, and material of value was also found in later reports on the Baltic and Canadian timber trade and the royal forests. The huge amount of testimony in these reports is fairly reliable in matters of fact, but the opinions are frequently distorted by personal interest or prejudice. The appendices to the reports also contain many official papers which are not available elsewhere.

Next to these reports, the *Calendars of State Papers*, in both the Domestic and the Colonial series, were most useful among the printed official source collections. The former, as has been said, preserve the dockyard correspondence which has been destroyed in the original, and they also have much information concerning forest policy and timber shortage. The colonial calendars in the America and West Indies series are invaluable for the study of the Broad Arrow policy and the colonial mast supply down to 1712, supplemented by other official collections mentioned in the list. Discounting the fact that the speakers frequently were not masters of the subjects on which they spoke, the *Parliamentary History* and *Parliamentary Debates* were useful at many different periods for opinions.

While the British official collections were naturally of the greatest service, the American colonial records were often useful for the study of the Broad Arrow policy from the colonial point of view, and there is one French collection which was of very great utility. The *Lettres, Instructions et Mémoires* of Colbert show what a well-conceived timber policy could be. They not only indicate the details of the French timber problem, but frequently contain an objective view of the English situation as well.

PUBLISHED ORIGINAL SOURCES—SEMI-OFFICIAL AND PRIVATE

This second category of printed original sources consists chiefly of the correspondence, diaries, or memoirs of men intimately connected with some phase of the timber problem. It also contains other material of a varied nature not published under government auspices. The field lacks sharp frontiers, for some of the works border on official sources, while the "life and letters" of some men might be classed as secondary works. This arrangement, however, seems to afford the greatest convenience.

The Navy Records Society has rendered a great service to students of naval history by publishing in useful form, with able editing, a large amount of naval source material. As the references throughout the work will indicate, many of these publications have been drawn upon for this study. Most helpful of all have been the three volumes of the *Barham Papers*, which contain the record of the activities and opinions of Sir Charles Middleton, later Lord Barham, who was very intimately associated with the timber problem from 1778 until 1806. The Naval History Society has undertaken a similar work in this country, and use has been made of their collection of the despatches of Admiral Graves. Several other collections of letters were useful, particularly Sir Harris Nicolas's despatches of Nelson. The two great Restoration diarists, by an odd coincidence, were both intimately associated with the timber problem. Reference has already been made to the great value of Pepys's revelations of the inner workings of the contract system. Evelyn had an important influence on the timber situation through the publication of his *Sylva*, but his diary has very little which pertains to the problem. The officials of Lloyd's on Fenchurch Street in London kindly gave me access to two rare old eighteenth-century copies of the Register, which threw much light on the durability of ships and the kinds of timber used in their construction.

SECONDARY WORKS

So many secondary works have been utilized in the preparation of this study that it is out of the question to discuss many of them beyond the brief comments upon some of the more important books consulted. It will be enough here to indicate what attention has already been paid to the naval timber problem, and how the subject has been treated.

This work represents the first attempt to make a thorough study of the naval timber problem in its entirety, since the investigations of the Commissioners of the Land Revenue in 1792, and even they had little interest in the mast supply. The general importance of the timber situation has been recognized by some writers, but only a few aspects of it have been treated in detail, and there has been practically no attempt at a correlation of the whole. The nearest approach to such a study is found in the short Göttingen doctoral dissertation of C. W. Pearson, entitled *England's Timber Trade in the Last of the 17th and the First of the 18th Century, more especially with the Baltic Sea*, which appeared in 1869. It is based almost entirely on secondary sources, however, and the author was inclined to push his theories too far without due allowance for other factors.

The only piece of thorough modern research in original sources devoted primarily to an important phase of the timber problem is Miss Eleanor L. Lord's *Industrial Experiments in the British Colonies of North America*, which gives an able description and analysis of the beginnings of the New England lumber trade and the inauguration of the Broad Arrow policy, particularly between 1696 and 1729. This study was written as a doctoral dissertation at Bryn Mawr in 1896, and was published in the Johns Hopkins Studies for 1898. It is based principally on the Board of Trade papers, and even in this field, so well covered, it has been possible to add considerable new material from the Navy Board and Treasury papers as well as from local sources.

In several other pieces of modern research, a chapter or so has been devoted to aspects of the timber problem. The Baltic intervention of 1715 has been ably handled by J. F. Chance, who takes full account of the importance of naval materials, and the earlier case of intervention has been treated with less reference to those materials by Guernsey Jones and Frank R. Harris. In the colonial field, Lawrence Gipson's chapter on "The Vice Admiralty Jurisdiction," in his life of Jared Ingersoll, and Lawrence Mayo's chapter on "The King's Woods" in his biography of John Wentworth, are valuable pieces of research. Thomas J. Wertenbaker describes well the need of relief from dependence on the Baltic in the opening chapter of his *Planters of Colonial Virginia*. Sir Henry T. Wood devotes a chapter in his *History of the Royal Society of Arts* to the efforts of that organization to overcome the shortage of naval timber. E. P. Stebbing gives a very good summary of English forest policy in his recent study of commercial forestry. Wiegner has made an excellent study of the contraband status of naval materials in his work on contraband of war, and Professor Cheyney describes well the beginning of England's policy of Baltic seizures. This same policy has been ably treated by Sir Francis Piggott, for a later period, in the *Quarterly Review.*

Some of the older works have considerable to say on certain phases of the work. The enforcement of the Broad Arrow policy did not escape the attention of the standard historians of the American colonies. Abbé Reynal has left an excellent summary of the relation of that episode to the Baltic situation. Laslett and Garraud each wrote a book dealing principally with the qualities of naval timber, while Oddy made a thorough study of the Baltic trade. Several other works of like nature could be mentioned, but the fact remains that none of these writers saw the timber situation in its broadest light, and none of them so exhausted their particular subject that much has not remained to be told of the relation of that subject to the naval timber situation. The regular naval historians have been particularly oblivious, or indifferent, to the timber problem. Charnock, James, and Mahan have recognized a part of its effects at certain periods, but several important effects of timber shortage, particularly the mast situation during the American Revolution and the relation of the "Timber Trust" to the shortage in the Napoleonic period, have completely escaped attention.

In the list of secondary works consulted, no separation of contemporary and later studies has been made. The contemporary works in particular vary widely in reliability. Many of the later books have been consulted principally for description or reference, though some are valuable for interpretation. Only the more important and pertinent works consulted will be included in the following lists, for the broad nature of the subject would make exhaustive enumeration altogether too extensive. The list of secondary works will be divided as follows:

1. Forestry and timber qualities.
2. Naval architecture and general shipbuilding.
3. English timber; growth, forest policy, and naval supply.
4. Baltic timber; growth, commerce, and foreign policy.
5. American timber; growth, forest policy, and naval supply.
6. Naval history and administration.
7. Periodicals.

Many works will fall under more than one of these headings, but each will be included in the classification where it applies most closely.

LIST OF IMPORTANT SOURCES UTILIZED

The asterisk indicates sources of particular utility.

A. BIBLIOGRAPHICAL AIDS

1. MANUSCRIPT SOURCES

*ANDREWS, C. M. — *Guide to the Materials for American History, to 1783, in the Public Record Office of Great Britain.* 2 vols., Washington, 1912–14.
Introduction gives very useful description of the various collections of archives and the bodies which produced them.

ANDREWS, C. M., and DAVENPORT, F. G. — *Guide to the Manuscript Materials for the History of the United States, to 1783, in the British Museum, in Minor London Archives and in the Libraries of Oxford and Cambridge.* Washington, 1908.

British Museum. — *Class Catalogue of MSS.*

HIGHAM, C. C. S. — *Colonial Entry Books, a Brief Guide to the Colonial Records in the Public Record Office before 1696* (Helps for Students of History no. 45). London, 1921.

JOHNSON, C. — *The Public Record Office* (Helps for Students of History no. 4). London, 1918.

LINGELBACH, W. E. — "Historical Investigation and the Commercial History of the Napoleonic Era" in *American Historical Review*, xix, 257–281. Analyzes printed sources also.

Oxford University, Bodleian Library. — *Catalogi Codicum MSS.*

PAULLIN, C. O., and PAXSON, F. L. — *Guide to the Materials in London Archives for the History of the United States since 1783.* Washington, 1914.

SCARGILL-BIRD, S. R. — *Guide to the Various Classes of Documents preserved in the Public Record Office.* 3d ed. London, 1908.
For the actual details of the naval papers, this must be supplemented by the catalogues in the office itself. The new guide by M. S. Giuseppi is more detailed, but it has not yet reached the subjects treated in this work.

*TANNER, J. R. — *Descriptive Catalogue of the Naval Manuscripts in the Pepysian Library* (Navy Records Society). 4 vols., London, 1903–23.
Invaluable for the period covered. Some of the papers given in full, others briefly calendared.

2. PRINTED SOURCES

*Admiralty Library. — *Subject Index of Printed Books; Part I, Historical Section.* London, 1912.

British Museum. — *Subject Index of Modern Works added to the Library of the British Museum, 1880–1920.* 9 vols., London, 1886–1922.

Library of Congress. — *List of References on Shipping and Shipbuilding.* Washington, 1919.

*New York Public Library. — *A Selected List of Works in the Library relating to Naval History, Naval Administration, etc.* New York, 1904.

——. *Naval Architecture and Shipbuilding, a List of References in New York Public Library.* New York, 1919.
These are also published in sections in the New York Public Library Bulletin for the respective years.

CHANCE, J. F. — *George I and the Northern War.* London, 1909, pp. xv–xviii.

CUNNINGHAM, WILLIAM. — *Growth of English Commerce and Industry.* 2 vols., London, 1903; ii, 704–738.

DEWAR, ALFRED C. — *Sources of Naval History in the Seventeenth Century* (International Historical Congress). London, 1913.

JOHNSON, EMORY, et als. — *History of the Domestic and Foreign Commerce of the United States.* 2 vols., Washington, 1915; ii, 352–386.

LORD, ELEANOR L. — *Industrial Experiments in the British Colonies of North America.* Baltimore, 1898; pp. 143–146.

MELVIN, F. E. — *Napoleon's Navigation System.* New York, 1919; pp. 378–413.

POELMAN, H. A. — *Bronnen tot de Geschedenis van den Oostzeehandel.* The Hague, 1917; vol. i.
Good bibliography on Baltic trade.

RECORD, S. J. — *A Bibliography of the Woods of the World* (*exclusive of the Temperate Region of North America*). New Haven, 1922.

ROBERTS, R. A. — *Reports of the Historical Manuscripts Commission* (Helps for Students of History, no. 22). London, 1920.

TEDDER, A. W. — *The Navy of the Restoration.* Cambridge (Eng.), 1916; pp. 192–230.

WIEGNER, MAX. — *Die Kriegskonterbande in der Völkerrechtswissenschaft und der Staatenpraxis.* Berlin, 1904; pp. ix–xxiv.
Various other works containing bibliographies on limited subjects will be noticed in the list of secondary works.

B. MANUSCRIPT SOURCES

I. PUBLIC RECORD OFFICE

Admiralty Papers.
Navy Board.
  In Letters.
    Abstracts of Letters from Admiralty.
    Deptford Letter Book.
    *Promiscuous.
  Out Letters.
    *Letters to Admiralty and Treasury.
  Minutes.
  Miscellaneous.
    *Contracts.
    *Correspondence on Cape of Good Hope Timber.

Admiralty Secretary's Department.
    In Letters.
      *Admirals' Despatches.
      *Captains' Letters.
      Letters from the Board of Trade.
      *Letters from the Inspector General of the Navy.
      Letters from the Governors of Plantations.
      Letters from Consuls.
      Letters from Custom House.
      *Letters from the Treasury.
      Letters from the Secretaries of State.
      Letters from Intelligence.
    Out Letters.
      Orders, Instructions and Letters from the Lords of Admiralty.
      Secretary's Letters.
    Minutes.
    List Books.
    *Digests of Correspondence.
    Index of Correspondence.

Accountant General's Department.
    Accounts.
      *Treasurers' Ledgers.
      *Various.
    Miscellaneous, Various.
      *Contracts.
      Lists of Ships.
      *Correspondence on Adriatic Timber.

Custom House Papers.
    Accounts — Imports and Exports, Ledgers.
      *General.
      *America (1768–73).

Treasury Papers.
    *In Letters.
    Out Letters.
    Minute Book.

Colonial Office Papers.
    Board of Trade Papers.
      Entry Books.
      *Calendars.
      Registers.
    Colonial Papers.
      *Massachusetts.
      *New England.
      *New Hampshire.
      Nova Scotia.
      Plantations General.

Foreign Office Papers.
  Austria.
  Denmark.
  *Prussia.
  *Russia.
  Sweden.
  Turkey.

State Papers, Domestic.
  Naval.
    *Letters from Admiralty.
    *Naval Commanders' Despatches.

Special Collections.
  *Chatham Papers.
  Rodney Papers.

2. ADMIRALTY LIBRARY

Corbett MSS.
  Digests.
    Naval Instructions, 1693.
    *Naval Stores (cir. 1725).
    Shipbuilding (cir. 1725).
Draft of Committee of Inquiry, 1609.
Report of Committee of Inquiry, 1618.
*Abstracts of Progress.

3. CAMBRIDGE AND OXFORD

Pepysian Library, Magdalene College, Cambridge.
*Pepysian MSS, *passim.*
Bodleian Library, Oxford.
  Carte Papers.
    74, Sandwich Papers, Sound, 1659.
  Rawlinson MSS.
    175–188, Pepysian Papers.

4. BRITISH MUSEUM

Additional MSS.
  *31, 191 — St. Vincent's Price List of Stores.
  *37, 275 — Wellesley Papers, correspondence on timber, 1804.
Stowe MSS.
  435 — Ship Registry Statistics, 1790–95.
  Many other scattering references.

5. OTHER COLLECTIONS

France, Archives de la Ministère de la Marine.
  Fond BB3, vols. 38, 39; Naval supplies during French Revolution.
Massachusetts Historical Society.
  Bowdoin-Temple Papers (Unpublished MSS) *passim.*
Harvard College Library.
  MS. Am. 819, Directions for cutting timber for a sloop of war.

C. PUBLISHED ORIGINAL SOURCES — OFFICIAL

GREAT BRITAIN

Acts and Ordinances of the Interregnum, 1648–60.
　Much detail on forest policy of period.
Acts of the Privy Council, 1542–1614.
　Useful for early English forest policy.
*Acts of the Privy Council (Colonial), 1613–1783.
　Several valuable long discussions of Broad Arrow policy.
Annual Register, 1758–.
*Calendar of State Papers, Colonial Series, America and West Indies, 1574–1712.
　Invaluable for trade in naval materials and Broad Arrow policy.
　First volume, 1574–1660, has simple designation, "Colonial Series," as it contains a few African papers.
*Calendar of State Papers, Domestic Series, 1547–1703.
　Also invaluable, containing full naval correspondence, including dockyard letters, as well as much material on forest policy.
　Naval civil papers omitted after June 15, 1673. See 1673 volume, preface.
Calendar of the Committee for Advance of Money, 1642–56.
Calendar of the Committee for Compounding, 1643–1660.
　These two series have occasional details on timber confiscation.
Calendar of Treasury Books, 1660–85.
Calendar of Treasury Books and Papers, 1731–45.
*Calendar of Treasury Papers, 1557–1730.
　Useful for forest policy in England and America as well as for naval credit.
Commons Reports (see *Parliamentary Papers*).
Historical Manuscripts Commission, Reports and Publications.
　No one collection was of any great value, but pertinent material was scattered through the whole series.
*House of Commons Journals.
　Useful principally for Land Revenue reports, *q. v.* under *Parliamentary Papers. Lords Journals* were of no service.
Journals of the Commissioners for Trade and Plantations, 1704–22.
　Occasionally supplements other collections on Broad Arrow policy.
*Letters and Papers, Foreign and Domestic, of the Reign of Henry VIII.
　Useful for early forest policy and Baltic trade.
Minutes of Courts Martial.
　Especially for trials of Keppel and Palliser in 1779.
*Parliamentary Debates, 1803–
*Parliamentary History, "1066"–1803.
*Parliamentary Papers.
　This general title is used in this work to cover the series of reports and other sessional papers which commenced in 1801. The references in the footnotes give first the date of the session, the number of the sessional paper, the volume for that session, and finally the page in the specified paper,

e. g., Parl. Papers, 1813–14 (115) vol. vii, pt. 2, p. 365. Prior to this series, the sessional papers had been published either in the journals of the houses or in the series of fifteen volumes, referred to in this work as *Commons Reports*, covering the period from 1715 to 1801. In the following list of "blue books" utilized in this study, all the papers are arranged in chronological order, in whatever source collection they may appear.

*Report from the Committee appointed to consider how His Majesty's Navy may be better supplied with Timber (1771); *Commons Reports*, vol. iii.

*Reports of the Commissioners appointed to enquire into the State and Condition of the Woods, Forests and Land Revenues of the Crown, and to sell or alienate Fee Farm and other unimprovable Rents.

First series, seventeen reports 1787–93, esp.,
   *3. English forest policy, Forest of Dean (*H. C. J.*, 1787–88, 559–632).
    5. New Forest (1788–89, 552–639).
    6. Alice Holt and Woolmer Forests (1790, 120–180).
    7. Salcey Forest (1790–91, 97–125).
    8. Whittlewood Forest (1792, 141–187).
    9. Rockingham Forest (1792, 188–229).
   10. Whichwood Forest (1792, 230–264).
  *11. Naval Timber (1792, 264–374).
   13. Bere Forest (1792, 1030–1061).
   14. Sherwood Forest (1792–93, 467–511).
   15. Waltham Forest (1792–93, 512–552).
   17. Surveyor Generalship of Woods and Forests (1792–93, 566–693).
   Second series, three reports, 1812–19.
    1. Plantation policy, 1812.
    2. Plantation policy, 1819.
The second series was published independently of the regular sessional papers. The first series was also published separately, as was the eleventh report for naval purposes, but references to *H. C. J.* are given for convenience. Frequent reference has been made to these reports in the text, the eleventh report being the most valuable single source for this study.

Reports from the Select Committee on Finance, 1797–98; *Commons Reports*, vol. xii.

*Reports of the Commissioners appointed by an Act of the 43rd Year of His Majesty's Reign intituled "An Act for appointing Commissioners to enquire and examine into any Irregularities, Frauds or Abuses, which are or have been practised by Persons employed in the several Naval Departments, etc." (Usually referred to as "the Committee of Naval Enquiry.")

Fourteen reports, esp.,
    1. Naval Storekeepers, Jamaica; 1802–03 (78), vol. iv.
    6. Plymouth and Woolwich Dockyards; 1803–04 (83), vol. iii.
   *9. Plymouth Dockyard; 1805 (1), vol. ii.
  *11. Navy Bills and Imprest Money; 1805 (47), vol. ii.
  *12. Contracts for Hemp, Masts and Fir Timber; 1806 (1), vol. iv.

Most of these reports are also printed, without complete appendices, in the *Parliamentary Debates*.

Reports of the Commissioners of Naval Revision.
Thirteen reports, esp.,
1. Dockyards, 1806 (8), vol. v.
2. Dockyards, 1806 (92), vol. v.
3. Dockyards, 1806 (312), vol. v.
4. Navy Office, 1809 (120), vol. vi.
5. Foreign Yards, 1809 (121), vol. vi.
6. Dockyards, Outports, 1809 (122), vol. vi.

Report of this committee on Naval Timber was not published. See text, Chapter X.

*Accounts and Papers presented to the House of Commons relating to Ships of War, etc., 1805 (152), vol. i.
Deliberately arranged to expose effect of timber shortage on the Navy during St. Vincent's administration.

Reports of the Commissioners appointed by Act 25, Geo. III, cap. 19, to enquire into the Fees, Gratuities, Perquisites, and Emoluments, which are or have been lately received into the several Public Offices therein mentioned. 1786–1788; 1806 (309) vol. vii.

*Minutes of Evidence taken before the Select Committee to whom the several petitions of the Shipbuilders and others, and also the Petition of the Agents of Owners of Ships built in the East Indies were referred; 1813–14 (115), vol. vii, pt. 1.
Thorough survey of the timber shortage and its relation to the Navy and merchant shipping.

*Report by the Lords' Select Committee appointed to enquire into the means of extending and securing the Foreign Trade of the Country and to whom were referred the several Petitions respecting the Duties on Timber; 1820 (269), iii, 381.

*Report from the Select Committee appointed to consider the best means of maintaining and improving the Foreign Trade of the Country and to whom the Report relative to the Timber Trade, which was communicated from the Lords in the last Session of Parliament, and the several Petitions respecting the Duty on Timber were severally referred; 1821 (186), vi, 1.

Report from the Select Committee appointed to take into consideration the Duties on Timber; and to whom several Petitions upon the Timber Duties, presented to the House in the present session, and a bill to provide for the better collection of the Duties on Wood, the produce of places in Europe, were severally referred; 1835 (519), xix, 1.

Report from the Select Committee appointed to enquire into Shipwrecks of Timber Ships, and Loss of Life attendant thereon, and whether any means can be adopted to reduce the amount thereof in the future; 1839 (333), ix, 223.
The above four reports contain a wealth of information concerning the Baltic and Canadian timber trades and the relative merits of the wood from the two regions.

Report from the Select Committee on the Woods, Forests and Land Revenues of the Crown; 1847–48 (538) (538II), (538III), vol. xxiv, pt. 1, pp. 1, 335; pt. 2, p. 1.

First Report from the Select Committee appointed in the following Session on the same Subject; 1849 (513), xx, 1.

Second Report from the same; 1849 (574), xx, 559.

Report from the Select Committee on the Steam Navy; 1849 (305), xxvii, 453.

Statements relating to the Advantages of Iron and Wood and the Cost of these Materials in the Construction of Ships for His Majesty's Navy, by Robert Spencer Robinson, Comptroller of the Navy, March 2, 1863; 1863 (83), xxxvi, 301.

Return of the Number of Ships added to the Royal Navy by Building or Purchase, stating the Tonnage of each Vessel in each Year from 1860 to 1866 inclusive: also a similar Return for all Ships, stating their Description and Tonnage withdrawn from the Royal Navy by Sale, Loss at Sea or otherwise during the same respective Years; 1867, xix, 487.

List of Vessels Launched, Broken up, Sold &c., from 1855; 1876 (297), xlv, 14.

Naval Estimates, *passim*, throughout the period.

Statutes at Large.

America

Connecticut

Public Records of the Colony of Connecticut, 1636–1776. 15 vols., Hartford, 1850–90.

Massachusetts

Journal of the House of Representatives of Massachusetts, 1715–27 (Mass. Historical Society). 7 vols., Boston, 1919–26.

Journals of each Provincial Congress of Massachusetts in 1774 and 1775, etc. Boston, 1838.

Acts and Resolves, Public and Private, of the Province of the Massachusetts Bay (Massachusetts Province Laws), 1692–1780. 5 vols., Boston, 1869–86.

Laws of the Commonwealth of Massachusetts, passed from the Year 1780 to the Year 1800. 2 vols., Boston, 1801.

Records of the Governor and Company of Massachusetts Bay in New England, 1628–86. 5 vols., Boston, 1853–54.

New Hampshire

Documents and Records relating to the Province of New Hampshire (also Towns and State of N. H.), 1623–1800 (Provincial and State Papers). 31 vols., Concord, 1867–1907.

New York

Documents relative to the Colonial History of the State of New York. 15 vols., Albany, 1856–87.

Nova Scotia
Calendar of Archives.
  Vol. ii, *Letter Books and Commission Book,* 1713–41.
  Vol. iii, *Minutes of His Majesty's Council,* 1720–39.

Rhode Island
Records of the Colony of Rhode Island and Providence Plantations in New England, 1636–1792. 10 vols., Providence, 1856–65.

United States
State Papers, Naval Series, vol. i.

FRANCE

Correspondance de Napoléon Ier; publiée par ordre de l'Empereur, Napoléon III. 32 vols., Paris, 1858–70.

Instructions sur les Bois de Marine et leur Application aux Constructions Navales, Ministère de la Marine. Paris, 1859.
Contains series of excellent colored plates illustrating timber diseases.

*Lettres, Instructions et Mémoires de Colbert, publiés d'après les Ordres de l'Empereur. 7 vols. in 9, Paris, 1861–73.
Gives best outline of a naval timber policy that can be found; interesting for contrast with contemporary English policy in every detail. See Index under *Bois de construction.*

SPAIN

Real Ordenanza para el Gobierno de los Montes y Arbolados de la Jurisdiccion de Marina. Madrid, 1803.

D. PUBLISHED ORIGINAL SOURCES — SEMI–OFFICIAL AND PRIVATE

ADAMS, JOHN QUINCY, *Writings,* ed. W. C. Ford. 7 v. New York, 1913–17.

*(Anon.). — *The Oeconomy of His Majesty's Navy-Office, containing the several Duties of the Commissioners and Principal Officers thereof,* by an Officer of the Navy. London, 1717.
Based on instructions for the Navy drawn up by the Duke of York in 1660, which in turn were based on instructions of 1638.

BARROW, SIR JOHN. — *An Auto-biographical Memoir of Sir John Barrow, Bart., late of the Admiralty,* etc. London, 1847.

BENTHAM, SIR SAMUEL. — *Naval Papers and Documents referred to in Naval Essays.* London, 1828.

——. *Services Rendered in the Civil Department of the Navy,* ed. Maria S. Bentham. London, 1813.

——. *Suggestions for the Better Management of the Civil Concerns of the Navy.* London, 1850.
Outlines interesting and valuable work of the Inspector General, with comments on defects in the timber supply.

BENTLEY, JOHN (Surveyor of His Majesty's Lands). — *A List of Woods, Underwoods, Timber and Trees felled and sold out of the King and Queen their Majesties Forrests, Chases, Parks, Manors and Lands in the Counties of Kent, Sussex, Surrey, Hampshire, Berkshire, and Middlesex for the Use and Service of Parliament.* (B. M. Thomason Tracts.) London, 1648.

BERNHARDT, G. DE. — *Handbook of Commercial Treaties between Great Britain and the Foreign Powers.* London, 1912.

*BURTON, THOMAS. — *Diary of Thomas Burton, Esq., Member in the Parliaments of Oliver and Richard Cromwell, from 1656 to 1659,* ed. J. T. Rutt. 4 vols., London, 1828.
Full accounts of debates on Baltic intervention policy.

Camden Society (after 1897, Camden Series, Royal Historical Society)
Clarke Papers, ed. C. H. Firth. 4 vols., 1891–1901.
Also useful in connection with first Baltic intervention.
Acts and Ordinances of the Eastland Company, ed. Maud Sellers, London, 1906.

Carnegie Endowment for International Peace. — *The Armed Neutralities of 1780 and 1800; a Collection of Official Documents, preceded by the views of the representative Publicists,* ed. J. B. Scott, New York, 1918.

COLLINGWOOD, G. L. N. — *A Selection from the Public and Private Correspondence of Vice-Admiral Lord Collingwood.* 4th ed., London, 1829.

Colonial Society of Massachusetts, Publications.

Connecticut Historical Society, Collections. — Vols. XV–XIX, *Law, Wolcott, Fitch* and *Pitkin Papers.*

CROMWELL, OLIVER. — *Letters and Speeches, with Elucidations by Thomas Carlyle.* 4 vols., New York, 1903.

DU MONT, JEAN, BARON. — *Corps Universel Diplomatique du Droit des Gens; contenant un Recueil des Traités d'Alliance, de Paix, de Trève, de Neutralité,* etc. 8 vols., Amsterdam, 1726–31.

——. *Supplement.* 5 vols., Amsterdam, 1739.

EVELYN, JOHN. — *Diary,* ed. H. B. Wheatley. 8 vols., London, 1900.

FARINGTON, JOSEPH. — *Diary,* ed. James Grieg. 5 vols., London, 1922–25.
References to cost of shipbuilding about 1800.

Hakluyt Society Publications
HAKLUYT, RICHARD. — *Divers Voyages Touching the Discovery of America and the Islands Adjacent,* ed. Jones, London, 1890.
STRACHEY, WILLIAM, GENT. — *The History of Travaile into Virginia Britannia* (1610), ed. R. H. Major, London, 1899.
Indicates attention of explorers to timber possibilities.

HOSTE, CAPT. SIR WILLIAM. — *Memoirs and Letters,* ed. Lady Harriet Hoste. 2 vols., London, 1833.

Lloyd's Register of Shipping. — *Registers:* London, 1764–66, 1775–76.

MARTENS, G. F. DE and C. DE et al. *Recueil des Principaux Traités d'Alliance, de Paix, etc. . . . depuis 1761 jusqu'à présent.* 2d ed., Göttingen, 1791–1835.

———. *Nouvels Supplements.* 13 vols., Göttingen, 1839-42.

Maine Historical Society, Collections.

Massachusetts Historical Society, Collections.

MEADOWE, SIR PHILLIP. — *Narrative of the Principal Actions occurring in the War between Sweden and Denmark.* London, 1677.

MELVILLE, HENRY DUNDAS, LORD. — *A Letter from the Rt. Hon. Lord Viscount Melville to the Earl of Aberdeen relative to the Management of the Civil Service of the Navy.* London, 1810.

———. **A Letter from the Rt. Hon. Lord Viscount Melville to the Rt. Hon. Spencer Perceval on Naval Timber.* London, 1810.

MUNDY, GODFREY B. — *Life and Correspondence of the Late Admiral Lord Rodney.* 2 vols., London, 1820.

Naval History Society
Letters of Rear Admiral Thomas Graves while in Command on the North American Station, 1780-81, ed. F. E. Chadwick. New York, 1910.

Navy Records Society
*Autobiography of Phineas Pett, ed. W. G. Perrin. London, 1918.

*Descriptive Catalogue of the Naval Manuscripts in the Pepysian Library at Magdalene College, Cambridge, ed. J. R. Tanner. 4 vols., London, 1903-23.
   Useful, though very brief, synopses of the naval papers, preceded by an excellent survey of civil service of Restoration navy.

Despatches and Letters relating to the Blockade of Brest, ed. John Leyland. 2 vols., London, 1899-1902.
   Indicate bad condition of ships on blockade duty, 1803-05.

*Hollond's Two Discourses of the Navy, 1638 and 1659, with Slyngsby's Discourse of the Navy, ed. J. R. Tanner. London, 1896.
   Intimate view of timber problem, especially from Hollond, who was Surveyor of Navy and, later, timber dealer.

Journal of Rear-Admiral Bartholomew James, 1752-1828, ed. J. K. Laughton and J. Y. F. Sullivan. London, 1896.

*Letters and Papers relating to the First Dutch War, 1652-1654, ed. S. R. Gardiner *et al.* 5 vols., London, 1899-1912.

*Letters and Papers of Charles, Lord Barham (Sir Charles Middleton), Admiral of the Red Squadron, 1758-1813, ed. Sir J. K. Laughton. 3 vols., London, 1907-11. (Referred to as *Barham Papers.*)
   One of the most valuable sources for this study, as Middleton was intimately associated with the timber supply from 1778 to 1806.

Letters of Admiral of the Fleet, John Jervis, first Earl of St. Vincent, ed. D. B. Smith. London, 1922, vol. i.
   Second volume, now in preparation, promises to have more of value on timber situation than the first, which extends to 1801.

*Letters written by Sir Samuel Hood (Viscount Hood) in 1781-23, ed. David Hannay. London, 1895.
   References to mast situation around Yorktown and in West Indies.

Naval Miscellany, ed. J. K. Laughton. 2 vols., London, 1902-12.

*_Naval Tracts of Sir William Monson_, ed. M. Oppenheim. 5 vols., London, 1902–14.
Quaint and pertinent observations on many phases of timber problem, cir: 1635.
Private Papers of George, second Earl Spencer, First Lord of Admiralty, 1794–1801, ed. J. S. Corbett. 4 vols., London, 1913–24.

*NELSON, HORATIO, LORD. — _Despatches and Letters of Vice-Admiral Lord Viscount Nelson_, ed. Sir Harris Nicolas. 7 vols., London, 1845–46.

——. _Memoirs of the Life of Vice-Admiral Lord Viscount Nelson_, ed. Thomas J. Pettigrew. 2 vols., London, 1849.

——. _Barker Collection of Manuscripts of and relating to Admiral Lord Nelson_, ed. Sir. J. K. Laughton. London, 1913.

New Brunswick Historical Society
*_Winslow Papers_, ed. W. Q. Raymond. St. John, 1901.
Correspondence of Sir John Wentworth and others in regard to shift of mast industry and Broad Arrow policy to New Brunswick.

New England Historical and Genealogical Society Register.

New Haven Colony Historical Society Papers
Ingersoll Papers. New Haven, 1921.
Details of attempt to sell Connecticut masts to the Navy.

PAPILLON, THOMAS. — _Memoirs of Thomas Papillon, of London, Merchant_, ed. A. F. W. Papillon. Reading, 1887.
Baltic timber supply during the Restoration.

*PEPYS, SAMUEL. — _Diary_, ed. H. B. Wheatley. 9 vols. in 18, London, 1901–05.

——. _Memoirs relating to the State of the Royal Navy of England, 1679–1688_ (1690), ed. J. R. Tanner. Oxford, 1906.
Diary gives invaluable intimate view of contract system, etc., while memoirs were written principally as an excuse for the rot of the 1677 fleet.

PIGGOTT, SIR FRANCIS T. and ORMOND, G. W. T. — _Documentary History of the Armed Neutralities of 1780 and 1800._ London, 1919.
Similar in substance to the Carnegie collection by Scott.

Prince Society
Edmund Randolph, including his letters and official papers etc., ed. R. N. Tospan, 7 v. Boston, 1898–99.

*RICHARDSON, WILLIAM. — _A Mariner of England; an Account of the Career of William Richardson, from Cabin Boy in the Merchant Service to Warrant Officer in the Royal Navy (1780 to 1819) as told by himself_, ed. Col. Spencer Childers. London, 1908.

*ROBINSON, CHRISTOPHER. — _Report of Cases argued and determined in the High Court of Admiralty._ 8 vols., London, 1801–12.
Contains several famous cases on contraband status of naval materials and indirectly gives many details of Baltic shipping.

*_Royal Society of Arts, Transactions._
Valuable records of planting of timber trees under stimulus of the Society's awards of prizes.

Royal Society, Philosophical Transactions.
Many learned papers on timber qualities, dry rot, shipbuilding, etc.

SAUMAREZ, ADMIRAL LORD DE. — *Memoirs and Correspondence of Admiral Lord de Saumarez. From original papers in the possession of the family,* ed. Sir John Ross. 2 vols., London, 1838.
Papers concerning intervention in the Baltic, 1808–12.

SMITH, CAPTAIN JOHN. — *Travels and Works of Capt. John Smith,* ed. Edward Arber and A. G. Bradley. 2 vols., Edinburgh, 1910.

*SMITH, REV. THOMAS. — *Journals of the Rev. Thomas Smith and the Rev. Samuel Deane, pastors of the First Church in Portland: with Notes and Biographical Notices and a summary History of Portland,* ed. William Willis. 2d ed., Portland, 1849.
Valuable details of Falmouth mast trade.

Sydney Papers, ed. R. W. Blencowe. London, 1825.
Correspondence of Algernon Sydney during Baltic intervention of 1859.

THURLOE, JOHN. — *Collection of the State Papers of John Thurloe,* ed. Thomas Birch. 7 vols., London, 1742.
Valuable for above episode.

TUCKER, JEDEDIAH S. — *Memoirs of Admiral the Right Hon. Earl of St. Vincent.* 2 vols., London, 1844.

WEEKS, LYMAN H., ed. — *An Historical Digest of the Provincial Press, Massachusetts Series,* vol. i (1689–1707). Boston, 1908.

WHITELOCKE, BULSTRODE. — *A Journal of the Swedish Embassy in the Years 1653 and 1654. Impartially written by the Ambassador Bulstrode Whitelocke,* ed. Henry Reeve. 2 vols., London, 1855.

D. SECONDARY WORKS

1. FORESTRY AND TIMBER QUALITIES

BOWDEN, AMBROSE. — *A Treatise on Dry Rot.* London, 1815.

BUREAU VERITAS. — *Rules and Regulations for the Building and Classification of Wooden Vessels.* Paris, 1911.

BURRIDGE, JOHN. — *The Naval Dry Rot.* London, 1824.

CHAPMAN, WILLIAM. — *A Treatise containing the Results of Numerous Experiments on the Preservation of Timber from Premature Decay.* London, 1817.

DODD, RALPH. — *Practical Observations on the Dry Rot in Timber, &c., with specifications for its prevention on board of Ships of War and Merchant Vessels, etc.* London, 1815.
Like the two preceding works, proposes special remedy for dry rot and throws light on instances of its prevalence in the Navy. Frequent inaccuracy and exaggeration.

*DUHAMEL DU MONCEAU, HENRI LOUIS. — *De l'Exploitation des Bois,* etc. 2 vols., Paris, 1764.

——. *Du Transport, de la Conservation et de la Force des Bois*, etc. Paris, 1767.
These two works form principal eighteenth century authority on forestry and naval timber.

ELLIOTT, SIMON B. — *Important Timber Trees of the United States.* Boston, 1912.

*FERNOW, BERNHARD E. — *A Brief History of Forestry in Europe, the United States and other Countries.* Toronto, 1907.
Best general history of forestry, by one of chief living authorities.

——. *Economics of Forestry.* New York, 1902.

GAMBLE, JAMES S. — *Manual of Indian Timbers.* London, 1922.

*GARRAUD, LÉOPOLD. — *Études sur les Bois de Construction.* Paris, 1852.
Very useful study of most aspects of ship timber, by naval constructor.

GEYER, PHILIP. — *Der Wald im nationalen Wirtschaftsleben.* Leipzig, 1879.

GOUJON DE LA SOMME. — *Des Bois propres aux Constructions Navales.* Paris (1803).

GUILLET, PETER. — *Timber Merchants' Guide. . . . Also, Plates representing the Figures of the Principal Pieces of Timber, used in building a 74-gun Ship of the Line, in Standing Trees.* Baltimore, 1823.

*HERBIN DE HALLE, P. ÉTIENNE. — *Des Bois propres au Service des Arsenaux de la Marine et de la Guerre.* Paris, 1813.

HOUGH, FRANKLIN B. — *Elements of Forestry*, etc. Cincinnati, 1882.

——. *Report upon Forestry (U. S. Department of Agriculture Report).* Washington, 1877.

HOWARD, ALEXANDER L. — *A Manual of the Timbers of the World, their Characteristics and Uses.* London, 1920.
Most useful general timber manual; good bibliography.

*KNOWLES, JOHN. — *An Inquiry into the Means which have been taken to preserve the British Navy from the Earliest Period to the Present Time, particularly from that Species of Decay now denominated Dry-Rot.* London, 1821.
Most accurate of the large number of contemporary works on dry rot. Written by a naval official.

*KRÜNITZ, JOHANN GEORGE, ed. — *Oekonomische Encyklopädie, oder Allgemeines System der Staats-Haus-u. Landwirtschaft, in alphabetische Ordnung.* 242 vols., Berlin, 1773–1858.
Long, thorough articles on *Abies*, i, 58–94 (1773); *Eiche*, x, 206–303 (1777); and *Holz*, xxiv, 457–949 (1784), with bibliographies.

*LASLETT, THOMAS. — *Timber and Timber Trees.* 2d ed., London, 1893.
Most valuable of all English works on timbers used for naval construction. Written by dockyard master shipwright.

LAYMAN, WILLIAM. — *The Pioneer, or Strictures on Maritime Strength and Economy . . . to which is added an Exposé of a Discovery for preparing Forest Trees for immediate Service and preventing the Premature Decay of Timber, Ships and all Structures wherein Wood is used.* London, 1821.

———. *Precursor to an Exposé on Forest Trees and Timber.* London, 1813.
Sweeping, often unsubstantiated statements concerning universal prevalence of dry rot in the Navy due to poor timber.

LINGARD, JOHN. — *A Philosophic and Practical Inquiry into the Nature and Construction of Timber, including an Investigation into the Causes and Origin of the Dry Rot.* London, 1819.
Also in Pamphleteer, xvi, 355–383.

*Lloyds' Register of Shipping. — *Rules and Regulations for the Construction and Classification of Wood Vessels.* London, 1920.
Appendix A gives complete specifications of relative values of various timbers for shipbuilding.

MARSH, GEORGE B. — *The Earth as Modified by Human Action.* New York, 1885.
Interesting chapter on forest conditions in many countries.

MAW, PERCIVAL T. — *The Practice of Forestry.* London, 1912.

MICHAUX, FRANÇOIS A. — *North American Sylva,* etc. 5 vols., Philadelphia, 1859–65.

MOHR, CHARLES. — *Timber Pines of the Southern United States (U. S. Forestry Division, Bulletin no. 13).* Washington, 1897.

NEWTON, GEORGE W. — *Treatise on the Growth and Future Management of Timber Trees and on other Rural Subjects. . . . Addressed to the Landed Proprietors of North Derbyshire.* London, 1859.

*PERING, RICHARD. — *A Brief Enquiry into the Premature Decay of our Wooden Bulwarks.* Plymouth Dock, 1812.

SARGENT, CHARLES S. — *Silva of North America,* etc. 14 vols., Boston, 1891–1902.

SCHLEIDEN, MATTHIAS. — *Für Baum und Wald.* Leipzig, 1870.
Conservation arguments against timber trade with historical examples.

*SCHLICH, WILLIAM. — *Manual of Forestry.* 5 vols., London, 1889–96.
Useful inclusive compilation on all phases of forestry, including translations of German works. Karl Gayer's *Forstbenützung* in vol. 5.

SCHWAPPACH, ADAM. — *Forestry,* tr. F. Story and E. A. Nobbs. London, 1904.

———. *Forstpolitik.* Leipzig, 1894.

SENILIS, JOHANNES. — *Pinaceae, being a Handbook of the Firs and Pines.* London, 1866.

SPAULDING, VOLNEY M. — *The White Pine* (revised and enlarged by B. M. Fernow, *U. S. Forestry Division, Bulletin no. 22*). Washington, 1899.

*STEVENSON, WILLIAM. — *Wood: Its Use as a Constructive Material.* London, 1894.

STONE, HERBERT. — *Timbers of Commerce and their Identification.* London, 1904.

TREDGOLD, THOMAS. — *Elementary Principles of Carpentry,* etc. 3d ed., London, 1840.

*WADE, THOMAS. — *A Treatise on the Dry Rot in Timber.* London, 1815.

WARD, H. MARSHALL. — *The Oak, a popular Introduction to Forest-Botany.* London, 1892.

——. *Timber and some of its Diseases.* London, 1889.

2. NAVAL ARCHITECTURE AND GENERAL SHIPBUILDING

(Anon.) — *Naval Expenditure from 1860 to 1866 and its Results.* London, 1867.

Typical of the controversial literature of that decade over the transition from wood to iron.

(Anon.) — *Shipbuilder's Repository, or a Treatise on Marine Architecture, the Theory and Practical Arts explained.* London, 1789.

(Anon.) — *Shipwright's Vade-mecum: An Introduction to the Principles and Practice of Shipbuilding.* London, 1805.

*ARTIÑANO Y DE GALDÁCANO, GERVAISO DE. — *La Arquitectura Naval Española (En Madera) bosquejo de sus Condiciones y rasgos de su Evolucion.* Madrid, 1920.

Excellent study of whole Spanish shipbuilding with much attention to timber and other problems common to all wooden navies.

BARRY, PATRICK. — *Dockyard Economy and Naval Power.* London, 1863.

——. *Dockyards and Private Shipyards of the Kingdom.* 2d ed., London, 1863.

BLAKE, RICHARD F. S. — *Descriptions of Various Plans for the Improvement of Naval Architecture.* London, 1833.

BUSHNELL, EDMUND. — *The Compleat Ship-Wright. Plainly teaching the Proportion used by Experienced Ship-wrights, according to their Custom of Building.* London, 1664.

BUSK, HANS. — *The Navies of the World, their Present State and Future Capabilities.* London, 1859.

Alarmist work, calling attention to French shipbuilding.

BUSLEY, KARL. — *Die Entwicklung des Segelschiffes.* Berlin, 1920.

*CHARNOCK, JOHN. — *An History of Marine Architecture, including a view of the Nautical Regulations and Naval History of all Nations, especially of Great Britain.* 3 vols., London, 1800–02.

Much valuable material for study of timber problem included in rambling account. Several valuable sources included verbatim.

CHATTERTON, EDWARD K. — *The Marvels of the Ship; the Story of the Development of the Ship from the Earliest Times.* London, 1921.

——. *The Old East Indiamen.* London, 1914.

——. *Ships and Ways of other Days.* London, 1913.

All of these works are popular in their nature but contain occasional descriptive material of value.

CLAXTON, CHRISTOPHER. — *Remarks on the Comparative Merits of Iron and Wood as Materials for Shipbuilding.* New York, 1845.

CONSTANCE, ADMIRAL SIR REGINALD. — *The Ship of Line in Battle.* London, 1912.

CORNEWALL JONES, R. J. — *The British Merchant Service.* London, 1898.

DOUGLAS, SIR HOWARD. — *Postscript to the Section on Iron Defenses.* London, 1860.

*——. *Treatise on Naval Gunnery.* 5th ed., London, 1860.
Arguments of principal opponent of introduction of iron.

*DUHAMEL DU MONCEAU, HENRI LOUIS. — *Élémens de l'Architecture Navale, ou Traité practique de la Construction des Vaisseaux.* 2d ed., Paris, 1758.
As valuable and authoritative as his works on timber. Many illustrations and diagrams, with good description of process.

DUPIN, CHARLES. — *De la structure des Vaisseaux Anglais, etc.* London, 1817.

*EDYE, JOHN. — *Calculations relating to the Equipment of Ships.* London, 1833.
Useful tables of dimensions and other specifications of various parts of warships.

*FINCHAM, JOHN. — *History of Naval Architecture, etc.* London, 1851.
More concise than Charnock; passages on ship timber used in British Navy.

*——. *Treatise on Masting Ships and Mast Making.* 3d ed., London, 1821.
Most useful work on general subject of masts.

*FORFAIT, PIERRE A. L. — *Traité Elémentaire de la Mâture des Vaisseaux.* 2d ed., Paris, 1815.
Similar to Fincham, written by Napoleon's first minister of marine. Good opinions on relative quality of timbers for masts.

GORDON, THOMAS. — *Principles of Naval Architecture. With Proposals for Improving the Form of Ships.* London, 1784.

*Great Britain, Board of Education. — *Catalogue of the Naval and Marine Engineering Collection in the Science Museum, South Kensington. With descriptive and historical notes.* 2 vols., London, 1911.
Valuable notes and illustrations of naval vessels at every period, with details of improvements in construction necessitated by timber shortage.

*GREEN, HENRY and WIGRAM, ROBERT. — *Chronicles of Blackwall Yard.* London, 1881.
History of principal private yard building ships for Navy.

GRIFFITHS, JOHN W. — *Shipbuilder's Manual.* New York, 1856.

HALSTED, EDWARD P. — *Iron Cased Ships.* London, 1861.

HAUSER, ALPHONSE. — *Cours de Construction Navale.* Paris, 1886.

HEYWOOD, THOMAS. — *A true Description of his Majesty's royal Ship built this Year, 1637, at Woolwich, in Kent to the great Glory of the English Nation, and not to be paralelled in the whole Christian World.* London, 1637.

HOSTE, PAUL. — *L'Art des Armées Navales; avec la Théorie de la Construction des Vaisseaux* (1727). Tr. O'Bryen, London, 1762.

HUTCHINSON, WILLIAM. — *Treatise on Naval Architecture and also the Management of Merchant Ships.* 4th ed., Liverpool, 1794.

KING, JAMES W. — *Report of Chief Engineer J. W. King, United States Navy, on European Ships of War and their Armament, Naval Administration, and Economy, Marine Constructions, Torpedo Warfare, Dock-yards, etc.* (U. S. 44th Congress, 2nd sess. Senate Executive Doc. 27) 2d ed., Washington, 1878.

KIPPING, ROBERT. — *Rudimentary Treatise on Masting, Mast-Making and Rigging of Ships.* 6th ed., London, 1861.

*KIRKALDY, ADAM W. — *British Shipping, its History, Organisation and Importance.* London, 1914.

*KNOWLES, JOHN. — *Elements and Practice of Naval Architecture, or a Treatise on Ship-building in Great Britain, with Appendix containing the Principles of constructing the Royal Navies as invented by Sir Robert Seppings.* 3d ed., London, 1822.
Best detailed contemporary study of shipbuilding around 1800.

LANG, OLIVER. — *Improvements in Naval Architecture.* London, 1847.

LOTT, YEAMAN. — *An Account of Proposals made for the Benefit of His Majesty's Naval Service.* London, 1777.

MAZAUDIER, M. — *Guide Practique d'Architecture Navale.* Paris, 1835.

(Mercator, *pseud.*). — *Copy of a Letter to Bilby Thompson, Esq. M. P. on the Navy Estimates shewing the Expense of building and repairing His Majesty's Navy from the year 1800 to 1820 with Remarks on the Adoption in His Majesty's Dockyards of Kyan's Patent Process for the Prevention of Dry Rot in Timber.* London, 1834.
Convenient tabulation of amounts spent by Navy for timber for construction and repairs, from Parliamentary Papers.

(MORGAN, WILLIAM and CREUZE, ALEXANDER). — *Papers on Naval Architecture and other subjects connected with Naval Science.* 4 vols., London, 1827–32.

MURRAY, ANDREW. — *Ship-building in Iron and Wood.* 2d ed., Edinburgh, 1863.

NICHOLS, JOHN. — *Methods Proposed for Decreasing the Consumption of Timber in the Navy with Observations on fastening Ships with Iron Knees.* Southampton, 1793.

*PAIXHANS, HENRI JOSEPH. — *Expériences faites par la Marine Française sur une Arme Nouvelle. Changemens qui paraissent devoir en résulter dans le Système Naval,* etc. Paris, 1825.

*——. *La Nouvelle Force Maritime, et Application de cette Force à quelques Parties du Service de l'Armée de Terre; ou, Essai sur l'état actuel des Moyens de la Force Maritime sur une Espèce nouvelle d'Artillerie de Mer, qui détruirait promptement les Vaisseaux de haut bord,* etc. Paris, 1822.
These works had important influence in the shift to iron.

PEAKE, JAMES. — *Rudiments of Naval Architecture*, etc. 2 vols., London, 1851.
Useful manual for the details of shipbuilding.

*PERING, RICHARD. — *On the Preservation of the British Navy when in a State of Ordinary*. Plymouth-dock, 1813.

———. *A Reply to some Strictures in the Quarterly Review (no. XIX) on India Built Ships to which are annexed Economical Recommendations for effectually preserving the British Navy on the Return of Peace*. Plymouth-Dock, 1814.

REED, EDWARD J. — *On the Modifications which the Ships of the Royal Navy have undergone during the Present Century*. London, 1859.

———. *Our Iron Clad Ships*. London, 1869.

———. *Shipbuilding in Iron and Steel*, etc. London, 1869.
Reed was in charge of naval construction of ironclads.

ROMME, CHARLES. — *L'Art de la Marine, ou Principes et Préceptes Généraux de l'art de Construire, d'Armer, de Manoeuverer et de Conduire des Vaisseaux*. Rochelle, 1787.

RUSSELL, JOHN SCOTT. — *The Fleet of the Future in 1862, or England without a Fleet*. London, 1862.

———. *The Fleet of the Future — Iron or Wood?* London, 1861.

———. *The Modern System of Naval Architecture*. 3 vols., London, 1864–65.
Ranks with Reed as a protagonist of iron ships; wrote in rebuttal to Douglas.

*SEPPINGS, Robert. — *On a New Principle of Constructing His Majesty's Ships of War*. London, 1814.
Important development in naval construction, due partly to need of great and compass timbers.

*SNODGRASS, GABRIEL. — *Letter to the Rt. Hon. Henry Dundas . . . on the mode of Improving the Navy of Great Britain*. London, 1797.
Wealth of information on naval timber problem. Snodgrass suggested patching up old ships of the line, as practiced in two wars, also use of iron braces and other improvements from his experience as builder for East India Company.

Society for the Improvement of Naval Architecture. — *Report of the Committee appointed to manage the Experiments of the Society. . . .* London, 1794.

(STEEL, DAVID.) — *The Art of Making Masts, Yards, etc. as Practiced in the Royal Navy*. 2d ed., London, 1816.

STIRLING, CHARLES. — *Letters on Professional Topics*. London, 1825.
Letters on dry rot and shipbuilding.

*SUTHERLAND, WILLIAM. — *Shipbuilders Assistant or Marine Architecture*. London, 1766.
Picture of English shipbuilding and timber situation, best for that immediate period.

WHITE, WILLIAM H. — *Manual of Naval Architecture.* 2d ed., London, 1882.

WILLSON, HUGH B. — *The Science of Shipbuilding, considered in its Relations to the Laws of Nature.* London, 1863.

WILSON, HERBERT W. — *Ironclads in action, a sketch of naval warfare from 1855 to 1895 with some account of the development of the battleship in England.* London, 1896.

3. ENGLISH TIMBER: GROWTH, FOREST POLICY, AND NAVAL SUPPLY

ANDERSON, JAMES. — *A Letter to the Right Hon. the Lord Duncannon and the Lords Commissioners of His Majesty's Woods and Forests shewing that a great proportion of the Timber used in Shipping is decayed before it is felled, and recommending to all Proprietors of Wood Lands to keep it and the land in proper condition,* etc. Southwark, 1834.

(Anon.) — A Dissertation upon the visible alarming Decrease and Consumption of Naval Timber in Great Britain, with correct Estimates of the enormous consumption in Timber for building the Navy and particularly East Indiamen, etc., by an Officer. London, 1787.

(Anon.) — An Earnest Address to the People of England containing an Enquiry into the cause of the great Scarcity of Timber throughout the Dominions belonging to His Majesty. With some hints towards more effectively securing and preserving the same, particularly that part of it applied in Ship-building, etc. London, 1766.
  Contains an interesting dialogue on the construction of a ship of the line, discussing each piece of timber and its part in the ship.

(Anon.). — *English Forests and Forest Trees, historical, legendary and descriptive.* London, 1853.
  Considerable material of value on administration of royal forests, based on Parliamentary reports.

(BLACK, JAMES). — Observations on the means of providing Naval Timber. London, 1807.

BROWN, JOHN CROUMBIE. — *Forests of England and the Management of them in bye-gone Times.* Edinburgh, 1883.
  Undiscriminating compilation, containing much information on royal forests.

CHOVEAUX, ANDRÉE. — La Forest of Dean (*Annales de Géographie,* an. 31, 215–233). Paris, 1922.

COOK, MOSES. — *Manner of Raising, Ordering and Improving Forest-Trees.* 3d ed., London, 1724.

COX, JOHN C. — *The Royal Forests of England.* London, 1905.
  Best general treatment, but emphasis mainly on mediaeval period.

EVELYN, JOHN. — *Sylva, a Discourse of Forest Trees and the Propagation of Timber in His Majesty's Dominions, as it was delivered in the Royal Society on the 15th day of October, 1662, upon occasion of certain Quaeries propounded to that illustrious Assembly, by the Honourable, the Principal Officers and Com-*

missioners of the Navy. Together with an historical Account of the Sacredness and Use of Standing Groves., ed. Alexander Hunter. 2 vols., York, 1786.
  Very important for its supposed influence on Restoration planting — discussed in text, Chapter III.

FISHER, ROGER. — *Heart of Oak, the British Bulwark, shewing, 1. Reasons for paying greater attention to the Propagation of Oak Timber than has hitherto been manifested*, etc. London, 1763.
  Valuable for its picture of timber scarcity at the end of the Seven Years' War. Written by Liverpool shipwright.

FORBES, A. C. — *Development of British Forestry.* London, 1910.

——. *English Estate Forestry.* London, 1904.

GILPIN, WILLIAM. — *Remarks on Forest Scenery and other Woodland Views* 4th ed., Edinburgh, 1834.

*(HALE, THOMAS). — *An Account of several New Inventions and Improvements now necessary for England, relating to Building of our English Shipping, Planting of Oaken Timber in the Forests. . . . Milled Lead for Sheathing,* etc. London, 1691.

HARRISON, WILLIAM. — Description of England (1577) in Holinshed, *Chronicles of England, Scotland and Ireland.* New ed., London, 1807–08.

LANGLEY, BATTY. — *The Landed Gentleman's Useful Companion, or a sure and easy Method of Improving Estates by Plantations of Oak, Elm, Beech,* etc. London, 1741.

LOW, DAVID. — *On Landed Property and the Economy of Estates.* London, 1844.

*MATTHEW, P. — *Our Naval Timber and Arboriculture.* London, 1835.

NAIRNE, DAVID. — Highland Woods, Ancient and Modern (*Transactions of the Gaelic Society of Inverness*, vol. 17). Inverness, 1891.

*(NAVARCHUS, pseud.). — *Considerations on the Scarcity of Ship-Timber submitted to the Right Hon. Charles Yorke, First Lord of the Admiralty.* London, 1811.

NICHOLLS, HENRY G. — *The Forest of Dean; an Historical and Descriptive Account,* etc. Gloucester, 1856.

*NICHOLS, J. — *Observations on the Propagation and Management of Oak Trees in General, but more immediately applying to His Majesty's New Forest in Hampshire.* Southampton, 1793?
  Written by naval purveyor for Portsmouth Dockyard.

NISBET, JOHN — *British Forest Trees and their Silvicultural Characteristics and Treatment.* London, 1893.

*——. The History of the Forest of Dean in Gloucestershire (*English Historical Review*, xix, 445–459). 1906.

——. *Our Forests and Woodlands.* London, 1900.

PEARSON, C. W. — *Historical Maps of England.* London, 1870.
  Special emphasis on early forests.

PONTEY, WILLIAM. — *The Forest Pruner: or the Timber Owner's Assistant; being a treatise on the Management of British Timber Trees.* Huddersfield (1805).

——. *The Profitable Planter. A Treatise on the Cultivation of Larch and Scotch Fir Timber,* etc. — Huddersfield, 1800.

*ROGERS, JAMES E. THOROLD. — *A History of Agriculture and Prices in England . . . (1259–1793), compiled entirely from the original and contemporaneous records.* 7 vols. in 8, Oxford, 1866–1902.
Section on timber prices and conditions in every volume.

SCRIVENOR, HARRY. — *A Comprehensive History of the Iron Trade Throughout the World from the Earliest Records to the Present Period.* New ed., London, 1854.
Useful for relation of iron smelting to timber supply.

SMITH, JOHN (GENTLEMAN). — *England's Improvement Revived: In a Treatise of all manners of Husbandry and Trade by Land and Sea.* London, 1673.

*STANDISH, ARTHUR. — *New Directions of Experience . . . for the Increasing of Timber and Firewood.* 2d ed., London, 1615.
Precursor of Evelyn in interesting landed gentry in planting oaks.

STEBBING, EDWARD P. — *Commercial Forestry in Britain; its Decline and Revival.* London, 1919.
Chapter on the history of English forest policy.

TOOKE, THOMAS and NEWMARCH, WILLIAM. — *History of Prices (1793–1857).* 6 vols. London, 1838–57.

**Victoria History of the Counties of England,* ed. William Page. Westminster, 1900.
One or more volumes for most counties. Forestry sections, especially for Sussex, Surrey, and Hampshire, contain a wealth of material useful for this subject. Maritime sections for certain counties, principally by Oppenheim, also of value.

*WOOD, SIR HENRY T. — *A History of the Royal Society of Arts.* London, 1913.
Chapter on "The Society and Forestry" dealing with the important and successful efforts to encourage private planting after 1757.

4. BALTIC TIMBER: GROWTH, COMMERCE, AND FOREIGN POLICY

AMNEUS, G. — *La Ville de Kristiania, son Commerce, sa Navigation et son Industrie, Revue historique.* Christiania, 1900.

ANDERSON, ADAM. — *An Historical and Chronological Deduction of the Origin of Commerce,* etc. New ed., 4 vols., London, 1787–89.
Much useful material, but most of it was also incorporated in Macpherson.

ANDERSON, ROGER C. — *Naval Wars in the Baltic during the Sailing-ship Epoch, 1522–1850.* London, 1910.

456

BIBLIOGRAPHY

Complete catalogue of naval events, but little interpretation or note of attendant circumstances.

(Anon.) — *General Remarks on our Commerce with the Continent, shewing our influence with the States of Russia, Prussia, Sweden and Denmark*, etc. London (1806).

(Anon.) — *An Inquiry into the state of our Commercial Relations with the Northern Powers, with reference to our Trade with them under the regulation of Licenses, the advantages which the Enemy derives from it*, etc. London, 1811.

*(Anon.) — *A Pocket Guide to the Riga Trade*. Hull, 1823.

(Anon.) — *Reasons humbly offered for passing the Bill for Encouraging and Improving the Trade to Russia*. London, 1699?

ATHERLY-JONES, LLEWELLYN A. — *Commerce in War*. London, 1907.
Good summary on various attitudes toward contraband status of timber.

AZUNI, DOMENICO A. — *Maritime Law of Europe*, tr. Wm. Johnson. 2 vols., New York, 1806.

BERESFORD, JOHN. — *The Godfather of Downing Street, Sir George Downing, 1623-84*. London, 1925.
Downing was minister to Holland at time of Baltic intervention of 1659.

BOSSE, EWALD. — *Norwegens Volkswirtschaft, vom Ausgang der Hansaperiode bis zur Gegenwart; mit besonderer Berücksichtigung der internationalen Handelsbeziehungen*. 2 vols., Jena, 1916.

*BREWSTER, SIR FRANCIS. — *Essays on Trade and Navigation*. London, 1695.

*——. *New Essays on Trade*, etc. London, 1702.
Interesting expression of opinion on relative merits of the Baltic and American supply of naval materials and other features of the Baltic trade.

BRISTED, JOHN. — *Resources of the British Empire*. London, 1811.

BROCH, OLE J. — *Le Royaume de Norvége*. Christiania, 1876.

BROUGH, ANTHONY. — *A View of the Importance of the Trade between Great Britain and Russia*. London, 1789.

BROWN, JOHN CROUMBIE. — *Finland: its Forests and Forest Management*. Edinburgh, 1883.

——. *Forestry in Norway*. Edinburgh, 1884.

*——. *Forests and Forestry in Poland, Lithuania, the Ukraine, and the Baltic Provinces of Russia, with notices of the Export of Timber from Memel, Dantzig and Riga*. London, 1885.

——. *Forests and Forestry of Northern Russia and Lands Beyond*. Edinburgh, 1884.
All these works, like his study of English forests, are mere compilations for the most part, but the Polish work in particular contains much of value.

Carnegie Endowment for International Peace. — *Extracts from American and Foreign Works concerning the Armed Neutrality of 1780 and 1800.* Washington, 1917.

CARY, JOHN. — *An Essay on the State of England in relation to its Trade.* London, 1695.

CAWSTON, GEORGE and KEENE, A. H. — *The Early Chartered Companies* (A.D. *1296–1858*). London, 1896.

CHALMERS, GEORGE. — *An Estimate of the Comparative Strength of Great Britain during the present and four preceding Reigns.* New ed., London, 1804.

*CHANCE, JAMES F. — *George I and the Northern War.* London, 1909.
Excellent diplomatic study of English intervention in the Baltic, 1714–21.

——. England and Sweden in the Time of William III and Anne (*English Historical Review*, xvi, 676 ff.). 1901.
Most of his other *E. H. R.* articles fully included in the general work.

CHEYNEY, EDWARD P. — *History of England from the Defeat of the Armada to the Death of Elizabeth.* 2 vols., New York, 1914–25.
Considerable attention devoted to Baltic trade, contraband, etc.

*CHILD, SIR JOSIAH. — *Discourse of Trade* (1664). New ed., London, 1751.
Valuable mercantilist work, with much to say on Baltic trade and timber, as well as on colonies.

CLOWES, SIR WILLIAM L. — *Mercantile Marine in War Time.* London, 1902.

COKE, ROGER. — *Reasons for the Increase of the Dutch Trade, Wherein is demonstrated from what Causes the Dutch govern and manage Trade better than the English,* etc. London, 1671.

*CUNNINGHAM, WILLIAM. — *Growth of English Industry and Commerce.* 2 vols. London, 1903.

DAMUS, RUDOLF. — *Geschichte der Stadt Danzig.* Dantzig (?).

DEARDORFF, NEVA RUTH. — *English Trade in the Baltic during the reign of Elizabeth.* New York, 1912.

(DEFOE, DANIEL). — *A Plan of the English Commerce, Being a compleat prospect of the Trade of this Nation, as well the Home Trade as the Foreign.* London, 1728.

DERAYMOND. — *Tableau . . . de l'Empire de Russie.* 2 vols., Paris, 1812.

*DRACHMANN, POVL. — *Industrial Development and Commercial Policies of the three Scandinavian Countries.* Oxford, 1915.

DROTTBROOM, GERHARD. — *Wirtschaftsgeographische Betrachtungen über die Wirkungen der Napoleonischen Kontinentalsperre auf Industrie und Handel.* Bonn, 1906.

GEE, JOSHUA. — *The Trade and Navigation of Great Britain Considered.* London, 1731.

*HARRIS, FRANK R. — *Life of Edward Montagu, K. G., first Earl of Sandwich (1625–72).* 2 vols., London, 1912.
Good passages on Baltic intervention in 1659, based on Carte MSS.

HAUTEFEUILLE, LAURENT B. — *Des Droits et des Devoirs des Nations Neutres en temps de Guerre Maritime.* 3d ed., 3 vols., Paris, 1868.

HAZLITT, WILLIAM, and ROCHE, HENRY P. — *Manual of the Law of Maritime Warfare.* London, 1854.
Chapter on naval stores as contraband.

HECKSCHER, ELI F. — *The Continental System, an Economic Interpretation (Carnegie Endowment for International Peace, Division of Economics and History).* Oxford, 1922.

HILL, CHARLES E. — *The Sound Dues, a Study in International Relation,* (unpublished thesis, Harvard University).

HOENIGER, ROBERT. — *Die Kontinentalsperre und ihre Einwirkung auf Deutschland.* Berlin, 1905.

IVERNOIS, SIR FRANÇOIS DE. — *Effects of the Continental Blockade upon the Commerce, Finances, Credit and Prosperity of the British Islands.* Tr. London, 1810.

JOHNSTON, ROBERT. — *Travels through part of the Russian Empire and the country of Poland along the southern shores of the Baltic.* New York, 1816.

*JONES, GUERNSEY. — *The Diplomatic Relations between Cromwell and Charles X, Gustavus of Sweden.* Lincoln, Neb., 1897.
Heidelberg doctoral dissertation. Very useful in connection with intervention in Baltic.

KIESSELBACH, W. — *Die Kontinentalsperre in ihrer ökonomischen politischen Bedeutung.* Stuttgart, 1850.

(KING, CHARLES). — *The British Merchant: a collection of Papers relating to the Trade and Commerce of Great Britain and Ireland.* 2d ed., 3 vols., London, 1743.

*KIRCHOFF, HERMANN VON. — *Seemacht in der Ostsee. Ihre Einwirkung auf die Geschichte der Ostseelander im 17 und 18 Jahrhunderts.* Kiel, 1907.

KLEEN, RICHARD. — *Lois et Usages de la Neutralité.* 2 vols., Paris, 1898–1900.
Discussion of ship timber as contraband.

LANE, MARGERY. — England and the Northern Powers, 1689–97 (*Royal Historical Society Transactions,* 3d ser., v, 157–191). 1911.

*LINDSAY, WILLIAM S. — *History of Merchant Shipping and Ancient Commerce.* 4 vols., London, 1874–76.
Valuable for several phases of this work; not only for Baltic trade, but also in the transition to iron ships in which the author played an active part.

(McCULLOCH, JOHN R., ed.) — *A Select Collection of Early English Tracts on Commerce.* London, 1866.

McCULLOCH, JOHN R. — *A Dictionary practical, theoretical, historical, of Commerce and Commercial Navigation.* New ed., London, 1869.
Large amount of statistical and descriptive material under headings of various countries and ports.

MACGREGOR, JOHN. — *Commercial Statistics, a Digest of the Productive Resources, Commercial Legislation, Customs Tariffs,* etc. 4 vols., London, 1847.

*MACPHERSON, DAVID. — *Annals of Commerce,* etc. 4 vols., London, 1805. Contains much in common with Anderson. Useful constantly for domestic and foreign commerce.

*MANLEY, SIR ROGER. — *History of the Late Warres in Denmark.* London, 1670.

(MARBAULT.) — *Essai sur le Commerce de Russie avec l'Histoire de ses Decouvertes.* Amsterdam, 1777.
Calls French attention to menacing British preponderance in Baltic trade, especially in naval materials.

MARIEN, THOMAS A. DE. — *Tableau des Droits & Usages de Commerce relatifs au Passage du Sund.* Copenhagen, 1776.

MARSHALL, JAMES. — *Digest of all the Accounts,* etc. London, 1833.
Useful statistical tables compiled from official papers.

*MELVIN, FRANK E. — *Napoleon's Navigation System — A Study of Trade Control during the Continental Blockade.* New York, 1919.
View of Continental System chiefly from French side. Helpful bibliography.

MUN, THOMAS. — *England's Treasure by Forraign Trade* (1664). New York, 1910.

*ODDY, JOHN JEPSON. — *European Commerce, shewing new and secure Channels of Trade with the Continent of Europe, detailing the Produce, Manufactures and Commerce of Russia, Prussia, Sweden, Denmark and Germany,* etc. London, 1805.
Most complete description of Baltic commerce. Valuable tables of port statistics are not included in the American edition, 2 vols., Philadelphia, 1807.

*PEARSON, C. W. — *England's Timber Trade in the Last of the 17th and First of the 18th Century, more especially with the Baltic Sea.* Göttingen, 1869.
Nearest approach to this study in purpose. Its limited period and secondary sources, together with an exaggerated argument, lessen its value.

PEEZ, ALEXANDER VON and DEHN, PAUL. — *Englands Vorherrschaft aus der Zeit der Kontinentalsperre.* Leipzig, 1912.

PETTY, SIR WILLIAM. — *Economic Writings,* ed. C. H. Hull. 2 vols., Cambridge, 1899.

PEUCHET, JACQUES. — *Bibliothèque Commercial.* 13 vols., Paris, 1802–15.
Useful collection of contemporaneous writings on commercial subjects from many sources.

*——. *Dictionnaire Universel de la Géographie Commerçante.* 5 vols., Paris (1799–1800).
Similar to Postlethwayt in plan. Much information on mast and timber trade under names of ports and countries, but occasional inaccuracy evident.

*PIGGOTT, SIR FRANCIS T. — Ships' Timber and Contraband of War (*Quarterly Review*, ccxxxvi, 110 ff.). 1921.

Good study of the relation of naval materials to the Armed Neutrality, though some of the naval papers used for this study were evidently not consulted. Shows recognition of many phases of the general timber problem. Some of Piggott's other works on international law touch on this subject.

PINKERTON, JOHN. — *Modern Geography.* Philadelphia, 1804.

POPE, CHARLES, ed. — *The Merchant, Ship-owner and Ship-master's Import and Export Guide, comprising every species of authentic information relative to Shipping, Navigation and Commerce.* 15th ed., London, 1831.

PORTER, GEORGE R. — *Progress of the Nation in its various Social and Economic Relations.* New ed., London, 1851.

*POSTLETHWAYT, MALACHY. — *Universal Dictionary of Trade and Commerce.* 2d ed., London, 1774.

Long, useful articles on naval stores and on the Baltic countries.

PRATT, FREDERIC T. — *Law of Contraband of War.* London, 1856.

PYKE, HAROLD R. — *Law of Contraband of War.* Oxford, 1915.

RALEIGH, SIR WALTER. — *Remains.* London (1681).

Collection of his writings. Good comments on Baltic timber trade.

ROBINSON, JOHN. — *An Account of Sweden.* London, 1694.

Refers to danger of dependence on Baltic.

ROSE, J. HOLLAND. — Napoleon and English Commerce (*English Historical Review*, viii, 677 ff.). 1902.

SCHMOLLER, GUSTAV F. VON. — *The Mercantile System,* ed. Ashley. London, 1896.

SHEFFIELD, JOHN B. HOLROYD, LORD. — *Strictures on the Necessity of inviolably maintaining the Navigation and Colonial System of Great Britain.* London, 1806.

*WIEGNER, MAX. — *Die Kriegskonterbande in der Völkerrechtswissenschaft und der Staatenpraxis.* Berlin, 1904.

Excellent historical sketch of the conflicting contraband theories regarding naval materials.

WHITWORTH, SIR CHARLES. — *State of the Trade of Great Britain in its Imports and Exports progressively from the year 1697.* London, 1776.

5. AMERICAN TIMBER: GROWTH, FOREST POLICY, AND NAVAL SUPPLY

*ABBOTT, WILBUR C. — *Conflicts with Oblivion.* New Haven, 1924.

Short study of Sir John Wentworth; also Monson and Pepys.

*ADAMS, NATHANIEL. — *Annals of Portsmouth.* Portsmouth (N. H.), 1825.

Many details of value on early mast cutting and trade.

*ANDERSON (DAVID). — *Canada; or a view of the importance of the British American Colonies . . . pointing out the . . . advantages which have been allowed to the Americans over our own Colonists.* London, 1814.

Reviews services of Canada in timber supply.

(Anon.) — *The Colonial Policy of Great Britain considered with Relation to her North American Provinces and West Indian Possessions, by a British Traveller.* London, 1816.

(Anon.) — *An Essay on the Trade of the Northern Colonies of Great Britain in North America.* Philadelphia, 1764.
Proposals for more utilization of timber resources.

*(Anon.) — *Letter to a Member of Parliament concerning the Naval Stores Bill.* London, 1720.
Review of advantages of American supply against precarious dependence on Baltic.

(Anon.) — *Observations on the Report of the Select Committee of the House of Lords relative to the Timber Trade, by a British Merchant.* 2d ed., London, 1821.

(Anon.) — *Observations on the Reports of the Select Committees of Both Houses of Parliament on the Subjects of the Timber Trade and Commercial Restrictions.* London, 1820.

(Anon.) — *Remarks on the Climate, Produce and Natural Advantages of Nova Scotia. In a letter to the Earl of Macclesfield,* London (1790?).
Advantages of new mast supply from New Brunswick.

*BATES, WILLIAM W. — Ship Timber in the United States (*in U. S. Dept. of Agriculture Report, 1866, 472–497*). Washington, 1866.

BEER, GEORGE L. — *Commercial Policy of England towards the American Colonies.* New York, 1893.

——. *The Old Colonial System, 1660–1754.* New York, 1912.

——. *The Origins of the British Colonial System, 1578–1660.* New York, 1908.

*BELKNAP, JEREMY. — *History of New Hampshire.* 2d ed., 3 vols., Boston, 1813.
Detailed account of Broad Arrow dispute in New Hampshire.

BISHOP, JAMES L. — *A History of American Manufactures from 1608 to 1860.* 3 vols., Philadelphia, 1866.

BRISTED, JOHN. — *America and her Resources.* London, 1818.

BURNABY, ANDREW. — *Travels through the Middle Settlements of North America.* 2d ed., London, 1775.
Contemporary description of lumbering and mast industry.

*CHAPMAN, LEONARD B. — The Mast Industry of Old Falmouth (*Maine Historical Society, Collections,* 2d ser., vii, 390–403).

COXE, TENCH. — *A Brief Examination of Lord Sheffield's Considerations.* Philadelphia, 1791.
Defense of American shipbuilding and timber.

DAVENANT, CHARLES. — *The Political and Commercial Works of that celebrated writer Charles D'Avenant, LL.D. relating to the Trade and Revenue of England, the Plantation trade, the East India trade and African trade.* Collected and revised by Sir Charles Whitworth. 5 vols., London, 1771.

*DEFEBAUGH, JAMES E. — *History of the Lumber Industry of America.* 2 vols. Chicago, 1906–07.
Wealth of undigested material from good sources on lumbering and timber trade in United States and Canada from the beginning.

DUNSKY, H. D. — *Statement on the present Timber and Deal Trade as regards Europe and the British American Colonies.* London, 1821.

*GIPSON, LAWRENCE H. — *Jared Ingersoll; A Study of American Loyalism in Relation to British Colonial Government.* New Haven, 1920.
Valuable chapter on the "Vice-Admiralty Jurisdiction" dealing with attempt to furnish Connecticut masts to the Navy.

*GOOLD, WILLIAM. — *Portland in the Past.* Portland (Maine), 1886.
Details of mast trade and relation of masts to burning of Falmouth in 1775.

*HANNAY, JAMES. — *History of New Brunswick.* 2 vols., St. John, 1909.
Long well-grounded account of development of mast industry in New Brunswick after Revolution.

HERTZ (HURST), GERALD B. — *The Old Colonial System.* Manchester, 1905.

(HOLLINGSWORTH, S.) — *The Present State of Nova Scotia,* etc. 2d ed., Edinburgh, 1787.

*HUMPHRIES, JOSHUA. — On the Naval Resources of the United States (*Port Folio,* Jan. 1814, 62–81), 1814.
Reply of one of America's leading naval architects, designer of the *Constitution,* to Congressional committee, dealing principally with relative qualities of different ship timbers and prevention of dry rot in relation to United States Navy.

*HUTCHINSON, THOMAS. — *History of the Province of Massachusetts Bay from 1691–1750.* 3d ed., 2 vols., Boston, 1795.
Full account of Broad Arrow dispute written by royal governor.

ISE, JOHN. — *The United States Forest Policy.* New Haven, 1920.

JACKSON, JOHN M. — *A View of the Political Situation of the Province of Upper Canada in North America.* London, 1809.

JOHNSON, EMORY, *et als.* — *History of the Domestic and Foreign Commerce of the United States* (*Carnegie Institution*). 2 vols., Washington, 1915.
First volume on colonial and revolutionary period. Uneven in quality.

KALM, PER. — *Travels into North America,* tr. J. R. Foster, 2d ed. London, 1772.
Contemporary picture of lumbering and mast industry.

KENNEDY, ARCHIBALD. — *Observations on the Importance of the Northern Colonies under proper Regulations.* New York, 1750.

KINGSFORD, WILLIAM. — *History of Canada.* 10 vols., Toronto, 1887–98.

LANG, ANDREW. — *Social England Illustrated, a Collection of seventeenth century Tracts.* Westminster, 1903.
References to early timber shortage and possible relief from American colonies, especially in "Britain's Bus."

*LITTLE, OTIS. — *The State of Trade in the Northern Colonies considered, with an account of their Produce, and a particular description of Nova Scotia.* London, 1748.

*LORD, ELEANOR L. — *Industrial Experiments in the British Colonies of North America.* Baltimore, 1898.
Most thorough single study covering an important part of the timber problem. See critical survey.

*LOWER, A. R. M. — *History of the Canadian Wood Trade.*
In preparation. Have compared notes with the author.

*MAYO, LAWRENCE S. — *John Wentworth, Governor of New Hampshire, 1767–75.* Cambridge (Mass.), 1921.
Chapter on "The King's Woods" deals with Wentworth's activities as Surveyor General.

*MURDOCH, BEAMISH. — *History of Nova Scotia, or Acadie.* 3 vols., Halifax, 1867.
Frequent reference to naval mast supply to France and England.

*Ontario, Province of. — History of Crown Timber Regulations (*Report of Minister of Lands, Forests and Mines, 1907,* Appendix 52, pp. 148 ff.). 1907.
Excellent detailed survey from original sources showing Broad Arrow policy in relation to previous French régime and later Canadian developments.

PALFREY, JOHN G. — *History of New England.* 5 vols., Boston, 1858–90.

PITKIN, TIMOTHY. — *Statistical View of the Commerce of the United States of America,* etc. New ed., Hartford, 1835.

*PREBLE, GEORGE H. — Vessels of War built at Portsmouth, N. H., 1690–1868 (*New England Historical and Genealogical Register,* xxii, 393–403). 1868.
Account of unsuccessful attempt of colonies to build warships for Royal Navy, with details of principal ships so built.

*RAYMOND, WILLIAM O. — *The River St. John.* St. John, 1910.
Valuable chapter on mast industry following shift of naval efforts to New Brunswick in 1779.

*RAYNAL (GUILLAUME T. F.), ABBÉ. — *A Philosophical and Political History of the Settlements and Trade of the Europeans in the East and West Indies,* tr. J. O. Justamond. 2d ed., 6 vols., London, 1798.
Excellent survey of mast situation in America in its relation to the Baltic trade.

REED, PARKER M. — *History of Bath and its Environs, Sagadahoc County, Maine, 1607–1894.* Portland, 1894.

*RIDLON, GIDEON T. — *Saco Valley Settlements and Families.* Portland, 1895.
Detailed descriptions in chapters on "Early Mills and Lumbering" and "Mast Pines and Masting" as carried on in the Saco Valley, which lies between Portsmouth and old Falmouth, the centers of the colonial naval mast supply.

ROSA, NARCISSE. — *La Construction des Navires à Québec et ses Environs.* Quebec, 1897.

SEWALL, RUFUS K. — *Ancient Dominions of Maine.* Bath, 1859.
Overemphasizes mast laws as a cause of the Revolution.

SEYBERT, ADAM. — *Statistical Annals (1789–1818).* Philadelphia, 1818.

*SHEFFIELD, JOHN BAKER HOLROYD, LORD. — *Observations on the Commerce of the American States.* 6th ed., London, 1784.
Influential argument against admitting American ships to privileges of British registry after Revolution. Disparages quality of timber in American ships.

*SULLIVAN, JAMES. — *History of the District of Maine.* Boston, 1795.

WEEDEN, WILLIAM B. — *Economic and Social History of New England, 1620–1789.* 2 vols., Boston, 1890.

*WERTENBAKER, THOMAS J. — *Planters of Colonial Virginia.* Princeton, 1922.
Opening chapter on naval materials as colonizing motive.

*WILLIAMSON, WILLIAM D. — *History of the State of Maine (1602–1820).* Hallowell, 1832.
Like Belknap, Hutchinson, and Sullivan, gives full account of Broad Arrow disputes.

*WILLIS, WILLIAM. — *History of Portland, from 1632 to 1864: with a notice of previous settlements, colonial grants and changes of government in Maine.* Portland, 1865.

6. NAVAL HISTORY, GENERAL AND ADMINISTRATIVE

(Anon.) — *An Answer to Mr. Pitt's Attack upon Earl St. Vincent and the Admiralty . . . on 15 March, 1804.* London, 1804.

(Anon.) — *Audi Alteram Partem, or the Real Situation of the Navy of Great Britain at the period of Lord St. Vincent's Resignation, being a reply to the misstatements,* etc., by an Officer of His Majesty's Navy. London, 1804.

(Anon.) — *A Brief Inquiry into the Present Condition of the Navy of Great Britain and its Resources.* London, 1804.
Pamphlets incident to the attack on St. Vincent's administration.

*(Anon.) — *An Inquiry into the Present State of the British Navy. Together with reflections on the late war with America, its probable consequences,* etc., etc., by an Englishman. London, 1815.

(Anon.) — *Naval Anecdotes for the years during which . . . the Earl of St. Vincent presided at the Board of Admiralty,* by a Recorder of Facts. London, 1805.
Virulent abuse of St. Vincent.

*(Anon.) — *Short accounts of the Naval Actions of the Last War with Observations on the Discipline and hints for the Improvement of the British Navy,* by an Officer. London, 1788.
Remarks effects of winds and storms on bad masts and hulls.

ANSON, WALTER V. — *The Life of Admiral Lord Anson, the Father of the British Navy, 1697–1762.* London, 1912.

BARNABY, SIR NATHANIEL. — *Naval Development in the Century.* London, 1904.

BARROW, SIR JOHN. — *Life of George, Lord Anson, Admiral of the Fleet, Vice-Admiral of Great Britain and First Lord Commissioner of the Admiralty, previous to and during the Seven-Years' War.* London, 1839.

——. *Life of Richard, Earl Howe, K. G., Admiral of the Fleet, and General of Marines.* London, 1838.

BEATSON, ROBERT. — *Naval and Military Memoirs of Great Britain from . . . 1727 to 1783.* 6 vols., London, 1790–1804.

*BENTHAM, MARIA S. — *Life of Brigadier General Sir Samuel Bentham,* K. S. G. London, 1862.
Wealth of detail on timber problem and civil service of navy, but "she attributed to him something more than his due."

*BLAGDON, F. W. (ARISTIDES). — *Naval Administration, a letter to the Earl of St. Vincent, K. B. etc., pointing out numerous instances of incapacity and misconduct in the present Board of Admiralty,* etc. London, 1804.
Most useful of the controversial pamphlets, and not entirely unreliable.

BRANDT, GEERAERT. — *La vie de Michel de Ruiter . . . où est comprise l'histoire maritime des Provinces Unies, depuis l'an 1652 jusques a 1676.* Amsterdam, 1698.
Useful contemporary picture of Dutch wars from Dutch side.

BRENTON, EDWARD P. — *Life of the Earl of St. Vincent.* 2 vols., London, 1838.
Has been called "quite untrustworthy except in respect to the correspondence."

——. *Naval History of Great Britain from the year 1783 to 1836.* New ed., 2 vols., London, 1837.
Offers many more interesting opinions than James on the same period, but is much less accurate.

BURROWS, MONTAGU. — *Life of Edward, Lord Hawke, Admiral of the Fleet, etc. With some account of the origin of the English Wars in the Reign of George II and the State of the Royal Navy in that period.* London, 1883.

CAMPERDOWN, ROBERT A., EARL OF. — *Admiral Duncan.* London, 1898.

CHEVALIER, ÉDOUARD. — *Histoire de la Marine Française depuis les débuts de la monarchie jusqu'au Traité de Paix de 1763.* Paris, 1902.

*——. *Histoire de la Marine Française pendant la Guerre de l'Independence Americaine, précedé d'une étude sur la Marine Militaire de la France et sur ses Institutions depuis le commencement du XVIIe siècle jusqu'à l'année 1877.* Paris, 1877.

*——. *Histoire de la Marine Française sous la Première République.* Paris, 1886.

*——. *Histoire de la Marine Française sous le Consulat et l'Empire.* Paris, 1886.

Most valuable French works on naval history as a whole. Good interpretation. Naturally considers condition and efficiency of English Navy. The works of Jurin de la Gravière, Tramond, and Troude contain less of value for this study.

*CLOWES, SIR WILLIAM L. et als. — The Royal Navy, a History from the Earliest Times to the Present. 7 vols., London, 1897–1903.
Standard comprehensive English naval history. Invaluable for reference but uneven in interpretation.

*CORBETT, SIR JULIAN S. — The Campaign of Trafalgar. London, 1910.
Excellent strategical study. Scarcely mentions timber situation which is noticed by Mahan and James.

———. England in the Seven Years' War — a Study in Combined Strategy. London, 1907.

*DERRICK, CHARLES. — Memoirs of the Rise and Progress of the Royal Navy. London, 1806.
Written by clerk in Navy Office. Contains valuable statistics and remarks from naval sources on shipbuilding and timber problem.

*DESBRIÈRE, ÉDOUARD. — Le Blocus de Brest de 1793 à 1805. Paris, 1902.

———. Projets et Tentatifs de Débarquement aux Îles Britanniques (1793–1805). 4 vols., Paris, 1900–02.

DUNCAN, ARCHIBALD. — The Mariner's Chronicle. 6 vols., Philadelphia, 1806.
Accounts of certain naval shipwrecks due to rotten ships.

*DUPIN, BARON CHARLES. — Voyages dans la Grande-Bretagne, entrepris relativement aux Services Publics de la Guerre, de Marine, des Ponts et Chausées, au Commerce et à l'Industrie depuis 1816. 2 vols., Paris, 1825–26.
Excellent analysis of the civil organization of the Navy in every detail in vol. ii, pt. 3.

FIENNES, GERARD. — Sea Power and Freedom; a Historical Study. New York, 1918.

*FRASER, EDWARD. — Famous Fighters of the Fleet. London, 1907.

*———. Fighting Fame of the King's Ships. London, 1910.

*———. Londons of the British Fleet. London, 1908.
Studies of individual ships by an Admiralty official. Very useful for this work because much information is included which is based on dockyard papers which have since disappeared.

GILLY, WILLIAM O. S. — Narratives of Shipwrecks of the Royal Navy between 1783 and 1849. Compiled principally from official documents in the Admiralty. 2d ed., London, 1851.

HALSTED, E. P. — Remarks and Information on the Peculiar Advantages afforded by the Port of Moulmein. London, 1843.

*HAMILTON, SIR RICHARD V. — Naval Administration. London, 1896.
Most useful study of the civil branch of the Navy.

HANNAY, DAVID. — Admiral Blake. London, 1886.

——. *Rodney.* London, 1891.

*——. *Short History of the Royal Navy (1217–1815).* 2 vols., London, 1909.
Best of the short histories of the Navy. Interesting and good interpretation with thorough treatment. Short bibliography at head of each chapter. Aside from Clowes and Jane, the other general histories such as Campbell, Charnock, Ekins, Marshall, Ralfe, Southey, and Yonge contained little that was of service.

JACKSON, SIR G. — *Naval Commissioners . . . 1660–1760, compiled from the original Warrants and Notices.* Lewes, 1899.
Personnel of Navy Board, with notes.

*JAMES, WILLIAM. — *An Inquiry into the Merits of the Principal Naval Actions, between Great Britain and the United States.* London, 1816.
Offers weak timbering and dry rot as partial excuse for defeats.

*——. *Naval History of Great Britain from the Declaration of War by France in 1793 to 1837.* New ed., 6 vols., London, 1902.
Foremost authority on that period for minute exactness of detail. Little general interpretation. References same as for 1878 edition.

*JANE, FRED T. — *The British Battle Fleet, its Inception and Growth throughout the Centuries.* London, 1914.
Valuable interpretation of effect of timber on changes in naval architecture.

*KEPPEL, THOMAS. — *Life of Augustus, Viscount Keppel.* 2 vols., London, 1842.
Contains some correspondence and much apology for his rôle in 1778.

KERGUELEN, TREMAREC Y. J. DE. — *Précis de la Guerre Present, des causes de la Destruction de la Marine et des Moyens de la retablir.* (Paris), 1796.

LAMBERT DE SAINTE CROIX, ALEXANDRE. — *Essai sur l'Histoire de l'Administration de la Marine de France, 1689–1792.* Paris, 1892.
Useful for contrast with English system; see also later study by Le Haneff.

LAUGHTON, SIR JOHN K. — *Nelson.* London, 1895.

*LEVY-SCHNEIDER, LÉON. — *Le Conventionnel Jeanbon Saint André, 1749–1813.* 2 vols., Patis, 1901.
Excellent study of Robespierre's minister of marine, based partly on naval records. Wealth of detail on timber situation during French Revolution.

LOW, CHARLES R. — *History of the Indian Navy (1613–1863).* London, 1877.
Account of Indian shipbuilding for Royal Navy with list of ships.

MACLAY, EDGAR S. — *History of the United States Navy from 1775 to 1902.* New ed., 3 vols., New York, 1902.

*MAHAN, ALFRED T. — *The Influence of Sea Power on History, 1660–1783.* 12th ed., Boston, 1896.
Landmark in naval history. Excellent interpretation in many phases connected with this study.

*——. *The Influence of Sea Power upon the French Revolution and Empire, 1793–1812*. 2 vols., Boston, 1893.
Even more useful than previous work. Took notice of condition of ships and the importance of naval materials in England's Baltic policy.

——. *The Life of Nelson, the Embodiment of the Sea Power of Great Britain.* 2 vols. Boston, 1897.

——. *Major Operations of the Navies in the War of American Independence.* Boston, 1913.
Adapted from Mahan's contribution to Clowes' *Royal Navy*.

——. *Sea Power in its Relations to the War of 1812*. Boston, 1905.

MASON, GEORGE C. — The British Fleet in Rhode Island (*Rhode Island Historical Society, Collections*, 1st ser., vii, 299–325).

*MAYDMAN, HENRY. — *Naval Speculations and Maritime Politicks: being a modest and brief Discourse of the Royal Navy of England, of its Oeconomy and Government . . . also necessary Measures in the present War with France.* London, 1691.

NEESER, ROBERT W. — British Naval Operations in the West Indies, a Study in Naval Administration (*U. S. Naval Institute Proceedings*, xl, 6). 1914.

OPPENHEIM, M. — *A History of the Administration of the Royal Navy and of Merchant Shipping in relation to the Navy.* London, 1896.
Thorough and valuable, but covers period to 1660 only. Projected later volumes never appeared.

PENN, CHRISTOPHER D. — *The Navy under the Early Stuarts and its Influence on English History.* Manchester, 1913.

RICHMOND, HENRY W. — *The Navy in the War of 1739–48.* 3 vols., Cambridge (Eng.), 1920.

ROBINSON, CHARLES N. — *The British Fleet.* London, 1894.
Less satisfactory than Hannay or Jane as a short study, but is one of the few writers to remark the last of the wooden ships.

RUSSELL, W. CLARK. — *Life of Admiral Lord Collingwood.* London, 1891.

SARGENT, WILLIAM L. — *Essays of a British Manufacturer.* London, 1869.
Essay on Samuel Bentham.

SINCLAIR, SIR JOHN. — *Thoughts on the Naval Strength of the British Empire.* London, 1795.

STEEL, DAVID. — *Naval Chronologist of the Late War, 1793–1801.* London, 1806.
This and other lists and compilations by Steel have occasional use.

TANNER, JOSEPH R. — *Samuel Pepys and the Royal Navy.* Cambridge (Eng.), 1920.

*TEDDER, ARTHUR W. — *The Navy of the Restoration.* Cambridge (Eng.), 1916.

THIERS, M. J. L. A. — *History of the Consulate and of the Empire of France under Napoleon*, tr. D. F. Campbell and J. Stebbing. 12 vols., London, 1893.

*WARREN, SIR JOHN BORELASE. — *A View of the Naval Force of Great Britain.* London, 1791.
  Makes numerous suggestions regarding the timber supply.

*WHEELER, H. P. B. and BROADLEY, A. M. — *Napoleon and the Invasion of England.* London, 1908.

7. PERIODICALS

American Historical Review.
Cumberland Gazette (Portland, Maine) 1789–91.
  Eastern Herald (Portland, Maine) 1794–96.
English Historical Review.
  Forestry Quarterly.
Naval Chronicle.
  New Hampshire Gazette and Historical Chronicle (Portsmouth) 1775–77.
  Niles' Weekly Register.
  Pamphleteer.
  Philosophical Review.
Quarterly Review.
  Revue Maritime et Coloniale.
  Timber Trades Journal.

INDEX

INDEX

Dantzig (Danzig), sources of timber supply, 140, 141; best organized timber trade, 146–149, 240, 328, 361; plank from, 153; important shipment of fir from, 325, 382, 388; under Continental System, 336–344; 25, 55, 56, ·151, 154, 161, 162, 195, 199, 275, 327, 402.

Darby, Adm. G., 306.

Deals, 9, 27, 146.

Dean, Forest of, 107–109, 117, 126, 129, 130, 132, 136, 138, 212, 322.

Deane, A. (later Sir), shipwright, 62, 79, 208, 212, 219–223, 227, 393, 399.

De Grasse, Adm. Comte, 309, 311.

Deptford Dockyard, 24, 57, 68, 69, 88, 123, 126, 208, 210, 214, 215, 218, 380, 403.

Denmark, and Baltic intervention, 164–176, 179, 180, 336, 337; 206, 215.

De Ruyter, Adm. M. A., 205, 216, 219, 222.

D'Estaing, Adm. Comte, 294–302.

De Witt (De With) Adm. W. C., 210, 211.

Dnieper, 141, 145, 146, 333.

Dockyards, location and description, 68–70; inspection of timber at, 40, 43, 71, 319, 320; corruption in, 72, 319, 320; compared to private shipyards, 78, 88, 92; "foreign" or colonial dockyards, 68, 289, 293, 299, 307, 330. And see Repairs, Shipbuilding and individual yards.

Dort (Dordrecht) timber trade at, 22, 142, 147, 157, 325, 326, 380.

D'Orvilliers, Adm. Comte, 294, 303–305, 386, 387.

Downing, E., 234.

Downing, Sir G., envoy to Hague, 156, 169, 171.

Drake, Adm. F. W., 312.

Dram (Drammen), timber port, 50, 142.

Drusina, secret service agent, 341.

Dry Rot, description, 11, 12; causes, 12, 13; efforts to combat, 14, 82, 101, 396; relation to durability, 84, 85; effect on navy, 161, 228, 313–315, 388, 392–397; examples of particular ships, 315, 394, 395.

Düna. See Riga.

Dunbar, Col. D., Surveyor General, 235, 257, 262, 266, 291.

Durability, of ships, 84, 85. And see Dry Rot.

Durmast Oak, 18.

Dutch. See Holland.

Dutch Wars, timber problem during, Chapter V; first, 204–211; second, 213–217; third, 218–224. And see Wars.

East India Co., rivals navy for best timber, 116, 134; 77, 80, 320, 366, 368.

Eastland. See Baltic.

Eastland Co., 155.

Elizabeth, forest policy, 123; Baltic policy, 166.

Elm, as naval timber, 25, 26, 38.

Embargo Act, 357; evasions of, 359.

Enclosure Movement. See Agriculture.

Eton, W., timber agent, 333.

Evelyn, J., 52, 130, 132, 431.

Exploitation of Forests. See Lumbering.

Falmouth (later Portland), Maine, mast trade at, 270–272, 347, 348; ends mast supply, 279; burned by British, 280, 309.

Ferrol, blockade of, 371, 374.

Fir, properties, 27; use in hulls of frigates, 27, 358, 361, 388–391; use for masts, 30, 31; effect of climate on quality, 30; use in Napoleonic emergency, 325, 356, 378, 382, 422; use for general building purposes, 120, 356; import statistics, 422. And see Pine.

Fisher, R., shipwright, author, 134.

Fishing, of masts. See Repairs.

Fiume, timber from, 331.

Foreign Policy, influence of naval materials on dual Baltic policy, 140; Baltic intervention policy, 164–182; debate on policy, 172; armed intervention, 166, 171, 174–188, 336; admission of dependence, 179; Baltic seizure policy, 182–199; description of process, 184; provokes Armed Neutrality of 1780, 189–193; cripples French navy, 195–198; Russian attitude toward building British warships, 329; diplomatic aid for timber supply, 329, 331, 332; Parga and ship timber, 333. And see Continental System, Contraband, Napoleon.

206, 326, 327, 339, 340, 358, 360. And *see* Contraband.

Neutrality, British attitude toward, 185. And *see* Contraband, Foreign Policy.

New Brunswick, development of mast industry, 291, 292, 346–349; Broad Arrow in 350; export statistics, 348, 356, 420–422; superseded by Quebec, 353; 192, 272. And *see* Canada, Nova Scotia, Forest Policy.

New England, Chapter VI; reasons for developing timber trade, 23, 233; timber and mast trade in, 207, 213, 233–280; commercial theories concerning, 238–240; opposition to forest policy, 254–267; end of mast trade, 276–280; trade after Revolution, 347, 348. And *see* America, New Hampshire, Maine, Forest Policy, Timber Trade.

New Forest, 68, 107, 108, 110, 132, 136, 322, 393.

New Hampshire, mast and lumber trade in, 233, 264, 273, 275, 347; legislature and Broad Arrow, 248, 267, 278; 253, 270. And *see* Portsmouth, N. H., New England, Forest Policy, Timber Trade.

Newport, dockyard at, 289, 299, 301.

New York, timber and mast trade, 233, 246, 273; 284; 347; dockyard at, 289, 299, 301, 310.

New Zealand, masts from, 364, 400.

Non-Intercourse Acts, 357–360. And *see* Embargo.

Norris, Adm. Sir J., 177, 178.

Norway, forests and timber, 31, 142; advantage of nearness, 151; 120, 145, 147, 156, 157, 159, 206, 215, 221, 337, 402, 420–422. And *see* Baltic Region.

Nottingham, Earl of, Lord High Admiral, 125. 127.

Nova Scotia, Broad Arrow in, 249, 259, 349, 350; early mast exports, 276; 290, 291, 346, 356, 420–422. And *see* Canada, New Brunswick.

Numbers, importance in naval war, 202, 385.

Oak, qualities for ship timber, 16; *Quercus robur*, 17; effect of climate and soil, 17, 18; Lloyd's rating of

various oaks, 37; the great ship timber, 38.

English, peculiar qualities, 19; national esteem for, 19, 20; rate of growth, 99; problems of maturity, 100, 112; rival economic demands for, 115–121; loss of supremacy, 325, 399; increasing use of substitutes, 403.

Baltic, qualities, 21, 22; first used for naval plank, 22, 153; sources of supply, 141; occasional use of larger timber, 161, 326; prejudice against, 14, 228.

American, excellent live oak neglected, 23, 358, 391; inferior white oak rejected, 14, 23, 243, 402; used in emergencies, 244, 354, 356, 420; relation to dry rot, 14, 392, 396.

Italian, 195, 400, 405.

Oil, analogy of timber problem to present quest for, xi, 164.

Onslow, Sir R., opinion on intervention, 173, 182.

Opdam, Adm. Lord, 169, 174.

Palliser, Adm. Sir H., 293, 303–305.

Palmerston, Lord, on wooden warships, 408.

Pappenburg, neutral port, 185, 339.

Parga, abandoned for ship timber, 333.

Parliament, influence of oak-owning members, xi, 63, 121, 322; appropriations for timber and shipbuilding, 39, 225, 410; debates on timber and shipbuilding, 161, 397, 403–409; legislation, on English forests, 118, 122, 128, 132, 137; on Colonial forests and naval materials, 248–251, 355, 402; on timber trade, 142, 156, 355, 402; investigations and reports, 134, 135, 397, 439–441.

Parry, E., mast agent, 277.

Pellew, Adm. E., 367, 371, 375.

Penn, Sir W., Navy Board, 208, 215.

Penobscot, 271, 272, 290, 349.

Pepys, S., illustrates contract corruption, 49–52; ix, 59, 63, 72, 213, 216, 218, 222, 228, 229, 431.

Peter the Great, of Russia, 141, 162, 178, 252, 345.

Pett, Christopher, 52, 212.

Pett, Peter, 73, 212, 215, 283.